MW01485599

CLASH OF EMPIRES IN

SOUTH CHINA

Clash of Empires in South China

THE ALLIED NATIONS' PROXY WAR WITH JAPAN, 1935–1941

Franco David Macri

University Press of Kansas

Published by the University Press of Kansas (Lawrence, Kansas
66045), which was organized by the Kansas Board of Regents and is
operated and funded by Emporia State University, Fort Hays State
University, Kansas State University, Pittsburg State University,
the University of Kansas, and Wichita State University

Library of Congress Cataloging-in-Publication Data

Macri, Franco David.
Clash of empires in South China : the Allied nations' proxy war with Japan,
1935–1941 / Franco David Macri.
p. cm. — (Modern war studies)
Includes bibliographical references and index.
ISBN 978-0-7006-1877-4 (cloth : alk. paper)
1. Sino-Japanese War, 1937–1945—Campaigns—China, Southeast.
2. World War, 1939–1945—Campaigns—China, Southeast. I. Title.
DS777.53.M2326 2012
951.04'2—dc23
2012026191

British Library Cataloguing-in-Publication Data is available.

Printed in the United States of America

10 9 8 7 6 5 4 3 2 1

The paper used in this publication is recycled and contains 30
percent postconsumer waste. It is acid free and meets the minimum
requirements of the American National Standard for Permanence of
Paper for Printed Library Materials Z39.48-1992.

To those who defended Hong Kong

in December 1941

Contents

List of Illustrations   ix

Acknowledgments   xi

Note on Romanization   xiii

1. Collective Security in Asia: The Global Significance
   of Hong Kong and Southern China   1

2. Clearing the Decks: Preparing for War in South China,
   1935 to July 1937   17

3. The Sino-Japanese War Begins: Proxy War in China,
   July 1937 to October 1938   37

4. The Trap Is Sprung: October 1938 to March 1939   89

5. Stalemate: March to October 1939   125

6. Impasse in Kwangsi and Japan's Failed Interdiction Strategy
   against Hong Kong: November 1939 to May 1940   176

7. Leveraging War and Peace:
May to December 1940   202

8. The Triumph of Collective Security:
Hong Kong, 1941   246

9. Empires Derailed: The War in South China,
September 1941 to January 1942   286

10. Collective Insecurity: The Demise of
Imperial Power in Asia   340

Notes   351

Bibliography   429

Index   441

Illustrations

Railways in China (1940)   24

Japanese army positions at Tehan, October 1938   56

Railway lines (1938) and supply lines (1939) in Kwangtung   62

Japanese army positions in Kwangtung, October 1938   94

Railway lines and roads in southern China, October 1941   108

Japanese operations in Hainan   112

Pearl River Delta   140

Shekki, 1944   142

First battle of Changsha, September 1939   167

Battle for Kwangsi, December 1939 to January 1940   182

Battle for Kwangsi, February 1940   185

Battle for Kwangtung, 20 December 1939 to 5 January 1940   192

Battle for Kwangtung, 6 to 20 January 1940   194

Japanese 23rd Army attack on Hong Kong, December 1941   309

Japanese offensive in Hunan, 24 December 1941   326

Japanese retreat in Hunan, 4 January 1942   330

Japanese retreat in Hunan, 11 January 1942   331

Newspaper cartoon about the third battle of Changsha   334

Acknowledgments

This book is the result of more than five years of work, and its completion would not have been possible without the fellowship and support of colleagues, mentors, and friends at the University of Hong Kong. Among these are Chris Cowell, Carol Tsang, Satoko Handa, Laura Verner, Michelle Tong, Qian Gang, May Wong, Kris Erskine, Anghard Fletcher, Paul Wenham, Dr. Gerald Sellinger, and Paul Spooner. They helped steer me through many of the complexities of the research, as did Dr. John Carroll and Dr. Priscilla Roberts. Deepest gratitude, however, is extended to my primary supervisor, Dr. Peter Cunich, whose advice and encouragement kept me motivated and focused. Additionally, it would not have been possible to complete this work without the studentship funding provided through the School of Graduate Studies. Thus, to members of the university, particularly those in the Department of History, I express my gratitude. I am similarly appreciative of Dr. Eric Chong at St. John's College and Vincent Chiu of the St. John's College alumni association. I also wish to thank Du Juan Juan at the Chinese University of Hong Kong and Liu Hai Xia at Beijing Normal University in Zhuhai for their friendship and guidance.

Others helped greatly along the way, in a variety of circumstances, and to each of them I extend many thanks. Friends in Canada who provided invaluable assistance and encouragement include Kevin Brown, Paul Buhagiar, Sam Jagpal, Michael Klar, Jonathan Knell, Nigel Mackey, Norm

McGlashin, Heather Nash, Jamie Ogle, John Pacheco, Karl Valaitis, and Dr. Tim Wilson. I was also quite fortunate to study Canadian military history under the supervision of Terry Copp at Wilfrid Laurier University, and to him I am grateful. In the United Kingdom, Dr. Ashley Jackson at King's College was very helpful; his advice and encouragement are greatly appreciated. Thanks are also due to Dr. Kristina Giannotta in Hawaii.

I would also like to acknowledge the *Journal of the Royal Asiatic Society Hong Kong Branch* for allowing me to use of one of my articles that appeared in 2010. A quote from my forthcoming article in the *International History Review* is also utilized. I would like to thank Mrs. Margaret Callan in Delta, British Columbia, for permitting me to reproduce one of her late husband's newspaper cartoons in chapter 9. Last, I am most grateful to Michael Briggs, Larisa Martin, and the staff at the University Press of Kansas for supporting this project and for their patience and assistance with the many questions and problems encountered along the way.

Note on Romanization

Due to language constraints, Japanese and Chinese individuals and places are identified by using the most common spellings in the primary source materials consulted. Individuals are identified by the family name first. When possible, the more modern Chinese pinyin equivalent is inserted following the first usage of the name.

ONE

Collective Security in Asia: The Global Significance of Hong Kong and Southern China

In most accounts of the Second World War, China has not attracted much attention, and this is particularly true of the region south of the Yangtse (Yangtze) River. When authors have considered China, it has been presented largely as an Allied liability of limited significance. One of the important reasons for this characterization was the weakness of China's military forces; by the end of 1941, this condition enabled the Japanese to conduct operations in the southwest Pacific without fear of defeat in East Asia. Because of subsequent Allied failures in the region, the idea persists that Chinese efforts against the Japanese army were hopelessly ineffective. Although there were many setbacks between 1942 and 1945 for which several powers shared responsibility, this view cannot be supported when the period from 1937 to 1942 is examined closely. During this time the Chinese survived the initial onslaught and ground their enemies down in what became a stalemate of attrition. Despite widespread expectations of failure, the Chinese were not defeated. It is fair to say that many internal problems were present—political, economic, and military—and that these limited China's potential for waging war. Yet elements of the Chinese army improved as the Sino-Japanese War unfolded, and the Chinese were able to hold the Japanese and defend key strategic areas. Of these, southern China was certainly of great importance. Throughout the war the defense of southern China was vital for the continuance of Chinese resistance, and several Japanese offensives were defeated there. Chinese success in the south was due to a variety of reasons, but the level of international interest and influence in the region was highly significant. The involvement of third powers, albeit covert, was greater in southern China than elsewhere because it was one of the last areas free from Japanese occupation where foreign military resources could enter the country. This situation was significant because it enabled several powers to use their logistical support for China as a way to influence the actions of others.

Had war not erupted in other areas around the globe, the crisis in China would likely have remained a regional problem. But as the global international order disintegrated, the Sino-Japanese War emerged as an increasingly consequential geopolitical contest. This occurred because several influential third-power officials saw the war's continuation as a useful way to limit Japanese aggression elsewhere. For some, the commonality of interests in China also served to create an environment where the alliance against the Axis could be consolidated. In time, this proved to be the case, especially in the south. China's logistical gatekeepers were the British in nearby Rangoon and Hong Kong, along with the French placed between them at Haiphong. It was through these portals that munitions from the United States entered and where most of the key strategic resources earmarked for the United States and the USSR were exported. Because of this situation, however, Western relations with the Japanese deteriorated greatly. By the end of 1941 Japan attacked the forces of both the United States and Great Britain, in part because of its problems in China, thereby ushering in the start of the Pacific war. With this escalation, global conflict reached unparalleled heights, and the anti-Axis alliance was finally forged. But this evolutionary process had been at work for quite some time. Starting with the British, several future Allied powers had attempted to pursue a policy of collective security in southern China as a way to compensate for an earlier faith in disarmament and the lack of military preparedness that ensued. By 1941, the war in southern China had become a significant consideration in the formulation of Allied grand strategy. Historically, China has not been given sufficient attention as an international arena that contributed to the expansion of a wider conflict. Hence, one goal in the pages that follow is to address this historical oversight and increase our understanding of the Second World War as a whole. Another is to demonstrate how the war in southern China helped accelerate the end of British and

Japanese imperial power, as each sought to challenge an array of enemies too numerous to fight successfully.

After years of tension and crises between China and Japan, the most serious of which involved the establishment of Manchoukuo, full-scale war erupted in July 1937. At first, many international observers expected the conflict to produce a short demonstration of Japanese military power and a quick Chinese capitulation. Certainly the Japanese believed that this would be the case, as their lack of planning or preparation attests. Until that time, senior Japanese military officers engaged in imperial expansion by exploiting Chinese political weaknesses whenever opportunities arose. In the process, they were also able to expand their own personal power. The aim for some was to create satrapies in northern China under their direct control.[1] Frequently, Japanese officers would act without authority from Tokyo and install themselves as the equivalent of new regional warlords. Until mid-1937 most Chinese opposition to Japanese encroachments was fragmentary and ineffective; thus, when the Marco Polo Bridge incident occurred in July, many Japanese thought that another opportunity for expansion was at hand. To their surprise, what began as a minor skirmish exploded into a full-scale war. Chinese forces at Peking (Beijing) were reinforced, and the Japanese position in Shanghai was seriously threatened the following month. At Shanghai, the best Chinese divisions in the army's order of battle were deployed. In leading China to war, Generalissimo Chiang Kai Shek (Jiang Jieshi) would have preferred more time to prepare the army, but delay in this case was unacceptable politically. Chinese nationalism could no longer be constrained, and the battle for Shanghai rapidly became an early major engagement of the war. The maelstrom of destruction that enveloped the city disabused many of the notion that the conflict would be swift or that the Japanese would easily emerge triumphant. Although Shanghai was eventually a battlefield defeat for China, the three-month-long struggle signaled to the world that despite the country's many political and economic problems, the Chinese people were capable of fighting, albeit in a limited way, the most powerful country in East Asia. Before the war ended several years later, however, tens of millions would die.

Chinese willingness to fight was undermined by the destruction of the army's best units at Shanghai and by the inadequacies of its remaining military forces. China's naval strength, for instance, was minuscule when compared with that of Japan. Chinese air defenses during the first four years of the war were of such poor quality that cities were frequently bombed with impunity. After Shanghai, it seemed that little could stop the Japanese advance. The Japanese wanted to make this clear at Nanking (Nanjing), but the atrocities committed there only served to unite the Chinese in hatred against them. Despite the deep-seated political divisions among China's leaders, events at Nanking helped ensure that the war would be both brutal and long. Although the Chinese retained a large army, the quality of its units varied greatly, and sufficient firepower was rarely available to fight effectively in a prolonged battle. There were several notable exceptions where the Chinese put up stiff resistance, including the battles of Shanghai and Taierhchuang (Taierzhuang), but overall, the Chinese army lacked sufficient stamina to mount sustained offensive operations. Instead, it generally retained a defensive strategic posture throughout much of the war.

Most major campaigns took place along or north of the Yangtse River, and this partly accounts for the lack of historical attention devoted to southern events. Northern China contained most of the country's industry, which made its occupation a Japanese strategic objective. Operations in the north were also relatively easy to support because the bulk of China's transportation infrastructure was located there. Since the Japanese relied heavily on mechanized forces, at least in comparison to the Chinese army, they were dependent on captured rail lines and waterways to advance farther inland and maintain their supply network. The problem facing the Japanese was insufficient troops to protect their lines of communication. As the war degenerated into a stalemate, the Chinese concentrated on waging guerrilla warfare against thinly held Japanese lifelines. Large-scale engagements were fought only when necessary. Difficult battles sometimes developed when Japanese divisions attempted to clear Chinese forces massed in mountainous base areas. During such campaigns, Japanese firepower and mobility advantages were often diminished or nullified, making a sustained defense feasible.[2] Despite such problems, the Japanese were sufficiently powerful to occupy much of the area they wanted in northern China and to hold it for as long as they wished. This was not so in the south.

The Chinese central government faced military as well as political problems, which made the defense of southern China most important for the republic's survival. In the south, the governments of Yunnan and Kwangsi (Guangxi) retained considerable political autonomy from Chungking (Chongqing). After the central government was pushed back into the mountainous stronghold of Szechwan (Sichuan), few areas that were still under Chiang's direct authority remained free from Japanese occupation. The loss of additional territory elsewhere would have undermined the Kuomintang's legitimacy to govern among China's regional leaders. Without a central government acting under the direction of Chiang's leadership, large-scale resistance likely would have ceased. This made defending southern provinces such as Hunan and Kiangsi (Jiangxi) a vital necessity. Chiang's mastery of Chinese politics also proved essential. Political factors were more influential in the war in China than in any subsequent theater of operations during World War II, but Chiang was generally able to maintain sufficient solidarity in government (with the exception of the communists far to the north in Shaanxi) to maintain resistance. He often did so by undermining or co-opting regional political opponents. From very early on, Chiang played political rivals against each other in Kwangtung (Guangdong) and Kwangsi, and in doing so, he was able to keep most of both provinces out of Japanese hands. Because southern China remained free (with the exception of Canton and a few other areas within easy reach of the Japanese navy), the country was able to continue the war. Given the innumerable problems in China, and given that most of them were the result of the country being at war with itself in one region or another since the revolution of 1912, it is remarkable that Chiang was able to maintain sufficient morale within the government and within the army to stave off defeat. Fortunately for China, Chiang's success in maintaining a relatively strong central government gave him greater credibility on the international stage, which in turn translated into greater prestige for himself and for the Kuomintang Party he headed at home.

In those regions still under Chungking's direct control, geographic and military factors were also advantageous in sustaining China's war effort. This was particularly important in the south. Below the Yangtse River, China stretches across some of the most varied terrain on earth. From the remote Himalayas to the more populated agricultural regions closer to the Pacific coast, distances were great, and the transportation infrastructure was limited or nonexistent. Once it became overextended, the Japanese army faced tremendous difficulties in making any further advances, but one of the most important provinces still barring its way to victory was Hunan. Rich agriculturally, Hunan's more mountainous southern region also contained large quantities of important rare earth metals, such as tungsten. This was also the case in neighboring Kiangsi, and together, these two provinces attracted considerable international interest as sources of strategic resources. The Japanese certainly understood the importance of Hunan, and between 1938 and 1942 they made three separate attempts to capture the provincial capital at Changsha in the hope of bringing the war to an end. These were not simply antiguerrilla campaigns or foraging expeditions; they were large-scale operations in which Chinese regulars emerged victorious. Hunan proved to be a wall against which the Japanese 11th Army battered itself apart, and many international observers took note. Because of its importance, Changsha receives much attention in this book.

After the fall of Hankow near the end of 1938 and the eventual reestablishment of the Chinese capital to Chungking, the war bogged down into a stalemate, but the chance of a negotiated peace was an ever-present possibility. Although an unaided Chinese victory was impossible, the conquest of China as a whole was also widely recognized as being beyond Japan's military capabilities. China's vastness limited the Japanese ability to occupy areas much farther inland and still maintain security over their lines of communication. With a large population and with significant international support behind them, the Chinese could afford to replace their losses and continue the war for a very long time. The only hope for the Japanese was to arrange a negotiated settlement. Divisions within the Chinese government and strains on Chinese morale made such a development possible, and officials of third powers paid close attention, looking for any signs of peace.

The Chinese received important external assistance because continuing the war became an objective of other powers. Prior to the spring of 1938, the Germans maintained a Military Mission in China to provide training on armaments purchased from German industry. In the course of their work, they helped forge the very effective divisions that fought the battle of Shanghai. As problems in Europe began to eclipse Far Eastern events, however, officials in Berlin started to see the Japanese as more useful potential allies. The German mission was therefore withdrawn. The Soviets were quick to take over where the Germans left off, as China was only one theater of potential Japanese expansion. With large military forces stationed in Manchoukuo and the home islands, the Japanese were eager to extend their influence and to control regions farther north or south. The threat to Siberia was therefore a constant source of anxiety in Moscow. Hence, the war in China grew in significance in the calculations of Premier Josef Stalin, and Soviet military aid began to pour into the country to keep the war from ending. Soviet advisers and pilots went to China in large numbers to strengthen the army's artillery arm and to bolster the ranks of the air force. After the war Soviet officers took credit for some of the operational victories in Hunan during 1939 and 1941.[3] Subsequently, all foreign military support provided to China by third powers was likewise intended to keep the Japanese bogged down in an endless cycle of attrition.

The war in China was a war for the control of supply lines, and this made southern China important in a fundamental way. With the exception of the road to the USSR, the Hunan-Kwangtung railway was the only significant line of communication to the outside world that remained in Chinese hands. Most of the essential military supplies that arrived in China passed along this corridor before reaching the armies of the 9th War Zone in Hunan. This accounted for Changsha's great significance, as it was located at the northern end of the line. The railway extended southwest into Kwangsi, where it expedited the movement of supplies from both the Burma Road and the French Indochina railway terminus in Yunnan. These routes converged at Kunming, where the road continued northeast toward the southern Chinese railhead at Kweilin. But the railway's greatest significance was that it connected Hunan directly to the only major Chinese seaport free from Japanese occupation: Hong Kong. Although the Burma Road has been cited elsewhere for its importance in sustaining the war, the line from Hong Kong to Changsha was more significant. This can be determined by comparing the useful tonnage figures for each throughout the war—a comparison that remains valid even after accounting for the Japanese occupation of Canton in October 1938. The same condition applies when the supply capacity of the Changsha–Hong Kong route is compared with that of the French railway line in northern Indochina. Hong Kong was an essential logistical component of the war, and to fully understand events, Hong Kong and southern China must be viewed together as a single military zone. Put another way, Hong Kong was an important Chinese city during the war; it was not a sleepy British imperial outpost. British involvement in the war grew deeper over time as a result of Hong Kong's importance, and this in turn influenced larger geopolitical issues. Because of this, Hong Kong features prominently in the following analysis as a source of considerable international friction.

An important reason why the Sino-Japanese War escalated international tensions was Japan's inability to stem the flow of military supplies entering China in the south. Anglo-Japanese antagonism was greatly aggravated because of the British policy of supporting the Chinese from their colonies. The Japanese needed to break the southern Chinese coalition and reduce China's logistical capacity, but the British helped prevent this. Failure to block the movement of war supplies within the Pearl River Delta caused the Japanese armed forces to increase their interdiction efforts in Kwangtung. They also attacked or seized other Chinese lines of communication, such as those in Kwangsi and Yunnan. But a maritime blockade proved to be futile so long as Hong Kong remained in British hands, and this placed the British at Hong Kong squarely in the sights of Japanese military leaders. Over time, a condition of low-intensity conflict enveloped Hong Kong, and as fighting spread across southern China, the British colony became a dangerous flash point, threatening to ignite an Anglo-Japanese war.

The war over China's lines of communication thus emerged as a larger international problem, but this certainly met with Chiang's approval. Securing active allies from abroad was always the cornerstone of Chinese strategy, and because of the supply situation at Hong Kong, the odds for success in this goal improved steadily. Chiang had reason for optimism: international interest and influence within the region remained strong, and the Japanese were both arrogant and reckless in their pursuit of imperial expansion. It was widely thought that, given enough time, other countries would become ensnared in the worsening crisis. The hope in Chungking was that the Japanese would eventually provide such a dangerous provocation to others that a powerful response would result. This scenario almost unfolded on several occasions, but Chiang had to wait several years before his goal would be reached.

Under increasing pressure in Europe, the British had few choices in responding to the worsening crisis in Asia. One option was to disengage from the region and demilitarize Hong Kong, but few wished to follow such a course due to the impact on British prestige. Another option would have been to adjust British foreign policy in Europe to a more neutral position and thereby enable the deployment of military forces for Far Eastern defense. Neither of these strategies was adopted. Instead, a proxy war in China was maintained, but direct material support in the form of munitions remained limited. Shortages in Britain were part of the problem. There was also a lack of faith in the Chinese government's abilities among most officials in London. Many in Whitehall were similarly wary of Chinese geopolitical ambitions, especially with respect to India. Thus, few were eager to provide military hardware. Support for China remained limited to loans and the continued transshipment of military supplies from other third powers through Hong Kong or Rangoon. Although British-made weapons were not provided as aid, the logistical support extended to China via Hong Kong and Burma made Britain's involvement highly significant. Until the United States became more directly involved in 1941, Britain's importance to China almost equaled that of the USSR. The Japanese understood this point clearly, and the dangerous situation at Hong Kong continued unabated as a result.

The kettle brewing at Hong Kong was heated further because those within the Foreign Office and the House of Commons who were most responsible for Far Eastern affairs saw the war in China as a useful means of finding more powerful allies in the struggle against Germany. Prior to the signing of the Nazi-Soviet Pact in August 1939, and even for some time thereafter, it was hoped that Soviet interest in China could be exploited to strengthen cooperation from the Kremlin. Risks were accepted in Asia because many continued to place great faith in the efficacy of collective security as a doctrinal solution to stem the aggression of fascist regimes. To induce greater diplomatic and military cooperation from Stalin, support for China was maintained, even as the risk to Hong Kong increased dramatically. Once it became obvious that this approach had failed, however, the British leveraged their support for China by interrupting the flow of munitions from Burma in the summer and fall of 1940. Yet British officials were not inclined to abandon their strategy, even if they temporarily shifted their aim away from the USSR. By the end of the year, the British were using their position in China to secure a more stable military partnership with the United States. Because of American interests, and particularly because of the attention paid to China by President Franklin D. Roosevelt, British policy was kept in step with U.S. policy. As the Americans increased their presence in Asia, so did the British.

Since collective security served as the doctrinal foundation for Britain's Far Eastern policy, its basic tenets and pitfalls require some clarification if the risks taken in southern China are to be fully understood. Collective security was often described by its proponents as a defensive arrangement adopted by democratically aligned countries to promote peace. Member states would cooperate in military affairs somewhat like an alliance, but theoretically, as equal partners.[4] An attack on one would be considered an attack against all. One problem with this traditional view was that the potential destabilizing impact of intervention in regional crises was frequently underestimated, and the possibility that intervention itself could be construed as an act of aggression was often overlooked. That was how the Japanese viewed the reinforcement of Hong Kong's garrison with Canadian infantry in the fall of 1941. Moreover, the potential for great powers to be drawn into conflict over relatively minor issues that they otherwise would have avoided or minimized was increased substantially; conversely, weaker states such as Canada were emboldened to take dangerous action.[5] Thus, collective security could instead be considered a policy that contributed to the escalation of world crisis toward total war. Moral and ideological considerations encouraged many British officials to act as global police. They became eager to challenge an excessive number of potential enemies from a position of military weakness in the hope of building an alliance against Germany. This was eventually accomplished, but for the British, the cost was unsustainable, and their ultimate victory was a Pyrrhic one. Moreover, the effectiveness of the alliance was constrained by Sino-British-Soviet mistrust, by internal Soviet repression, and by Stalin's lack of reciprocity.[6] Ideological factors, such as an antipathy toward nationalistic governments, and economic considerations, such as some Western officials' desire to expand and dominate neoliberal trading blocs, also impeded cooperation. Collective security failed to deter the Axis, and it failed to promote global security. Nevertheless, many officials in London maintained faith in its effectiveness, despite the inherent dangers.

The British, however, were not the sole advocates of collective security in China. Most U.S. officials wanted the war to continue, as they hoped to deter Japanese aggression. Many in the State Department, for example, believed that if the Japanese were fully occupied fighting in China, they would be less likely to expand farther south toward the Philippines. President Roosevelt and members of his cabinet shared in the ideological conviction of collective security's value, at least ostensibly, but despite their democratic rhetoric of equality, White House officials were determined that any coalition in China would be established under U.S. leadership. Moreover, as time wore on, Roosevelt came to see deterrence as only one potential goal. By increasing foreign military support to China as the international situation deteriorated, it was thought possible and eventually desirable to pressure the Japanese into stepping up their efforts in China or to focus their attention farther south. Thus, by the summer of 1941, the United States had already increased its presence and influence in China with the deployment of Military Missions and the introduction of Lend-

Lease material support. Most important was the arrival of the American Volunteer Group (AVG) under the command of Colonel Claire Chennault. Although the AVG, otherwise known as the Flying Tigers, was at first a quasi-mercenary force, it was a highly visible symbol of the American air-power that would follow in the event of a wider war. Once the Pacific war began and the British were pushed out of Burma, U.S. influence in China was uncontested by the spring of 1942.

Aside from Britain, smaller Western powers with forces in the Far East served as U.S. clients, albeit under the illusion of maintaining sovereignty. With respect to the reinforcement of Hong Kong in the fall of 1941, it has been widely assumed that Canada was simply a loyal British Dominion following instructions from London, but this is far from accurate. Although Canadian military policy remained wedded to that of Great Britain due to organizational and logistical considerations, after the fall of France, Canada's foreign policy shifted, aligning with that of America. This has been demonstrated by several Canadian historians, but the larger ramifications of such a transformation on Allied Far Eastern strategy remain unexplained.[7] As American involvement in China's affairs increased steadily following Roosevelt's reelection in 1940, Canadian involvement in China began. Hong Kong was reinforced with Canadian infantry instead of British troops because Canada's policy of military intervention in China originated from inside the White House. Thus, in addition to the AVG and Lend-Lease aid, the other important but underrecognized example of Western support to China was Hong Kong's reinforcement with Canadian troops. This topic is covered in detail in subsequent chapters.

Providing greater urgency to Anglo-American efforts was the near destruction of the Soviet Red Army and the potential for a Soviet defeat. Because of the problems with Chinese morale and the persistent possibility of peace, the decision to reinforce Hong Kong's garrison was undertaken by the Canadian government with the goal of maintaining Chinese resistance. It was a diplomatic gesture aimed at bolstering Chinese morale, with the primary objective of providing indirect support to the Soviet Union at a time when the Red Army faced destruction. Ottawa's decision to take such a step was made when the situation in the USSR appeared to be most critical—at the beginning of the battle for Moscow. The deployment kept Japanese attention fixed on China and southern operations, thereby enabling Stalin to transfer a sizable percentage of his Far Eastern forces westward. In this light, sending Canadian troops to Hong Kong was one of the most significant symbols of Western support to China prior to the outbreak of the Pacific war.

The ensuing Anglo-American military disaster was partly the result of this policy, and the most damaging consequences were felt initially at Pearl Harbor and Hong Kong in December 1941. But Allied leaders saw the outcome differently. The main purposes behind strengthening the Anglo-American commitment to China in the latter half of 1941 were to provide indirect support to the Soviets' Far Eastern flank and to solidify the alliance. Thus, officials at the highest levels in both Washington and London considered the result a success. The battle of Hong Kong should serve as a reminder, however, that the cost in lives made collective security in Asia an expensive proposition, especially for smaller powers such as Canada. Collective security was embraced during the 1930s to compensate for the effects of disarmament, but dangerous pitfalls awaited democratic societies that pushed an aggressive foreign policy from a position of military weakness. Nevertheless, advocates of disarmament were often the same officials who supported armed intervention against aggressors, but only against those with whom they were ideologically opposed. Western governments' dereliction of responsibility in the prewar years—allowing their military forces to degrade—meant that combat effectiveness had to be acquired over time, and only after hard-won battle experience had been absorbed. The development of an effective combined-arms warfare doctrine was fully realized only in 1943. Because of such a contradictory stance, Hong Kong became a military liability, yet instead of demilitarization, officials in London and Washington decided to defend the colony against Japanese attack, even though the chances of success were remote. Results across the Far East under such circumstances were easy to predict. Commonwealth casualties were high, and easy victories were absent once the fighting began.

Adherence to such conflicting policies also undermined the principles of responsible government on which much of Western civilization was based. Official attempts to downplay or conceal military deficiencies, as occurred during the Canadian Royal Commission of Inquiry on Hong Kong, may have been politically expedient in terms of maintaining public support for the war, but they ultimately helped erode governmental credibility and legitimacy. The same can be said for concealing the purpose behind the colony's reinforcement. The garrison was sacrificed purportedly to maintain Britain's position in the Far East, but there were other reasons behind the decision to reinforce Hong Kong that the public had a right to know.

Instead, these were clouded from view, thereby spurring a culture of secrecy in government inimical to the preservation of free and democratic societies. Political and diplomatic issues associated with the battle of Hong Kong therefore need to be considered jointly with military affairs so that the cost of applying collective security in the Far East can be more accurately assessed, both in terms of the lives lost and in terms of the damage inflicted by such precedents on the democratic process in the West.

Our understanding of the significance of southern China during the war has remained limited for a variety of reasons. Most historians have examined the wartime history of Hong Kong largely from a British military perspective, and less attention has been devoted to questions of foreign policy. Much research has been based on cabinet or military documents, primarily from the War Office and the Admiralty. This helps us understand Hong Kong's role as an element of the Singapore strategy and why the War Office was eager to limit British military commitments to the Far East, but it fails to fully explain why Hong Kong was reinforced in the fall of 1941. For this, Foreign Office records are essential. Additionally, historians have often overlooked the role of both the Soviet Union and Canada in China. A greater problem is that many documents have remained classified as secret for more than fifty years by the governments of both Great Britain and the United States.

Many of the documents used in this study originate from U.S. and British officials serving in Asia, as well as from lower-ranking officials working at Whitehall. These have been included in large number because Anglo-American policy in Asia during this period tended to be formulated and driven by such officials. Guidance from Washington and London was often deficient. Political figures and strategic planners in both capitals had many pressing issues to contend with, and the Far East was typically ranked low on the list of strategic priorities. Some authors have noted previously that Far Eastern affairs were often conducted within a policy vacuum that necessitated independent thinking and initiative by Anglo-American officials on the ground.[8] Franz Schurmann, for one, has explained how in this situation distance and geography made the development of different forms of warfare, compared with those used in the European theater of operations, inevitable. In the process, U.S. military officers enjoyed considerably more independence in both planning and action than their counterparts based in Europe. Littoral warfare in the Pacific emphasized airpower and fast-moving naval forces acting in concert with highly mobile infantry (either by sea or by air). Conversely, European operations were governed by the army and were concentrated geographically. Large, powerful armored formations dominated operations in a system more conducive to centralized planning and control.[9] Existing service loyalties from the prewar period also tended to be eclipsed in the Pacific by loyalties to regional commanders.[10] This autonomy in planning and action led to the development of competing military policies in the postwar period to meet the challenges posed by the onset of the Cold War. Containment of the Soviet Union was applied in Europe using the army and strategic nuclear forces, whereas rollback was adopted in Asia by the navy and the air force after the communists seized power in China. This eventually led to war in Korea and Vietnam. The origin of this process, however, was evident in China as early as 1941, and it included British officers as well as American ones. This is seen most clearly with Major General Arthur Edward Grasett, the general officer commanding British forces in China during most of the period in question. Consequently, documents originating from officials in the region form the bulk of those consulted for this study.

Before proceeding, a comment on this book's organization is in order. Material is presented chronologically. Chapters 2 and 3 lay the foundation by illustrating how the strategic value of southern China rose substantially following the outbreak of the Sino-Japanese War. This was a result of the completion of the Hunan-Kwangtung railroad in 1936. Chapters 4 through 6 detail the Japanese response to Great Britain's support for China, particularly from Hong Kong, and how the war escalated by spreading across Kwangtung, Hainan, Hunan, and Kwangsi. The development of Anglo-Japanese low-intensity conflict at Hong Kong is also described. Chapter 7 is largely concerned with the divergence in British and Soviet foreign policies and objectives in China in the wake of the Nazi-Soviet Pact, and how this almost brought the war in China to a close. Chapters 8 and 9 explain the full geopolitical significance of Hong Kong and southern China in the period after the German invasion of the Soviet Union. The reinforcement of Hong Kong is addressed in chapter 8 as a product of U.S. foreign policy, and the crescendo of violence in southern China during the battles at Changsha and Hong Kong is examined in chapter 9. These chapters also emphasize how the region was treated as an integrated Allied theater of war.

This book was written to develop a clearer picture of the global significance of southern China as it affected Allied grand strategy. In doing so,

Hong Kong can now be seen as a vital element in sustaining Chinese resistance against Japan. This state of affairs assumed greater importance when the Soviet Union faced military defeat in the west. But before the arguments and evidence are unfolded, a final comment is necessary to clarify one of the underlying themes. In examining British and American objectives and policies, and in uncovering how southern China became significant in the provision of indirect support to the Soviet Union, difficult questions are raised about Anglo-American war aims. The garrison at Hong Kong was destroyed in the process of providing aid to Stalin, but the USSR had effectively been an ally of Nazi Germany until just a few months before the reinforcement. The situation that developed at Hong Kong during the latter half of 1941 indicates that the Western governments were willing to risk their own forces to aid a totalitarian dictatorship that operated on a par with their enemies. This brings the necessity of the war into question. War aims are not the central focus of this book, but because Hong Kong was reinforced under these circumstances, and because those making the decision knew that the mission had virtually no chance of success, the value of such an enterprise becomes an issue of debate. This is especially so, given that the governments involved kept the truth about the reinforcement and the battle from public scrutiny. It is a contention of this study that although the Western Allies likely helped prevent the end of Chinese and Soviet resistance in 1941 by maintaining the transshipment of military supplies into China from Hong Kong and Burma, Allied strategy failed to provide for long-term global security. The decision to reinforce the colony was both unnecessary and ignoble.

It is hoped that this material will clarify an important element of the Second World War that has thus far received insufficient attention. From 1937 to the end of 1941, southern China became a zone of escalating violence that helped ignite the Pacific war. This occurred because several third powers found the conflict useful in influencing Japanese policy. Instead of deterring the Japanese, however, the opposite effect was produced. Because of their common interests in China, third powers also considered it possible to influence international relations in Europe. As the Western governments applied the doctrine of collective security in southern China, they hoped to establish a similar arrangement with Stalin against Hitler. But with a continuous flow of military supplies entering China, Hong Kong's significance as a nexus of international conflict in Asia grew steadily. Ultimately, when these issues helped spark the Japanese offensive in southern

China in December 1941 against both Changsha and Hong Kong, the Japanese defeat in Hunan only stiffened Chinese resolve and prevented a termination of the war. Moreover, although the battle of Hong Kong at first appeared to herald Japanese victory, it combined with the attack on Pearl Harbor to constitute one of the greatest strategic blunders of the Second World War. The Japanese engaged an array of enemies possessing enormous potential power, and once this power was harnessed, the destruction of Japan was assured. However, the price paid by Britain during the opening stages of the conflict meant that ultimate victory in 1945 came at a prohibitive cost.

TWO

■

Clearing the Decks: Preparing for War in South China, 1935 to July 1937

Chinese resistance during the Sino-Japanese War (1937–1941) was surprising to many Far Eastern observers, but the Chinese determination to continue was encouraged by third powers that provided military equipment and training. By supplying the Chinese army with large quantities of weapons during the conflict, the USSR used the Chinese to fight a proxy war against the Japanese. Similarly, but less aggressively, Great Britain allowed Hong Kong to be used as a transshipment point for munitions arriving from abroad. Hong Kong thus became a militarily strategic center in East Asia in the war against Japan. This situation was partly a product of the prewar consolidation of power in the hands of the Chinese central government under Generalissimo Chiang Kai Shek, as well as a divergence of British Far Eastern strategic goals between the Foreign Office and the military. In preparation for war, the Chinese central government improved its logistical network in southern China, and the region became a bastion of resistance in order to keep war supplies moving northward in 1937. In 1936 the Chinese greatly enhanced their military capabilities by completing major infrastructure improvements such as the Hankow-Canton railway, which served as the only all-rail link between central and southern China. The completion of this railway also increased the Chinese central government's authority over Kwangtung, allowing Chiang Kai Shek to control military operations within the province and fight the war in an area of British economic and military interest. This was similar to the strategy he employed at Shanghai in 1937. For its part, the British Foreign Office encouraged Chinese resistance by allowing Hong Kong to be used as the primary Chinese military supply source once the war began. Prior to the outbreak of war, however, diplomatic and economic steps were taken as early as 1935–1936 to stiffen Chinese resolve to challenge Japanese expansion in northern China. In the process, British foreign policy began to exceed the level of support that could be provided by British military forces. The British thus adopted a confrontational diplomatic posture from a position of military weakness, and this eventually led to a Japanese military attack on Hong Kong in 1941. Although Japanese aggression had the greatest impact on upsetting the established order in Asia, British and Chinese geopolitical maneuvering contributed to the outbreak of the Sino-Japanese War, as well as to its subsequent escalation into a war of global consequence.

The Canvas of War:
Geography and Politics in South China

One of the most important ways in which the Chinese government prepared for war was by improving transportation networks. In 1934 the total length of rail lines in China amounted to 18,000 kilometers, two-thirds of which were national railways; 2,400 kilometers were private railways, and 3,300 kilometers were foreign owned. Two years later, hard-surfaced highways totaled 43,521 kilometers in length, and there were 65,979 kilometers of dirt roads.[1] Most of this fell under Japanese control soon after the start of the war, but the establishment of the Hankow-Canton railway in 1936 was a signal event that gave the Chinese their only all-rail link to the sea through the south. For the first time, central and northern China were directly linked by a rapid transportation system to the south's most important commercial region at Canton and the British colony of Hong Kong.[2] It was an impressive engineering feat, and it proved to be commercially successful partly because it offered travelers some remarkable scenery as the railroad cut through difficult mountainous terrain. An American missionary, R. D. Rees, described it in early January 1937: "The journey is a most picturesque one, especially on the new section over the border between the two provinces. The line runs for hours up a deep gorge, the track being cut out of the side of the gorge and the river running down below."[3] A trip from Changsha to Canton took approximately thirty-three hours, and passenger trains heading south ran twice a week on Tuesday and Friday nights at 2300 hours.[4] The primary significance of the Hankow-Canton railway, however, was that it would become the core military lifeline of the south China front.

Southern geographic features presented many construction challenges, which explains why so few road and rail systems had previously been built in this region. The two great arterial lines in China that served as principal routes of commerce were the West and Yangtse rivers, terminating in the deltas near Canton and Shanghai, respectively. Between these areas lies a distinct region dominated by a series of southwest-to-northeast ridges culminating westward in a high axial range. The mountainous area north of the West River forms the watershed for both the West and the Yangtse rivers. Spurs from the ridges near the coast run toward the sea, with low areas appearing at various river mouths such as at Swatow (Shantou), Amoy (Xiamen), Foochow (Fuzhou), and Wenchow (Wenzhou). The coastal provinces are thus physically isolated on the landward side by sharply mountainous and forbidding terrain. These areas of China were largely undeveloped, with few or no lines of communication between them. People in areas separated by relatively short distances spoke dialects so different that mutual understanding was sometimes difficult or impossible.[5]

Because the mountainous terrain presented serious transportation problems, it also proved to be a formidable military barrier resulting in political divisions between the central government and the provinces of Kwangtung and Kwangsi.[6] Despite the fact that the people in the former spoke Cantonese while those in the latter spoke a dialect of Mandarin, geographic factors imposed a practical unity on Kwangtung and Kwangsi that had long been recognized farther north. Both provinces were intimately linked economically and politically, making the region a primary base of official opposition to Nanking since the early days of Chiang Kai Shek's national regime. With regard to internal administration and provincial aims, each province had gone its own way, but in terms of the broader political scene, they were generally considered together.[7] The completion of the Hankow-Canton railway greatly improved China's physical infrastructure, and this eventually proved to be invaluable to the Chinese army's logistical network. However, the railway was initially viewed as a political and economic threat to the independence of General Chen Chi Tang in Kwangtung, as well as General Li Tsung Ren (Li Zongren) and his Muslim second-in-command, General Pai

Chung Hsi (Bai Zhongxi), in Kwangsi. The Kwangsi government was considerably more efficient, responsible, and popular with the people than was the central government of Chiang Kai Shek, and this helped fuel a strong spirit of political independence across the region.[8] These southern Chinese leaders are often described as the "Kwangsi Clique."

Chinese political factions such as the Kwangsi Clique made centralized political control and unified military resistance against Japan difficult to achieve, and divisions between the central government and southern Chinese factions eventually had a significant impact on the security of Hong Kong as well. A clique in China was unlike a Western party; it was more fluid and had less organization, and there was little concern for ideology. It most closely resembled the military factions of Japan. Personalities counted for more than principles, and personal relationships based on quasi-feudal loyalty were the glue that bound followers to their chief. The power of the cliques was derived from the possession of solid support, such as that given by an army or a party machine, or from the personal prestige of members. No clique could hope to secure unlimited power. Its aim was to secure control of part of the governmental machine, such as an army or a ministry. Warfare between the cliques was tempered by an old Chinese tradition of compromise and a willingness to share power while sparing the "face" of opponents—a tradition that in some ways compensated for the notable absence of the rule of law. Acts of violence and unbridled aggression did take place and sent shock waves through the political organism, but these episodes did not occur very frequently; when they did, they elicited surprise, since the violence was often successful.[9]

Although the Chinese government was authoritarian, it generally posed no ideological threat to regional leaders because the power was somewhat diffused throughout the ruling upper class. Determining which star was in ascendance at any given time, however, was not always easy. A peculiarity of the struggle among the cliques was its concealment from view. Every now and then, the personal stock of some leading figure rose or fell sharply; then there would be a sensational dismissal, and political power would shift in one direction. But it was often unclear precisely what had happened. Secrets and speculation were clogged by the number of different rumors that followed every change in political relations. In this atmosphere, Chiang was not an all-powerful dictator. His position resembled that of a Caesar or Pompey in Rome or the tyrant of an Italian medieval state. He had to juggle, maneuver, and balance groups and conciliate individuals by the gift of patronage. His orders might have been obeyed, but if they were inconvenient and were not related to matters of the first magnitude, they would sometimes be lost or forgotten. Further complicating the situation was the fact that China was still immersed in civil strife, and during the revolution, many of the institutions that commanded obedience by the tradition they embodied had vanished. It was the personal prestige and individual power of Chiang Kai Shek that kept the central government functioning. Amidst this chaos, many foreign observers maintained that some form of dictatorship was necessary, despite its disadvantages. Thus, after years of conflict with Nanking, the southern generals defended their autonomy to the utmost extent and concentrated their efforts on maintaining the region's economic and political stability. This soon made Kwangsi the best-governed province in China.[10]

Central governmental authority was also resisted because of the rich deposits of strategic minerals in southern China and the revenue they generated for provincial governments. Many of these metals were found in the southern portion of Hunan. The most important was tungsten (wolfram), amounting to 90 percent of Chinese production. China also accounted for approximately 60 to 70 percent of the global production of antimony, half of which was exported to the United States. Manganese and molybdenum were present in substantial quantities as well. Large tin deposits were mined by General Lung Yun in Yunnan (combined with the tin from Hunan, production equaled 8,000 tons per year). Manganese was located in Kwangsi and Kwangtung, whereas Kiangsi and Kwangtung also contained a great deal of tungsten.[11] These strategic materials helped provide southern provincial governments with the necessary resources to run relatively effective and popular administrations.

During the mid-1930s Chiang Kai Shek increased his efforts to consolidate control over the various tungsten-rich regions. His first objective was to occupy Kiangsi after the ejection of the communists. This was accomplished with the installation of General Yu Han Mou from Kwangtung as his representative. The Long March of the Chinese Communist Party under Chairman Mao Tse Tung (Mao Zedong), which lasted from 1934 to 1935, began in this region. While General Yu was in control of the Kiangsi tungsten mines, he amassed great personal wealth and cemented his loyalty to the Kuomintang and to Chiang Kai Shek personally. It was not long before Yu became a prominent and controversial figure in the Chinese government in terms of influencing the future of Kwangtung and Hong Kong.[12]

Another factor that led to Kwangsi's and Kwangtung's disaffection with the central government was Chiang's failure to counter the steady expansion of Japanese control over northern China. Japanese officers such as General Itagaki Seishiro, chief of the Mukden Special Service Agency, and Major General Doihara Kenji, also of the Kwantung Army's military intelligence arm, were able to consolidate their position in Manchuria, and by 1935 they began work to establish the puppet Hopei (Hebei)-Chahar Political Council over the provinces of Suiyuan, Chahar, Jehol (Rehe), Hopei, and Shantung (Shandong). The Japanese strategy of pitting northern regional warlords against each other often succeeded by utilizing bribery, subversion, and terror.[13] They were able to maintain "a measure of control over North China by the instigation of incidents with resultant military intervention or threat of such intervention."[14] Doihara also built up a considerable opium distribution network throughout northern China and Manchuria.[15] One example of the intimidation tactics used against the Chinese was the construction of a Japanese army barracks and armored fighting vehicle (AFV) motor pool in the Chapei district of Shanghai; regular armed patrols were dispatched from this facility and sent throughout the city. A Canadian diplomatic report described this installation:

In the very heart of the most densely populated quarter the Japanese have raised a four-storied barracks of heavy steel and concrete construction. This building which is some 400 feet in length provides living quarters for a considerable garrison and houses in addition a formidable fleet of armoured cars, mobile guns, and tanks. On all sides a fire-area has been cleared and machine gun emplacements are reported to have been constructed to enable the defenders to cover every angle of approach. Solid steel doors and shutters add to the defensibility of the barracks. Issuing from this building the Japanese troops hold periodical manoeuvers, particularly for their mechanized units, through the crowded Chinese streets. Needless to say the necessity of avoiding Japanese tanks and of watching Japanese troops practice bayonet charges in their business streets does nothing to reconcile the Chinese inhabitants to the presence of their detested enemies.[16]

Because of Japanese expansion and intimidation in north China, anti-Japanese sentiment had grown strong across the country, but the leaders in Kwangsi and Kwangtung were perhaps the most vocal on this issue, and they wanted Chiang to take a more confrontational approach. Chiang, however, continued to bide his time with the Japanese, intending to accomplish the destruction of the communists first.[17]

Chinese Strategy: Military Logistics and the Dismantling of Southern Independence

In late 1935 and early 1936 two events engineered by Chiang Kai Shek precipitated a political crisis that seemingly threatened to wreck his government and fragment the country, yet the opposite effect was produced. In response to ongoing international criticism, Chiang began to suppress China's opium trade as an element of the New Life Movement. This act heightened the political friction that already existed between the central government and many provincial leaders.[18] Reporting on conditions in the north, U.S. military attaché Lieutenant Colonel Nelson Margetts noted, "The traffic in narcotics in China is enormous. . . . Travellers from Shensi Province reported seeing poppy fields reaching clear to the horizon."[19] In March 1936 U.S. military attaché Colonel Joseph Stilwell reported that "Jehol is one vast poppy field," and it was estimated that 90 percent of the global opium supply originated in China.[20] Opium was grown mostly in outlying provinces, so Chiang's antidrug campaign was designed to increase centralized power by taking revenue out of the hands of provincial officials. The impact on Kwangsi and Kwangtung was tremendous because great quantities of opium were shipped through the region into Burma, Indochina, Thailand, Hong Kong, and the Malay states. General Lung Yun was the independent general in charge of Yunnan, and as such, he made a fortune dealing in opium. Opium use was also common among Yunnan's regiments, although this was not the case in Kwangsi.[21] The redirection of the opium trade hit the Kwangsi and Kwangtung provincial leaders hard, destroying much of their revenue and thus threatening their autonomy.

The second event impacting Chiang's relations with Generals Chen, Pai, and Li was the completion of the Hankow-Canton railway (see figure 2.1). A primary reason for its construction was to facilitate the transportation of military supplies for the Chinese national army, but it presented a problem to Kwangsi and Kwangtung leaders. Over a period of several years, the German Military Mission had achieved some remarkable results in training the Chinese army, but as this transformation progressed, southern leaders grew more concerned that these improvements would facilitate the spread

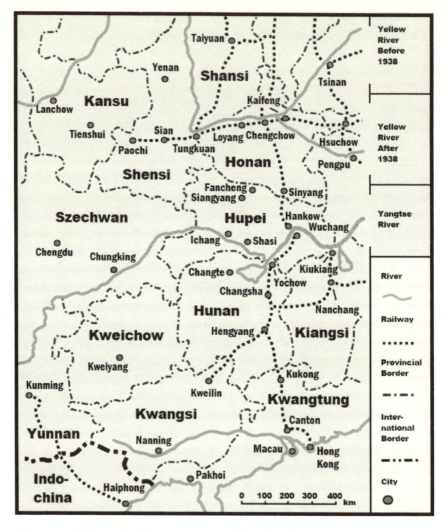

Figure 2.1. Railways in China (1940). (Based on data from NARA, RG 165, M1444, reel 11, Report No. 9842 by Captain F. P. Munson, 11 January 1940.)

of central governmental authority. Completion of the railway meant that good-quality troops could be rapidly deployed against Kwangsi and Kwangtung, constituting a direct military threat to their independence. Consequently, the redirection of Yunnan opium to the Yangtse River in 1935 and the establishment of the Hankow-Canton railway in 1936 caused the Kwangsi and Kwangtung generals to embark on a war with Nanking. Chiang Kai Shek immediately sent 600,000 troops to Hunan to counter them in June 1936.[22]

The 1936 Kwangtung-Kwangsi rebellion was a watershed event in the central government's consolidation of power over China's southern provinces. It also laid the foundation for Chiang's successful strategy of escalating the war with Japan and entangling third powers in it. During the first half of the 1930s, Chen Chi Tang was the political and military leader of Kwangtung, and up until 1936, he worked with Chiang Kai Shek. But according to one British official, "the co-operation had always to be purchased, for he was not so much Chiang's supporter as his rival . . . he was only half-hearted in co-operating with the Central Government troops, his one determination being to retain hold over Kuangtung against his rivals and equally to prevent Chiang's domination from being extended to Kuangtung."[23]

In 1935 the double threats posed by Japanese expansion and the increase in the central government's authority caused much attention to be given to "the question of defence, and on the completion in the summer of 1936 of the track of the Hankow-Canton Railway, the clash between Canton and Nanking became inevitable."[24] On 10 June 1936 Chen Chi Tang issued a circular telegram denouncing Chiang Kai Shek. He called for the nation to embark on a war against Japan, and his forces subsequently invaded Hunan. By 25 June General Pai and General Li both sided with Chen, and they soon dispatched Kwangsi armies to join his rebellion. There was no such favorable response from Yunnan, Szechwan, or elsewhere; Chen's financial position was weak, and it was difficult to buy the additional support needed to make the rebellion a success.

Chiang Kai Shek had deeper pockets, and this tipped the balance in his favor. General Yu Han Mou, who had been born in the Kwangtung town of Kaoyao, was originally part of this group of southern generals, but on 9 July he flew to Nanking with several Kwangtung air units and defected to the central government.[25] Yu's betrayal of Chen destroyed the southern coalition and ended any possibility of Kwangtung's independence. His defection, however, was generally considered to be "the greatest single factor in the avoidance of civil war between Canton and Nanking in 1936."[26] For about another month, the Kwangsi armies faced the central government's forces in Hunan, and some minor skirmishes were reported, but by 8 August General Li and General Pai ended their challenge and agreed to support the central government.[27]

Chiang sought a relatively bloodless peace with Kwangsi and Kwangtung because of the ever-present threat of the Japanese army. But he helped ensure that the two provinces remained politically disunited by showing leniency toward the Kwangsi leadership and somewhat harsher treatment toward Kwangtung officers. Generals Li Tsung Ren and Pai Chung Hsi retained their positions in Kwangsi following this incident, as Chiang sought to maintain national unity. Reconciliation talks proceeded during September, and Kwangsi remained a quasi-independent region.[28] Following the outbreak of war with Japan, these officers continued to support the government, and both Li and Pai became prominent generals. Pai eventually became Chiang's right-hand man as deputy chief of the General Staff.[29] Throughout 1938 Kwangsi troops fought in the north in defense of Hankow, and Kwangsi leaders were paid $2 million per month in exchange. Railway construction from Hunan to Kwangsi also began.[30] Despite these developments, other Kwangsi leaders remained distrustful of the central government until the war's end.

Kwangtung: Origins of a Combat Zone

As noted, Chiang dealt with Kwangtung officers somewhat less benevolently, and the continued presence of national army troops in the province deepened Cantonese disaffection with the central government. For his loyalty to Chiang, General Yu was made head of military forces and pacification commissioner in Kwangtung after General Chen fled to Hong Kong. Chen remained in Hong Kong until the war started in July 1937, when he was rehabilitated in another effort by Chiang to strengthen Chinese unity against the Japanese invader. Chiang took additional punitive steps to reduce Kwangtung's independent power, further cutting provincial revenues. One example was the suppression of Cantonese casino operations in Shumchun (Shenzhen), at the border with Hong Kong. Shumchun, home to a luxury gambling resort, had easy access to Canton via the Kowloon-Canton railway and had captured a good percentage of Macau's gambling revenue.[31] Underpinning these events in Kwangtung was a current of popular regional separatism and resentment; in time, this produced a degree of political apathy among some Cantonese following the Japanese invasion and occupation of Canton in October 1938.

Thanks to the administration of his loyal Cantonese subordinate General Yu, Chiang derived several military and diplomatic advantages by assuming direct control over Kwangtung. First, regional defense considerations were subordinated to national interests; thus, all military supplies coming into China from Hong Kong remained in Chiang's hands. Powerful, independent regional officers would have kept a considerable amount of this material for themselves, challenging his authority yet again. In later years, this is what happened with General Lung in Yunnan. Second, relatively good-quality Cantonese military forces could be deployed elsewhere during important campaigns. In the fall of 1938 four Cantonese divisions proved their worth in the Hankow campaign during combat operations at Tehan, south of the Yangtse River near Nanchang. The Japanese 101st and 106th Divisions were both badly hurt in their battles with Kwangtung forces. The deployment of Cantonese troops to central China also made it easier for Chiang to maintain control of their home province using weaker units of limited combat value.[32] Third, because the central government could deploy its own troops into Kwangtung, Chiang could ensure that the province became a greater international concern by maintaining the Pearl River Delta as an active war zone adjacent to Hong Kong for a protracted period. After the Japanese invasion of south China began in the fall of 1938, Chiang ordered his military forces to withdraw north into the Kwangtung mountains, and the smuggling of war supplies into China was temporarily disrupted by the occupation of Canton. War supplies from Hong Kong soon started moving, however, through Mirs Bay up to Waichow (Huizhou) and then on to the Hankow-Canton railway at Kukong (Shaoguan, Shiuchow, or Shuikwan), where Yu reestablished his base. Consequently, a constant state of war was maintained near and within the British colony, with the aim of straining Anglo-Japanese relations. The resulting tension escalated the war by directly involving Britain in a low-intensity military conflict with Japan for more than four years. Major General F. S. G. Piggott of the British embassy in Tokyo noted that it was fairly well understood, even among Japanese officers, that Chiang Kai Shek was not displeased to have the Japanese army posted on Hong Kong's doorstep. Fighting the war in areas of international economic interest was a strategy Chiang employed wherever possible, and this was demonstrated at Shanghai in the summer and fall of 1937 and in Kwangtung until 1941.[33]

Japanese Strategy: Stumbling Off to War

Japanese strategy in China was much less focused than Chiang's and occasionally counterproductive. Interservice rivalry was a problem within the military command structure of most countries at the time, but nowhere was this more pronounced than between the Imperial Japanese Army and Navy. Japanese army officers such as General Itagaki of the Kwantung Army and Tojo Hideki, Kwantung Army chief of staff, considered war with the USSR to be inevitable within five years, and they were eager to consolidate their country's expanded position in north China.[34] They did not wish to see a protracted war develop in China. Japanese naval officers were more intent on seeking objectives in the south. Captain Nakahara Yoshimasa, a cruiser captain who was later promoted to admiral as head of the War Guidance Office of the Navy General Staff (in 1940), was one of those pressing for a strategic advance south at this early stage. According to one account, his future moniker would be "King of the South Seas."[35]

One of three significant crises in China during the last half of 1936 showed that the lack of a unified Japanese strategy was a contributing factor in starting the Sino-Japanese War and that Japanese actions led to the involvement of third powers. These three events consisted of an attack on a Japanese consulate at Chengtu in August, anti-Japanese riots and subsequent deaths at Pakhoi (Beihai) in western Kwangtung in September, and the rout of Japanese-controlled Mongolian cavalry in the Suiyuan incident later that year.[36] The Pakhoi incident was the most serious of these because it occurred in an area of British and French economic interest. In response to several riots and killings, the Japanese navy landed marines and temporarily occupied Hainan Island, which positioned them along the lines of communication between the British in China and the French in Indochina. Anglo-French shipping passed through this area between Haiphong and Hong Kong, and in addition to provoking war with China, the presence of Japanese naval and air units at Haikow raised international concern about potential interference with maritime traffic. Tensions eased only after the Japanese army forced the navy to withdraw from Hainan so that it could remain focused on checking Soviet influence in the north.[37] The Pakhoi incident was one early example of how Japan's lack of a unified strategy had

the potential to involve Britain and France in the Sino-Japanese dispute unnecessarily, when Japan's primary interests lay elsewhere. This counterproductive situation would emerge again in Kwangtung once the war began.

British Foreign Policy: Choosing Sides

British Far Eastern policy and military strategy prior to the Sino-Japanese
War were originally based on diplomatic neutrality and remained largely
defensive. However, Japanese expansion into north China caused the British Foreign Office and Treasury to adopt a more interventionist approach
in support of China. Primarily for economic reasons, a stronger China was
considered more important to British interests than an unrivaled Japan,
and Sino-British relations gradually improved. Yet initial steps were limited
because British strategic priorities were identified elsewhere, and the country was militarily weak. Europe was the primary area of interest, followed
by the Middle East. In the Far East, however, the British were still motivated to protect imperial and economic interests. British investment in
China totaled $1.8 billion and accounted for 57 percent of the total foreign
commitment. The United States had investments equaling $220 million,
while France and Germany had invested $180 million and $140 million, respectively.[38] The Colonial Office, the War Office, and the Admiralty similarly prepared for a defensive posture in the Far East, and their plans were
based on the Singapore strategy, but unlike the Foreign Office and the
Treasury, their efforts remained rooted in a more neutral foundation. Two
major events marked a point of divergence in policy between these departments of government: the Chinese currency crisis of 1935, and the Sian
(Xian) incident of 1936.

In September 1935 the British made one of their first cautious moves to
counter Japanese advances in China when senior Treasury official Sir Frederick Leith-Ross arrived in Shanghai to become economic attaché to the British
embassy in Peking and head of the British Economic Mission to China. This
also led to one of the first links between Hong Kong and the Sino-Japanese
dispute. Leith-Ross had been sent to China to help solve the Chinese currency crisis and to improve the British trade position at Japanese expense.
Because of British military unpreparedness, however, avoidance of war with
Japan still remained a fundamental principle of British foreign policy.[39]

The Chinese silver shortage was a result of President Roosevelt's failed
attempts to dampen the effects of the Great Depression in America.[40] His

silver policy wrecked the previously favorable Chinese exchange rate, and exports plummeted. However, this crisis provided the British with an opportunity to influence Sino-Japanese affairs. Silver flowed out of the Chinese ports of Shanghai and Canton as the U.S. government became the metal's largest purchaser. Hugh Keenleyside, a Canadian diplomat posted to Japan, had visited China and explained how the crisis impacted Sino-Japanese relations:

> The silver policy of the United States Government has been the last and one of the most severe blows from which the financial and commercial structure of China is suffering and this action of the President and Congress of the United States may very possibly have the ironic result of forcing China to bow more quickly and more completely to the tremendous pressure that is now being exerted upon that unhappy country by Japan. Even Canton, the centre of the most peaceful and most prosperous districts of China, and the centre also of the Anti-Japanese Movement, has been forced to recognize the inevitable and to abate the southern Government's official policy of antagonism to Japan.[41]

The Japanese were eager to exploit the situation and offered financial relief in the form of a currency loan in exchange for the transfer of additional sovereignty in provinces such as Shantung. In an effort to quell the rising level of anti-Japanese propaganda emanating from Kwangtung and Kwangsi over these and other issues, General Doihara visited officials in Canton in April 1935 to threaten them into line. This had the added effect of creating a war scare in Hong Kong, as residents thought the city was about to be attacked along with Canton. Keenleyside noted the impact on Hong Kong's residents:

> It is difficult to understand upon what basis the apprehensions of the people of Hong Kong are founded unless it is due merely to a realization of the fact that in the event of such a war their territory would be the first point of attack and that their imaginations have been so excited by this fact that balanced judgement has become impossible. This war atmosphere was not apparent in any other city visited.[42]

Fear of invasion was still premature.

Although an Anglo-Japanese war was not imminent, Hong Kong soon became a nexus to the Sino-Japanese dispute. U.S. Consul General C. Hoover reported to Secretary of the Treasury Henry Morgenthau that the Chinese were to blame for the situation because of their illegal smuggling of silver into the colony. This violated an earlier agreement between the British and the Chinese, signed in April, to end the export of silver from China, but Chinese banks in Hong Kong continued to engage in this business. Hong Kong thus served as a useful financial center, which helped aggravate the Chinese silver crisis. This gave the British Treasury, with Foreign Office approval, an opportunity to intervene as China's quiet ally, offering credit against Japanese economic and diplomatic pressure. By November, Leith-Ross's efforts to increase British intervention were largely successful, and the Chinese accepted his assistance in stabilizing the currency. In retaliation, the Japanese navy initiated smuggling operations from Hong Kong and Formosa in order to undermine the authority of the Chinese Maritime Customs Service and cut the Chinese government's revenue by up to one-third.[43] Hong Kong thus became a center for Sino-Japanese economic warfare as early as 1935, and this ultimately had a negative impact on Anglo-Japanese diplomatic relations.

Another opportunity for the British to strengthen their growing partnership with the Chinese presented itself in late 1936 during the Sian incident. The Young Marshal Chang Hsueh Liang (Zhang Xueliang) kidnapped Chiang Kai Shek during the latter's visit to Sian in December in an attempt to destabilize the central government for the benefit of the Chinese Communist Party (CCP).[44] Mao had encouraged the kidnapping in order to strengthen his own position, but unfortunately for Mao, Stalin was anxious to use China as a bulwark against Japanese ambitions in Siberia. As the threat to Chiang Kai Shek's life was quite real, Minister of Finance H. H. Kung summoned the Russian chargé d'affaires and informed him that if Chiang was killed, China would side with Japan and help invade Russia in any future war.[45] Kung's threat had the desired effect. Stalin exerted his influence over the CCP to help end the incident, but he did not act alone. William H. Donald, the Australian adviser to Chiang Kai Shek, also played an important role in securing his release. Several years after the incident, B. E. F. Gage, a consul general at Nanking in 1937, noted: "Those who were in China in 1937 & 1938 remember with gratitude his [Donald's] patriotism and helpful attitude towards H. M. Embassy. He has played a big part in the life of the Chiang Kai-shek's & it should not be forgotten that it was mainly his influence with the Young Marshal (Chang Hsueh-liang) that enabled Chiang Kai-shek to get away with his life from Sian in 1936."[46] The Foreign Office presented Donald with an award for his role in the affair.

The Sian incident was thus an important event whereby Sino-British relations were improved by the covert action of a British Foreign Office asset.

British Military Strategy: False Security

In the military sphere, cooperation was established between Great Britain and China. This too helped improve relations between the two countries, but only on a limited scale. British Far Eastern military strategy was defensive and was still somewhat in step with British foreign policy, but it was similarly flawed in that it had the potential to encourage Japanese aggression. Plans for operations north of Singapore were centered on Hong Kong, but these were intended only for imperial defense; these operations were unrelated to any role the colony might play within China. Military policy of the 1930s was formed in a climate of disarmament and could not support a strong defense of the Far East, nor could it support an aggressive foreign policy. Germany was assumed to be England's primary threat, and in any future European conflict, Britain would require military support from its empire, rather than the reverse. The British Empire was militarily overstretched, and the so-called Singapore strategy was developed to compensate for this military weakness. Singapore was established as the primary naval base in the Far East, and sizable British naval forces were to be deployed from home waters in the event of a crisis.[47] The primary objective remained the protection of Australia and New Zealand, but ultimately, the Singapore strategy proved hollow for the defense of Far Eastern interests.

The more permanent elements of Britain's South China Fleet based at Hong Kong were not very strong; they included five gunboats of the West River Flotilla and the 2nd Motor Torpedo Boat Flotilla, with HMS *Tamar* serving as naval headquarters. Until 1940, Hong Kong also served as the base for a cruiser squadron, but the Royal Navy's function in China was largely diplomatic. In May 1935 Royal Navy units at Hong Kong and Chinese naval units conducted joint antipiracy actions near the colony's territorial waters. British destroyer patrols also worked with Chinese naval patrols at Bias Bay, with the *Hai Chi* serving as flagship for three cruisers and 200 Chinese marines. Additional military cooperation of a minor nature also began when Lieutenant Colonel W. Dawson was attached to instruct at the Chinese School of Military Mechanisation at Nanchang.[48]

In the event of war with Japan, the plan in 1939 was to relieve the garrison at Hong Kong 90 days after the arrival of the main battle fleet at Singapore. This unrealistic interval was raised to 130 days by 1941. The Singapore strategy was maintained because there were few military alternatives to address what was essentially a diplomatic problem. The British were drifting toward war with too many enemies, and their military weakness only encouraged their adversaries.[49] Britain thus had several options to adequately defend the empire: (1) confront fewer enemies in Europe and strengthen military forces in the Far East, (2) demilitarize Hong Kong, or (3) deter the Japanese with the illusion of strength provided by the Singapore strategy. The third option was selected, but it proved to be counterproductive because it had little deterrent value. A false sense of security stemmed from British overconfidence and an underestimation of Japanese military capabilities—views held by many in London. These were later reinforced by Japan's lack of success in China.[50] Instead of deterring Japanese aggression, the Singapore strategy invited attack; it maintained a weak British military presence at Hong Kong, but southern Kwangtung was a region where the possibility of conflict could only grow stronger. The actual result in late 1941 and early 1942 was the loss of Hong Kong followed by the loss of Singapore and the deaths of tens of thousands. The only military force that had deterred the Japanese from attacking until that time was the U.S. Navy's Pacific Fleet.

To maintain British prestige, Hong Kong was not demilitarized, even though the colony was expected to become a battleground. Between 1934 and 1937 the British Chiefs of Staff decided that air and ground forces for operations north of Singapore were unavailable and that the growth of Japanese airpower made the likelihood of relieving Hong Kong more remote. Although the Singapore strategy had become less viable, the utility of defending Hong Kong was still seen in its role as an outpost that could draw away forces that might otherwise be used against Singapore itself. Thus, the Admiralty and the War Office took some measures to strengthen Hong Kong's fixed defenses but did not address the real problem of increasing the size of the ground forces or their mobile firepower to a satisfactory level. Improvements were made largely in anticipation of a naval attack. The general officer commanding British forces in China, Major

General A. H. Bartholomew, estimated that the garrison needed to be raised to seven battalions of infantry and still required five fighter squadrons to augment Royal Air Force No. 715 Reconnaissance Squadron. Approved defense expenditures by the end of 1936 included £20 million (US$97 million) for facilities, such as construction of a new headquarters and barracks at Stanley. Naval fortifications and gun improvements began in late 1936 after the expiration of the Washington Naval Agreement. One thousand mines were unloaded at the Hong Kong dockyard during June 1937—the first such shipment in many years. More ten-inch guns were also landed. Construction on Stonecutter's Island provided gas- and bomb-proof subterranean shelters for 3,000 people. There was also a small but insufficient increase in the size of the field artillery. By the time Governor Sir Andrew Caldecott left Hong Kong in April 1937 (succeeded by Governor Sir Geoffry Northcote), the cost of defense improvements amounted to £8 million, but serious deficiencies remained in the event of a landward attack from the north. Nevertheless, with these limited improvements, Hong Kong remained an imperial outpost and the first line of defense in the Far East.[51]

Aside from physical deficiencies, there was also a lack of understanding among officers serving in the colony as to the seriousness of Britain's situation at Hong Kong, and this too encouraged Japanese antagonism. One example occurred during the colony's military maneuvers held in March 1937—an event that undermined the value of the newly constructed defense works. Much of the exercise was directed against a possible naval assault, and four infantry battalions of Hong Kong's ground force also participated: the Welsh Fusiliers, the Royal Irish Rifles, the Seaforth Highlanders, and the Kumaon Rifles. They were supported by the Hong Kong and Singapore Royal Artillery, plus men from the Royal Engineers and the Hong Kong Volunteer Defence Corps. All these units participated, but they were inadequate to fully man the main defense line in the New Territories, known as Gindrinkers' Line. This problem was compounded by the requirements of simultaneously defending against an attempted amphibious landing. Just one month after the annual defense exercise was held, the Chiefs of Staff in London recommended continuing the policy of defending Hong Kong in case of attack, but they also recommended sending ground reinforcements; the latter suggestion was not acted on.

The main problem with the maneuvers, however, was the presence of a certain Major Ohira of the Imperial Japanese Army, who had been invited to attend by one Colonel Harrison. Colonel Lance Dennys at the War Office noted that an official Chinese request to send their own observers had been refused. This created unnecessary friction with the Chinese government and caused it to question British intentions in the region, especially as the reason given for the refusal was related to security. Prior to the start of the maneuvers, Captain Charles R. Boxer of army intelligence was so concerned about the looming breach of security posed by Ohira's presence that he informed Major General F. S. G. Piggott, military attaché in Tokyo, that Ohira would have access to almost all defense installations. Boxer noted in frustration that the Japanese would never let a British officer see their fortified defenses situated around Japan or Formosa. Despite the security threat, Ohira's invitation was not canceled because the British did not want to offend the Japanese army.[52] Thus, because of the 1937 military maneuvers, the Japanese had a full understanding of how the British intended to defend Hong Kong against an attack.

The Hawser Is Fastened

Up to the outbreak of war in July 1937, the Japanese continued to extend their influence in China, and the British and Chinese governments responded in a variety of ways. The Chinese prepared for war with infrastructure expansion projects and political coercion of regional governments. Railroad construction provided rapid, direct ground transportation to south China and Hong Kong for the first time. This, in turn, precipitated a political crisis engineered by the central government that allowed Chiang Kai Shek to consolidate his grip on south China.[53] Increased control over Kwangtung meant that in the event of any future Japanese military operations near Hong Kong, Chiang could control the pace of Chinese logistical operations in the region to better his chances of involving England directly in the war.

For their part, the British sought to protect their interests by slowly and quietly improving diplomatic and economic relations with the Chinese, but also by avoiding direct conflict with the Japanese. The Singapore strategy provided the illusion of security, since British Far Eastern policy lacked a realistic appreciation of Japanese military capabilities. Hong Kong's landward defenses thus remained weak. Ultimately, however, Hong Kong's strategic importance was not based on its role as an imperial outpost. Hong Kong was strategically important because of its large port facilities and because of the new railway connection to central China via Canton. With strengthened Sino-British relations, Hong Kong would become a source of military supply for the Chinese army and a vital lifeline for Chinese survival in the Sino-Japanese War.

■

THREE

The Sino-Japanese War Begins: Proxy War in China, July 1937 to October 1938

With the outbreak of the Sino-Japanese War in July 1937, China assumed greater significance on the world's diplomatic stage, but aside from the Soviet Union, most other countries lacked clear objectives or policies for responding to events. For several powers, China appeared to be a significant bulwark against further Japanese expansion, and the Soviet Union extended material aid in support of the Chinese army and air force. In this way, Stalin used Chinese military forces to fight a proxy war of attrition against the Japanese army. The British Foreign Office also began to see the Chinese army as a means of waging a proxy war against Japan. With the war in Spain ongoing, some in the Foreign Office, under the leadership of Anthony Eden, saw China as a useful vehicle to promote the establishment of a collective security agreement with the Soviet Union; thus, vast amounts of war supplies were allowed to be transshipped from Hong Kong into free China. From the outset of the Sino-Japanese War, the Hankow-Canton railway was the most vital Chinese military lifeline, since the port of Hong Kong became the primary source of war materials from abroad.

In contrast to the Foreign Office, Britain's military services remained focused on the preservation of imperial security and endeavored to limit commitments by maintaining Hong Kong's status as an outpost of the British Empire. These contradictory policies led to a discussion in Whitehall during August 1938 on a Chinese-inspired scheme to encourage greater

British intervention with the purchase of the New Territories. This plan ultimately stalled, but it remains useful in demonstrating how conflicting Far Eastern objectives among various governmental departments in London impeded the formulation of a useful strategy to meet the challenge posed by Japan. In short, after years of disarmament, Foreign Office objectives increasingly outdistanced military capabilities, and as the country's foreign policy became more confrontational, its Far Eastern military strategy became less effective.[1]

Japanese strategic planning also lacked uniformity. From the battle of Shanghai onward, Japanese army commanders continued to expand the scale of the war on their own initiative; simultaneously, a variety of diplomatic efforts were mounted to impose peace. Because of the threat posed by the USSR, Japan had originally hoped to limit military commitments in China, but the strength of resistance surprised many senior officials. To end the war quickly, the navy conducted an aggressive aerial and naval interdiction campaign along China's lines of communication to neighboring areas. Although southern Chinese ports were blockaded, foreign shipping could still enter and depart from Hong Kong, so the colony became the warehouse through which the greater part of all munitions and supplies to the central government passed.[2] Chinese resistance continued despite the grave losses sustained, largely because of this constant flow of supplies.

The transshipment of military supplies from Hong Kong to the Chinese army was a significant factor that contributed to the outbreak of the Pacific war. To secure greater international support, especially from Great Britain, Chiang Kai Shek fought the war in areas of foreign economic interest, and the use of Hong Kong as a strategic military logistical center was an element of this strategy. Its port capacity and connection to central China by rail caused Japanese officers to perceive the British colony as a significant obstacle to victory. Strained Anglo-Japanese relations were the result, and preliminary moves to effect Hong Kong's isolation started with the political destabilization of Kwangtung. Chinese morale was often under great strain, and during 1938 the Japanese strove to eat away at the Chinese central government's legitimacy by neutralizing the province of Kwangtung both politically and militarily. In doing so, they hoped to sever Chinese lines of communication. Violence spread across the province by air and by sea, and a state of low-intensity conflict with Britain blanketed the region surrounding Hong Kong. Japanese frustration over their growing military difficulties led to an increasingly violent blockade, and as the war progressed, Hong Kong's military function as the primary Chinese supply depot helped escalate the conflict from a regional problem into a devastating war of global destruction. Upon its conclusion, Japan lay prostrate, while British exhaustion led to a forfeiture of empire. Southern China was the trap that ensnared them both.

Chinese Strategy:
Escalation and Third-Power Intervention

Hong Kong's transformation from peacetime entrepôt to military supply base was not accidental; it resulted from a shift in British foreign policy in support of China against Japan, alongside a separate planned consolidation of power by the Chinese central government over Kwangtung. With British cooperation from the summer of 1937 through the fall of 1938, the Chinese transformed the Pearl River Delta into a vital conduit of military supply. Japanese military forces were quick to respond, attacking Chinese supply lines from the air and at sea. Over time, the escalation of violence across the Pearl River Delta produced a corresponding increase in friction between the British and the Japanese, and eventually the operation of this logistical network from Hong Kong provoked a Japanese invasion of the region in October 1938. The Japanese occupation was not unforeseen by the Chinese, however, nor was it entirely undesired by the central government.[3] By invading Kwangtung, Japanese and British military forces came into close proximity, and the potential for direct conflict between the two powers steadily grew. Bringing this situation about was a Chinese strategic objective, and in order to drag the British into the war, Kwangtung had purposely been kept in a state of military unpreparedness, thus encouraging the Japanese to invade.

Throughout the course of the war, Generalissimo Chiang Kai Shek sought to meet the threat posed by Japan by employing foreign military experts to train and equip his inadequate forces. The Chinese army varied in quality from unit to unit, but it was generally inferior to the Japanese army and was capable of only limited offensive operations under the most favorable conditions. Many problems plagued the Chinese army, but the most serious was the ineptitude of much of its leadership, compounded by a lack of modern equipment and doctrine. Much of it was a malnourished nineteenth-century force that was largely incapable of combined-arms operations until 1943–1944, and then only on a very limited scale.[4] Opium addiction was another problem that destroyed the Chinese army's fighting ability. Provincial leaders required large numbers of troops for the collection of opium (as a form of taxation), but these men often served as their own best customers, and the drug was regularly used as pay. In 1936 U.S. military attaché Colonel Joseph Stilwell wrote, "This intimate connection between opium and militarism is a cause of two of China's great sorrows—the tremendous size of her so-called armies and their utter worthlessness for national defense."[5] Almost every account of the Sino-Japanese War describes this dismal state of Chinese military affairs, but some units trained by the German Military Mission under General Baron Alexander von Falkenhausen were good enough to fight the horrendous battle of Shanghai in 1937 until they were finally destroyed by superior Japanese firepower.

Chinese military organization requires some explanation, as unit designations can be misleading. In general, Chinese units were much smaller than forces with similar designations from other combatant nations. Most Chinese divisions numbered between 5,000 and 7,000 men, whereas a division in most other armies would comprise about 15,000 to 18,000 men. Furthermore, Chinese divisions usually went into battle lacking any useful field artillery, relying instead on mortars for added firepower. At a higher level, Chinese armies approximated the size of most Japanese divisions, but they still lacked adequate fire support for offensive operations. Some historians have designated Chinese armies as corps-level formations, but the use of the term *armies* has been maintained here to ensure continuity with the bulk of the sources consulted.

Chiang Kai Shek fought the Japanese partly to legitimize the authority of his national government, but also because Japanese militarists had become too aggressive and arrogant in China to be left unchecked. The battle of Shanghai, however, was a very costly affair. It was the first major clash following the Marco Polo Bridge incident. Beginning in August 1937, the Japanese landed a brigade at the city to protect their economic and political interests. To drive them from their initial lodgment, the Chinese army attacked with nine of its best-trained divisions. The Japanese reinforced their position by landing two additional divisions supported by heavy artillery and naval gunfire; these were augmented with large numbers of tanks and aircraft. The battle lasted about two and a half months and involved a total of eighty-five Chinese divisions against ten Japanese. Chinese and Japanese military forces became locked in a struggle that eventually cost the Chinese army approximately 400,000 men and 10,000 well-trained junior officers. Seventy-nine divisions out of the total 180 in the army's order of battle had been smashed. Many of China's heaviest weapons, including 150mm artillery, were also destroyed. When Chinese losses are compared with Japanese dead, numbering 40,000, the impact of Japan's naval transport and gunnery advantages becomes clear.[6] Chinese losses at Shanghai made it essential to import great quantities of weapons if resistance was to continue, and the British Foreign Office obliged by allowing the weapons trade at Hong Kong to proceed.

Chiang Kai Shek fought at Shanghai partly in the hope of gaining international support. Caught in a salient at Shanghai were a number of British troops stuck in the Chapei district; many of them had been bombarded, and about twenty men were killed. Although officially neutral, British forces became involved in the struggle by sustaining casualties. Some of the troops at Shanghai included volunteers living in the city who had been called out to man the barricades around the British concession, but they also included the Royal Welch Fusiliers, who had been rushed north from Hong Kong aboard the French Blue Funnel ship *Maron*. Six Royal Navy vessels escorted them on their journey.[7] Hong Kong thus served as a relatively secure base for British military forces to deploy from. Although Chiang's strategy of involving foreign powers had the potential to escalate the war at an early date, direct overt military intervention by other nations was not yet forthcoming.

The Japanese lacked an effective strategy to deal with determined resistance, and this problem was a fundamental factor in expanding the war. The Japanese General Staff did not wish to fight a protracted war in China because their primary concern was still the Soviet Union and the destruction of communism. They wanted to secure a rapid victory using a limited force of only fifteen divisions so that readiness could be maintained for operations in Siberia.[8] According to the U.S. naval attaché in Tokyo, "Japan aimed at and hoped for a quick and decisive victory, to overthrow the government of China without need of a long campaign embittering to the Chinese people themselves, [but] the plan for a quickly terminated action failed."[9] The prime minister, Prince Konoye Fumimaro, had been assured by the army that China could be beaten and forced to negotiate within three months, but Shanghai was an exceedingly difficult battle. Hence, the subsequent advance along the Yangtse River by General Matsui Iwane and the Central China Expeditionary Army was conducted with utter ruthlessness largely because of Japanese embarrassment at not concluding peace.[10] The China Expeditionary Army marched farther upriver with no clear idea of how to achieve victory, and the subsequent occupation of Nanking was meant to terrorize the Chinese into submission.

Terror and genocide proved to be counterproductive substitutes for the lack of strategic planning. Atrocities were committed throughout the region between Shanghai and Nanking, resulting in widespread devastation. Millions of people were driven from the area, and many were killed.[11] A U.S. naval intelligence report from Tokyo noted: "Atrocities have been numerous . . . the conduct of the hostilities has been such as to arouse Chinese hatred and resistance, [which] have in a degree of intensity [been] surprising to Japanese plans [and] its methods have been unnecessarily frightful . . . Chinese hatred [has] largely escaped the Japanese mind."[12] The slaughter and mayhem in Nanking during December 1937 and January 1938 were the result of several factors, but one of the most significant was the propensity of officers in the field to exceed their authority by taking independent action that widened the scope of the war.

Nanking exemplified how the lack of a coordinated strategy among field commanders and other officials combined with outright insubordination to render Japanese efforts self-defeating. General Matsui did not restrain officers such as Prince Asaka Yasuhiko, who ordered the savagery at Nanking, although it was his duty and responsibility to enforce discipline. U.S. assistant military attaché Major David Barrett also explained that the only beneficiaries of Japanese barbarism were the communists: "The net result of Japan's 'holy war' to insure the peace of the Orient by stamping out communism in China has apparently been to place the Chinese Reds in a position many times more favorable than they could ever have hoped to attain . . . before the outbreak of hostilities."[13] Incidents such as the strafing and wounding of British ambassador Sir Hughe Knatchbull-Hugessen while driving from Nanking to Shanghai in August 1937, in addition to the attacks on HMS *Ladybird*, HMS *Bee*, and USS *Panay* in December, were similarly inspired.[14] These actions, however, threatened to ignite war with Britain and America. Ultimately, the net result of Japanese barbarity was to produce strategic failure as Chinese resistance was encouraged and the war eventually bogged down into stalemate.

Major Barrett also reported on dangerous Japanese army attitudes after Matsui made comments in January 1938 regarding the transshipment of munitions from Hong Kong:

The Japanese Government has requested its officials, both at home and abroad, to moderate anti-British utterances. . . .

Among several extremely interesting, if not startling, statements made by General Matsui . . . was the following: "Considering the growth and development of our own country, it is inevitable that Japan should expand in China. Lack of appreciation of this situation on the part of Great Britain may, I am afraid, lead to unnecessary conflict between the two countries."

General Matsui pointed out that no doubt of Great Britain's ardent support of the Kuomintang regime could be entertained in view of the way she had supplied China with arms and supported the Chinese currency in such an effective manner that the exchange rate continued to hold up. . . .

General Matsui did not hesitate to imply that to all intents and purposes he was the Japanese Government in Central China at the present time, as is indicated by his statement concerning the Customs. "Originally I had it in mind," said the General, "to take over the Shanghai Customs right away, but as the *Panay* and *Ladybird* incidents occurred, I thought it better to treat the question on more moderate lines, and to have the matter talked over with the Customs authorities on a more conciliatory basis. Negotiations have been going on, but it seems to me that they are taking too much time and, if so, I may have to revert to my original attitude. . . ."

The significance of General Matsui's interview with Mr. Woodhead lies not in what he said, but in the fact that a military commander of a nation in which the civil [government] is supposed to maintain at least a shadow of power could make such statements and get away with it.[15]

This kind of undisciplined bravado was compounded by a lack of organizational uniformity in objectives and policy, and these twin problems were mimicked in southern China, where Japanese naval aggression eventually proved to be even more counterproductive.

By 1938, Chiang Kai Shek adopted a longer-range strategy of gradual withdrawal, and the spread of guerrilla warfare was intensified. Space was traded for time as the army retreated north and west following the defense of Hsuchow (Xuzhou).[16] The danger with this strategy, however, was withdrawal into political irrelevance. A year into the war, Colonel Stilwell wrote:

On the Chinese side, the spirit to fight to the last is of the utmost importance, but to an observer it appears that coupled with this spirit should go the determination to make a stand before the Chinese armies are driven back to the point where the Japanese can afford to ignore them. After all, a government maintained with difficulty in the mountain fastnesses of Szechuan and Kweichow or in far-distant Yunnan can very easily lose the aspect of a real China, and assume the appearance of a rebel faction fighting against a country, even though Japan-dominated, which because of its size and population must be considered as the real China by most of the world.[17]

Chiang had few good options, and the Chinese delegation to the League of Nations appealed for international assistance. During the first half of 1938, Chinese morale plummeted as the Japanese army continued its advance, but Chiang issued a statement that the country was determined to resist the Japanese. For resistance to continue, the Chinese army had to avoid total destruction, buy time for the redeployment of China's industrial base, and prepare other defensive strongholds, such as at Hankow.[18] To accomplish these goals, the continued importation of weapons was essential.

Infrastructure problems made the implementation of Chiang's strategy difficult. After 1937, the number of internal land routes available to the Chinese for the transportation of munitions and equipment decreased greatly. Many railways and roads were lost to the advancing Japanese or were washed out by heavy rains. Road and rail transportation in central and western China were virtually nonexistent, making the early movement of China's industrial plant to Chungking an almost impossible task. The logistical problems involved in moving industries out of Hankow and farther inland during 1938 were aggravated by the lack of available shipping capacity. Equipment and workers piled up on docks, awaiting transport or air attack. Yet despite these problems, 134 factories had been moved west by September 1938. Most of these were for the production of mechanical equipment, metal goods, chemicals, and electrical equipment. Water transportation allowed 17 percent of China's industry to be salvaged after shipment to Szechwan and Hunan. River transportation also had an impact on battlefield tactics, as it was often the only efficient way to move men and material around the country. Because of this, the control of railways and rivers dominated Japanese operational planning.[19]

Although China's infrastructure was poorly developed in many regions, it was especially poor in the south. Hong Kong was a valuable exception, and access to its port facilities was a distinct advantage. Oil installations included large facilities for companies such as Standard Oil, Texaco, and Asiatic Petroleum. First-class roads ran to the Chinese border, and several important factories had been built along the western route. Kai Tak aerodrome was also economically and logistically significant. Air transportation in and out of Hong Kong had grown rapidly since 1936, with many airlines making it a gateway city to the Far East.[20] The most important factor that made Hong Kong so vital to Chinese survival, however, was its connection to the only direct rail line running across the south China front to Hankow.

Without the railway, it is unlikely the Chinese would have been able to continue the war. The amount of material transshipped along this network was immense, and Sino-British relations grew stronger as a result of their cooperation. In June 1938 a U.S. Army officer reported, "The Chinese are bringing more munitions and war supplies into China than ever before. The Hong Kong Harbor has never in its history berthed so many steamers. . . . Notwithstanding the recent intensive bombing . . . of Canton and other sections of the Hong Kong–Hankow Railway, traffic continues to move over this important artery."[21] Many sympathetic foreign civilians also understood the importance of the railway and could see its impact on Chinese morale. One missionary noted in December 1937, "China would be helpless if she did not possess this line which now . . . has its southern terminus in the great port of Hong Kong."[22]

During the first sixteen months of the war, 60,000 tons per month were brought in through Hong Kong, and more than 700,000 tons reached Hankow. British ambassador Sir Horace Seymour reported in 1944 that, according to a central government spokesman, China had imported 1.5 million gallons of gasoline through Hong Kong during 1938, before the invasion of south China, whereas 1 million gallons had come through Burma in 1940. To put this volume of traffic into context, 2,500 tons of aviation fuel were required to keep 100 aircraft in the air for combat operations each month (360,000 gallons of aviation fuel equal approximately 1,000 tons). This rate of supply was maintained despite the ubiquitous corruption in China, which was only made worse by the Military Affairs Commission and the South-West Transportation Commission. The latter agency, run by Chiang Kai Shek's brother-in-law Dr. T. V. Soong, was responsible for the Chinese portion of the railway north of Canton. Still, the

Hong Kong–to–Hankow supply line surpassed all other logistical networks in terms of the amount of material delivered to the Chinese army, almost to the end of the war. In contrast, construction of the famed Burma Road was not begun until October 1937 and was not completed until late 1938.[23]

The Japanese often failed to appreciate that their attacks on the railway helped strengthen Sino-British relations. By 1938, Japanese air strikes against the line north of the colony were common occurrences. Damaged engines and wagons could be found periodically along the line, and most of the bomb damage was on the southern portion. An air defense early-warning network was established to help protect trains in transit, and during alarms, trains were often shunted into forested areas that provided overhead concealment. To help keep the railway operational, the Colonial Office and the Foreign Office approved a Chinese request in May 1938 to build a locomotive repair yard within the New Territories.[24] Because of the assistance provided by Great Britain through Hong Kong, China was able to continue the war, and Sino-British relations grew stronger. This feeling was expressed during a 2 September 1938 visit to Hong Kong by Kwang-tung governor Wu Teh Chen, otherwise known as "Iron City Wu" for his prior service as mayor of Shanghai. In a speech delivered on the roof garden of the Hong Kong Hotel in October 1938, Wu stated, "Great Britain and China are like brothers."[25] In time, this growing collaboration brought a Japanese response.

Although the British provided important support to China, Soviet military aid between August 1937 and June 1941 was more substantial and much less covert. Stalin wanted a protracted war in China in order to keep the Japanese army engaged and thus prevent an invasion of Siberia. Unlike the British, however, he furnished the Chinese directly with the weapons necessary to fight it. In April 1937 Stalin promised Chiang military hardware and assistance in the event of a Japanese attack on China, and the Sino-Soviet Non-Aggression Pact was signed that August. A barter agreement was also negotiated, and the trade of munitions for strategic materials such as tungsten and antimony was quickly begun. Sun Fo, chairman of the Legislative Yuan and son of Sun Yat Sen, traveled to Moscow via Hong Kong in January 1938 to arrange for increased aid, and the barter agreement itself was formalized in June 1940.[26]

The principal method of bringing Soviet supplies into China was from Turkistan through Sinkiang (Xinjiang) to Lanchow (Lanzhou). Chinese raw materials returned either the same way or between Hong Kong and

Vladivostok. Altogether, there were five routes from the trans-Siberian railway that brought material into and out of China, starting in 1937. Traversing these routes were approximately 20,000 camels, each of which made two to three trips per year. The number of camels reportedly increased to 50,000 by 1940, and each beast could carry about nine five-gallon cans of gasoline, or just under 300 pounds, for a distance of twenty-four miles each day. Several hundred trucks eventually augmented this camel capacity, raising the average amount of material brought into China by this route to 2,000 to 3,000 tons per month.[27]

From 1937 to 1941 the level of Soviet supplies imported into China remained substantial and included light and heavy artillery, in addition to hundreds of aircraft. Soviet air units were also committed to the war, and the initial group sent in November 1937 included four fighter squadrons and two bomber squadrons. By the end of December, China had received approximately 250 aircraft, and 400 more had been ordered. Two hundred Soviet airmen arrived at Nanchang on 12 January 1938, and two weeks later, on 26 January, an all-Soviet air raid on Japanese air bases at Nanking was credited with destroying more than 30 Japanese aircraft. Three hundred additional air and ground personnel arrived by 15 April 1938. Soviet air units usually operated independently of the Chinese air force, and they established their own aircraft factory in Kansu (Gansu). The problem for the Chinese central government, however, was the politically subversive activity the Soviets engaged in while stationed in the country, but Chiang deemed this a price worth paying. With the support already provided up to May 1938, some Chinese officials felt that direct Red Army ground intervention might also be a possibility.[28] Chinese hopes for increased Soviet involvement on the ground were indeed fulfilled during the 1939 battle at Nomonhan along the Mongolian border.

During 1937 and 1938 Chiang was successful in gaining limited international assistance, and he had already managed to gain a degree of direct military intervention from the USSR. With British and Soviet support, Chiang was able to continue the war despite the devastating losses at Shanghai. Amidst a deteriorating diplomatic situation in Europe, Anglo-Soviet support remained strong, as the possibility of peace in China was a constant worry to British and Soviet foreign policy makers alike. To increase British involvement, however, Chiang took steps to exploit the rising level of violence and destruction then occurring in Kwangtung and transform the Pearl River Delta into a more dangerous war zone.[29]

The Destabilization of Kwangtung and
the Question of Chinese Morale

The Japanese intensification of military operations in China paralleled unsuccessful regional and bilateral political efforts to bring the war to an end. Because of the Chinese army's unexpected determination and ability to resist at Shanghai, the military logistical situation in Kwangtung and Hong Kong soon became a problem for the Japanese to confront. The struggle between the Chinese central government and the Japanese armed forces to control the ground lines of communication between Hong Kong and mainland China led to great political instability and civil strife. The policy of divide and rule through puppet administrations was already established in many parts of occupied China, and an attempt to replicate another such government in Kwangtung was the objective of a failed coup d'état in February 1938.[30] Soon thereafter, the Japanese intensified their aerial and naval interdiction operations, leading to the terror bombing of Canton in the spring. Combined with this escalation, Japanese political machinations created a power vacuum that undermined popular Chinese support for the war.

The Chinese government was faced with a difficult situation in Kwangtung, but through ruthless calculation, Chiang was able to turn the tables on both his enemies and his potential allies. By purposely keeping Kwangtung militarily weak while maintaining political control, he was able to erode provincial autonomy and simultaneously raise the level of Anglo-Japanese friction. This served the dual strategies of eliminating Kwangtung's independence forces and increasing Britain's involvement in the war. The price was Kwangtung's destabilization and an increase in social disorder. This, in turn, encouraged a Japanese invasion of the province in the fall of 1938, as the ability to resist such a move was greatly undermined. However, it was a price Chiang was willing to pay.

Kwangtung's morale was eroded throughout 1938 by a series of threats that increased the sense of isolation among many living in the province. The most obvious of these was the threat of invasion, which the Japanese had already contemplated in January 1938. Fifty thousand troops had been loaded onto naval transports for an assault at Bias Bay, but events at Tsingtao (Qingtao) interrupted the operation, and the troops were redirected northward instead. To keep the Chinese off balance, the Japanese navy made a small landing north of Macau on 16 January 1938 with a force of about 600 men, but this was merely a reconnaissance of coastal defenses. Still, their arrival stoked the fear of invasion among many in the region until the unit was withdrawn on 20 January.[31]

Invasion anxiety was justified according to U.S. naval attaché Commander H. E. Overesch. During a tour of the province with the British and French military attachés in May, Overesch estimated that 100,000 Chinese troops were present in Kwangtung, but official claims that Bocca Tigris defenses had been strengthened with artillery were proved false. Bocca Tigris guarded the approach to Canton on the east side of the Pearl River Delta, but the fortifications were equipped with only a few old French 75mm guns. British Captain J. V. Davidson-Houston of the Shanghai military intelligence section also traveled to Bocca Tigris in July 1938 and noted that Chinese defenses consisted of conspicuous casements for guns located on the eastern shore and on an island to the west, but these were unsupported by infantry fortifications.[32] The general conclusion among foreign observers was that physical installations in Kwangtung were inadequate to defend against a Japanese invasion.

As a military solution for Kwangtung was postponed, the Japanese navy chose to deal with its problems using political methods, and one approach was an attempted coup set for March 1938. Japanese commanders established puppet governments in other parts of China to administer occupied areas while enhancing their own personal power and autonomy from higher authorities. In 1938 the North Chinese Provisional Government was based in Peking, while another puppet regime governed Manchuria. The new Reformed Government of the Republic of China was also established in Nanking. This administration was eventually amalgamated with the Provisional Government to form a larger puppet regime under the leadership of Wang Ching Wei in 1940. In 1939 Wang would use Cantonese nationalist sentiment to increase support for his administration in Kwangtung by promising limited political and military autonomy under his leadership. His national government ultimately failed because the Japanese continued to ignore the growing importance of nationalism in the rest of China, and their limited support for Wang only pushed Chiang Kai Shek further into the arms of third powers, thereby increasing his credibility among many Chinese.[33]

Nevertheless, a Kwangtung coup attempt held great potential to wrest the province from the control of the central government and thereby disrupt the movement of war supplies from Hong Kong. On 3 February the

British were informed of the closure of the Pearl River by Japanese naval officers, and the next day several warships sailed past Hong Kong to bombard Bocca Tigris, but these efforts were in support of a coup that had already failed. The nucleus of the revolt was within the Peace Preservation Corps, and the entire operation was foiled on the night of 2–3 February by the actions of an individual named Li Fook Lam. Aside from Li, the primary coup agents in Canton were Chen Chung Fu and Hsi Chao Tzu, and the Japanese had supplied them with $6 million to organize and instigate the revolt. With Li's defection, the Japanese lost their money and a chance to establish a puppet government in Kwangtung. In response, martial law was declared in Canton, the Pearl River was closed for over a week, and the coup was violently suppressed by General Yu Han Mou. At the time, General Yu was the leader in Kwangtung who was most loyal to Chiang Kai Shek, and he controlled all the central government's regular military forces in the province. Hundreds were arrested, and several individuals were executed, along with a Japanese national. Swift retribution thus ended the plot, but the resultant political instability caused many military, political, and social problems that festered for the remainder of the war.[34]

Kwangtung's political situation had already worsened with the start of the Sino-Japanese War, and existing ideological divisions became deeper as a result of the coup. Many wished to fight the Japanese, but a large number still wanted to resist the central government's authority, even though the coup had essentially dashed hopes for future independence. Some pragmatists were willing to make a political or economic arrangement with whoever could provide security and a modicum of order. Watching events closely were the Hakka minority living near Hong Kong and in the New Territories, whose sympathies were with the communists. The violence and uncertainty created by the coup had a long-term demoralizing effect on the population as a power vacuum was created in some areas and lawlessness became widespread; this situation was made worse by the withdrawal of 20,000 Kwangsi troops through Wuchow (Wuzhou). Japanese disinformation sowed additional seeds of discord by publicizing Chinese disunity. Disturbances in Canton were said to be the result of a power play between General Yu Han Mou and Governor Wu Teh Chen, and the coup was rumored to be an attempt by Generals Li Chi Shen and Chen Chi Tang to eliminate General Yu.[35] With the province fractured politically, there was little cohesion or effective leadership to resist the Japanese invasion when it finally came in the fall.

Following the failed coup, the three men in charge of the government in Canton were Governor Wu, Mayor Tseng Yang Fu, and General Yu, and they more or less ensured that most of Kwangtung remained politically loyal to the central government for the remainder of the war. But with the province loosely under the control of these men, the economy suffered greatly. Over time, corruption and inflation soared, and the people justifiably became more apathetic toward fighting the war.[36] The governor of Kwangtung and the mayor of Canton were described by Captain Davidson-Houston as unscrupulous men interested primarily in self-enrichment. Personal jealousies among themselves and General Yu prevented the establishment of a strong or cohesive political leadership, and this further diminished the military readiness of the province.

On a national level, contact between the central government and the Japanese was never completely severed, and the prospect of a negotiated settlement was kept alive by the Chinese peace movement. Those who wished to arrange peace had varying degrees of influence with Chiang throughout the course of the war. Discussions were renewed after the Kwangtung coup when Kao Tsung Wu and Tung Tao Ning, of the Chinese Foreign Ministry's Asian Bureau, were sent to Nagasaki to meet with Japanese officials. In March they met again with Nishi Yoshiaki at the Repulse Bay Hotel in Hong Kong, along with Matsumoto Shigeharu, who was a personal friend of Prince Konoye. Another significant participant was Finance Minister H. H. Kung; in June 1938 he also sent his personal secretary, Chiao Fu Sa, to Hong Kong to meet with Japanese Consul General Nakamura Toyokazu. These talks lasted until September but ultimately failed because the Japanese insisted on Chiang's resignation. Chiang held fast, despite the poor state of Chinese morale, because he still had combat forces in the field and a continuous supply of material from Hong Kong and French Indochina. He continued to fight in the north and regrouped his armies for the defense of Hankow.[37]

A few Japanese officers, including the former governor general of Korea, General Ugaki Kazushige, understood that a political solution was the best way to end the war and that peace negotiations had to be conducted with Chiang Kai Shek's representatives directly, rather than propping up a collection of unpopular satraps. Potential allies understood this as well. With Japanese consent, Adolf Hitler ordered Ambassador Oscar Trautmann to try to secure a peace arrangement between China and Japan in December 1937. Hitler's goal was to avert any improvement in Sino-Soviet relations, but Trautmann's efforts came to nothing. In February 1938 General Matsui was ordered home because of the embarrassment caused by Chiang's rejection of the peace terms, as well as his own failure to pursue the routed Chinese army after Nanking. He was replaced by General Hata Shunroku.[38]

Prime Minister Konoye also began to see the destruction of the Kuomintang and the establishment of puppet regimes as unrealistic objectives. Consequently, a change was made in the cabinet, and General Ugaki assumed the post of foreign minister on 26 May 1938. He would hold the job for four months. Ugaki wished to secure better relations with Great Britain because he knew that the war's continued prosecution would further damage Japan diplomatically and also stretch the country's resources. To accomplish his goal, Ugaki held numerous discussions with British embassy officials in Tokyo and elsewhere, including Ambassador Sir Robert Craigie and Major General F. S. G. Piggott, the British military attaché and Ugaki's personal friend. One of the main Japanese demands during these meetings was for Great Britain to stop the transshipment of war supplies from Hong Kong. Craigie had previously recommended a termination of the war supplies trade at Hong Kong, but by September, the Craigie-Ugaki talks had not produced an agreement.[39]

Disagreement on objectives and strategy among Japanese leaders undermined Ugaki's efforts. In May 1938 Ishii Itaro, chief of the War Ministry's Asian Bureau, had released a report outlining reasons to pursue direct negotiations with the Kuomintang, and Ugaki had adopted the report's recommendations. Ishii believed that Japanese army commanders in China were the main obstacle to peace because they acted in their own interests and saw China as a colony to be exploited. Most wished to continue fighting, and while Ugaki was negotiating for peace, subversion and assassination were expanded in scale. Chinese puppet hit squads were dispatched from Hong Kong on missions to kill Chinese central government officials in Shanghai and other cities. Some Japanese army commanders in China intensified their military operations and became overtaxed in their commitments. Ugaki ultimately failed in his efforts to arrange peace because army hard-liners pushed for military solutions to their problems. In June, Konoye reported to the emperor that there was no unity among Japanese commanders or within the cabinet. A few months later the new ambassador, Sir Archibald Clark Kerr, found himself in agreement with his French counterpart in Chungking when he commented that the Japanese army was running its own foreign policy and that the Japanese embassy in China had shifted from its role as an honest peace broker between third powers and the Japanese military to a position of subordination. International diplomatic tensions in China increased accordingly. General Ugaki quit his office shortly after the breakdown of discussions with Craigie, and the Japanese adjusted their efforts toward the establishment of a puppet national government at Nanking.[40] The invasion of south China was launched in October 1938, beginning a new and dangerous stage of the war.

Within this diplomatic cloud, it was the Chinese central government that emerged victorious in Kwangtung. It generally maintained control over most of the province, and the continued transshipment of war supplies from Hong Kong was assured. Yet, because of the political instability and increased lawlessness in Canton, some of the imported war material had to be diverted around the city. Minor delays were experienced as weapons were moved overland to the east through Waichow before being loaded onto trains in northern Kwangtung. By taking such a circuitous route, supplies passed through General Yu's 12th Group Army in areas that were firmly controlled by the central government. The amount of supplies transiting Kwangtung remained high, but what mattered most was that the new routes established east of Canton would serve the Chinese army well after the Japanese invaded and occupied the city later that year. As the movement of weapons continued under their noses, Japanese frustration and anger only deepened, and the strain on their relations with the British increased accordingly. Stirring Anglo-Japanese animosity, however, was one of Chiang Kai Shek's main objectives in Kwangtung.

During 1938 several interrelated military events transpired that also threatened to make resistance in Kwangtung more tenuous. First were the losses suffered by the Chinese air force in the battle for air superiority over the Yangtse River. The air force started the war with twenty-three squadrons, or approximately 250 obsolete aircraft, but by September 1937 they had acquired additional planes from the United States so that 600 were ready for operations. To maintain a supply of replacement pilots, an air force training school at Liuchow (Liuzhou) was moved to Mengtze after being bombed, but there was also another school in operation at Yunnanyi. Soviet airpower in China by this time amounted to about 300 aircraft, and many of these were I-15 and I-16 fighters. In contrast, the Japanese could deploy more than 2,100 aircraft and produce another 300 per month. Of these, 1,223 were from the army, and the navy possessed 860. Because the army tended to concentrate on the north, the Japanese navy conducted the majority of air operations in central and southern China.[41]

Air dominance was ceded grudgingly, and the Chinese initially achieved a measure of success in defeating Japanese long-range naval bombers operating from Formosa and Japan. The navy was responsible for most of the strategic bombing at this stage of the war because army air units, which were used largely for air superiority or to provide tactical ground support, lacked the necessary aircraft and doctrine for such missions. In July 1937 the Japanese bombed a Chinese city for the first time at Hangchow (Hangzhou), and the Chinese shot down six Japanese bombers. Each year thereafter, Air Force Day was observed in commemoration of the event. After the fall of Shanghai, Japanese naval air units based themselves at captured airfields near the city and concentrated on the destruction of Chinese air defense centers near the Lower Yangtse, such as at Nanchang in December 1937. Casualties mounted as operations shifted west toward Hankow. On 29 April 1938 a relatively large air battle occurred over the city involving approximately forty-eight Japanese aircraft (eighteen bombers and thirty fighters) against sixty to eighty Chinese and Soviet I-15 and I-16 fighters. Many losses were inflicted on both sides, but exact numbers are difficult to determine. In later years Major General Claire Chennault wrote that in this particular battle, the Soviets and Chinese ambushed the Japanese and destroyed more than fifty aircraft. During the summer of 1938 the Chinese air force managed to check the Japanese air offensive in central China, and Chennault considered this air campaign a significant Japanese disaster. The cost to the Chinese, however, was unsustainable, and operations were curtailed from midsummer to October 1938.[42] An aerial war of attrition was a contest the Chinese could not win.

The Yangtse ground offensive had a negative impact on national morale as well as in Kwangtung, and this campaign was significant in that it greatly eroded Chinese military power. Through the summer and fall of 1938, the Japanese army continued its western drive in central China, and during the course of this offensive, the political wedge between Kwangtung and the central government was driven deeper. Cantonese soldiers were committed to a difficult battle north of Nanchang, and although they inflicted many casualties, they sustained numerous casualties themselves, resulting in sharp criticism from Kwangtung. Military readiness in the province was further eroded because of this offensive, and a Japanese army invasion of southern China was encouraged when the central front at Hankow began to collapse.

The subsequent occupation of Canton, coinciding with the fall of Hankow, was a serious blow to Chinese morale and represented a dangerous escalation as war conditions near Hong Kong only worsened.[43]

Hankow was politically significant because Chiang was attempting to build a coalition government there in 1938 to strengthen central governmental authority. He also sought to unify the country by restoring normal relations with southern Chinese officials, and he achieved a measure of success. A Foreign Office report noted that Kwangsi leaders "are still working in the closest harmony with General Chiang Kai-shek." In turn, Generals Li Tsung Ren and Pai Chung Hsi tended to limit some of the more autocratic tendencies of the Kuomintang. Open political debate was encouraged, as was a free press, and General Tai Li's (Dai Li) secret police directed most of their attention to Japanese sympathizers. At Hankow, the formation of a more democratic government inclusive of China's many political factions promised to take root. This new united front produced a sense of political optimism across the country, and many provincial soldiers were deployed along the Yangtse River to defend the new capital. Kwangsi and Kwangtung forces had already been sent north by the spring of 1938, and Cantonese troops under the command of Generals Hsueh Yueh and Ou Yang Chen were committed to battle in Kiangsi, near the town of Tehan, from June until October. These troops had already been replaced at home by weaker units of the 12th Group Army under the command of General Yu Han Mou near Kukong. In early September 90,000 of Yunnan's troops had also been trained and were ready to fight, while a slightly larger number remained in the south.[44] By upholding this Chinese version of collective security, these provincial troops represented an increased regional commitment to centralized control.

The battle of Tehan, fought in the mountains north of Nanchang, was one of the few military events of the Japanese offensive that gave the Chinese reason for optimism. In supporting the drive on Hankow, Japanese units on the south bank of the Yangtse River attempted to isolate Chinese forces in the region west of Lake Poyang, but in October 1938, amidst rough terrain, the Japanese 2nd, 101st, and 106th Divisions were badly hurt in battling Cantonese divisions (see figure 3.1). Because of Japanese logistical limitations, the use of rail lines and waterways normally constrained their operations, and when fighting occurred at a distance from these fixed lines of supply, the Chinese often had excellent opportunities to stage damaging counteroffensives against overextended lines of communi-

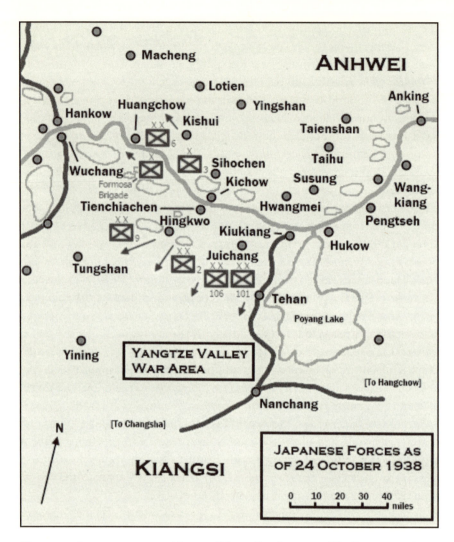

Figure 3.1. Japanese army positions at Tehan, October 1938. The Japanese unit identified with a "3" is an element of the 3rd Division (i.e., it is not the 3rd Regiment). (Based on data from TNA, WO 106/5356, HKIR No. 22/38.)

cation. These opportunities were usually not well exploited, but in this instance, Generals Ou and Hsueh were credited with the destruction of two regiments by employing large-scale flank attacks as the Japanese advanced south from the river in two parallel columns. Specifically, General Ou's 4th Army was responsible for destroying the Japanese 147th Regiment of the 106th Division. The use of such attacks against Japanese lines of supply at Tehan foreshadowed China's victories on a larger scale in the important battles for Changsha.[45]

Foreign military observers took note of these events and reported cautiously optimistic appraisals of Chinese military capabilities back to their respective governments. British military intelligence officers at Hong Kong noted that the Japanese "encountered much stiffer opposition and the capture of Tehan was only effected after very heavy fighting, with correspondingly severe losses on both sides."[46] Captain Charles Boxer and Captain H. Chauvin confirmed initial reports of victory during a visit with the 4th Army in the spring of 1939. Boxer described the 4th Army as having a fighting spirit and morale somewhat greater than a Japanese reserve division and noted that General Ou "was the most impressive Chinese senior officer I had yet met, and gave the impression of being a real fighting soldier."[47] The two captains were invited to examine many captured weapons, in addition to the 147th's Regimental War Diary. Colonel Poon, a Japanese-speaking officer of the Chinese 4th Army's military intelligence section, informed the British officers that the Japanese 13th Regiment (of the 6th Division) had likewise been destroyed near the Yangtse River: he had seen their captured regimental flag as proof. Boxer subsequently wrote that the Japanese had never lost a battle flag in either the first Sino-Japanese War of 1894–1895 or the Russo-Japanese War of 1904–1905. After inspecting this material, Boxer and Chauvin admitted that "the Chinese claims for a victory on the 'double tenth' at the Teian front last year possess more substance than this office and G 'I' Shanghai were willing to admit at that time."[48] According to Japanese documents, the use of chemical weapons at Tehan did not prevent defeat, but this evidence prompted Boxer and Chauvin to warn about the possible use of gas in a future attack against Hong Kong. U.S. officials such as Major Barrett also commented on the victory at Tehan: "This office has long been of the opinion that Japanese tactics in the present hostilities constantly invite major disaster and one may have occurred in this instance."[49]

At Tehan, the Chinese achieved a rare military victory, and because of this, the battle had the potential to restore some measure of political confidence and acceptance of the central government in Kwangtung. Political divisions between the central government and Kwangtung only worsened, however, as the many casualties sustained did not prevent the fall of Hankow. Moreover, while Cantonese troops fought and died south of the Yangtse River, many perceived that Chiang had used provincial troops at Tehan to preserve the strength of his own units. A Hong Kong military intelligence report noted: "He has been freely accused of sacrificing provincial troops to keep his own divisions intact, and a growing antagonism to him has been noticed in Kwangtung. The four Cantonese divisions have been fighting very gallantly on the Tehan front but are liable to be suborned by defeatist propaganda spread by reinforcements from their native province."[50]

To be fair, Canton was the center of the anti-Japanese movement in south China, and Chiang fought the war partly at the insistence of many regional leaders, especially those from Kwangtung. This left Cantonese officials with little cause for complaint about the losses incurred; nevertheless, widespread sentiment against central authority spiked yet again in Kwangtung.[51] In the end, Tehan was overshadowed by larger events, and with only a few weak divisions under the command of General Yu to defend Kwangtung, there was little opposition when the Japanese invaded the province on 12 October 1938.

By then, the fall of the capital was also imminent. Firepower and mobility advantages accounted for the success of the Japanese offensive, and Hankow's fate was sealed when the fortress city of Tienchiachen was lost to the 6th Division on 29 September 1938. By 21 October the Chinese army began to withdraw from the Hankow region, and the capital was eventually moved to Chungking. Units north of the Yangtse retreated upriver and along the road to Shasi. Those farther south retreated west upriver or toward Changsha. The Chinese General Headquarters was established at Hengshan, Hunan. Chiang left Hankow on 24 October 1938, and the city fell to Japanese forces the following day. At this point, it was decided to defend Hunan with the greatest determination to protect what remained of the lines of communication to the south. Surviving Cantonese troops from Tehan had been withdrawn into Hunan, while General Yu maintained control in Kwangtung with weak central government forces.[52]

The fall of Hankow was a Chinese political and military disaster. During the offensive the Chinese army suffered more than 1 million casualties, including 80 percent of the officer corps. These casualties totaled more than those absorbed over the next seven years combined. No medical treatment was available for wounded men, and the Chinese army was permanently affected by these losses. The central government never recovered the same level of military strength or political cohesion it held during 1938, and prominent political figures such as Wang Ching Wei defected soon afterward to form the puppet national government in another attempt to broker peace.[53]

Throughout 1938 several political and military events had a detrimental effect on Cantonese morale, and Kwangtung's ability to resist the impending Japanese assault was diminished. Japanese attacks on Chinese lines of communication brought the war to Hong Kong's doorstep, and low-intensity conflict with Britain began to spread across the Pearl River Delta. The failed coup in February produced civil strife across the province and led to a government that was more corrupt than its predecessor. Disaffection with central authority grew stronger, and Chiang's attempt to alleviate provincial grievances with a more democratic form of government at Hankow failed as military setbacks mounted along the Yangtse River. Compounding this problem was the deployment of Cantonese ground forces to Tehan, north of Nanchang. Although they acquitted themselves well, losses were heavy, and many Cantonese felt that Chiang had sacrificed their troops while safeguarding his own. The net result of these problems was to elevate both fear of the Japanese and disaffection with the Chinese central government. Kwangtung's possible defection had already become sufficiently apparent to raise concerns among British authorities at Hong Kong, such as Governor Sir Geoffry Northcote. Thus, Northcote traveled to Canton in July in an effort to shore up morale and demonstrate British diplomatic support for Chiang Kai Shek.[54]

Blockade and Low-Intensity Conflict in the Pearl River Delta

The Japanese military services and the government in Tokyo often failed to coordinate strategy in the Sino-Japanese War, causing the conflict to escalate toward the disastrous war of annihilation with Britain and America. Until 1941, south China was the incubator where this problem grew worse. The Japanese did not officially declare war on China in 1937 because the U.S. Neutrality Act would have resulted in a termination of trade, including the importation of necessary war materials such as oil. Had they done so, foreign vessels would have been legally barred from entering Chinese waters.[55] A blockade was nonetheless established by the Japanese navy when it saw an opportunity to participate more fully in the war by patrolling the coastal waters of south and east China in search of Chinese war supplies. Seeking victory through blockade, which included aerial interdiction of lines of communication from Hong Kong to China, the navy adopted a more aggressive posture and, in doing so, contributed greatly to the creation of low-intensity conflict in and around Hong Kong. The colony thus became a focal point of Anglo-Japanese confrontation, and another step was taken toward igniting the Pacific war.

Anger toward Great Britain mounted after the British took the lead in condemning Japanese actions at the League of Nations. Japanese officials in Tokyo and China worked at cross-purposes, however, as the navy intensified hostilities near Hong Kong while some elements within the army tried to reach a diplomatic understanding with British officials. On 16 January 1938 Japanese navy minister Admiral Yonai Mitsumasa publicly demanded cabinet unity in an all-out war in China.[56] This was followed by a proclamation by home minister Admiral Suetsugu Nobumasa, who wanted his government to officially declare war against the Chinese in order to strengthen the blockade of south China. The Canadian minister to Japan reported to Ottawa that "the Home Minister, Admiral Suetsugu, and other high naval officers, advocate this step, mainly for the purpose of blockading more effectively the China coast especially in the vicinity of Hong Kong."[57] Major Barrett reported that the admiral had said, "China in the present struggle was relying on British aid through Hongkong, and as Japan could not stand indefinite resistance from China, the sources of resistance must be cut off."[58] Suetsugu added, "If Japan comes to clash with Great Britain, that cannot be helped. If the British were to cease to assist China, it would be a very good thing for the Orient."[59] In February 1938 the Japanese press began to label the British as merchants of death, compelling Anthony Eden to respond in the House of Commons that British exports of munitions to China between June 1937 and January 1938 had amounted to only £134,338.[60] This did little to ease tensions.

During the period from July 1937 to October 1938, the war was brought to the Pearl River Delta as the Japanese navy began to isolate Hong Kong through aerial and naval interdiction. This onslaught against Kwangtung was much less dangerous geopolitically than a full invasion of Hong Kong would have been, but it still resulted in deaths among the colony's residents, and it raised the level of Anglo-Japanese friction. The primary objective in Kwangtung from August 1937 until October 1938 was the disruption of the Chinese logistical network, and the most important element was the railway system. Air operations were also politically motivated, as witnessed during the terror bombing of Canton during the spring of 1938. Conducted by long-range naval bombers operating from Formosa and by aircraft from the fleet carrier *Kaga*, the assaults inflicted substantial damage on the city.[61] Attacks throughout the rest of Kwangtung also grew in frequency, and British nationals' anger toward the Japanese mounted as the level of casualties rose and commerce was disrupted. Over time, this contributed greatly to the buildup of British resentment and the forging of local determination to retaliate.

Tactics of the aerial interdiction campaign emphasized the use of unescorted bombers directed against hard targets on land, such as railway bridges, in addition to attacks on soft targets, including civilian aircraft, junks, and trains. In 1937 Japanese aircrews were still inexperienced and skills were not well developed, so squadrons often missed their targets. Aircraft regularly overflew the city of Kongmoon (Jiangmen), northwest of Macau, on their way to bomb Canton or the Hankow-Canton railway, as it served as a useful navigation point, but it also gave the Chinese valuable advance warning. On 6 October 1937 one typical raid comprising three squadrons overflew Kongmoon at an altitude of 3,000 feet at 10:00 AM, and by 10:30, reports from Canton confirmed that they had continued north to attack the railway. One of the squadrons returned an hour later to its carrier near the coast. Due to the fear of Chinese antiaircraft fire (limited as it was), the Japanese frequently bombed from higher altitudes, with much imprecision.[62]

The primary type of aircraft used in these attacks was the carrier-based seaplane operating from one or two small carriers patrolling along the Chinese coast. These vessels approximated the size of a cruiser and could usually carry about a dozen biplanes. The ships would anchor for several days, often at Hainan or Weichow Island (twenty-five miles south of Pakhoi), and a relatively protected beach would be selected as a refueling and rearming point for the planes unloaded at the beginning of the first day's missions. About 100 men would be landed as ground crews and defense forces to service the aircraft. Seaplanes conducted several missions each

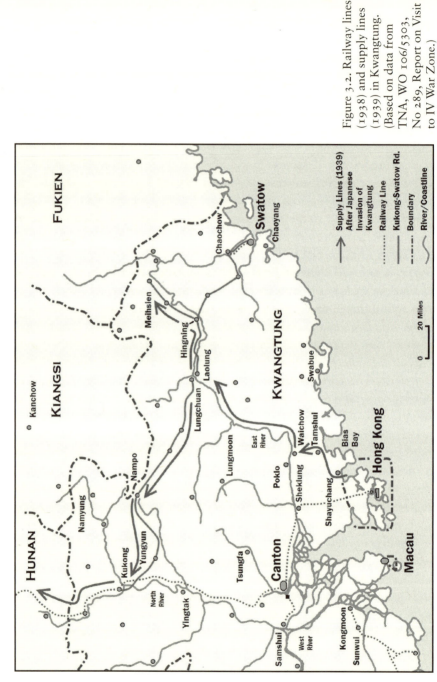

Figure 3.2. Railway lines (1938) and supply lines (1939) in Kwangtung. (Based on data from TNA, WO 106/5303, No 289, Report on Visit to IV War Zone.)

day and were usually armed with 100-pound bombs; crews provided mission reports to the senior officer ashore after landing. By operating from Weichow and Hainan, these carriers positioned themselves astride the shipping lanes between Hong Kong and French Indochina, and the threat to third powers was also made clear.[63]

One of the most important targets of the campaign was the large bridge at Sheklung, located about halfway between Canton and Hong Kong, along with another bridge situated about 120 miles north of Canton at the town of Kukong (see figure 3.2). The first strike launched against the Kukong bridge took place on 31 August 1937, but this mission ended in failure. Only residents of the town were hit, resulting in many civilian casualties. Many other attempts followed throughout the fall and winter, with equally poor results. Kowloon-Canton railway (KCR) trains were also attacked. During October 1937 at Nam Sheh, about 5 miles south of Sheklung, a squadron of eight Japanese seaplanes killed two people—one soldier and a small girl. One hundred passengers aboard the train ran for cover before strafing and bomb attacks wounded another two.[64]

Bombing of the KCR became a regular occurrence, and although loss of life continued, the air war against Kwangtung produced some unexpected results on civilian morale. One Canadian missionary wrote, "Great credit is due to repair crews and train crews. . . . Such courage on the part of workmen in China would not have existed a few years ago."[65] A few months later in Canton, Royal Navy officers were surprised by the self-sacrifice and efficiency of the city's fire brigade and rescue personnel, who remained on duty throughout.[66] In general, air strikes against Chinese rail lines were not very effective in slowing the movement of supplies to points farther north, but the Japanese were persistent.

During October 1937 frequent attacks were launched across the West River region, especially in the area surrounding Kongmoon. It was not long before many towns south of the city along the Sunning railway also became targets. Government facilities and bridges were usually singled out, but terror bombing was also conducted. Train attacks were regular occurrences but still remained largely ineffective, with delays usually limited to several hours. Farther south toward the coast, the town of Toishan was bombed in December. Toishan was a rather prosperous area, since many Chinese living in America and Canada originated from this part of Kwangtung, and family remittances from overseas accounted for a great deal of the region's wealth. Because of this, the Japanese navy used marines to occupy Toishan on more than one occasion over the next several years. Attention was also directed against the Kwangsi road network running northeast from French Indochina. Strangely, Kongmoon was one of the few cities to avoid initial bombardment, and one missionary, the Reverend Duncan McRae, speculated that the reason might be due to the fact that two of the characters used in spelling Kongmoon were used in the name of Emperor Hirohito. Kongmoon was also a source of vegetables for the Japanese navy, and at this stage of the war, cholera remained a bigger problem there than Japanese bombers.[67]

After the aborted Japanese invasion of Kwangtung and the failed coup d'état in February, the Japanese consul in Hong Kong, Nakamura Toyokazu, stated in April 1938 that intensive air raids were the only way Japan could prevent the importation of war materials into China. He also noted, "Chiang will never sue for peace and Japan must use stronger measures to defeat his government."[68] The terror bombing of Canton from May to June was greatly intensified, with the Japanese navy's long-range Mihoro Air Group pounding Canton regularly from bases in Formosa, along with units from the *Kaga*. The large numbers of civilian casualties shocked many foreign nationals, who believed the Japanese bombing of Canton was primarily meant to terrorize the population. This charge was brought before the League of Nations as early as March, but the international reaction remained limited.[69]

Civilian targets were most commonly hit, and as the death toll climbed, sympathy for the Chinese grew among many foreigners. A missionary for the United Church of Canada reported on an earlier raid: "At one, thirty in the afternoon (in clear daylight) . . . Japanese planes dropped six bombs on a residential area killing not less than three hundred persons, mostly women and children. When the bombing stopped Dr. Bates . . . brought out wounded and dying."[70] Dr. F. Bates ran a hospital in the eastern part of Canton near Tien Ho airfield, which had been heavily bombed for several days. Many dead and wounded from nearby residential areas were discovered shortly after. In mid-June 1938 the YMCA was targeted repeatedly, and one raid killed hundreds just outside its doors. Several thousand had been killed in Canton not only by bombing but also by low-level strafing. Many more had been wounded. Passenger boats plying the West and Pearl rivers were likewise strafed. On another occasion a sewing factory was hit, killing scores of young women. Incendiary munitions were used, and KCR stations were attacked, killing many others. Canadian doctors Victoria

Cheung, Jack Lind, and Richard Cockfield treated many of the wounded and sent reports of these incidents to the United Church in Toronto. There had been 400 air strikes throughout Kwangtung up to that time, and air raids on Canton continued into July. Of the original 1.3 million residents of that city, only 600,000 remained by summer's end.[71] Many had moved to the relative safety of Hong Kong, creating additional security problems for the colonial government.

During the Canton air raids, people tried to move close to the Anglo-French concession of Shameen Island (Sand Bank) to avoid being hit, but this often proved futile as the Japanese navy demonstrated its willingness to attack third-power targets with regularity. Shameen was often hit by bombs and machine gun fire. Many Chinese were strafed in the canal between the concession and the city. To prevent people from seeking refuge there, the concession gates were often kept closed.[72] On 8 June 1938 Ambassador Sir Robert Craigie protested Japanese belligerency and the numerous over-flights of Shameen: "The Japanese attacking aircraft have in many cases flown over Shameen, and on one occasion an aeroplane passed directly over the British Consulate-General, at a height of barely 600 feet. Moreover when the locomotive sheds at Wongsha Station were hit from over 10,000 feet on 5th June the bombs passed directly over Shameen."[73] Japanese naval commanders were not greatly concerned about British complaints.

Craigie also expressed his government's displeasure at the large loss of life among civilians, but again, Japanese authorities were not greatly worried. A news article reported that in response to diplomatic protests, the Japanese "agreed to pay the French government approximately $100,000 for damage caused to the French cathedral at Canton during air raids last week," but observers estimated that the damage totaled four times the sum the Japanese were willing to pay.[74]

Not all the raids launched against Canton were indiscriminate. Directed attacks against specific rail facilities such as Wongsha Station were carried out with the aim of destroying military infrastructure. Colonel Stilwell noted that some of the most severe bombing in Canton was designed to interrupt rail supplies from Hong Kong so that the Japanese would not have to "commit themselves to land operations in South China, operations which cannot but further strain the already . . . tired resources of Japan."[75] These attacks usually failed, and although Wongsha Station itself was partially damaged, railway operations were not significantly disrupted. Nor were supplies impeded in Hunan or Kiangsi to any great degree, and the branch line south of Chuchow (Zhuzhou) remained in use to supply the forward battle areas near Nanchang. To compensate, the Japanese navy bombed Swatow in June 1938, and the port of Amoy had been seized in May. Namao Island (near Swatow) was also occupied as a springboard for future operations in Kwangtung.[76]

The Japanese navy's air assault on Canton was designed to aggravate political divisions between the central government and the Kwangtung independence faction, and in this, the Japanese were successful.[77] Because most of the Chinese air force was busy over Hankow, there were conspicuously few air units available to defend against Japanese attacks. The lack of Chinese air defenses greatly worsened the rift between north and south. Those few air units available in Kwangtung were of mixed quality, as one example provided by Hong Kong military intelligence well illustrates: "Colonel Ng, who was shot down and killed while flying a 'Gladiator' early in October, 1938, at Namyung (North-East Kwangtung) was at the time leading a flight of three aircraft, but as soon as they met the Japanese formation the other two aircraft turned back and their pilots 'bailed out.' Colonel Ng accounted for two Japanese aircraft before he himself was shot down."[78] In addition to the lack of fighters, antiaircraft guns and ammunition remained scarce in Canton because of the earlier coup attempt. Chiang's lack of trust in local Kwangtung commanders (except for General Yu) prevented any strengthening of air defense units. The city had three batteries of four three-inch guns, several Soviet 37mm guns, and one battery of three 120mm guns, but all these weapons lacked sufficient ammunition due to rivalries among the civil and military leadership, in addition to the distrust of the central government.[79] Chiang's statement that "today's sacrifices will pave the way for tomorrow's victories" did little to improve matters.[80] Kwangtung newspapers printed many grievances about this state of affairs and about Chiang's hollow-sounding promises that southern air defenses would be strengthened.

While the air war in Kwangtung intensified, many were dismayed at the limited official response by Great Britain, as the country's foreign policy remained based on the avoidance of open war with Japan. Oscar Thomson, a Canadian doctor in Canton, wrote to a colleague in May: "Even the Japs must be amazed themselves and British prestige is at zero. The Japs would not have dared bomb the Kowloon (Hongkong) Canton railway. Partly British owned and British financed—had Britain showed some spirit."[81]

Japanese air attacks against railways continued, and when these were conducted close to Hong Kong, they became a potential source of military conflict. Hong Kong's growing isolation raised the anxiety of British residents and officials alike, and it was not long before the conflict's intrusion into areas close to Hong Kong caused a divergence in outlook between British officials in the region and those making policy in London. In time, this divergence caused Hong Kong officials to act independently, both diplomatically and militarily. Henceforth, this problem was a significant factor in the slow escalation of Anglo-Japanese conflict.

The air war against south China also included attacks against aircraft flying out of Hong Kong, with Japanese air units occasionally violating the colony's airspace. These events caused alarm among residents and provoked additional protests by Ambassador Craigie in Tokyo. In one incident a Royal Navy aircraft from HMS *Eagle* encountered Japanese naval anti-aircraft fire off the coast of Hong Kong in November 1937. The attack was described as a legitimate accident by the Japanese, who stated that the officers aboard the vessel in question thought they were firing in self-defense. In December 1937 fifteen Japanese bombers overflew Lantau Island and the Taikoo docks. A protest was lodged in Tokyo, and more antiaircraft guns were delivered to Hong Kong in response. Air action against civilian aircraft also caused great indignation among Hong Kong's residents. The two prominent airline companies flying out of the colony were the China National Aviation Corporation (CNAC) and Eurasian Aviation Corporation. In August 1938 Japanese naval aircraft shot down a CNAC plane near Macau, killing sixteen of the nineteen occupants. The Japanese were attempting to assassinate a prominent Chinese official whose life was saved by a last-minute change in travel plans. The following month two Eurasian aircraft were forced down—one in Kwangtung and the other near Hankow.[82]

Ultimately, the Japanese air campaign was successful in creating greater political divisions in China, but the cost was an increase in diplomatic friction with Great Britain and France, pushing both these powers closer to Chiang Kai Shek. Japanese air attacks on military depots in Canton caused the Chinese army to rely on alternative lines of communication that bypassed the city. As with the earlier coup attempt, these routes proved strategically useful, since the Chinese refined their ability to move large quantities of material around Canton to the railroad in northern Kwangtung. More important, once the Japanese army invaded south China in October 1938, the disruption of these supply lines from Hong Kong intensified, and the potential for conflict between British and Japanese military forces increased over time.

The Japanese were loud in their criticism of British aid and, in conjunction with the air campaign, began naval interdiction operations against Chinese vessels plying the waters near Hong Kong.[83] Attacks were conducted against junks carrying military supplies from Hong Kong to coastal China. Aside from merely impeding supply, another objective was to secure British agreement to terminate their support altogether. Ultimately, Japanese officials hoped to intimidate the British into recognizing greater Japanese authority in China.

During the first year of the war, attacks on Hong Kong junks and other vessels were limited in frequency compared with later years, but they were violent and constituted a direct provocation to British authorities. The first of these was recorded in September 1937, when a Japanese submarine sank eleven junks. Most of the people aboard these vessels were killed, including many women and children, and almost all of them lived in Hong Kong. The Japanese claimed that they had been forced to return fire when the junks attacked their ships. On 11 December 1937 a Japanese destroyer fired on a Chinese customs cruiser inside Hong Kong's territorial waters. This violation of British sovereignty was followed by the intrusion of two additional destroyers that entered the area to tow the vessel away. Japanese sailors also landed on a British-controlled island and stole property. Diplomatic pressure failed to produce any noticeable results, and an armed Japanese motor trawler again violated Hong Kong's waters to attack four more junks on 11 February 1938. Nonetheless, Ambassador Craigie continued to make representations in Tokyo throughout the winter. In February 1938 the SS *Asian* was seized and taken to Bako in the Pescadores (west of Formosa), but the ship was eventually released. There was a temporary lull during March and April, but large numbers of Japanese vessels appeared near Hong Kong in May to coincide with the terror bombing of Canton. In May 1938 a Chinese sampan was destroyed by an armed Japanese motor trawler in Hong Kong territorial waters, and a junk was seized. In these attacks one of the sampan's crewmen was decapitated, and the entire junk crew was killed.[84]

Smaller patrol vessels such as destroyers, motor torpedo boats (MTBs), or trawlers were used by all sides in the Kwangtung naval war because of their better speed and mobility and because of the risk posed by deploying larger ships near the coast. Small vessels were also more suited for stopping and boarding junks and were easier to conceal in coastal inlets. Japanese main-force units were sometimes deployed to south China from the Marianas in support of coastal operations; these usually consisted of one or two cruisers accompanied by a flotilla of four or five destroyers. One or two carriers plus four or five fleet auxiliaries would also be on station at such times.

Chinese tactics in the Hong Kong junk war were well suited to advancing their strategy of involving Great Britain in the conflict. The topography of the Kwangtung coast enabled the Chinese to utilize their meager naval forces to the fullest, thereby provoking Japanese retaliation near and within Hong Kong waters. While being interviewed by a British newspaper reporter, a Portuguese air force officer stationed at Macau stated that the Japanese had begun their naval attacks because Chinese MTBs had been using the junks as cover to approach Japanese warships. This officer reported that one Chinese MTB had sunk a Japanese seaplane carrier near Macau with a quick torpedo shot using these tactics. The Chinese MTB and all the accompanying junks had then been sunk by the destroyer escort.[85] Regardless of the actual outcome, simply by attempting an attack of this kind near Hong Kong, the Chinese advanced their strategy by extending the war into areas of British military and economic interest. Attacks on junks effectively expanded the blockade to include Hong Kong's food supply and recklessly damaged Anglo-Japanese relations because this was the most likely reason for British and Japanese naval forces to come into direct conflict. Of the three military services stationed at Hong Kong, it was the Royal Navy that, despite its limited size, had the only real ability to project power outside of the colony's boundaries. The violence of these attacks held the greatest potential for triggering an Anglo-Japanese confrontation at sea should Royal Navy forces intervene in defense of Hong Kong junks. Protection of the Hong Kong fishing fleet became such a serious problem that it almost led to open warfare during the summer of 1941.

Like the bombing of the railroads and Canton, the attacks on Hong Kong junks created a great deal of anger among the colony's residents, as well as in Kwangtung. Some of the criticism regarding the lack of official reaction was expressed by missionaries working in the region. Dr. Thomson wrote in May 1938: "Foreigners and Chinese here cannot understand why Britain allows the Japs to persecute and destroy the Hongkong fishing fleet—the personnel of which were born in Hongkong territory—live there, are there registered and pay taxes."[86] A month later he added that the Japanese navy "seems to delight in destroying the South China and Hong Kong fishing fleets. . . . Many foreigners have watched the Japanese warships attack, sink or set the junks on fire. Why? Why are they given no protection by the British warships in Hong Kong?"[87]

One reason for British restraint was a lack of clarity about who the Hong Kong government was responsible for. Many of the fishermen and traders plying the waters between Hong Kong and Macau were residents of Hong Kong as well as Chinese nationals. Where did the British government's responsibilities start and end? Questions of governmental responsibility were intertwined with questions of nationality and identity. Over time, these attacks caused the Chinese government to become more involved in Hong Kong's internal affairs, and by 1941 it insisted on the establishment of a consulate in the colony.[88]

From the outset of the Sino-Japanese War, Hong Kong served as the most significant source of supply for the Chinese army, and the Japanese were quick to respond. Aerial interdiction of Chinese lines of communication both in Kwangtung and at sea resulted in a state of low-intensity conflict in the Pearl River Delta between Japanese and British military forces. Anglo-Japanese diplomatic relations worsened as British sympathies, among both residents and officials, became more supportive of the Chinese. In time, colonial officials' frustration grew over the inability to protect the Hong Kong Chinese against what was considered Japanese piracy. Hong Kong officials began to assume greater initiative and independence of action in countering Japanese aggression, but in 1937 and 1938 they continued to follow London's lead. They limited the use of their resources to rescuing Chinese crews when possible and continued to monitor Japanese naval activity closely. For four and a half years, however, the transshipment of war supplies from the colony was not interrupted by British officials, and much of this traffic was carried in Hong Kong junks. Although there were many factors behind the start of the Pacific war, the end of this practice was one of the reasons the Japanese attacked the colony with a direct ground assault in December 1941. As will be seen, the invasion of Kwangtung in October 1938 was one of the major steps toward this cataclysmic result.

British Far Eastern Policy:
Collective Security in East Asia

British Far Eastern policy during 1937 and 1938 was not well defined, and the resulting policy vacuum helped escalate Anglo-Japanese tensions. This

CHAPTER THREE

ultimately contributed to the diminution of British power. Problems in China were often regarded as an unwelcome diversion from what were considered more important events in Europe.[89] Although British policy seemed to be based on the protection of imperial interests, ideological considerations shared by many government officials and parliamentarians in London were inimical to the formulation of a sound strategy in China.

During the 1930s many believed that only through disarmament would a new world order be peacefully imposed on nations; more specifically, they held that collective security should be maintained without arms.[90] Many idealists, often found within the House of Commons, increasingly shared propinquity with influential personages more closely aligned with private policy councils such as the Royal Institute of International Affairs—an organization pursuing the centralization of global economic and political power under Anglo-American control.[91] Sir John Brenan was another senior official at the Foreign Office who thought that Japanese exhaustion in China made the rise of a socialist regime in Tokyo both possible and desirable.[92] Being antinationalistic in its worldview, the USSR was starting to be seen as a potential ally in the looming war with Germany, despite the shared tactics of the Nazi government and the damage inflicted on millions of people by Stalin and the NKVD.[93] A good number of officials also held strong communist sympathies, and, according to Major Barrett, some British embassy and consular officials in China, including Ambassador Clark Kerr, were fervently pro-Soviet. These officials strongly and regularly encouraged the approval of all possible assistance to China.[94] Others, such as Donald Maclean of the Cambridge Five, along with John Cairncross and Captain J. King at the Foreign Office, were outright Soviet agents or assets.[95]

Under the leadership of Anthony Eden from 1935, the Foreign Office began pushing the government to adopt a more confrontational posture against the fascist dictatorships, even though Britain was still militarily weak. Britain was being steered into a period of protracted warfare it could not afford against enemies that were too numerous to contain. In February 1938 Prime Minister Neville Chamberlain reasserted some cabinet control over foreign policy, causing Eden to be replaced by Lord Halifax. This brought renewed emphasis for conciliation with Germany.[96] A notable observer of international relations during this period—one who would play a role in the fate of Hong Kong during the war—commented on the significance of the changes taking place in the British government.

In London for the Imperial Conference in May 1937, just before his visit with Hitler, Prime Minister William Lyon Mackenzie King of Canada noted: "This is indeed a moment of change in British politics. We are crossing the Great Divide—whether into storms and disaster or into a re-ordering of world affairs, no one can say; one can only pray that it may not be the former."[97] British High Commissioner to Ottawa Sir Francis Floud reported Mackenzie King's views to London following Eden's departure in 1938: "He was solidly in support of Mr. Chamberlain's policy of seeking agreement with Italy and Germany. He naturally regretted Mr. Eden's resignation but he said that he had realised when in London last summer that there would be little hope of any agreement with Mussolini or Hitler so long as Mr. Eden was at the Foreign Office."[98] By challenging the Japanese in China, British Far Eastern policy makers accepted the inherent risk to imperial security, but they did so with the aim of influencing Soviet foreign policy in Europe.

Eden was just one of many officials who chose to ignore the incongruity of selecting Stalin as a potential ally. Those who were paying attention to the Far East, especially within the Foreign Office, continued to push for increased British support to China even after Lord Halifax assumed duties as foreign secretary in February. Informal collective security in China was a precursor to what many hoped would become a more structured arrangement in Europe. Thus, during 1938, while most of the government was focused on Germany, the Far Eastern Section of the Foreign Office quietly brought Britain's China policy into line with that of the USSR. Over time, a de facto Anglo-Soviet collective security arrangement developed in East Asia as each nation used China to wage a proxy war against Japan. This kept the Japanese army away from more vital areas of economic or military interest, such as Vladivostok.

The problem Whitehall faced was that military weakness rendered diplomatic confrontation much less effective, but at least in Europe, British foreign policy rested on the combined strength of the French army and the Royal Navy. To compensate for military weakness in China, the British also attempted to parallel their diplomatic efforts with those of the United States in order to maintain the appearance of wider collective action even while it was still in its infancy. In this way, the Japanese were kept guessing as to how much international support Britain actually possessed.[99] Conversely, the extension of aid to China was considered useful to increase American involvement in Far Eastern affairs.[100] Without substantial military forces in place, however, Anglo-Japanese antagonism was the likely outgrowth of an ambiguous Far Eastern strategy that transformed Hong Kong from an imperial outpost into a strategic Chinese logistical base. So long as Germany was considered Britain's primary threat, empire defenses could not be strengthened. The result of this unaltered situation at Hong Kong was likely to be the ensnarement of Britain's limited military forces in south China and the exhaustion of British power in an enlarged conflict. British foreign policy provided indirect support to the Soviet Union in China, but the weapons trade from Hong Kong threatened to enlarge the war.

Thus, British assistance to China continued covertly after battles at Shanghai and Taierhchuang encouraged the Foreign Office to maintain its support. J. Thyne Henderson wrote of the Chinese determination to fight: "The Chinese Government have shown themselves capable of putting up a much better defence than was expected. It is also now clearer that our interests in China have better chances of favourable treatment under a Chinese regime than under a Japanese."[101] To maintain the appearance of neutrality, however, and because of rearmament difficulties at home, direct British arms sales were kept to a minimum, and military supplies transported on American or British vessels could not be transshipped along the KCR; weapons carried on third-power vessels, such as those from Germany, were able to proceed unhindered. Since there had been no declaration of war, the British saw no need to place an embargo against either side, and the weapons trade was allowed to continue in Hong Kong without interference. Eden was supported in this by Chamberlain as early as 6 October 1937. Aid to China was also encouraged by officials in the region, including the acting governor of Hong Kong, N. L. Smith, and Consul General Robert Howe at Shanghai.[102]

Alternatives to maintaining covert support for China were few but present. One option would have been to terminate the flow of war supplies from Hong Kong into China in an attempt to improve Anglo-Japanese relations. This is what Ambassador Craigie recommended in Tokyo. It was his considered opinion that relations with China could be salvaged at a later date. Those in the Foreign Office, such as Henderson and permanent undersecretary Sir Alexander Cadogan, however, thought Craigie was too optimistic about maintaining peace in the long term, especially in the face of continued Japanese military success.[103]

Another alternative was to withdraw military forces from the region altogether. This was considered prudent by Colonel Gordon E. Grimsdale as early as 1934, when the Far Eastern Combined Intelligence Bureau was established.[104] Like Grimsdale, Major General A. E. Grasett, future general officer commanding (GOC) in China, had also determined that it was unsound to defend Hong Kong with the limited forces available. He came to this conclusion while at the Imperial Defence College in Camberley. After assuming duty in the colony in November 1938, Grasett's opinion reversed dramatically, but until that time, demilitarization was still considered viable by some. Demilitarization was not a very popular idea in London, however; it was considered an unnecessary and dishonorable sacrifice of British prestige.[105]

A third course of action would have been to strengthen military forces in the Far East and concentrate on the defense of the British Empire and the Dominions. But this could have been accomplished only after a diplomatic realignment toward neutrality in Anglo-German relations. Martin Brice reflected on this problem in his memoirs of Royal Navy service in China: "It was all very well for the Foreign Office to explain that ships were needed to back up foreign policy: it would help if the Foreign Office could reduce the number of our enemies. In the meantime we must cut our cloth according to our limited pocket."[106]

To effectively challenge Japanese expansion, preparations for war in the Far East would have required full Chinese military cooperation. A joint Sino-British defense plan for operations in the Pearl River Delta and for southern China in general might have been a useful deterrent to Japanese aggression if it had been formed without delay. In the event of war, it might have made a defense of Hong Kong more tenable. Instead of these options, however, the British decided to simply continue supporting the Chinese army by allowing the transshipment of supplies at Hong Kong.[107]

British Far Eastern policy gradually became more confrontational, but military strategy was never sufficiently adjusted to either deter Japanese aggression or adequately defend the empire. China was starting to be seen as a potential ally, yet Hong Kong was still largely considered an outpost of Singapore—an encumbrance to be held as long as possible in the event of war. In July 1937 the Committee of Imperial Defence (CID) took some initial steps in forming an appreciation of Hong Kong that better addressed the colony's new function as a Chinese military supply base, but demilitarization was still discounted, primarily because of its impact on British prestige. Significantly, the effect on Chinese morale was also discussed, and a CID memorandum noted: "We wish to emphasize the importance which

CHAPTER THREE

we attach in the event of war against Japan, to the co-operation of the Chinese, which is likely to be forthcoming only if we maintain our position at Hong Kong."[108] This position was reaffirmed by the CID when it met one year later in July 1938, but without reinforcements for the Far East, British military strategy in Asia remained inadequate to maintain the security of the empire.[109]

The Chiefs of Staff had determined by mid-1938 that as long as munitions and supplies continued to move from Hong Kong into China and its military defenses remained weak, the situation virtually compelled the Japanese to stage an operation to neutralize or capture the colony. Nevertheless, optimism prevailed because they thought that even in this scenario, Hong Kong "would fulfill the proper function of an outpost by drawing off forces which might otherwise be used against Singapore. Moreover, operations by our Fleet in support of the invested garrison might offer the best chance of bringing on a Fleet action against the Japanese Navy, which would be all to our advantage."[110] Although the CID recognized the likelihood of a Japanese attack on the colony, British army forces at Hong Kong were not strengthened until November 1941, with the arrival of two Canadian infantry battalions. It was hoped that the Japanese would be deterred from attacking by the potential power of the U.S. Pacific Fleet.

The limited strength of Royal Navy forces stationed in Hong Kong reflected this reality, and most vessels were withdrawn by the end of 1940. The China Station order of battle included the 5th Cruiser Squadron, with the cruiser HMS *Cumberland* arriving at Hong Kong in April 1938. This vessel was replaced by HMS *Kent* in September. The 21st Destroyer Flotilla and the 4th Submarine Flotilla were also present, in addition to a handful of gunboats of the West River Flotilla and the 2nd MTB Flotilla. In March 1938 Hong Kong's gunboats consisted of HMS *Tarantula*, *Robin*, *Seamew*, *Cicala*, and *Moth*. These generally patrolled the West River, and their main ports of call were Hong Kong, Canton, Kongmoon, Wuchow, Samshui (Sanshui), and Macau. Royal Navy activity in south China was concerned primarily with protecting British economic interests and suppressing piracy, but gunboats also assisted diplomats in the course of their duties and hoisted the Union Jack during official functions, such as the annual Flotilla Pulling Regatta at Canton from 18 to 21 March 1938 and Empire Day on 24 May. Chinese gunboats and the French gunboat *Argus* also participated in British celebrations at Canton, and the Royal Navy responded in similar fashion. By December 1941, only the destroyer HMS *Thracian* plus a few gunboats and MTBs remained in Hong Kong, ready for battle.[111] The most useful naval units employed by the British to investigate Japanese attacks and conduct patrols in and around Hong Kong were the faster vessels, such as destroyers and MTBs, but the paucity of warships throughout the Far East greatly limited the navy's overall ability to deter Japanese aggression.

In the event of war, British strategy called for the relief of Hong Kong by sea within 90 days of the commencement of hostilities, but the strength of Japanese airpower eventually caused a change of opinion that increased this time to 130 days. Hong Kong lacked the ability to provide for its own air defense because there was insufficient room to build an airstrip free from potential Japanese ground bombardment. The Gindrinkers' Line was the basis of British defense plans for the New Territories, but Kai Tak airfield and Kowloon were both within artillery range from many points along that position.[112] Several large airfields at Canton could have been supplied overland from Burma, but the use of these airfields would have required overt Sino-British military cooperation, which was never fully developed.

After the arrival of Governor Sir Geoffry Northcote in October 1937, the defense plan for Hong Kong was reviewed, and GOC Major General A. H. Bartholomew decided not to request additional reinforcements for the colony. A new battle plan was adopted instead. By July 1938 the Gindrinkers' Line had been abandoned as a defensive position, and the only resistance that would be offered in the New Territories was sabotage and demolitions along the Japanese line of advance for up to forty-eight hours after the commencement of hostilities. Defense of the colony was to be made only on the island itself, but the main problem went unresolved. Lack of troops and mobile artillery meant that the garrison was unable to defend Hong Kong against a determined assault. Ground forces in Hong Kong included only four infantry battalions plus the Hong Kong Volunteer Defence Corps (HKVDC), which approximated the strength of another reinforced battalion. In January 1938 the HKVDC comprised about 70 officers and 1,000 men. Taking one kilometer per battalion as the maximum frontage that could possibly be covered by infantry at a basic level of training and experience (during the battle of Okinawa, veteran U.S. Marine battalions covered about half a kilometer), the number of battalions defending Hong Kong was less than half that needed just to man the eleven-kilometer Gindrinkers' Line, let alone man a perimeter defense of Hong Kong Island against an amphibious assault or provide for an operational reserve. Over-confidence based on the lack of Japanese success in defeating the weaker Chinese army resulted in an underestimation of Japanese military capabilities, and this was a significant factor behind the decision not to adjust the garrison's strength or to seek greater military cooperation with Chiang.[113]

Besides a lack of numbers, defense-oriented tactical training was another factor that handicapped the garrison. Hong Kong military forces were ultimately defeated in December 1941 because few officers fully appreciated the combat advantages of coordinated fire and movement that benefited an attacker in modern war. Colonel Lindsay Ride, future head of the British Army Aid Group (BAAG), felt that the garrison never practiced for realistic operations. Only defensive exercises of withdrawal were conducted, and the idea of employing counterattacks against high-ground positions captured by enemy forces was not fully considered. This helped build a fatalistic outlook and sapped any latent offensive spirit that might have existed within the garrison. Consequently, an aggressive defense was never really contemplated or planned for prior to the attack, and in December 1941 the defenders had great difficulty retaking all-important elevated terrain whenever it was lost to the Japanese.[114] As Colonel Ride commented at the time, "Hong Kong never got down to real war until it was too late."[115] Ride also noted that the government was "rotten" and failed to provide the necessary impetus to prepare the colony for war. Despite the inadequate defense situation at Hong Kong, the colony was still expected to function as a logistical base for Chinese military supplies. Over time, this provoked a Japanese attack.

The lack of uniformity between British Far Eastern foreign and military policies was also due to conflicting organizational aims and objectives. After Governor Northcote's arrival in the colony, confusion surfaced in both Hong Kong and London over an issue of great future significance that highlighted the ambiguity of Britain's wartime strategy in China. Early in 1938 the British were presented with the possibility of purchasing the New Territories from China, which would have negated the need to hand back the colony at the termination of the lease agreement in 1997.[116] This development was important in 1938 for several reasons. First, it showed how the divergence in strategic planning within Whitehall was mirrored by a split in political objectives between London and colonial officials at Hong Kong. The lack of a consensus on strategy with Hong Kong officials only deepened as time went on, and this divergence became a factor in escalating the Sino-Japanese War. Second, this issue reaffirmed that the level of British wartime support for China would remain limited in scale. Over time, the hypocrisy of proffering moral encouragement for continued Chinese resistance without providing substantial overt military aid caused Sino-British relations to strain to the breaking point. Third, the decision not to purchase the New Territories showed that British strategy in China was not greatly influenced by imperial concerns.

The idea to purchase the New Territories was first broached by Sir Shouson Chow, who in December 1937 was leader of the Chinese National Bonds Subscription Branch Society in Hong Kong.[117] This organization was headed by T. V. Soong for the purpose of raising war revenue for the Chinese central government. Between January and February 1938 Madame Chiang Kai Shek (Soong Mei Ling), her siblings Soong Ai Ling (wife of Finance Minister H. H. Kung) and Soong Ching Ling (wife of Sun Yat Sen), and T. V. Soong had all been gathered in Hong Kong at about the same time the attempted coup in Kwangtung collapsed and peace talks with the Japanese began. At some point between February and early April, Chow approached Governor Northcote to discuss the idea of a purchase agreement or lease extension between Great Britain and China with regard to the New Territories. Although British sovereignty over Hong Kong Island had already been established in perpetuity, the lease expiry date set for the New Territories was 1997, and it was felt that retaining control of the island was impossible without controlling the New Territories.[118] On 13 April 1938 Northcote informed the secretary of state for the colonies, William Ormsby-Gore, about the proposition and stated his reasons why it should be approved:

> The new territories are essentially necessary to Hong Kong from the economic as well as the defensive point of view. Retention of Hong Kong is essentially necessary to Great Britain—and, indeed, to the Empire—economically speaking; and all the more so in view of Shanghai's jeopardy: it is equally necessary to China from a standpoint of defence, as the present hostilities have demonstrated. China in her *present* mood would recognize the latter point: when the renewal of the lease comes up she may not be so disposed.[119]

Nigel Ronald at the Foreign Office commented in mid-May that Ambassador Clark Kerr had recently recommended the provision of some form of concrete material assistance to the Chinese, whose losses had been heavy and who desperately needed money to shore up their currency and purchase additional munitions.[120]

During the spring of 1938 the purchasing scheme gathered momentum in Hong Kong, and the Foreign Office in London expressed interest. The plan was strongly supported by the commander in chief of China Station, Vice Admiral Sir Percy Noble, and Ambassador Clark Kerr expressed enthusiasm for a lease extension.[121] Governor Northcote was most enthusiastic about the proposal from the beginning and wrote to the new colonial secretary, Malcolm MacDonald, on 11 June 1938 in full support of it: "The volume of trade along the Hong Kong–Hankow railway is certain to grow steadily when China is again in a position to develop her south-western provinces. Moreover, it may be asserted safely, I think, that Great Britain's prestige in this part of the world rests to a very large extent upon the fortunes of this colony."[122] He also noted why the opportunity had to be seized at that time:

> It is unlikely that at any future time China will be more deeply impressed by the advantage accruing to her through Hong Kong being possessed by a strong foreign and friendly Power than she is at present; and, secondly, although sixty years of the lease's currency have still to run, the injurious effect upon British trade and capital of a prospect of non-renewal of the lease would be operative many years before the actual date of expiry of the lease.[123]

The price being considered was £20 million. Northcote continued to press urgently for acceptance of the proposal following his visit to Canton aboard HMS *Tarantula* on 23 July 1938, noting that Sir Shouson Chow and Sir Robert Kotewall had both agreed to act as intermediaries with the Chinese government to facilitate any agreement and that time was likely running out if they wanted a favorable response from the Chinese.[124] By July 1938, the greatest pressure for a purchase agreement or lease extension was coming from British officials in China, especially Northcote, while those in London outside the Foreign Office remained cautiously observant of further developments.

In London, Lord Halifax agreed with MacDonald about the need for an interdepartmental meeting to settle this issue. On 26 August 1938 the Colonial Office hosted such a meeting, but the result did little to improve

Britain's position in East Asia.[125] In attendance were H. R. Cowell (chairman), F. J. Howard and P. Rogers of the Colonial Office, Sir John F. Brenan of the Foreign Office, D. J. Wardley and E. G. Compton of the Treasury, Captain G. K. Bourne of the War Office, Major G. W. M. Grover and C. G. Jarrett of the Admiralty, and Wing Commander R. M. Foster from the Air Ministry. Arguments for and against the deal were made, but it was ultimately rejected on several grounds. The chief concern was that such a deal would provoke a Japanese response, and a previous loan for China had already been rejected for the same reason. In addition, it was thought that in the event of Chinese capitulation to Japan, a puppet Chinese government would not recognize the agreement. The Air Ministry, War Office, and Colonial Office representatives were essentially neutral or cool to the scheme, while the Admiralty appeared somewhat lukewarm. The Foreign Office expressed a measure of greater interest.[126]

The War Office and the Air Ministry were well aware of the lack of resources available to defend Hong Kong and were not inclined to push for an increase in their commitments to the region. Without greater resources to defend Far Eastern possessions, it was logical that they would not fully endorse the proposal. The Foreign Office expressed support not because of any imperialist ambitions but because the deal presented an opportunity to strengthen Chinese resistance. The final decision was made by the Treasury, however, which simply stated that the price was excessive. Thus the deal was shelved, and any immediate material assistance to China remained an unlikely prospect. Nigel Ronald succinctly summarized British policy following the meeting: "I am sceptical as to whether pusillanimity, tempered with hypocrisy, pays as a policy in the long run."[127] It was still hoped that the Chinese would maintain the war effort as best as they could, but Sino-British relations were not improved as a result of this decision. Similarly, it did nothing to improve Anglo-Japanese relations, as British objections to Japanese expansion in north China continued to lack credibility so long as the British maintained a colonial presence at Hong Kong.

This issue remained on the back burner until just after New Year's Day in 1939, when the governor again wrote to the Colonial Office and urged that the matter be reconsidered. The fall of Canton to Japanese forces in October 1938 seemed to have shut the door to any positive response from Chungking, but Northcote still thought there was a chance for its acceptance. One of the principal reasons he revived the proposal was the military factor involved:

I have throughout this correspondence kept to the economic argument and kept off that of defence but I feel that I should add this. If Inquiry goes to show that the commercial importance of Hong Kong does *not* justify the expenditure that would be necessary to procure a long extension of the lease, then this Colony must be regarded as a wasting asset; for it is undeniable that it cannot continue to exist into the next century as a British Colony without the extension. In that case surely the following questions arise as riders:

(1) Is it worth H.M.G.'s while to spend many millions of pounds fortifying a wasting asset?
(2) Would it not be wiser to demilitarize the Colony at once?

Northcote summarized his position and that of the scheme's supporters as follows:

(1) Hong Kong's survival into the next century is of prime importance to the future of British trade in China.
(2) Unquestionably that survival depends upon retention by Great Britain of at least part of the New Territories.
(3) The whole issue is one which demands instant consideration.[128]

Sir Shouson Chow continued his efforts for another month or two, and Northcote noted that Chow had been "in the employ of the Chinese Government for some 30 years, I believe, and rose to high rank. His unsought advice on this matter has always impressed me as significant."[129] But after the fall of Canton, the chances that London would approve an official approach to the Chinese government were virtually nil. Brenan indicated his altered position on 23 February 1939: "The Governor is asking the Government to be a good deal more farsighted than it is in the nature of democratic governments to be."[130] Essentially, this was the problem affecting British foreign policy overall. On 8 March 1939 he added, "If anything was to be done it should have been while the Chinese were still in control of Kwangtung. It is too late now."[131]

For the same reason that Northcote thought it wise to demilitarize Hong Kong, the military services did not wish to purchase the New Territories. There were insufficient military forces available to defend the British Empire as long as Germany was considered the primary threat. That being the case, there was not much point in increasing commitments to defend the colony. Again Northcote wrote, "As I view it, the issue is in no sense of the term a domestic issue but in every sense an imperial one. Hong Kong has no material interest other than the furtherance of British trade; as a fortress she is a liability and she has no territorial assets. If the Treasury's attitude is such as you appear to suggest then we may as well close this file finally."[132] With that, the scheme to purchase the New Territories was dead.

Had foreign policy objectives been more focused on defending the empire, Britain's position in the Far East and China might have become much stronger, especially with the establishment of an overt military agreement with the Chinese. This, in turn, would have helped direct Japanese ambitions north against the USSR, but this was not a Foreign Office objective. Furthermore, Hong Kong's political future might have developed differently. But in 1938 and 1939 a demonstration of British resolve to defend Hong Kong, if combined with real military strength, at least had the potential to deter further Japanese aggression and impose a salutary effect on the Sino-Japanese War.

Instead, Hong Kong continued to function as a transshipment point for Chinese war supplies, while the colony's ground forces remained weak. These policies were the result of divergent organizational objectives in Whitehall, and they only encouraged the Japanese view that the British army "is very good at Tattoos and displays, but not at much else."[133] The compulsory service bill signed by Governor Northcote in the spring of 1939 was an attempt to show resolve, as exhibited in a letter written to Sir Henry Moore in May:

> I am convinced that the more that we shew our determination not to be driven off our perches in China the more respectful the Japanese will become: and Hong Kong is among the bigger of the local perches. Why should not the announcement of the intention to introduce compulsory service here be as effective vis-à-vis the Japanese as the announcement of that policy for Great Britain was in Europe?
>
> Even Chiang Kai-shek, as the Foreign Office can tell you, was not sure until Clark-Kerr's recent visit that we meant to defend Hong Kong "a l'outrance" and he derived much comfort from the assurance that we were. Is it not possible that the Japanese are thinking along the same lines?[134]

Ultimately, Hong Kong's compulsory service legislation could accomplish only so much; it was a Band-Aid solution at best. A few more troops without greater firepower did not alter the fact that the garrison and the colony had become sacrificial pawns in an increasingly dangerous game.

By allowing the transshipment of military supplies at Hong Kong, Chinese resistance was encouraged, and the British remained satisfied that the Japanese could be kept away from other areas of greater strategic importance. Their actions closely followed those of the Soviet Union, albeit less aggressively, and the Chinese army effectively became a proxy military force that was used against Japan. The decision not to purchase the New Territories meant that direct British assistance to China at this stage of the war would remain limited, but several military and diplomatic incidents that followed had the effect of increasing Anglo-Japanese friction and ultimately expanding the scale of the war. One of the most significant of these was the invasion of Kwangtung in October 1938. Military weakness at Hong Kong did not deter the Japanese from taking this step, but the colony itself was not yet attacked, due in part to the fluid diplomatic situation in Europe and the threat of retaliation posed by the United States. Armed with this hope, the British transformed Hong Kong into an important Chinese military supply point, but this represented an escalation of the Sino-Japanese conflict toward a wider war that the British would be unable to manage.

Alternative Lines of Communication: French Indochina and Macau

During the first year of the war, the only real alternative to Hong Kong as a southern point of entry for Chinese military supplies was Haiphong in French Indochina. This was due to its connection to Yunnan along the railway to Kunming. By mid-1938, the Chinese had already begun several large-scale infrastructure construction projects in south China, including the extension of rail lines from Hunan through Kwangsi to branch lines of the French railway running north from Hanoi. Improvements on the Yunnan portion of the Burma Road were also finished on 29 December 1938. The Indochina-Yunnan railway, however, remained the most significant artery aside from the route through Hong Kong. The rail line had been in operation for more than thirty years, and its construction had taken nine years to complete, with many deaths adding to the cost. Yet the main problem with the line was that it extended only as far as Kunming. From there, material had to be transported by a variety of means over a very poor transportation network before reaching its final destination. Later in the war, General Chennault noted that it took six weeks for mules to travel between Kunming and Kwanghan (Guanghan) carrying supplies delivered via Burma and the Himalayan Hump air route. Despite the existing transportation problems in Yunnan and Kwangsi in 1938, 200 tons of munitions and fuel traveled north daily over some of the most difficult terrain in China—regions that included tropical forests, forbidding mountains, and large, swift-moving rivers. By way of comparison, the Hankow-Canton railway hauled ten times as much material over the same period. Even after the occupation of Canton, the amount of useful supplies brought in through Hong Kong and Waichow after bypassing Canton ranged between 1,500 and 5,000 tons per month.[135]

The main difference between these two routes was that the railway from Haiphong ceased to carry any war material once the Japanese occupied northern Indochina in September 1940, whereas Hong Kong remained a source of supply until the outbreak of the Pacific war. Until its occupation, however, the volume of material transiting Indochina remained substantial, and a U.S. Army report noted that Haiphong "is breaking all incoming cargo tonnage records."[136] The majority of supplies consisted of petroleum, oil, and lubricants (POL); trucks; cotton yarn; and piece goods. At the outbreak of war in July 1937, the French government ordered Haiphong closed to the shipment of arms, under pressure from the Japanese, but it delayed the implementation of this order until after the fall of France in June 1940.[137] One reason for this delay was the original Sino-French railway agreement signed in 1903, which stipulated, "If China is at war with a foreign country, the railway will not observe the rules of neutrality but will be entirely at the disposal of China."[138] The problem for France was that the Indochina line was owned entirely by French interests up to Kunming. An attack on it at any point could be considered an attack on a third power. Another political concern limiting its value to Chiang was that the railway helped support the independence of General Lung Yun, head of the government in Yunnan, from central governmental authority.[139]

The railway was useful in other ways, such as helping to establish some of the air defense infrastructure that made Yunnan an important base of operations for Chinese and American air units later in the war. A French-staffed pilot school was first established in the spring of 1938 at Kunming to help train Chinese pilots and provide some degree of defense for the railway. Personnel from a training unit based at Hangchow were assigned there, along with twelve to fifteen large Dewoitine fighters, but the program met with limited success. By June 1938, a Curtis Wright aircraft assembly plant in Canton was also moved to Yunnan. Curtis Wright's agent in China, William Pawley, had requested to build an assembly plant in Hong Kong for Chinese production, but the proposal was repeatedly rejected in London as late as June 1940 to avoid antagonizing Japan. Pawley therefore established a plant at Loiwing in Yunnan, near the Burmese border, in early 1939.[140] These facilities required their own airfields, logistical network, and skilled personnel to operate them effectively, most of which remained available for later use.

Closer to Hong Kong, the Portuguese colony of Macau served as another limited conduit of supplies due to its proximity to the West River. But because it lacked a sufficiently large harbor, it played a subsidiary role relative to Hong Kong. Under these circumstances, junks carrying war supplies routinely traveled between the two colonies. Attacks on junks transiting the western side of the Pearl River Delta, however, were motivated by considerations other than the interdiction of munitions. Japanese efforts to destabilize Kwangtung civil society and to limit potential military resistance against invasion were facilitated by the distribution of opium via Macau.

The Kwangtung opium trade was an additional problem for the British because it encouraged the Japanese to escalate hostilities. Much of the global opium production in 1937 and 1938 came from Korea, Manchoukuo, Persia, and northern China, but Macau was a major conduit within the Japanese distribution network. By way of example, in April 1938 an armed Japanese military vessel transported 80,000 kilograms of raw opium from Persia to Macau, where it was escorted by Portuguese troops through the city to the Banco Nacional Ultramarino. Opium use was widespread in occupied China, and the practice was encouraged by Japanese employers, who often paid workers partially or wholly in opium; those workers who complained were routinely fired. Japanese naval officers were engaged in the smuggling of opium in addition to other commodities, and the attacks on Hong Kong junks constituted an effort to discourage competition.[141] With limited military forces at their disposal, Portuguese officials at Macau had little choice but to accede to Japanese pressure to cooperate, whether they wished to or not.

The presence of Japanese naval forces in southern China created anxiety among Portuguese officials, so authorities in Hong Kong and Macau increased their interaction, with the aim of presenting a more united front of third powers. Shortly after the failed Kwangtung coup in February 1938, the British senior naval officer of the West River Flotilla paid a visit to Macau and met with Governor Artur Tamagnini de Sousa Barbosa; courtesies were also exchanged with Commodore Rebello. A twenty-one-gun salute was fired from HMS *Tarantula*, and this was returned by the colonial fort. Luncheons and dinners were held over several days, and relations between the two colonies were strengthened. Governor Barbosa was enthusiastic about improving Anglo-Portuguese collaboration in the region, and a subsequent visit by Lieutenant Commander D. L. C. Craig aboard HMS *Seamew* occurred in May. On this occasion, Royal Navy officers met with the governor, several of their opposite numbers, and the commissioner of police, Captain Carlos de Souza Gorgulho.[142] In the end, no long-lasting defense arrangements were completed, but the Portuguese did pledge to encourage Macanese traders to continue transporting foodstuffs from the West River into Hong Kong.

Anglo-Japanese Low-Intensity Conflict at Hong Kong

From the start of the Sino-Japanese War, the colony of Hong Kong increasingly drew the attention of the great powers as military conflict escalated throughout the Pearl River Delta. This was due to the continuous flow of weapons and war material from Hong Kong into free China via Kwangtung. Several factors combined to help spread the war from central China into the south.

Political intrigue in Kwangtung weakened governmental authority and damaged popular morale, which in turn encouraged the Japanese to invade. Public anxiety about this eventuality had grown due to a series of destabilizing incidents, including a failed coup, the withdrawal of effective Cantonese military forces, and Japanese interdiction campaigns that culminated in the terror bombing of Canton. Amidst the wreckage of the Cantonese political battles with both Chiang Kai Shek and the Japanese were the crushed regional aspirations for independence. This did no harm to Chiang, however, as the cost of losing Canton to Japanese occupation was greatly reduced. Moreover, the benefits of deepening Great Britain's involvement in the south China logistical war more than offset the estrangement of any limited (or more likely nonexistent) Cantonese readiness to accept centralized political authority.

For their part, the British helped escalate the conflict by reacting to the war without a uniform strategy, as reflected in the decision not to purchase the New Territories. Military authorities understood the limitations of the power they could exert in East Asia, but the Foreign Office opted to pursue a more aggressive foreign policy than could reasonably be sustained. Seeking to promote collective security with the Soviet Union, Foreign Office officials allowed the movement of military supplies from Hong Kong into free China in order to fight a proxy war intended to impede Japanese military incursions elsewhere. In bringing British foreign policy in line with that of the Soviet Union, albeit less aggressively, the British still hoped to avoid direct military conflict with the Japanese. Their lack of military strength at Hong Kong, however, made this an increasingly difficult scenario to manage as the Japanese were roused to respond. The result of this strategy was the loss of military forces and prestige in the Far East and the prolongation of global war. Upon its conclusion, the Japanese Empire was destroyed, but British power had been sacrificed to the United States and the USSR.

Prior to the invasion of southern China, the Japanese continued to stumble into a wider war because they too lacked a clear, unified strategy among the navy, the army, and the government in Tokyo. The army generally sought to limit the conflict to the north in order to concentrate on the primary enemy: the Soviet Union. The navy looked for glory by advancing in a southerly direction, and many naval commanders were eager to spread the war into Kwangtung. But there was no unanimity within the Japanese armed forces and the government on the crucial question of how to settle the war politically—whether to negotiate with Chiang Kai Shek or establish a set of puppet governments. In Kwangtung they tried to do both and accomplished neither. Hence, the state of low-intensity conflict established between Great Britain and Japan steadily deteriorated in and around Hong Kong, making the war in China—and in Kwangtung in particular—a greater international problem as time progressed.

Control of southern China was the key to victory for both sides in the Sino-Japanese War because it contained the lifeline that enabled the Chinese to continue their struggle. The major components of the vital logistical system in this region were the Hankow-Canton railway, the KCR, and the British colony of Hong Kong. Without Hong Kong, it is doubtful that the losses suffered at Shanghai could have been recouped or that a strong defense along the Yangtse River toward Hankow could have been sustained. Because of this supply network, the Chinese were able to exact a steep price from the Japanese army and continue the war. Consequently, China became a quagmire that sapped Japanese military strength, but the ensuing stalemate only spurred Japan to embark on a suicidal war against Anglo-American forces in December 1941.

FOUR

■

The Trap Is Sprung:
October 1938 to March 1939

In October 1938 the Sino-Japanese War escalated with the Japanese invasion of Kwangtung. This move was designed to cut British support for
China, but it had the opposite effect of provoking a semiunified Anglo-
American economic response. The invasion of south China brought the
war to Hong Kong's door, and the potential for conflict between British
and Japanese military forces rose dramatically as a result. After the simultaneous fall of Hankow, the occupation of the rest of south China emerged
as the next Japanese strategic objective. With Chinese armies defending
Hunan from their base at Changsha, Hong Kong remained a vital source
of supply for continued Chinese resistance. The Canton-Changsha railway
was the primary link to the south, and because of Hong Kong's importance, it was the most significant military transportation system left in free
China. This logistical situation continued even after the fall of Canton—an
event Chiang Kai Shek anticipated as part of his effort to fight the war in
areas of foreign interest. Hong Kong was the most suitable place for this
strategy to be implemented because the transit of military supplies through
the Pearl River Delta was a provocation the Japanese army could not
ignore. Its response created several crises in Anglo-Japanese relations, including the Lo Wu bombing incident in February 1939. Although the occupation of Canton appeared to be a grave military setback, it was an

essential element of Chiang's strategic plan to involve Great Britain directly as an overt cobelligerent against the Japanese.[1]

Third-power involvement in the Sino-Japanese War increased during this period, and a chance to achieve peace in late 1938 was discarded. In addition to the shipment of German and American weapons through Hong Kong, loans were again extended to China as part of a coordinated Anglo-American Far Eastern effort to challenge the Japanese more aggressively. Cooperation between the British and Americans began to coalesce following the fall of Canton and Hainan, partly because of the growing threat to their Asian interests, but early collaboration also coincided with the resumption of Anglo-Soviet discussions about the establishment of a collective security alliance in Europe against Hitler. Stalin's support for Chiang was maintained to ensure Soviet Far Eastern security, and one of the more important functions of British assistance to China remained the provision of indirect support to the USSR. Because of these factors, the Anglo-Soviet proxy war against Japan was intensified, with Hong Kong serving as its primary base of supply.

The Invasion of Kwangtung and Occupation of Canton: October to December 1938

As summer turned to fall in 1938, Japanese military operations reached a crescendo along the Yangtse River, and the southern plan to isolate Hong Kong was implemented. By invading Kwangtung, however, the Japanese became ensnared in a dangerous trap. The Japanese decision to invade southern China was made after the Munich Agreement was signed and hostilities with the Red Army were terminated in the border clash at Changkufeng near Vladivostok. With Manchuria apparently secure, Soviet intervention during Japanese southern operations appeared less likely. Preliminary military action against Kwangtung began with aerial bombardment of Chinese lines of communication. An unopposed landing at Bias Bay commenced on 12 October 1938, followed by a rapid march across the Weiyeung District north of Hong Kong. The virtual isolation of Hong Kong was complete once Canton was occupied less than two weeks after operations began. General Yu Han Mou, commander of the 12th Group Army, was held responsible for the military defeat by both Chinese and foreigners alike, but to better understand Chiang's strategy, it is necessary to examine Yu's role closely.[2] Ignominies surrounded General Yu following his rapid withdrawal from Canton, yet there is evidence that charges of cowardice and treason were made without a full appreciation of the facts.

Early in October 1938 air operations in Kwangsi and Kwangtung, which constituted most of the 4th War Zone under the overall command of General Chang Fa Kwei, were stepped up against Chinese lines of communication. The most frequent targets were rail and road bridges along the Hankow-Canton ailway and the Kowloon-Canton railway (KCR). The most valuable of these was the new large bridge located at Sheklung (Shilong), about halfway between Canton and Hong Kong.[3] Although these raids were frequent and severe, the initial bombing results were ineffective largely because Chinese antiaircraft fire, though weak, caused attacks to be made at high altitude. Yet persistence produced results, and by 11 October, the KCR was forced to suspend traffic. Air strikes continued, and the following day a Hong Kong military intelligence officer reported that "nearly the whole of Kwangtung's communications were bombed—a total of 115 planes in 14 relays dropped 246 bombs on road and rail junctions, stations, etc."[4] With the railway disrupted, the likelihood of Chinese reinforcements arriving from Hunan to assist in the defense of Canton was diminished.

On the night of 11–12 October a Japanese invasion convoy of at least sixty transports entered Bias Bay and was sighted by both the Chinese Watching Service and the merchant vessels SS *Lalita* and *Sagres*. Some large-scale naval activity had been expected in the region because many transports had already been reported farther northeast along the coast. Japanese naval forces of the South China Fleet (5th Fleet) had been augmented for this operation with the aircraft carriers *Kaga*, *Ryujo*, and *Soryu*. The cruiser *Jintsu* was also attached, as well as the 2nd Destroyer Squadron. An additional seaplane carrier was dispatched to Bocca Tigris and the Pearl River, along with the 8th Cruiser Squadron. The Japanese Combined Fleet, minus destroyers and carriers assigned to the 5th Fleet, was also in the region at Amoy.[5]

On 12 October the Japanese invasion of south China began at Bias Bay with a 4:00 AM bombardment of Outaokang (Aotou) and Hachung. Japanese ships owned by the OSK and NYK lines carried the men and equipment of the 5th, 18th, and 104th Divisions, and unopposed landing operations commenced at 4:30. One beachhead was established at Outaokang by elements of the 18th Division, along with two regiments of the 5th Division. From Outaokang, a good road ran to Tamshui (Danshui).

A second beachhead was secured at Hachung by elements of the 104th (Reserve) Division, where a cart track led to the Canton-Swatow road farther inland. Plans were also made for one regiment of the 5th Division to land northwest of Hong Kong near Bocca Tigris and join the remainder of the division after its westward move north of Hong Kong via Sheklung. The initial forces landed at Bias Bay totaled about 30,000 men; they were quickly followed by an additional 20,000. Overall, it was a small invasion force for such an ambitious undertaking.[6]

Japanese movement through the province was swift due to a lack of Chinese resistance, and by the evening of 12 October, the 18th Division had already advanced 10 kilometers inland. Cantonese divisions had previously been sent north to fight at Tehan, leaving only two Chinese divisions—the 151st and 153rd, plus attached local militia—in Kwangtung as part of the 12th Group Army under the command of General Yu Han Mou. It was not possible to reinforce Kwangtung rapidly because the only troops available were located in Kwangsi, and they had to march on foot or take slow river transport.[7] Poor communication and a lack of coordination greatly contributed to the 12th Group Army's ineffectiveness.

The first potential points of defense were located at Tamshui and Pingshan, but the Japanese met no opposition. A British officer commented on the overall lack of Chinese resistance: "Pingshan where the Sai Kong River is deep and broad, and the bridge is of flimsy construction was wholly undefended. There were some entrenchments at Tamshui held by regular troops who bolted at the first signs of the enemy's approach."[8] Tamshui was occupied on 13 October, and aside from some sniping, there was little combat. While the main Japanese force occupied Tamshui, the flank guard seized the transportation hub at Lungkong, which cut the main road network between Hong Kong, Waichow, and Tungkunghsien.[9]

Japanese forces continued to advance on Canton without pause, and Waichow was severely bombed from 12 to 14 October. One Japanese aircraft was lost during these attacks; a few days later, antiaircraft fire brought down four other planes over Kukong and Canton (two at each city). But by this stage, there was virtually nothing left of the meager Chinese air forces in the 4th War Zone, and Japanese losses were minimal. For months the Waichow region had been prepared with trenches and concrete pillboxes, but like at Tamshui, most of the Chinese 151st Division retreated as soon as the Japanese approached. One unit that did not receive its withdrawal orders in time was the 12th Group Army's armored battalion, which was destroyed along the road at Waichow. The loss of this valuable unit was a frustrating blow, as there were few armored fighting vehicles available to rebuild it. Waichow was occupied on 15 October, and its airfield was quickly put into service as a Japanese forward base.[10]

The Japanese continued onward and crossed the East River unopposed at three points. Their eastern column crossed at Wonglik and continued west past Poklo on 16 October. The bulk of the 5th Division marched cross-country to Sheklung and captured the town on 19 October, but its important railway bridge had already been blown up by the retreating Chinese the day before. After more than a year of air strikes, it was the Chinese who delivered the final blow. A good road ran from Sheklung to Tungkunghsien, past the Bocca Tigris forts to Namtau. The 5th Division continued to march southwest along this road to capture Bocca Tigris on 21 October (see figure 4.1). The forts surrendered without firing a shot, and the remaining Japanese regiment (scheduled to assault the area the following day) landed without incident. A few smaller Chinese units attempted to defend strongpoints along the railway with some determination, but the Japanese bypassed these positions without difficulty.[11]

Chinese forces withdrew quickly from Canton on the night of 20–21 October, and in accordance with Chiang's scorched-earth order, they destroyed much of their equipment and many facilities. The provincial capital was soon transferred to Kukong, along with Canton's civilian administration. As an indication of the relative ease with which the invasion forces advanced through Kwangtung, Japanese tanks passed through Canton without infantry support on the afternoon of the twenty-first; the infantry arrived the following day and found the burning hulks of empty buildings and rubble. The entire city had been evacuated, and government buildings and installations that were not destroyed by Japanese planes were instead blown up by retreating Chinese soldiers.[12] U.S. Consul General Irving N. Linnell commented on the situation: "The Chinese withdrawal from Canton was so hurried that stores, munitions, anti-aircraft guns, and railway rolling stock had to be left behind in the yards of the Wongsha station, the terminal of the Canton-Hankow line."[13] The station was completely destroyed on 21 October, but the fires there continued to burn, spreading the damage elsewhere. "Fires and ensuing explosions of carloads of munitions, ammunition dumps and aviation gasoline destroyed the whole Wongsha area. . . . Fires . . . broke out in other areas. They burned . . . unchecked for days, destroying most of the wholesale district of

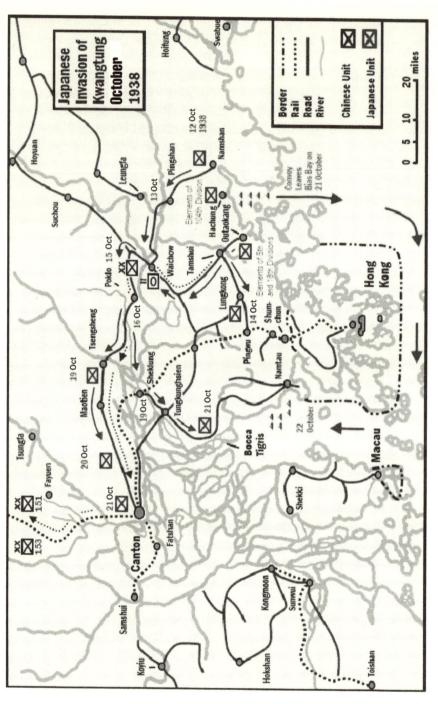

Figure 4.1. Japanese army positions in Kwangtung, October 1938. (Based on data from TNA, WO 106/5356, HKIR No. 22/38.)

Canton." Linnell added, "Canton will not recover for years from the damage it has suffered through fire, looting, and the destruction of the livelihood of its people."[14] Although Chinese troops did not engage in much looting, many of the 20,000 to 30,000 civilians who remained in the city did so, as they were among the poorest residents.

With about 50,000 Japanese troops in Kwangtung, there were only enough units to hold Canton and sections of the East and West rivers. After securing the city, Japanese forces spread out toward Kongmoon in the south and west into Samshui, situated at the confluence of the West and North rivers. In doing so, they were able to control all inland water traffic and trade. Samshui was occupied on 30 October, and West River communications with Kwangsi were cut off. Chinese civilians now had to move overland to avoid Japanese forces. To the north and east of the city, both Tsungfa and Waichow were occupied, but some of the troops posted to these areas were quickly withdrawn. When the operation ended, the bulk of the 5th Division was positioned from Sheklung to Bocca Tigris, the 18th Division occupied the Canton area, and the 104th (Reserve) Division was based between Waichow and Pingshan.[15] By mid-November, most of the Japanese naval vessels that took part were withdrawn to the Marianas after regrouping at Amoy (Xiamen), but the *Kaga* remained in the Gulf of Tonkin to continue bombing targets in Kwangsi.

The rapidity of the Chinese collapse surprised many foreign observers and reinforced the widely held view that the Chinese were of limited value as a potential ally. In particular, General Yu Han Mou was widely accused of being grossly incompetent. Ambassador Sir Archibald Clark Kerr noted that the Chinese abandonment of Canton "without any resistance caused considerable surprise and speculation, especially as the . . . [terrain] . . . is naturally favourable to the defense and . . . elaborate preparations" had been made.[16] Captain Charles Boxer placed the blame for the debacle on "the inept Yu Han Mau and his still more incompetent Chief-of-Staff (who was directly responsible for the faulty troop dispositions which resulted in the loss of that city)."[17] Captain H. Chauvin was less critical of Yu, noting that his genuine concern for the welfare of his men was an indication of competent leadership; Chauvin suggested that Yu's subordinates were more likely the problem.[18]

U.S. assistant military attaché Major David Barrett commented that the presence of Prince Chichibu as part of the invasion force indicated that widespread political divisions in Kwangtung had already been successfully exploited to eliminate resistance. Chichibu's accompaniment of the troops in south China strongly suggested that the Japanese knew in advance that there would be no real fighting.[19] Commander H. E. Overesch, the U.S. naval attaché to China, also surmised that Canton had been set up to fall:

(2) The thrust of the Japanese Expeditionary Force into South China may be given a place as one of the most swiftly executed attacks in history. The speed with which the main objectives were reached, the fall of Canton, after a completely unexpected lack of resistance, left everyone, including military observers, gasping in astonishment. It is honestly believed by this office that the whole situation can be summed up in the statement that only two people knew that South China was not going to be defended. One of these was General Chiang Kai-shek and the other—the Japanese Intelligence Service! In no other way can the sudden and unexpected withdrawal of the Chinese forces be explained.

(3) In no other way can the decisive thrust of an intentionally small Japanese force be explained. If major resistance had been expected in South China, Japan would never have embarked upon the invasion with the limited force that is now known to have been assembled. Nor would this force, after landing, have proceeded so rapidly, disregarding the dangers of tremendously extended lines of communication, unless it was known beforehand exactly what was to be expected.[20]

British officers at Hong Kong reported in similar tones: "The Japanese accepted the risks of landing with a comparatively small force on an open beach. Before them was a march of 150 miles through difficult country with several serious river crossings. At Waichow it was known that elaborate concrete fortifications existed and that . . . a formidable fighting force could have opposed them. Yet they confidently expected to capture Canton at one swoop, and were not disappointed."[21] Clearly, it was well understood that the Chinese had abandoned Canton.

Subversion and the employment of fifth columnists played a role in the collapse. The Japanese spent a great deal of time and money buying the support of many disaffected junior officials, in addition to ordinary fishermen in the Bias Bay region to act as guides. The Japanese navy knew the location of minefields in Bias Bay and swept them in advance. Fishermen in this area often resorted to piracy when the opportunity presented itself, so they had little compunction about helping the Japanese, provided the price was right. Several Kwangtung officials also attempted a coup at the outset of the invasion by naming Marshal Li Chai Sum as the new provincial commander, but Governor Wu Teh Chen sided with General Yu, who remained steadfastly loyal to Chiang throughout. Yu's 12th Group Army remained solidly within the central government's camp, even though it failed to fight the Japanese in any meaningful way. Foreigners such as Consul General Linnell, however, were disappointed that Li had not assumed command in place of Yu.[22]

There was widespread speculation that corruption had been a factor in weakening morale prior to the invasion. A military intelligence officer in Hong Kong reported on this state of affairs: "The first really serious blow to Chiang Kai Shek's prestige was struck by the farcical collapse of the Cantonese defence. . . . The methods employed by the Japanese showed that they were fully aware of the complete rottenness of the Provincial administration. The crookedness of the officials is typified by the horns of the emblem of their capital, the city of Rams."[23] Before the assault, Governor Wu repeatedly and publicly denied that an invasion was imminent, despite evidence to the contrary originating in Shanghai. The invasion was an open secret, and more than forty troop transports, loaded with men, were known to have sailed. In previous weeks, authorities had assured the people of Kwangtung that there was no possibility of an attack because the Japanese did not have enough troops available in China to stage such an offensive. As a result, many people in the region were caught unprepared.[24] Wu continued to deny the threat to Canton even after the assault had begun; he and others had embezzled more than 40 percent of the defense fund earmarked for munitions, and they needed to buy time until the evacuation north was completed. This corruption affected popular morale, and the Cantonese who remained in unoccupied Kwangtung refused to cooperate with further revenue-collection schemes. Many junior public officials grew hostile to their superiors. From Hong Kong, Commander J. M. Sturgeon reported: "There was a very strong anti Chiang Kai Shek feeling in Canton which was not being checked by those in authority. People had contributed generously to the war chest, both voluntarily, and by salary cuts, and yet not a single aeroplane appeared for the defence of Canton."[25] Canton's rapid fall was thus a product of corruption and the lack of munitions and troops.

The most serious issue, however, was the suspected treason of General

Yu Han Mou himself—a suspicion shared by many Chinese and foreign officials. One of the first to vent their anger was Major Barrett, who reported that opinion on this issue was unanimous: "The ease with which the Japanese took Canton was due to a sell-out on the part of Yu Han-mou, Pacification Commissioner of Kwangtung and supposedly in charge of its defense."[26] In condemning Yu as a traitor, Barrett also cited Yu's earlier conduct against his former chief, General Chen Chi Tang, in 1936 and the lack of readily available troops as evidence of his treachery. Barrett continued: "In the end no outside general appeared to save the day and such commanding as was done was done by Yu Han-mou. Since the debacle, Yu has at least had the decency not to attempt an explanation of his wretched showing, which is the only commendable thing he has done since the landing."[27] British officers in Hong Kong likewise noted their disgust. They believed Yu was a traitor because of his actions in 1936, but also because they thought he had almost turned on Chiang in February 1938. "It is probable that only the fear of the Generalissimo's reprisals kept him from turning traitor at the moment of the abortive New Year Coup d'état. A Japanese garrison to protect him from his own countrymen was not too great a price to pay for continuance in office."[28]

Adding to the speculation was the U.S. naval attaché in Tokyo, who reported the possibility of a ¥30 million payment from the Japanese to General Yu for his cooperation.[29] Even missionaries were suspicious. A Canadian clergyman wrote: "It is all still a mystery. Someone sold out Kwangtung."[30] This rumor persisted for some time.[31]

At first glance, betrayal seems like a plausible reason for the ease with which the Japanese took Canton, but it does not adequately explain events, even if Yu did accept money from the Japanese. Corruption was endemic throughout the Chinese army, and trading with the enemy was common once a war zone became somewhat static. In the circumstances of the Sino-Japanese War, being paid by the enemy to execute an existing plan would have been viewed as good business. As seen elsewhere in China, discipline involving lesser problems, such as incompetence or simply gross stupidity, was meted out frequently by Chiang. Many Chinese generals paid with their lives for failing to follow orders. One of the most serious offenses a Chinese general could commit was to be disloyal to the generalissimo, and executions were commonplace among the Chinese high command. General Chan Shu Tang was executed in early October for his failure to bring the

81st Division into battle and for the fall of Techow in Shantung. General Fu Tso Yi of the 35th Army killed himself in anticipation of court-martial and execution. Generals Feng Chan Hai and Wan Fu Lin of the 53rd Army were executed in September 1937 for their failure along the Peking-Hankow railway at Paotingfu. Li Fu Ying of the 61st Army was shot for losing control of north Shansi (Shanxi). General Han Fu Chu was arrested on 11 January 1938 for cowardice and executed for the disasters at Nanking and Shantung.[32] A U.S. officer noted, "His death could be said to mark the complete liquidation of the troublesome Shantung situation, in addition to standing as a warning to the few remaining northern warlords."[33] Others met a similar fate.[34] Chinese generals were executed for less significant setbacks than the loss of Canton, yet Yu was not disciplined for his retreat. Instead, he was given command of the 7th War Zone following its creation in 1940. He also rose to very high rank during the postwar period. Clearly, General Yu did not act against Chiang Kai Shek's instructions when he destroyed and abandoned Canton.

What Chiang sought in Kwangtung was the preservation of central governmental authority in the unoccupied areas of the province, rather than a costly defense of Canton that he knew would be unsuccessful.[35] The generalissimo ordered Yu's withdrawal to limit the growth of regional political power and to keep Kwangtung's defection contained to areas of Japanese occupation. Commander Overesch reported this:

Chiang Kai-shek, above everything else, knew that most of the Kwangtung and Kwangsi divisions, originally available in South China, had been sent North to the Yangtze Valley for the defense of the Wuhan area. He knew also that General Yu Han-mou, whom he had appointed to command the troops in South China, was neither a good politician nor a good general and hardly to be entrusted with the important work of organizing new armies or defending important areas. Chiang had apparently arrived at the decision that, for military and political reasons, the southern troops were of more importance under his own direct command, than they were in attempting to defend South China. The statement that political reasons may have been responsible is not to be lightly dismissed. One of Soong's henchmen admitted that with all forces concentrated in the North, the last possibility of anyone making a separate peace had been eliminated.[36]

Overesch added that General Yu had tried to secure reinforcements from other areas almost up to the time of the invasion. He had been promised 150 trucks to help in his defense, but Japanese bombing of the Hankow-Canton railway limited rail traffic during early October. By keeping the military forces in Kwangtung under the control of the central government, any move by the Cantonese to create a new independent regime outside of Japanese control could be put down by force. A similar scenario arose in February 1945 following the collapse of south China during Operation Ichigo.[37] On that occasion, Yu stated publicly: "Our mission in this War Zone is dual in nature; one is to strengthen the cooperation between the army and the party so as to match the new developments of the war."[38] According to a report by the Office of Strategic Services (OSS), Yu's loyalty to Chiang remained strong throughout the Sino-Japanese War.[39]

Of even greater importance than maintaining Chinese political unity with Kwangtung was Chiang's overall strategy for fighting the Japanese. The abandonment of Canton did not interfere with Chinese strategy as long as the Japanese occupation forces remained in close proximity to the British. Over time, Chinese war supplies such as POL would be transported into free China under Japanese noses from nearby Hong Kong, greatly increasing the potential for military confrontation between Britain and Japan. The British military attaché to Japan, Major General Piggott, explained that Chinese resistance was being maintained with supplies from Hong Kong and that this situation had become an embarrassment to Japan. Piggott added that it was widely understood, even in Tokyo, that Chiang Kai Shek wanted the Japanese army planted on Hong Kong's doorstep.[40] Chiang had originally fought at Shanghai in order to bring the war to areas of foreign economic interest, but in Kwangtung he lacked the necessary military forces and political control to wage another large-scale battle. Thus, he withdrew from Canton to maintain the rest of the province as an active theater of operations over a prolonged period. Chiang chose to abandon the city in order to drag Great Britain into the war.

Chiang was somewhat disappointed about the way operations unfolded, especially the tempo of events. Yu did not develop sufficient local militia or guerrilla forces to delay the Japanese advance or at least provide the appearance of resistance.[41] Several months prior to the invasion, General Tsai Ting Kai, the "hero of the 19th Route Army," had requested weapons and ammunition to equip 15,000 militiamen, but he received only a motley collection of antiquated weapons for about 5,000 men just before the attack. When these finally arrived, he refused to follow Yu. Instead of presenting a show of resistance, the rapidity of the Chinese withdrawal made Canton's abandonment obvious. Overesch commented, "It was apparently his [Chiang's] intention to maintain the illusion of a strongly defended South."[42] In this, the Chinese failed, and the repercussions were felt at some distance from Kwangtung. Acting Consul General C. E. Whitamore reported, "The speedy loss of Canton and the conviction that the Japanese victory in the South had been secured by bribery had consequently a most damaging effect on morale in Hankow and undoubtedly accelerated the abandonment of the city's defences."[43] Consul General Linnell felt the same way.[44]

The impression left with foreign military officers also had far-reaching repercussions. Captains Boxer and Chauvin traveled through unoccupied Kwangtung during the spring of 1939 and visited the 4th War Zone's group armies. These included General Yu's 12th Group Army headquartered at Samma, in the mountains southeast of Kukong, and the newly attached 9th Group Army commanded by General Ng Kei Wai from his headquarters at the recently vacated Swatow. The latter included General Ou Yang Chen's Cantonese 4th Army, which had fought with efficiency and skill at Tehan. General Hsia Wei and the 16th Group Army were not visited.[45] The Boxer-Chauvin report contrasted the combat capabilities of the 9th and 12th Group Armies, and their conclusions had a negative impact on Chiang's ability to forge closer military cooperation with the British. It was noted that Yu's 12th Army had lost all its heavy equipment and artillery in the debacle at Canton (including 146 antitank guns). They had virtually no heavy weapons of any kind except for a handful of old 40mm Vickers antiaircraft guns, but these lacked vital sighting equipment. The 12th Group Army's artillery battalion could not make effective use of these weapons because the brigade commander refused to provide the battalion with the necessary supplies. The few competent officers available, including those with foreign training, were not utilized to any great degree, while most of the others devoted their time to the pursuit of graft. The 12th Group Army had virtually no discipline, and there was little respect for the officers. One saving feature was a relatively high level of morale due to the fact that General Yu had sufficient leadership skills to make the welfare of his troops a primary concern. In contrast, the 9th Group Army under General Ng was highly disciplined, and it included Cantonese and Hakka veterans of all ranks who had fought on the Nanchang front.

Upon concluding their visit to the 4th War Zone, Boxer and Chauvin reported their observations and made recommendations with regard to future Sino-British military cooperation—a relationship that Chiang and many Chinese officers wished to develop:

> If such a scheme of direct Chinese military co-operation ever does materialise, then our own authorities should have a decisive voice in the selection of what Chinese forces should be so employed. Of the Chinese troops in the IVth War Zone which borders on this colony, the 9th Group Army would probably be a valuable asset to the defence, but the 12th Group Army (with the exception of certain individual officers and units) would almost certainly be a dangerous liability.[46]

Despite Yu's very friendly disposition toward British and American officers, the fall of Canton caused British officials in Hong Kong to view the Chinese as ineffectual military partners.[47] Undoubtedly, General Yu was loyal to Chiang Kai Shek and followed his orders without question. But Chiang's reliance on Yu in Kwangtung and the decision to abandon Canton without a fight were both factors that impeded the development of overt military cooperation with the British.

Creating Anglo-Japanese Friction at Hong Kong: The Shataukok Incident

Following the loss of Hankow and Canton, Chiang Kai Shek hoped to increase third-power intervention by demonstrating an improved capability to resist. Since the number of provinces under the central government's authority had shrunk considerably, Chiang needed military victories to secure allies and justify his government's claim of leadership. He also had to undercut the momentum of those wishing to make peace with Japan. In 1939 his two most important allies were Britain and the Soviet Union, and southern China provided the best region for cooperative relations to develop further. By this stage in the war, retreat had become a less viable strategic option. Consequently, greater emphasis was placed on guerrilla warfare in occupied areas against Japanese lines of communication. But defense of the remaining railway system, bringing valuable weapons and fuel from the south, was critical to protect the rice-growing region of Hunan. Thus, maintaining a conventional defense of northern Kwangtung became a vital necessity, as did the defense of Changsha. This situation was well understood by the Soviets. Hence, there was significant collaboration with Red Army advisers during the first battle of Changsha in August 1939.[48] To increase British involvement, the Chinese also endeavored to fight the war as close to Hong Kong as opportunity would allow. With the Japanese stuck in Canton, and with the ongoing use of Hong Kong as a supply source, greater strain was placed on Anglo-Japanese relations.

In the immediate aftermath of the fall of Canton and Hankow, China's military situation became desperate, causing Chiang to take more drastic measures in dealing with foreign officials. Resistance was thought to be possible for an additional year, as approximately 40 percent of the supplies already received from abroad had been cached in various locations around southern China. Chinese military forces were still self-sufficient only in the production of light infantry weapons. Many of these were produced in Chuchow and Siangtan (Xiangtan), along the railway south and east of Changsha. Troops from Kwangsi also received weapons and munitions produced from their own arsenals. But more supplies were needed, and Chiang wasted no time in pressuring the British for increased assistance. On 6 November 1938, at the Chinese General Headquarters established at Changsha, Chiang met with Ambassador Clark Kerr, whom he had summoned during the retreat. After sixteen months of war, Chiang demanded to know whether the British would supply direct military or economic assistance; if they did not, he threatened to end his cooperation. This tactic became a regular feature of Chiang's diplomacy with third powers. Although the threat was often downplayed in London and Washington, the time came in 1941 when it was not so easily sidestepped. But in late 1938 the forcefulness and anger of Chiang's ultimatum resulted from his genuine frustration over China's grave military situation. More than ever, Chiang needed weapons and allies. Although this was not an easy ultimatum for the British to ignore, Whitehall found little incentive to challenge the Japanese further at this stage of events. Their refusal to provide immediate overt assistance thus temporarily soured Sino-British relations.[49]

Chiang's demands for increased British aid coincided with his forceful insistence that leadership among his own generals be improved. Determined to fight, he confronted the leadership problems in the army. At the time of his meeting with Clark Kerr, following the loss of Hankow, Chiang was not only visibly angry but also disgusted over the unwarranted burning of

Changsha by General Feng Ti. Feng had panicked and destroyed the city prematurely, fearing a Japanese advance south from Hankow. The destruction of Changsha spurred Chiang to redouble his efforts, and evidence of his resolve was demonstrated not only by periodic court-martials and executions but also by his critical rebuke of Chinese generals at the Nanyue military conference held in late November 1938. Chiang demanded that commanders demonstrate greater professionalism as well as aggression. He also ordered staff officers to improve the quality of their performance.[50]

Within a month, Chiang commenced military operations near Hong Kong in order to provoke an Anglo-Japanese diplomatic crisis. After the fall of Canton, the Japanese consolidated their position in and around the city, but they lacked sufficient troops to fully garrison many areas farther afield. The situation was made worse by the withdrawal of the 5th Division to Tsingtao. Thus, in November Chiang ordered the 12th Group Army to secure the region north of Canton near Tsungfa and to maintain pressure along the East River near Waichow. Samshui on the West River was also attacked by troops marching south from Yingtak (Yingde). More important, troops of the 151st Division headquartered in the Pingshan district were tasked with the resumption of logistical operations between Hong Kong and Waichow. Hence, the better part of a regiment (about 1,000 to 1,500 men in the Chinese army) under the command of Lo Kuan began moving large quantities of ammunition from Hong Kong into Kwangtung. The 151st Division did not comprise Chungking's finest soldiers, but they were adequate to cause problems for the Japanese and a consequent loss of face. Lo Kuan was better known for his earlier work as the "Pirate King" of Kwangtung, but his troops were able to conduct guerrilla warfare and sabotage with some degree of competence.[51]

On 26 November 1938 a serious incident tested Anglo-Japanese relations when Japanese ground forces marched to the colony in pursuit of another Chinese regiment, also of the 151st Division. After battling the Japanese north of the border, this force retreated into the village of Shataukok on the far eastern end of Hong Kong's frontier, but part of it ran into the colony itself across the KCR bridge at Shumchun. Japanese troops followed, crossing the border as well as the bridge, and in two different areas they hoisted a flag on British-controlled territory. The 1st Battalion, Middlesex Regiment, was immediately ordered to take up positions along the border. The Japanese troops left about twenty minutes after being confronted by British military officers, without further incident. At

Shataukok, however, the Japanese paused because the village straddled the boundary. Due to the topography, an attack would have involved crossing British territory. Negotiations ensued between Brigadier Reeve and Japanese officers at the Shumchun casino, before being continued in Tokyo. The final agreement, reached several days later, brought a Japanese withdrawal and the internment of 850 Chinese soldiers under British control. Although the Shataukok incident was quickly defused in a professional manner, the Chinese troops remained in British custody at the expense of the Hong Kong government until December 1941 (during the battle of Hong Kong they were used as stretcher bearers, but lacking disciplined leadership, they created as many problems as they solved).[52] Many other border incidents would not be resolved so smoothly.

In response to these early border problems, British authorities prohibited the transshipment of munitions from Hong Kong directly into China at the beginning of 1939, but these supplies were still allowed to be sent on to Haiphong and Rangoon. The Burma Road had been completed, and munitions were able to proceed from there. Fuel, trucks, and spare parts were also quite important, and they continued to be sent into China directly from Hong Kong, much to the annoyance and anger of Japanese officers. Chiang's efforts to create trouble in Anglo-Japanese relations had minimal early results, but the potential for greater friction increased as the war progressed through 1939. It would be another three years before Britain became a full participant in the war as a Chinese ally, and although the British were well aware of Chiang's strategy to involve them directly in the war, limited support at Hong Kong continued. It would not be long before American involvement was also forthcoming.[53]

Lines of Communication:
Hong Kong, Burma, and French Indochina

It is useful at this stage to examine the relative strengths and weaknesses of the various lines of communication into China. In doing so, Hong Kong's significance with respect to increasing Britain's involvement in the Sino-Japanese War can be better understood. When the actual tonnage for each route is examined, it becomes clear that Hong Kong remained the most prominent supply center available to the Chinese army. At the end of 1938 the Japanese had reason to be confident of victory with the capture of Hankow and Canton, but as the war descended into stalemate, the reason for Japanese frustration over Chinese resistance becomes more discernible after a close examination of the logistical role of Hong Kong.

During 1939 there were four major lines of communication available to transport war supplies into China. The first of these was the northwest route through Sinkiang. Approximately 2,000 to 3,000 tons of war material entered China each month from the Soviet Union via Sinkiang. By April 1941, the total value of these supplies was estimated at US$200 million.[54] The other routes were the Burma Road, the French Indochina railway (including the Kwangsi road network), and the route from Hong Kong via Waichow.

Under construction from the fall of 1937 to late 1938, the Burma Road became an important line of communication for Chinese military supplies after the fall of Canton and even more so following the collapse of French Indochina. Many problems, however, impeded operations, including corruption, the operating practices of T. V. Soong's South-West Transportation Commission, and the annual fall monsoons. The British closure of the road from July to October 1940 also caused serious diplomatic tensions in Sino-British relations. When combined, these factors limited the route's capacity.[55]

The simple inefficiency of road transportation through rough terrain was another factor limiting the usefulness of Burma. U.S. assistant military attaché Captain Edwin M. Sutherland noted in August 1939 that heavy transportation costs and landslides contributed to a reduction in traffic. During the rainy season, capacity fell to between 60 and 100 tons daily. Even under normal conditions, a minimum of 25 to 30 percent of the fuel carried on the Burma Road was consumed in transit. The 710-mile trip from Lashio to Kunming took an average of one week to complete. Hopes were placed on the construction of a new railway to parallel the road, but this project was stalled as late as 1941 due to a lack of rails and difficult labor conditions.[56]

In the spring of 1939 U.S. Army assistant military attaché Captain F. P. Munson reported that almost no munitions were being transported into China via the Burma Road, and only a fraction of estimates was managing to arrive from Indochina. Plagued by inefficiency and later by Japanese air strikes, the Burma Road ultimately ended up providing an average of only 3,000 useful tons per month (of all supplies, including POL).[57] This figure was confirmed in a report written by Ian Morrison for the Foreign Office in June 1941:

The amount of freight leaving Lashio has rarely exceeded 7,000 tons monthly. . . . Of this 7,000 tons, approximately 30 per cent is taken up by the gasoline required for the long hauls to the north, 25 per cent represents commercial freight and 15 per cent smuggled goods. Of goods directly required by the Chinese government for the prose-cution of the war against Japan, it is highly doubtful if more than 3,000 tons monthly ever enters China by this route. The organisation is chaotic, with control divided between the military and the civil au-thorities, between the central and the provincial governments. The drivers of the lorries are inexpert, undisciplined and arrogant. . . . Large numbers of lorries are lost through accidents, large numbers are out of action through a chronic shortage of spare parts, much time is wasted at the ferries which are badly organised.[58]

Others also reported that 3,000 tons per month was the realistic limit of the Burma Road's effective capacity. Previous estimates anticipating total deliveries of between 10,000 and 20,000 tons per month had been grossly optimistic.[59]

Until the summer of 1939, the French Indochina railway was of greater value to the Chinese than the Burma Road, but this route also had many problems. Although 200 tons of material traveled northwest daily, problems such as fuel shortages and a lack of wagons at Kunming developed by midyear, thereby preventing the Chinese from exploiting the railway's full potential. To alleviate congestion, 10 to 15 percent of all supplies leaving Haiphong were sent northeast from Hanoi into Kwangsi rather than north-west to Yunnan. In moving through Kwangsi, supplies were hauled by road or trail to Kweilin, where they were then transported by rail to Changsha (see figure 4.2). Supplies were also sent through Nanning and other Kwangsi road routes via the Kwangtung coastal city of Pakhoi and the French-controlled enclave of Kwangchowan; however, fearing another Japanese in-vasion similar to Kwangtung, General Pai Chung Hsi destroyed part of the road network in January 1939. On an international level, Franco-Japanese relations began to deteriorate as early as November 1938, when the Japanese threatened to invade Hainan if the French did not terminate munitions ship-ments from Haiphong. Although the French issued an order to stop the movement of weapons, the shipment of aviation fuel and other supplies con-tinued unimpeded. Consequently, a six-month to one-year backlog of Chi-nese supplies began to accumulate on the docks at Haiphong.[60]

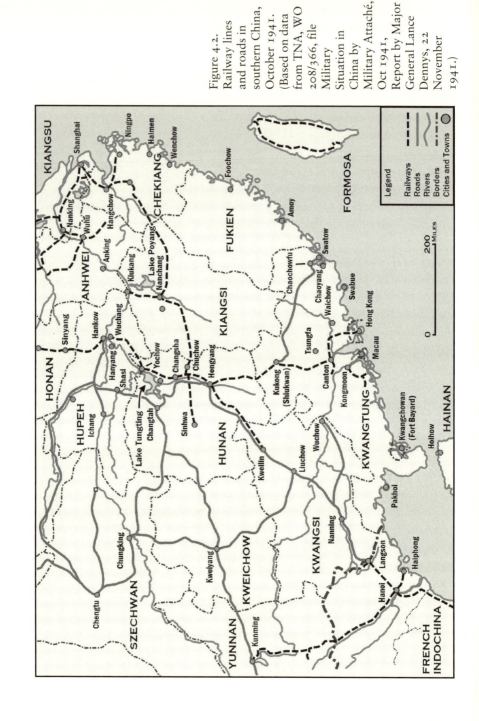

Figure 4.2. Railway lines and roads in southern China, October 1941. (Based on data from TNA, WO 208/366, file Military Situation in China by Military Attaché, Oct 1941, Report by Major General Lance Dennys, 22 November 1941.)

Legend
- Railways
- Roads
- Rivers
- Borders
- Cities and Towns

KIANGSU
Shanghai
Ningpo
Haimen
CHEKIANG
Wenchow
Nanking
Wuhu
Hangchow
FOOCHOW
ANHWEI
Anking
Klukang
Lake Poyang
Nanchang
Sinyang
HONAN
Hankow
Wuchang
Lake Loyang
KIANGSI
FUKIEN
Amoy
Hanyang
Shasi
Yochow
Changsha
Chuchow
Chaochowfu
Swatow
Chaoyang
Waichow
Ichang
HUPEH
Lake Tungting
Changtah
Sinhwa
Heng/yang
Tsungfa
Swabue
Kukong (Shiukwan)
Hong Kong
Canton
Macau
Kongmoon
KWANGTUNG
Chungking
HUNAN
Kweilin
Liuchow
Wuchow
Kwangchowan (Fort Bayard)
Kwelyang
KWEICHOW
KWANGSI
Pakhol
Holhow
HAINAN
Chengtu
SZECHWAN
Nanning
Langson
Hanoi
Haiphong
YUNNAN
Kunming
FRENCH INDOCHINA
FORMOSA

0   200
MILES

Once the occupation of Hainan Island was complete in February 1939, matters became more complicated as Japanese air units began to operate virtually at will throughout much of southern China. Airpower became a serious threat to Chinese logistical operations north of the Indochina border. Long-range air strikes against the Indochina railway at Kunming remained infrequent, but the road network leading through Kwangsi was heavily bombed. Built-up areas such as Liuchow, Nanning, and Pakhoi became popular hunting grounds for Japanese pilots. With new air bases in Kwangtung, air operations were also intensified in April 1939 along the coast as far north as Chekiang (Zhejiang). Japanese airpower was making itself felt across southern China, but this was especially true in Kwangsi. By the end of 1939, the usefulness of the Indochina railway had diminished. Japanese pressure against French authorities increased during 1940, and traffic in fuel and armaments was terminated by the middle of that year.[61]

In contrast to routes involving the USSR, Indochina, and Burma, war supplies continued to travel from Hong Kong to China until December 1941. The quantity of material transported between 1937 and 1938 alone was so great that the Chinese army was able to rebuild after the damage sustained at Shanghai. Even after the fall of Canton, materials such as fuel and spare parts were sent to China from Hong Kong through Waichow or after being transshipped to coastal ports such as Swabue, Swatow, Foochow, and Ningpo (Ningbo).[62] In October 1940 Major R. Giles of Hong Kong's military intelligence section described how these materials were moved into China primarily from Waichow and the East River to Kukong or by following a secondary route along the East River into Kiangsi:

All imports from Hong Kong find their way to the East River and move up that to Laolung/Lungchuan. Laolung is the main entrepot on the East bank, but three arches of the concrete bridge carrying the road across the river have been broken by bombs and so Lungchuan (8 km downriver) is used as a road head on the West bank. From Lungchuan the road runs 80 km to Chunghsiu, where it divides, one branch going 245 km to Hsiukwan, and the other 140 km to Lungnan leading to Kanchow. From Laolung the road leads to Hingning and Meihsien, with one branch towards western Kiangsi (Juikin) and the other into Fukien. All these roads are in a shocking state though there are not far short of 1,000 trucks operating on them. The cargo moving up the East river consists of salt, piece goods, motor spares (I saw one large junk load filled entirely with new tyres), kerosene, gasoline, cigarettes and hardware. Coming down it consists of tea, wood oil and wolfram.

Chekiang, Fukien and Kiangsi have been relying on Ningpo and other coast ports for foreign supplies. Kwangtung and Hunan draw on Hong Kong. Shiukwan at the southern end of the Canton-Hankow railways is the bottle neck [sic] through which 90% of the Hong Kong exports to China pass.[63]

These routes can be seen in figure 3.2. Reports are conflicting, but for most of the three-year period between November 1938 and November 1941, an average of 3,000 tons per month was maintained in this manner.[64] Four months later, Giles commented that the volume of material moving along "the important Mirs Bay–Waichow route to Free China . . . was . . . comparable[,] according to some qualified observers, to that over the Burma Road."[65]

When all factors are considered from 1937 until the end of 1941, Hong Kong was the most significant supply source in China's war effort. This situation helps account for Japanese hostility against the colony and their invasion of southern China.

The Invasion of Hainan

Initial satisfaction over the battlefield successes of October 1938 led to Tokyo's announcement of a "New Order in East Asia" in November 1938—a policy to drive Western influence from China. Because of this development, and shortly after rejecting Chiang's ultimatum, the British began to reconsider their level of support. Another factor in this decision was Chiang's determination not to capitulate. The Japanese army's triumphs at Canton and Hankow failed to bring victory, and because Japanese forces were overextended, stalemate began to envelop them.[66] Insufficient troop strength and a limited resource base restricted their strategic options, and morale began to drop. Major Barrett noted, "Observers generally agree that the Japanese are heartily sick of their Yangtze Valley and South China campaigns."[67] Consequently, Prime Minister Konoye Fumimaro and his cabinet resigned in January after failing to reach a peace settlement with the Chinese.[68] While the Japanese army continued to fight the Chinese unsuccessfully throughout 1939, the navy stepped up its air attacks in northern provinces such as Shansi, bombed Chungking, and waged a brutal littoral warfare campaign along south China's coast. This offensive was directed primarily against China's lines of communication to Hong Kong, and the level of violence in the colony rose sharply throughout the year. The major development, however, was the invasion of Hainan in February 1939. Already poor, Anglo-Japanese relations were further damaged as a result of this move.

A few months after the fall of Canton, Vice Admiral Kondo Nobutake, commander of the Japanese 5th Fleet, was given responsibility for the invasion of Hainan, but the operation was ultimately counterproductive.[69] The assault on the island was initially executed to extend the range of Japanese airpower over Chinese lines of supply in Kwangsi; it was not intended as a preparatory element of an advance farther southward, but it did encourage such a move. Once the Japanese were established in the region, the temptation to occupy Indochina grew larger, as such an action became easier to support by air from the newly developed bases in Hainan. In this sense, the invasion of Hainan was a direct threat to the Western powers and provoked an unwelcome diplomatic reaction that resulted in strengthened Chinese ties to the West. But the invasion was also a failure because the movement of military supplies from Hong Kong was never significantly interrupted—a situation made worse by the corruption of Japanese officers. Moreover, the brutality exhibited during the operation was at variance with the army's professed desire to improve relations with the southern Chinese, and this in turn undermined efforts to reach a peaceful settlement of the war.

The assault on Hainan began on 10 February 1939, and the occupation proceeded quickly. Naval forces included the fleet carrier *Kaga*, the seaplane equipped cruiser *Myoko*, and more than ten other warships from their base in the Marianas; bombardment of the island began in December. Ground forces included a composite group of approximately two regiments drawn from the 18th and the 112th Divisions as well as the Formosan Force; these were augmented by two tank companies. Most of these troops were part of the Canton garrison and were under the command of Major General Tanaka Hisaichi, chief of staff of the 21st Army. The Formosans had been fighting along the Yangtse River near Hankow in December 1938, but were redeployed to Canton in January 1939. The initial assault forces landed without opposition and established themselves rap-

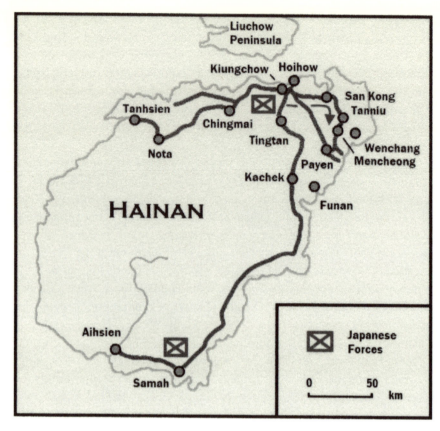

Figure 4.3. Japanese operations in Hainan. (Based on data from TNA, WO 106/5356, HKIR No. 5/39 by Captain C. J. Edwards, 28 February 1939.)

idly within a forty-mile radius of Hoihow. A smaller area in the south at Samah Bay was also secured. Only the Chinese 159th Division and the 9th Independent Brigade had been posted to Hainan for its defense, under the command of General Wong Ngai, but they had been withdrawn shortly after the fall of Canton, leaving a weak, motley collection of local militia in their place. They retreated with General Wong to the interior to conduct guerrilla warfare after the invasion began.[70]

In the north, one mechanized column started the Japanese advance from the capital of Kiungchow and moved southeast along the coast. After arriving at the town of Mencheong, they reinforced popular enmity by rounding up approximately 150 people and machine-gunning them. Operations by the Formosan Force against Chinese guerrillas continued into March. An air base was constructed at Mencheong, and soon more than 100 aircraft were based there. Within a week of the initial assault, however, all immediate objectives had been secured, and the Japanese navy's main fleet units, such as the *Kaga* and the 29th Destroyer Flotilla, departed Hainan for Japan—mission accomplished.[71] The invasion is illustrated in figure 4.3.

The occupation of Hainan was a significant escalation of the logistics war in southern China. Once Hainan was secured, air-base construction was begun to accommodate land-based aircraft, but it soon became evident that Japanese naval forces could now block maritime traffic to and from the Gulf of Tonkin with ease. Despite Japanese statements that the disruption of Chinese lines of communication was their sole preoccupation, the threat posed to third powers became more pronounced.[72] One published announcement indicated that logistical factors had been the primary reason for the invasion, but its threat to occupy Kwangsi was also highly provocative. Captain C. Edwards at Hong Kong quoted the Japanese statement as it appeared in the Chinese press:

> The attack on Hainan Island is within the scope of non-occupation of territory and no verbal explanation with the British and French Government. If the Chiang Regime continues to carry on its war of prolongation Japan will vow to occupy Hainan permanently. . . . If Britain and France continues [sic] to assist Chiang, Japan will not only occupy Hainan Island but also give the South West regions military occupation.
>
> The occupation of Hainan Island is a military necessity and no explanation is necessary that we have no ambition over it. If Britain and France do not wake up from their nightmares we will take the necessary steps to bar the policy of helping the Chiang Regime. The Japanese Empire does not mind the collective of Britain, France and America against her but will proceed undaunted towards her aim.[73]

In conjunction with the May 1938 occupation of Amoy, a port sitting astride Hong Kong's lines of communication to the northeast, the invasion of Hainan allowed the Japanese to establish more permanent naval and air facilities, isolating Hong Kong to the west.

Lieutenant General Ando Rikichi:
A New Approach

Although some of the usual brutality was evident among Japanese troops during their first few days in Kwangtung, British officials from Hong Kong observed that the Japanese army made a considerable effort to adopt a less hostile approach in dealing with Cantonese civilians than had been witnessed elsewhere during the war.[74] The Japanese army's initial pacification efforts in Kwangtung relied less on terror and more on building peaceful relations where possible.

In November 1938 Commander J. M. Sturgeon of Hong Kong's military intelligence section traveled to Canton and witnessed Japanese troops conducting themselves with greater discipline than he had seen previously. Their change in behavior was due to the leadership of Lieutenant General Ando Rikichi, the general officer commanding the 21st Army (also known by this point as the South China Expeditionary Force). As the former military attaché in London, he spoke English well. He was also a personal friend of Major General Piggott in Tokyo. Ando's methods were considerably more moderate than those of many of his fellow officers, and he strove to build better relations with the Cantonese from an early date. In this regard, Ando was a notable exception in China. At the outset of the invasion, Ando was commander of the 5th Division, but he was appointed commander of all Japanese army forces in south China after his predecessor, Lieutenant General Furusho, suffered a stroke in November.[75]

Following his visit, Commander Sturgeon reported his observations to the War Office, where they were received with much interest and concern:

> That the Japanese authorities must have taken particular care in their selection of troops for operations in Kwangtung is borne out by many facts.
>
> (1) Nearly all the Gendarmerie, appear to be reservists they are certainly of a type superior to the normal infantry. Many are well educated, pleasant mannered, and a very reasonable proportion speak either English or Cantonese.
> (2) The infantry, who are of a lower type (many cannot read) are not allowed into Canton City, this is in the interests of avoiding trouble.

(3) Many Formosans are to be found among the troops, both of the Gendarmerie, and of those infantry permitted to enter the city. These are very similar to Chinese in character, and nearly all speak Chinese. The writer has seen several groups of Chinese and Japanese sitting and chatting in the most friendly manner.

(4) The first Japanese officer to appear at the British concession was the former manager of M.B.K. in Shameen, he greeted warmly the Superintendent of Police who met him.

(5) There had not been, up until 15/11/38 even a suggestion of any "incident," and all foreigners are impressed by the good manners of Japanese sentries.

(6) The writer, on several official tours of the city has never met with anything but courtesy and politeness.[76]

Sturgeon noted that Japanese conduct in Canton was such a striking contrast to that in Nanking and Shanghai that there must have been a change in policy. The Japanese seemed eager not to impair relations with third powers, and in view of the proximity of Hong Kong, this was particularly so with Great Britain. Sturgeon added: "Whatever the reason, it is an extremely pleasant surprise, and this policy is already having its effect in Canton where the Chinese populace is responding, and is learning to trust the Japanese, and where everyday sees welcome signs of changes towards normal life."[77] The last statement was of greatest interest to officials in London because it showed that the Japanese had adjusted their civilian administration policies to achieve some degree of victory from the ground up.

Acting Consul General Whitamore also reported that the Japanese had entered Hankow in a more disciplined manner.[78] The problem for the Japanese was that it took a year and a half to develop this understanding, and many senior officers did not posses Ando's vision.

On the day of the Japanese invasion of Hainan, the British assistant military attaché to Japan, Major G. T. Wards, traveled from Hong Kong to Canton aboard HMS *Moth* for a meeting with General Ando. Wards wanted to learn more about Japanese intentions in south China and hoped to improve relations. They met the following day (11 February 1939) at the Japanese headquarters in Canton, and Wards found the general to be both cordial and professional. Also attending the meeting were two staff officers: Captain Yano and Lieutenant Colonel Ohira Hideo. The conversation was informative, and some of Ando's more significant comments revealed that the Japanese occupation of Canton was primarily a result of the military logistical situation in southern China; it was not directed against third powers. Ando informed Wards that "the role of his army as given him on taking over command is to stop the supply of munitions through South China, nothing more, and he intended to confine himself to this and not bother in any other affairs."[79] Later in the interview, Ando revealed that communism remained the primary threat to China and to the Far East in general and that a change in policy toward Chinese civilians had been implemented to deal with this. Wards reported, "To my enquiry as to the progress of the war and as to his opinion on future events, General Ando replied at some length. He first of all admitted that things could not be settled by war alone, and it is very necessary from now on to try to create a better feeling between the Chinese and Japanese peoples."[80] Wards commented that the poor discipline of Japanese forces had thus far been counterproductive, making victory difficult and damaging Anglo-Japanese relations, but Ando explained that relations would improve after victory was achieved. As a means of reassurance, Ando reiterated that Japan's main priority in south China was the termination of military aid and supplies to free China.

In time, the general's administrative policies toward the Cantonese helped establish a puppet regime in Kwangtung, but Ando was overly optimistic about Japanese chances for success. By the end of his meeting, Wards could confidently report that Japanese ambitions in China did not yet include war against Britain, at least as far as General Ando was concerned. The general stated that he did not have any plans for further large-scale operations, but some other ports might be occupied. Most future military efforts would take the form of aerial interdiction against southern Chinese roads and railways. Significantly, Wards noted that Ando appeared somewhat fatigued and lacked a full appreciation of Japanese limitations. Although the Japanese had initially expected a war of short duration, he and others were surprised at the strength of Chinese unity. Ando also felt that time was on Japan's side and that it could carry on the war indefinitely. At the end of the meeting, Ando surmised that there was still a chance to settle the war in China to the satisfaction of all, provided Japanese face could be maintained. Wards reported:

As a parting message General Ando impressed on me that the only way in his opinion to save China from being "bolshevised" is for England, U.S.A. and France to stop giving aid to Chiang Kai-shek. My answer to this was that Chiang Kai-shek is nothing to us, all we desire is that our interests and rights in China be respected and we naturally intend to do what we can to preserve these interests and rights. In any case, I added, the Japanese Government have stated that they will not deal with Chiang Kai-shek. Is this really so or not? To this General Ando replied that it is so but there would be no objection to Chiang Kai-shek going into retirement for a while and returning to power a little later on after peace has been declared.[81]

Wards felt that General Ando was sincere and that Japanese ambitions in south China were strictly focused on wrecking the Chinese logistical system that was sustaining their resistance. Because Hong Kong did not appear to be in any immediate danger, the British continued to allow supplies to pass freely through the colony.

Ando's hopes began to unravel less than two weeks later through the insubordinate actions of personnel in his own army. This type of conduct often made it difficult to implement Japanese strategy, but it was usually a problem only when it occurred among senior officers. In the Lo Wu incident, which occurred on 21 February 1939, it was lower-ranking officers who were responsible for straining Anglo-Japanese relations. On that date, recently arrived pilots at Canton attacked the New Territories. A Japanese army squadron of nine twin-engine bombers (Mitsubishi Type 97—Sally) entered Hong Kong airspace from the south. From an altitude of 500 feet, the squadron bombed a KCR train, a bridge, and a customs office. A railway station was also strafed, killing a Sikh policeman and eleven Chinese and wounding four others.[82] There was excellent visibility that day, and more than one pass was made to complete the mission. The main target of the attack was the bridge at Lo Wu, but the entire area was easily identified as British territory. Targets were hit up to a mile south of the border in an incident witnessed by Governor Northcote from his home and by 2nd Battalion, Royal Scot officers at the Lo Wu training camp, which was overflown by the raiders. This was not an accidental bombardment; it was a deliberate provocation for war by elements within the 21st Army. In response, Ambassador Sir Robert Craigie lodged a protest in Tokyo, and the issue was resolved locally in Hong Kong during meetings held in early March among Northcote, Major General Grasett, Captain Charles Boxer, and Major General Tanaka Hisaichi. Northcote reported that the Japanese apologies appeared to be sincere, and $20,000 was agreed on as suitable compensation.[83]

Emotions ran high in Hong Kong, and from this point forward, relations between colonial officials and the Japanese began to develop somewhat independently from London. The Japanese attempted to ease tensions at a dinner party held at the U.S. consulate in Canton on 10 March. Consul General Okazaki informed British Consul General A. P. Blunt that one of the pilots had been imprisoned immediately after the Lo Wu incident, and the general officer commanding army air forces in south China lost two years' seniority and 20 percent of his pay for six months; his chief of staff received the same punishment for one year. This gesture was welcomed, but it had little long-lasting effect. Disappointment and anger in the colony, among Chinese and non-Chinese alike, were substantial, but Ambassador Craigie advised that it would be best not to press the Japanese further. Because of the attack on Lo Wu, fear of even greater crises became more common throughout the colony, and both Governor Northcote and General Grasett felt frustration and anger with the passage of events.[84] By 1941, their feelings were much more pronounced and led to the adoption of more intransigent attitudes toward the Japanese than Whitehall was willing to permit. Moreover, Grasett in particular would demonstrate an affinity for independent action on several occasions over the next two years, and Anglo-Japanese relations worsened as a result. But as early as February 1939, the Lo Wu incident demonstrated that Hong Kong was a source of considerable friction in Anglo-Japanese relations and that armed conflict could easily result between the two powers, despite the best wishes of higher authorities. Just four months after the Japanese invasion of south China, Hong Kong had become a flash point that threatened to ignite war between Britain and Japan, and colonial officials' attitudes began to harden against the Japanese.

The invasion of Kwangtung isolated Hong Kong, and the seizure of Hainan effectively threatened to isolate southern China, but Japanese victory could no longer be achieved solely through military power. Improved Sino-Japanese relations were required, but the time for a military solution was running short. Victory on the battlefield was becoming less possible as Japanese forces were constrained strategically by a lack of resources and operationally by the need to maintain combat forces in close proximity to rail and riverine transport to ensure adequate supplies. This limited the amount of territory that could be controlled effectively, as well as the location of future operations and the manner in which they could be conducted. The military stalemate was mirrored by the lack of progress politically. Moderate pacification efforts, such as Ando's, had come late and were threatened by the impatience of others. Soon his policy of conciliation would not extend past the confines of Canton. As the stalemate in China dragged on, the Japanese continued to search for a way out of their predicament and waited for new opportunities. Wards reported, "The policy hitherto followed of setting up puppet Governments in the controlled areas supported by military force, excellent in theory, has so far proved unworkable in practice, and the impression is that the actual policy now being pursued is an opportunist one."[85] Opportunities would arise from European events.[86] In the meantime, after the invasion of Kwangtung and Hainan, Japanese military endeavors in south China concentrated on the destruction of China's logistical network. But the biggest problem remained: Hong Kong was an integral component of that network.

Challenging Japan:
A Collective Response to Thwart Peace

Soon after the fall of Canton and Hankow and Chiang's ultimatum to Clark Kerr in October 1938, the British and Americans intervened directly and collectively using economic warfare. Peace in China would have been an unwelcome development, so loans were extended as a counterattack against the change in Japanese methods. The Chinese were desperate for external financing, and in August 1938 they began negotiations for a $20 million loan with Kuhn, Loeb and Company in New York to pay for additional war supplies.[87] The U.S. government's loan of $25 million was announced in December 1938, and within a month after the bombing of Lo Wu, a British loan for £10 million was also approved for material aid and to help stabilize the Chinese currency. These actions disrupted Japanese attempts to undermine the Chinese economy, which created much animosity and the crisis at Tientsin (Tianjin) later in 1939.[88] The two governments coordinated the issuance of these loans, but this was denied publicly to limit political opposition in the United States. Some have argued that the reason for direct Anglo-American intervention was the invasion of south China, the occupation of Hainan, and the threat this posed to their interests farther south. Combined with Japan's announcement of the New Order in East Asia, these factors undoubtedly played a role in the decision. Another consideration, however, was the provision of indirect support to the USSR while a collective security arrangement against Germany was being discussed. Economic intervention in China was also viewed by Foreign Office officials as a means of fostering greater cooperation with the United States at a time when the Americans were rearming (e.g., the aircraft production program ordered by Roosevelt in late 1938).[89] For the British, closer relations with the United States were considered most useful with regard to European affairs, but because of American interest in the Far East, China was a region where improved relations could be developed most effectively.

It is significant to note that ideological factors continued to dominate Far Eastern policy in London, and the British loan helps explain the decision not to purchase the New Territories. At the time the British government extended the £10 million loan to China, Sir John Brenan's initial support for the purchase of the New Territories had faded, and he terminated the deal. Purchasing the New Territories would have been an imperial measure, and in the Foreign Office, the concept of imperialism did not pass ideological muster. The loan to the Chinese government was selected as an alternative method of maintaining the war effort because it prevented the political isolation of the Chinese Communist Party (CCP). Brenan wrote that Sir Shouson Chow, the relatively senior Kuomintang official who had originated the scheme, was "out of touch" with the government in Chungking and his further advice was not needed, but this excuse was disingenuous.[90] Brenan and others in the Foreign Office wished to address the Chinese morale problem without driving a British imperial wedge between the Kuomintang and the CCP, and the loan helped accomplish this. A purchase agreement would have alienated the CCP and some segments of U.S. public opinion, but if necessary, complaints from the latter quarter could have been challenged with a glance toward the U.S. presence in the Philippines. Whitehall's decision was not based on a desire to preserve a balance of power. Realists would have used their money to secure more than just another war and would have purchased the New Territories when the opportunity arose. By extending the loan without concessions at Hong Kong, the British demonstrated that the political aspect of this issue superseded other considerations.

Because of the loan, China remained a war zone that the British could exploit, but to continue to do so, the political dimensions had to be carefully monitored from several angles. Aside from the Kuomintang-CCP problem, or the puppets associated with Wang Ching Wei, there were many in the central government who wanted to make peace with Japan. In November 1938 morale was so low in the new capital that Colonel Stilwell expected the Chinese to collapse within six months, and this was reported to Washington. Many officials, such as Finance Minister H. H. Kung, were weary of war yet remained loyal to Chiang Kai Shek. Japanese peace proposals to Chungking in December 1938, however, were based on terms that the British considered most conciliatory. The loans were subsequently announced to counter Japanese advances, and in doing so, there was cause for Anglo-American optimism.[91] In south China, General Ando's troops controlled the area in and around Canton, and despite the moderation displayed by both the general and his men, their occupation was still widely resented. In February 1939 at Kongmoon, Canadian missionary Duncan McRae wrote, "Great efforts for peace are being made by the Japanese but there is no hope apart from a complete withdrawal of her forces."[92] So long as Chiang held firm in his determination to fight, the peace party in Chungking could be contained, and once the loans were made, there was some degree of confidence in Washington and London that the war could be kept active.

The British and Americans had other reasons for optimism, including the political situation in occupied China. The absence of a cohesive Japanese political strategy in dealing with Chinese surrogates helped prolong the war. Wang Ching Wei and his followers had recently defected because they understood that only the communists would benefit from a protracted war, and as head of a large national government in occupied China, he sought to achieve a somewhat equitable peace with Japan.[93] In Kwangtung, small businessman Chi Chi Ching was appointed chairman of the Canton Chamber of Commerce as an initial step in the creation of a southern arm of the Wang administration (the Kwangtung Peace Commission), but Japanese attempts to encourage people to return to Canton and begin economic renewal met with limited success. Wang's position had been eroded by the resignation of Prime Minister Konoye in mid-January after failing to reach a peaceful settlement with Chiang.[94] The new government made little initial progress in securing popular support because it lacked autonomy and any real military force with which to exert its authority. Moreover, U.S. and British loans had given Chiang Kai Shek great credibility across China while simultaneously undercutting morale in Wang's government. Following Konoye's resignation, senior Japanese army officers made the situation more difficult by boosting support for several regional puppet officials in areas under their direct control, but these administrations had little popular appeal. Across the country, people had few inducements to support a collection of weak Chinese political figures serving under Japanese tutelage, especially when they were subjected to economic discrimination in business and in labor.

Additional problems for the Japanese included the lack of a unified military strategy, combined with an increase in disciplinary problems. Japanese army forces in garrison at Canton were not entirely reliable, and 2,000 Korean troops reportedly revolted during February 1939.[95] Poor discipline in the army damaged Japanese prestige, along with Ando's credibility, but more significant were the actions of the Japanese navy. The differences in army-navy policies and strategies were reflected elsewhere in China, but the impact of Japanese interservice rivalry was tremendous in Kwangtung. The navy was largely responsible for creating havoc throughout the West River region, thereby undoing much of what Ando had tried to accomplish with his policy of restraint. The reasons for the navy's preoccupation with the West River were twofold. First, south China was an area where the navy could best contribute to the war at the strategic level by attacking Chinese lines of communication. Second, topographic features of Kwangtung's West River best suited its tactical capabilities. The lack of interservice uniformity with respect to policy and operations resulted in an endless cycle of violence in the Pearl River Delta that kept the Cantonese from rallying to support the puppet administration. Over time, Japanese military operations not only alienated the Chinese but also had a direct negative impact on the security of Hong Kong, which steadily exacerbated Anglo-Japanese relations.

The Chinese, for their part, gained some limited advantage in their attempts to influence international relations. Closer ties with Britain and America had been established, and relations between British and Chinese officers in the 4th War Zone were strengthened. However, the desire to build greater military cooperation in defense of Hong Kong was not yet reciprocal because the British needed to avoid open war with Japan and lacked confidence in Chinese military capabilities.[96] They thought Chinese army morale was sufficient to sustain guerrilla operations, and this was considered satisfactory for British aims. Lack of enthusiasm in Whitehall for greater immediate cooperation was further dampened by the lack of Chinese military discipline. Rampant piracy by guerrillas against civilian vessels, for example, quickly resurfaced along the West River. Chiang's strategy of weakening Kwangtung's military forces and abandoning Canton did little to inspire British confidence in their ally.[97] Although Britain was slowly becoming more entangled in the war, Chiang's strategy had its share of deficiencies.

In the end, economic warfare in China produced limited results for Britain outside of East Asia. British discussions in Moscow during 1939 did not result in closer Anglo-Soviet collaboration. Despite British appeals, the German occupation of Czechoslovakia in mid-March gave Stalin sufficient cause to abandon collective security. Although the British had redoubled their efforts to establish an alliance with the USSR during this period, the ultimate result was the signing of the Nazi-Soviet Pact on 23 August 1939.[98] The provision of economic aid to China was only temporarily useful in improving relations with Stalin, although it did help promote long-term collective security with Washington. A British-mediated settlement of the Sino-Japanese War would have removed the main obstacle to improved Anglo-Japanese relations and redirected a great deal of Japanese attention against the USSR, but in the House of Commons and the Foreign Office, the desire for stronger relations with Stalin against Hitler superseded imperial considerations. British aid to China was therefore continued in the hope of exploiting any future reversal in Soviet policy, but the chance to attain peace in China had been discarded in early 1939.

Digging In

During the winter of 1938–1939 the war in China became a larger international problem, but most of the great powers lacked clear strategies to face it. Japanese frustration at the duration of the war resulted in the invasions of Kwangtung and Hainan, with the aim of cutting the movement of war supplies across southern China from Hong Kong and French Indochina. But the invasion of Kwangtung represented a dangerous military escalation, as ground operations along the Hong Kong border and aerial bombardment of the colony soon followed. Low-intensity conflict started to envelop Hong Kong, and with Japanese forces stationed at Canton, further conflict with the British became increasingly likely.

Japanese aggression during this period also produced a diplomatic response from third powers that was somewhat collaborative. The Anglo-American loans to China in 1939 were economic counterattacks aimed at thwarting Japanese peace efforts. Following the invasion of Hainan, the

United States became increasingly concerned about the threat to the Philippines and elsewhere in the southwestern Pacific, and this helped foster greater Anglo-American cooperation in support of Chiang Kai Shek. With a volatile diplomatic situation in Europe, collective action was also intended to support the USSR, but Anglo-Soviet cooperation against Germany was not forthcoming. In similar fashion, the British remained unenthusiastic about overt military cooperation with the Chinese, preferring the maintenance of a proxy war in place of a more concrete arrangement.

While the British and the Americans coordinated their efforts to continue the war, the Japanese missed their chance to secure peace. After a year and a half of hostilities, the Japanese had seemingly made some political progress with the defection of Wang Ching Wei, but continued Chinese resistance after the fall of Hankow led to the resignation of Prime Minister Konoye and the institution of a more hard-line regime. Impatience also produced poor military discipline at all levels, and a confused political agenda for occupied China was the result. The Japanese undermined their own position and, ultimately, further strained Far Eastern international relations.

In Chungking, Chiang's strategy of securing overt third-power military involvement had taken some steps toward fulfillment. In 1939 Anglo-Soviet support remained limited, but there was sufficient assistance to ensure the continuation of the war. In the process, southern China became the most significant theater of operations, with the railway from Changsha to Kwangtung and the port at Hong Kong being the most important strategic objectives for keeping the Chinese army alive. The invasion of south China marked the first major escalation of the war since Shanghai that threatened to involve third powers, but for Chiang, Canton was expendable because it brought Britain and Japan closer to war.

FIVE

■

Stalemate: March to October 1939

As war clouds gathered in Europe, the impact of the conflict in China on the conduct of international relations became more pronounced. The Sino-Japanese War also increasingly affected the grand strategy of several great powers. Since China's survival depended on the importation of military supplies from abroad, the region south of the Yangtse River had become one of the most important theaters of the war. Until the Japanese attack on the United States in December 1941, control of the southern Chinese railway between Hunan and Kwangtung remained a vital condition for victory, and because of this, the cities of Changsha and Hong Kong became strategic military objectives of global significance by the fall of 1939.

The pivotal period for Japan in the Sino-Japanese War was the summer and fall of 1939. Aside from the easy occupation of Hainan in February and the capture of Nanning in November, most military operations ended in defeat. Because of the political impact, three of the most important battles were Nomonhan in Mongolia, Changsha in Hunan, and Shekki (Shiqi) in Kwangtung (Shekki and Chungshan [Zhongzhan] are sometimes used interchangeably in the documents to refer to the same location, but Shekki is used here to identify the capital city of the Chungshan district, the area north of Macau). Taken together, the Japanese loss of prestige was great, and the psychological impact on the Chinese encouraged further resistance.

Nomonhan ensured that Soviet material assistance to China continued, although it diminished in scale over the next two years; this was followed by the battle for Changsha and the smaller yet equally significant battle for Shekki. Because of these three battles, the inauguration of the new Wang Ching Wei government was delayed, but a critical opportunity to secure a workable peace was discarded. Strategic stalemate failed to induce the British to end their vital support of Chiang Kai Shek from Hong Kong, despite the humiliations imposed on them at Tientsin and a temporary halt in Anglo-Soviet Far Eastern cooperation. Military reverses in the summer and fall of 1939 marked a turning point in Japanese fortunes in China, and the final result was an escalation of the conflict with the invasion of Kwangsi. Henceforth, after the fall of France in June 1940, the Japanese temptation to seize Indochina became too great to resist, and a reckless advance farther south was encouraged.

Anglo-Japanese relations became further strained as the Japanese blockade against China and Hong Kong was strengthened. Disruption of the supply of war materials remained the paramount concern of the Japanese, while food became a weapon used against Hong Kong. Littoral warfare in south China spread along the coast, culminating in the occupation of Swatow and Foochow. Closer to Canton, the blockade had far larger ramifications as it produced the battle of Shekki. In Hunan the battle of Changsha was more vital for Chinese survival, but without supplies from Hong Kong, the Chinese army could not have persevered. In response to these defeats, the Japanese applied greater direct military pressure against Hong Kong in the form of recurring attacks on the colony's fishing fleet, and army units returned to position themselves along the frontier. Throughout all this, Anglo-Japanese relations were further impaired by British ambassadorial misconduct, as revealed in the David Kung incident, and by an increased British covert military presence in Kwangtung. These developments contributed to an escalation of diplomatic tensions at Tientsin.

The Japanese had become increasingly frustrated by the Chinese supply situation rooted in Hong Kong, but a strengthened blockade was ultimately counterproductive. It was not only militarily ineffective; it also provoked greater British involvement in the war and promoted Anglo-Soviet cooperation. So long as a Soviet alliance remained a British objective, however, Hong Kong was a hostage to Japanese ambitions, and the longer the Sino-Japanese War lasted, the more British options diminished.

Food as a Weapon in the Pearl River Delta:
January to March 1939

From Toishan in the south to Samshui at the juncture of the West and North rivers, the western half of the Pearl River Delta was an important region to control, given its status as "one of the most highly developed agricultural areas in the world."[1] As such, its production accounted for much of the region's wealth, and it was an important source of food for both Macau and Hong Kong. This was particularly true of the Sze Yap district surrounding the city of Toishan, west of Macau. Almost 90 percent of Chinese living in North America at that time came from this region, and remittances from abroad increased the district's prosperity. This resulted in a high population density, with Toishan having about 950,000 prewar inhabitants. Because of these factors, control of the lower West River became a priority for the Japanese navy. Interlaced with its numerous waterways, the region had additional topographic features that allowed the Japanese to exploit their many tactical advantages during combat operations. With their arrival in October and November 1938, food quickly became a weapon used not only against Cantonese civilians in the province but also against Hong Kong and Macau. Japanese marines often seized harvested crops and other goods in raids that increased in frequency throughout most of 1939. War exacerbated the problems created by Chinese corruption, and as illegal commercial trading with the Japanese developed, starvation became endemic along the lower West River within a few short years.[2]

By January 1939, the Japanese had already stepped up their intimidation of Kwangtung by increasing the frequency of air strikes and ground operations throughout the Pearl River Delta. Air attacks against the region's roads and towns targeted both civilians and militia forces. The city of Shekki in particular (population 250,000), on the Chungshan River eighteen miles east of Kongmoon, attracted a great deal of unwanted attention. Ground attacks continued along the West River, and much of the Chinese river traffic came to a standstill, but the Japanese encountered more resistance than they had originally anticipated. Strangely, the one place left unmolested until late January was Kongmoon, but it was finally bombed on the twenty-seventh. Later in the war the city became a rest and recuperation center for wounded Japanese soldiers.[3]

During a pause in operations at the end of January, the Japanese army held discussions in Macau with Chinese regional leaders such as Chung-shan's district magistrate General Chang Wai Chang (Cheung Wai Cheung), hoping to bring an end to the fighting and enlist support for the new government in Canton. These meetings occurred on 29 January and 5 February 1939, and Japanese terms would have allowed Chinese officials to retain their positions; a commercial treaty was also offered as an inducement for cooperation.[4] Negotiations ended in failure. The Chinese blamed Japanese barbarity and the loathsome nature of several of their negotiating officers, such as one Lieutenant Wada Shinzo, a Kempeitai officer and "pseudo-dentist" convicted of war crimes by British authorities after the war.[5] The first Japanese response to the breakdown in negotiations came from the air, followed in March 1939 by numerous ground operations along the West River. Army units and marines were accompanied by their Chinese puppet allies, whose only real utility was the looting of civilians. This monthlong operation met with even greater resistance. Part of the reason for the lack of Japanese success was the paucity of available troops; there were only 25,000 in the entire province for the dual missions of conducting offensive operations and maintaining an effective garrison in Canton.[6]

To the residents of Macau and Hong Kong, one of the more disquieting elements of the March offensive was an amphibious landing by two companies of Japanese troops on Lappa Island, near the border of Macau, and their attack against Portuguese colonial military forces located just outside the colony. The Macau incident was a Japanese attempt to better control the inner harbor, and it coincided with efforts to purchase property and generally manipulate the Macanese economy in late 1938 and early 1939.[7] In this brief clash, East African colonial troops did not offer prolonged resistance, and they retreated in good order back to Macau.

Portuguese ground forces were not strong in number and were supported by only three or four Osprey reconnaissance planes, one gunboat, and an understrength battery of five field guns.[8] A February visit to the garrison by Major G. T. Wards of the British army revealed that the available forces were not meant for sustained combat. With only a single Mozambique battalion divided into four rifle companies and one machine gun company totaling about 800 men, plus 100 Sikh policemen, Macau invited attack. Wards's comments indicate that the strength of the infantry was found among the noncommissioned officers and the men:

CHAPTER FIVE

My general impression was that with the exception of the Portuguese officers, the troops looked clean, well clothed and equipped, and well disciplined.

The state of cleanliness of both the barrack room and the weapons was of a high standard, especially as, the visit being unexpected, they could not have been prepared for any special inspection.

As for the Portuguese officers they looked slovenly and lazy and a direct contrast to everything else seen.[9]

Because Macau was a conduit for food into Hong Kong, as well as another route by which war supplies entered China, the Japanese were likely to bring greater pressure against the British by increasing their grip on Macau. Unfortunately for the Portuguese, and also for the British, Macau had become another potential flash point that threatened the stability of international relations in the Far East.

Sinking into a Quagmire:
March to May 1939

From the spring of 1939 onward, Japanese aims in south China included building popular support for their new puppet administration in Canton while eroding British support for Chiang Kai Shek from Hong Kong. In both these objectives they failed. As a result, the Japanese navy increased its patrols along the south China coast once Hainan had been secured in order to restrict the transshipment of war supplies from Hong Kong to Swatow and Foochow. Both these cities would be occupied by the end of the summer in operations supported by powerful naval forces based at Amoy. After failing to gain greater support for their Chinese administration in Kwangtung during the first three months of 1939, Japanese marines and army units resumed their attacks throughout the Pearl River Delta, with combat becoming severe during May and again from July to September. These operations were directed primarily at cutting the food supply into Hong Kong.[10] The near complete breakdown in Anglo-Japanese relations impacted Hong Kong during August, when Japanese army units took positions along the frontier and closed the border to China. Throughout all this, the Japanese air war over China continued with great ferocity, especially at Chungking. With large bases available at Hainan and Canton, aerial interdiction against Chinese lines of communication to Hong Kong and

French Indochina was greatly increased, although this effort remained largely ineffective.

Building popular support for the new administration in Kwangtung was difficult. At Canton, the Japanese formed a twenty-five-mile-radius defense zone with a no-man's-land between the two sides, but with up to 200,000 guerrillas reportedly located in Kwangtung, Japanese ground forces patrolling the region often met with opposition. Fighting in Chungshan resumed during March, causing Japanese morale to deteriorate. The 4th War Zone, and especially Kwangtung, was weak both politically and militarily, but Chiang Kai Shek maintained control. He ensured resistance throughout the province by keeping the bulk of his meager regular forces intact under General Yu Han Mou north of Canton and by fighting the Japanese aggressively in Chungshan using General Chang's militia. Although Chinese guerrillas were of varying quality and were certainly a large part of the province's banditry problem, they were far too numerous for the Japanese to eliminate. Anarchy was common in much of the province, including Canton, and due to the lack of effective political control, people were slow to return to the city out of the fear of violence from all sides. By June 1939, somewhere between 500,000 and 700,000 people had returned, but half the businesses remained closed.[11]

Japanese ground operations at this time coincided with China's failed nationwide April offensive. Along the North and East rivers, the net military results were inconclusive, but civil instability persisted. Twelve thousand men of General Yu's 12th Group Army, including elements of the 151st, 152nd, 154th, and 159th Divisions, attempted and failed to capture Tsengcheng in early April. At Shihlingpu, north of Canton, the Japanese also defended against the Chinese 151st, 152nd, 154th, 157th, 158th, and 160th Divisions. Chinese forces had little chance of success in attacking large garrisoned cities or towns owing to a lack of air and artillery support. To avoid squandering Yu's forces, neither of these attacks was pressed with great determination. Yet, with only 25,000 men to maintain security over occupied areas, the Japanese were similarly unable to make military gains; they could not venture far from their base at Canton in any great strength. Somewhat surprising to Hong Kong residents, then, was the 10 April 1939 landing of Japanese troops at the western end of the colonial frontier at Namtau, but these troops quickly proceeded north and away from the border.[12]

Combat occurring south of Canton was normally small in scale (company or battalion level) and usually inconclusive, but the Chungshan district became an increasingly deadly arena as the war of attrition dragged on. The thought persisted among many Japanese officers that peace could be imposed more easily after victory on the battlefield.[13] Because of their unexpected failure to establish a stable puppet government in the province, preparations for larger military operations were begun in April. A Hong Kong military intelligence report explained that the movement of war supplies continued to be a main source of frustration: "A very respectable volume of traffic was flowing up the back reaches by this route from Hong Kong and Macau, but even if the Japanese succeed in stopping up these particular holes, it will doubtlessly seep through by some other ways in due course."[14] Fanning the flames was the increasingly determined leadership of General Chang Wai Chang and the Japanese desire to maintain prestige by defeating him. In the second week of April 1939, Captains Charles Boxer and C. J. Edwards traveled to Chungshan via Macau to investigate the situation. They reported to the GOC in China, Major General Grasett, that the Japanese were making preparations for larger offensive operations. Numerous hospital ships had been collected in the area in anticipation of significant casualties, and Japanese infantry patrols were more frequent northwest of Macau. As an indication of their growing difficulties, Japanese reinforcements supported by substantial airpower and naval gunfire were required near Kongmoon to defeat an increasingly determined Chinese counterattack between 19 and 22 April 1939.[15]

Japanese frustration with the stalemate across China resulted in an expanded long-range aerial bombardment campaign to the interior. Szechwan was hit hard by Japanese naval bombers from May 1939 onward, and Chungking was often targeted from newly acquired air bases at Hankow. The British embassy was badly damaged after being hit on 4 May 1939, and the French embassy was similarly bombed on 3 August 1939. Other important centers in Szechwan and along the Yangtse River were also targeted frequently. In one particularly heavy raid at Ichang on 8 March 1939, more than 1,500 people were killed. Unfortunately for the Chinese, their air force was badly defeated in the defense of Szechwan, and a total of about 800 aircraft had been destroyed since the start of the war. What units remained were in disarray or were being flown by a handful of Soviet pilots. Chinese air defenses were very limited in strength while the air force rebuilt itself with planes acquired from the Soviets and the Americans.[16]

In reaction to the Japanese air offensive, the Chinese received greater international material assistance. In March 1939 the U.S. War Department began to reassess its Pacific war preparations, with specific attention devoted to the reinforcement of the Philippines in the event of a U.S.-Japanese crisis. The following month, 200 aircraft were sold to the Chinese for $9 million, but there were substantial delays in delivery. After the German occupation of Prague, the Soviets also grew more concerned about the threat posed by the Japanese army in Manchuria, and they signed a deal with Sun Fo on 5 April 1939 for the delivery of additional aircraft plus 800 pilots and ground crew personnel. This action coincided with a renewed effort by the British Foreign Office to form an alliance with Stalin after a brief hiatus from earlier discussions. In East Asia, Japanese strategy remained opportunistic, and the Japanese reaction to European events during the spring and summer became increasingly anti-British. What they continued to strive for, however, was a break in the military and political deadlock with a significant military victory.[17]

The Occupation of Swatow and Foochow:
Summer 1939

With more than 1 million men in the field and approximately 100,000 dead, the Japanese had few ideas on how to bring the war with China to an end. The Japanese had rejected joining the Axis Pact in the spring of 1939, and they would not decide until September 1940 which grand strategy to pursue. In the meantime, it was a question of whether to advance north or south. Until a decision was made, the British continued to allow the movement of war materials into China. In March 1939, for example, 32,000 tank shells and 80 million rounds of small-arms ammunition originating from Germany passed through Hong Kong to Rangoon, followed in July by another 10 million rounds labeled as machine accessories. The latter went directly to free China from Hong Kong on board the SS *Bertram* in exchange for tungsten. In response, the Japanese continued to monitor European events, but China and Hong Kong were further isolated with the occupation of Swatow and Foochow.[18]

One of the major problems thwarting the establishment of a Chinese government in the occupied regions of south China was the lack of a uniform strategy—a result of Japanese army-navy rivalry. The highly aggressive posture adopted by Vice Admiral Kondo Nobutake and the Japanese 5th Fleet failed to correspond with General Ando Rikichi's policy of restraint. Personal ambition and greed among senior Japanese officers also prevented the establishment of a politically cohesive strategy, as many commanders continued to favor regional puppet governments over a single administration headed by Wang Ching Wei.[19] Poor Japanese civil-military relations compounded the difficulties. In Canton, Japanese officials openly expressed their complaints in this regard, even to foreign missionaries. One of these missionaries was Dr. Oscar Thomson, who noted that many Japanese felt that the lack of direction was leading to a wider war. He explained to a colleague how the Japanese consul had told him that the consul's own lack of communication and understanding with the military was making his job much more difficult, especially in dealing with the British.[20]

Impatience among Japanese commanders was one of the reasons for these problems, but the cruelty exhibited all too frequently by troops outside of Canton was also a constant drag on whatever limited political progress was made. Captain Edwards reported: "Of all of Japan's mistakes none has been so foolish or done more to lose her the war than the apparent inability to prevent, if not the actual incitement of her soldiers to behave as pure savages. Especially during the early days of the war murder of large numbers of innocent civilians under revolting conditions, looting, arson and wholesale rape were the normal corollary of every Japanese advance."[21] Continued cooperation between the Chinese central government and the communists was the first result of Japanese cruelty. Increased political awareness among many Chinese was another. Edwards continued: "It turned even the uneducated Chinese peasant, who normally neither knows nor cares who rules him, so he can cultivate his field in peace, into an active enemy of Japan, either as a guerilla or as the guerilla's friend."[22] Many Chinese also shared the fatalistic view that, having survived for two years on their own with limited aid from abroad, time was on their side. An acquaintance in Chungking once told Edwards: "We do not expect to beat Japan to her knees, but we think we can drag her down with us."[23] So long as the Chinese army remained along the Yangtse River and in Hunan, there was less need for capitulation. Hatred of the Japanese remained a relatively constant variable in the equation of Chinese morale, and resistance would continue, provided Hong Kong supplied the Chinese army in Hunan.[24]

Commerce offered a chance for the Japanese to achieve their political and diplomatic objectives, but few Japanese officers understood this as well as General Ando or the British. Several foreign observers noted the possibility of establishing peace over time if the Japanese military services restrained their more aggressive elements and adopted less brutal methods.

Foreign missionaries and military officers based these opinions on years of observation of Chinese culture and the Chinese affinity for trade. As the war progressed, their predictions of the gradual emergence of peace through military stalemate and static deployments were substantiated by events. Major David Barrett was one of the most prescient regarding this eventuality.[25] In areas where Japanese aggression was curbed, trading with the enemy grew more common, given the desire of many Chinese—both in and out of uniform—to return to a normal life. By 1944, a de facto peace had grown out of this widespread economic reality in many parts of China, but by then, it was too late to help the Japanese. It was already an established reality in some parts of north China and in Manchuria as early as the summer of 1939. Although the development of Sino-Japanese trade in areas of static warfare had the potential to undermine Japanese military discipline over time, the possibility of peace developing in occupied and adjacent areas was an issue of great concern to officials in London tasked with managing affairs in China. This scenario was considered most undesirable by the British, whose objective was the prolongation of the war, not peace.[26]

After the Pearl River was effectively closed, much commercial trade passed from Hong Kong into China to the north through Swatow and Foochow. Several nontreaty ports such as Wenchow were opened to international economic activity, but trading with the enemy soon became commonplace along the entire Kwangtung and Fukien coastline. Trade was often conducted with the navy, and this business continued in great volume even under the threat of occasional bombardment and invasion; however, the Chinese endeavored to avoid provoking an attack on Foochow and Swatow by restricting imports there to nonmilitary goods. Helping them maintain peace was the fact that tungsten mined from Kiangsi was the most important commodity sold to the Japanese at Swatow (tungsten mines near Toishan were an additional factor in drawing the navy's interest toward Macau). But Admiral Kondo's impatience over the ongoing political trouble in Kwangtung and the logistical situation in Hong Kong resulted in periodic bombardments of Foochow and Swatow throughout the spring.[27]

Littoral warfare along the coast increased tensions between Japanese and Hong Kong officials, as these operations often directly affected British naval forces and civilian maritime vessels. Admiral Kondo's arrival in Amoy during the first half of May did not ease Anglo-Japanese friction. He had come to personally oversee events in the region following the assassination of a Chinese puppet official in what became known as the Kulangsu incident. As in Foochow and Swatow, aerial bombardment became common in the area around Amoy from the beginning of May onward, and an air base was established there to accommodate additional units. Naval reinforcements were also received.[28] On 14 May 1939 a severe aerial attack on Swatow was conducted with aircraft from three Japanese warships, including the heavy cruiser *Myoko*. These attacks involved British vessels and were reported on by Hong Kong military officers:

> While air-raids have been carried out by all units, including "Myoko," "Nagara," "Natori," and "Kamikawa Maru," the most brutal and destructive attacks are the work of aircraft from the flagship "Myoko." The most wanton act of all was the machine-gunning of sampans by "Myoko's" aircraft at Swatow on 14th May. "Folkestone" reported that two sampans within 200 yards of the ship were attacked and ten casualties sustained including several dead. Two children were treated by "Folkestone's" Medical Officer but one, a girl aged 16, subsequently died. "Folkestone" also reported the machine gunning of the Nanchai ferry which caused 24 casualties including 8 killed and "Thracian" has reported similar cases.[29]

Royal Navy vessels were in Swatow to assist British ships that had been stopped due to the blockade. Just prior to the *Folkestone*'s report, the SS *Sagres* had been seized off the Fukien coast and brought to the Pescadores Islands. The Royal Navy prevented additional seizures by its prompt intervention on behalf of other British ships.[30]

By June, Japanese anger directed against the British in southern China had grown, although with less intensity than that seen at Tientsin. Air attacks along the coast were followed by an amphibious landing at Swatow on 21 June to isolate Hong Kong further. For this operation, a Japanese army mixed brigade that included Koreans and elements of the Formosan Force, all supported by the recently arrived seaplane carrier *Chiyoda*, was landed to occupy the city. By 9 July 1939, this brigade had secured the port and most of the immediate area after meeting stronger than expected Chinese resistance and sustaining approximately 200 casualties. Consul Matsudaira in Swatow explained to a British maritime officer that all third-power shipping was henceforth restricted to one ship per week because of the high volume of war material passing through the port. The Japanese included trucks and rice from Hong Kong as contraband.[31]

The occupation of Swatow had little impact on the Chinese military supply situation. Captain John Stapler of the USS *Tulsa* noted, "British coastwise shipping is keeping up [the] struggle against the closing of the ports and is endeavoring to find out-of-the-way places where vessels can stop."[32] Closer to Hong Kong, Kondo attempted to hit the Chinese economically with a small ground assault on the salt distribution center at Swabue, but this attack was repelled between 18 and 21 July 1939. Salt was one of the few commodities left that generated revenue for the Chinese government, and disruption of the salt trade was as much of an economic goal of the Japanese as was their attack on the Chinese currency at Tientsin.[33]

Kondo soon turned his attention to Foochow. His forces had periodically bombarded the port throughout the spring and summer, and its occupation was completed by 1 August 1939. The bombardment and mining of other ports as far as Wenchow in Chekiang (Zhejiang) were also under way by September, but the net result was of little military utility. By the fall of 1939, Kondo had failed to block the movement of war supplies from Hong Kong into free China.[34]

In consolidating their newly acquired positions, the Japanese installed puppet administrations in both Foochow and Swatow, but ultimately, little was gained politically. Once it was established, the Japanese navy tried to tighten the south China blockade by increasing the frequency and strength of surface patrols in Bias Bay. They also encouraged anti-British demonstrations among the Chinese at Swatow. On 7 August 1939 a party from HMS *Tenedos* landed to safeguard the British consulate from a potentially violent mob, but the situation was defused without great difficulty. Although anti-British sentiment among Japanese officers was becoming more pronounced in south China, personal profit still seemed to play a more prominent role in their decision making. By way of example, Admiral Kondo arrived in Swatow on 10 September 1939 to discuss how much money Chinese business interests would pay him in exchange for permission to ship goods to America.[35] Aside from such business arrangements, little else was accomplished by Kondo's coastal war northeast of Hong Kong. Had trade been conducted with fewer bombs from his fleet, perhaps the results would have been more profitable for Japan.

Following the Cantonese political rebuff in Chungshan, the Japanese intensified their military operations throughout the entire Pearl River Delta during the summer and fall of 1939, but they remained unsuccessful in terminating the war. An acceptable peace in occupied Kwangtung could not be imposed. Aggressive patrolling against Chinese irregulars south of the East and West rivers continued; simultaneously, the Japanese hoped to keep General Yu's 12th Group Army divisions from infiltrating from the north. As summer turned to fall, the forces of both sides converged on Shekki, but repeated Japanese attempts to capture the city met with failure. The Chinese defended the birthplace of Sun Yat Sen with great determination, and although the fight for Shekki was small in scale compared with other significant battles, its political impact helped prolong the war. Combined with the defeats at Nomonhan and Changsha, the Japanese Pyrrhic victory in Chungshan only strengthened the Chinese in their resolve to continue fighting. The military victory required for the inauguration of the Wang Ching Wei government continued to be elusive.

Japanese plans also involved maintaining pressure against Hong Kong, and this escalated the conflict. From June to October 1939 the Japanese army appeared on Hong Kong's border in strength, but General Ando was careful to ensure that his forces respected British sovereignty and avoided direct confrontation with the colonial garrison. Admiral Kondo was much more aggressive in attacking Hong Kong's lines of communication, especially toward the West River, and his forces brought the war directly into Hong Kong by both air and sea. Kondo's desire to exploit the British preoccupation with the crisis in Europe caused the low-intensity conflict enveloping Hong Kong to expand.

With General Yu's 12th Group Army and General Ng Kei Wai's 9th Group Army ready to attack any thinly held positions outside of Canton, it was difficult for the Japanese army to gather sufficient forces to fight effectively at a distance. Consequently, the Japanese navy's marines and their Chinese allies fought much of the summer battle for control of the Pearl River Delta. Support for the Chungshan campaign was extended as early as March, with airfield expansions and railway improvements near Kongmoon and Canton and on Sanchau Island (during August). The Chinese were expected to defend the region with weak militia forces made up largely of peasant farmers, but for added assurance, the navy reinforced the 5th

Fleet with several seaplane carriers, such as the *Mizuho* (with its fifteen-aircraft capacity), during April and May. The 5th and 23rd Destroyer Flotillas were replaced by the 9th and 45th Destroyer Flotillas, respectively. Along the West River the Japanese also had an advantage in gunboats, including the *Saga, Enoshima,* and *Ento.* General Ando's army at Canton likewise received reinforcements, but the bulk of his infantry consisted of elements of several divisions, including the 18th, the 104th, and the Formosan Force under Major General Iida Shojiro. Iida later commanded the Imperial Guard Brigade at Nanning in 1940 and the 15th Army in Burma. In all, there were approximately 50,000 Japanese troops in the region during the first week of June, with the 18th Division under Major General Kuno Seiichi guarding the East River and the 104th under Major General Hamamoto stationed along the North and West rivers. The Formosan Force had three full regiments supported by AFVs and engineers at Canton, Fatshan, and Samshui; part of this unit also defended Bocca Tigris. An artillery regiment was positioned at each of these places (as well as at south Hainan and Swatow), and each of these garrisons was augmented with a marine battalion and Chinese puppet troops. Because of the general manpower shortage, towns such as Samshui and Sheklung were usually garrisoned by only one or two companies totaling 200 to 300 men.[36]

In order to protect Canton adequately, the 21st Army could provide only limited assistance to the Chungshan offensive; it focused most of its attention to the north of Canton and in areas along the East River, close to the city. In contrast, General Chang Wai Chang could defend the region effectively because his militia forces were supported from western Kwangtung. To keep the Japanese in place at Canton, help was available from 16th Group Army, from Yu's weaker 12th Group Army in the north, and, if necessary, from Ng's more effective 9th Group Army positioned in southwest Kiangsi. Kwangsi reinforcements also arrived along the West River to strengthen Kwangtung's western defenses; these included the 64th and 69th Armies under Lieutenant General Hsia Wei. The westernmost base of operations was located at Wuchow on the Kwangsi-Kwangtung border, and it was defended primarily by Kwangsi troops. Many fortifications were constructed during June. More forces were positioned farther downriver at Koyiu (Shiuhing), along with ten Chinese MTBs to protect the river boom located there. Because these were the gateways into Kwangsi, both cities were bombed often by Japanese aircraft, and a 26 July 1939 raid on Wuchow resulted in over 1,000 casualties.[37] With these forces available throughout the province, the Chinese were able to exploit any opportunities that arose when the Japanese reduced their garrisons to support offensive operations in Chungshan.

Airpower was used to begin the assault on the Chungshan district in May and June, and raids continued throughout the summer. Many towns were bombarded, and Chinese farmers were often strafed while working in their fields or transporting their produce to Shekki. During this first phase, interference with the region's agricultural production remained the primary objective. This was confirmed by Hong Kong military intelligence when officers of the *Saga* informed Governor Barbosa that food shipments into Macau were going to be reduced to provide only for the needs of his colony. In July, Japanese naval officers informed Portuguese mariners that food from Shekki could be shipped only to Macau or Swabue, not to Hong Kong.[38]

Ground operations began by mid-June 1939, and these were once again carried out with companies of marines and Chinese puppets patrolling the West River Delta. However, these forces were insufficient to defeat the unexpectedly determined guerrillas, who were reinforced by regulars during July. According to a Canadian missionary, the Reverend Tom Broadfoot, the Japanese made very little headway near Kongmoon and Sunwui and were constantly harassed by Chinese central government forces. Japanese river and ground patrols continued throughout the month, and reinforcements were brought in from Swatow.[39] "Severe fighting" was reported by U.S. Army Captain Edwin Sutherland in the area between Sunwui and Shekki on 16 July, against the Chinese 152nd Division.[40] Broadfoot commented on the situation near Kongmoon that same day: "Fighting proceeds in and around Kong Moon as it has now, for many weeks. The Japanese are making no progress and are losing men and material."[41] A Japanese marine battalion assaulted and captured the town of Kishan, along the eastern coast of Chungshan district, on 27 July, but the following advance met strong resistance at Shekki, and the attack on the city ended in failure. The Reverend Harry Wittenbach, an Australian missionary, described what he saw that day:

July 1939 for Chungshan was a continuance of air raids and conflict. I was able on July 10th to take my family to Hongkong and to spend a fortnight with them in the peace and cool of Shatin bungalow before returning to my work. While on my way to Shek-kei, on July

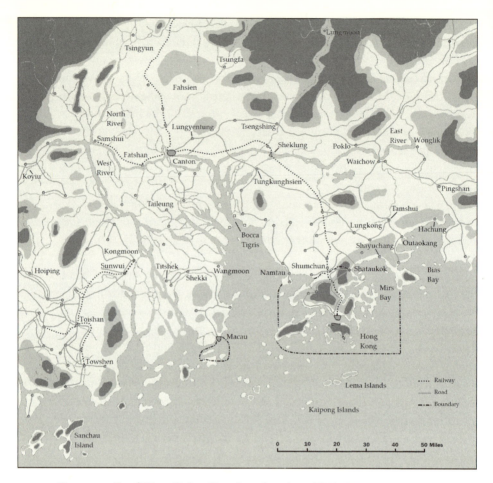

Figure 5.1. Pearl River Delta. (Based on data from TNA, WO 106/2384.)

27th, I narrowly escaped a bombing raid. Two Japanese planes attacked a village through which I had just passed and I spent half-an-
hour sitting in a field of turnips while the planes, after dropping their
bombs, circled around machine-gunning the village and the adjoining
roads. The journey to Shek-kei involved a bicycle ride of twenty miles
over mutilated roads or a forty mile ride by circuitous roads in better
condition—either a very strenuous trip in mid-summer. I made the return journey in a day.[42]

To deal with the troublesome situation, the Japanese increased their troop strength in Kwangtung by dispatching two additional divisions to Canton from Formosa. By the end of July, this brought their total strength in the province to about 75,000 men. Some success was achieved with the capture of Kongmoon, Kowkong, and Sunwui once they arrived (see figure 5.1).[43]

Even with the loss of these cities, and despite the near death of General Chang on 3 August 1939 during a Japanese attack at Wangmoon (on the eastern shore of Chungshan district), the Chinese grew more resolute. Counterattacks increased in both frequency and strength, and on 3 August near Kongmoon, a Japanese column including twelve tanks and a cavalry battalion was ambushed, with many killed. Because of this resistance, the Japanese political program in support of the new Wang Ching Wei national government was given a rocky start. The arrival of poorly disciplined reinforcements did little to help, as looting became commonplace. Less than a week later, on 9 August, Wang and Ando met in Canton, but this failed to produce positive political results because most southern Chinese generals failed to rally to Japanese calls for unity and peace. Although Ando agreed to permit autonomous Chinese police and militia forces and agreed that all Chinese officials in occupied Kwangtung would retain positions of power, Wang's public radio appeal to launch a new national government based in Canton fell flat among both the Chinese military leadership and the general public. Wang's message of "Canton for the Cantonese" had little attraction in the face of the Japanese navy's pacification methods in Chungshan.[44]

Urban areas such as Shekki were bombarded regularly by Japanese artillery and aircraft as the fighting continued throughout August and September. By 26 September, three increasingly severe assaults on Shekki had been defeated in succession; the third had been augmented by almost two army battalions transferred from the Hong Kong border. Hong Kong military officers took note of the Chinese ability to defend the hometown of Sun Yat Sen and sent their observations to London. They reported that the Japanese had lost a tremendous amount of prestige due to their repeated defeats at the hands of Chinese "farmer soldiers," but most importantly, they noted the political result: the Cantonese had failed to respond to Wang Ching Wei's call for unity with his new national government.[45]

Pressure for a quick victory began to mount on Japanese commanders

Figure 5.2. Shekki, 1944. (NARA, RG 341, entry 217, box 824, MIPI File No. 69404, aerial reconnaissance photo, 4 October 1944.)

from within the army and from businessmen who were anxious about the Pearl River's closure to civilian traffic. All previous Japanese attempts to take Shekki had failed due to limited troop strength and an overreliance on weak Chinese allies. Yet a victory at Shekki was required to save face, and the final assault began on 6 October 1939. Three columns advanced on the city, supported by air and naval gunfire. A full Formosan brigade was landed at Tieshih (Titshek) and advanced on Shekki from the west, while two marine battalions advanced from the east starting at Wangmoon on the coast. Another group came in from the north.[46] Waterborne forces took full advantage of the river bisecting Chungshan district (see figure 5.2).

Following two days of heavy combat, the Japanese finally occupied Shekki on 8 October 1939, and the 2,000 remaining Chinese withdrew when they ran out of ammunition. The defending force sustained a total of 2,600 killed and 350 captured. It was a bitter pill to swallow—withdrawing from the birthplace of Sun Yat Sen just before the "Double Tenth" anniversary of the revolution—especially after the Cantonese victory over Japanese forces at Tehan on the same anniversary in 1938. Nonetheless, it had been a hard-fought battle, and the campaign had dragged on, despite all expectations, for a large part of 1939. Most of the fighting had been done by Cantonese forces, while Kwangsi troops maintained security over Chinese lines of communication. Despite holding much of the lower reaches of the West River, the Japanese victory was short-lived, and they withdrew from Shekki after only two days of occupation. The Chinese under General Chang Wai Chang quickly returned as soon as the occupiers left.[47]

Although much smaller in scale than the major battles occurring elsewhere during the summer and fall of 1939, the battle for the Chunghsan district was significant, in that it helped upset Japanese plans to inaugurate the national government of Wang Ching Wei. Captain R. Giles of the Royal Marines reported this to London:

The only reason they occupied Shekki was to retrieve the loss of "face" resulting from their previously unsuccessful attacks on the Chungshan district with Marines and Puppet troops. But although strategically sound, it was a tacit admission since it implied that they have not sufficient troops to garrison all the points they capture. The political effect therefore greatly encouraged the Chinese, especially as it coincided with the turn of the tide at Changsha and the air raids over Hankow. Japanese efforts to install a puppet government proved abortive, and the Chinese under General Cheung Wai Cheung reoccupied the town as soon as they had left.[48]

It also proved that the Chinese could defend Kwangtung militarily for a protracted period if they chose to. This, in turn, supports the view that the rapid withdrawal from Canton in October 1938 had been a deliberate element of Chiang Kai Shek's strategy, not an act of treason by General Yu. The Japanese loss of prestige in Kwangtung followed much larger defeats in July in both Shansi and Hupeh. Morale problems intensified among Japanese forces as a result of the military stalemate, and the disasters suffered in Mongolia and Hunan from August to October only compounded Japanese difficulties.[49]

Nomonhan (Khalkhin Gol): August–September 1939

The battle of Nomonhan had a large psychological effect on the Chinese, and when the effect of Nomomhan was combined with that of the battles of Chungshan and Changsha in south China, the political impact was tremendous. Throughout much of the Sino-Japanese War, Anglo-Soviet support to China was somewhat coordinated, but this assistance was sometimes shaped by conflicting strategic and political interests. Often, British and Soviet efforts occurred simultaneously, but support was usually increased or decreased by one to influence the other. Both countries supported the Chinese to keep the Japanese from expanding north or south, but since much of the British economic activity along the Yangtse River had already been eliminated, Hong Kong was the only place where British interests in China remained relatively strong (economic activity there amounted to 2 percent of British trade).[50] Although a free Hong Kong remained a vital concern for Chinese survival, as far as British imperial security was concerned, it was merely an outpost for Singapore. Siberia was of much greater strategic importance to the Soviet Union, and these realities were reflected in the level of support each country provided to China.

The Soviet-Japanese battle of Nomonhan provides a case in point. As Stalin moved toward Hitler in August 1939, the ferocity of the Mongolian battle increased. Stalin's first concern in Asia was to maintain the proxy war in China by reassuring the Chinese of his continued support. As the battle was heating up, U.S. Army Captain Edwin Sutherland reported on Soviet objectives in Mongolia: "The aim of the Soviets in this war is to give the Chinese just enough aid and encouragement to keep them from accepting any Japanese peace proposals that may be forthcoming. The Russian Military Attaché, Combrig Ivanov, indicated this."[51] In countering the diplomatic effects of the Nazi-Soviet Pact and the Tientsin crisis, Nomonhan served as a useful tonic in boosting Chinese morale, and Japanese peace offers directed at Chungking were thwarted, once again, in part because of the Japanese defeat at the hands of the Red Army. The battle of Nomonhan was more than just another border clash: it was the largest foreign intervention of the Sino-Japanese War and a key element of Stalin's evolving Far Eastern strategy.

Early in 1939, after the occupation of Hainan, Japanese army commanders felt secure enough in the north to reinforce south China in anticipation of operations along the coast. At that time, it appeared that the Soviets and the Japanese had come to some kind of diplomatic understanding, as demonstrated by the signing of a fishery agreement in April. Some British officers in Hong Kong thought that additional Japanese units might be pulled from Manchuria for service elsewhere,[52] but these concerns were short-lived. Following Hitler's move into Czechoslovakia, when French and British officials renewed their interest in collective security with Moscow, the Soviets began to intervene more directly on the ground in the Sino-Japanese War. Since May 1939, Soviet-Japanese border friction in Mongolia had grown more serious, and the military situation deteriorated over the course of the summer. Consequently, by August, the Japanese army's desire to provoke trouble with Britain was temporarily lessened. One demonstration of this change was the termination of the crisis at Tientsin at the end of July. Then, during the first half of August, seven Japanese divisions were transferred out of the Yangtse River valley for duty farther north. But as the Nazi-Soviet Pact was being signed on 23–24 August 1939, the Japanese 6th Army was encircled at Nomonhan near the Mongolian border. Red Army forces completed the 6th Army's destruction by the end of the month. Although casualty totals vary, depending on the source, some place the number of Japanese casualties as high as 50,000. This battle was a significant intervention on the part of the Soviets, but Chinese hopes for greater involvement were overly optimistic. Aside from elements of its Far Eastern forces, the Red Army was incapable of conducting large-scale offensive operations effectively because of Stalin's purges in 1937 and 1938. Nevertheless, Japanese withdrawals from central China caused a dangerous shortage of troops on the eve of the first battle of Changsha, which took place in late September and early October and represented another humiliating defeat for Japan in a year of noteworthy defeats.[53]

Coinciding with discussions of an Anglo-Soviet alliance, Soviet military supplies to China increased, but in an odd turn of events, Stalin boosted Soviet commitment even further as negotiations with the British stalled and a deal with Hitler became a possibility. Soviet artillery and air advisers were posted as far south as Kweilin as the Japanese navy began an aerial interdiction campaign against Chinese lines of communication to French Indochina. Naval transfers from Leningrad to Vladivostok included the passage of eleven warships via Panama during July, followed by the appearance of 150 aircraft at Lanchow. An additional squadron arrived at Chungking during August. Loans worth $150 million were also negotiated on 10 August 1939 to counter Japanese economic pressure at Tientsin; these coincided with a British loan of £5 million.[54]

Unfortunately for the Chinese and the British, the battle of Nomonhan marked the turning point of Soviet aid to China. Following the Nazi-Soviet Pact, Soviet assistance was gradually reduced until it was terminated in 1941 with the German invasion of the USSR. During the early summer of 1939, Soviet military operations in Mongolia helped support the British position at Tientsin while negotiations were under way in Moscow for a collective security alliance. But when discussions with the British and French stalled by the end of July 1939, the ferocity and scale of the battle were greatly increased, and the destruction of the 6th Army helped convince the Japanese that future expansion southward against British interests would be more profitable than an attack into Siberia. After Stalin's alliance with Hitler was signed in August 1939, a Japanese advance to the south became a Soviet strategic objective, not only for national security but also as a means of providing indirect support to Germany.[55] Consequently, the intensification of the battle at Nomonhan was directed as much against the British as it was against the Japanese. Officials in London had previously considered aid to China via Hong Kong to be useful as long as the USSR remained a potential ally. Nevertheless, the British continued their support throughout 1939 and into 1940 in the weak hope of a Soviet reversal of policy.

Soviet aid continued, but on a diminishing scale, following the alliance with Hitler and the outbreak of war in Europe. Stalin still wished to keep the Japanese mired in China, but from this point forward, both the Japanese and the Soviets sought to maintain official neutrality in their diplomatic relations, in part to continue the shipment of raw materials to Germany. This led to a change in Anglo-Soviet diplomatic relations in the Far East. As part of their aerial counteroffensive, Soviet raids were carried out against Hankow shortly after the October debacle at Changsha, and this helped keep the Japanese off balance while trying to recover from their losses. By November, Lanchow had become a larger external Soviet base, with barracks for 1,000 Red Army troops and 1,000 air force personnel. Weapons arsenals were also being operated under Soviet supervision. But despite the continued assistance to China, Soviet attitudes toward Britain and France had become problematic. Soviet propaganda directed at China highlighted French military limitations and suggested that the French army would be outflanked by a German advance through Belgium.[56] Propaganda against Poland was also meant to undermine British prestige and demonstrate Soviet solidarity with Germany. Captain Edwards in Hong Kong reported to London some examples of this trend: "The merciless hunting-out and shooting of Polish 'officer-scum' is recounted in a vivid and peculiarly revolting manner. There are detailed accounts of the alleged atrocities committed by Polish officers upon the defenders and downtrodden workers. 'Fat Priests' are described as preying on the people."[57] Vitriolic radio attacks worsened with the Soviet attack on Finland in December: "The 'Anglo-French Imperialists' are blamed for egging-on the Finnish, 'scarecrow militarists and their clownish government.'"[58] In the Far East, the change in Soviet attitude was first physically witnessed at Vladivostok by British ship masters, whose crews had previously been allowed ashore with few restrictions. When the SS *Hauk* docked at Vladivostok following the Nazi-Soviet Pact, the contrast could not have been greater. In this case, a Chinese crew suffering from beriberi was forced to remain on the ship, and several crewmen died. An autopsy was performed on the deck by Soviet officials, and the headless corpse of one man was left there to rot for another day.[59]

The battle for Nomonhan was also significant because it lent Soviet military and diplomatic support to Chiang Kai Shek when a Sino-Japanese peace again seemed possible. It simultaneously strengthened the Chinese communists' morale. After the destruction of the 6th Army, whatever unity of command the Japanese possessed continued to fragment. Steps were taken to restore discipline among their own leadership, and the Japanese then concentrated on building greater support for Wang Ching Wei. The reckless independence of commanders in Mongolia was mimicked farther south in Nanking, where a plan to assassinate Wang was revealed. His death would have promoted the maintenance of regional puppet regimes, which would have better preserved the autonomous power of independent-minded senior officers. The shift in support to Wang began in late September and early October, following a change in command in Manchuria and central China. Lieutenant General Umezu Yoshijiro was appointed to command the Kwantung army in place of Lieutenant General Ueda Kenkichi, and Lieutenant General Nishio Toshizo assumed command of the China Expeditionary Army.[60] Greater discipline and unity in command were demanded from Tokyo at a time when Soviet influence in China was at its height, but also when the potential to exploit British weakness following the outbreak of war in Europe had become too appealing to ignore.

Low-Intensity Conflict at Hong Kong

On 18 August 1939 the British Chiefs of Staff determined that it would be virtually impossible to relieve Hong Kong in the event of hostilities with Japan. Yet the following month they opted to continue the war in China, even though peace was possible and it would be in their interests to arrange it.[61] Japanese anger over this ongoing situation had been directed at Hong Kong as well as Tientsin. While commanding the 27th Division at Tientsin, General Homma Masaharu insisted that British support for China was the major factor in prolonging the war. This opinion was shared by British officers such as Captain Edwards in Hong Kong, who wrote in August 1939: "Although the U.S.A. and Russia are in some ways giving more support to China at the present moment than ourselves, there is no doubt that the Japanese are right to a great extent when they blame us for the efficacy of China's continued resistance."[62] The navy's blockade was somewhat successful in curbing the food supply from Chungshan into the colony, but friction with British military officers was building because of such action.

Anglo-Japanese conflict was becoming more of a problem in the air. Other than for reconnaissance missions, the Royal Air Force's few Walrus and Vildebeeste biplanes at Hong Kong were of little combat value; this became evident during the Lo Wu incident, when Japanese pilots flew over the colony with no fear of interference. Attacks on aircraft flying into or out of Hong Kong, such as occurred in August 1938, were a constant threat, and more aircraft were forced down during the blockade. Civilian pilots also had to worry about being hit by antiaircraft fire from Japanese warships. For example, the Imperial Airways aircraft *Delia* was fired on near Hong Kong on 31 January 1939. Another Imperial Airways plane, the *Dardanus*, was attacked on 8 November 1939 while flying from Hong Kong to Bangkok; three naval fighters forced it to land at Weichow Island in the Gulf of Tonkin, but no casualties were reported. Colonial airspace violations resumed only a month after resolution of the Lo Wu incident when three Japanese naval aircraft overflew Castle Peak while en route to their ship located west of Lin Tin Island. In April, four Type 96 Japanese bombers from Sanchau Island flew through Hong Kong airspace at Deep Bay, and on 29 April, HMS *Cicala* was buzzed at Black Point by three of the same type of aircraft. Three monoplanes made a mock dive-bombing attack on a police station on Lantau Island on 8 May. Macau was similarly intimidated when a squadron of Japanese bombers overflew the city on 2 July while returning to their base at Sanchau. To make their intentions clear, Japanese Consul General Okazaki met with British Consul General Blunt at Canton on 1 June 1939. Okazaki threatened that Japanese air units would attack any air base where Chinese aircraft were operating, including Kai Tak in Hong Kong.[63]

At sea, the Japanese made their presence felt more strongly by periodically attacking junks and regularly stopping and searching British-owned ships just outside Hong Kong's territorial waters. After the invasion of south China, junk attacks by motor launches from armed Japanese trawlers resumed in January, interfering with Chinese tungsten-smuggling operations. Japanese warships frequently intercepted merchant vessels plying the waters of south China to search for war supplies. On 8 February 1939 the SS *Wosang*, carrying British military attaché Lieutenant Colonel C. R. Spear at the outset of his famous journey to the north, was traveling from Hong Kong to Haiphong when it was stopped by the heavy cruiser *Myoko* and examined under searchlights. Seven trucks on the ship's deck were carefully investigated. In April, Colonel Gordon Grimsdale noted that on a return trip to Hong Kong from Shanghai aboard the SS *Ranpura*, he and several other British officers, including an admiral, became incensed when their vessel was stopped just outside Hong Kong's territorial waters while on its regular run. Four Hong Kong Royal Navy MTBs responded by aiming tubes at the Japanese cruiser while the boarding party was still reviewing the *Ranpura*'s log. Grimsdale and the Royal Navy officers donned their dress uniforms in case a serious incident developed, but the confrontation ended peacefully. On 25 July 1939 the British vessel *Haitan* was holed by a mine along the Fukien coast and had to limp into Hong Kong for repairs.[64]

Other serious confrontations at sea occurred during September, after ground combat in Chungshan had intensified. While covering a fleet of troop transports located in Bias Bay on the night of 12 September, HMS *Dorsetshire* discovered the carrier *Kaga*, along with the *Myoko*, conducting night landing exercises and aimed its searchlights on the *Kaga*. Many Japanese army troops were situated north of the colony from mid-August until early September, and it was widely feared that the navy was preparing to make a diversionary amphibious landing as a prelude to a larger naval assault on Hong Kong itself. Instead, the Japanese navy stepped up its attacks on junks from September to October.[65] Captain Edwards reported that the objective was still the disruption of Hong Kong's food supply:

Six occupants left their own junk in a dinghy on observing Japanese aircraft firing at another junk anchored ahead of them.

Two aeroplanes then attacked the dinghy killing 3 female occupants, the remaining three, including a child aged one were wounded.

Several attacks occurred between 9th and 22nd September.

The junks attacked were usually burnt and in some cases members of the crew drowned, in others bayoneted. In one case M.T.B. 10 rescued a junk's crew of 7 after they had been in the water for about 1 hour and their junk burnt.

The *R.F.A. Pearleaf* picked up the crews of three junks in the vicinity of Hong Kong, 8th October.

Two Junks had been gutted and the three crews placed in the remaining disabled junk. The Japanese are reported to have told them that, "if they were again found to be taking food to Hong Kong they would have their throats cut."

(The junks were reputed to have come from Santao and were carrying potatoes, ginger and a little rice.)[66]

Hong Kong officials considered this increase in aggression during September to be a manifestation of the Japanese navy's sense of diplomatic ease-

CHAPTER FIVE

ment caused by the start of the war in Europe—a most welcome event for the Japanese following their initial shock over the Nazi-Soviet Pact.[67]

Anti-British sentiment had grown strong in 1939, and increasingly impatient officials demanded that greater pressure be exerted on Hong Kong from the ground. In July, Shiratori Toshio, Tokyo's ambassador to the USSR, commented on the situation: "It is well known that at present the Chiang regime is supported by two pillars. These are, of course, Great Britain and the Soviet Union. If one of these two pillars were to be removed, the China Incident could probably be settled."[68] Thus, the Japanese began military operations along the Hong Kong border in August with the aim of better interdicting the importation of war materials and controlling the exportation of wolfram (tungsten), much of which had been diverted to Hong Kong after the occupation of Swatow.[69]

In the early-morning hours of 16 August 1939, General Ando landed a mixed brigade of Formosans and elements of the 18th Division, supported by AFVs, artillery, and cavalry, at Namtau. Parts of the 23rd Brigade (18th Division) also marched down the coastal road from Bocca Tigris. When combined, the total strength of the force was about 6,000 men. Because of an earlier agreement between Ando and Grasett (reached after the Shataukok and Lo Wu incidents), the Japanese provided a forty-eight-hour warning of the impending operation. They rapidly moved inland after a Chinese regiment withdrew and then began to advance along the Hong Kong border. In response, the British deployed troops to the frontier, and bridges in the New Territories were dismantled. Roads were also mined, barbed-wire barricades were erected, and the colony was placed on a war footing. After conferring with Japanese army officers, however, no serious problems developed. By 21 August, the Japanese reached Shataukok at the other end of the border; a partial withdrawal totaling 1,800 Formosans was carried out on 27 and 28 August, although the area of occupation was extended along the coast of Mirs Bay. One reason for the abrupt end of the operation was the signing of the Nazi-Soviet Pact and a very brief Japanese reversion toward neutrality vis-à-vis Great Britain.[70]

Some of the troops withdrawn were sent on to Chungshan, but the bulk of the 55th Regiment under the command of Colonel Nakajima Tokutaro remained at Shumchun and was headquartered at Namtau. This regiment had some support weapons, including 37mm and 70mm mortars, but it also had a battery of 75mm guns for extra firepower. The nearest Japanese unit was the remainder of the 23rd Brigade posted to the north at Sheklung, but the 55th Regiment made no attempt to link with the brigade since the Chinese had already destroyed the KCR. Because the 55th Regiment lacked greater support or a land line of communication to Canton, it was not considered an immediate threat to Hong Kong. Chinese forces at Waichow also posed a threat to the 55th's flank. This operation along the colony's border was the first ground action to involve Japanese army units in such close proximity to Hong Kong since the Shataukok incident of November 1938. As such, it created a war scare among Hong Kong's residents and foreign missionaries living in Kwangtung.[71]

An original purpose of these border operations was to intimidate British officials.[72] The timing of the event coincided with the worsening situation in Europe. Captain Edwards reported that the move had been ordered from Tokyo:

> An open secret [was] that the comparative moderation of the South China Expeditionary Force in the anti-British campaign being waged by the Japanese army in China, was provoking serious dissatisfaction in Tokyo. Both the G.O.C. Lt-Gen. R. Ando, and the Consul-General Mr. Miyazaki, had limited the anti-British campaign in Canton to press attacks, and great pressure was being brought on them to do something more drastic. They were eventually compelled to give way, but even so acted with relative caution and moderation up to the last moment. A further obvious purpose of the Japanese move, was that it enabled them to place a screen of troops along the frontier, behind which a striking force could be assembled for a quick blow against Hong Kong, if Japanese intervention should materialise in connection with the anticipated outbreak of war in Europe.[73]

The presence of secondary objectives, such as a guerrilla training school at Pingwu just fifteen miles north of the border and several Chinese radio transmitters located at Shataukok, also attracted Japanese attention to the colony.[74]

In conjunction with this operation, the Japanese launched several serious attacks between August and October to the north of Canton at Tsungfa and Fahsien, partly to reduce the Chinese army's strength near Canton, but also as retribution for the stubborn Cantonese refusal to align themselves with Wang. But these attacks ran into stronger than anticipated defenses established by General Yu's 12th Group Army, resulting in little appreciable gain. Many casualties were sustained, including the deaths of three senior Japanese commanders. The Japanese could not afford to become greatly entangled, however, because the potential for a Chinese counterattack posed an ever-present danger. Chinese forces were watchful for any chance to threaten Canton, and they conducted guerrilla raids against forward posts almost nightly. Yu's 12th Group Army maintained the defense of Waichow, with large numbers of troops awaiting opportunities to occupy vacated towns or strongpoints along the East River closer to Canton or in the region just north of Hong Kong.[75]

Fighting between Japanese and Chinese forces southeast of Canton was stepped up at the end of September once the Japanese decided to exploit Britain's difficulties arising from European events. To make Hong Kong's isolation more effective, the Japanese landed additional troops at Namtau and advanced eastward along the border between the night of 29–30 September and 3 October, but on this occasion, combat against Chinese forces ensued. There was no direct British involvement, but with the war now being fought along the colony's frontier, the potential for such a scenario resurfaced. This action was timed to support the inauguration of the new national government under Wang Ching Wei. The Japanese had hoped that by isolating China from Hong Kong even further, Wang's new government could more easily be established by 10 October.[76]

The Chinese response to the landing came on the night of 30 September–1 October 1939, when the 20th Regiment of the 151st Division attacked Japanese positions along the border with Hong Kong. One reason for the operation was to boost Cantonese morale in Hong Kong as part of the larger effort to erode political support for the Wang Ching Wei government. But another military objective was to indirectly assist the Chinese forces fighting desperately at Chungshan by preventing Japanese reinforcements from Shumchun. The Chinese attacks were well timed but were not pressed with determination, and the Japanese counterattack began during daylight. Hong Kong officers of the 1st Kumaon Rifles witnessed a company-level assault by Japanese troops on a hill just outside Shataukok, and the battalion commander reported on the tactical capabilities of each side. Both made effective use of terrain to aid movement, and Japanese automatic weapons and mortars were very accurate, even though few Chinese casualties were sustained. Japanese noncommissioned officers were described as being of excellent quality, and they proved to be the decisive factor in the engagement. Both Japanese and Chinese troops moved unhurriedly and without great élan, and a sense of caution intended to limit casualties was evident, but the Chinese held their ground stubbornly, even though they lacked sufficient automatic weapons and mortars. Over several days, the Chinese regiment was pushed up the KCR for some distance away from the border, and combat operations came to an end.[77]

Like elsewhere in China, Japanese tactical combat advantages failed to produce tangible military and political results in Kwangtung. Despite their best efforts, they were unable to fully isolate Hong Kong, and as the disaster at Nomonhan unfolded, the Japanese sought to bring the Tientsin crisis to an end while they quickly made peace with Stalin. To help achieve these goals, the government of Prime Minister Hiranuma Kiichiro was replaced by the Abe Noboyuki cabinet on 30 August 1939, and the former naval attaché to Britain, Vice Admiral Takasu Shiro, was appointed the new commander of the 5th Fleet, replacing Vice Admiral Kondo. In line with these developments, Japanese troop strength was reduced at Hong Kong, and changes were made in the Japanese army leadership to ease tensions with the British. Among those who continued to demand the termination of support to China, however, Britain remained the primary target of Japanese hostility because of Japan's dependence on U.S. trade and fear of the Red Army. Britain was also the weakest power among the group and was most vulnerable at Tientsin and Hong Kong. Although anti-British activity was reduced, many Japanese officers did not support changes to their political strategy in China. Thus, the formal establishment of Wang Ching Wei's national government was held in abeyance in favor of maintaining regional and subordinate Chinese administrations.[78]

Undermining Diplomacy:
British Covert Warfare

As early as the spring of 1939, and in response to the Japanese presence in Kwangtung, the British began to increase their support for China, moving from simple assistance in the transshipment of munitions to stronger direct military and intelligence ties. This escalation coincided with ongoing negotiations for an Anglo-Soviet alliance. Conscription was introduced in Hong Kong in July to double the size of the Hong Kong Volunteer Defence Corps to about 2,500 men (this force included an armored car platoon, a mechanized company, a motorized machine gun platoon, and a company of field engineers), and authorization was granted for the destruction of all oil stocks if the colony came under attack. Stonecutters Island was already an important global signal intelligence center, but Hong Kong's role as a base for British intelligence and special operations in China was soon expanded in a variety of destabilizing ways.

It was during this time that the GOC in China, Major General Grasett, began to exert considerable influence on the course of British strategy in Asia. Grasett personally directed the expansion of Britain's military role in the region by first developing greater professional links with the Chinese army, often with the aid of military intelligence officers such as the recently promoted Major Charles Boxer. Meetings with Chiang Kai Shek and other Chinese officials during May resulted in the reaffirmation of an offer for 200,000 Chinese troops to defend Hong Kong. Although this offer was rejected in London after the signing of the Nazi-Soviet Pact, Boxer made several trips to Chungking in July and October 1939, as well as in August 1940, for the purpose of building greater military coordination. This occurred despite Grasett's orders from the War Office in July 1940 not to engage in direct negotiations with the Chinese out of fear of provoking a Japanese attack.[79] These discussions and other efforts helped lay the foundation for a future military alliance, and this process did not go unnoticed by the Japanese.

Prior to the outbreak of war in Europe, senior Hong Kong civilian and military officials met with allied colleagues to coordinate strategy. Aside from strengthening military relations with the Chinese, Grasett worked closely with the French, and from 22 to 27 June 1939, French and British officers met in Singapore. They agreed to maintain covert support for China and sent recommendations to London for air reinforcements. Those in attendance included Major General Grasett, Air Vice Marshal Sir J. T. Babington, Admiral Jean Decoux, and Lieutenant General Martin.[80] During the height of the Tientsin crisis, Grasett conferred with his French counterpart in that city on 5 July to formulate a more coordinated strategy. They decided not to offer military resistance in the event of a Japanese attack on Anglo-French concessions; rather, they would withdraw their forces into the U.S. zone if permission was granted.

Once war against Germany was declared, Grasett developed a tendency to formulate British Far Eastern foreign and military policy on his own initiative. Given his family's lengthy history of military leadership and command, followed by his own previous experience in Asian affairs and intelligence, it is easy to see how this came about.

A brief review of Grasett's background is useful at this point to better explain the general's actions at Hong Kong. Born in 1888, he was the son of prominent Toronto importer Arthur W. Grasett, a partner in the firm Wyld, Grasett and Darling.[81] His uncle was Colonel Henry Grasett, Toronto's chief of police from 1886 to 1920 and commander of the 10th Royal Grenadiers against the forces of Louis Riel at Fish Creek and Batouche during the Northwest Rebellion of 1885.[82] Grasett's grandfather, also named Henry, was born in Gibraltar; he moved from Montreal to Toronto in 1833, when he was a twenty-five-year-old Anglican minister and the city's population was 9,000. Shortly after his arrival, Reverend Grasett was appointed the garrison chaplain and later became the dean of Toronto in 1867. General Grasett's great-grandfather served in the Peninsular War and was sent to Montreal in 1813 or 1814 to become deputy inspector general of hospitals in Quebec with the rank of major general.[83] The surgeon's father-in-law was Captain Stevenson, a dragoon officer who also served in Spain under Wellington. Many other distant and closer relatives had military experience, including Grasett's brother Sidney.[84]

Grasett's military career began at Royal Military College in Kingston, Canada, where he was known to his friends as Teddy.[85] He left Canada for service with the Royal Engineers in either 1909 or 1910 and fought with the British army in France during the First World War. Physically brave, Grasett was awarded the Distinguished Service Order and the Military Cross and was mentioned in dispatches on five different occasions. After the war he served in many different places, including the Northwest Frontier of India from 1921 to 1923. Grasett graduated from both the Staff College at Camberley in 1920 and the Imperial Defence College in 1931; he returned to the latter and served as a General Staff officer from 1935 to 1937.[86] In 1932 he was appointed head of the Intelligence Staff in India. That same year he returned home to visit his family and was quoted a few years later by a Toronto newspaper for ironically predicting that the "influence of Mahatma Gandhi was not of the lasting character and would soon wane."[87] Grasett's career was described in the same article: "Before receiving high rank in India, the new O.C. at Hong Kong had wide experience, and acted in a variety of capacities. For two years he patrolled lonely frontiers, executed diplomatic missions and held various commands. He dealt with foreign propaganda effectively, so report says from England, and his labors have been rewarded."[88] From 1937 to 1938 Grasett served as brigadier of the General Staff, Northern Command, until being posted to Hong Kong as GOC British forces in China.[89] With this background of service, often in remote places lacking basic communications, Grasett undoubtedly had to rely on his instincts without the benefit of guidance from above. By the late 1930s, he had become an individualistic and determined commander who relied on his own personal judgment in making decisions at Hong Kong.

On the civilian side of Hong Kong's administrative ledger, Governor Northcote also grew more determined to confront the Japanese. By the spring of 1939, he abandoned his earlier suggestion for demilitarization. With the introduction of conscription, he began to emphasize to the Colonial Office that a "bold front" in defense of the colony was important for the maintenance of Chinese resistance.[90] On this issue, Foreign Office officials surprisingly considered Northcote somewhat aggressive: "We concur generally in his views about the 'bold front'—all that we lack is the courage to assume it."[91] By 1941, both Grasett and Northcote would exert greater control over British foreign and military policy in East Asia than the Foreign Office was prepared to allow; officials such as A. L. Scott eventually grew worried that they might start a war with Japan precipitately.[92]

In 1939 the formation of a small special operations detachment under the command of a fellow Canadian, Major Francis Kendall, was a significant Grasett initiative. Z Force was tasked with conducting sabotage and guerrilla warfare operations behind enemy lines in the event of a Japanese attack on the colony. During the battle for Hong Kong, members of Z Force carried out their assignment to the best of their ability and evacuated Admiral Chan Chak, along with other important figures, to free China via Mirs Bay and Waichow. Major Kendall was a mining engineer who had worked in Kwangtung between 1931 and 1939 before being recruited by British authorities as an intelligence agent in southern China. He had many close personal connections with the Hakka communists north of Hong Kong, one of whom was his wife. Because of this, Kendall was able to establish a very effective network of contacts stretching from Hainan to Swatow, and throughout the Sino-Japanese War, he was engaged in the organization of communist guerrilla bands for operations in Kwangtung. By 1941, Lieutenant General Vasily Chuikov would be commander of the Soviet Military Mission to China, and in his memoirs he praised the British intelligence net in Kwangtung and its contributions throughout the Sino-Japanese War.[93]

Naturally, the British employment of Kendall did not improve Sino-

British relations at Chungking. His activities ran afoul of Chinese intelligence, headed by General Tai Li, and his work with the communists created a great distrust of British motives. Kendall was a factor in the expulsion of John Keswick's China Commando Group in 1942, once Z Force had been rolled into that organization after the fall of Hong Kong. In 1943 the OSS sought to employ Kendall, who was described as one of Britain's "most reliable agents" within the Special Operations Executive (SOE). During this period, Kendall cooperated a great deal with the OSS—an organization thoroughly compromised by the Soviet NKVD. The following year he continued his work with the SOE by training North American Chinese in California and British Columbia for planned operations in Malaya and south China, but the war ended before many tangible results were realized.[94] In 1939, however, Kendall was already a significant tool in the British clandestine effort to aid the communists, and in this role, he had the full support of General Grasett.

It is significant that, like the Japanese, the British disagreed on how to proceed both diplomatically and militarily with the Chinese. This also did little to ease Anglo-Japanese relations. Grasett was strongly anti-Japanese, but serving under him was Colonel Gordon Grimsdale, who had assumed command of the Far East Combined Bureau (FECB) in April 1939. The FECB was an intelligence unit directly responsible to the War Office in London, and as such, Grimsdale shared the War Office's view that the Japanese should not be provoked with overt aid to China. Grimsdale's services were sought by the British Military Mission to the Soviet Union in December 1941 because of the threat from Manchuria, and he was considered the "greatest expert on the Japanese Army."[95] In 1939, however, the divergent views of Grasett and Grimsdale on British strategy in Asia resulted in a disjointed approach in dealing with the Japanese. Consequently, the two officers often clashed as Grasett endeavored to strengthen ties with Chiang Kai Shek while Grimsdale stressed the need for caution and diplomacy. Grimsdale noted in his memoirs that Grasett's attitude had a negative influence on Britain's relations with Japan, and this feeling was strengthened after his meetings with General Ando on 3 May and at the end of August 1939.[96]

Anglo-Japanese diplomacy was often conducted at a local level by both sides, and Grimsdale attempted to maintain friendly relations. Despite strains in the relationship at Tientsin, Grimsdale thought Britain's position in the Far East could best be maintained through negotiations with officers such as Ando. During an August visit to Canton, a dinner was held where both Grimsdale and Boxer were honored guests, and Ando used this occasion to reassure them about Japanese objectives. Grimsdale noted that Ando appeared to be an honest, quiet professional whose sole concern was to stop the movement of military supplies from Hong Kong to China. Ando also reemphasized that the communists were the greatest threat to East Asia. Grasett took a dim view of Grimsdale's contact with Ando, and because of their differences, Grimsdale's movements in China were soon restricted. Without much support from the War Office, his usefulness quickly diminished. It was not long afterward that the FECB was transferred to Singapore.[97]

Grimsdale's caution was necessary because there were many strategic and diplomatic problems to confront in 1939, aside from the tensions at Hong Kong. The Tientsin crisis and the arrest of British military attaché Colonel Spear were the two most serious thorns in Anglo-Japanese relations; these situations were created partly by an increasingly reckless Foreign Office that almost led to an early Anglo-Japanese war. In May, after traveling through communist-controlled areas and holding discussions with CCP Chairman Mao Tse Tung, the outspokenly anti-Japanese Spear was arrested on charges of espionage and held at Kalgan. The Japanese made it clear to Spear that his release was directly related to the fate of the Tientsin negotiations, and this included a satisfactory response to their demands for the cessation of British economic warfare in China. The barricades established at Tientsin at the end of 1938 had been transformed into a full-blown blockade by June 1939 for a variety of reasons, including the likelihood of war in Europe, but the British wanted to continue playing for time. Some of their reasons included the worsening economic situation in Japan, Japanese pacification difficulties in China, a hardening of U.S. opinion against Japan, and, most important, the potential power of the Red Army.[98]

The lack of unity on policy in London exacerbated the strain on Anglo-Japanese relations. Although attitudes within the Foreign Office were largely anti-Japanese, the cabinet, the War Office, and the Chiefs of Staff continued to favor a much less confrontational approach until August 1939, due to Britain's limited military power. Many military officers were reluctant to rely on Chinese military collaboration in challenging Japan due to the abandonment of Canton in October 1938. A good number thought that Prime Minister Neville Chamberlain's praise for Ambassador Craigie and his ability to resolve the situation at Tientsin was well placed.

Craigie succeeded in moving the negotiations to Tokyo, while General Piggott maintained peaceful relations with the ill-tempered Homma in China. It was during this crisis that Chamberlain complained that the anti-Japanese bias in the Foreign Office had worsened the situation as the summer wore on.[99] With few exceptions (such as R. A. Butler), many in the Foreign Office were disappointed by the eventual retreat over Tientsin, but others, especially within the military, were quite relieved. Nigel Ronald's attitude following the signing of the Anglo-Japanese agreement in July was typical of those in the Foreign Office: "Everybody's eyes are likely to be more opened when General Piggott has gone. He is a worthy man, but he has always been as complete a dupe of the Japanese as his brother was of the Nazis."[100] Piggott, like the Chiefs of Staff, was simply more aware of British military limitations and what the final cost of antagonism toward Japan would be. More important, he knew who would be paying the bill. In Hong Kong, despite the signing of the Anglo-Japanese agreement on 23 July 1939, officers had little optimism about the prospects of a lasting peace, and as the blockade in south China continued, they thought the Japanese would persist in their efforts to starve them out.[101]

Maintaining support for the USSR in China was another factor associated with the Tientsin and Spear problems, and this was evident during the David Kung incident in Hong Kong. On 25 September 1939 the Nathan Road offices of the Central Trust China Corporation were raided by Hong Kong police, who were searching for illegal Chinese government radio transmitters. This company was responsible for military supply procurement in Hong Kong and was headed by General K. C. Tang and David Kung, the son of Finance Minister H. H. Kung. Besides the transmitters, the police found code books, ciphers, weapons, money, and messages, some of which were munitions orders intended for Berlin. The documents revealed that Kung headed an organization in Hong Kong named Nam Chim She, which controlled assassination squads based in the French concession at Shanghai. Their targets were Japanese officers and Chinese puppet officials in the British concession. Kung was personally involved in the assassination of Wang Ching Wei's nephew Shum Sung and with the collection of intelligence on Ambassador Clark Kerr, but the primary objective of the assassination teams was to create havoc in Britain's diplomatic relations with Japan. Governor Northcote was greatly angered by this situation because he did not want Hong Kong to be used too openly as a Chinese military base of operations. Chiang's Australian adviser, William

Donald, soon emerged to calm the crisis, advising Kung not to incriminate himself publicly because of the harm it would cause to Sino-British relations and the possible disruption of future military cooperation (i.e., the ongoing negotiations regarding Chinese army relief forces for Hong Kong). By November the crisis was resolved quietly, with the return of Kung and Chinese government ciphers to Chungking. In an interesting postscript to this incident, after studying economics at Harvard, David Kung personified an improvement in Sino-British relations by serving briefly as a Guards officer in Lord Mountbatten's South East Asian Command in 1944.[102]

Death squads, however, were only one element of this incident impacting Anglo-Japanese relations during 1939. British duplicity uncovered by the Japanese was another. During the raid, the police found six official British government documents that had been stolen from Clark Kerr by his Chinese language teacher (whom the ambassador had employed until March 1939), all taken from his Shanghai residence. The sixth document revealed British plans to prolong the war in China indefinitely by establishing direct military cooperation with the Chinese. This document detailed discussions between Clark Kerr and Chiang Kai Shek regarding the Chinese offer of 200,000 troops for the defense of Hong Kong; it also outlined a British proposal to train Chinese guerrillas. This sort of breach in security was unprofessional and improper on the part of Clark Kerr, and the Foreign Office assumed that the information had already fallen into Japanese hands. Proof of Sino-British collusion against them, in the face of official denials to General Ando and others, was a direct cause of the furious Japanese escalation of tensions at Tientsin and the establishment of a full blockade against the British concession. The Japanese made certain that the British understood this by informing Colonel Spear of their knowledge during his imprisonment at Kalgan.[103] In outlining the problem, A. L. Scott noted a Soviet connection as well:

No. 6 reports a conversation between Sir A. Clark Kerr and C. K. S. in which inter alia the latter urged that we sh'd include the Far East in the scope of the understanding which it was then hoped to negotiate with Russia and sh'd initiate joint consultations with China for action in the Far East, offering to help in the defence of Hong Kong with 200,000 men.

No doubt copies of these documents have been passed by Sir A. Clark Kerr's Chinese teacher to other govt's than the Chinese, including the Japanese. That the Japanese are in possession of the information contained in No. 6 seems to be borne out by the statement on p. 18 of Col. Spear's report on his detention at Kalgan just received in which he says, "Kobayashi (on 22nd June) added that from information in possession of the Japanese it had come to their notice that Gt. Britain intended to train a body of Chinese troops to oppose the Japanese indefinitely."

Evidently Sir A. Clark Kerr has not been observing the instructions regarding security measures contained in the secret circular Y 414/414/650 of 1st April 1937.[104]

Clark Kerr's security lapse was either simple negligence or a deliberate act, but either way, it certainly helped prolong the war in China. As was often noted by Wang Ching Wei, the primary beneficiaries of a protracted war were the Chinese communists.[105] The ambassador was "very sympathetic with the Communists," and by helping to redirect Japanese attention southward and away from Siberia, this incident also benefited the Soviets.[106] Despite the severity of the problem, there were no negative repercussions on Clark Kerr's professional career, and following his appointment as ambassador to the USSR in early 1942, he became a personal friend of Stalin.[107]

The breakdown in Anglo-Soviet talks about an alliance was followed by significant shifts in international relations, starting with the signing of the Nazi-Soviet Pact in August 1939.[108] Anglo-Japanese relations were affected positively, albeit temporarily, as friction between the two countries eased. The Anglo-Japanese agreement, a deal Chiang Kai Shek publicly labeled a "Far Eastern Munich," was signed once it became clear that Stalin would not join an alliance with Britain.[109] Subsequently, the Chinese became suspicious of British intentions when the latter rejected Chiang's offer of troops for the defense of Hong Kong. The British obviously had less reason to cooperate with Stalin in defending the Soviet Far Eastern flank once he became an ally of Hitler. The Japanese soon realized this, and the Nazi-Soviet Pact was the primary factor in their suspension of the anti-British blockades. In London, the Committee of Imperial Defence had already determined that the defense of Hong Kong depended on the assistance of Chinese troops, but it settled for an arrangement based on indirect support from the Chinese in the form of guerrilla warfare, rather than any direct conventional move on Hong Kong or Canton. This was the foundation of the policy that led to the formation of the China Commando Group and Detachment 204. British and French garrisons were withdrawn from Tientsin in November, but British support for China continued with the transshipment of war supplies such as POL from Hong Kong through nearby Mirs Bay.[110] Although British intrigue resulted in retreat at Tientsin, Hong Kong remained a key element in China's survival, and the colony helped turn the proxy war against Japan into a deadly military stalemate by October 1939.

With the outbreak of war in Europe, the War Office altered its position to bring itself more in line with that of the Foreign Office, as China came to be seen as a potentially useful ally against the Japanese. War Office personnel were now more inclined to use the Chinese as a lever in discouraging a Japanese southern advance, but unlike officials in the Foreign Office, military officers were concerned that China would drift too far under Soviet control if British support were to end. They viewed the strategic situation in terms of a balance of power. This decision came during a difficult period in Europe but at an opportune moment in the Far Eastern crisis: the Japanese had failed to find a military solution in Kwangtung (in August), and their peace offensive in China was fully under way. The Chinese expressed a desire to end the war at this time, and any substantial reduction in military assistance from either Great Britain or the Soviet Union was likely to encourage a Chinese peace agreement with the Japanese. Consequently, military leaders recommended no involvement in the mediation of peace between the Japanese and the Chinese; instead, they thought the war should be encouraged by maintaining the covert system of supply at Hong Kong and Burma. It was noted, "On balance therefore it appears desirable, from our point of view, that hostilities should continue in China."[111] On 26 September 1939 the cabinet accepted the War Office's recommendation, and a British mediation effort in the Sino-Japanese War did not materialize.[112]

Leading up to the Nazi-Soviet Pact, British foreign policy in China also began to parallel that of the Americans, who were showing a greater willingness to become more directly involved in the Far East. The Americans would gradually increase their opposition against Japan to establish a global liberal economic order. Chinese fears of diminished support after the outbreak of war in Europe were eased by this change. The Foreign Office had not completely abandoned the idea of Soviet cooperation in Asia, but with the Americans slowly increasing their support for China, the U.S. Pacific Fleet became a more powerful consideration in confronting Japanese ambitions. From 12 to 14 June 1939, secret Anglo-American naval talks were held with President Roosevelt in Washington on joint strategic planning for the Pacific. Both the Philippines and Hong Kong were considered outposts that could buy time in the event of a Japanese attack. But the Americans remained cautious in their commitments because U.S. military officers had reported that British economic warfare in China was inviting a direct military confrontation with the Japanese at Hong Kong—a situation the British would be unable to cope with. British weakness at Tientsin, combined with the Soviet-Japanese truce after Nomonhan, likewise caused some Americans to surmise that British support might fade over time. It was understood that when the United States applied full economic sanctions against Japan (e.g., cutting oil supplies), war would become an immediate probability, and full U.S.-British cooperation would be vital to meet a Japanese offensive effectively. Nonetheless, British support to China remained sufficient to encourage greater U.S. involvement, and the appointment of American logistical specialists in support of T. V. Soong's South-West Transportation Commission along the Burma Road reflects this. Hence, British and U.S. foreign policies began to move slowly in unison toward war with Japan. The knowledge that the U.S.-Japanese commercial treaty was due to lapse in a few months and the public announcement by U.S. Ambassador Joseph Grew in Tokyo that America would not relinquish any of its rights in China helped reassure anxious Chinese, while giving the Japanese further reason to pause and reassess their relations with third powers. Modifications to the Neutrality Act in Washington, allowing easier access to American munitions, had a similar effect.[113]

Until Anglo-American cooperation coalesced, however, the British assumed an increased level of involvement in the war in China by enhancing special operations and intelligence capabilities. This too damaged Anglo-Japanese relations. In the summer and fall of 1939 Sino-British relations were similarly tested by British assistance to the communists. These developments were the products of an inconsistent foreign policy that lacked a clearly defined level of commitment to Chungking. Until the outbreak of war in Europe, there was little consensus on this issue at Whitehall and even less with British officials on the ground in the Far East. Amidst this confusion, some, such as General Grasett, tended to follow their own instincts, receiving only haphazard guidance from London. Hong Kong thus became more than a vital Chinese military lifeline; it became the center of British intrigue and covert warfare that generated substantial Japanese enmity, and the chance for peace in East Asia afforded by the Nazi-Soviet Pact was discarded.

The First Battle of Changsha:
September and October 1939

Significant military defeats had already been meted out to Japanese forces during 1939, and after receiving orders from Tokyo to end the war, another serious setback was soon experienced in Hunan. The first battle of Changsha lasted from 14 September to 8 October 1939 and resulted in 30,000 Japanese casualties, while Chinese losses were estimated at 20,000. This costly defeat boosted Chinese morale and prevented the Japanese from achieving total victory in 1939. Hunan's rice crop and its natural resources such as tungsten and antimony were valuable strategic assets, but more important, Changsha was one of the few major transportation hubs and military supply depots left in Chinese hands.[114] Because of its location at the northern end of the railway from Kwangtung, its loss to the Japanese most likely would have resulted in the fall of Hunan and might have brought an end to Chinese resistance. Instead, supplies transported north by rail helped make the battle a Chinese strategic victory.

Japanese preliminary moves commenced with the fall of Nanchang earlier in the spring of 1939. The Japanese navy had to assist the army's advance through Kiangsi at that time owing to the strong resistance encountered—a defense that was supported by Chinese and Soviet air units.[115] The first attempt to take Nanchang did not bode well for an advance into Hunan. On 26 March the Chinese waited for advance Japanese elements to reach halfway across the Kan River Bridge before blowing it up. Nanchang fell the following day, however, and this badly disrupted the supply of munitions and reinforcements to Chinese guerrilla forces operating in Anhui and Chekiang. Chinese defenses stiffened after the fall of Nanchang because any further loss of territory toward Hunan would have worsened the guerrillas' supply situation to the northeast and east.

Geographic considerations made Changsha a likely objective because the Japanese were dependent on rail and riverine transport for supply. Although there were several important Chinese military facilities to be defended in Hunan, the most important strategic objective was the railway from Changsha to Kwangtung. A large Japanese military base was located about halfway between Hankow and Changsha at Yochow (Yueyang), and that city became the jumping-off point in all four battles waged for Changsha. Yochow had fallen to the 9th Division in late 1938, as Japanese forces consolidated their position at Hankow. Prior to 1939, railway lines had extended north from Changsha to Yochow before being destroyed by the Chinese, but because of the lack of alternative infrastructure in the region, this remained the primary axis of advance. Just south of Changsha was another railway line branching east to Nanchang, which made eastern Hunan and Kiangsi a more distant secondary front. Japanese naval units and transports could also outflank Chinese defenses north-northwest of the city by advancing across Tungting Lake and along the Hsiang River. Thus, in September 1939 the Japanese converged on Changsha from the east (Nanchang), north (Yochow), and north-northwest (Tungting Lake).[116]

In defending from the north, the Chinese enjoyed several terrain advantages. From Yochow, the railway bed crossed several difficult rivers, including the Milo, before passing to the west of Tamoshan, a mountain that dominated the line. The very limited road network in this area had also been destroyed by the Chinese, and during rainy periods, the entire region turned into a sea of mud. Since the Japanese depended entirely on mechanical transport for the maintenance of their lines of communication, it was impossible to supply their advance forces adequately or defend the entire 160 kilometers between Yochow and Changsha. Moreover, the infantry was heavily dependent on artillery and AFVs for support, most of which were virtually useless in this region.[117]

The bulk of six Japanese divisions of the Central China Expeditionary Force under Lieutenant General Yamada Otozo participated in the campaign. These included the 3rd, 6th, 13th, and 33rd Divisions of the 11th Army, under Lieutenant General Okamura Yasuji at Yochow, and the 101st and 106th Divisions, which advanced from Kiangsi. The 6th, 13th, and 33rd bore the brunt of the fighting north of Changsha and sustained the greatest casualties during the retreat. Opposing Okamura were Generals Chen Cheng, Guan Lin Cheng (Guan Linzheng), and Hsueh Yueh (Xue Yue), who established a defense in depth consisting of four lines along a thirty-kilometer front using approximately fifty divisions of the 31st and 33rd Group Armies. Reinforcements from Kwangsi were also dispatched north.[118]

The Japanese launched their attack on 14 September, and by the twenty-third they had broken through the third defense line a little more than halfway to Changsha (see figure 5.3). In most major battles against the

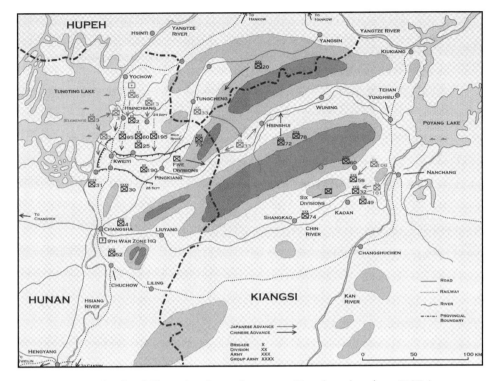

Figure 5.3. First battle of Changsha, September 1939. (Based on data from NARA, RG 165, M1444, reel 11, Report No. 9799 by Captain Edwin M. Sutherland, 29 September 1939.)

Chinese, Japanese forces achieved victory because of Chinese weaknesses in leadership and firepower. These deficiencies usually forced a withdrawal, but Japanese tactics invited defeat at Changsha once the Chinese counterattacks, which started on 1 October, were directed against their overextended lines of communication. Gaps in the Japanese rear were penetrated by Chinese units, and their supply lines across several major river crossings were threatened.[119] Units caught too far forward advancing on Changsha were thus forced to terminate the offensive and attack Chinese forces that had moved against their flanks. They had to fight their way back along the route of advance in order to prevent a disaster. From the heights of Tamoshan, a handful of Chinese artillery crews were aided by Soviet advisers, and they bombarded Japanese forces to good effect. The

Japanese 11th Army was able to extricate itself from a dangerous situation, but the first battle of Changsha ended as a significant Chinese victory.

Undaunted, the Japanese used the same battle plan, with only minor alterations, for three of the four attacks against Changsha, but it was not until 1944 that they finally succeeded. General Hsueh Yueh, who was still only the acting commander of the 9th War Zone, was confirmed in his position after the victory. He had earlier predicted that the Japanese would attack Changsha because they needed to atone for the debacle at Nomonhan, and his record thus far augured well for the future defense of Hunan.[120] In Hong Kong, Captain Giles proved equally prophetic: "The possibility of another Japanese drive on Changsha, or of an attack on Shasi and Ichang, must always be reckoned with; but such a move would probably be undertaken to divert attention from far more serious operations in South China than for any other purpose."[121] This was indeed the case when the third battle for Changsha was fought from December 1941 to January 1942 to provide indirect support for the attack on Hong Kong.[122]

Changsha was a timely victory for the Chinese for several reasons. Militarily, the Japanese defeat proved once again that the war had become a stalemate. The Japanese army was absorbing about 10,000 casualties per month, and with the exception of Hainan, its military record in 1939 had been one of failure. Diplomatically, Changsha boosted Chinese morale when future Soviet support began to look uncertain. Chiang had grown concerned about Stalin's invasion of Poland, and there were rumors that the Soviets were negotiating with the Japanese in Shanghai to make a peace deal at Chinese expense.[123] Although international attention was focused on Europe, Chiang had to defend Hunan at all costs in order to retain his government's legitimacy and prestige among foreign powers. At this juncture, the Japanese were forced to review their strategic options. U.S. military attaché Lieutenant Colonel William Mayer noted this situation:

The Japanese position has deteriorated markedly in the last few months. The notice of the abrogation of our treaty and Ambassador Grew's speech in Tokyo have indicated to Japan our "unfriendly" stand. The Russo-German pact was a definite blow. The outbreak of the European war, which might have been of great benefit to Japan had she not been engaged upon her China venture, now makes her economic stability practically dependent upon the Americas. The

Nomonhan operations and the Changsha reverses have been serious assaults upon Japan's military prestige.[124]

The Japanese began to look southward for expansion opportunities, since the British were concentrating most of their energy and military forces in Europe. However, the victory at Changsha reassured both the British and the Americans that the Chinese were determined to maintain resistance.

The most significant aspects of the battle, however, were of a domestic political nature. At the start of the year, much of north China was already in Japanese hands, and few provinces remained under the control of the central government. Among these, political loyalty was a constant problem. Chiang Kai Shek's government could not afford to lose any additional provinces, or it would become politically irrelevant. But there was also great pressure on the Japanese to support the establishment of the Wang Ching Wei government with a military victory against Chiang.[125] Several foreign military attachés reported on the significance of the battle in relation to these problems. Captain Edwards sent his observations from Hong Kong:

> There is no need to believe even a tenth of the spectacular Chinese claims, but the fact remains that the Japanese offensive was a complete failure. The results—like the objective—of this battle are of greater political than military importance, but it could not have come at a better time from the Chinese point of view. The Japanese have lost an enormous amount of prestige by their premature disclosure that Changsha was their objective, and by their previous references to it as the "doomed capital." The Chinese on the other hand have been heartened to a degree quite unjustified by the purely military significance of the operation, and the Wang Ching Wei faction correspondingly discredited. The recall of Gen O. Yamada, formerly G.O.C. of the Central China Expeditionary Force, may also be connected with the Changsha fiasco.[126]

Colonel Mayer likewise reported on the political impact of Changsha:

> Reports from Tokyo indicate that political purposes behind the Japanese drive on Changsha were first to strike a decisive blow at Chinese morale, which was considered to be at an exceptionally low ebb, and

second, to use the victory celebration following the expected fall of Changsha to herald the launching of the new Wang Ching-wei puppet regime. It was hoped that this victory would swing many wavering Chinese over to the Wang fold and make Chinese in general amenable to Japanese peace overtures. It was to be the final military stroke of the war. The attack backfired . . . giving the Japanese another serious set-back to add to their increasing difficulties. In addition to the Japanese losses in personnel, material, and prestige, the resultant beneficial effect upon Chinese morale will materially hamper Japanese political intrigue in China.[127]

Following the reverses elsewhere in China, including, albeit on a much smaller scale, the difficulties experienced by the Japanese in Kwangtung, the defeat at Changsha was a watershed event. Over the next two years, the Japanese took increasingly desperate measures to end the conflict in China, and this ultimately involved them in a war with the British and the Americans.

Although Chungshan was taken on the same day that the battle of Changsha ended, the result in Kwangtung was of small comfort, considering that Japanese marines and army troops had battled provincial militia forces throughout most of the summer.[128] The defeats north of Canton at Tsungfa and Fahsien against General Yu's weaker 12th Group Army also meant that the Chinese lines of communication from Hong Kong to Kukong remained open, and military supplies continued to move north along the railroad from Kwangtung at about the same rate (or greater) as along the Burma Road. But unlike in Yunnan, these supplies were not being siphoned by regional leaders. In this way, Hong Kong kept the Chinese army alive in Hunan, and by the 1939 Double Tenth anniversary of the Chinese revolution, Japanese forces had remarkably little to show for their efforts. Following the defeats at Nomonhan and Changsha and the stalemate in Kwangtung, 1939 can rightly be considered a year of significant failure leading to Japan's ultimate destruction. This was becoming clearer to many Japanese officers, as Dr. Thomson noted in mid-October 1939: "We were told that a number of high Japanese military officers had a conference recently in the hotel opposite the Canton Hospital. One of the employees reported that they were very discouraged at the military situation, and actually wept!"[129] In the fall of 1939 the Chinese were still capable of fighting, and more important, they were resolved to do so. Unfortunately, while Wang Ching Wei continued his negotiations with the Japanese, the opportunity for peace was missed. Between August and October, there was the potential for a gradual withdrawal of Japanese forces from southern and central China.[130] The British could have helped broker this peace, and it would have been a sensible option after Stalin embraced Hitler as his ally and together they swallowed Poland.

Kwangsi: Prelude to Invasion

Following the breakdown of peace efforts in September and the serious reversal at Changsha, the Japanese redoubled their attempts to interdict the transportation of war supplies into free China by increasing the pressure on Kwangsi. Before leaving China in October, Vice Admiral Kondo publicly indicated where the Japanese were likely to strike next. Although most of the major seaports had already been neutralized (aside from Hong Kong), port facilities at Pakhoi (Beihai) in western Kwangtung were still fully functional. Pakhoi tied into the Kwangsi road network, which also connected French Indochina to the important railhead at Kweilin. By isolating Pakhoi and occupying Nanning, the Japanese could block a considerable amount of supplies coming north from Haiphong, as well as intensify the bombardment of the Indochina railway and the Burma Road in Yunnan. Thus, as a prelude to the amphibious assault at Pakhoi and the invasion of Kwangsi in November 1939, Japanese air interdiction of Chinese lines of supply was intensified during the summer months. Concurrently, efforts to build Chinese support for the Wang Ching Wei government continued.[131]

The Chinese had greatly expanded road and railway construction in south China during 1939, and Kwangsi served as a useful adjunct to the French Indochina railway to Yunnan. Before the outbreak of war, virtually nothing in southern China could have been considered a useful military road; it was the area least developed for mechanical transportation. But the Chinese had been building an average of twenty miles of new road per day, so that by July 1939, almost 7,500 miles of road had already been constructed and another 5,000 miles was planned. In Yunnan, a 530-mile portion of the Yunnan-Burma railway was another important project under way at the time, but even with 100,000 laborers, completion was not expected until sometime between 1942 and 1944. Until then, several thousand South-West Transportation Commission trucks operating on the Burma Road had to suffice, but corruption and incompetence limited the amount of material delivered by this route.[132]

These new transportation routes were vital, not only to meet Chinese army requirements but also to maintain French cooperation. By August 1939, backlogged supplies at Haiphong already required at least six months to clear, and with the onset of war in Europe, the Chinese were afraid the French would confiscate their supplies. In April, Ambassador Clark Kerr traveled to Haiphong from Hong Kong aboard HMS *Delight* and reported that Haiphong was full of merchant ships, with a two-week delay just to unload. French officials could not keep up with demand. The China United Transportation Company was attempting to establish a trucking service to relieve the congestion at Haiphong through Kwangsi. Many roads in western Kwangtung had been destroyed following the occupation of Canton, and the company's operations from Kwangchowan had already been suspended. Kwangsi was a useful place to resume business because the French kept the Hanoi-Kunming railway in operation, and they also continued their naval patrols along the coast.[133]

The French navy monitored the sea between the Gulf of Tonkin and the Paracel Islands using two cruisers, the *Lamotte Picquet* and the *Suffren*, in addition to several other vessels. Vice Admiral Jean Decoux also maintained close contact with British officials in Hong Kong following the outbreak of war, and the gunboat *Argus*, under Lieutenant Commander Ruyneau de Saint George, was stationed at the colony to help preserve the French presence up to Canton. Decoux and the British also agreed to have French naval vessels continue twice-daily contact with Stonecutters Island to report on operations and problems.[134]

Japanese air units did not let Chinese supply operations in Kwangsi and western Kwangtung continue unmolested. Airpower, however, was proving to be militarily ineffective and politically counterproductive. During the first half of April 1939, targets in Kwangsi were bombed, and some missions were launched against Yunnan. Air strikes increased in intensity and frequency beginning in July and reached their highest levels during August. In Kwangtung, much attention was paid to the area around Pakhoi on the Liuchow peninsula, as well as the North River closer to Canton. Operations continued throughout the summer, and Japanese aircraft were able to strike more deeply into south China once their main bases at Weichow Island and Hainan were reinforced with larger numbers of aircraft (Hainan had received 160 planes by 25 August), but these ultimately had little effect.[135]

Transportation routes were also politically significant because they facilitated greater internal cooperation and unity between Chungking and the south; this was another reason they attracted Japanese attention. General Lung's loyalty was an important consideration for Chiang, as the governor controlled the Burma Road. Even under normal circumstances, the road's potential military effectiveness was lowered by Lung's grazing of transported munitions, combined with the graft extorted by provincial officials. Yet the province remained a viable if less than perfect supply route to Chungking partly, and ironically, because of these factors. Another reason for Lung's loyalty to the Kuomintang was the U.S. and British loans to China, along with the growing sense of Chinese nationalism within his officer corps. In Kwangsi, powerful generals such as Pai Chung Hsi and Li Tsung Ren were more politically reliable at this time, and because the railway line from Langson in French Indochina to the railhead at Kweilin was nearing completion by the end of 1939, Chinese political cohesion would likely grow stronger.[136] To counter this trend, the Japanese considered air attacks on southern transportation routes to be useful.

The same rationale underpinned the bombing of Chungking. Terror bombing operations against the capital continued without resistance during June, after the Chinese air force had been forced to withdraw. Chinese morale was slightly improved with the addition of 25 French Dewoitine fighters, plus 150 aircraft and 14 Soviet pilots who arrived at Lanchow on 13 August 1939. With these Soviet and French reinforcements, the defense of Chungking was restored, and Japanese casualties in the air continued to climb slowly (Japanese losses were heavy throughout the war, totaling approximately 2,200 aircraft, with somewhere between 300 and 800 lost over Mongolia). Despite their best efforts, Japanese terror bombing became increasingly futile, as it only unified the people and built a spirit of resistance that had not existed before. By the end of the year, with little to show for all the effort expended, the Japanese escalated the war in December with an amphibious assault in the Gulf of Tonkin.[137]

War without End

Militarily and politically, 1939 was a year of strategic defeat for the Japanese as the war settled into a stalemate. The Japanese army was stretched thin on the ground and could not make any new major advance without risking its existing garrisons or lines of communication. The debacle at Changsha was proof of this reality. Changsha demonstrated Chinese determination and an ability to resist Japanese forces using conventional forces, not just guerrillas. Taken together, the military setbacks at Nomonhan, Chungshan, and Changsha greatly undermined support for Wang Ching Wei at a time when peace in China was possible.[138] Out of frustration, the Japanese rebounded from the numerous military disasters with the invasion of Kwangsi in November 1939, but even after their initial success in occupying Nanning, any further advance north was stopped by Kwangsi and central government forces. The stalemate continued, and a quadrilateral defense zone was effectively established in south China, based on the four cities of Chungking, Changsha, Hong Kong, and Kunming. Defense of this region was necessary for Chinese survival, and Chinese resistance was the means chosen by the British and the Soviets to keep the Japanese army bogged down in great numbers. Although this zone was partially penetrated at Canton, the Chinese army could be maintained so long as war supplies from Hong Kong continued to bypass Canton to the east through Waichow. If the Japanese were to have any chance of victory, they would have to clear the Changsha-Canton railroad. They would make three more attempts to do so before the war was over, two of which occurred in 1941. The latter of these was executed in support of the assault on Hong Kong during the opening moves of the Pacific war.[139]

In defending Hunan, the Chinese army was supplied from the opposite end of the railway in Kwangtung and along the Burma Road to Rangoon. Interdiction of war materials continued to be an element of Japanese strategy, and the state of low-intensity conflict at Hong Kong was maintained while Anglo-Japanese relations worsened. The Japanese army patrolled the border, and the navy continued to attack the Hong Kong fishing fleet. The blockade was strengthened with the occupation of such ports as Swatow and Foochow. This intensification of the conflict culminated in the hard-fought battle for Chungshan. Increased pressure was placed on the Soviets and the British to terminate their support of Chiang Kai Shek, but in both cases the Japanese failed. Victory at Nomonhan was the Soviet response, and following the Hitler-Stalin pact, their military victory sent the message that any future Japanese expansion should occur in the south against British interests. On balance, Nomonhan was beneficial to China but a setback for Great Britain. When Japanese military defeats in China are tallied, along with the occupation of Poland by the Red Army, it is clear that the fall of 1939 was a lost opportunity for the British to mediate a useful peace agreement. Instead, hope was based on the ideal of collective security and the possibility of a change in Soviet foreign policy. To this end, the British opted to continue their Far Eastern war from Hong Kong while concentrating their resources in Europe against Germany. In following such a course, the British chose to wage a proxy war that increased their commitments to Asia, but without stronger military ties to China, it was a war they would be unable to finish.

■

Impasse in Kwangsi and Japan's Failed Interdiction Strategy against Hong Kong: November 1939 to May 1940

One of the most significant outcomes of the battle of Nomonhan in August 1939 was the redirection of Japanese strategic attention south. This policy was expressed by the announcement of the Greater East Asian Co-Prosperity Sphere in December, but after a year of defeat on the battlefield, Japanese ambitions remained unfulfilled. Army morale had deteriorated since the start of the war, and a successful campaign was needed to restore confidence among both the military and the people at home. With limited resources, a major ground offensive into the key regions of Szechwan or Yunnan was not feasible, but during the winter of 1939–1940, the Japanese thought it would be possible to sever the remaining lines of communication that kept the Chinese army supplied and thus win the war quickly. These lines included the Burma Road, the French Indochina railway to Yunnan and Kwangsi, and the Hong Kong–Changsha route via Mirs Bay, Waichow, and Kukong. The Japanese also hoped to achieve a reduction in Soviet military aid to Chungking by improving relations with the USSR.[1] Thus, in November 1939 General Ando Rikichi's 21st Army was given the task of seizing Kwangsi to deepen China's isolation and pressure the central government to end the war. But as elsewhere in China, Japanese ambitions once again exceeded available resources. The Chinese were able to contain this move into Kwangsi while continuing to use Hong Kong and the Burma Road as conduits of supply. These routes were sufficient to sustain Chinese resistance even in the face of increased pressure both in the air and at sea.

By the spring of 1940, the occupation of Nanning proved to be a chimera. As a result, many Japanese reached the end of their endurance in seeking to solve their problems solely within China. Although Sino-Japanese efforts to arrive at a peaceful settlement increased throughout the year, after the fall of France, the Japanese resolved to challenge the Western powers directly by preparing for an advance into the southwestern Pacific. In the interim, the strategic value of Hong Kong only grew once Kwangsi's supply capacity was reduced, and because Hong Kong and Burma remained open, Chinese determination to continue the war did not break. In turn, the occupation of Hong Kong soon became a Japanese strategic objective.[2]

The Invasion of Southern Kwangsi: November 1939 to April 1940

Japanese desperation over their inability to eliminate China's military logistical capacity remained a primary factor in the conflict's escalation. Therefore, Kwangsi was targeted for several reasons to break the deadlock. For one, Kwangsi's defenses were weak, but more significantly, sporadic aerial interdiction had proved inadequate to reduce Chinese supply, due to the limited number of air bases available and the very long distances to many targets, especially those in Yunnan. Kwangsi's own road and rail carrying capacity from the French Indochina border was another consideration, as these lines were being rapidly upgraded. Politically, the Japanese were quite desperate to achieve a military victory after the Changsha debacle in order to regain prestige and boost popular support for the Wang Ching Wei administration in occupied China. It was also hoped that an invasion would aggravate existing political divisions within the Chinese central government and impair its relations with regional southern leaders such as Generals Pai Chung Hsi and Li Tsung Ren of Kwangsi, as well as General Lung Yun of Yunnan. When taken together, these factors encouraged the Japanese to make the occupation of Kwangsi their immediate objective in November 1939, but by winter's end, victory remained as distant as ever.[3]

The Chinese did not expect a Japanese ground offensive deep into Kwangsi, and the limited degree of road destruction, along with the paucity of military forces, reflected China's general military weakness across the south. Largely because of political considerations, there were no more than six divisions in all of southwestern Kwangtung and Kwangsi to meet the Japanese invasion. Kwangsi divisions were widely dispersed, with the 1st Division at Kweilin and the 2nd Division at Nanning and Shangsze. The latter was supported by the 12th Artillery Battalion, which included four 75mm guns and one 100mm gun. The 3rd Division was located at Liuchow, while the 4th and 5th Divisions were posted to Wuchow on the Kwangtung border and to Lungchow, near Indochina, respectively. But once the invasion was under way, military necessity overshadowed political problems, and Generalissimo Chiang Kai Shek was able to send an initial force of 100,000 reinforcements into Yunnan and Kwangsi. Central government troops arrived piecemeal in Kwangsi; the first of these included the 135th Division near Nanning (46th Army Headquarters), while the 170th Division was sent to Kweihsien (Guixian or Guigang; 16th Army Headquarters), a point midway between Nanning and Wuchow along the West River. Three central government divisions had also been positioned in southwest Kwangtung prior to the assault: the 175th Division was located at Pakhoi, and the newly formed 19th Division, which bore the brunt of the attack, was posted to the Yamchow coastal district (also known as Chinchow [Qinzhou]). The 188th Division was also in the region. Of all these forces, however, less than half the 50,000 men in Kwangsi were committed to battle, and just as the Bias Bay pirates had been paid to guide the Japanese army along its routes of advance on Canton in 1938, similar preparations were made in Kwangsi. One reason for the lack of resistance was that another offensive directed against Changsha was expected, but this never materialized.[4]

Japanese forces were similarly limited due to the widespread fighting occurring throughout China at the time. Only two Japanese divisions of the 21st Army were earmarked for the invasion; the 5th Division returned once again to south China from its base at Shantung, and the Formosan Force, by this time redesignated as the 28th Division, was brought in from Canton. On 15 November 1939 these forces landed at various points in western Kwangtung along Chinchow Bay, northwest of Pakhoi, under difficult high-wind conditions, but they were supported by powerful vessels such as the carriers *Agaki* and *Kaga* and the battleship *Fuso*. Seventy ships were deployed, and of these, approximately fifty were infantry transports. An additional Japanese marine regiment was landed near Pakhoi, although the port itself remained unoccupied for the time being.[5]

Initial combat after the landings was brief. The Chinese did not defend in strength owing to Japanese airpower and naval gunfire advantages. Japanese lodgments were quickly secured, and all arms functioned in a coordinated, effective manner. Weak Chinese ground forces in the vicinity, primarily those of the 19th Division, were brushed aside easily, and the bulk retreated north up the road past Nanning and into the mountains. Within five days of the landings, the Japanese cleared their beachheads and followed the Chinese up to the Kwangsi border; by 24 November 1939, they were in control of Nanning. According to a missionary living there, General Ando's forces entered the city without creating additional mayhem and captured several Chinese AFVs in the process. The entire operation to secure Nanning took ten days to complete. Shortly thereafter the Japanese consolidated their position by constructing a belt of fortified posts several kilometers from the city. Unfortunately for the Chinese, a mobile column later struck west toward the French Indochina border near Dong Dang, where much of the 5.5 million gallons of stockpiled POL at Chehnankuan and Lunge was destroyed.[6]

Similar to the case of Canton the year before, foreign observers speculated about Chinese actions as the Japanese rapidly advanced 100 miles inland over rough terrain but met little resistance. Nanning was the obvious objective because it was a major communications hub along the West River to French Indochina, and its occupation would result in the loss of a major road artery connecting the Hanoi railway line to Kweilin. It would also provide the Japanese with a useful air base, allowing them to increase attacks on the railway in Yunnan and the new Burma Road. The frequency and intensity of air strikes directed against these targets grew quickly starting in late December 1939. Because of the similarities to the 1938 invasion of Kwangtung, and because the Chinese did not seem overly concerned about this latest setback or how it complicated China's supply situation, it was widely suspected that the lack of resistance was deliberate. U.S. military attaché Colonel William Mayer noted that the ambivalent attitude among many Chinese officials may have been connected to the fact that General Pai had remained in central China for three days after the landings before going to Kwangsi to deal personally with the situation in his home province. Information is limited, but Pai did keep half his forces out of combat, and it is likely that he did so in an attempt to preserve some degree of political autonomy from Chiang Kai Shek, given that the arrival of central government reinforcements potentially threatened his position.[7] Even though he had to accept Chiang's forces, Pai knew from the recent political history of Kwangtung that it would be beneficial to preserve some of his own strength.

Several factors contributed to the Chinese reverse, and British Royal Marine Major R. Giles commented on these from Hong Kong:

> There are various explanations for this disgraceful debacle, so reminiscent of the inglorious Canton campaign, but all the specious Chinese excuses may be boiled down to these. Firstly they never really expected that the Japanese would have sufficient men, equipment, or courage to undertake an operation of this magnitude; consequently they were quite unprepared when the blow fell, though proclaiming their eagerness and readiness for battle until the last minute. Secondly, the reported destruction of all roads and bye-paths in this district had evidently not been properly carried out, as otherwise the Japanese could never have covered the 100 odd miles to Nanning in ten days, as they did, bringing with them Mountain Artillery into the bargain. Thirdly—and perhaps most importantly—the Kwangsi Warlords, Pai Chung Shi and Li Tsung Jen, have always been so jealous of their provincial autonomy that they have never permitted Central Government troops to enter the province, although they have sent large contingents of their own men to fight in Central and North China.[8]

When the invasion occurred, the Chinese took the assault to be a feint to cover the expected offensive against Changsha, which never took place. Because of this, many Kwangsi troops were defending Hunan when they were needed at home. Previous Japanese operations in Kwangtung also diverted Chinese attention from their primary objective at Nanning.[9] The loss of Nanning was an embarrassing setback, but the Kwangsi generals, under the nominal authority of 4th War Zone commander General Chang Fa Kwei, were able to maintain some degree of independence throughout the war because of their hesitance in committing their troops to battle in November 1939.

An unknown quantity at this time was General Lung Yun in Yunnan, and although the invasion of Kwangsi damaged Chinese logistical capabilities, the Japanese occupation of Nanning carried some potentially useful political benefits for Chiang Kai Shek. With the Japanese established in

Kwangsi, an invasion of Yunnan became possible, and Lung's reliability was once again tested. Lung was strongly tempted to reach some sort of peace with the Japanese, and Yunnan's defection would have greatly undermined China's ability to continue the war. Kunming was an important Chinese logistical center for supplies heading north from both Burma and French Indochina, and it possessed some of the few important bases that were still available to the Chinese air force. Yet Chiang's reinforcement of the province had the potential to threaten Lung's authority, and the presence of central government forces ultimately kept the Yunnanese leader in line. Militarily, they also strengthened Yunnan's defenses as the Japanese, and especially General Ando, considered invading the province. This threat remained constant throughout the occupation of southern Kwangsi, but the extremely difficult terrain and lack of troops prevented its implementation.[10]

Chinese counterattacks began in Kwangsi in December, coinciding with the failed nationwide winter offensive. The subsequent campaign in the region surrounding Nanning turned into a difficult struggle for both sides. Although Nanning was not recaptured, the Chinese prevented the Japanese from venturing much farther inland. On 5 December 1939 the Japanese 5th Division under Lieutenant General Imamura Hitochi advanced to a position twenty-five miles northeast of the city and captured the strategically important Kunlunkwan Pass. Possession of this pass was essential for any further move into the interior of Kwangsi (see figure 6.1). But exceptionally heavy and determined Chinese counterattacks soon blunted this drive, and by the beginning of January, the Chinese under General Pai pushed the Japanese back to Nanning. Kunlunkwan Pass changed hands four times during the process. In a sign that the Chinese were worried about these recent developments, the valuable semimechanized 5th Army was deployed from Kweichow (Guizhou) to help retake the city; however, its participation did not lead to success, even after sustaining more than 16,000 casualties. British military officers expressed concern over this unit's commitment to battle, as there was little confidence in the Chinese ability to defend it from enemy air strikes. At the beginning of January, Major Giles noted, "Unless therefore the Chinese have the sense to withdraw these forces, it can only be a matter of time before they are caught massed on a road by the Japanese bombers like the Cantonese motorised brigade near Waichow in October 1938."[11] Unfortunately for the Chinese, there were many dangers in the air.

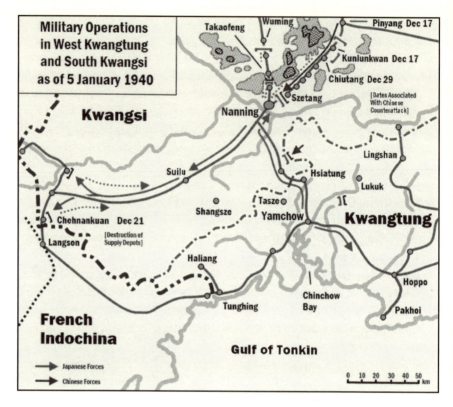

Figure 6.1. Battle for Kwangsi, December 1939 to January 1940. (Based on data from NARA, RG 165, M1444, reel 11, Report No. 9842 by Captain F. P. Munson, 11 January 1940.)

Repeated frontal assaults on Nanning's fortified defenses by the Chinese army were supported by Chinese and Soviet air units, but their combined strength was insufficient to alter the situation. Part of the problem was that Chinese air force losses had been heavy in 1939, and few aircraft were available for Kwangsi.[12] Those that were sent proved to be worse than in-effective in an air campaign described by Giles, for one, as a "complete fi-asco."[13] Heavy antiaircraft fire resulted in inaccurate bombing, and on at least one occasion, a Soviet squadron attacked friendly ground forces. Approximately fifty Japanese fighters were based at Nanning to maintain air superiority, and most of their attention was directed toward the Soviet pilots based at Liuchow and Kweilin. Air-to-air combat was frequent, but with the exception of a small victory by Soviet pilots over Liuchow on 1

CHAPTER SIX

January 1940 (several aircraft were shot down), the Japanese maintained complete aerial dominance and were able to fly continuous ground support missions virtually at will. Another factor contributing to Chinese deficiencies was the quality of Soviet airmen. Personnel included a mixture of new pilots and veterans from Spain, but tours of duty were limited to three months, with training being the primary consideration. Nevertheless, as an indication that losses were substantial, wounded pilots were flown out of the region aboard CNAC aircraft when military transport was unavailable.[14] Throughout the struggle for Kwangsi, Sino-Soviet airpower failed to worry the Japanese, and losses were heavy. Conversely, Japanese airpower and firepower advantages remained significant, but these were of little value in helping the army break out of the fortified base at Nanning.

In conjunction with the battles being waged at Nanning, Chinese guerrilla forces converged on the Japanese line of supply that snaked along the slender mountainous road running between the city and Kwangtung's southwest coast at Yamchow. Some of the lessons arising from the Japanese 11th Army's defeat at Changsha in early October had not yet been learned, and the force sent to Kwangsi was greatly understrength for its mission. Two divisions were inadequate to both fight effectively at Nanning and protect a tenuous 100-mile line of communication to the sea, and the battle for the road threatened to drag the expedition into a trap. Each day, Nanning was supplied by heavily escorted convoys of approximately 100 vehicles from Yamchow. Initially, these convoys had little difficulty getting through, as they were often assigned air cover, and when Chinese forces engaged in road destruction, traffic was usually impeded for only about forty-eight hours.[15] But as the frequency of Chinese attacks continued to increase, this artery became a dangerous problem for the Japanese.

After realizing his error in sending an inadequate number of troops, General Ando reinforced Kwangsi in January 1940 from units fighting north and northeast of Canton. These forces included elements of the 18th Division (originally from Kyushu), an additional Formosan brigade, and a Guards Mixed Brigade, raising the strength of the Kwangsi force to 3.5 divisions, or about 50,000 men. Most of these units had recently been engaged in a diversionary offensive in central Kwangtung, and this move left Japanese forces in that province similarly understrength. But the situation in Kwangsi demanded immediate assistance. The Guards brigade quickly became involved in heavy fighting upon its arrival, just to maintain security between Yamchow and Nanning. Initial losses included a battalion commander.[16] U.S. Army Captain Earl Mattice noted that in late January 1940 a Japanese security detachment tried to clear an area northeast of Hsiatung, about one-third the distance north from Yamchow, but "the Chinese fell upon this column and cut it to pieces."[17] Despite their unexpected aggression, the Chinese were unable to sever the line completely, but the Japanese were equally unable to push the Chinese out of their logistical zone of operations.

Undeterred, the Japanese resumed operations farther north in another attempt to secure the Kunlunkwan Pass. This offensive, which began on 26 January 1940, was also designed to break up a Chinese force of thirty to thirty-five divisions, or almost 200,000 men, now massing in the region for another counterattack on Nanning. At least sixteen Chinese divisions had been transferred from north China during late January and early February, and on 1 February, Chiang Kai Shek flew into Kwangsi to investigate matters for himself. Chinese reinforcements were largely concentrated into four groups: the 75th, 78th, 92nd, and 156th Divisions (among others) northeast of the Kunlunkwan Pass at Pinyang (twelve divisions in total); the 145th, 301st, 302nd, and 303rd Divisions farther northwest at Shanglin; the 2nd, 13th, 17th, 45th, 84th, 93rd, 103rd, and 135th Divisions to the west of Pinyang at Wuming; and the 110th, 115th, 155th, 156th, and 175th Divisions east of Pinyang at Litang. Pinyang was the primary Japanese objective, and to bypass Chinese defensive positions along the road, Japanese forces began their attack from Nanning by utilizing the same infiltration tactics along small paths and trails that they had used in the earlier advance on Nanning from the coast.[18]

The Japanese kicked off the offensive from Nanning by attacking along the northeast road to Pinyang and sending elements of the 18th Division and the Guards eastward to hook around the main Chinese defenses. This eastern column crossed the West River at Yungshun on 29 January 1940, before heading north to attack Pinyang. By 2 February, the town was in their hands, with the Kunlunkwan Pass sandwiched between the two Japanese columns. A Chinese countermove on the vacated Yungshun allowed them to reoccupy the town, thereby cutting off the Japanese force at Pinyang, but the Japanese continued onward nonetheless. They were able to maintain their attack because most of the Chinese defenders at Pinyang withdrew farther north to Chienkiang after taking heavy casualties. The following day at Kunlunkwan, the Japanese converged on the pass from both directions and met strong resistance, but in the end, one and a half

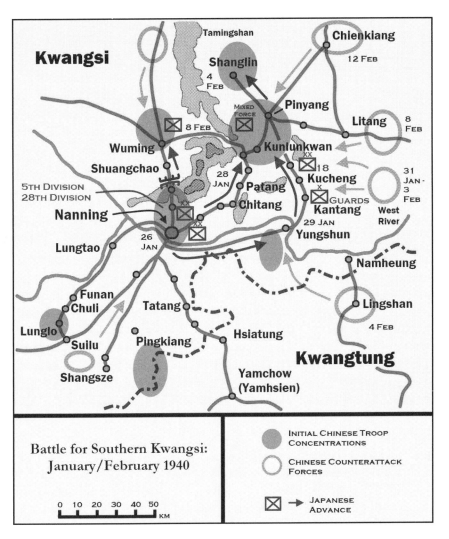

Figure 6.2. Battle for Kwangsi, February 1940. (Based on data from NARA, RG 165, M1444, reel 11, Report No. 9856 by Captain Earl Mattice, 6 March 1940.)

Chinese divisions were wiped out. Within a few days, the road from Nanning to Pinyang was entirely in Japanese hands. An additional Japanese column had also advanced on Wuming from Nanning at the start of the offensive, and it captured the town on 8 February. All seemed well for the Japanese, but that same day a large Chinese counterattack hit them on their flanks and succeeded in blocking the Nanning-Pinyang road. Faced with this significant danger to their rear, discretion prevailed over valor, and on 11 February the Japanese at Pinyang began a partial pullback south. After sustaining many losses, they were content to halt and maintain a defense of Kunlunkwan Pass (see figure 6.2). While this was occurring, General Ando flew into Nanning from Canton to better assess the situation, but from mid-February onward, the northern Nanning front turned relatively static as both sides consolidated their positions and regrouped.[19]

By 15 February 1940, the Japanese felt confident that they had disrupted Chinese plans for a counterattack on Nanning, and they redeployed their forces. Ando was placed in command of the newly formalized South China Expeditionary Force, and a partial withdrawal from Kwangsi soon followed. The South China Expeditionary Force encompassed all units in southern China thereby replacing the 21st Army. In the fall of 1939, however, prior to its official establishment, units in Hainan and Kwangtung were already known collectively as the South China Expeditionary Force. Troops from about one and a half divisions, including soldiers of the 18th Division, traveled back down the road to Yamchow and boarded naval transports for a return to Kwangtung. This move was completed by the first week of March. Those units that remained included the 5th Division and elements of the 28th Division, plus the Guards Mixed Brigade. In covering this partial withdrawal, a Japanese regiment struck Chinese units southwest of Nanning to disrupt their impending move against the road to Yamchow; this operation was followed by a similar difficult attack southeast toward the coast. To push the Chinese further off balance, the Japanese occasionally struck out in brigade strength from their base at Nanning to disperse potentially dangerous Chinese troop concentrations. These expeditions were not of any great distance or duration, but when possible, the Chinese usually attempted to block their line of retreat back to the city. One of these Japanese operations was launched in a westerly direction on 1 April 1940. The coastal port of Pakhoi was also assaulted and occupied for a week by Japanese marines during March, but most of their actions consisted of security sweeps and punitive expeditions against Chinese civilians

CHAPTER SIX

or military forces threatening the line of communication between Nanning and the sea; the marines usually met considerable Chinese resistance. The ensuing stalemate persisted for most of the year, until the Japanese finally withdrew from Kwangsi in October. This transpired after northern French Indochina had been occupied and the need to block Chinese lines of communication through Nanning was obviated.[20]

Soon after the initial capture of Nanning, the Japanese were able to expand air operations against the Chinese strategic lines of communication crossing Kwangsi and Yunnan. The principal routes targeted were the Burma Road and the French Indochina railway. Japanese formations as large as thirty-nine heavy bombers were assigned to single missions, and these aircraft were based at airfields near Yamchow and Pakhoi. From 30 December 1939 until 19 February 1940, Japanese army and navy bombers based in Kwangsi hit the railway line to Indochina on thirteen different occasions from altitudes ranging between 6,000 and 12,000 feet. Most attacks were concentrated against tunnels and bridges from the Indochina border to a distance of eighty kilometers inside Yunnan.[21] Captain Mattice noted that in January the Japanese had announced their intention to bomb the railroad "out of existence."[22] The Chinese reacted by intensifying road construction work in Yunnan and by employing waterborne transport when possible to cross rivers.[23]

Although the winter air offensive against the Yunnan railway did not succeed, the Japanese did create a great deal of damage, but more to their diplomatic relations with the French and the Americans than to the railway. One of the principal reasons for this friction was the 1 February 1940 bombing of the French-owned Lace Bridge, located just inside the border in Yunnan. Although the bridge itself was undamaged, Major Barrett explained in graphic detail why the attack provoked international anger: "The bombing of February 1st resulted in a ghastly slaughter of passengers on a train which was passing through a tunnel near the mouth of which the bombs fell. The force of the explosion caused the locomotive boiler to burst and reduced the coaches in the tunnel almost to splinters. Many persons were literally cooked to death by the steam."[24] Approximately eighty-five people were killed, including five French citizens. The crew of HMS *Falcon* was leaving China at the time because some Royal Navy gunboats were being withdrawn or decommissioned, and these men witnessed the event. They provided a detailed account of the evacuation of casualties to Hong Kong military intelligence officers.[25]

The Lace Bridge bombing was one of the more gruesome episodes of the air campaign, but just as in the 1938 bombing offensive against the KCR, the physical damage inflicted did not permanently interrupt rail traffic. Repairs were made rapidly during the evenings, and material such as gasoline continued to travel northwest, transported by barge and by other means around obstacles where necessary. Bombardment of the railway brought diplomatic protests from the French, but for the time being, the Japanese were more concerned about potential trouble with the United States. Hence, the frequency of Japanese attacks against the line diminished shortly after mid-February. Regardless of the reduction in Japanese raids, Washington grew more anxious about Japanese ambitions after the occupation of Kwangsi, and the United States extended a $20 million loan to China in March 1940. At this stage of the war, the Japanese in south China were still focused on cutting Chinese lines of communication, not on expanding farther south. That would soon change, but until the situation in Europe was altered, American concerns could not be completely dismissed.[26]

The Japanese were also unable to influence the leadership in Yunnan, meaning that they were unsuccessful in breaking General Lung Yun's alliance with Chiang Kai Shek. Despite the increased threat to Yunnan, the lack of antiaircraft units to defend the railway, or Lung's disinclination to accept central government troops in the province, he remained loyal to the anti-Japanese camp in Chungking. Because of these diplomatic and political factors, POL continued to travel into Yunnan via the Indochina railway.[27]

The Japanese invasion and occupation of Kwangsi was an unprofitable military venture, despite initial Chinese military incompetence. Early in the war the Chinese had anticipated an invasion of the region, but because of political friction and poor planning between Kwangsi and the central government, there were limited forces available to defend the province. The Japanese temptation to attack was only encouraged once Kwangsi forces were sent north to fight in Hunan, leaving a numerically deficient army. For the ridiculous ease with which Nanning was initially captured, and for his failure to retake it, General Pai was recalled from the battlefield and demoted. But the Japanese had underestimated the Chinese ability to contain them once the campaign was under way. Despite Japanese efforts to clear the region, they were unable to occupy any area of significance outside of Nanning and had considerable difficulty maintaining their line of communication to the coast. In the ensuing struggle for control of this artery, both sides suffered many casualties.[28]

Japanese civilian pacification methods in the region between Nanning and Yamchow also proved counterproductive, and these operations further demonstrated that General Ando's policy of conciliation did not extend very far beyond Canton. Major Barrett reported from Chungking the unintended impact the Japanese were having on Chinese morale and what this augured for the future:

> The undersigned has ventured to point out to some of his Chinese friends upon whose discretion he can depend that probably the best friend China has in the world today is the Japanese Army, for it is the Japanese Army which has caused the birth of a new and at least partially united China, and it is the Japanese Army which, if it continues on its present course, will probably eventually bring about the downfall of Japan.[29]

Until that happened, Chinese resistance continued as military supplies entered China from Hong Kong as well as through Yunnan via Burma and French Indochina.[30]

Although the backlog of material at Haiphong had increased, the Chinese war effort was not greatly impacted by the occupation of Nanning. The greater problem for the Japanese was the growing anxiety among the Western powers and the diplomatic friction created by Nanning's occupation. The invasion of Kwangsi was accepted in many foreign quarters as evidence of Japanese preparations for expansion farther south, and an increase in the frequency and severity of air strikes against the French Indochina railway did not ease rising tensions with Paris, especially after the bombing of the Lace Bridge. All things considered, the Japanese invasion of Kwangsi was not worth the cost.

Stalemate in South-Central Kwangtung: The Battle for Kukong, December 1939 to March 1940

Prior to the late December 1939 Chinese counterattack against Nanning, the Japanese reinforced their positions in Kwangtung and launched a diversionary offensive in the central part of the province in an attempt to divert Chinese forces from Kwangsi. Japanese troops on the border with

Hong Kong were withdrawn for this attack, and the net result of these developments was to increase Hong Kong's effectiveness as a Chinese supply center. The withdrawal of two battalions from the Hong Kong border was welcomed by British officials, as it reduced the potential for conflict with the Japanese army while simultaneously creating an opportunity to ease the colony's refugee problem.[31] But this respite from Japanese pressure was only temporary, as Major Giles informed London: "Japanese authorities stressed that their troops would return if Hong Kong should again be used as a centre for the import of arms and munitions into China, and expressed the hope that the colonial government would do its best to stop any smuggling of arms over the border."[32] During this period, the Japanese navy maintained the blockade at sea and continued its ground campaign against the rich agricultural region on the western side of the delta. A more serious problem for colonial officials and for the British in general was the rapid collapse of the French in June 1940. Japanese army officers were emboldened by this event and assumed a more bellicose posture; they were determined not only to terminate the movement of Chinese military supplies but also to exploit the opportunity presented by European events to expand their areas of occupation farther south. Thus, an Anglo-Japanese war became increasingly possible, and the threat to Hong Kong became more dangerous.

To draw Chinese forces away from Kwangsi, General Ando launched a diversionary offensive in Kwangtung on 20 December 1939. Its objective was to destroy General Yu Han Mou's 12th Group Army headquartered in the mountainous region surrounding Yungyun, southeast of Kukong. In accounting for the apparent weaknesses of General Yu's army, the plan seemed sound enough, but as the threat to the Japanese line of communication in Kwangsi increased, the Kwangtung offensive had to be aborted. After their easy advance through Kwangtung in October 1938, confidence was high among Ando's command. Consequently, only a limited number of forces was actually committed to the attack. Three columns began the advance from their starting points north of Canton to envelop Yu's troops in what was supposed to be a ring of steel. To accomplish this, Ando ordered the Guards Mixed Brigade, recently arrived from Japan, to strike hard north from the center at Tsungfa. On the left, much of the 104th Division (including the 107th Infantry Brigade), which had been in garrison at Swatow, Fatshan, and Samshui, was ordered to push up the Hankow-Canton railway and the North River to capture the town of Yingtak, eighty miles north of Canton. The 104th's garrison duties were assumed by the new 38th Division headquartered at Fatshan; this unit had recently been formed at Nagoya and arrived in November 1939 under the command of Lieutenant General Fujii Yoji. It would eventually assault Hong Kong in December 1941. On the right were elements of the 18th Division starting from Tsengsheng. This division was ordered to envelop Yu's forces after passing through Lungmoon, farther northeast. Originally, the 18th Division had been dispersed in garrisons at Tsengsheng, Shumchun, and Namtau, and two of its battalions had been spread out along the Hong Kong border, but like the Guards, part of this force had to be redeployed to Kwangsi in the midst of what became a costly retreat.[33]

These three groups of the South China Expeditionary Force began the advance in Kwangtung simultaneously. Initially, all went according to plan, but partly because of unexpected resistance in the mountains, they were unable to achieve victory.[34] Some preliminary combat had already occurred during the week prior to the offensive. Dr. Thomson noted there was "heavy fighting up the north and west rivers," but General Yu quickly withdrew his forces north to prevent their encirclement, enabling them to defend the approach to Kukong.[35] Approximately fifteen Chinese divisions were available for the defense of Kwangtung, including the 151st, 153rd, 154th, 157th, 159th, 160th, 168th, 187th, and 7th Cantonese. Attacking on the left, the Japanese 104th Division marched on Yingtak and occupied the town on 29 December 1939 (see figure 6.3). In the center, the Guards took Langkow on 26 December and, after some difficulty, captured Lutien on 2 January 1940. On the right, the Japanese 18th Division met with greater success, reaching Lungmoon on 25 December and capturing Yungyun, 110 miles northeast of Canton, on New Year's Eve.[36] From there, the terrain to Kukong was less difficult to traverse. An advance on the city would have been somewhat easier to conduct, but the Chinese once again moved against the overextended Japanese flanks to cut their lines of supply to Canton. A general withdrawal from central Kwangtung therefore began on 1 January 1940. The bigger problem, however, was that the Japanese position in Kwangsi had become dangerously threatened, and reinforcements were needed immediately from Kwangtung to stabilize the situation between Nanning and the coast.[37]

Before help could be sent to Kwangsi, the Japanese had to extricate themselves from their problems in Kwangtung. Maintaining pressure during the South China Expeditionary Force's retreat, the 12th Group Army

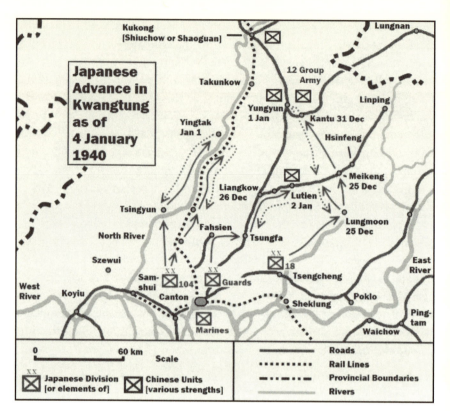

Figure 6.3. Battle for Kwangtung, 20 December 1939 to 5 January 1940. There were three Japanese moves north of Canton. (Based on data from NARA, RG 165, M1444, reel 11, Report No. 9849 by Captain F. P. Munson, 11 January 1940.)

advanced closely behind, and several units managed to work their way around the Japanese to become blocking forces at key points. In the east, the retreat of the Japanese 18th Division was delayed at Lungmoon on 10 January 1940; the troops had to fight their way into the town, but once this was accomplished, they continued their move, passing through Tsengsheng on the nineteenth. In the center, the Guards traveled back down the Canton-Kukong highway, passing through their original starting positions at Tsungfa on 10 January, but they were forced to fight their way into Shenkang farther southwest. Heavy fighting developed there on 19 and 20 January. Along the river and the railway line, the Chinese kept constant pressure on the 104th Division until it halted just north of Canton at

Hsinkai. By the time the Japanese finished their withdrawal, the positions they occupied were closer to Canton than they had started from (see figure 6.4). In the end, the Japanese Kwangtung offensive lasted for about a month, but it was even more futile than the occupation of Nanning. Instead of diverting the Chinese, Ando had to break off his attack in Kwangtung to save his position in Kwangsi. Casualties amounted to 6,000 Japanese and 13,000 Chinese, but there was little to show for it. The war in Kwangtung remained deadlocked.[38]

General Yu's defense of Kwangtung showed that the Chinese strategy of securing direct British involvement was still in effect. In contrast, even with limited troop strength, General Ando still thought the destruction of the Chinese 12th Group Army was possible. What surprised many observers was General Yu's ability to put up a useful defense. Part of the reason for Yu's unexpected competence in battle was his preparation to face such a challenge. Chinese villagers had practiced their evacuation over several months, and many were able to move quickly, before the arrival of Japanese troops. Thus, the Japanese were forced to withdraw partly because of a general lack of supplies. Nothing was left for the Japanese army to use. All the food was dispersed away from the line of advance, and there were no people available to repair the roads. In battle, Yu was forced to rely on some of the poorest-quality troops in the Chinese army, but even so, he managed to avoid encirclement and maintained the bulk of his forces intact. By advancing with insufficient troops, General Ando gambled that he could use long, extended columns with exposed flanks to envelop the Chinese, just as Lieutenant General Okamura Yasuji and the 11th Army had hoped to do during the first battle of Changsha in October 1939. But in an echo of Changsha, once the Japanese advanced into the rougher terrain farther north, much of their firepower advantage was lost when they were limited to the use of mountain artillery.[39] Fortunately for Ando, Yu lacked sufficient firepower of his own to exact a greater toll during the retreat. Oddly, by February 1940, once Ando's withdrawal was complete, Yu chose to discontinue his attack. An assault on Canton would have been costly, but his forces were closer to the city than ever before. Moreover, with the Japanese South China Expeditionary Force heavily engaged in Kwangsi, it was unlikely that conditions for an attack would ever be more favorable. Yet Yu halted his forces just short of the city and gave the Japanese a chance to regroup. Even a failed attack would have provided indirect support to Chinese forces fighting in Kwangsi. Instead, Yu was content

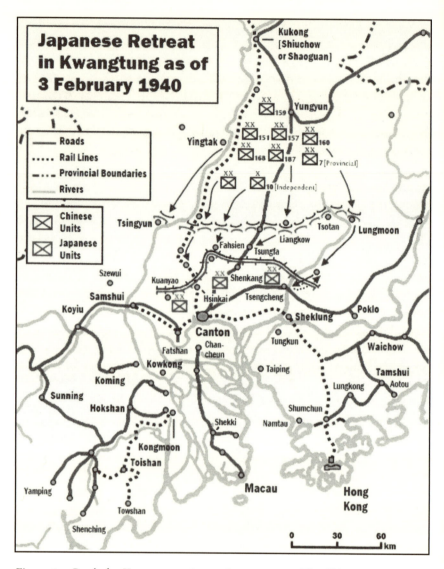

Japanese Retreat in Kwangtung as of 3 February 1940

Kukong [Shiuchow or Shaoguan]

Roads
Rail Lines
Provincial Boundaries
Rivers

Chinese Units
Japanese Units

Yungyun

Yingtak

159
151 157 160
168 187 7 [Provincial]
10 [Independent]

Tsingyun
Tsotan Lungmoon
Fahsien Liangkow
Tsungfa

Szewui
Kuanyao Shenkang
Samshui
Koyiu Hsinkai Tsengcheng
Sheklung Poklo

Canton
Chan-cheun Tungkun Waichow
Fatshan Taiping
Kowkong Tamshui
Koming Lungkong Aotou
Sunning Shumchun
Hokshan Shekki Namtau

Kongmoon
Toishan
Yamping Macau Hong Kong
Towshan
Shenching

0 30 60 km

Figure 6.4. Battle for Kwangtung, 6 to 20 January 1940. The Chinese counteroffensive and final positions are shown. (Based on data from NARA, RG 165, M1444, reel 11, Report No. 9849 by Captain Earl Mattice, 3 February 1940.)

to keep the Japanese frustratingly contained close to Canton, while military supplies still tauntingly entered China from Hong Kong.

Blockade of Hong Kong:
November 1939 to June 1940

Kwangsi had been invaded to strengthen the blockade against China, but Japanese plans were once again thwarted, largely because the Chinese continued to use Hong Kong. Japanese forces redeployed from Hong Kong and from places such as Swatow were urgently required elsewhere for combat, but with an open border, the blockade was greatly weakened. Out of desperation, the Japanese attempted to make the most of this development by promoting themselves as good neighbors. Proclamations emphasizing their desire for improved relations with British officials were tempered, however, by Major General Tsuchihashi Yuichi, Ando's new chief of staff for intelligence, who, while passing through Hong Kong, informed his hosts that he hoped to see a termination of their gasoline exports to China.[40] The Japanese also relied on weak Chinese puppet troops to make up the shortfall in available manpower, but their utility was minimal at best. These forces were aided by Japanese naval and marine units when possible, but overall, the ability to maintain the blockade was diminished during the winter of 1939–1940.

Although Japanese army officers' attitude toward the British in south China had soured during the fall of 1939, this situation temporarily improved after the invasion of Kwangsi began. This was also true of the navy following Vice Admiral Takasu Shiro's appointment as commander of the Japanese 5th Fleet. Takasu was the former naval attaché to Great Britain and a friend of General Ando, yet his replacement of Vice Admiral Kondo Nobutake on 10 October 1939 did not result in any reduction of violence against Chinese civilians near Hong Kong.[41]

After a year of occupation, Ando's conciliatory approach to the Chinese had essentially evaporated. Attacks against civilians throughout the region had become more severe, especially along the West River and throughout the Chungshan district. As a reprisal for Chinese guerrilla attacks, the town of Kun Shaan, in occupied territory near Canton, was bombed and strafed by Japanese aircraft in early December 1939, and more than 100 people were killed. Ground combat involving the Japanese 38th Division also occurred in December near Kongmoon and was resumed in February

1940 with greater ferocity. The city itself had previously been assaulted on 29 March 1939. Heavily battered Shekki likewise became the object of Japanese attention once again, and British residents speculated that the Japanese needed a face-saving victory following their difficulties in Kwangsi. Food was also becoming increasingly scarce, as disrupting Hong Kong's supply of agricultural goods remained the primary goal of Japanese activities in the region. Because of the deployment of Chinese forces elsewhere, Shekki was left undefended in March 1940, and many civilians were unable to flee before the Japanese troops arrived. Looting, rapes, and executions occurred during the city's occupation.[42]

Macau likewise received its share of intimidation during March, when Japanese units again occupied villages on the eastern side of Lappa Island, overlooking the inner harbor. These units did not stay for long, but smaller groups of armed Japanese troops entering Macau on leave and for other purposes created many problems. Merchants were often paid in military yen, civilian houses were searched, and several Chinese were kidnapped. A levy of $400,000 per month was also placed on the city, all with the aim of securing Portuguese recognition of the puppet government in Chungshan district. The following month, Macanese police reoccupied the villages on Lappa Island, but these units were attacked by Japanese and Chinese puppet troops on 24 April 1940, forcing their withdrawal back inside the colony.[43]

Despite the open border at Hong Kong, Japanese interdiction efforts were maintained at sea. By the end of 1939, most Royal Navy vessels had already been withdrawn from the Far East for service in the Mediterranean or home waters, and the China Squadron flag was transferred to Singapore in May 1940. Hence, Japanese navy pressure against Hong Kong and along the south China coast was persistent, both offshore and along the Pearl River, with little interference. Beginning in mid-December 1939 and throughout much of 1940, the Pearl River was periodically closed to foreign traffic so that the Japanese could support ground operations up the North and West rivers, but conveniently, this action also disrupted British commercial activity inland.[44] A stop-and-search policy directed against British and other third-power shipping continued just outside the colony's territorial waters, but officers and men from HMS *Liverpool* returned the favor, boarding the Japanese liner *Asama Maru* close to Japan and detaining twenty-one Germans in January.[45] The potential for a dangerous naval confrontation also existed in Hong Kong itself, as the harbor was closed

　　　　CHAPTER SIX

for approximately five hours that same month due to the presence of an unidentified submarine. More menacing were the continual attacks against Hong Kong junks. In one instance during March 1940, a group of fifty junks positioned two to five miles from Kit Shek were attacked by Japanese naval vessels at about 4:00 AM, with most of the boats being destroyed. A favorite area for the Japanese to strike was in the vicinity of Lin Tin Island and San Mei, and these attacks continued throughout the year. Chinese lines of supply to and from Hong Kong also came under increasingly frequent aerial bombardment. A carrier strike was made against Shayuchang in the Mirs Bay region on 13 April 1940, resulting in the deaths of approximately 120 Chinese; this was followed by additional strikes launched in early May. These were quickly extended north to Tamshui, Waichow, and other points along the East River.[46]

Following the battles for Kwangsi and Kwangtung, General Ando strove to stabilize his positions on the ground, and the South China Area Army resumed the task of supply interdiction and garrison duty in Canton. Farther east, a growing Chinese threat to Japanese and puppet forces at Swatow was confronted in March, when the 136th Infantry Regiment of the 106th Division was transferred from the central Yangtse region to strengthen the city's defense. In the first week of May, additional Japanese infantry and armor arrived at Canton as reinforcements for central Kwangtung, thus allowing the Japanese 38th Division to reestablish the Canton defense zone by battling its way into Tsungfa on the eighteenth. Aside from this action, south China remained relatively quiet between April and May, and the 136th Regiment was soon withdrawn from Swatow to Japan. The Japanese 18th, 38th, and 104th Divisions continued to occupy the area surrounding Canton, while the Imperial Guards Brigade, along with the 5th and 28th Divisions, kept control of Nanning and the road to Yamchow.[47]

Since many Japanese ground units of the South China Expeditionary Force were operating within the interior of Kwangtung and Kwangsi, weak Chinese puppet troops were utilized to plug the holes along the coast. By January 1940, approximately 6,000 Chinese had been recruited into the Kwangtung puppet army under the ostensible overall command of Cantonese General Lay Chan Ming, but about 70 percent of the officers and noncommissioned officers were Japanese personnel. The remainder were Chinese junior officers supplied by an officers training school in Canton, a facility that provided candidates with two months of instruction. Although the school was clean and the troops were seemingly well disciplined, much of the training was rudimentary, and the Chinese central government was able to infiltrate it with ease.[48]

Japanese hopes for the Kwangtung puppet army were short-lived. Military results were unimpressive, and the army's combat record did little in the short term to enhance Japanese prestige among the population. Initially, these forces were also of limited value in bolstering the new Wang Ching Wei government, which was officially established on 1 April 1940. Leading up to this event, Chinese puppet troops under the command of General Huang Ta Wei had advanced into south Fukien in December 1939 to clear the Amoy region of central government forces, but they were stopped by local Chinese militiamen, who dispersed the entire puppet force. Huang made another attempt on 12 February 1940 with about 3,800 puppet troops supported by Japanese warships, including an aircraft carrier. His force landed near Amoy, but after battling the Chinese 75th Division, Huang quickly withdrew. A second landing was made on 17 February near the International Settlement on Kulangsu, but on the afternoon of the twentieth, after some indecisive fighting, half the puppet force defected, taking 1,500 rifles and many of their machine guns with them. Out of the total original force, about 800 casualties were sustained, including several Japanese advisers. To conclude this farce, General Huang was arrested by Japanese officials and detained in Amoy. The value of the weapons lost was estimated to be about $1 million (Chinese dollars [CD], or fapi), and the Chinese government paid each defecting soldier $100 if he was armed and $50 if he was not. A similar effort in June to clear a region near Swatow met with equally dismal results. Early one morning, in a town near Swatow, a Chinese puppet battalion was attacked by central government forces and compelled to withdraw, but during the retreat toward Swatow, the troops were mistaken for Chinese guerrillas and machine-gunned by Japanese forces; 120 of the puppet force were killed. Japanese patrols later reoccupied the town, where they meted out reprisals by using local farmers for bayonet practice.[49]

Despite the violence inflicted on rural civilians by Japanese military forces, they were able to recruit puppet soldiers in Canton due to the dismal state of the economy and the lack of political stability throughout the rest of the province. In Canton there was still a sliver of order that was not apparent elsewhere in the region. It was partly because of this that two British officers reported some acceptance of the Japanese army among the

population. Most of the Canton garrison was well disciplined and quar-
tered in the eastern part of the city near the airfields, away from civilians.
Encouraging enlistment were the twin problems of unemployment and inflation. About 30 percent of the preinvasion population remained in the
city, trying to eke out an existence; only a few businesses were open, and
inflation made the cost of living seven times what it had been at the start of
the war. Office clerks made between $200 and $300 per month, while a
pair of shoes cost $100, a suit went for about $200, and a room cost $100
to $200. Rice was also very expensive. Food riots developed on occasion,
and approximately 100 deaths per day were attributed to starvation. With
the Pearl River repeatedly closed, and with most of Canton's industry in
ruins, there were few options available to alleviate the problems of Canton's poor. Compounding their difficulties was the widespread distribution
and consumption of opium, brought into the province by the Japanese. Dr.
Thomson furnished information about the opium problem to both U.S.
Ambassador Nelson T. Johnson and Lieutenant Colonel William Mayer
during their visit on 21 February 1940, corroborating intelligence already
in the hands of U.S. officials. Opium and gambling dens were easy to find,
and the Japanese used the revenue generated for their personal enrichment
and to help pay the costs of occupation.[50] Consequently, a few Chinese
made the best of their situation by enlisting in the Kwangtung puppet army
merely to survive.

Others sided with the communists, despite periodic atrocities committed
by their troops. One such incident occurred in Hopei (Hebei) in June 1940,
when 500 farmers were buried alive for failing to comply with demands.[51]
Prior to this, when Canton fell to the Japanese in November 1938, a Chinese communist guerrilla unit had been formed along the KCR, between
Sheklung and Shumchun. This unit, under the command of former seaman
Tsang Shang, initially consisted of two battalions. Shortly after its formation, the unit broke away from the central government's guerrilla forces
and declared its communist loyalties. This was possible because Tsang had
been sent to take command of the East River force by the New 4th Army.
Over time, and with the involvement of Major Francis Kendall, this force
grew in strength and became known as the East River Column or the East
River Brigade. Throughout 1939 the Kwangtung communist force continued to train and recruit additional members while avoiding entanglements
with either the Japanese or the Chinese army. But on 9 March 1940,
amidst the chaotic social and military situation following the Chinese and

Japanese battles north of Canton, the Chinese army launched an attack against one of the communist battalions that had seized the opportunity to occupy Tamshui and Pingshan.[52] The attack was carried out in an effort to maintain Chinese army lines of communication to Hong Kong. Lacking adequate firepower, the communists withdrew from Tamshui and retreated to the mountains of eastern Kwangtung, where they remained until late 1941.[53]

By April 1940, after combat operations diminished across southern China, the Japanese once again concentrated their energies and resources on the blockade, but the commitment of scarce Japanese infantry to Kwangsi left General Ando and the South China Expeditionary Force with gaps too numerous to fill. Supplies entered the country easily from Hong Kong, ensuring the colony's status as a principal strategic center. POL and other military stores also continued to move into China from Burma and French Indochina, despite the Japanese occupation of Kwangsi and the intensified air campaign against Chinese lines of communication in Yunnan. Because of the general shortage of troops, the Japanese tried to maintain the blockade with Chinese puppet infantry, but these units were generally unreliable in combat, and results were poor. Their lack of combat power, however, was somewhat offset by their potential political value. Over time, they might lend a degree of credibility to the Wang Ching Wei administration, increasing Japanese leverage against Chiang Kai Shek during future peace negotiations. Militarily, however, neither the occupation of Kwangsi nor the expansion of the puppet army was sufficient to deal with the Chinese logistical problem. Thus, the stalemate in China continued.

A Time to Weigh Options

Amidst this impasse, the prospect of peace was once again advanced, but Chiang Kai Shek preferred to bide his time as his strategy of involving third powers slowly progressed. Bitter experience on the battlefield had molded part of the Chinese army into a more effective fighting force, but significant improvements were still required in leadership, staff work, and the technical branches before it would be able to defeat the Japanese. Unfortunately for the Chinese and the British, the necessary changes were not expected to occur soon enough. Furthermore, without a navy, it was impossible for the Chinese to break the Japanese blockade. Although many foreign observers were surprised by Chinese endurance, it was widely understood that the Chinese could not achieve victory on their own. Reflecting on this situation, Major Giles noted that Chinese strategy depended on greater foreign intervention:

These elementary truths are perfectly clear to the Generalissimo, but he has never seriously considered driving the Japanese north of the Great Wall with his own unaided military might. On the contrary he has always based his continued resistance on the supposition that sooner or later, Britain, the U.S.A. or Soviet Russia would intervene on China's behalf; not necessarily by force of arms, but with such drastic economic or political measures as would force Japan to withdraw.[54]

For their part, the Japanese did little to improve diplomatic relations with the Western powers. During the winter of 1939, the Japanese concentrated on cutting the Chinese lines of communication in Kwangsi and Yunnan, but by the end of spring 1940, the Japanese began to seek other ways of bringing the war to an end. Because of their failure in China, Japanese strategy evolved into a more ambitious program of conquest at the expense of the French. Overshadowing Chinese events was the worsening situation in Europe, and after the fall of France, the opportunity to occupy Indochina as a solution to Japan's problem seemed too good to ignore. Peace negotiations were supported throughout the year, but war against Britain and the United States had become a more widely acceptable option. The road to victory would be sought farther south, but unfortunately for all, it was a road to ruin.

■

SEVEN

Leveraging War and Peace:
May to December 1940

The spring and summer of 1940 proved to be a transitional period of great significance, with the fall of France ushering in far-reaching changes. Powers on the defensive, such as China and Britain, were able to leverage the possibility of peace to secure greater international support, since the French defeat created a power vacuum in the Far East that was quickly exploited by Japan. The Japanese began to see an advance into the southwest Pacific as a solution to their problems in China, and although Sino-Japanese peace negotiations were occurring at very high levels, war with the Western powers became accepted as necessary. From the Soviet Union, Stalin was emboldened to attack neighboring states as he aligned himself closely with Hitler.[1] More isolated than at any other period of the war, the British lacked the necessary resources to continue fighting, so the War Cabinet, armed with a new prime minister, was forced to consider the possibility of making peace with Germany. This course was rejected, but with their grand strategy in tatters, the British temporarily restricted their commitment in China to increase American and Soviet cooperation against the Japanese. Facing the threat of war in the Far East, the British closed the Burma Road but hoped that by making such a move, others would take the lead in opposing the Japanese. This drastic measure was employed as Stalin made it abundantly clear (by August 1939) that collective security was dead and as U.S. diplomatic and military support for Britain was lagging.[2]

Yet, as Britain stood alone, the United States started to assume a leadership role against the fascist dictatorships. From this point forward, British power steadily declined, as manifested by the establishment of a U.S.-Canadian security alliance. This shift was an important factor behind the decision to reinforce Hong Kong in 1941 with Canadian troops.

British strategic options remained limited, but China was still an area where pressure could be exerted on the USSR and the United States, since both saw the continuation of the Sino-Japanese War as essential to their interests. With the French driven out of the war and northern Indochina occupied, only three avenues into China remained open to maintain Chinese resistance. The Soviets controlled the northwest route into Sinkiang, but the British still held the keys to the all-important doors at Rangoon and Hong Kong. The British thus maintained their influence in China through Hong Kong, when all other southern routes, including the Burma Road, had been closed. The strategic value of the colony as a military supply center was greatly enhanced during this period, as was its geopolitical significance. Barring any fundamental diplomatic or military changes on the part of Great Britain or Japan, the colony's seizure would remain a Japanese strategic objective, even at the cost of war with Great Britain and the increased likelihood of war with the United States.

The Sino-British Coalition in Retreat

The fall of France on 25 June 1940 was a pivotal event, affecting the course of the war in both Europe and Asia. Japanese hopes for victory had been wrecked on the battlefield at Changsha in October 1939, and the establishment of the Wang Ching Wei government was delayed because their prestige had been thoroughly undermined. Part of the problem was that until mid-1940, Japanese strategy had been opportunistic and lacked a clear direction. They hoped to bring the war in China to a close by cutting Chinese strategic lines of communication, but beyond that, the overall inconsistency in planning grand strategy was an impediment to Japanese efforts and often produced political instability at home. Abrupt shifts in foreign policy usually followed the installment of a new faction in power, and reactions to changing geopolitical conditions were often aggressive and hasty. Needless friction was thereby created in relations with other powers, more so after the fall of France.[3] With an eye on Indochina, hardline officers returned to power in Tokyo and increased the pressure on Britain to end its support of China; simultaneously, they continued to push the Chinese central government to make peace. Both London and Chungking were stretched to their limits of endurance, but each continued to fight in the hope of securing greater international cooperation. Once that was accomplished, however, the cost was high, and Britain grew weaker as a result. Within the British Empire, Canada became less of a Dominion and more of an American protectorate. For their part, the Japanese began to see a southern strategic advance and a war with the West as the only path to victory. Thus, amidst the turbulence stemming from the French defeat, preparations were begun to move the war onto a much larger stage.

In Europe, the strategic situation for Great Britain was most discouraging, but this did not bring an end to the war. With France in defeat, the British army was forced to evacuate the Continent at Dunkirk between late May and early June, but only after losing all its heavy weapons and vehicles. During the battle, German armored forces had been ordered to halt on 23 May 1940, and this helped make the British withdrawal possible. After the war, Sir Basil Liddell Hart was informed by various German commanders, including Field Marshal P. L. E. von Kleist, that Hitler had issued the order in the hope of securing peace with Britain once the French had surrendered.[4] Hitler's ambitions did not include the conquest of Great Britain.[5] John Lukacs commented on this in his examination of the struggle between Hitler and Churchill in mid-1940: "There is no question that Hitler wished for an alliance with Britain, or at least for the neutrality of the latter. . . . It is wrong to believe that, as late as 1940, Hitler wanted 'world domination.' He wanted to rule Europe."[6] German peace proposals were subsequently discussed in the cabinet throughout 1940 (and after), with Prime Minister Winston Churchill and Foreign Secretary Lord Halifax positioned on opposite sides of the issue until the latter was dispatched to Washington as ambassador.[7] The crux of the problem was the insufficiency of British resources to fight a protracted war past the end of the year. Industrial and economic weakness impeded the country's war effort. With few interests in Europe and its dependence on trade, what Great Britain required above all else was peace.[8] In contrast, Germany's autarkic structure ensured that the country could sustain itself in war for a longer period and render a British blockade useless. The best that could be managed, while still preserving Britain's global independent position, was perhaps a limited war, but certainly not a protracted war of annihilation. Under such conditions, British exhaustion and collapse were assured.[9]

Despite being hindered by material deficiencies, the British had several strategic options. During the battle of Britain, the Royal Air Force (RAF) demonstrated its ability to defend the country from any potential German invasion. But the defeat of Germany was beyond British capabilities. After the fall of France, neutrality in Europe was a sensible foreign policy option that recognized British military limitations. In the Far East, withdrawal from Hong Kong was also a realistic course. Alternatively, given Britain's economic and industrial shortcomings, a limited war against the Japanese would have been much more feasible with China as an overt ally. Chiang's offer of 200,000 troops for the defense of Hong Kong was still on the table, as it had been since early 1939.[10] To challenge the Japanese and keep China fighting, an alliance with the Chinese centered on the defense of Hong Kong, or along a Kunming-Changsha axis, was possible, but in the end, British Far Eastern forces were destroyed during the winter of 1941–1942 in what can be described as a humiliating debacle.

It was largely because of Churchill that there was no change in policy, and as war with Germany progressed, war with Japan drew close. With or without victory, Britain's days as a global power were cut drastically short, and the security of the empire was imperiled. Authors such as Correlli Barnett, Bernard Porter, and others have demonstrated this in great detail.[11] Barnett noted that during the summer of 1940, "England's existence as an independent power" was lost.[12] The only hope of victory rested on American entry into the war, but even with this eventuality, British power would be diminished greatly.[13]

A clear manifestation of this situation was Canada's geopolitical shift toward the United States. Many supporters of Prime Minister Mackenzie King's Liberal government distrusted British imperial motivations, and even before the outbreak of war they had begun to look to America for guidance and leadership in steering Canada through world events. Some influential party members and allies were associated with the Canadian Institute of International Affairs (CIIA), headed by Escott Reid until 1938. Reid later served as a Canadian representative to the United Nations' 1945 conference in San Francisco. The CIIA was a private body that formulated policy recommendations for government consideration, and one of its goals was the strengthening of U.S.-Canada relations. It also supported propaganda projects within the United States aimed at bringing that country into the war.[14] The CIIA collaborated closely with the Department of External Affairs, and its members included senior officials such as Hugh

Keenleyside. In stark tones, Keenleyside described Canada's situation in a July 1940 policy document: "Co-operation with Washington is going to be either voluntary on Canada's part, or else compulsory; in any event it is inevitable."[15] Fighting for the British Empire was not an agreeable option for many people within this circle; waging war as a junior partner in a coalition dominated by the United States was more palatable.[16]

Much of the impetus for strengthening U.S.-Canadian relations came from those working together in the CIIA and from other forums.[17] Adherents of collective security eagerly rallied under American leadership to establish what Jonathan Utley only partially identified as the primary aim of the war: a global liberal economic order based on trade.[18] Unfortunately, it was to be supported by nondemocratic, supranational, political and economic authority. On 24 June 1939 the Third Conference on Canadian-American Affairs was held at Canton, New York, under the auspices of the Carnegie Endowment for International Peace (the second conference had been held at Queen's University in Kingston, Ontario, on 30 June 1937). It was directed by Dr. James T. Shotwell. Representing America among approximately 150 influential individuals were Professor Owen Lattimore, former undersecretary of the treasury Roswell Magill, and future secretary of state John Foster Dulles. Colonel Charles P. Stacey took some time away from Princeton to represent Canada, as did Brigadier General H. D. G. Crerar, then commandant of the Royal Military College at Kingston. They were joined by the widely read journalist Grant Dexter and Professor A. R. M. Lower from Winnipeg.[19] On this occasion Dulles delivered a well-received paper entitled "A North American Contribution to World Order," and Stacey presented a Canadian perspective titled "Defence and External Obligations."[20] Amply financed forums such as this one helped influential people on both sides of the border share ideas and discuss methods for changing the global distribution of power. Consequently, by 1940, Mackenzie King's government and the Department of External Affairs contained many individuals, including himself, primed to adjust Canada's international position toward America.

After the fall of France, Canada's shift toward the United States accelerated. Washington's representative in Ottawa, Jay Pierrepont Moffat, informed the State Department on 23 June 1940: "Canada is at a crossroad. She is about to intensify to the full her war effort and knows that it must be redirected. She is all prepared to direct it along American lines if we give her any encouragement."[21] Fear of a British collapse under the weight of

German invasion was a prime topic of discussion during the personal telephone diplomacy conducted between President Franklin Roosevelt and Prime Minister Mackenzie King, as was the threat posed by Japan. Early in July, Oscar D. Skelton, the undersecretary of state for external affairs, informed Mackenzie King that if Japan entered the war, Canada would be unable to defend itself without the help of U.S. forces. Because of the crisis in Europe, the two leaders, meeting in upstate New York, agreed to form a military alliance in defense of North America. The Ogdensburg agreement was signed on 17 August 1940, leading to the formation of the Permanent Joint Board of Defence (PJBD).[22] What was truly significant about this event was that the United States entered into a military alliance with a country that was already at war. This was an important consideration when Hong Kong was reinforced with Canadian infantry in the fall of 1941. Some Canadian officers, such as Brigadier General Maurice Pope, the future vice chief of the General Staff and senior Canadian member of the PJBD, saw no military necessity for the new arrangement. Nor did the new chief of the General Staff, General Crerar, consider a German invasion likely.[23] Nevertheless, the agreement went forward.

Roosevelt was eager to sign the agreement because it would increase American involvement in the war. Another objective was the ability to control the British fleet in the event of surrender. Within weeks, conscription legislation was passed in the United States, followed by a deal with Great Britain involving the exchange of destroyers for bases. Roosevelt was assured that if the Germans occupied Britain, the Royal Navy would continue the war from Singapore.[24] Having embraced collective security, Mackenzie King also wanted U.S. intervention, and he needed to reassert control in his own foreign service by quelling lingering doubts that the war was not being fought for the sake of empire. In 1939 there was still considerable popular resistance to a declaration of war; nationalist spirit was strong in many parts of the country, and it was assumed that colonial attitudes dominated the issue. Widely held opposition in Quebec was particularly worrisome, but the Ogdensburg agreement helped nullify much of this.[25] Canada's shift initially angered Churchill and other British officials, but once they realized that the possibility of American intervention had substantially increased, their discomfort dissipated.

Mackenzie King sought to assuage the British by having Canada serve as the linchpin (or bridge) in bringing the United States and Britain together as the basis for a "new world order"—an arrangement he enunciated during his Mansion House speech in London on 4 September 1941.[26] Being a Harvard alumnus and former lecturer, and given his associations with such prominent and intimate friends as his previous employer John D. Rockefeller III, Mackenzie King's worldview was based on a corporate liberal ideology that was transnational in scale.[27] Utley explained how this position, shared by FDR, served as a primary factor in the United States' eventual participation in the war: "What really worried Roosevelt and Hull was the loss of whole sections of the world to an autarchic economic system controlled by Germany or Japan. This was a question not of a few supplies, but of the preservation of a world order that had brought unparalleled prosperity for the industrial nations in general and the United States in particular."[28]

The question of who actually prospered remains a matter of debate. Nevertheless, Mackenzie King's alignment with FDR and his policies, which were also supported by a majority of those in the foreign policy circles of the eastern establishment, was no great surprise. As early as October 1936, Mackenzie King had explained to Rockefeller that although he was not too concerned about war in the immediate future, the world needed another international political body, besides the League of Nations, to manage global affairs.[29] That is partly why, in the summer of 1940, Mackenzie King did not consider the shift in power created by the establishment of the PJBD to be an abandonment of Great Britain. Indeed, from the summer of 1940 until America's entry into the war, Canada functioned as the linchpin in forging a transatlantic alliance. Yet by then, Canada had also been strategically positioned under an American umbrella, and the limited influence it temporarily exerted quickly receded with the growth of American hegemony. In this case, ideology did not trump power. Canada's flight into the American orbit was just the first of several. Next in line was Australia in 1942.

Despite having limited interests or resources in Asia, the Canadian government soon became involved in Chinese affairs because of its contacts within organizations such as the CIIA and the PJBD. Keenleyside, for example, was the Canadian secretary of the PJBD, and he was on friendly terms with Major General Clayton Bissell, who was also on the board. Bissell later commanded the 10th Air Force in the China-Burma-India theater, and the two men corresponded on a first-name basis.[30] Lacking a national intelligence agency, Ottawa gathered information not only through regular communication with American officials and academics but also through people on the ground in China, such as United Church of Canada (UCC) missionaries based in Toronto. Future presidential envoy to China Owen Lattimore visited the UCC Foreign Mission Council in March 1939 to discuss Far Eastern affairs with the Reverend Jesse Arnup. He and others in the church had considerable experience in China, and on at least one occasion, Arnup corresponded with Soong Mayling (Madame Chiang Kai Shek). Both Arnup and Lattimore were on friendly terms with Keenleyside, and Lattimore advised him in the spring of 1942 on the selection of Canada's first ambassador to China.[31] Prior to this, Canadian involvement in China grew to include the provision of military hardware and the reinforcement of Hong Kong. By fulfilling external alliance obligations in China, in part through such contacts, Canada helped maintain the anti-Axis coalition and align British and American Far Eastern policy. Few paid much attention to Canadian affairs, however, as there were issues of greater importance around the globe. This was especially so in Japan.

As occurred in Britain with Churchill's rise to power, a cabinet crisis emerged in Tokyo in 1940 largely because of the failure to achieve victory in China. In January a stop-gap cabinet headed by Yonai Mitsumasa assumed control of the government, much as the Abe Noboyuki cabinet had done the previous August in the wake of the Nazi-Soviet Pact. Soon thereafter, in February 1940, the overall commander of Japanese forces in China, General Nishio Toshizo, was replaced by the war minister, General Hata Shunroku, partly because of the large number of casualties sustained during the Chinese winter offensive, but also to signal Japan's willingness for rapprochement with the USSR.[32]

The Japanese army was being subjected to greater domestic criticism than at any time in the past, and the reasons for this situation were reported to the War Office from Hong Kong:

The North China Garrison which seized upon the Lukouchiao incident of July 1937, to put in practice their long-cherished designs on North China, never dreamt that they would involve their country in a major war, the issue of which is still uncertain after two and a half years. The result of this miscalculation is now becoming painfully apparent. Although early predictions of a collapse of the Japanese economic structure have been falsified, the burden of the war is becoming increasingly difficult to carry.[33]

Few were eager to assume leadership of the government. In Hong Kong, Major Giles noted that the army, which had "landed Japan in her present predicament and should logically be responsible for getting the country out of the mess, is equally loath to come forward and attempt to solve the muddle of its own creating."[34] Not only did peace remain elusive, but Japanese repression and drug peddling had reduced the population to such a state of poverty and malnutrition that even occupied China was unable to function as the profitable market for Japanese exports visualized in the original schemes of exploitation.[35]

Underpinning Japan's political troubles were the great divisions on military grand strategy that persisted among the country's civil-military leadership. This problem contributed to the prolongation of the war and encouraged reckless behavior among field commanders. Relations with third powers were frequently made worse as a result. In general, three groups advocated three different strategies. The first, which included General Hata, General Nishio, and Hata's chief of staff, General Itagaki Seishiro, desired a southward attack as soon as the European war presented such an opportunity. The second group comprised some of the older army commanders, such as General Count Terauchi Hisaichi, and General Yanagawa Heisuke of Nanking infamy, as well as many prominent Japanese business leaders who wanted to finish the war in China at all costs and fix the economy. General Ushiroku Jun, commander of the South China Expeditionary Force at Canton in late 1940 (following Ando's departure), was part of the third group, which sought to attack Siberia when the opportunity presented itself.[36]

Among these groups, recognition of the need to end the war in China varied in degree, but overall Japanese hopes were placed on the Kiri Project to establish peace with the Chinese. As was so often the case, Japanese efforts again proved counterproductive. Peace overtures received their strongest support throughout 1940 in these high-level discussions conducted directly with the Kuomintang in Hong Kong and Macau. The Japanese offered to withdraw to areas north of the Great Wall in a bid to end the war, but Chiang Kai Shek remained cool to their proposals. As long as Chiang continued to receive support from abroad, time was potentially on his side, and he believed a guerrilla warfare strategy could keep the Japanese bogged down in northern and central China.[37] The Japanese threatened recognition of the Wang Ching Wei regime to keep negotiations active, but most influential Westerners, such as future U.S. ambassador John L. Stuart, believed that Chiang was resolved to continue fighting. Although not yet officially recognized, the Wang government was itself a confession of the Japanese failure to beat Chiang into submission, and it only served to harden opposition against Japanese designs. Some diplomatic personnel thought Chiang might accept peace, but only if it were negotiated by President Roosevelt. Yet the majority expected the new national puppet government to end in failure, and because neither the Japanese nor the Chinese were strong enough to win on their own, they thought the war would continue until either the USSR or the United States intervened militarily. Major Barrett was one Western official, however, who warned that without greater foreign intervention, whether economic or military, the stalemate would continue for some time and eventually end in an undeclared peace. In time, events almost proved him correct. Had the Japanese adapted themselves to promote greater trade, occupied China might have been pacified more easily, making some semblance of victory possible.[38]

The new national puppet government was inaugurated on 30 March 1940 in Nanking. Although Tokyo withheld formal diplomatic recognition while the Kiri Project continued its work, the move was diplomatically provocative, and it increased the strain on international Far Eastern relations. The presence of the Japanese Combined Fleet under Admiral Yamamoto Isoroku at Amoy for four days from 30 March to 2 April was a limited but contributing factor to this strain. The Japanese fleet included seven battleships, four carriers (*Akagi, Soryu, Hiryu,* and *Ryujo*), five cruisers, and approximately eight destroyer flotillas (twenty-seven destroyers), plus submarines and numerous ancillary vessels. The presence of such an intimidating naval force was meant to demonstrate Japanese support for the new government. Two weeks later, Admiral Takasu and the emperor's naval aide-de-camp met with Wang Ching Wei during their visit to Canton.[39] Since the Chinese central government lacked any substantial naval forces of its own, the deployment signaled a challenge to foreign powers, particularly the United States, to stay out of Chinese affairs. A $20 million American loan to China had been approved on 7 March 1940, and this display of force was a powerful response. The Americans returned the gesture by holding a Pacific fleet exercise near Hawaii during May, and upon its conclusion, they retained the fleet at Pearl Harbor—a permanent redeployment from its former base in California. Along with other factors, this gunboat diplomacy encouraged the Japanese navy to begin planning a preemptive strike on the U.S. fleet the following year.[40]

As added leverage in forcing the Chinese central government to come to terms, the Japanese began the most serious air assault of the war, with Chungking as the target. Operation 101 was a high-altitude terror-bombing campaign instigated by General Itagaki; his aim was to weaken Chinese morale by deepening the country's sense of isolation. Chungking was bombarded with great frequency from May to November 1940 in the hope of breaking popular support for the war, and one mission alone accounted for more than 10,000 deaths.[41] Conducted primarily by Japanese naval wings 13 and 15, the initial missions consisted of approximately 27 aircraft; these grew to include more than 100 aircraft, but tactics varied, so multiple smaller missions were also carried out on some days. Incendiaries were used, beginning with the 190-plane raid on the night of 19–20 August. Overall, in purely arithmetic terms, the Japanese exchanged one ton of bombs for every Chinese killed. In addition to bombs, they dropped leaflets comparing death in Chungking to peace in occupied China. The Japanese expended great effort in this campaign, including the employment of women as part of their aircrews. At the end of June, a dead female radio operator was found in the wreckage of a bomber brought down by antiaircraft fire near Chungking. Weak Chinese air units defended the capital until September and were able to shoot down about one or two aircraft per mission, but after the arrival of the new Japanese Zero, Chinese fighters were driven from the sky, and with the exception of a few antiaircraft guns, the city was left virtually unprotected.[42]

The bombing of Chungking did have a negative impact on Chinese morale, but it also damaged relations with other powers. Hankow served as the initial base of operations until the Japanese occupation of Ichang in mid-June, and more than 200 heavy bombers were based there. Being 500 miles from Chungking, Hankow's utility lay in its geographic position, but it was also situated 650 miles from Hong Kong, and this threat was noted by British officers. The results in Chungking made the potential for future damage to Hong Kong painfully obvious. However, there were more than enough immediate problems to tackle, without looking ahead. The wounding of British nationals and attacks on British-owned property were added to the growing list of grievances compiled by the ambassador, and numerous protests were delivered in Tokyo. Damage to foreign embassies was also a recurring problem; the Soviet embassy was bombarded on 11 June 1940, and the British and French were similarly hit on 24 June. German diplomats received the same treatment on 13 September. Yet the Japanese were not greatly worried about the diplomatic fallout from these attacks, and the bombing achieved some desired results. By October, public sentiment had grown for Chiang to come to terms with Japan. Public morale became such a concern that Chiang told Colonel Chennault that he might be compelled to accept Japanese peace terms because he had no way left to defend the public against aerial bombardment.[43]

The fall of France created greater logistical problems for China, but Chiang would eventually have reason to be encouraged by political and military developments in Japan. With Anglo-French forces defeated first in Norway and then in France, Japanese hard-liners were quick to seize control of the government and embrace a southern strategic military agenda. The more moderate triumvirate of Admiral Yonai Mitsumasa, Admiral Yamamoto Isoroku, and Admiral Inoue Shigeyoshi was outmaneuvered, resulting in the collapse of the Yonai cabinet in July 1940. Prince Konoye Fumimaro reemerged as the head of the government, and Matsuoka Yosuke assumed the post of foreign minister to strengthen ties with Germany.[44] Greater British and American intervention was still only a hope among Western officials, but as Japan drew closer to Germany and made preparations to move south, Anglo-American intervention became increasingly possible.

For the time being, however, Britain remained weak, while cracks in the empire grew wide. The power vacuum created in East Asia following the collapse of the French greatly added to British troubles by emboldening the Japanese, but Tokyo's second cabinet crisis of the year brought internal conflicts on strategy into public view. Although a southern advance had been selected as the basis of a Japanese grand strategy, divisions between the military services and within the government persisted. This encouraged some field commanders to take reckless action, as was soon witnessed in Indochina. Meanwhile, Japanese aggression in the air over Chungking and elsewhere intensified, placing a greater strain on Anglo-Japanese relations. Amidst these problems, the Chinese continued to participate in high-level peace negotiations with the hope of gaining greater international support. The British would use similar diplomatic tactics in Europe to accomplish the same goal vis-à-vis the United States and the USSR, and during the summer, the Japanese helped push them in that direction. Given the fundamental divergence of interests and the mutual antipathy engendered by Britain's cooperation with China and Japan's sympathy with Germany, a frontal Anglo-Japanese clash was becoming increasingly likely. Ending the war in China as quickly as possible remained a Japanese strategic goal, and doing so required that the movement of Chinese military supplies be stopped at the source. Hence, encouraged by Britain's strategic situation, the capture of Hong Kong became a primary Japanese military objective, a fact well understood by British officers in Hong Kong.[45]

Hong Kong: The Fulcrum of War

From 1937, the Foreign Office utilized the war in China to improve Anglo-Soviet relations, but like Japan, the country's Far Eastern policy lacked uniformity, as the War Office continued to view Hong Kong as a dangerous liability. Few resources could be spared for Far Eastern interests, and the colony's defenses remained weak.[46] But following the signing of the Nazi-Soviet Pact, the British Foreign Office started to adapt its position to better reflect existing military limitations. U.S. concern over Far Eastern affairs also became more pronounced in an evolutionary process that greatly accelerated after Roosevelt's reelection in November 1940. Substantial material support for Britain would eventually increase, at considerable cost, but until that time, Britain alone shouldered much of the responsibility for challenging Japanese expansion in Asia. During the summer of 1940, however, the Chinese and Americans grew more anxious about Britain's stamina and its ability to continue to resist. One means of determining British resolve was to assess the posture they maintained at their hazardous base at Hong Kong. At a time of great peril, Hong Kong was not demilitarized, and it started to become more of a Far Eastern nexus, drawing the attention of all the great powers. Although still officially regarded as an expendable outpost of Singapore, it remained a military center of global significance so long as the war in China continued and the number of avenues into the country diminished.

Following the invasion of Kwangsi and the Japanese declaration of the Greater East Asia Co-Prosperity Sphere in November 1939, the prospect of war between Britain and Japan had increased. Until then, the Far East had been considered an area of only tertiary priority in British grand strategy. Hong Kong was a dangerous military outpost because it was encumbered with diplomatic and military commitments disproportionate to its physical defenses. Although the British temporarily eased tensions with the Japanese following the withdrawal of French and British garrisons at Tientsin in November 1939 and the resolution of the Tientsin silver problem in

April 1940, the fall of France and Italy's entry into the war greatly damaged Britain's global military position. With the loss of the French fleet, the British concentrated more of their resources on protecting their lines of communication in the North Atlantic while contesting the Mediterranean Sea, but this left little for Far Eastern defense.[47] The Singapore strategy was no longer feasible, and there was no prospect of reinforcing Hong Kong, even though the British fully realized that it was likely to be the first point of attack by the Japanese. This problem was noted in a Chiefs of Staff Far Eastern appraisal dated 13 August 1940: "In view of the traditional Japanese method of step by step advance it is thought that her first action would be on our garrisons in China including attacks on or at least blockade of Hong-Kong, all without declaration of war."[48] Despite the threat, Hong Kong would not be demilitarized, partly because of the adverse impact this would have on British prestige. Cabinet records on this decision have often been quoted elsewhere.[49] The Chiefs of Staff noted, "In the event of war, Hong Kong must be regarded as an outpost and held as long as possible. We should resist the inevitably strong pressure to reinforce Hong Kong, and we should certainly be unable to relieve it. Militarily, our position in the Far East would be stronger without this unsatisfactory commitment."[50] The military services were aware of their deficiencies in the Far East, but tragically, Prime Minster Churchill maintained an exaggerated view of Singapore's strength as a fortress. Furthermore, as Peter Lowe has noted, Churchill's "single-minded concentration on Europe and the Middle East" meant that the Japanese threat was not fully appreciated at the highest level of government.[51]

As Britain's global situation deteriorated, the prospect of U.S. collaboration against the dictatorships began to grow, and Hong Kong became a yardstick whereby the Americans and the Chinese could measure British reliability in challenging the Japanese. The British were not inclined to accept a formal alliance with China at this stage, but they were also unwilling to abandon their Asian interests altogether. So long as Hong Kong was not demilitarized, the British signaled their willingness to fight Japan, if they must. Since the Americans also wanted the war in China to continue, a firm British posture at Hong Kong was useful in encouraging greater U.S. involvement in the war. The prospect of U.S. participation helped buoy Chinese morale after earlier British retreats, such as at Tientsin, had made the likelihood of Western support seem remote.[52] The Chinese remained concerned that British weakness might lead to an agreement with the Japanese at Chinese expense, but maintenance of a garrison at Hong Kong precluded the possibility of complete abandonment.

Unlike the Chinese, some U.S. military officers were not too concerned about British intentions in China; however, they were less than optimistic about the ability of the Hong Kong garrison to hold against a determined Japanese ground attack. In the Philippines, Lieutenant Colonel Henry C. McLean of U.S. military intelligence submitted a report on this topic in June 1940:

Three redoubts, or fortified points, have been fortified at Sleepers Knoll, Unicorn Ridge and Smugglers Ridge. The chief of staff stated that the garrisons of these were only 1 company each which seems incredible. These had been estimated as at least a battalion. Although this is a very strong position, it is believed this could be taken by a night assault because of its being so thinly held. All the ground to the north has been carefully plotted so that the guns on Hong Kong Island could search that area. It is believed, that the artillery is insufficient to be critically effective.

The British expect to be forced off that line and to retire to the south across the channel known as Victoria Harbor, there to defend the island of Hong Kong to the last. No heavy guns with permanent emplacements are in Leased Territory, as they would expect to lose them all. Guns of all calibers are in position on Hong Kong Island. The British will run the risk of having very heavy losses in crossing Victoria Harbor. . . .

Large sums of money have been lavished on the defense of Hong Kong. It is believed this will prove futile because of the insufficiency of troops to hold the line north of Beacon Hill and to properly garrison the Island of Hong Kong and to eject by counter attack [sic] any landing parties which might get a footing on the island. . . .

The British are prepared to sacrifice by destruction the splendid city of Hong Kong rather than let it fall into Japanese hands. . . .

If the Japanese make a determined attack on Hong Kong in sufficient strength it can not [sic] last over two months.[53]

Some British officers also expressed anxiety. In May 1940 Major Giles commented on Japanese perceptions: "The Japanese have a low opinion of the British Army as a fighting force. They are fully aware of their own inherent advantages in having local naval and complete air superiority, and do not consider that the reduction of Hong Kong presents a particularly difficult military problem."[54] Hong Kong was not strongly held, but McLean added some positive comments regarding the military leadership:

General Grassett is the general officer commanding in Hong Kong. He is a very able officer, much respected in the British army and formerly Operation Officer for the Indian Army at Delhi.

Colonel Neville is chief of staff in Hong Kong; is also a very able officer. Just before his appointment in Hong Kong was Secretary of the Imperial General Staff in London.

All of the above information was obtained from General Grassett and Colonel Neville and from the War Plan which the writer was permitted to see; as well as inspection of the defenses.[55]

Grasett was undoubtedly eager to challenge the Japanese, but in mid-1941 he would gamble the security of Hong Kong to do so.[56] In the interim, American and Chinese concerns about Britain became more pronounced as the year progressed.

During subsequent Anglo-American strategic planning meetings, U.S. officers, attempting to ascertain Britain's ability to wage war in the Far East, asked their British counterparts how long Hong Kong could hold if attacked. The new Dominions secretary, Lord Cranborne, informed the Canadian government of the British response:

The United States representatives addressed a series of questions to the Chiefs of Staff. With regard to the Far East they enquired regarding the strength of Hong Kong and were told the fortress should be able to resist a siege for a considerable time. They were emphatically assured, in response to another question, that it is very much in our interests that the United States main fleet should remain in the Pacific.[57]

Naval issues aside, American and Chinese anxieties were not eased by the long-delayed British refusal (in July) of Chiang Kai Shek's offer of 200,000 troops for the defense of Hong Kong.[58]

Because of the fall of France, Japanese belligerence directed against Britain greatly increased during the spring and summer of 1940, as they attempted to terminate external support for China while expanding territorially. British grand strategy was in disarray once the French army had been defeated and Britain faced both Germany and Italy with only the Dominions as allies.[59] But Britain refused to demilitarize Hong Kong, hoping to maintain Chinese resistance and thereby encourage greater American involvement in international affairs. In this, the British were successful. The Japanese, in turn, made Burma, Hong Kong, and French Indochina the immediate objects of their attention.

The Burmese Gambit

One of the most difficult tests of British endurance in China came during June and July 1940, when the Japanese demanded that the Burma Road be closed and that military supply shipments from Hong Kong be terminated. Until late 1939, many in Whitehall believed that the war in China was a useful way to minimize the threat to British Far Eastern interests elsewhere. For some, especially those in the Foreign Office, the hope was that common cause with Stalin against Japan would lead to improved Anglo-Soviet relations in general. Out of a sense of desperation, however, the British temporarily became willing to adjust to the global military situation. To avoid war with Japan, the British closed the Burma Road, but in doing so, the potential for a Sino-Japanese peace was exploited, with the aim of ending Britain's isolation. In this, the British were only half successful: American support against both Germany and Japan expanded, but Stalin remained Hitler's ally. Nevertheless, American support was sufficient to maintain Britain's war effort, and the war in China would be used to expand U.S. commitment further over time. This was facilitated by reopening the Burma Road in October 1940, but during the intervening period, the British were able to hedge their bets, despite Japanese intimidation, by maintaining the covert movement of Chinese supplies from their vulnerable position at Hong Kong.[60] In this way, China remained a useful lever that could be equally applied against both the Soviet Union and the United States.

The Japanese demanded the termination of British support for China, under the threat of war, starting with the fall of France. Munitions had not been allowed into China from Hong Kong since January 1939, but the Japanese regarded POL and spare parts as contraband and therefore included these military supplies in their new demands. French restrictions on the Indochina railway were already being implemented, and as Japanese troops again deployed along Hong Kong's border, the British agreed to close the Burma Road for a three-month period starting on 18 July 1940. Ambassador Sir Robert Craigie negotiated the agreement in Tokyo and was in favor of the move because he understood Britain's military situation and because he thought the Burma Road served Chinese interests ahead of Great Britain's. He also advocated a rapprochement with Tokyo at this time, noting that the Americans were not yet willing to carry the diplomatic or the military load in the Far East and that it would be possible to encourage a peace accord for China. Sino-British relations could be repaired at a later date. Additionally, Japanese attention would be redirected against the Soviet Union.[61] By the first week of July, the War Cabinet and the chief of the Imperial General Staff, Sir John Dill, agreed with Craigie's recommendation to make concessions to the Japanese; they thought the situation in Europe was too dangerous to risk open war with Japan. Craigie's advice was accepted in this instance, but even though the Burma Road was closed and the British garrison at Shanghai was withdrawn three weeks later in August, the placement of Japanese inspectors in Hong Kong was refused. Despite these retreats, the Chinese were not abandoned completely; POL and other essential supplies were allowed to move into China surreptitiously from Hong Kong, just as before.[62]

To weaken Chinese morale and bring about a collapse of Chiang's government, the Japanese also redoubled their military efforts. The closure of the road was a serious blow to the Chinese, as aviation fuel and spare parts were urgently needed to defend Chungking not only from aerial bombardment but also from a ground offensive being fought in Henan. Some foreign observers thought a Chinese collapse was possible, given the increased pressure on Chiang after General Itagaki launched his attack in May 1940, with Ichang as his primary objective. Ichang was situated farther west along the Yangtse River, and it controlled the water transportation system of Szechwan. The Japanese 13th Division captured the city on 11 June after a twelve-day advance that involved very heavy fighting and many casualties on both sides. After the fall of Ichang, the Japanese offensive was expected to continue against Chungking, in combination with moves against Kwangsi, Yunnan, and Shensi to finish the war. In preparation, General Chen Cheng was appointed in August to command the newly created 6th War Zone, covering the approach to Chungking; however, any Japanese offensive against the capital would have been extremely difficult owing to the vulnerability of Japanese lines of communication to Chinese flank attacks.[63] Because of these factors, Itagaki limited his advance to Ichang, but as the city was only 240 miles from Chungking, its fall made the Japanese aerial campaign much more efficient; the newly acquired air bases substantially reduced flight time. The loss of Ichang also greatly complicated the Chinese logistical situation by disrupting the movement of military supplies between the railroad at Changsha and Szechwan. The defeat at Ichang, along with the failed winter offensive, the closure of the Burma Road, and an inflationary economy, had a very negative impact on the Chinese will to continue the war.[64]

Running perpendicular to Japanese military efforts was the Kiri Project, which seemed to be having a degree of success. Chiang Kai Shek and General Itagaki were scheduled to meet in Changsha in August to elevate discussions, but this was called off when the existence of the peace talks was leaked to the public. It is possible that Chiang was merely playing for time, hoping to delay Japanese recognition of the Wang Ching Wei government, but the peace faction within the Kuomintang was not inconsequential and could not be entirely dismissed. Chiang himself was determined to fight, but the potential for Chinese capitulation increased after the Burma Road was closed.[65]

In Britain, morale was also low; concern in Washington over a potential British collapse soon resulted in greater American intervention. One of Churchill's first priorities following his assumption of power in May 1940 was to develop his personal relationship with the U.S. president, but by closing the Burma Road, he was also able to leverage Britain's Far Eastern policy against the Roosevelt administration. By doing so, Churchill effectively employed one of the few methods available to increase American opposition against both Germany and Japan. Keeping China in the war was essential to American plans, but because of the upcoming election, Roosevelt was wary of increasing U.S. involvement in the Far East too quickly.[66] The U.S. government's public criticism of the British decision to close the Burma Road therefore did not accurately reflect private foreknowledge and approval, and the hypocrisy of American complaints about the closure was noted by many, including officials in Hong Kong. Some in Whitehall, such as historian George Sansom at the Foreign Office, hoped that economic sanctions would soon be leveled against Japan, fully realizing that such a course of action would eventually lead to war. The July 1940 embargo on aviation fuel and scrap iron instigated by Treasury Secretary

Henry Morgenthau (in Secretary of State Cordell Hull's absence) was one of the first steps in this direction.[67] Across the Atlantic, many U.S. military officers already considered Britain a de facto ally, and secret Anglo-American staff talks were held in August 1940 to formulate a joint grand strategy. These talks centered on the "Rainbow 5" plan, which was the basis of the Germany-first strategy employed when the United States entered the war. A full transition to American leadership in China would have to await the arrival of the U.S. Military Mission in August 1941, under the command of Brigadier General John Magruder. His mission's task was to supervise the distribution of Lend-Lease material.[68] But the initial moves in 1940 formed the basis for subsequent U.S. intervention, and they were sufficient to keep Britain fighting.

Equally if not more significant, the British decision on Burma was meant to pressure Stalin. By June 1940, British strategy in East Asia had started to assume a degree of uniformity, as both the War Office and the Foreign Office sought to limit commitment in China. Until August 1939, the Foreign Office had attempted to build a collective security arrangement with Stalin to encourage Soviet collaboration against Hitler. But with the signing of the Nazi-Soviet Pact, Stalin became Hitler's loyal, if junior, ally.[69] The war in China had been supported from Hong Kong with the goal of providing indirect protection to the Soviets' Far Eastern flank. Once the Hitler-Stalin pact was signed, British foreign policy underwent a gradual reversal. Anglo-Soviet relations were greatly strained as Stalin supplied Hitler with considerable amounts of strategic resources and joined his ally in attacking neighboring states. The extermination of Polish officers in the Katyn Forest mimicked the war of annihilation being waged against the Russian people by the NKVD. The invasion of eastern Poland, along with the Winter War in Finland, caused widespread resentment, prompting the British government to condemn Soviet actions at the League of Nations and to belatedly approve the release of more than 100 aircraft for the Finnish air force. Stalin's friendship with Hitler caused some cabinet and military officials in London to consider the Soviets and the Nazis enemies of equal standing.[70] Few options were available to confront the Berlin-Moscow axis, but when the British closed the Burma Road, Chinese morale was pushed to the breaking point. Had peace been secured, the possibility of a Japanese attack into Siberia would have greatly increased. Stalin needed to sustain the war in China, and he wanted British cooperation to achieve this goal.[71] Stalin had reason for concern because there were many dangers confronting him, and the British were able to play on his fears.

Naturally, Stalin was anxious to reduce his reliance on British cooperation, and this was gradually accomplished by improving Soviet-Japanese relations. The possibility of such a development was reported from Hong Kong as early as January 1940:

The poor showing of the Red Forces in Finland must not be taken entirely at its face value, since the Russian armies are neither trained nor equipped for fighting in such difficult country in arctic conditions. They put up a very different performance against the best Japanese troops in the spring and summer of last year at Nomonhan. But it is nevertheless fairly certain that Stalin cannot fight a war on two fronts; and if his present Finnish or future Balkan adventures are going to involve him as an active participant in the European war, the present slight possibility of an agreement with Japan at China's expense will become a strong probability.[72]

Ambassador Craigie reported Tokyo's view of Anglo-Soviet relations, which supported this analysis. Japanese press reports emphasized that the war in China was more important for Soviet security than it was for the British, and they noted that diplomatic efforts should be directed toward Moscow rather than London. Translations were sent to London: "Russia regards continuation of Chungking's resistance as in her defence interests and is absolutely opposed [to] any weakening of that resistance. Molotov said to have stated if England abandons support of Chungking, Russia will continue supplies. . . . Russia thus holds key to solution since though England may desire amicable settlement with Japan, she is also most anxious for improved relations with Russia."[73] German success in France, however, complicated Stalin's position, as he had counted on a war of long duration.

London officials were also considering German peace proposals at this time, and Stalin's anxiety grew accordingly. Unencumbered with war in the west, Hitler could easily turn his attention east, so when the possibility of an Anglo-German peace emerged, the British closed the Burma Road in the hope that Stalin could be restrained. For his part, Stalin very much wanted a southward Japanese strategic advance, but he remained cautious about pushing Britain into making a deal with Germany. This partly accounts for the delays that occurred during the Soviet-Japanese neutrality talks. Although privately antagonistic to the USSR, the Japanese were eager to exploit Britain's weakness by carrying on discussions with the Soviets. But Stalin was also aware that the new Japanese cabinet was more aggressive than its predecessor, and some members, such as Army Minister Tojo Hideki, had not dismissed the idea of challenging Soviet power.[74] Amidst these many variables, China remained one of the few areas where the British could still apply pressure on Moscow.

Despite the impending British retreat over Burma, the need to keep up the appearance of Anglo-Soviet cooperation was deemed vital in London, even though it no longer had any basis in reality. One Foreign Office official commented: "Our position in the Far East is admittedly insecure, but the insecurity will be increased once the Japanese are sure that we have nothing in common with either the USSR or the USA."[75] Four days after the road was closed, J. W. R. Maclean clarified the new policy in China:

Nothing that we say to the Soviet Government is likely to have the slightest effect on their policy in the Far East. Nor do I see that we should in any way help matters in Moscow by raising the question of the Far East. In point of fact there is no real community of interests between ourselves and the Russians in this region. As I understand it, our policy at this moment is to promote a reasonable settlement of the "China incident" and to find a satisfactory basis for our own relations with Japan. The Soviet Government on the other hand are undoubtedly anxious to keep the war going between China and Japan for as long as possible, and, if an opportunity offers, to make trouble between ourselves and the Japanese. Clearly then, the Far Eastern problem offers no real basis for Anglo-Soviet co-operation, and it would be likely to do more harm than good if we were to raise it in our conversations with the Soviet Government.[76]

Out of growing concern, the Americans entered the fray. Secretary of State Cordell Hull proposed that the British seek greater Soviet assistance in pressuring the Japanese, but the British were not interested.[77]

The British were not inclined to trust Soviet intentions unless Stalin was prepared to alter his position with Hitler. This view was expressed by Sir John Sterndale Bennett on 20 July 1940: "It has been suggested that we should make an attempt to work in more closely with Russia over the Far Eastern problem. The advantages of this course from the point of view of our general relations with Russia requires further discussion. From the purely Far Eastern point of view it is difficult to see what we are likely to gain by such a course."[78] Ambassador Ivan Maisky in London attempted to deal with the problem on 16 July by approaching Parliamentary Undersecretary of State for Foreign Affairs R. A. Butler. He expressed his government's great concern about British efforts to secure peace between the Chinese and the Japanese, but Butler was evasive, simply informing Maisky that the British government had no concrete proposals to achieve this goal. Maisky then sought to restore British support for the Chinese by suggesting that a £7 million loan be extended to China, along with an additional £8 million from the Americans. Butler duly passed on this request, with no result.[79] The British had become amenable to the idea of easing their Far Eastern problem at Stalin's expense, and attempts at cooperation with the Soviet Union were finally terminated with the closure of the Burma Road.

Unsurprisingly, British opinion on challenging the Soviets was not universal. Several significant individuals in the House of Commons, such as Labour's Sir Stafford Cripps, as well as Foreign Office officials, such as Ambassador Clark Kerr, were still determined to be supportive of Soviet actions, despite Stalin's alliance with Hitler.[80] Cripps was enthusiastically pro-Soviet and had written articles in defense of Stalin's invasions of Poland and Finland.[81] But unlike Sir Oswald Mosley and other British fascists who were imprisoned for their political activity, Cripps was selected to be the new ambassador to Moscow on 20 May 1940. He was given the job because of his communist credentials, and his objective was to weaken German-Soviet relations. To help accomplish his mission, Cripps was instructed to inform his Soviet colleagues that the British government would recognize Stalin's mid-June seizure of the Baltic states.[82] He also informed Molotov and others in October and November 1940 that the British cabinet was deliberating on Hitler's peace proposals, which, if accepted, would obviously encourage a German invasion of the Soviet Union.[83] But in his limited number of meetings with Soviet officials during the year, Cripps achieved few tangible results. He was not well received at the Kremlin, where it was thought that his influence with the cabinet and the Foreign Office was limited. Cripps failed not because of a lack of personal effort but simply because Britain had little to offer.[84]

In the future, after the tide of war had turned, Cripps's successor would be Ambassador Archibald Clark Kerr, who would have much greater success in gaining Stalin's favor. By that time (1942), Britain and the Soviet Union were allies, so his job was easier, but his own ideological outlook certainly aided him in his work. His views were known to many Western officials inside China, and Cripps himself commented on them during his stopover in Chungking on his first trip to Moscow in February 1940. According to Cripps's biographer, Peter Clarke, "Cripps heartily approved of the British ambassador, Archibald Clark Kerr, who was 'most advanced in his views & very sympathetic with the Communists.'"[85] On 1 March 1941 Lieutenant Colonel David Barrett (promoted in October 1940) also commented on Clark Kerr:

A noteworthy aspect of the present relations between the National Government and the Communists is the apparent indifference with which the representatives of the Soviet Government here appear to contemplate the alleged grievances of the Communists. The Soviet Ambassador stated not long ago to a member of this Embassy that his Government had no intention of interfering in the internal affairs of China particularly as far as relations with the Communists were concerned.

The Chungking representatives of the British Government, however, appear definitely in sympathy with the Communists. Communist sources claim that the British Ambassador has on several occasions exerted pressure on the Chinese Government to refrain from oppressing the Communists. Whether this is true or not, the British Ambassador has on several occasions told the writer that he considered the National Government unduly alarmed over the ability of the Communists to threaten the present set-up in China, and he hoped that the Kuomintang would not attack the Communists until the war with Japan had been won.

The Press Attaché of the British Embassy, Mr. James Bertram, is frankly in sympathy with the Communists, and appears to use every possible opportunity to further their interests.[86]

Evidence of this can be seen in Clark Kerr's opposition to London's tungsten embargo against the Soviet Union.

The British tried to apply pressure on the USSR by using the Burma Road and Hong Kong as choke points against the flow of strategic materials leaving China. But meddling with Sino-Soviet relations in this way produced marginal results. Sino-Soviet barter agreements called for Soviet military hardware and pilots to be exchanged for tungsten and other strategic resources at a financial ratio of ten to one, favoring the Chinese.[87] Stalin's alliance with Hitler ensured that many Chinese resources arriving in the USSR were actually sent to Germany to be made into munitions for use against British troops. By January 1940, Soviet vessels plying Pacific waters caught the attention of British officials, and those entering Rangoon and Hong Kong, such as the *Salenga* and the *Vladimir Mayakovsky*, were temporarily detained while export controls on Chinese tungsten bound for the USSR were considered.[88] This situation continued throughout 1940, and after the fall of Ichang, it became quite difficult to transport tungsten overland from Hunan and Kiangsi north into the Soviet Union. After May 1940, the French also embargoed the transportation of these materials through Indochina, leaving the British in control of the sole remaining lines of communication through Hong Kong and Burma. Curtailment of Chinese exports to the USSR was maintained until the German invasion in June 1941. Until that time, Clark Kerr's persistent appeals to the Foreign Office to help the Chinese meet their commitments to Stalin failed to significantly alter the British position.[89]

Faced with the prospect of supporting the Chinese on their own, the Soviets redoubled their military efforts to keep the war from ending. During August 1940, the Chinese communists launched the One Hundred Regiments Campaign in north China, in support of the central government forces fighting around Ichang. This was the only major offensive the communists conducted during the war, and it was carried out because morale in Chungking had deteriorated to such a low level that the idea of a peace settlement became too attractive to ignore. As Soviet influence became stronger in Chungking, Chiang and others also grew increasingly anxious about their growing dependence on Stalin.[90] They also became more critical of the lack of support from the West.

In the end, closing the Burma Road had little influence on Stalin, but the British were able to somewhat restrict the movement of strategic materials to Germany via Vladivostok. The closure did, however, help increase American involvement in global affairs as a British partner. This provided sufficient encouragement for the British to continue the war in Europe, but at the expense of the empire's Far Eastern defenses and the security of such allies as Australia and New Zealand. Lacking adequate military strength in Asia, Britain remained greatly exposed at Hong Kong, and the Japanese started preparing for war with the Western powers. Planning began for an attack on Hong Kong, but first, the Japanese seized the opportunity presented by the capitulation of France and invaded northern Indochina.[91]

Taking the Plunge:
The Invasion of Northern French Indochina

With Japanese officers now planning for war with the United States and Great Britain, the fall of France provided a rare chance to expand south territorially and simultaneously eliminate a significant line of supply into China. Greatly encouraged by German success in Europe, the Japanese hoped to move against the French before an Anglo-German peace could be negotiated. The occupation of northern Indochina began on 22 September 1940 as the first major step in Japan's southern strategic advance, yet once again, lack of discipline at high levels antagonized the Western powers and escalated diplomatic tensions.[92] The Japanese decision to join the Axis Pact compounded the effect. Fortunately for the French, their colony at Fort Bayard—otherwise known as Kwangchowan (Guangzhouwan)—near Pakhoi, was left relatively unmolested due to its limited logistical capacity. In contrast, Hong Kong grew more significant as a Chinese source of military supply while becoming an increasingly dangerous Far Eastern flash point.

Facing catastrophic problems in Europe, the French lacked military strength in Indochina, and the Japanese did not require a large army to occupy the northern half of the region. Heading the colonial government was Vice Admiral Jean Decoux, who had commanded French naval forces in the Far East until replacing the anti-Vichy Georges Catroux as governor-general on 24 July 1940. His available ground forces consisted of twenty-four battalions of the Tonkin Division, five battalions of the Annam Brigade, and sixteen battalions of the Cochin-China and Cambodian Division. European troops numbered 12,000 out of the total 120,000 dispersed throughout the colony. French AFVs were negligible, amounting to twenty-four medium Renault 1918 tanks, of which only two were operable; airpower was also minimal at eighty-two aircraft, but at least twenty-five of these were modern Morane 406 fighters. More positively, gun batteries at Doson and at Camranh Bay were considered strong. Against these forces, elements of the six divisions constituting the Japanese South China Expeditionary Force under General Ando Rikichi were available for operations, and those involved prominently included the 5th Division and Formosans from Kwangsi under Lieutenant General Nakamura Aketo, along with part of the 104th Division in Canton. Other units employed were drawn from north China, including elements of the 26th and 110th Divisions.[93] All of these were supported by the 2nd China Expeditionary Fleet (replacing the 5th Fleet in late 1939) under the command of Admiral Takasu.

Agreements negotiated with French officials during the summer of 1940 allowed Japanese inspection of the embargo as a preliminary step to an unopposed Japanese occupation, but as with many best-laid plans, problems soon developed. Despite these agreements, arranged in large part by General Nishihara Issaku, head of the Japanese inspection unit in Hanoi, other Japanese officers created needless embarrassment for both the Konoye government and the army as soon as the invasion began. Insubordination was exposed as a serious problem in General Ando's command during the 22–25 September battle of Langson near the Kwangsi-Indochina border. General Nakamura and officers of the 5th Division were most eager to fight the French, and they ignored orders not to initiate combat during their advance from Kwangsi. In violation of the occupation agreement, the French battalion at Dong Dang was attacked, and about thirty of all ranks were killed. Among the dead was the battalion commander, Lieutenant Colonel Louvet. Nakamura achieved nothing with his dishonorable conduct except to damage his government's relations with third powers, the most important of these being the United States.[94]

Hoping to receive assistance during the crisis, the French appealed, unsuccessfully, to the Americans for aircraft. There had been some reason for optimism, since Roosevelt had threatened in August to tighten the economic embargo against Japan in order to deter any aggressive action directed southward against the Netherlands East Indies; however, no support was extended to Hanoi due to political concerns over the government's reliability.[95] Fighting was brought to a close by a diplomatic agreement reached within a few days, but the manner in which this transpired was as odious to foreign officials as the attack itself. British officers in Hong Kong paid close attention to events in Indochina for several good reasons and described the affair to London (partly to encourage additional support for the Dutch): "Under the most miserable conditions, the Governor-General, Vice-Admiral Decoux, decorated Major-General Nishihara, the outgoing head of the Japanese Military Inspectorate, with the Order of the Dragon of Annam. Senior Japanese and French officers also banqueted daily in Hanoi, whilst French prisoners and wounded were rotting in the sun at Langson."[96] Although the French were not held prisoner for long, the British could see how Langson might serve as a discouraging premonition of events at Hong Kong.

Nakamura's actions reflected the confusion among Japanese strategic planners amidst the scramble to determine how best to react to the pace of European events while the war in China was still unresolved.[97] The navy and army were at odds over the tempo of challenging the Western powers directly, and Nakamura demonstrated the lingering persistence of disunity within the army itself. To remedy this, he and the senior commanders of the South China Expeditionary Force were disciplined for their conduct, as Army Minister Tojo Hideki reasserted Tokyo's control.[98] General Ando shouldered much of the blame for the affair, as Nakamura's attack was ultimately his responsibility. Owing to his overall rise in frustration, Ando himself also became more aggressive and reckless. At one point, he sought additional forces to make a difficult attack into Yunnan in conjunction with the occupation of northern Indochina. Some foreign nationals living in Kwangtung suspected that during a previous trip to Tokyo, Ando had pressed hard for the closure of the Burma Road as well as the invasion of French Indochina.[99] Observing events, U.S. Army Captain F. P. Munson laid the blame for the affair squarely at Ando's feet:

The fact that General Nishihara's agent failed in his mission is not surprising and shows all the more clearly the lack of unity in the present Japanese chain of command. That General Nishihara represented the Tokyo government made little or no difference to General Ando, who probably had his own plan to invade Yunnan via Tongking and thought by committing his forces to action he would force the Tokyo government to recognize his course. It is also possible that the news of the signing of the agreement had not reached the commander at Lungchow, but in that case it would seem the messenger would be authorized to explain this to the Japanese commander, and when the fighting continued it showed too clearly that General Ando either did not like the terms of the agreement or had made up his mind to ignore it anyway.[100]

After being summoned by the emperor, Ando was held responsible for the actions of the 5th Division and was replaced by Lieutenant General Ushiroku Jun; Nakamura was sacked to make room for Major General

Nishimura Takuma.[101] The South China Expeditionary Force was later redesignated as the Japanese 23rd Army in 1941.

Just as disconcerting as the absorption of northern Indochina was the announcement on 27 September 1940 that Japan had joined the Axis. But again, this move was counterproductive. The Japanese signed the pact to end their diplomatic isolation and to forestall any possibility of an Anglo-German compromise peace. The Japanese also hoped to deter the British from reopening the Burma Road and to stave off further economic sanctions by the Americans.[102] It produced the opposite effect.

The Americans reacted to the German-Japanese alliance in a variety of ways, the net result being to encourage the British by providing increased support. First the Americans tightened the fuel and scrap-iron embargo against Japan; then, in October, all U.S. nationals in China were ordered to evacuate. The embargo was also tightened in part because the Japanese were buying as much fuel as possible in the United States and then loading it onto German ships in Japan. China received more support when a $100 million loan was approved in November. With American power stirring behind them, the British found the Japanese shift toward Germany to be an excellent excuse to revert to a more confrontational foreign policy. They reopened the Burma Road in October, at the end of the three-month agreement. Victory in the battle of Britain was another factor behind this decision, and although the British military situation was still difficult, the prospects of an Anglo-German peace were correspondingly reduced. With the Americans beginning to assume the leadership role in confronting Japan, the reopening of the road helped make Anglo-American strategy in the Far East more uniform while strengthening their bilateral relations. Britain's goal from this point forward was the formation of a defense alliance among the United States, the Netherlands East Indies, and itself.[103] Previously, the Burma Road had served as a means of pressuring Stalin, but in the end, the British found it to be more effective in swaying their new potential senior ally. U.S. intervention in the global crisis started to gain momentum, and after Roosevelt's reelection in November, it greatly accelerated.

By November 1940, events also produced a positive impact on Chinese morale. But even though the war was escalating into a larger conflict with greater American involvement, the limit of Chinese endurance remained difficult to determine.[104] Hong Kong intelligence officers noted that if

China was to continue as an ally, Anglo-American support would require constant reinforcement:

> The air has been full of peace rumours and there are good grounds for believing that the Japanese are now making a special effort to come to terms with Chiang Kai Shek as well as with Soviet Russia, and for the same reason. On the other hand there is no doubt that the Generalissimo and the majority of those in power at Chungking are resolved to continue the struggle if only they can be sure that the USA and Britain will intervene on China's behalf in the long run. They realise that we can do nothing to help them now; but they also realise that it is impossible for China to expel the Japanese with her own unaided might. Chiang has always fought this war and rejected all previous offers of peace, in the belief that eventually the victorious Democratic Powers would induce Japan—whether by economic pressure or by force—to let go. It is probable that he still retains this belief; but if by any chance he does not, then he may well be tempted to conclude at any rate an armistice with Japan. In this connection a continued display of Anglo-American firmness vis-à-vis Japan will do much to reassure him.[105]

This problem grew more acute as time passed. It became most severe during the invasion of the Soviet Union, when the German offensive was being pushed hard against Moscow in the fall and winter of 1941. Had the Japanese been free to invade Siberia at that time, Allied grand strategy would have fallen apart. It is ironic, then, that along with the departure of Soviet military attaché General Pavel Rybalko on 10 September 1940, military support for China was partly withdrawn by the USSR as a result of Soviet-Japanese neutrality negotiations.[106]

The most significant result of the invasion of French Indochina was the emergence of the United States as the dominant Chinese ally. This eventually translated into considerable increases in American material support, but the costs were steep. Moreover, the damage to the Chinese economy caused by the war only perpetuated the lowering of popular morale. It also increased the level of influence exerted by Washington over Chungking, which in turn had a negative impact on Chinese sovereignty. By way of example, aircraft were desperately needed because the Chinese air force had

been virtually wiped out after the appearance of the Zero, but the procurement costs were tremendous. Expenditures for such items were covered
with gold reserves, which until this time had been sufficient to back approximately 70 percent of all Chinese notes, but inflation became more of
a problem as gold transfers were common and the printing of excess notes
remained high at $150 million (CD) per month.[107] Consul General A. J.
Martin commented on this from Chungking: "A special plane took gold
from Chungking to Hongkong on 1st August, the value being estimated at
about £150,000."[108] Despite growing inflationary pressures, Chiang managed to maintain Chinese resistance largely because of his own prestige
among the people and because of their widespread hatred of the Japanese.
Major Giles illustrated this point for London by quoting a letter written by
an unnamed British traveler. After commenting that the high price of rice
had hit the poorest in Chinese society hardest, the writer noted:

> The Generalissimo stands supreme and penetrates to the furthest re-
> gions. Take, for instance, Ningpo. In Ningpo there is one God, and
> he alone is God—the dollar. That is notorious throughout China. It
> recently cost the 7th Day Adventist Mission more to ship a truck
> from Shanghai to Ningpo at Mr. Yu Ya Ching's rates than it cost to
> ship a similar truck from Shanghai to Rangoon. No good citizen of
> Ningpo would willingly abide the slaughter of such a golden goose.
> After the Japanese withdrawal from Chinhai at the mouth of the
> Ningpo River, it was believed that the renewal of steamer sailings
> from Shanghai could be "arranged"; and so it could, easily, were the
> matter left to local Sino-Japanese interests. But to the horror of the
> Ningpo merchants, Chiang Kai Shek ordered that mines were to be
> laid in the Yung (Ningpo) River and, such is his authority, the order
> was carried out without audible demur.[109]

War is good business, and trade held the potential to bring the conflict
to an end, but Chiang effectively retained control of its direction. Unfortunately for the Chinese government, it was becoming more reliant on Western loans as the war continued to expand.

With growing Western intervention, peace in China became less likely,
at least temporarily, and the Japanese prepared for further offensives. After
the aborted Chiang-Itagaki meeting, the Kiri Project virtually died, and in
November the Japanese recognized the new Chinese national government

under Wang Ching Wei in Nanking. Although the Japanese move negated the possibility of peace in the short term, recognition of the Wang government was a way of managing the war while preparations for a southern advance gathered momentum. The navy minister, Admiral Oikawa Koshiro, former head of Japanese naval forces in China, had already ordered preparatory fleet mobilization measures in September, including the stockpiling of resources as a preliminary step. In the army, a general reorganization in November included the adoption of a triangular divisional system in place of the previous square system. The excess regiments were used to form five new divisions, which augmented Japanese littoral warfare capabilities.[110]

The Japanese also redeployed. Substantial forces briefly remained in French Indochina as a garrison, but the army withdrew from Kwangsi in October, as the need for its occupation had been removed. By December, there were still approximately half a dozen divisions attached to the South China Expeditionary Force, but the 28th and 5th Divisions, having endured prolonged combat in Kwangsi, as well as malaria and dysentery, were withdrawn for rest and reorganization. They were replaced by the 15th and 26th Divisions, which were deployed to Swatow and Hainan, respectively. Only 6,000 Japanese troops remained in northern Indochina by the end of the year.[111]

In the meantime, Japanese efforts to break Chinese resistance were strengthened by exploiting their new strategic position from the air. Burma had become more important for Chinese communications, and Kunming had been turned into a significant air base, so French Indochina airfields were utilized to attack the Burma Road more aggressively than ever before. Japanese facilities included the airfield at Laokay (Lao Cai) near the Yunnan border and other air bases closer to Hanoi, such as the Gia Lam civil airfield; the base at Phulangtong, thirty-three miles northeast of the city; and Phuto, a base situated along the railway. One result of this new air campaign was the bombing of the aircraft assembly factory at Loiwing near the Yunnan-Burmese border on 26 October 1940, causing more than sixty Chinese casualties.[112] Arrogant contempt of Western weakness was expressed by Captain Kamei Chudo of the navy's special mission to Indochina when he stated, "British circles would not have dreamed that Japanese bombers would visit the outskirts of the Himalayas when they decided to reopen the supply route."[113]

The Chinese also redeployed and reorganized. Nanning was reclaimed, and 200,000 Chinese troops were sent to the Yunnan-Indochina border to prevent a Japanese move northwest. Kwangsi had already been reinforced during August with five additional divisions and a regiment of heavy artillery equipped with twenty-seven 150mm German guns (three or four guns per company).[114] A Chinese army leadership struggle in May resulted in major organizational changes. The 7th War Zone was created in Kwangtung by October 1940 under the leadership of General Yu Han Mou. To accomplish this, most of Kwangtung was removed from the control of Chang Fa Kwei in the 4th War Zone. This clarified the reality of the leadership situation in southern China by strengthening Chungking's control.[115]

The invasion of French Indochina was a major step forward on the part of the Japanese toward war with the West, as was joining the Axis Pact.[116] American reaction was swift, and international support for China increased accordingly. American money and a resumption of military traffic along the Burma Road helped offset the loss of the Indochina railway, and the Chinese were able to continue the war. But like Britain, China would be under U.S. domination. In addition to Burma, Hong Kong continued to serve as a significant base of Chinese support. With the occupation of Indochina, Hong Kong's importance increased once again—a fact well understood by the Japanese.

Escalation at Hong Kong

With control firmly established over northern Indochina, and with the air war picking up steam over Yunnan, the Japanese army returned its attention to the neglected Chinese logistical situation in Kwangtung. During the occupation of southern Kwangsi, the Japanese army had been hard-pressed to confront the Chinese at any great distance from Canton, and the noose around Hong Kong had frayed.[117] This was remedied after the withdrawal from Kwangsi. Although the Japanese were preparing to move into the southwest Pacific before concluding the war in China, they continued the pressure against Chinese lines of communication to maintain the country's isolation. The Burma Road and Hong Kong were the only routes still functioning in this capacity southward. Of the two, Hong Kong was more exposed, and Anglo-Japanese friction remained a dangerous problem that was only made worse by the lack of a uniform military policy among local British colonial officials.

Larger Japanese designs for a southward advance raised the strategic value of southern China, and this increased the potential for turning the low-intensity conflict at Hong Kong into an open Anglo-Japanese war. Victory in China depended on clearing the Hankow-Canton railway of Chinese forces. Hence, closure of the Burma Road in combination with the occupation of Hong Kong was now considered essential.[118] Because of the capitulation of France, air attacks were intensified against the railway lines in southern China, and after a temporary lull, Hong Kong military officers assumed that they might be attacked at any time. London was informed of their concerns and observations: "The capture of Hong Kong, together with the Foreign Settlements at Shanghai and Tientsin, would be a crushing blow to the political and economic side of Chinese resistance, and might even prove fatal. So long as these centres of anti-Japanese feeling and action remain, Japan can never hope to achieve complete success in China. This opportunity to eradicate them may not recur."[119] In addition, in early June the Soviets and the Japanese had signed an agreement officially ending the Nomonhan dispute of 1939, making a southern advance more viable. Accordingly, by June 1940, the South China Expeditionary Force assembled plans for a direct invasion of Hong Kong, and Japanese troops were once again deployed along the border for the purpose of restoring the landward blockade. Their assigned task was to stem the movement of Chinese military supplies, but the arrival of these forces was primarily meant to be an act of intimidation. On 21 June 1940 the Japanese 124th Regiment (18th Division) under Colonel Nomizo landed at Namtau and advanced east, with air support, along the frontier to Shataukok. The Mirs Bay supply point for Hong Kong at Shayuchang was occupied and burned on the twenty-seventh. With the return of Japanese ground forces to Hong Kong's landward frontier, food supplies became strained. This new threat was not ignored; all women and children were ordered to leave the colony on 1 July 1940, with mixed results.[120]

The immediate British concern was somewhat diminished by the limited number of Japanese troops that actually appeared, but a feeling of unease persisted among some colonial officials. This was fueled on 24 June 1940 when officers of the 1st Kumaon Rifles witnessed a fight for the control of Shumchun, as the Japanese clashed with elements of the Cantonese 159th Division.[121] Although potentially dangerous to the colony's security, this event provided another useful opportunity to assess Japanese and Chinese infantry tactics. A report written by Major Giles indicated that not all British military officers were willing to underestimate Japanese army capabilities:

> Both sides made good use of ground, and fire and movement were well coordinated. As in the case of the similar skirmish which was witnessed and fully reported by O.C. 1st Kumaon Rifles last November, there was a total absence of the "human bullet" spirit on the part of the Japanese; but on the other hand they worked forward over exposed ground very well, and covering fire was given as and when (but for no longer than) was necessary. The unprepossessing appearance of the Japanese troops on our frontier should not blind us to the fact that they are by no means so untrained as their appearance would indicate.[122]

He added that the Japanese soon began to improve the road network immediately north of the colony to Canton. This was necessary preparation for any future attack on Hong Kong. Significantly, Major General Grasett took note of these and subsequent developments and informed London that war could break out at Hong Kong at any time. In a bid to bring this about, the Chinese attacked Japanese ground forces again at Shumchun on 18 and 19 September, as well as at other locations closer to Canton.[123]

The Japanese also increased pressure by tightening their grip on outlying coastal areas. Both the Swatow and Amoy regions were reinforced for upcoming ground operations during the summer. Hainan was reinforced, causing some foreign observers to speculate that the Japanese were making preparations for an invasion of the Dutch East Indies. Air bombardment throughout Kwangtung was intensified from July into the fall, although a less than convincing display of strength was applied against the Chekiang supply lines to Ningpo.[124] This was reported from Hong Kong at the end of July: "Farcical operations for tightening the Japanese blockade of Ningpo and other areas of the Chekiang coast, petered out in the usual welter of rival claims of sweeping victories, accompanied by the passing of considerable sums of hard cash to ensure a Japanese withdrawal."[125]

Additional troops arrived along the Hong Kong border in August, following the first group in June. The arrest of British nationals in Japan that same month created further anxiety among British military officers. Reinforcement of the 124th Regiment along the Hong Kong border by the

137th Regiment under General Hara Mamoru showed that the Japanese were fully determined to enforce the blockade with renewed vigor. The 137th Regiment (of the 104th Division) brought the total number of Japanese troops adjacent to Hong Kong up to 5,000. It would not take many more to make the threat of invasion credible, and a zone of occupation five miles north of Hong Kong to Pokut was established to support such action. Road improvement continued, and an amphibious landing area was prepared at Deep Bay for future use. Officers in Hong Kong thought the Japanese might also be preparing for a move against the Chinese 153rd, 157th, 159th, and 165th Divisions located around Waichow, but it was soon determined that the Japanese reinforcement of the region was only meant to strengthen the blockade. As a countermove, the Chinese reinforced Waichow with an additional two divisions during November.[126]

Japanese aggression displayed in south China and elsewhere further strained Anglo-Japanese relations. Air attacks on civilian airliners, for example, had become more frequent and deadly. One of the more brutal incidents was also a cause of great Japanese embarrassment: on 7 July 1940 they shot down an Air France plane carrying two of their own Indochina inspectors who were monitoring French compliance with the embargo against China. Other nations such as Canada also felt the brunt of Japanese hostility, as evidenced by the bombing of the SS *Empress of Asia* on 14 September 1940 near Japan. Closer to Hong Kong, Japanese antiaircraft gunners stationed at the Namtau airfield were quick to shoot at British and Chinese aircraft flying nearby, even if the planes were inside British airspace. On 13 September a CNAC DC-2 was hit shortly after leaving Kai Tak airfield, as was an RAF Vildebeeste on the twenty-seventh. Both were inside Hong Kong airspace. Two civilian airliners were shot down during October 1940. One of these, a CNAC plane, was attacked near Kunming on the twenty-ninth. Nine of the fourteen people aboard were killed, including the pilot, W. C. Kent, after the aircraft was grounded and strafed.[127] Major Giles described the attack:

The China National Aviation Corporation 12-ton Douglas DC-2 14 passenger airliner "Chungking" No. 39 (formerly the "Kweiling" No. 32, the same aircraft which was shot down by Japanese naval fighters in the Pearl River Delta near Macao on August 24th, 1938, and which, after repair carried out the initial flight on the Chungking-Rangoon air service), left Chungking for Kunming shortly after noon on 29th October, 1940. As Yunnan province was under air alarm the pilot cruised around the northern part of that province waiting for the "all-clear" to be given, but after some time decided to continue to Kunming. The aircraft was carrying two pilots, one radio operator, one air hostess, and ten passengers. As the aeroplane approached Tchangyi (Tsunyi), 75 miles north-east of Kunming the radio operator sent the message, "sighted Tchangyi." This was at 1432 hours and immediately afterwards the aircraft was intercepted and fired at by five Japanese aircraft. The last message received was, "Am trying to land." After the plane had been forced down the Japanese aircraft dropped bombs on the aerodrome and continued to fire their machine-guns at the aeroplane, which was destroyed by fire. Of the ten passengers, seven were killed, two were wounded and one was uninjured. The pilot and stewardess were also killed.[128]

Japanese attention had been drawn to the company because CNAC was a significant blockade runner and was partly owned by the Chinese government. CNAC was used to export strategic materials; this included a deal in which 300 tons of tungsten were flown into Hong Kong from Namyung, near the Kiangsi border, every month.[129] Perhaps the Japanese wished to corner the market at Ningpo.

Lack of airpower throughout East Asia prevented any kind of deterrence of these attacks. The British were hard-pressed to reinforce the Far East because of the battle of Britain, and by November 1940, the Chinese air force had been smashed over Chungking, leaving only about 30 aircraft spread throughout the country. To defend their interests, the British estimated they required 336 aircraft to cover Malaya, Singapore, Borneo, Australia, and the Netherlands East Indies. In August 1940 they only had 88 in the entire region, few of which were useful fighters. The Dutch were similarly hard-pressed with 144 aircraft, only 24 of which were fighters. After several months without any deliveries to China, Stalin sent 40 I-16 fighters in early December 1940, but Chinese problems extended beyond a lack of aircraft. Persistent logistical difficulties plagued them as well. Six million gallons, or about 18,000 tons, of aviation fuel were arriving in China annually, but that was only enough to keep about 40 fighters and a similar number of bombers in the air. As for other supplies, half the total entered the country from the frequently interdicted route from Hong Kong via Tamshui and Waichow. In contrast, the Japanese had 170 well-supplied aircraft on Hainan, 12 at Sanchau, plus 30 more at Canton. Nanning based an additional 36 planes until October, and there were many other aircraft available in central and northern China. Aside from these air forces, the Japanese navy temporarily increased its carrier strength patrolling off the coast of Kwangtung during September, while the army kept busy in Indochina.[130]

As part of the blockade of Hong Kong, the Japanese also resumed ground operations in the western part of the Pearl River Delta; additional motivations were the acquisition of loot and to provide training. Shekki had already been reoccupied in March, and since the Sze Yap district had previously been identified as an area of interest, the city of Toishan was finally taken in late October 1940. Transportation was difficult in the region. The railway between Toishan and Sunwui had been destroyed through a combination of bombing and Chinese guerrilla activity, so there were few mechanical means of reaching the city. Even so, army units were able to converge on Toishan from the northeast using riverboats starting near Sunwui. Cavalry approached overland from the south through mountainous passes, after being landed at Kwonghai Bay. The force from Sunwui included at least two small gunboats, and the infantry was towed toward the city in rafts. The cavalry's march was aided by fifth columnists dressed as monks. Even though no Chinese army units were available to defend the region, the city was heavily bombarded, and Japanese forces occupied Toishan without difficulty. Although the occupation was not of great duration, the blockade was once again extended, resulting in a curtailment of food supplies to Hong Kong. The 38th Division and the 2nd Guards Independent Mixed Brigade arrived in the Chungshan district shortly thereafter, in December.[131]

With Japanese army units deployed throughout the Pearl River Delta, British officials in London and the Far East grew more anxious about a possible attack on Hong Kong, but with limited resources, hopes for greater security were placed on improving military cooperation with potential allies and augmenting special warfare capabilities in southern China. The greatest sense of relief came from the reelection of President Roosevelt. Hope for expanded U.S. intervention was founded on the belief that American public opinion was becoming increasingly pro-British as European countries continued to fall under German domination, and secret Anglo-American military discussions during August produced similar optimism. To encourage collaboration in Asia among the British, Dutch, Chinese, and Americans, Air Chief Marshal Robert Brooke-Popham was appointed in October 1940 as the new British commander in chief, Far East Command, based in Singapore. To British disappointment, however, the Americans did not attend the Singapore Defence Conference held that same month because of the upcoming election. Nevertheless, Brooke-Popham got on with his work, and one of his first tasks, supported by Churchill, was to develop a special warfare training program with the Chinese. He quickly prepared for the establishment of such units as Detachment 204 and the China Commando Group, both under the direction of the Special Operations Executive, which was formed in July.[132]

Brooke-Popham's arrival also encouraged General Grasett in Hong Kong to push for greater British commitment in China. Earlier in the year a British propaganda office had been opened in Hong Kong to counter Japanese radio broadcasts.[133] Grasett and others thought Britain needed a better propaganda campaign in both China and Japan, since publications containing illustrations of happy soldiers with their girlfriends or of women in air raid shelters sent the wrong message, unlike German propaganda which featured tanks and victory parades. Hong Kong intelligence officers explained this to London:

Our own representatives in Tokyo are fully alive to the necessity for careful selection in the type of propaganda which should be sent to Japan, and have requested London to avoid, as far as possible, the sending of photographs depicting the democratic habits of their Majesties, soldiers kissing their sweethearts, and others of this kind, which though popular in America and the Dominions are highly incongruous and un-military to Japanese eyes. Photographs of U-Boat personnel in uniform as prisoners of war, would go a long way to counteract similar German efforts; whilst action pictures of troops, naval units engaged in anti-submarine work etc. should also be distributed on a lavish scale. Best of all however are photographs of aeroplanes of all types. The Japanese dove of peace has long since developed a tendency to resemble a twin-engine bomber; and a study of the Japanese pictorial press for the last year or two reveals the undisputable fact that pictures of aeroplanes, in action or on the ground, are more popular than anything else. Japan is becoming air-minded at a phenomenal rate, and the more we can do to convince her that we are a first-class nation in the air, the better for our prestige.[134]

CHAPTER SEVEN

More significantly, Grasett requested permission from the War Office to form an independent commando in Hong Kong. He wanted a unit that could be used to counterattack Japanese forces in the event of war, but the scheme was shelved because the commando had to be created from local resources. Then, in October, Grasett revived a previous request from February 1940 (submitted after the War Office extended Hong Kong's period of relief) regarding regular infantry reinforcements for the colony.[135] This request, however, was at variance with the views of Governor Northcote, and it demonstrated Grasett's tendency to act independently of external authority.

Without altering the military situation at Hong Kong, the cabinet's rejection of Grasett's request struck a middle ground between the general and the governor by maintaining the status quo. Because of a medical problem, Northcote returned to England in August 1940 and stayed until March 1941.[136] One of his first actions upon arrival in London was to inform Whitehall that he had reversed his opinion on Hong Kong's defense policy, and he recommended that the colony be demilitarized. His appeal was considered, but the War Cabinet concluded that American support was now more likely in the event of an attack on British forces, and demilitarization would have a negative impact on U.S. policy.[137] The reasons for rejecting Northcote's advice were varied, but most significantly, the Chiefs of Staff believed that as long as Hong Kong could be used to bring America into the war, demilitarization was unjustified. They stated:

The retention of the garrison and our avowed intention of defending our territory:—
(a) Would cause the Japanese to hesitate before attacking it.
(b) Would encourage the USA to take a firm line. Its gallant defence might be an important factor in bringing them into the war.
9. In fact the possible loss of prestige due to the fall of Hong Kong in war even with all its attendant horrors would have less serious results than the loss of prestige from its demilitarisation under present conditions.
10. We therefore are firmly of the opinion, with which we understand the Foreign Office are in agreement, that demilitarization is out of the question at the present time. In the event of war Hong Kong must be regarded as an outpost and held as long as possible.[138]

Hong Kong officials were ordered to stockpile food and supplies for a protracted siege, as the colony (not just China) would now be used to influence American foreign policy in Britain's favor. This was a significant problem; in the event of a Japanese attack, provisions would be needed for more than 2 million civilians, many of whom possessed unknown loyalties.[139]

Refusal of Grasett's appeals did not prevent him from seeking greater collaboration with the Chinese, which he did on his own authority. When diplomatic tension with the Japanese was at its height over the Burma Road crisis in July, the War Office ordered Grasett not to engage in direct talks with the Chinese and thus give the Japanese reason for additional complaints. Grasett ignored this order and sent Major Charles Boxer to Chungking in August to gather intelligence on Japanese troop deployments. In October, after the departure of Governor Northcote, Grasett established a joint Sino-British radio intelligence network based in Hong Kong for the stated purpose of providing early warning of Japanese air operations from Canton airfields. In addition to Hong Kong's air defense requirements, teams placed in Hainan and the Bocca Tigris were established to identify Japanese army and navy movements.[140]

Grasett informed the War Office of his actions after the fact, explaining that Chinese military personnel would be required to work in Hong Kong: "Chinese can read Japanese Naval and military air force codes, but that as their operators use unorthodox system of signals it will be necessary for Chinese operators to man Hong Kong terminals."[141] In developing this link with the Chinese army, Grasett was acting on his own, and he did not notify colonial civilian authorities. Major General E. F. Norton was serving as the officer administering the government in Northcote's absence, and he downplayed the significance of the issue when he communicated with the War Office in November:

Arrangements made by G.O.C. designed purely to improve military intelligence naturally attempted to establish some measure of warning in war of approach of hostile aircraft. At present we can expect no warning of air raids and in view of vulnerability of Hong Kong to air attack and teeming Chinese population exposed such warning is a vital factor.

G.O.C. himself has been conducting secret conversations with the Chinese on this question and has arranged for necessary wireless sets and Chinese operators using a Chinese code to be accommodated in military premises and under military supervision. There are no administrative problems which concern the Colonial Government. On political side as arrangements made are purely of a military character, for reasons of secrecy G.O.C. has not informed the Colonial Government. They are in fact merely extension of existing intelligence system employing Chinese agents for reasons of defence and therefore have no political significance.[142]

The radio net was not merely an extension of the existing intelligence system. It was something new, and it had considerable diplomatic significance. Grasett increased British involvement in the war against Japan on his own initiative, and the radio net established that the British and Chinese were acting as active military allies, albeit in a limited manner.

Significantly, Ambassador Clark Kerr had been notified from the beginning and gave the project his full endorsement, as Grasett explained in October:

Chinese delegation consisting of Major-General Colonel and Air Force Officer arrived as personal emissaries of Generalissimo with instructions to cooperate with us to the full. Discussions held on (A) possibility of organising air raid warning system on lines found so effective at Chungking and elsewhere and (B) speeding up of intelligence reports from likely centres of Japanese troop concentrations forming potential threat to colony. . . .

Although this arrangement has been kept strictly secret and is in fact solely designed to improve our local intelligence and secure vital air raid warning, it does constitute closer contact with the Chinese which would seem inevitable since Japan has joined the Axis and former reasons for keeping Chinese at arms [sic] length have now lost much of their validity. The Generalissimo is giving this matter his whole-hearted personal support and I have acted throughout with the full approval of the Ambassador.[143]

Grasett may have had the approval of the ambassador, but his plan should have been discussed at a higher level. Neither Grasett nor Clark Kerr was authorized to determine British foreign policy. The plan should have been approved in London by the departments involved before its implementation.

One of the reasons Grasett acted independently when the opportunity presented itself was that he and the colonial government held opposing views on Hong Kong's defense policy. Governor Northcote, for one, most certainly would not have approved. Following the discovery of a Chinese intelligence organization in Hong Kong during the David Kung incident in 1939, an angry Northcote had expressed his adamant opposition to the Chinese using Hong Kong as an intelligence base, but Grasett ignored this once the governor had left the colony and the government was being administered by Norton and the ailing colonial secretary N. L. Smith. After Northcote's return to Hong Kong, another clandestine Chinese radio transmitter was discovered on 19 May 1941 on Robinson Road, under the control of Shum Hang Chung. Shum was conducting counterintelligence operations in Hong Kong, Shanghai, and Macau for the Kuomintang, and his group had been operating for three years. Northcote was similarly distressed, and although he wanted to expel the Chinese agents involved, he followed Clark Kerr's advice and refrained from doing so to avoid further diplomatic embarrassment. Instead, the British responded with an official diplomatic protest delivered by Clark Kerr.[144] Northcote certainly would not have supported Grasett's scheme to establish a Sino-British radio net centered on Hong Kong; he would have viewed it as a provocative move. Thus, Grasett took the initiative, implemented his plan, and, in his own way, advanced British involvement in the Sino-Japanese War.

In fairness to Grasett, the cabinet had already decided to use Hong Kong as bait to bring America into the war, and his actions can reasonably be seen as an officer making the best of his military situation, given the meager resources available to him. But in the fall of 1941, during the reinforcement of Hong Kong, Grasett again showed that he was trying to escalate the war on his own initiative—in this case, by involving Canada. He was successful in both instances. In the interim, official British policy remained unchanged: Hong Kong would not be reinforced, nor was there any intention to resist a Japanese occupation of southern Indochina militarily. Unfortunately for the British, their Far Eastern strategic plans became known to the Japanese after the SS *Automedon* was sunk on 11 November 1940 in the Indian Ocean by a German surface raider. A copy of the August 1940 Chiefs of Staff Far Eastern strategic assessment fell into German hands as a result.[145] Armed with the information contained in this document, the Japanese continued to pursue a southern advance strategy without undue worry about British resistance. Military pressure was conse-

CHAPTER SEVEN

quently maintained against Hong Kong. Japanese naval forces patrolled the waters adjacent to the colony, and from May to December 1940 they carried out forty-one known attacks on junks. Grasett's frustration would mount as the blockade continued because his options for response remained limited. By the summer of 1941, he was willing to risk open war by challenging Japanese naval vessels directly with the meager forces he had available.[146]

Shifting the Load

After the occupation of southern Kwangsi failed to end the war, the Japanese sought solutions for their problems elsewhere. The French defeat produced fundamental changes in Japanese grand strategy, as it seemed to provide a unique opportunity to tighten their grip on China. It was a watershed event. The invasion of Indochina was the first step in the Japanese advance to the southwest Pacific, and preparations for war against both Britain and America were begun. With the absorption of northern Indochina, the importance of Hong Kong and Burma as conduits for sustaining Chinese resistance greatly increased, and Hong Kong's military situation deteriorated because its occupation had now become a primary Japanese objective. With diminishing diplomatic options in the Far East as the war against Germany continued, the British were somewhat successful in leveraging their support for China as a means of encouraging greater international cooperation against their enemies. The cost, however, was a further weakening of their global position, as manifested by the transfer of Canada into America's orbit. But success in Washington was not paralleled in Moscow, and Stalin remained a loyal partner of Hitler. Nevertheless, with a temporary closure of the Burma Road, China kept fighting despite intensified Japanese efforts to arrange peace, and this was accomplished in part because of Hong Kong. Against this backdrop, British military policy for the colony remained virtually unchanged, notwithstanding the best efforts of senior colonial officials to alter it. Lacking an alliance with China and remaining militarily weak, Hong Kong invited Japanese attack. In such an event, the War Cabinet and the Chiefs of Staff hoped to use Hong Kong to bring America into the war.

EIGHT

The Triumph of Collective Security: Hong Kong, 1941

By the end of 1941, the United States assumed the lead in the anti-Axis coalition, and this transition developed partly in the Far East. Britain had already scaled back its proxy war in China after the temporary closure of the Burma Road in the summer and fall of 1940, yet under changing geopolitical conditions, the conflict remained a potentially useful tool with which to influence other great powers. Important adjustments occurred in mid-1941, making the latter half of the year the most crucial period of the Second World War. Two major events were the German invasion of the Soviet Union and the release of the Maud report in Britain, a document that confirmed the feasibility of producing an atomic bomb within the projected time frame of the war.[1] Anglo-American grand strategy depended on the continuation of Soviet resistance, but this appeared unlikely, given the near destruction of the Red Army. Because it was not possible to provide immediate direct assistance to Stalin, it was considered essential to increase support to China as an indirect method of securing the Soviet Far East. China therefore became the most significant area affecting Allied plans in East Asia, and because of this, Hong Kong completed its transformation into a globally significant strategic objective.

As the Far Eastern crisis deteriorated throughout 1941, American opposition to Japanese ambitions steadily grew. The Japanese were desperate to end the war in China and began to view an advance to the south as a means of terminating Allied material support transiting Burma and Hong Kong. Occupation of southern Indochina was the first step in this direction, and the blockade of Hong Kong was also tightened. Anglo-Japanese tensions only worsened in the Pearl River Delta, where localized brinkmanship threatened to erupt into open war. The American oil embargo was a response to this Japanese expansion, and it was an ultimatum that could not be ignored in Tokyo. The pace of Far Eastern developments quickened accordingly. Anglo-American weakness invited attack; the British lacked forces to spare for Far Eastern defenses, and President Roosevelt's ability to intervene was restricted by Congress. American financial power proved effective as a temporary substitute for real military support, and it ultimately ensured the country's dominant position in the burgeoning anti-Axis alliance. Potential allies were kept in the war, but unfortunately for the British, this came at the expense of imperial power. An erosion of Chinese sovereignty also began, as American aid was followed by interference in domestic political affairs. In time, American military assistance became dependent on the central government's cooperation with the communists, and it would eventually be supplied only under direct American supervision or control. Whereas aid to the Soviets would be given unconditionally, support to others would not.[2]

As China became central to the Far Eastern crisis, Canada emerged as a useful Anglo-American agent that helped bind the anti-Axis alliance in Asia. With the Permanent Joint Board of Defence in place, along with the Hyde Park and Lend-Lease agreements sustaining the Commonwealth war effort, the stage was set for Canada to take a more active role in the Pacific. The primary Canadian actor that ushered in this development was Prime Minister Mackenzie King. The prime minister had visited Hong Kong in 1909 during a roving diplomatic mission to China and Japan on behalf of the government then headed by Sir Wilfrid Laurier. Since that time, Mackenzie King had remained well versed on Far Eastern affairs, and he saw the region as a useful arena where Anglo-American cooperation could be strengthened.[3] Because Hong Kong was vital for the Chinese war effort, and because continuation of the Sino-Japanese conflict was increasingly important for the maintenance of Soviet resistance against Germany, the colony became a more volatile Anglo-Japanese flash point. To encourage Chinese resistance and help satisfy British and American obligations, Canadian troops were sent as reinforcements for Hong Kong, but the move ended in unmitigated military disaster. Part of the reason for this outcome was that the Allies were less concerned with assisting the Chinese than with aiding Stalin, and this information was suppressed from the public at the highest levels. More important, as a manifestation of Allied collective security doctrine, the Canadian deployment did little to deter further conflict. Instead, the Japanese viewed it as a direct provocation.[4]

Change of Command: Lend-Lease and
U.S. Assumption of Coalition Leadership

America's leadership of the anti-Axis coalition began with the reelection of President Roosevelt in November 1940. It was an evolutionary process that often involved Canada. Popular opposition to war remained strong in the United States, but the push for military intervention continued unabated from the White House and from much of the American foreign policy establishment. With his political base secure, Roosevelt proceeded to build an anti-Axis coalition. This was largely accomplished with the enactment of Lend-Lease in March 1941, since economic warfare was still the primary American method of influencing geopolitical events, but the charade of American neutrality became increasingly transparent after Lend-Lease legislation came into force. Britain was virtually bankrupt by this stage of the war, and Prime Minister Churchill was desperate to bring America into the conflict. Once this was accomplished, however, the decline of Britain's autonomous power was greatly accelerated. Nevertheless, British intelligence operations and coercive propaganda efforts in the United States were intensified and supported by America's new military ally to the north. Canada was thus a useful partner in cementing the Anglo-American alliance. With North America secure from invasion, Canadian reinforcement of Great Britain was greatly encouraged, with U.S. naval support being provided on at least one occasion for the deployment of an armored division across the Atlantic.[5] As wartime circumstances developed, Canada found itself playing the role of middleman to deepen U.S. involvement in China. Due to army expansion, there was a general shortage of munitions in the United States, but Roosevelt seized on Canadian overproduction of light infantry weapons as a useful resource to meet Chinese requirements. The shipment of Canadian Bren guns to China lent additional weight to U.S. assurances of support to Generalissimo Chiang Kai Shek, and it demonstrated that Canada's China policy originated in the White House. Canada, under Mackenzie King's leadership, helped Churchill and Roosevelt bring America into the war, and Roosevelt launched Canada's official involvement in China.

After the battle of Britain and Roosevelt's reelection, the British cabinet was united in the decision to continue the war against Germany, yet this did not alter the fact that the country was facing financial ruin. Prophetic warnings by the British Treasury about the consequences of large-scale military spending were becoming clearer by the spring of 1941, when Britain's gold reserves fell to US$12 million. This deteriorating situation had triggered a forthright statement to the press by Lord Lothian a few months earlier, in November 1940.[6] According to John Charmley, the British ambassador to America remarked, "Well, boys, Britain is broke; it's your money we want."[7] The following month, Churchill informed Roosevelt that the United States had to assume the costs of maintaining the war; otherwise, Britain would be compelled to terminate hostilities. Roosevelt's adviser, Harry Hopkins, was dispatched to London to provide assurances of full American support and a pledge that they would win the war together, but American aid would not come cheaply.[8] Following a review of British assets, Roosevelt remarked to Secretary of the Treasury Henry Morgenthau, "Well, they aren't bust—there's lots of money there."[9]

The first $7 billion of the Lend-Lease program addressed immediate needs, yet those in London with knowledge of the agreement were angered by its terms; they thought Britain was being robbed. During 1940, half a billion pounds had been raised and spent when an American warship was sent to Cape Town on 23 December 1940 to pick up £50 million of gold. Concern seemed to be justified, as a large portion of Britain's final reserve had been relinquished. More financing would be extended through Lend-Lease, but hopes for an American gift were short-lived. Eventually, less encumbered aid emanated from Canada in early 1942, when $1 billion was donated to ease Britain's plight.[10] By that point, however, British decline was past the point of no return.

Lend-Lease was also designed to enrich American business. One noteworthy example was China Defense Supplies, a corporation that supplanted the Universal Trading Corporation soon after the Lend-Lease bill was signed into law by the president.[11] The company was headed by Chiang Kai Shek's adviser and brother-in-law Dr. T. V. Soong, and its purpose was to procure weapons and munitions for Chinese military forces. Almost every plane, rifle, or bullet sent into China from America was bought and sold by China Defense Supplies. Barbara Tuchman noted, "The business generated by Lend-Lease through China Defense Supplies was even more lucrative than most military procurement operations. It made the fortunes of the Americans involved in the group and added to Soong's, which through his previous tenure as Minister of Finance and chairman of the Bank of China was already considerable."[12] Using the Lockheed Aircraft Corporation as an example, it cost almost $80,000 to buy a Hudson bomber, not including the propeller and engine, which cost an additional $30,000. There was plenty of money to be made, provided one had the right connections. Omitted from the Tuchman rebuke was the fact that the president's uncle, Frederic Adrian Delano, was also a member of the board.[13] Delano was born in Hong Kong on 10 September 1863, and the family made much of its original fortune on the opium trade. War was also good business, and, not to be outdone by their forebears, the president and his family did what they could to profit in Asia by supplying the Chinese with weapons. This was not the sole or even the most important factor shaping Roosevelt's wartime policy, but personal considerations cannot be entirely dismissed as irrelevant.

Notwithstanding the economic situation, prominent personages in the Commonwealth remained eager to continue the war and deepen American involvement. By 1941, even earlier skeptics such as Lord Halifax saw U.S.-Canadian relations as a useful arena where this objective could be developed. British cabinet members such as Churchill, South African Prime Minister Jan Smuts, and press baron Lord Beaverbrook (Max Aitken from Canada) all earnestly desired a greater propaganda effort in the United States, but the Canadian prime minister and his allies south of the border were more cautious about such moves.[14] One of these allies was the president's son, James Roosevelt. The younger Roosevelt was a leading figure in the Office of the Coordinator of Information, along with William Donovan and James Warburg. This agency preceded the OSS and worked closely with British Security Coordination, an intelligence organization in North America headed by Canadian businessman William Stephenson. Direct American intervention in the war remained the paramount objective among British officials working in British Security Coordination and elsewhere, and in this they were aided by the Canadian government.[15]

Propaganda work was coordinated with the Canadian legation in Washington, and military collaboration was also arranged. In January and February 1941, for example, James Roosevelt sought Mackenzie King's help in establishing a pilot training facility in California. It would be run on a cooperative basis with Canada's Commonwealth air training program, which

CHAPTER EIGHT

was already in operation. During the summer, Donovan traveled to Canada to strengthen propaganda efforts, and this led to the establishment of a Canadian department within his agency.[16] Mackenzie King understood the president's reluctance to fully engage Congress for an open declaration against Germany, and both leaders were hesitant to aggressively publicize Commonwealth military efforts in the United States. President Roosevelt wanted to enter the war gradually, following the imposition of retaliatory measures against Axis military action, and he thought the less attention focused on Anglo-American or U.S.-Canadian cooperation, the better. He hoped war could eventually be waged without a formal declaration, once the anger of American voters had been sufficiently roused.[17]

America's domination of the Commonwealth was advanced with the signing of the Hyde Park agreement on 21 April 1941. Written partly by Canadian Deputy Minister of Finance Clifford Clark and Secretary Morgenthau, the agreement streamlined war production between the United States and Canada by integrating economic and industrial resources. Just as the PJBD had created greater military and diplomatic cooperation between the United States and the British Commonwealth, the Hyde Park agreement expanded this collaboration into the field of economics. This "free trade" agreement was a product of the personal diplomacy regularly conducted between Roosevelt and Mackenzie King, and it increased North American wartime industrial production by ensuring that Commonwealth Lend-Lease purchases could be made in dollars borrowed from Wall Street and guaranteeing that the United States would purchase Canadian overproduction.[18] Hence, the further loss of British sterling was prevented, while greater profits were accrued in New York.

Like the PJBD, the Hyde Park agreement signaled a shift in Canada's foreign policy that pulled the country farther away from Great Britain and into America's orbit. It was applauded in political circles on both sides of the border because of the expanded military and economic interdependence of the two countries. Even before America officially entered the conflict, this relationship was upheld as a positive model for the preservation of world peace that could be duplicated elsewhere during postwar reconstruction.[19] Apparently, Mackenzie King became somewhat discouraged later in the year, commenting in his diary on the linkage created between the Federal Reserve and the Bank of Canada to facilitate subsequent transactions: "I confess I begin to look on that institution [the Bank of Canada] as being part of the Empire of Finance."[20]

With financing arranged, Allied strategic planning proceeded full steam ahead. It was agreed during Anglo-American discussions (the ABC-1 talks) held in Washington from late January to early March 1941 that the war in Europe would have priority over the Pacific. The air campaign over Germany would be intensified while the British held in the Mediterranean against any further Axis advance. The recommendation from Singapore was that if Malaya, the Dominions, or the Netherlands East Indies were attacked by Japanese forces, both the United States and Britain should declare war. It was also recognized that one of the first points of attack would be at Hong Kong. Global areas of responsibility were defined, and because of the weight of American power, the British indicated that they would follow America's lead and not make any further concessions to Japan.[21] A conference report explained the Allied strategy being formed:

> If Japan does enter the war, the Military strategy in the Far East will be defensive. The United States does not intend to add to its present Military strength in the Far East but will employ the United States Pacific Fleet offensively in the manner best calculated to weaken Japanese economic power, and to support the defense of the Malay barrier by diverting Japanese strength away from Malaysia. The United States intends so to augment its forces in the Atlantic and Mediterranean areas that the British Commonwealth will be in a position to release the necessary forces for the Far East.[22]

Henceforth, Europe was the primary theater of operations, and America was the dominant partner. This report was also significant because it made any reinforcement of Hong Kong an element of Allied grand strategy rather than solely a British maneuver.

East Asian events had already tested the spirit of Anglo-American resolve. Roosevelt's main goal was for China to continue fighting and tie down as many Japanese troops as possible. However, after the New 4th Army incident, and despite reliable information that the Chinese Communist Party was largely responsible for exploiting the underlying political friction, grossly unequal pressure was applied against Chiang Kai Shek by making additional support dependent on the cessation of internal conflict. Farther south, a war sparked by Japanese subterfuge was waged in December 1940 and January 1941 between the French in Indochina and Thailand. This war extended Japanese influence onto Malaya's doorstep once Thailand became essentially a Japanese satellite later in the year.[23]

Other serious incidents had the effect of encouraging the development of a Japanese southern strategy. One of these was the signing of the Soviet-Japanese neutrality pact by Stalin and Foreign Minister Matsuoka Yosuke in April 1941.[24] A Japanese strike to the south was now much more feasible, and Matsuoka's bellicosity had already raised anxiety. When speaking to Japanese provincial governors, he reiterated complaints about Hong Kong's military logistical role. He stated, "As to China, it was unavoidable that third Powers' interests should suffer, 'particularly if those interests are being used as bases to resist our military operations in China.'"[25] According to a military intelligence report from Hong Kong, the foreign minister issued additional threats:

[Matsuoka] broadly hinted that continued British and American aid to the Chiang Kai Shek regime may lead Japan to invoke the 3rd clause of the Tripartite Pact which would automatically bring her into the war. This may be—and probably is—only bluff; but the fact remains that under steady German pressure and with Prince Konoye's admitted lack of control over the extremists, Japan is drifting into a position wherein she will have no option but to fight. Such at least is the opinion of one of the leading Japanese firms in Hong Kong, which has received instructions to send back unostentatiously to Japan all members of its staff who are not indispensable, in view of the fact that American participation in the war is regarded as only a matter of time.[26]

Army-navy discussions in Tokyo built momentum for the acquisition of southern Indochina as a preliminary move. Subsequent military preparations indicated that the Japanese might soon strike south toward Malaya and Singapore. In response, the British cautiously paralleled the Americans' latest $50 million loan to China by finalizing a smaller £5 million credit that had originally been planned in late 1940.[27]

During the second round of Anglo-American strategy discussions held in April 1941, China was still relegated to a position near the bottom of strategic priorities, although the desirability of increasing support to Chiang was recognized. The Middle East, Greece, and Turkey were regarded as a single strategic theater of much greater significance than China, and when General Erwin Rommel pushed east in North Africa, the British position in Egypt was far from impregnable.[28] Defeat in the desert was expected, and very few resources could be spared to augment Far Eastern defenses. The Americans also wished to concentrate forces against Germany, and in May 1941 one-quarter of the U.S. Pacific Fleet was transferred from Hawaii to help escort convoys during the battle of the Atlantic. Chief of the Imperial General Staff, General Sir John Dill, tried to convince Churchill that Singapore should be made a higher British priority, but Churchill did not expect a Japanese attack during the first half of 1941, and he remained determined to concentrate on Egypt. Since American military leaders did not see Britain's Asian possessions as strategically vital to Allied interests, they were not willing to make any commitment to defend Singapore.[29] Nevertheless, it was agreed that China should receive greater material assistance than it had obtained in the past.

As the United States assumed command of the anti-Japanese front, the foundation was laid for China to become a U.S. sphere of interest. Loans had thus far provided sufficient inducement to prolong the war, but to prevent any possibility of its cessation, and to thereby keep the Japanese army engaged, Roosevelt considered it useful to expand America's influence and presence in China.[30] One of the first actions taken was to send a personal representative to Chiang. Roosevelt selected Lauchlin Currie, his Canadian-born economic adviser and former board member of the Federal Reserve, to strengthen his connection to Chungking. Roosevelt's emissary was a primary architect of the Lend-Lease plan as it pertained to China, and his first recommendation was to quickly increase military aid. In addition to his White House duties, however, Currie was a Soviet intelligence asset, and while traveling through Hong Kong during March, he conferred with Ernest Hemingway.[31] It was about this time that Hemingway conducted a tour of the 7th War Zone in Kwangtung while working for the U.S. Treasury, and he met with General Yu Han Mou in Kukong. His subsequent writing emphasized the need to maintain external Western support in order to keep China in the war. Hemingway was also a friend of Morris "Two Gun" Cohen, another former Canadian who was both a general in the Chinese army and an international arms dealer. During the year, Currie would be instrumental in helping to establish an American Military Mission under Brigadier General John Magruder in Chungking, as well as the U.S. Army Air Force (USAAF) Mission under Brigadier General Henry

CHAPTER EIGHT

Claggett. He was also essential in obtaining increasingly scarce aircraft for the American Volunteer Group (AVG).[32]

Although the Americans concentrated on using the Burma Road to sustain the war effort in China, Hong Kong did not escape their attention, and the U.S. service chiefs soon began to push the British to reinforce their position within the colony.[33] Like Currie, President Roosevelt's son had also been sent on a mission to Hong Kong and Chungking. Staying approximately three days in each city, Captain Jimmy Roosevelt arrived in Hong Kong on 26 April 1941 wearing his Marine Corps uniform to demonstrate publicly America's commitment to China. Roosevelt toured the colony with the governor and discussed the military situation with Canadian-born Major General Grasett. At that time, Grasett was working with the U.S. military attaché, Colonel William Mayer, to establish an American attaché office within the colony, ostensibly to better administer official finances. This was accomplished during May, without the initial approval or knowledge of the American ambassador, Nelson Johnson.[34] Both Grasett and the commander in chief, Far East Command, Air Chief Marshal Sir Robert Brooke-Popham, had previously requested reinforcements for Hong Kong, but their appeals had been rejected by the Chiefs of Staff and by Churchill. Undoubtedly, the question of reinforcing Hong Kong soon reached the president's ear following Jimmy Roosevelt's departure from China in early May. As a point of interest, the president's son next appeared in Crete, where he joined the island's evacuation by Sunderland flying boat about thirty-six hours ahead of the German airborne assault.[35]

Following Roosevelt's trip, Canadian diplomatic and military involvement in China was initiated. Because of the U.S. Army's expansion program, one of the biggest obstacles to the provision of Lend-Lease support was the scarcity of surplus munitions. China's greatest need was for small-arms ammunition, but no U.S. plants produced the necessary 7.9mm rounds. After consultations between Currie and C. D. Howe, Canada's minister of munitions and supply, and after Lord Beaverbrook's discussions in London with Canada's minister of defense, J. L. Ralston, the answer was found at the John Inglis plant in Toronto, touted as the world's largest production facility for automatic weapons. Surplus Bren guns were made available for shipment to China, and the scheme was expanded from an original 500 weapons to an order for 15,000 more by October 1941, a figure that was 43 percent of Canada's total Bren gun production at the time.[36] The shipment of Canadian Bren guns to China lent additional weight to

U.S. assurances of support to Chungking, and in the process, the Canadian government was once again part of the linkage deepening America's involvement in the war. Howe explained this development in a letter to Ralston:

> In the matter of materials, we are dependent to a considerable extent on the goodwill of the United States. A shortage of steel exists in that country, and we are dependent on steel from that country to the extent of 25 per cent to 30 per cent of our requirements. It has been necessary on two or three occasions to invoke the good offices of the President in order that we can maintain our place as buyers of steel in that market.
>
> In the matter of supplies to China, the President, through his assistant, Mr. Lauchlin Currie, told me that, in return for the help of his office, he would expect us to give him some help in arranging urgently needed supplies for China. I therefore have contracted for certain material where our productive equipment promises to be in excess of our commitments either to Canada or to Britain. Any commitment we have made for China has the reservation that we must first meet both these prior commitments.
>
> It also must be kept in mind that we have received large orders from the United States for equipment to be lease-lent to Britain, and that our usefulness to supply equipment to Britain has been greatly enlarged by that process. It seems to me that Britain should be the last to object to our doing something for the United States, when Britain has been so greatly helped by the United States in stepping up Canadian production.[37]

Howe also indiscreetly told Winnipeg reporter Grant Dexter that, "apart from Empire points Washington is paying for these shipments but this is strictly confidential."[38] In 1944 it was noted by General Brehon Somervell, head of the U.S. Army's Services of Supply, that Canadian production of light automatic weapons such as Bren guns, Sten guns, and pistols had been arranged largely for China's benefit.[39]

The main difficulty with the Canadian munitions plan was actually delivering supplies under the chaotic transportation conditions in southern China and Burma. The situation was aggravated by the heavy bombing inflicted on Chinese lines of communication in Yunnan and Kwangtung by

Japanese aircraft based in northern Indochina and Canton.[40] A Japanese press spokesman stated that raids carried out on Kunming and against the Burma Road were very successful, with hundreds of trucks stranded at a destroyed bridge over the Salween River; the navy's "Wild Eagles" claimed responsibility.[41] With periodic intensity, these attacks continued through the first half of the year. In late April, one raid on Kunming resulted in damage to the British consulate; during the summer, the city's power station was destroyed, as was another important bridge to Kweichow. Japanese air units were also taking a toll on CNAC planes flying in and out of Kunming.[42]

Since Chinese airpower was all but wiped out by the fall of 1940, the Americans created the AVG to defend against Japanese air units, but they needed British help to do so. According to AVG commander Colonel Chennault, it was primarily because of the support from Roosevelt's cabinet, especially Morgenthau and Secretary of the Navy Frank Knox, that the "Flying Tigers" became a reality. Once the Burma Road was reopened and Roosevelt was reelected, Chiang sent Chennault and General P. T. Mao, head of the Chinese air force, to the United States in search of replacement aircraft over the winter of 1940–1941. With White House assistance, 144 Vultee aircraft were diverted from Britain and Sweden and allocated to the Chinese air force; more significantly, in April 1941 Roosevelt authorized the release of pilots from American military forces for service in the AVG. Coinciding with the arrival of 150 Soviet fighters in China, 100 P-40 Tomahawk fighters were also diverted from Britain to equip the AVG. By the beginning of June 1941, the personnel and aircraft were assembled and began to be deployed to China via Hong Kong.[43] This White House initiative was a significant escalation of American involvement in the war.

Internal British opinion on the release of these aircraft demonstrates that Western intervention in China during the first half of 1941 was not a British priority. The driving force behind such action came from Washington. In February 1941, while diversion of the P-40s was being arranged, Berkeley Gage at the Foreign Office noted:

In view of the fact that we consider it an absurd waste of good material to send these ultra-modern machines to the Chinese, who are unlikely to have pilots trained to fly them, I think it is a lot to ask us to use the subterfuge suggested by Mr. Soong to protect them on their way, especially as the Japanese know all about the transaction. I think that we should refuse to do so. If the ship is intercepted by the Japanese it will be unfortunate, since they will be able to make use of the aircraft against us. But the number is not great and their capture might be a lesson to the United States on the futility of sending good material direct to the Chinese, who are incapable either of protecting it en route or using it effectively on receipt.[44]

Nigel Ronald noted:

The whole behavior of the US administration over this strikes me as lacking in consideration to us and demanding a lamentable want on their part of any sense of proportion. But it is obviously no use returning to the charge over this particular parcel. . . . I feel, however, that the left hand of the administration can have little idea of what the right is doing and that, if we could continue to call attention to this in the gentlest and politest possible way at some favourable opportunity, we might at least minimize the chance of this sort of thing recurring.[45]

A. L. Scott commented on where British strategic attention was fixed: "We do not wish priority to be given to Chinese requirements over Greek."[46] An unidentified official commented: "The upshot is that 100 of our aircraft & 470 of our guns are to be wasted."[47]

The British agreed to the release of the aircraft, despite their misgivings, only because of U.S. pressure. This was explained to Ambassador Clark Kerr on 24 March 1941:

Our present Far Eastern policy, is to avert war with Japan unless forced upon us i.e. to avoid action which would be unnecessarily provocative to Japan, but to keep in line with the United States Government and to maintain Chinese powers of resistance. Scheme has been examined in the light of these considerations by Chiefs of Staff who are disposed to recommend it to His Majesty's Government provided it is quite clear that the United States Administration are in favour.[48]

Ironically, it proved to be one of the better military investments made by the British during the war.

By the spring of 1941, American leadership of the anti-Axis coalition was increasingly firm, and initial moves were taken to intervene more directly in China. Outside of Asia, the Sino-Japanese War had largely become a White House concern, and until the German invasion of the USSR, it was no longer a British priority. Military resources were marshaled to defend southern lines of communication while the White House kept the increasingly dangerous situation in and around Hong Kong under close observation. In North America, Canada served as a winch to pull the Anglo-American alliance together.[49] Through Canada, weapons and money flowed east across the Atlantic, while intelligence efforts and special operations chiseled away at domestic American opposition to war.[50] Canada also helped fulfill American commitments in China, which eventually led to the establishment of strong personal and diplomatic relations between Ottawa and Chungking. It was because of the White House and the personal diplomacy between Roosevelt and Mackenzie King that Canada became involved officially in Chinese affairs. In the long run, the establishment of Sino-Canadian diplomatic relations did not translate into great material changes in China, as the prime minister had originally hoped, but the moral support was certainly a limited factor in building cohesion within the alliance. Altogether, these developments were manifestations of Roosevelt's vision of Allied collective security, yet more time was needed to build up sufficient forces in the Far East to meet an increasingly likely Japanese attack.[51] This effort failed, however, because the British were dragging their heels. Significant wartime geopolitical events soon outpaced Anglo-American deployment arrangements, and Axis victories in both the USSR and Indochina threatened to derail Allied strategy before it could be fully developed and implemented.

A Base Openly at War:
Blockade and Conflict at Hong Kong

By 1941, the Sino-Japanese War was stalemated, and the Japanese were desperate to isolate Hong Kong from free China.[52] Japanese strategy underwent significant changes as the country's leadership began to see the occupation of more distant regions as a solution to the problem. In the summer, war with Britain and America became an acceptable option. As a preliminary move, Hainan was reinforced and a submarine base was completed on the south shore of the island.[53] Following the German invasion of the Soviet Union, the Japanese advanced into southern Indochina and reinforced Manchuria in preparation for additional moves either south or into Siberia. On land and at sea, the blockade of China was also significantly tightened, with Anglo-Japanese friction at Hong Kong escalating to dangerous levels. Senior British Far Eastern officials also helped escalate the conflict by increasing their country's involvement at a more accelerated pace than London was inclined to accept.[54] Relying on meager military resources, officials at Hong Kong began to aggressively challenge Japanese naval forces in defense of the colony's fishermen. The low-intensity conflict that had been brewing in the region for several years became more brutal and destructive and threatened to spark an open Anglo-Japanese war in July.

For approximately one week during early January 1941, the recently appointed Brooke-Popham visited Grasett in Hong Kong. During the winter, both officers had requested two infantry battalions as reinforcements for the colony, claiming that these would be useful in tying down Japanese forces that could otherwise be deployed elsewhere. They also claimed that reinforcements would serve as a useful deterrent against further Japanese aggression.[55] The prime minister conferred with his military adviser, Major General Hastings Ismay, as to the soundness of such a move. In an oft-quoted passage, Churchill wrote:

> This is all wrong. If Japan goes to war with us, there is not the slightest chance of holding Hong Kong or relieving it. It is most unwise to increase the loss we shall suffer there. Instead of increasing the garrison it ought to be reduced to a symbolic scale. Any trouble arising there must be dealt with at the Peace Conference after the war. We must avoid frittering away our resources on untenable positions. Japan will think long before declaring war on the British Empire, and whether there are two or six battalions at Hong Kong will make no difference to her choice. I wish we had fewer troops there, but to move any would be noticeable and dangerous.[56]

The Chiefs of Staff denied the requests but reiterated that Hong Kong was considered an outpost to be held as long as possible. In the event of war, relief by sea was thought to be most unlikely, and a reinforcement of two infantry battalions was insufficient to increase the deterrent value of the garrison. Demilitarization had also been ruled out because of the negative impact on Chinese morale as well as on continued American collaboration.[57] After the reinforcement of Hong Kong was considered during the January–February 1941 Anglo-American strategy discussions, however, the Chiefs of Staff informed Brooke-Popham, "Should present discussions in Washington or any major change in situation alter our estimate of the position we will reconsider."[58] In Singapore, American, Dutch, and British officers also planned for war, but they recognized that time was required to build up strength.[59]

Many of China's military supplies passed through Hong Kong, but as an outpost of the British Empire, the colony would obviously be one of the first points of attack in any Japanese offensive south. For the Chinese, Hong Kong was an absolutely vital component of their logistical network, as well as a relatively safe haven for families and assets. Even during the Japanese occupation of Canton beginning in October 1938, Hong Kong remained as militarily significant as the Burma Road. Supplies such as fuel and spare parts bypassed Canton as they were transported from Hong Kong through Mirs Bay north to Waichow and then north-northeast along the East River to the Kukong-Swatow highway. From there, the majority of supplies were forwarded northwest to the Hunan-Kwangtung railway at Kukong, while the remainder were sent north along secondary roads directly into Kiangsi.[60] Aside from its importance to China, Hong Kong was also the center for British intelligence in the region. From Hong Kong, British officials were in contact with General Tai Li's agency in Chungking, Wu Teh Chen's organization in Kwangtung, and the Chinese Communist Party through Chu Teh. They also worked with Colonel N. V. Roshchin of the Soviet Military Mission, headed by Lieutenant General Vasilii Chuikov.[61]

Because of the situation at Hong Kong, additional friction was created in Anglo-Japanese relations, and the Sino-Japanese War underwent a dangerous escalation. The Japanese decision to advance south was intended to bring the war in China to an end. They believed that without Western economic, moral, and material aid, the Chinese would have ended their resistance, and this was the primary reason for the blockade and the final attack on Hong Kong in December.[62] According to British military intelligence officers, the link from the colony was vital: "Goods from Hong Kong pour into the interior and a considerable export trade in wood-oil, Tungsten and other products of 'Free China' is also carried on."[63] The War Office passed this information along to the Far Eastern Department at the Foreign Office, noting that Chinese resistance could be maintained only if supplies continued to enter China from British-controlled areas.[64] Officers of the Japanese 23rd Army, which made the attack on Hong Kong, commented on the importance of this situation to Allied occupation personnel in Japan after the war. The 23rd Army's intelligence chief, General Shimoda, stated:

> The outbreak of the Pacific War did not alter the main objective of our operations against China, which consisted of the overthrow of the Chiang Kai-shek regime. We were going to bring further pressure upon them by exploitation of the gains in the battle to the South. . . . With the success of our operations in the South and the capture of Hongkong, we were determined to route out all enemy foreign influence from China by confiscating their concessions, rights and interests. The Chungking Govt. thus cut off from the support of British and U.S. Allied Powers, would receive a fatal blow both psychologically and materially. If we were to follow up our military success by adequate political and administrative measures, the Chiang Kai-shek regime would ultimately surrender.[65]

Even without a Chinese surrender, however, the war had the potential to end without Chiang's consent by a more or less open Japanese rapprochement with Wang Ching Wei.[66]

Anglo-Japanese friction had already turned the Pearl River Delta into a more deadly arena prior to the Japanese attack on Hong Kong in December; ground combat throughout the region became more pronounced following the Japanese withdrawal from Kwangsi. Elements of the Japanese 38th Division maintained control throughout the West River Delta, with bases at Fatshan and Chungshan, and the fighting expanded twenty miles northwest of Canton. Aside from the disruption of agricultural production, the 38th Division conducted foraging raids on towns near Kongmoon in search of loot, frequently murdering and raping civilians in the process. East of Canton, two Chinese divisions, including the 157th, had been sent to reinforce Waichow in November 1940; in Canton itself, the Japanese reinforced the 18th Division under General Hyakutake soon thereafter. Chinese guerrilla activity increased through the spring along the West River and north of Canton. Assassinations and bombings were rife, and Japanese authorities often declared martial law in response. As a prelude to Japanese operations along the North River, the South China Expeditionary Force had been reinforced, and the defense zone surrounding Canton was extended. Fighting resumed at Tsungfa between General Yu Han Mou's 7th War Zone forces and the 104th Division under General Ito Takeo. Consequently, Japanese losses in the region continued to number between 200 and 300 men each month.[67]

Japan's presence was also felt from the air. Pilots of the 5th Air Regiment based at Canton supported ground actions and interdicted lines of communication to Hong Kong. Heavy bombardment of the Mirs Bay–Tamshui logistical route occurred regularly. In these operations, the 5th Air Regiment was assisted by aircraft flying from carriers such as the *Mizuho*, which were often positioned in Bias Bay. They had little success in halting Chinese supplies, however, usually because of poor weather conditions. Occasional airspace violations created anxiety, such as on 26 November 1940, when six planes overflew the colony in conjunction with a small ground reconnaissance of the north shore of Mirs Bay. CNAC losses also accumulated during this period, as fuel and tungsten continued to be flown between free China and Kai Tak airfield. This air traffic attracted much attention from Japanese fighters, but because most flights were conducted at night, losses were limited. Japanese air units did not have a completely free hand, however, and they sustained a serious loss on 5 February 1941. An aircraft carrying ten senior officials to Indochina was shot down near Shekki at the town of Tan Moon, killing all aboard. Among the dead were Supreme War Councillor Admiral Osumi Mineo and Rear Admiral Hikojiro Suga. More significantly, plans for future southern operations were captured by Chinese guerrillas and sent to Chungking.[68]

In March the Japanese conducted many seaborne raids along the Kwangtung coast to cut other supply lines and, in the process, provide troops with additional training in amphibious operations. These operations included the 229th and 230th Regiments of the 38th Division under Lieutenant General Fujii Yoji, the latter of which was landed at Pakhoi. Both regiments would see heavy combat during the attack on Hong Kong later in the year. Other units simultaneously increased the Japanese presence in the region just north of Hong Kong. After assuming command of the 124th Brigade (18th Division) from Major General Hara Mamoru, Major General Suefuji Tomofumi continued to post a number of units along the frontier and thereby maintained the landward blockade.[69]

A major interdiction effort against Hong Kong was mounted during January and February 1941. On 17 January an initial marine detachment supported by the carrier *Hiryu* advanced along the coast of Mirs Bay, with the objective of blocking the Chinese line of communication from Hong Kong to Tamshui. This was followed on 4 February with a landing farther east in Bias Bay by 2,000 troops of the 38th Division under General Kawaguchi Kiyotako. Another force landed northwest of the colony at Namtau on 7 February. A 1,000-man detachment of the 124th Regiment under Suefuji marched north from Shumchun and converged on Tamshui, along with the Kawaguchi detachment, which had moved up from Bias Bay. The total number of Japanese troops positioned north of Hong Kong was estimated to be about 8,000 men. Tamshui was occupied on 6 February without resistance; this resulted in the loss of a large amount of military supplies, including fuel that had been stockpiled awaiting shipment north to Waichow. Tungsten destined for the United States was also seized. Despite these Japanese moves, Chinese smugglers were able to transport 1.5 million gallons of fuel using junks over alternative routes from Hong Kong during the first half of 1941.[70]

After failing to achieve their goals, several Japanese ground units occupying towns scattered along the Kwangtung coast were withdrawn by the middle of March for deployment northeast and for operations farther inland in Kwangtung. Where possible, the void was filled with Chinese puppet troops, such as those of the 20th Division under Lieutenant General Li Au Yat. There were approximately 20,000 of these men in Kwangtung, but training and equipment remained minimal. New Japanese raids began on 1 April 1941 when the 115th Regiment (18th Division) left Tamshui and linked up with an amphibious assault force at Swabue under the command of Vice Admiral Sawamoto Yorio. Ground operations in the vicinity of Swatow were also stepped up, but several towns and cities farther along the coast in Fukien and Chekiang still faced extended occupations. Elements of the Japanese 18th, 28th (Formosan), and 5th Divisions were used against Foochow, Wenchow, and Ningpo. Heavy artillery was landed at Bocca Tigris and Namtau; the latter was also reinforced with infantry. The small airfield constructed there saw some activity when pilots used it to practice dive-bombing.[71]

Air attacks against inland Chinese supply routes became more frequent in advance of a move against Waichow. Units from the 18th and 38th Divisions occupied the town during May, but the Chinese 152nd and 160th Divisions moved south to divert these forces by threatening Japanese units positioned along the Hong Kong border. Finding resistance just north of

CHAPTER EIGHT

Waichow, and with their position at Shumchun under threat of attack, the Japanese broke off contact and evacuated the town, withdrawing west along the river. With approximately 6,000 to 7,000 men still scattered at various locations along the Hong Kong border, they wanted to be able to support these forces if necessary.[72] Fortunately for the British, these troops lacked sufficient strength to mount an attack on Hong Kong.

British military officers nevertheless sought to ease some of the tension building along the border. By this time, the elderly Lieutenant General Katajima, commander of the 18th Division, had established his headquarters at Shumchun to better study the approaches to Hong Kong. This was the first time an officer of that rank had been posted so close to the colony. In mid-June Major Charles Boxer entered into negotiations with Katajima to curb Chinese puppet agitation at Shataukok. A Japanese infantry company under Captain Sekiya had been encouraging Chinese to throw rocks at British police patrols, and they repeatedly cut the boundary wire. A gambling racket was also creating disorder. During Boxer's meeting with Katajima, the atmosphere was friendly, and the general agreed to deal with the problem personally. Brigadier Peffers and Major Boxer were then invited to accompany Katajima on an inspection of one of his companies commanded by Lieutenant Mori at Shumchun. In their presence, Katajima ordered the men to cease interfering with British patrols and to move gambling dens away from the border. But as General Grasett reported to London after Boxer's return, the lingering problem was junior officers' tendency to ignore orders they did not agree with, and the problems at Shataukok persisted.[73]

The Japanese 2nd Fleet also underwent a change of leadership, and the level of aggression displayed at Hong Kong increased significantly. On 17 May 1941 Vice Admiral Niimi Masaichi assumed command of the 2nd China Expeditionary Fleet from Vice Admiral Sawamoto Yorio, who had served in that position since the beginning of the year but had recently been appointed vice minister of the navy. On 30 May at Amoy, Niimi conferred with the commander in chief of the Japanese fleet in China, Admiral Shimada Shigetaro, and the blockade at Hong Kong grew increasingly dangerous. On 10 June Niimi landed troops less than five miles south of Hong Kong territorial waters on the Chinese-controlled Lema and Kaipong island groups, and the occupation continued throughout the summer. Henceforth, attacks on Hong Kong junks became more deadly than ever before, and British merchant shipping was intercepted and searched with greater regularity. Ships as large as cruisers were involved in these attacks.

On one occasion the *Izuzu* reportedly attacked junks and had several vessels in tow. Aircraft were also seen strafing junks.[74]

The Japanese were successful in disrupting the colony's food supply because the fishing fleet remained in port, but local colonial officials soon retaliated. In the sixty attacks reported during this round of conflict, at least fifteen people were killed and three were wounded. In response, General Grasett almost precipitated an overt Anglo-Japanese war by using six requisitioned Chinese Maritime Customs vessels to challenge Japanese naval forces directly. On 18 July 1941 shots were fired from a ship of the HMS *Cyclops* class to ward off a Japanese submarine; the Pearl River had already been partially mined by other Royal Navy vessels.[75] Just prior to this event, Grasett had indignantly explained the deteriorating situation to Britain's ambassador in Japan, Sir Robert Craigie:

I fully concur that this is a most dangerous practice. Could Minister of Marines notice be called to this and reminded that we are at war with two other powers both of which are using submarines for indiscriminate warfare and the fact that though a submarine may be flying a Japanese flag it might well be a ruse de guerre and must not be taken as a security that she will not be fired on if she attempts to stop British ships.[76]

He later added: "If the Japanese navy wished to avoid incidents [the] easiest way to achieve this is to remove their patrols from proximity of Hong Kong observing that this is a British Naval Base and we are in a state of openly declared warfare."[77] Grasett's confrontational actions threatened to ignite open war with Japan.

Whitehall's reaction followed Craigie's recommendation against further retaliation. He noted: "The danger of a locally provoked incident is, in fact, greater in the case of Hong Kong than in that of other British possessions in the Far East."[78] The Foreign Office supported his position, with A. L. Scott commenting: "In this case Sir R. Craigie talks sense, and the governor of Hongkong and his military advisers talk wildly."[79] Gerard Gent at the Colonial Office had written earlier: "Local retaliatory measures at Hong Kong seem to us to be unwise. . . . We should not like to see Hong Kong incited or permitted to start a local war of reprisals with Japan."[80] Thus, on 19 July 1941, the day after the incident occurred, Grasett's command in Hong Kong was terminated.[81] On his way back to England,

Grasett stopped in Ottawa to meet with General Harry Crerar, the Canadian army chief of staff, and they discussed the possibility of sending Canadian infantry to Hong Kong. Governor Northcote departed soon after Grasett, but he had been preparing for his retirement as early as June.[82]

The Japanese grew more desperate after failing to sever Chinese lines of communication to Burma and Hong Kong, but it was the German invasion of the USSR that provided a chance to break the impasse in south China once again. With the survival of the Soviet Union in doubt, the opportunity to threaten Anglo-American forces farther south with an occupation of the rest of Indochina seemed too good to ignore. Thus, many troops, including much of the 104th Division, were withdrawn from Kwangtung to conduct the operation, which began on 24 July. The largest mobilization of forces in Japanese history was also begun at this time. Reinforcements were sent to Manchuria to seize any favorable opportunity for an attack into Siberia. After being stripped for southern operations, the South China Expeditionary Force was disbanded (in June), and the 23rd Army was left in its place with three understrength divisions, one mixed brigade, and two infantry regiments to hold positions in Kwangtung. Troop reductions left approximately 5,000 men positioned along the Hong Kong border, and anarchy returned to areas that were temporarily abandoned, such as Chungshan.[83]

Violations of British sovereignty at Hong Kong subsequently worsened. The Japanese warned British officials that they had issued orders to shoot anyone approaching Hong Kong, Swatow, or Canton, and during August, twelve Chinese were shot while attempting to cross the frontier. Two sampans were also seized inside British territorial waters in Mirs Bay. The Chinese crews were released after protests were lodged. In September, Japanese aircraft entered the colony's airspace on two occasions. A bomber overflew Fanling on the twelfth, and a few days later, a flight of three aircraft crossed over Shataukok in a less flagrant violation. More blood was spilled at the end of October when a Japanese soldier fired at three Chinese boys driving cattle across the frontier near Shumchun. One was well inside British territory when he was shot in the head and subsequently died. Echoing the earlier submarine incident, a Japanese naval vessel carrying troops and several senior commanders entered the colony's waters in October to conduct a reconnaissance of the defenses. It was stopped by MTB No. 8 after machine gun rounds were fired across the bow. The Japanese prepared to repel boarders, but discussions on the MTB resulted in a withdrawal of the offending ship.[84]

The last round of Japanese ground action in Kwangtung prior to the attack on Hong Kong itself was conducted during September and October. Unlike previous operations earlier in the year, this offensive was launched primarily as a diversion to aid the beleaguered Japanese 11th Army in Hunan. The second battle of Changsha was a significant Japanese reverse that resulted in many casualties. In rendering aid from Kwangtung, the 23rd Army at Canton attacked north along the railway, hoping to draw Chinese divisions south, but it ran out of steam after an advance of approximately 100 kilometers. Closer to the coast, Japanese attention was fixed once again on the towns of Tamshui and Toishan. The latter had become a depot for tungsten transiting the West River. As was the case elsewhere in Kwangtung, Toishan had been occupied before, but this attack was more brutal, causing much damage and many casualties. What made the September attack on Toishan most notable, however, was the use of chemical weapons. Although outlawed by the Washington Armament Treaty of 1922, the use of chemical weapons was on the increase in China, and British officials in Asia feared that the Japanese might use them at Hong Kong.[85] There was less concern in London, however, as indicated in an early 1942 comment by a Foreign Office official: "The Chinks no doubt are ill-prepared against it & so it pays. The Japs have told us they won't use gas if we don't."[86]

The effects of these raids were devastating to the local population. Living conditions in Kwangtung were already dangerous, with robbery, inflation, and cholera being constant threats to those too impoverished to flee. Places such as Toishan and Tamshui soon faced serious food shortages, and famine became a difficult problem for many as the war progressed. As an additional affront, wheat sent to China as American Red Cross aid was seized by Japanese troops in Chungshan and Toishan, only to be sold at a high price in Canton. Compounding these problems was the continued widespread cultivation and distribution of opium.[87] The British consul in Swatow noted that the Japanese were financing their occupation by selling narcotics: "Around Swatow the fields are full of opium."[88] Macau remained a primary distribution base for the region, but Hong Kong likewise served as a useful opium conduit. Powerful criminal figures such as Tu Yueh Sheng (Du Yuesheng), also known as "Big Eared Tu," were able to develop networks as far away as Canada and America well into the postwar period.[89]

Throughout 1941, Kwangtung became increasingly violent. The Japanese inability to terminate the movement of military supplies from Hong Kong ensured that the war could continue indefinitely. Because of their failure to achieve peace, the Japanese grew more desperate and prepared to fight the additional enemies they blamed for their predicament. Encouraged by the German invasion of the USSR, the occupation of south Indochina was a significant step in this direction. British Far Eastern officials were also angered by the worsening crisis, and their impatience with Whitehall's restraint almost led to open warfare in July. Hong Kong had become the most dangerous flash point in the Far East, and local officials were removed in an attempt to prevent premature war. American intervention was still desired, but until that occurred, every effort was made in the Far East to maintain the Soviet Union as a belligerent ally. Thus, Anglo-American support for China assumed a much higher priority in the latter half of 1941.

A Faithless Gesture:
The Reinforcement of Hong Kong

After the fall of France, Canada accelerated its shift into the orbit of the United States, and American strategic problems increasingly became associated with Canada. This was the case in China, where U.S. interests were strongest among the wartime allies, except for the Soviet Union. Both the British and the Americans considered the continuance of the Sino-Japanese War necessary to keep the Japanese army engaged and away from other more strategic areas; this was especially so after the German invasion of the USSR.[90] Within this scenario, Canada's role in Far Eastern affairs emerged as a globally significant component of Anglo-American Far Eastern strategy. It was also another manifestation of Roosevelt's approach to the implementation of collective security.[91] Initially conceived in the White House, Canadian policy was based on the provision of military support as a means of maintaining Chinese morale. The essential elements involved the sale of munitions, but also the deployment of combat forces to Hong Kong in the fall of 1941. The crucial timing of these events, concurrent with Operation Barbarossa, meant that Canada's official presence in China was begun and maintained to provide indirect military support in defense of the Soviet Far Eastern flank, but this information was suppressed at the highest levels of government.

Political factors influenced the war effort more significantly in China than in any other theater of operations, and during the latter half of 1941, the maintenance of Chinese morale became a constant concern of Western leaders, especially as the bombing of Chungking intensified during the summer.[92] Japanese leaders had good reason to suspect that Chinese morale was shaken; it had been severely tested over the course of the war, and because of this, the peace faction was a significant force in Chinese politics that could not be ignored. British military attaché Brigadier General Lance Dennys commented on the situation on 25 October 1941:

China still fervently hopes for war between Japan and the democracies, as providing the best chance of winning their own war. A Japanese move against Siberia would not suit her book so well, unless she was certain that the democracies would then come in on Russia's side. The Chinese General Staff have two main fears, firstly that Japan may come to some compromise with the democracies which will leave her free to concentrate all her efforts against China; secondly that a complete Russian collapse may occur and open up communications between Germany and Japan via Siberia, which the General Staff feels would put both the democracies and China in a very bad position in the Far East. It is probable that a Russian collapse would be followed by the exertion of strong pressure by the "peace party" to come to terms with Japan.[93]

Ian Morrison at the Foreign Office noted his concerns:

Everything, for the moment, hinges upon the outcome of events in Europe. China today is sitting on the sidelines. But if things go badly, it is possible, indeed probable, that this second group . . . [the peace party] . . . will assert itself. And in the hostility which these Chinese leaders as well as the Japanese feel for the communists, may be detected what will perhaps be the face-saving solution to this struggle, the union of the two participants, to eliminate a common enemy.[94]

Years of defeat compounded by the incessant bombing of Chungking had made the Chinese weary of war, and as the global military situation became more critical, Anglo-American policy makers became increasingly concerned over the prospects for continued Chinese resistance.[95] Sir John Sterndale Bennett at the Foreign Office noted in July: "[The] Chinese should be provided with additional aircraft defence. If the Japanese raids on Chungking continue at the present rate without any effective defence being put up, it is quite possible that the Chinese may crack and we cannot afford to see them crack at this stage."[96]

The new U.S. ambassador, Clarence Gauss, informed the State Department that "Chinese resistance to Japanese aggression is largely based on the Chinese expectation that sooner or later Japan will clash with other powers having interests in the Far East."[97] In search of additional support, Chiang often exploited the potential for a Sino-Japanese peace in his communications with both Churchill and Roosevelt.[98] His requests for increased aid grew more forceful in 1941, as American peace talks with Japanese Ambassador Nomura Kichisaburo continued throughout the year.

Chiang's appeals became most insistent when an apparent threat to Yunnan developed in November, following a buildup of Japanese forces in northern Indochina. The Chinese were anxious because U.S. warnings to Japan about an attack on Yunnan had not been included in the Washington discussions. Chiang likely exaggerated the severity of the military threat against the Burma Road, but intelligence gleaned from the Japanese consul in Hong Kong and elsewhere indicated that peace between China and Japan remained a possibility. To the Chinese, it looked as though a deal might be made in Washington at their expense, and after the temporary closure of the Burma Road in 1940, followed by the signing of the Soviet-Japanese nonaggression treaty in April 1941, they had good reason to be concerned. Following the German invasion of the USSR, neither Roosevelt nor Churchill wished to take any more chances in China; therefore, support for the AVG was stepped up, while the Philippines were reinforced with additional B-17 bombers.[99]

Germany's invasion of the Soviet Union was the most critical event of 1941, as Soviet military reverses encouraged the Japanese to adopt a more aggressive posture. Soviet losses were staggering, amounting to more than 2 million casualties, 5,000 tanks and aircraft, plus an additional 9,500 guns by the end of October. After observing early Red Army defeats, the Japanese Imperial Council decided at a meeting held on 2–3 July 1941 to move south, and the seizure of southern Indochina was the first step in preparation for future operations. Roosevelt responded by embargoing oil exports to Japan and freezing Japanese assets.[100] Lord Halifax commented on these measures to Foreign Minister Anthony Eden in mid-1942:

That the United States Government had, in fact, imposed a total blockade upon Japan by an adroit exploitation of its freezing order was scarcely appreciated by the general public. It is worth recording that the Governments of the British Commonwealth and of the Netherlands East Indies followed the United States' lead in this forward policy without asking for any prior military guarantee. The United States public do not to this day understand how severe were the measures of economic pressure imposed upon Japan, and still believe implicitly in the official doctrine of the Japanese "stab in the back" at Pearl Harbour.[101]

Although many saw the embargo and the subsequent announcement of the Atlantic Charter as a virtual declaration of war, Allied leaders wanted the Japanese to fire the first shot.[102] In Ottawa, Mackenzie King shared this view, but he still wanted the Americans to commit themselves further. He also remained anxious that "British militarists in the Orient" might start a war prematurely, before Congress was willing to authorize American participation.[103]

The Japanese also approved plans to attack the USSR, but these were held in abeyance due to the size of the Soviets' Far Eastern army. Foreign Minister Matsuoka and War Minister Tojo Hideki advised an immediate attack into Siberia, but after signing the nonaggression pact with Stalin, the Japanese had been embarrassed by the German invasion and were unprepared for offensive operations in the north. Nevertheless, they were anticipating a reduction of Red Army units because reinforcements were badly needed against the Germans to prevent Soviet defeat, which was widely expected on all sides. If a significant number of Siberian divisions were transferred west, a Japanese attack northward became a distinct possibility. In such an offensive, the Soviet Union would likely be defeated, and this was to be prevented at all costs.[104] Although Allied intelligence confirmed by early October that the Japanese had decided not to attack Siberia, it was also clear that they would seize the opportunity if conditions developed to make such a course more promising. A significant problem, however, was the lack of willingness to share this information with the Chinese, as security in Chungking was poor.[105]

Western political figures were worried about the Soviets' ability to continue the war.[106] Mackenzie King's comments are useful to consider because they demonstrate why someone who feared the domestic political repercussions of conscription would be motivated to sacrifice ground troops in a forlorn military venture in Asia. After Kiev had been encircled in mid-September, along with almost 700,000 men, Mackenzie King began to note some of his fears. On 9 October 1941 he wrote, "I am really haunted by the horror of the Russian situation. It is the worst thing the world has ever witnessed in the nature of slaughter."[107] The following day he added, "I have never felt so anxious since the war began about this situation than I do about the Russian[s] at the present time. Germany's might is proving to be terrific."[108] On 16 October 1941 Mackenzie King recorded his comments to the cabinet:

I pointed out there were signs of considerable trouble on the horizon. Some fomenting the conscription issue; others, march on Parliament by farmers to demand $1. a bushel of wheat; others stirring up labour. That with Russia and Japan on the verge of war, the whole situation might get very unsettled. The minds of the Canadian people might get very unsettled and the whole situation get easily out of hand.[109]

Extending Allied aid to the Soviet Union was greatly desired, and China was a theater where indirect support could be provided swiftly.

The timing and pace of global military events made China the central issue in Far Eastern affairs during the latter half of 1941, and Canada's involvement in Asia took a major step forward.[110] After leaving Canada, Major General Grasett met with the Chiefs of Staff in London on 3 September 1941 to present his proposal for the Canadian reinforcement of Hong Kong, stating that an attack could be expected at any time. He added: "Everything possible had been done to assure General Chiang Kai Shek that the garrison intended to fight to the last man."[111] A reinforcement of Hong Kong by two battalions would help in this regard, but not simply because it would strengthen the garrison. As a political gesture, it would seemingly demonstrate Allied solidarity and commitment to China, and the potential effect on morale throughout the "whole of the Far East" was emphasized in the cabinet.[112]

That same day, as the noose was beginning to tighten around Kiev, Churchill received an urgent telegram from Stalin, demanding a second front in Europe and significant quantities of material aid. Due to material shortages, fulfilling his requirements would prove difficult, but without such assistance, Stalin warned that the USSR would be unable to continue the war.[113] Concurrently, however, Stalin was waging a domestic war against the Russian people, with up to 1 million NKVD men working on internal security. Their duties consisted largely of managing mass deportation, organized terror, and genocide.[114] Nevertheless, on 29 August Churchill informed Stalin that he was anxious to render additional support to Chiang Kai Shek as an immediate stopgap.[115] The cabinet was determined to help Stalin in any way possible, and the most vocal voice for support was that of the minister of aircraft production, Lord Beaverbrook. According to Brian Farrell, Beaverbrook once remarked: "Anything that furthers Russia's effort in the war is worth any price, no matter how high."[116] Because of Britain's military weakness, Churchill upheld his rejection of Stalin's persistent demand for a second front, but he told Soviet Ambassador Ivan Maisky, "If by our action we could draw the weight of attack off Russia we would not hesitate to take such action, even at the risk of losing 50,000 men."[117] On 13 September 1941 Stalin acknowledged Britain's inability to open a second front in France but made an alternative suggestion: "Perhaps another method could be found to render to the Soviet Union an active military help?"[118] Appeals for British divisions to fight inside the southern USSR were considered but ultimately dismissed.[119] According to Peter Clarke, in response to pleas from Ambassador Sir Stafford Cripps in October for acceptance of such a plan, Churchill stated, "It would be silly to send two or three British or British-Indian divisions into the heart of Russia to be surrounded and cut to pieces as a symbolic sacrifice."[120]

While visiting Britain from 20 August to 7 September, Mackenzie King was present for numerous cabinet discussions involving the destruction occurring in the Soviet Union. His visit also coincided with Grasett's meeting with the Chiefs of Staff. In lending diplomatic support, Mackenzie King delivered a speech at the Mansion House on 5 September in which he called for increased American involvement in the war and for the establishment of a new world order to be led by Britain and the United States. After returning to Ottawa, the prime minister reported to his cabinet that the British military were not optimistic about the Soviets' capacity for long resistance. At the same time, Grasett's request for Canadian reinforcements for Hong Kong was approved by the British Chiefs of Staff, and it was immediately submitted to Churchill. The Canadian government was officially notified on 19 September 1941.[121]

The British request was then considered by the Canadian cabinet.[122] During a meeting on 2 October:

Mr. King expressed the view that Canada should do whatever was possible for the U.S.S.R., in the present critical circumstances. Stalin's requests to the U.K. government for the despatch of British expeditionary forces to the Continent had, of necessity, been refused by the U.K. government. This made it all the more important to aid in other ways, and Canada should adopt all means within her power of assisting and encouraging Russia.[123]

During this meeting, final approval was given for the reinforcement of Hong Kong. In the Soviet Union, Army Group Center launched Operation Typhoon to begin the battle for Moscow.[124]

Just over a fortnight later in Tokyo, the Konoye cabinet fell owing to the failure to reach an agreement with Roosevelt, and the aggressive prime minister, General Tojo Hideki, assumed leadership of the government.[125] A *New York Times* editorial surmised that the likelihood of war had increased greatly as a result. It noted, "as long ago as 1937 he [Tojo] declared that Japan must prepare to fight China and Russia simultaneously. His advent to a position of power at this crucial time in the Battle for Russia cannot help but be a matter of concern."[126] Compounding the problem, Stalin began to transfer a significant portion of the Red Army's Far Eastern forces westward in the latter half of October. When Soviet spy Richard Sorge reported from Tokyo that the Japanese had chosen to advance south, approximately ten divisions, along with 1,000 tanks and aircraft, were withdrawn from Siberia, and these reliable units were thrown against the Germans. As the force ratio in Manchuria began to shift toward the Japanese, a surprise offensive into Siberia remained a distinct possibility.

Against this backdrop, C Force left Vancouver aboard the SS *Awatea* on 27 October 1941 and arrived in Hong Kong on 16 November.[127] A few days before its departure, Dominions Office telegram M-337 arrived in Ottawa to fully explain the importance of the deployment as an application of collective security in Asia. In this document, Lord Cranborne provided the primary rationale:

Since our conversation with Mr. Hull, Japanese Government has fallen, apparently on issue of Washington conversations and conduct of affairs has been put into extremists hands. It is therefore necessary, in conjunction with United States Government, to take stock of situation having regard to (a) the stimulus which German advance on Moscow is giving to those in Japan in favour of early action and (b) the effective pressure of our economic embargo on Japan.

(2) It is possible direction which Japanese will take is southwards, e.g. into Thailand, and we have had an urgent appeal from Thai Prime Minster for cooperation. . . . Japan knows, however, that this choice is likely to bring her into collision with ABCD front. This risk is less in the north where Japan had already a strong concentration of military forces. Japan may also hope that departure of Government from Moscow and consequent weakening of its authority may lead to some disintegration of Soviet forces in Siberia. We have [to] reckon therefore with possibility of an attack upon Russia in the fairly near future.

(3) Even though there is little effective action that we could take in this eventuality (and you should make it clear that we have taken no decision on the point) it is desirable that we should enter into consultation with the United States Government at once. So long as our Russian Allies are resisting Germany in the west it is important that we should not weaken or discourage their resistance by a failure to support them to the best of our ability in the Far East. We have also to consider position of our Dutch Allies and effect on spirit on Netherlands East Indies if we were to fail the Russians.[128]

He went on to clarify that Allied Far Eastern policy was being formed in Washington:

We have been well content to leave handling of Japanese problem to the United States and to follow United States in their policy of maximum economic pressure. Prime Minister made it clear moreover in his broadcast of August 24th that should their attempt to reach a peaceful solution fail we should arrange ourselves by their side. This remains the position. While as stated above, positive action by ourselves alone is unlikely to be very effective, we are prepared to support any action however serious which the United States may decide to take.[129]

CHAPTER EIGHT

As this message makes clear, Soviet Far Eastern security was an important consideration behind the deployment of C Force, as was following America's lead.

At the end of October, only four days after C Force set sail from Vancouver, another Dominions Office telegram arrived in Ottawa. In it, Cranborne communicated a change in Whitehall's appraisal of the situation, based on updated intelligence from Japan:

> His Majesty's Ambassador at Tokyo considers indications of a Japanese attack on Russian line somewhat decreasing since August. . . .
>
> Sir Robert Craigie adds that this view relates merely to situation as he sees it today and would naturally cease to apply if there were to be a complete collapse of the Soviet armies in the west, or any serious weakening of their forces in the east.[130]

Whitehall's message to Ottawa reveals that anxiety over Soviet survival had diminished somewhat since C Force's deployment had been approved. However, it remained strong, pending further developments in front of Moscow. In any event, C Force had already left Canada for Hong Kong by the time of this reappraisal.

While C Force was in transit, Mackenzie King reflected on the importance of its mission:

> I do not know of any day when I have felt a greater concern about the outcome of the war than today. It is now perfectly clear that Japan intends to fight and that, very soon. China has made it quite clear that without further assistance, she cannot hope to effectively resist and that her resistance will end unless such assistance is speedily given. If China's resistance falls and breaks, Japan will have a free field, no enemy at her rear in Asia, and will be able to go after both the British and the Russians but what is worse is that a break in Chinese resistance will probably mean a break in Russian resistance.[131]

C Force was sent to Hong Kong to help prevent this scenario.

Mackenzie King was not confused over the threat posed to the colony. Nor is ignorance plausible concerning Churchill's view that there was "not the slightest chance of relieving it."[132] Mackenzie King was certain that war with Japan was inevitable in 1941, and he commented on this many times.[133] He did so once in August, during a conversation with reporter Grant Dexter, who subsequently related this information to his boss in private correspondence: "Official information shows that Japan is feinting both north and south. King thinks the blow will strike southward, but if Russia crumbled up in Europe, it would be into Siberia. One point on which the P.M. is quite emphatic is that 'Japan is planning to go a long way now'—it will be a shooting war before long."[134] Much of Mackenzie King's information came from Roosevelt, as Dexter noted on 7 November 1941: "Roosevelt told him that war between United States and Japan regarded as certain and almost certain to come within 30 days."[135] On Friday, 5 December 1941, Mackenzie King made another highly prescient entry in his diary: "The situation is tenser than ever, and I shall be amazed if, before the week is out, war does not take place in the Far East, possibly Sunday."[136] On cue, the disastrous battle of Hong Kong began almost simultaneously with the attack on Pearl Harbor and ended on Christmas Day.

Domestic political fallout was not long in coming, and statements by senior Canadian officials show that the deployment of C Force was a diplomatic issue of significance as well as a military affair. Under heavy criticism, Mackenzie King wrote that the decision had been made in support of American objectives: "Our political enemies were taking the ground out from under our feet through our not having power under the Mobilization Statute to even move men across the border to the United States or into Newfoundland or to an Island on the Pacific though we had mutual obligations with the States to defend each other."[137] General Crerar explained to the Royal Commission of Inquiry, headed by Sir Lyman Duff, that the deployment was similar to the British action in Greece. The British had intervened in the Balkans as a demonstration of their commitment to Turkey, with the aim of maintaining that country's neutrality. The alternative hope of arranging a solid Balkan bloc encompassing Greece, Yugoslavia, and Turkey met with failure.[138]

Mackenzie King wanted to make public the contents of telegram M-337 in order to explain his reasons for the deployment of C Force explicitly and to blunt parliamentary furor over his cabinet's decision, but his appeal was rejected in London.[139] Under similar political fire, Churchill was advised by General Hastings Ismay in June 1942 that "the less said on this subject the better."[140] He added, "It would not be in the public interest to give any further information on this subject."[141] In 1948 Prime Minister Clement Attlee rejected another Mackenzie King request to publish the contents of telegram M-337 after the release of Major General Christopher Maltby's postwar report of the battle reignited the issue in Ottawa. Out of five telegrams identified in correspondence between External Affairs and Whitehall, telegram M-337 was singled out specifically by the Dominions Office and Attlee because it identified the Soviet crisis as being a fundamental reason behind the deployment.[142]

There were several reasons for official silence. First, motivations had to be concealed to maintain public support for the war. It would have been politically inconvenient to explain why soldiers had been sent on a forlorn mission that was widely expected to fail in defense of a dictator whose despotism paralleled Hitler's. Thus, Canadian troops had been dispatched to Hong Kong ostensibly as a deterrent against further Japanese aggression, but War Office correspondence with Sterndale Bennett and others at the Foreign Office clarified that the deterrence explanation "should be treated for publicity and propaganda purposes."[143] Because of C Force's limited strength, its deployment was not an act of deterrence; it was instead a provocation. Moreover, few were eager to announce that the propaganda value of the garrison's destruction would be increased in the United States by the participation of Canadian troops. Second, disclosure would have created unwanted diplomatic trouble. Any mention of encouraging the Chinese or impressing the Americans was to be minimized because the deployment was not solely a British maneuver. Sir John Brenan noted, "The American authorities are obviously objecting to exaggerated publicity by us about their part in the joint defence programme."[144] F. E. Evans added, "Commentaries should, I suppose, avoid any suggestion that the arrival of these forces represents pursuit of a joint Anglo-U.S. policy."[145] Five days prior to C Force's arrival in Hong Kong, officials in London received a rude shock when a front-page article in the *Daily Telegraph* indicated that the colony would be transformed into a vital bastion "of democratic defence" after consultations with American authorities had resulted in the deployment of Canadian soldiers.[146]

Anglo-American strategic discussions about southern China continued throughout the year. After agreeing to a Europe-first strategy during secret talks held in Washington from late January to early March 1941, U.S. officials stated that they would concentrate their forces in the Atlantic so that Commonwealth units would be available for the Far East. The primary military objectives in defending Hong Kong were to deny use of the port facilities to the Japanese for as long as possible and to draw off forces from an attack on Singapore. Officers in theater, however, held on to the dangerous premise that it would be possible to keep Hong Kong open as a forward base of operations.[147] They were optimistic that an overland relief of the colony could be mounted by the Chinese army. Faith in such a plan was strengthened following a 10 October 1941 meeting between Chiang Kai Shek and General Dennys. According to Catherine Baxter, Chiang stated firmly during the meeting that Hong Kong "was just as much China's battle as it was Britain's."[148] Japanese officers shared that view, and they designed their offensive for southern China accordingly. They would support their attack on Hong Kong with a corresponding attack on Changsha.[149]

Due to limited Allied resources, reliance was placed on small guerrilla and commando units, supported by airpower, to operate in conjunction with Chinese regular forces in any potential relief of a siege at Hong Kong. As part of this plan, the AVG was based in Kunming to provide air defense for supplies transiting the Burma Road. Initially, two RAF squadrons were to be sent to Kunming and Kweilin for the same purpose and to support ground operations closer to Hong Kong, but their deployment was canceled later in the year. Guerrilla forces led or dominated by British personnel, such as Detachment 204 and the China Commando Group, were to be supplied overland from Kunming, and they were to fight in collaboration with Chinese regular army units in Hunan and Kwangtung. It was hoped that heavy bombers based in the Philippines might also become available to support Asian mainland operations should they be required. In Hong Kong itself, the garrison was supposed to hold for as long as possible and link up with Allied relieving forces, if able. Odds for success were not rated highly in London or Washington, but belated arrangements were made to coordinate with the Chinese.[150] Had such a plan been cultivated in 1938–1939, prior to the outbreak of war in Europe, it might have deterred Japanese aggression if supported by sufficient British military strength. Once war against Germany was under way, however, the lack of available resources for Far Eastern defense doomed it to failure.

Momentum for the development of the Hong Kong relief plan was generated from military commanders in the region. In the process, they contributed substantially to strengthening military ties with China and facilitating greater U.S. involvement in the war, though still on a limited scale. British Far Eastern officials eagerly outpaced Whitehall in establishing military links with the Chinese and in presenting a firmer front to the Japanese. Although Whitehall remained quite cautious on this issue to avoid provocations, senior commanders in the field, such as Grasett and Brooke-Popham, pushed the limits of official restraint when confronted with operational problems firsthand. General Grasett demonstrated this by establishing, on his own initiative, a joint Sino-British radio net in late 1940. Prior to this he created Z Force, a small special operations unit to fight behind enemy lines.[151] In December 1940 Grasett instructed General Dennys to develop plans with the Chinese for fully coordinated operations between their military forces and British units at Hong Kong. Through the spring and summer of 1941, both Brooke-Popham and Dennys engaged in discussions with Chinese officers along these lines; coordination with the AVG was also included. Until the German invasion of the USSR, Whitehall was cool to the idea of collaborating with China, and although limited cooperation was accepted for the relief of Hong Kong, the offer of Chinese troops for Burma was rejected in London until 23 December 1941.[152] By then, it was too late.

Enthusiasm for the Hong Kong relief plan peaked in October, after the second battle of Changsha and the Chinese attack on Ichang. At that time, General Dennys reported that the Chinese army was incapable of sustaining large-scale offensives but was capable of limited offensive action under favorable conditions if assisted by Allied airpower. As the military situation in the Soviet Union became more serious, some resources were delivered and positioned for use by Allied air and special operation forces in southern China. In July a Sino-British agreement was reached for the deployment of Detachment 204, and by September, the force was ready. In addition, 700,000 gallons of aviation fuel were delivered to storage depots in China for use by the AVG, and the deployment of that unit was accelerated. The diversion of additional aircraft, beyond those already allocated, was still discouraged by London.[153] There are also indications that in the fall of 1941, Colonel Mayer was working on the formation of a small U.S.-led special operations group to fight alongside Detachment 204. For instance, the future commander of Merrill's Marauders, Captain Frank Merrill, was present in the colony during October 1941 for approximately one month, working out of the American attaché's office. With the start of the Pacific war, Mayer requested that personnel from the USS *Tulsa* be trained at Maymyo, Burma, and molded into an American commando company.[154] The commander of C Force, Brigadier General John Lawson, followed this trend soon after his arrival and requested an additional battalion to transform his unit into a full brigade group. He told the new

GOC China, Major General Christopher Maltby, that additional reinforcements "will be thrown at us," and the Chiefs of Staff began to lean in that
direction. Lawson also discussed plans with Captain E. J. Hudson, commander of the U.S. Navy Asiatic Fleet Southern Patrol, while visiting the
USS *Mindanao* on 1 December 1941. It was Whitehall's reluctance to cooperate with the Chinese throughout much of the year, however, that hindered full implementation of joint action.[155]

Over time, Anglo-American strategy underwent several alterations, but
its essence remained the same: Hong Kong was fixed as the strategic objective in southern China. During 1942, General Joseph Stilwell embraced the
XYZ plan, which was implemented with the objective of immobilizing Japanese forces, but China's liberation was also meant to support the Pacific
campaign. X and Y Forces included Chinese divisions in India and Yunnan, respectively, and these saw action in Burma. Once the Burma Road
was reopened, the focus of operations would shift east of Kweilin, where
Sino-American Z Force units would drive on Hong Kong. With Hong
Kong secured, supplies could then be delivered north to the Yangtse River
and beyond. This plan was temporarily abandoned in 1944 because of Japanese success during Operation Ichigo, but it was revived under General
Albert Wedemeyer to become Operation Carbonado in 1945.[156]

Until that time, Canada in many ways served as an Anglo-American
proxy in the Far East, but the real objectives behind such a role remained
concealed. The reinforcement of Hong Kong did not greatly affect military events in China at the operational level, but the geostrategic impact
was not altogether insignificant. It was the principal mission of General
Dennys to prevent a Sino-Japanese peace as the Far Eastern crisis deteriorated. Following his discussions with Chiang in the summer of 1941 concerning joint military action at Hong Kong, his position became more
credible with the arrival of C Force. After the war, Brooke-Popham stated
that the Chinese had clearly understood the importance of Hong Kong for
their own supplies, and had they not been convinced of British determination to defend it militarily, they might have come to terms with the Japanese beforehand. Ironically, Mackenzie King would not have reinforced
Hong Kong simply to defend the British Empire, as demonstrated by his
government's refusal to reinforce Australia and the Falkland Islands during the winter of 1941–1942, but he did so with less hesitation to aid
Stalin.[157] Another disaster unfolded eight months later at Dieppe, with
equal obfuscation, when, according to Brigadier General Denis Whitaker,

CHAPTER EIGHT

Roosevelt suggested that Churchill make a "sacrifice landing" in France for the very same reason.[158]

As the Allied disaster in Burma unfolded in February 1942, Mackenzie King expressed some of his views in his diary after a discussion with Lieutenant General Andy McNaughton, commander of the Canadian army in England:

[According to McNaughton] the three areas that, above all, needed to be protected today were, first, Great Britain itself; if Britain went the whole show would go. Second, the Gulf of Azov, the control of the passage to the Caucuses. Third, the Burma Road to China. While it would be a serious thing to lose Singapore, he doubted if General Wavell would be over-concerned about that loss, because as a naval base, it was not functioning anyway. What he would be concerned about was the Burma Road, which was the only means of keeping supplies going to China. If those supplies were stopped, China might drop out of the picture, which would be very serious indeed. It was a relief to my mind to hear him so describe the relative significance of Singapore. He, of course, regards the whole situation as very critical. I, personally, feel it is worse at the moment than it has been at any time, with the single exception of the early attack upon Britain.[159]

This statement shows that Mackenzie King was clearly more concerned about events in China than he was about Singapore, and it was due to this anxiety that C Force was dispatched to Hong Kong to strengthen Chinese morale.

Whether the Chinese would have quit the war remains a mystery. More important was the fact that Allied leaders believed it was possible, and on this question, they were not willing to gamble during the fall of 1941. In the end, Grasett was awarded the Order of the Red Banner for his service.[160] Presumably, this came about following Clark Kerr's reassignment to the USSR in 1942 and his advocacy of the general to Stalin. The Order of the Red Banner was one of the most coveted decorations for bravery in the Red Army, but it was also bestowed on foreign NKVD agents for their outstanding performance on "special tasks."[161] Based on Grasett's history, it seems unlikely that he was a Soviet agent, although the possibility does exist. It is more plausible that he was simply acting aggressively on his own initiative in a manner that was unnecessarily reckless and counterproductive. In this affair, however, the general did not act alone. Others were involved in the decision to reinforce Hong Kong, and the ultimate responsibility rests with Mackenzie King.[162] As Canada's prime minister and external affairs minister, he was the official most responsible for the deployment, as well as for the undemocratic concealment of the reasons behind it.

Toward the Abyss

Once Roosevelt was reelected, American intervention in the war evolved steadily throughout 1941, and this transpired at the expense of British wealth and power. Contributing to this process was Mackenzie King and the Canadian government. Canada acted as a catalyst in forging the transatlantic alliance, but the country also served the same function in Asia. Until the German invasion of the Soviet Union, China was not a great priority in either London or Washington, but as the Red Army was being destroyed, Anglo-American strategic plans became more dependent on the continuation of the Sino-Japanese War. In all likelihood, a two-front war inside the USSR would have ended in an Axis victory; thus, neither Roosevelt nor Churchill would allow the Japanese army to deliver the death blow by attacking the Soviet Far East.

The problem, however, was Chungking's lack of faith in Allied assurances of commitment and support. The British were never eager to ally themselves fully with the Chinese, and in any event, they had few forces to spare for a meaningful military effort. Roosevelt tried to do more but was encumbered by the democratic will and the lawful authority of Congress to remain neutral. Loans provided sufficient inducement to keep the Sino-Japanese War from ending, but as diplomatic maneuvering at China's expense once again appeared during the Nomura-Hull negotiations in Washington, Chinese patience with their unreliable allies may have reached the breaking point.

British weakness at Hong Kong did nothing to assuage their fears, as the colony had become a strategic center of global significance. Without the use of the port, Chinese resistance would have been much more difficult, but more important, if the British and the Americans would not defend their own interests in southern China, the Chinese could reasonably assume that their promises were utterly worthless. Another problem was that the violence building around Hong Kong threatened to spark a war before

CHAPTER EIGHT

America was sufficiently committed, and with only weak military forces available, British officers in the region were making this situation worse. At this point, Mackenzie King entered the fray. Guns were sold to China to help Roosevelt out of a bind, while Canadian troops were dispatched to Hong Kong to demonstrate Allied commitment, but ulterior motives guided this development. Western political leaders were less concerned about aiding their Chinese allies than about supporting the USSR, and the net result of Allied efforts was to protect Stalin in the Soviet Far East. The application of collective security doctrine at Hong Kong ultimately did not provide any useful deterrence against Japanese aggression south; instead, it produced the opposite effect by helping to ignite the Pacific war.

NINE

■

Empires Derailed:
The War in South China,
September 1941 to January 1942

Lack of clear Japanese strategic planning greatly contributed to the outbreak of the Pacific war. Until 1941, the Japanese enlarged their empire by
reacting to opportunities created by Anglo-French military weakness.
Moves such as the occupation of northern French Indochina were also conducted primarily to sever China's external lines of communication. Conversely, the invasion of southern Indochina was a more ambitious and
aggressive empire-building endeavor meant to extend Japanese hegemony
throughout Asia, and it heralded the onset of the long-expected advance
south against other Western colonial powers. In preparing for such a move,
the Japanese were hesitant to join their German partners in invading the Soviet Union. Leaders in Tokyo had decided to wait for a reduction of the Red
Army's Far Eastern forces while building up their own strength in Manchoukuo; once the Soviets were sufficiently weakened, the opportunity to
invade Siberia might then be seized. In the meantime, a southward offensive
against Anglo-U.S. forces was approved, and preparations were carried out
while the Hull-Nomura negotiations continued in Washington.[1]

Concurrently, the Japanese continued to look for military solutions to
deal with their problems in China, but those efforts proved counterproductive. Chinese morale was under great strain, partly due to the ongoing discussions in Washington, and the Japanese thought that by seizing the rice
bowl of Hunan while simultaneously cutting lines of communication to

British-controlled areas, victory would be assured.[2] Thus, during the fall and winter of 1941, two important battles were fought for the control of Hunan, with the goal of knocking China out of the war. The Japanese hoped that the fall of Changsha would finally discredit the Chinese sufficiently on the international stage to prevent further third-power intervention, but after four years of war, elements of the Chinese army had become more combat-effective than anticipated. Consequently, Chinese military victories in the second and third battles of Changsha were significant geopolitical events, as they encouraged additional foreign aid that sustained the country as an active belligerent. With the Japanese army contained, the resulting military stalemate ensured that indirect Allied support for the Soviet Far East was not disrupted. In preventing a two-front war from developing in the USSR, the south China front became a globally significant theater of operations during the latter half of 1941 and early 1942.

Japanese failure in the second battle of Changsha, fought during September and October 1941, also accelerated the onset of war against Britain and America. Faced with gridlock in China and a crippling American oil embargo, the Japanese attacked the Western powers on 7 December 1941 with the expectation of fighting a war for limited objectives. They hoped that through the rapid seizure and fortification of forward positions in the Pacific, the Allies would balk at the cost of a prolonged campaign of reconquest and quickly sue for peace.[3] By acting on this assumption, the Japanese committed one of the greatest strategic mistakes of the war.

The Sino-Japanese War finally reached its crescendo with the combined offensives at Hong Kong and the third battle of Changsha, and this culmination of the conflict opened the door to a vastly worse struggle. With the start of the Pacific war, both cities were attacked as twin objectives of the same plan, the goal of which remained the termination of the war.[4] Both were in the same theater of operations, and the railway linking Kukong and Changsha made Kwangtung and Hunan mutually supportive regions. This internal line of communication was a tremendous Chinese advantage. Most of the supplies that had been entering China from Hong Kong were transported overland to the railhead and then sent north to the 9th War Zone forces defending Hunan. Armies based in the province could also be easily moved south to defend northern Kwangtung, as needed. Getting troops to Hong Kong, however, was a different matter. Infrastructure problems north of the colony made the movement of military forces difficult, and this contributed to a premature surrender on 25 December 1941.

Yet Japanese success at Hong Kong was insufficient to offset the disaster inflicted on the 11th Army under Lieutenant General Anami Korechika in Hunan. The third battle of Changsha was the only major battle of the period that resulted in an Allied Far Eastern victory, and because of this, Chinese morale was sustained at a time when the country's physical isolation became virtually complete.

The British policy on Hong Kong was counterproductive as well, although to a lesser degree. By inviting Japanese attack, Britain greatly hastened the decline of its global power. The British were unable to meet the threat in the Far East because they were heavily engaged in Europe and North Africa. Thus, in a relatively short time, they too would be eclipsed by American hegemonic power. The expedient of waging a proxy war to contain the Japanese was prejudicial to their imperial longevity and to the maintenance of global power. Because of the flow of military supplies through Hong Kong and into China, low-intensity conflict in the Pearl River Delta escalated to become another significant factor leading to an open Anglo-Japanese war. The British, however, were slow to fully integrate both Hong Kong and south China as a single theater of operations into their Pacific war strategy, and the colony surrendered within three weeks of the opening attack. Lack of mutual trust prevented full coordination with the Chinese, despite initial steps taken toward joint military action. The relief of the garrison by the Chinese army was therefore delayed, and the early fall of Hong Kong on Christmas Day shattered expectations. Defeat also produced sufficient animosity among many Chinese to prevent military cooperation between the two countries for the remainder of the war.

By 1942, the Americans assumed a dominant role in China. Catalyzing this transition in part was the Canadian war effort. American commitment increased steadily during 1941, and in early 1942 China effectively became a U.S. sphere of influence. Allied military reverses in Asia meant that President Roosevelt was largely limited to extending financial and diplomatic support to the Chinese, but at his behest, Prime Minister W. L. Mackenzie King ensured that Canadian military hardware was made available to bolster Chinese morale.[5] Canadian diplomatic assistance was also considered useful, coming at a time when Allied prestige was low and Generalissimo Chiang Kai Shek was hoping to make China the dominant power in Asia. As Chiang moved to support Indian leaders in their bid to gain independence from Britain, Mackenzie King offered his full backing as a leading

CHAPTER NINE

figure in the British Commonwealth. Amicable Sino-Canadian relations were established during the war as a result of the personal diplomacy conducted between Mackenzie King and China's foreign minister, T. V. Soong, and their discussions helped foster a close friendship between them.[6] The impact of these issues on Chinese morale was limited, but they show that Canadian efforts in China, and the defense of Hong Kong itself, were not aimed at promoting British imperial ambitions. Canada was supporting U.S. foreign policy.

The Second Battle of Changsha and the Battle of Ichang: Twilight of Soviet Support for Chungking

While the Germans were inflicting great destruction on the Soviet Red Army, Allied strategy for Asia was being formulated, with the aim of diverting Japanese attention southward by increasing material support for China in Yunnan, Hunan, Kwangsi, and Kwangtung. In the event of war with Japan, some British and American military officers in the Far East hoped to keep Hong Kong open as a forward base of operations astride Japanese lines of communication in the South China Sea. As part of this strategy, American long-range airpower was based in the Philippines, as was the AVG in Burma. At this time, the British strengthened their position at Hong Kong, while Soviet advisers under the command of General Chuikov continued to thwart Japanese ambitions in Hunan.[7]

In the second battle of Changsha, Chinese and Soviet artillery officers in the mountains north and west of the city inflicted considerable damage on the Japanese 11th Army, as 9th War Zone forces under General Hsueh Yueh attacked the exposed Japanese flanks to cut their lines of communication. During this battle, General Chuikov also assisted Chinese leaders by directing a decisive strategic counterstroke at Ichang.[8] The second battle of Changsha in September and October 1941 was the high point of Soviet success in southern China. Hunan was kept out of Japanese hands, and military supplies for 9th War Zone forces continued to arrive from British-controlled areas. As a result of their victory, Chinese morale was buoyed, and the country continued the war. Stung with defeat in Hunan, Japanese determination to cut off external sources of aid to China coalesced into a final decision to wage war against both Britain and the United States. Taken together, the second battle of Changsha and the Chinese counterattack at Ichang were significant geostrategic events. Allied cooperation in south China enhanced Soviet Far Eastern security, but this ultimately came at British expense in Hong Kong and elsewhere.

Following the invasion of southern Indochina, the Imperial General Headquarters in Tokyo approved an offensive in Hunan. General Anami's objectives were to capture the important city of Changsha and destroy Chinese military forces within the province. In doing so, the Japanese hoped to bring the war in China to a final conclusion, but Anami was a highly aggressive officer whose zeal and persistence were betrayed by an overconfident recklessness that resulted in Japanese defeat. By exceeding the 11th Army's capabilities, Anami suffered a reverse that only stiffened Chinese resolve. U.S.-Japanese peace negotiations were under way in Washington at the time, and attempts to demonstrate China's military worthlessness as a potential American ally were partly undone by Anami's ineffective leadership.[9]

With only a handful of provinces left unoccupied by Japanese forces, Hunan was an important region for sustaining Chinese resistance. It was one of the principal rice-growing areas of the country, in addition to being a significant source of manpower for the army. Strategic resources needed by the Allies were found in abundance, with tungsten being one of the more important.[10] Railway lines also made Hunan the nexus of south China's transportation infrastructure. Politically, it was vital for Chiang to keep Hunan from falling into Japanese hands, since it was one of the few provinces in free China still directly under the control of the central government. However, doubts about the loyalty of several provincial leaders persisted. Yunnan, for example, remained largely autonomous under the leadership of General Lung Yun. General Chang Fa Kwei in Kwangsi and officials in Szechwan similarly continued to exhibit an independent attitude, despite the grip of centralized power held by Chiang. Hunan was one of the few provinces that remained more or less loyal to Chungking, even under the leadership of the Cantonese General Hsueh, and it would stay that way throughout 1941 and 1942. Hunan had been defended with determination in 1939, and in two rare instances when artillery superiority was mustered, greater efforts were exerted in the fall and winter of 1941 to keep the province out of Japanese hands yet again.[11]

Bilateral Sino-British military cooperation for the defense of south China was hindered by mutual mistrust.[12] Aside from assisting the Soviets, the British had other reasons for keeping the war in China active. The threat posed to India was one of the most significant, but British anxiety was not directed solely toward the Japanese. A. L. Scott at the Foreign Office made note of this a month before the outbreak of war in the USSR: "It will not be long before the Chinese persuade themselves that they have won the war unaided . . . and [begin] actively promoting anti-Imperialist movements in adjacent countries—we do not want Japan therefore to be utterly crushed."[13] Imperial sentimentality was not the guiding principle behind this policy, but India was still considered useful in the war against Germany. It was only after Stalin switched camps that China became more desirable as an ally, and British support slowly increased. Several military training facilities, including a guerrilla warfare school at Manchiang, had been established in places such as Kiangsi to strengthen Sino-British cooperation. The development of forces such as Detachment 204 and the China Commando Group soon followed. Chiang, however, was similarly suspicious of British motives, and these units were prevented from reaching their full potential. They were supplied with the poorest-quality recruits, and, being largely ineffective, these units did not greatly enhance Sino-British military cooperation.[14]

Confidence in Chinese military capabilities was not high among foreign military officers in either London or Washington, with recent setbacks along the Yellow River providing little reason for optimism about future operations. Nevertheless, there was some faith in Chinese military capabilities among a few high-ranking individuals, including British military attaché Major General Lance Dennys (also head of the British Military Mission). Combat effectiveness within the Chinese army was never uniform, but units stationed in Hunan and Yunnan tended to be of better quality than those posted elsewhere in the country. Being closely involved with arrangements to increase military cooperation, Dennys had inspected many Chinese army units in the south, including the 5th Army, which was earmarked for service in Burma. Fitness, equipment, and morale were at relatively high levels, but there was a significant shortage of artillery.[15] Another optimist was Major K. Millar, who included some prophetic comments in a report he wrote in July:

It is only when one compares the China of ten or even five years ago with the China of today, that it is possible to appreciate what tremendous progress has been made under the most difficult conditions. This comparison affords a fair measure of the progress which can, and I think will, take place in the future.

Another point which must be borne in mind is that Chinese methods, although to us they may appear to be clumsy and inefficient, are often the most effective when dealing with Chinese conditions. Attempts at super-imposing purely Foreign methods, generally end in failure.[16]

Dennys and Millar still considered the Chinese army incapable of offensive action, but they did not discount its potential. Their observations were also sent to Washington and appeared to be widely circulated.[17]

Allied success in south China centered on the defense of Hunan; this was partly due to the province's topography, which played to Chinese strengths. Since 1939, the Chinese had been preparing their defenses, as Dennys reported to the War Office: "The country to the North of Changsha is moderately hilly and intersected by rivers running East and West into the Siang Kiang which form good defensive positions. All roads running North from Changsha and the railway between it and Yoyang have been destroyed by the Chinese."[18] The all-important road and rail center at Hengyang ensured that the Chinese could exploit their interior lines of communication. Reinforcements could easily be dispatched north to Changsha or south to Kwangtung, as needed. Hengyang was also the location of the 9th War Zone headquarters, so its defense was augmented by a valuable armored regiment comprising forty-four medium and twenty-six light tanks.[19] Most important for the defense of Hunan, however, was the city of Changsha, situated south of Tungting Lake (Dongting Lake). Because the city was located at the northern end of the railway lines stretching from Kukong and Kweilin, it was relatively easy for supplies entering the country to reach armies in the field. The significance of Hunan was reiterated to Whitehall by General Dennys on 25 September: "The threat to Changsha and possibly Henyang must not be overlooked. Occupation of the latter place would interfere with our plans."[20] American military intelligence officers also took note of this problem.[21]

In contrast, conditions in Hunan made a Japanese offensive a difficult endeavor. South of the Milo River, Japanese motorized and mechanized units were unable to move; only infantry and horse-drawn transport could navigate the narrow and broken trails that interlaced the innumerable rice paddies. The Japanese 11th Army also had limited forces available. General Anami selected three divisions plus elements of two others to begin the offensive. These forces included the 3rd, 4th, 6th, 13th, and 33rd Divisions, with the 40th held in reserve; they would be supported by four lower-quality independent brigades guarding their lines of communication. With two years to rebuild, the 9th War Zone order of battle included close to twenty-five Chinese divisions by the time the Japanese began their attack. These were organized into ten armies—the 4th, 10th, 20th, 26th, 37th, 58th, 72nd, 74th, 79th, and 99th—which in turn constituted the 31st and 33rd Group Armies.[22] Anami's march through Hunan was going to be a hazardous undertaking.

Prior to the commencement of the September operations, the Japanese made some preliminary moves. An air offensive over Szechwan took a heavy toll on the Chinese air force, and a series of costly setbacks were experienced at Chengdu during the spring and summer months. Japanese naval aircraft also shifted away from their summer assault on the Burma Road in Yunnan to concentrate on targets situated between Hengyang and Changsha. After ground operations north of the Yellow River in Shansi were successfully concluded in June, the Japanese also built up their strength near their base at Yochow.[23]

The offensive was launched on 16 September 1941. The initial advance south went well enough, as the Chinese had anticipated only a foraging expedition, and the weight of the attack caught them somewhat off guard. Chinese forces north of the Milo River were outflanked and quickly fell back without offering any serious resistance. The Japanese hoped to avoid a repetition of the 1939 fiasco by supporting the attack with additional forces. Thus, the 33rd Division on the far left advanced eastward through the neighborhood of Tungcheng and Pingkiang. The Chinese had achieved victory two years before by debouching from this hilly terrain into the Japanese flank, thereby forcing a retreat. Japanese units advanced in three main columns on the eastern side of the Hankow-Canton rail line, with an additional column consisting solely of the 4th Division to the west. The right and center wings crossed the Milo River from 21 to 23 September, and the subsequent breakthrough to Changsha occurred from 25 to 27 September. These forces were aided by an amphibious assault by a battalion of infantry on the south shore of Tungting Lake, and approximately two battalions of the 4th Division entered Changsha itself on 27 September without much difficulty.[24]

Despite wild claims made by Chinese officials, there was no fighting whatsoever inside the city or in the immediate area. Reports of Japanese airborne landings were equally false and were later properly identified as supply drops. Part of the Japanese 6th Division secured the eastern approach to Changsha, while a cavalry detachment of the Japanese 3rd Division made an enveloping move around the city to take the important rail and road junction thirty-five miles farther south at Chuchow. Two years after the initial attempt, Changsha was finally occupied, but the prize was rapidly abandoned.[25]

With the Japanese 33rd Division delayed near the Kiangsi border and the bulk of the 11th Army across the Milo River, three Chinese armies emerged from the eastern hills and descended on the extended left flank starting on 24 September. This move was much more successful than the initial defense. Chinese forces were able to regain positions north of the Milo River, and after taking many casualties, they managed to block Japanese lines of communication for four days. Anticipating such a move, the Japanese unleashed the 40th Division to disrupt the Chinese counterattack. Approximately 180 aircraft were also committed to provide ground support, but the Chinese had advanced with "unusual vigour" and inflicted considerable damage on Anami's forces. Contributing to Japanese problems were the dismal weather conditions, which limited the value of airpower. Rain had already prevented Japanese armor and heavy artillery from keeping up with the initial assault, and poor weather persisted from 24 to 29 September. In fact, an early blizzard hit the region on 26 September. Partly because of the Chinese success in cutting the overstretched Japanese supply lines, Changsha was abandoned after only four days of occupation.[26]

By the start of October, Japanese forces were in full retreat. The 11th Army sustained many casualties as it fought its way through Chinese blocking forces positioned along the Milo River and areas farther north. Compounding their difficulties, Soviet and Chinese artillery units entrenched atop Tamoshan (approximately 25 kilometers north of Changsha) maintained a relatively constant bombardment. To prevent further damage, the 23rd Army launched a diversionary attack at Canton to keep General Yu Han Mou's 7th War Zone forces from deploying up the railway into Hunan. The 23rd Army advanced along the North River starting on 22 September, but the offensive came to a halt two weeks later after reaching a position approximately 100 kilometers north of the city. While combat in Kwangtung continued, the 11th Army eventually crossed the Milo River, and Japanese forces returned to their starting point at Yochow by 8 October. Except for a few wounded troops, evacuation through Tungting Lake was prevented, despite the deployment of about thirty gunboats; the Chinese navy had mined much of the lower Hsiang River to Changsha.[27]

The Chinese army had many deficiencies, but several factors combined to make the second battle of Changsha a scarce but much-needed victory. In addition to better troop quality, leadership in the 9th War Zone was of a higher caliber than in many other regions of the country. General Hsueh was competent and sufficiently aggressive to challenge the Japanese successfully on several occasions. Although initially surprised at the scale of the attack, when it became clear that Changsha was threatened, Chiang ordered that the city be held, and the General Staff's defense plan, made with Soviet advice, was quickly implemented. General Chuikov made his presence felt during the planning and execution of this defensive strategy, which played well to Chinese strengths and exploited Japanese logistical weaknesses. He and his staff were joined by British officers. Once the battle was under way, however, Chinese counterattacks north of Hunan by 6th War Zone forces under the command of General Chen Cheng and 5th War Zone Forces under General Li Tsung Ren had the greatest influence on the outcome because the Japanese position in central China became seriously imperiled.[28]

While the battle raged in Hunan, Soviet advisers encouraged the Chinese to launch an offensive against the reduced garrison at Ichang. This strategically important city was located to the northwest, near the eastern end of the Yangtse River gorges, and the Chinese attack was primarily meant to divert Japanese pressure from Hunan. Anticipating a Japanese offensive against Changsha, the Chinese began preparing for a Yangtse River offensive during the summer, with reinforcements, including artillery, being deployed farther upriver. The normal strength of the 11th Army garrison in the region between Hankow and Ichang was three divisions and two brigades, but General Anami reassigned one-third of the units defending this region to operations in Hunan. A large-scale Chinese attack was not expected, and the city of Ichang was foolishly left with a garrison of only two battalions totaling approximately 2,000 men, with very little artillery to support them. Ichang was ringed by eighty concrete fortified positions, but after these were manned, few troops remained to form any useful reserve.[29]

After a few days of delay and strong Soviet urging, two divisions of the 5th War Zone launched the operation on 26 September, attacking Japanese posts north and northwest of Ichang. The Chinese had the unusual experience of finding themselves with equality in artillery strength—and at times, a local superiority. This allowed them to capture more than twenty of the Japanese posts early and reach the walls of the city. Heavy fighting soon spread farther south in the 6th War Zone, and Chinese morale soared with the experience of success. By 8 October 1941, the Chinese army forced its way inside Ichang itself, and the 5th and 6th War Zone armies linked up between the Yangtse and Han rivers. Chinese morale continued to climb as they captured more than fifty of the fortified Japanese posts and threatened the Japanese position at Hankow. By this point, the battle was still going well for the Chinese. They had also forced the Japanese army to abandon its offensive in Hunan. Elements of the Japanese 13th and 39th Divisions were rushed to Ichang as reinforcements for the beleaguered garrison. The Japanese attempted to distract the Chinese farther north with an attack in Honan (Henan), but this had little effect.[30]

The turning point occurred during the heaviest fighting between 8 and 10 October, as Soviet advisers encouraged the Chinese to push home the attack. After several uphill assaults, the Chinese bent the Japanese line, but as Ichang was about to be taken, a strong counterattack with recently arrived reinforcements hit their northern flank. Heavy air strikes and, more ominously, a large-scale use of chemical weapons supported this attack. Mustard gas and phosgene were employed, and more than 1,000 shells weighing twenty to fifty pounds each were fired into Chinese positions. The battle of Ichang marked the heaviest use of gas in the war, with munitions impacting an area 2,000 yards long by 1,500 yards wide. Chinese troops had no defense against chemical weapons, and gas casualties numbered approximately 1,350, of which 750 were killed.[31] Japanese chemical weapons attacks had been on the increase since July 1940, but occurrences had generally been scattered and of limited intensity. General Magruder noted, "Attacks in August and October Nineteen Forty One were concentrated and heavy."[32] Against this pressure, Chiang broke off the attack and ordered a westward withdrawal from Ichang. The Sino-Japanese War was stalemated once again.[33]

Although the heavy employment of chemical weapons was a significant development in the war, there were larger geopolitical factors behind Chiang's decision to withdraw from Ichang. Chinese military spokesmen stated that the withdrawal was intended to preserve their forces from the effects of further combat, but these explanations were not widely believed. Foreign observers, especially the Soviet advisers who had helped plan the attack, resented the outcome and expressed their displeasure to British and

CHAPTER NINE

American counterparts. With the battle for Moscow under way, a reduction of conflict in China was of great concern to Stalin, and the Soviets complained loudly. At the 14th Military Attaché Conference, Colonel Bedniakoff stated that Chinese field commanders had opposed the order to withdraw. The Chinese had superiority in artillery, terrain, and position, and morale was high. The withdrawal had been ordered despite the likelihood of retaking Ichang, and it had been done as a political, rather than a military, maneuver.[34] The withdrawal from Ichang was meant to remind President Roosevelt that while Japanese-American peace talks continued in Washington, a termination of hostilities in China remained a possibility, and Chiang expected better support.

Other foreign military officers commented on the significance of these events, including military intelligence personnel in Hong Kong: "The Chinese came within an ace of success in their attack on the heavily reduced garrison, although their offensive was a rather belated one. According to the Soviet A.M.A., now in Hong Kong, the attack was called off when the Chinese had mopped up the majority of the outlying defences and were in an excellent position to break into the city itself."[35] Lieutenant Colonel James McHugh of the U.S. Marine Corps, among others, reported to Washington that the Chinese did not inflict greater damage on Japanese forces along the Yangtse River because they did not want to discourage any planned offensives into the USSR or against the British and Americans to the south.[36] He snidely added that a close analysis of the situation revealed "that maybe the Chinese were not as stupid and fatuous as they appear to have been."[37] Chiang maintained the security of Hunan, but his withdrawal of forces at Ichang was a signal and a threat to Allied leaders that he was serious about receiving additional support from abroad. It is useful to note that the timing of the withdrawal corresponded with the assembly of Canadian forces for Hong Kong. Ultimately, in the fall of 1941, Chiang used the battles in Hunan and Hupeh as leverage in maintaining pressure on his allies.

Notwithstanding Chiang's withdrawal order, some Allied officers in the region were sufficiently impressed with Chinese military abilities to comment favorably on their performance. General Chuikov claimed that the Chinese had seized the initiative and executed a bold strategic counterstroke at Ichang, inflicting an estimated 10,000 Japanese casualties. Chuikov commented on deficiencies in the Chinese army leadership but stated, "They were capable of waging vigorous defensive operations (so-called offensive defense) and . . . they were capable of scoring victories in limited-scale offensive operations."[38] Lieutenant Colonel McHugh reported to Washington that either the Japanese had underestimated Chinese strength and overestimated their own prior to the attack on Changsha or, alternatively, the commander in chief of the China Expeditionary Force, Field Marshal Hata Shunroku, "with equal stupidity initiated the campaign without prior approval from Tokyo."[39]

British officers were similarly encouraged by the overall outcome and recommended that further support be extended to China.[40] One of the most outspoken was General Dennys, who remarked that foreign perceptions of the Chinese army needed adjustment:

> The Changsha and Ichang operations, which took place in September and early October[,] were of considerable military and political importance. The practice of the Chinese press and foreign news agencies in Chungking of "writing up" the Chinese Army and publishing extravagant claims of Chinese victories for every action fought is too well known to require any comment, except to say that it does more harm than good. On the other hand there is a noticeable tendency on the part of our intelligence organisations in the Far East to pour immediate scorn, sometimes without waiting for full information, on any military achievements claimed by the Chinese, on the analogy of "can any good come out of Samaria?" This does no good either.[41]

This reasoning was similar to General Chuikov's. Dennys continued:

> The Chinese, with the assistance of Russian advisers, did what they are popularly supposed to be incapable of doing—namely, coordinate a strategic plan in two separate areas. The co-ordination was not by any means perfect, for the Ichang offensive started several days late, but it was none the less [sic] a major factor in effecting the hurried Japanese withdrawal from Changsha.

> (b) The Chinese Army is capable of offensive action under favourable circumstances. At Changsha circumstances were favourable because the Japanese were overconfident and had a bad line of communication owing to their failure to open up the river. At Ichang conditions were favourable because the Japanese had no marked

superiority in artillery and their air force was fully occupied elsewhere. There is little doubt that the Japanese were completely surprised by the Chinese offensive, having believed them incapable of anything but passive defence. For obvious reasons Chinese offensives must be infrequent and on a limited scale for some time to come, but their nature and scope can be increased if the Chinese Army can be given air support and/or more equipment.

(c) The Japanese failure to bring up reinforcements to the Ichang battle points to considerable exhaustion after the Changsha operations. The Russian advisers are convinced the Chinese could have taken up their old positions along the Han River and mopped up any Japanese troops to the West of it. This seems a reasonable assumption. It is equally reasonable to assume that, in that case, the Japanese would have had to stage a larger scale counter attack [*sic*] against them.

(d) The effect of both operations on Chinese morale has been good and it must be disturbing to the Japanese General Staff, at this juncture, to get practical proof that the Chinese Army is improving.[42]

As the senior British officer in Chungking, Dennys's report carried considerable weight.

Dennys's views on the second battle of Changsha and the battle of Ichang were important because they fueled the belief among some Allied officers in the region that Hong Kong could be held in the event of an Anglo-American war with Japan, since it seemed possible that Chinese forces could relieve the garrison. As events transpired, his assessment of Chinese capabilities may have been correct, but for the plan to succeed, many more troops would have to be posted somewhere closer to Hong Kong, perhaps at Waichow, before the battle started. Chinese assistance was not greatly desired in Whitehall, however, because British officials did not wish to incur further obligations to China. According to Andrew Whitfield, after the fall of Hong Kong, David MacDougall of the War Department's Hong Kong Planning Unit wrote: "The feeling was that Britain would rather have lost the colony than accept Chinese help. For my own part, I agree with them."[43] Prior to the German invasion of the USSR, British support for China remained lukewarm, but greater (if still limited) cooperation began to coalesce in Sino-British military planning after the second battle of

Changsha.[44] Guerrilla warfare and Allied airpower would be used in cooperation with regular Chinese army units in Kwangtung and Hunan, but effective Sino-British collaboration for the defense of Hong Kong itself was slow to develop. Unfortunately for the men of the garrison, officials in Whitehall were still dragging their feet.

The Japanese launched the offensive in Hunan for several reasons. Seizure of the provincial rice harvest was one factor. Aside from replenishing their own stocks, capturing large quantities of rice was a form of economic warfare that could damage Chinese morale by increasing economic pressure on the population. Rice hoarding in Szechwan was already making inflation such a serious problem that Chiang outlawed such practices under the threat of severe punishment. Yet the Hunan offensive was not merely another rice raid, and the augmentation of Japanese food supplies was only a secondary motivation. According to General Chuikov, the battle was fought to convince the British and the Americans that the Chinese were weak and valueless as allies, whereas Chiang desperately needed a victory to convince them otherwise. In this, Chiang was successful, at least in the eyes of Allied officers in China such as General Dennys. Anami hoped that by capturing Changsha and destroying 9th War Zone forces, it would be possible to remove the Chinese threat to Hankow and physically link Japanese positions in the central and southern parts of the country. The Japanese were also eager to counter Chinese propaganda that withdrawals along the Yangtse River were being made in preparation for an attack on the USSR. In the final tally, however, the stakes were much higher. An official Japanese military announcement clarified that the second Hunan offensive against Changsha was launched to solve their problems in China. The Japanese wanted to end the war before they began their advance to the south, and in this objective they failed.[45]

The Battle of Hong Kong and the Third Battle of Changsha: Rupture in Sino-British Relations

Unable to knock China into submission, the Japanese adjusted their strategic plans by preparing for war against the Western powers and reinforcing the 23rd Army for future operations in Kwangtung. In fulfillment of Chiang's hope, the attack on Hong Kong finally completed the metamorphosis of the low-intensity conflict in the Pearl River Delta into a full-scale war that included Britain and America. Yet the battle of Hong Kong was the penultimate act in the Japanese army's strangulation of China; the coup de grace was almost delivered during the Burma campaign shortly thereafter. By January 1942, Allied strategy in southern China had started to unravel, but the battle of Hong Kong was the crescendo of a crisis that set the stage for a new and vastly wider catastrophe. In bringing Japanese offensive power south, Soviet Far Eastern security was enhanced, and when events at Hong Kong were tallied with the simultaneous attack on Pearl Harbor, the result was a tremendous strategic defeat for Japan. In launching the Pacific war, the Japanese immediately engaged a coalition of enemies without the slightest chance of achieving long-term success.[46] Although the scale of Japanese folly was assuming greater proportions, their actions did not mitigate the consequences of Allied recklessness in the reinforcement and defense of Hong Kong.

The Japanese assault on the British colony was only half the offensive in southern China—the other half being the third battle for Changsha. Both these battles were part of the same operational plan to complete China's isolation and thereby force its surrender. In early 1942 the Chinese remained hopeful of direct large-scale Anglo-American intervention, but Allied reverses in the opening stages of the expanded conflict made this impossible. This, in turn, greatly damaged Chinese morale. With the fall of Hong Kong, British wartime influence in China effectively came to an end, but the impact of Japanese victory was nullified by their defeat in Hunan as China remained a belligerent power. The third battle for Changsha prevented Chinese morale from breaking completely for two reasons. First, it was the only major Allied victory during the first six months of the Pacific war, and it demonstrated China's value as a military ally both at home and abroad. Second, although the Chinese finally fought as a coalition partner, on this occasion they were able to beat the Japanese almost unaided in a large-scale defensive engagement. Partly due to these events, the war in China became an element of the Pacific war.[47]

On 6 November 1941 the Imperial General Headquarters ordered the 23rd Army to ready itself for an attack on Hong Kong, and plans were coordinated with the navy. The Japanese 2nd Fleet designated a small force to assist in the isolation of Hong Kong and prevent reinforcement or escape, while the 11th Air Fleet in Formosa supplied units of the 21st and 23rd Air Flotillas to ensure air superiority and provide ground support.[48] Some changes in command of the 23rd Army were made in advance of operations: Major General Kuribayshi Tadamichi, former military attaché in

Ottawa, assumed his new duties as chief of staff from Major General Kato, and Lieutenant General Sano Tadayoshi was appointed commander of the 38th Division. Overall command of the 23rd Army still rested with Lieutenant General Sakai Takashi.[49] During the summer, the number of troops at Canton and its immediate area had fallen to about one and a half divisions, but this was raised to almost four divisions, or approximately 60,000 men, some of them reinforcing the area just north of Hong Kong. This meant that the strength of the Japanese army in Kwangtung had returned to the springtime levels observed prior to the commencement of operations in southern Indochina. Hainan was also strongly reinforced with units destined for other regions farther south.[50]

Aside from the 38th Division, the 23rd Army order of battle included elements of the 18th Division, positioned along both the East River and the Hong Kong border, as well as the 104th Division, which was based largely in Canton and along the North River. After its arrival, the newly activated 51st Division was handed responsibility for the lower East River. Smaller elements of the 28th Division reinforced Chungshan, Namtau, and Bocca Tigris after being withdrawn from Foochow in September and spending some time in the Marianas for rest and recuperation. More worrying for Hong Kong was the arrival of several battalions of siege artillery, which were also landed at Bocca Tigris and Namtau. These units were equipped with 150mm and 240mm guns and were part of the 23rd Army artillery group under the command of Lieutenant General Katajima. In garrison at Hainan, Swatow, and Chaoyang were units of the 19th Mixed Independent Brigade.[51]

By 26 November, the decision had been made in Tokyo to wage war against Britain and America, and General Sakai prepared to deploy his army for the assault on Hong Kong. On 1 December the bulk of the 38th Division began moving from Samshui and Foshan toward the British colony. Advance elements were already positioned at Shumchun, along with some of Katajima's heavy artillery from Namtau. Road repair was intensified, and tanks were seen moving east through Canton. Final fortification work on the line of defense running east to west approximately fifteen miles north of the city was also completed, resulting in the addition of several thousand pillboxes. The 66th Infantry Regiment of the 51st Division, otherwise known as the Araki Detachment, marched on Tamshui to protect lines of communication against the Chinese ground forces that were expected to attempt a relief of the garrison. The 104th Division similarly braced itself at Canton. Many Chinese puppet soldiers and Formosans had already been sent into Hong Kong to join other fifth columnists once the battle was under way.[52]

Even though the Japanese made little effort to conceal these deployments in Kwangtung, some British officers misread their moves. Most noteworthy was the new GOC China, Major General Christopher Maltby. In contrast to his predecessor, Major General Grasett, Maltby was not as alert to the threat posed by the Japanese army, nor did he heed the reports issued by his intelligence staff. RAF reconnaissance flights of the area provided intelligence on Japanese movements, as did Chinese radio detachments located at Bocca Tigris, but Maltby was not overly alarmed by the Japanese deployments. As Japanese reinforcements continued to arrive, he informed the War Office that the frontier was relatively quiet. He speculated that Japanese units in the region were likely training for operations against Thailand or making preparations for an advance up the East River. Given previous complaints that the British had violated agreed-on no-fly zones, the Japanese initiated their own naval reconnaissance flights over the colony's fortifications on 4 December 1941, but Maltby remained confident that there was little reason to worry.[53]

Maltby had been misinterpreting events for some time, and his poor judgment was an unfortunate encumbrance on the defenders. As early as 23 October, the head of military intelligence at Singapore had shown concern about the general's laxity in reporting Japanese moves. A telegram was sent to express this concern and to clarify Maltby's responsibilities in an attempt to improve the flow of information and ascertain the true extent of the danger facing Hong Kong:

> Concentration of approximately one division has been taking place in Bocca Tigris Namtau area for at least ten days but no identifications received here. Assume you are doing your best through your own sources and not relying solely on S.I.S. to whom I have already made strong representations here. Standard required is that you should know name of every commander of major unit within 48 hours of landing and no effort must be spared to reach and maintain this standard.[54]

As late as 3 December 1941, Maltby thought the 38th Division had been sent to Indochina, and he remained confident that the Japanese were still preparing solely for an attack farther south. Maltby sent a telegram to the War Office that day and noted: "Despite flood of local rumours that Japanese intend attacking colony in near future there are no concrete signs of this and present Japanese dispositions in Frontier Area indicate balance of movement in last few days outward. Although Japanese Consul General urged all Japanese to evacuate yesterday only thirty three did so and one hundred and seven still remain."[55] The following day he estimated that there were three Japanese divisions positioned in south China with support, but he was certain these were insufficient for a powerful attack against the colony. In contrast, the Americans were more circumspect about Japanese moves, and the USS *Mindanao* departed Hong Kong for the Philippines on 4 December (it was last reported to be anchored off Bataan on 31 March 1942).[56]

The day before the battle began, Maltby sent another appraisal of the colony's situation, after ignoring what turned out to be timely intelligence reports of the arrival of large numbers of Japanese troops eight miles to the north.[57] Maltby reported:

> Two independent frontier sources report 10 to 20000 Japanese troops expected to arrive Namtau Shumchun area Dec. 4th (?5th) preparatory to attack on colony.
>
> 1. SIS sources have similar reports. So far no substantial reinforcements are known to have arrived in this area although independent Bocca-Tigris source states 20,000 men left for Namtau during last 4 days in Dec.
> 2. Above reports are certainly exaggerated and have appearance of being deliberately fostered by Japanese who judging by their defensive preparations around Canton and in frontier area appear distinctly nervous of being attacked. It is considered they are disseminating these reports to cover up their numerical weakness in South China although some (?reinforcement to) skeleton Japanese force in frontier area is extremely likely in near future. M.T. traffic on Namtau-Shumchun road notably increased in last 48 hours and 206 loaded lorries proceeding to latter place on 5th Dec.[58]

Thirty minutes later he added the following:

CHAPTER NINE

Bocca-Tigris W/T set now functioning again reports 20,000 men majority infantry and artillery with 4,000 horse arrived from direction of East River between 1st. and 4th. December and proceeded down coastal road towards Namtau.

2. Above is probably grossly exaggerated version of recent troop movements eastward from Canton reported in my 1678 of 4th. December and he has been asked whether his report is hearsay or eye-witness.
3. Same source also reports Japanese are issuing shells and S.A.A. in Bocca-Tigris which are being sent same destination.[59]

At the Foreign Office, A. L. Scott's wry response was recorded on a file jacket a few days later. He wrote that the reports were "not 'grossly exaggerated' at all, as it turned out!"[60]

Both Hong Kong and the American fleet at Pearl Harbor were attacked on 7 December 1941, and the long-anticipated Japanese advance into the southwest Pacific was begun. The date in Hong Kong was actually 8 December, due to the difference in time zones and the bisection of the Pacific Ocean by the International Date Line. The bombardment of Kai Tak airfield marked the opening phase of the battle. A squadron of dive-bombers of the 45th Light Bomber Regiment, along with three squadrons of fighter escorts, succeeded in destroying most of the civilian aircraft there, as well as all five RAF reconnaissance planes still parked on the ground. Much of the damage was caused by the fighters during numerous low-level strafing runs, as the only air defense available was the fire from three light machine guns. Wing Commander Ginger Sullivan had limited options to protect his aircraft. Kai Tak airfield was too short to accommodate modern fighters, and there were no antiaircraft guns positioned there. Hong Kong antiaircraft defenses as of November 1941 included only sixteen heavy and two light guns of the 5th Anti-Aircraft Regiment, Royal Artillery, and these were primarily defending the port facilities. When a handful of mobile antiaircraft troops finally arrived, they were too late to offer any useful assistance. Despite these opening losses, CNAC was able to make sixteen flights on the night of 8–9 December and evacuate 275 people. One of the more prominent was Green Gang leader Tu Yueh Sheng.[61]

More dangerous were British deficiencies in infantry and artillery. After General Maltby learned that Canadian troops would be sent as reinforcements for his garrison, he revived the 1938 defense plan, which was based on the deployment of two brigades—one on Hong Kong Island, and the other on the mainland north of Kowloon. The Mainland Brigade was under the command of Brigadier General Cedric Wallis, who had been appointed after the departure of Brigadier Reeve in mid-November. Wallis's brigade consisted of three battalions of infantry: the Royal Scots, the 5/7th Rajputs, and the 2/14th Punjabs. It was deployed along the Gindrinkers' Line without sufficient reserves. The other brigade was positioned on Hong Kong Island and included the Middlesex Regiment along with C Force, together commanded by Canadian Brigadier General John Lawson. Several Hong Kong Volunteer Defence Corps (HKVDC) companies further strengthened the brigade. The Middlesex Regiment manned the fortified posts constructed near the waterline to defend against amphibious assault, but maintaining a perimeter defense along the shoreline meant that the establishment of an effective reserve was still a problem.[62] Artillery forces were also limited in strength, and of the sixty-five guns, only twenty-eight were mobile. These belonged primarily to the 1st Medium Regiment of the Hong Kong and Singapore Royal Artillery, and only four gun troops with 3.7-inch mountain guns (four guns apiece) were available to be positioned behind the Gindrinkers' Line.[63]

Maltby's defense plan was inadequate for the situation; his forces were too thinly spread, making the Gindrinkers' Line vulnerable to aggressive night infiltration tactics. The Gindrinkers' Line was more than ten miles long, and each battalion had to cover a frontage of approximately 5,000 yards—about five times the normal requirement. Maltby did not have sufficient forces to defend the line, nor did he have effective reserves to counterattack the Japanese in strength.[64] Fortified positions along the line, such as the Shingmun redoubt, were considered sufficiently strong to hold the Japanese for at least a month, and by defending the colony this far north, it was hoped that a measure of control could be maintained over the Jubilee Reservoir. Although much of the colony's water came from the reservoir, its retention was not absolutely vital, owing to the existence of alternative sources. According to U.S. Army attaché Major Reynolds Condon, who led Commonwealth troops during the battle, water supplies were not a critical problem. In a postbattle report he wrote: "In the city the water supply had failed due to bursting of exposed mains. This was not as serious as might be imagined since the population promptly reopened long unused wells as well as making use of several running streams."[65]

CHAPTER NINE

General Sano's 38th Division began ground operations by crossing the border and rapidly advancing south. Sano held the initiative and had the advantage of being able to concentrate his forces at a point of his choosing. Major General Ito Takeo, former commander of the 104th Division, was in charge of the 38th Division's infantry group. He originally deployed the 228th Regiment, under Lieutenant Colonel Doi Teihichi, and the 230th Regiment, under Lieutenant Colonel Shoji Toshishige, as the western assault group. They were supported by three battalions of mountain artillery. The 229th Infantry Regiment, under Lieutenant Colonel Tanaka Ryosaburo, constituted the eastern group. The advance went forward without great difficulty (see figure 9.1). Sensibly, there were no British forces of consequence deployed along the frontier, and despite Maltby's earlier misinterpretation of Japanese intentions, the garrison was not caught by surprise. Some demolition and sabotage work had been carried out by Z Force and other small detachments, resulting in minor delays to the Japanese.[66]

By the night of 9 December, a large reconnaissance force of the 228th Regiment had positioned itself for a surprise attack on the Gindrinkers' Line, and the vital Shingmun redoubt was overrun on 10 December at about 0100 hours. At least a company was required to defend the position properly, but with only a platoon of the Royal Scots in place, the position fell after a brief period of combat. Inadequate artillery and insufficient patrolling may have contributed to the rapid fall of the post, and the Royal Scots were forced to withdraw to Golden Hill, with the Japanese following behind. The loss of the position was not their fault, however, as Lieutenant Colonel Simon White and the Royal Scots had been given an impossible task.[67]

During the morning of 10 December, it was clear that the Gindrinkers' Line had been cracked. After some hard fighting for Golden Hill during that day and the next, General Maltby ordered the evacuation of the mainland, with the exception of the 5/7th Rajputs, who were sent to defend the Devil's Peak peninsula. Devil's Peak dominated Lye Mun Passage on the eastern end of the harbor, and its retention would make a Japanese amphibious assault on the island impossible at the narrowest and most likely point of attack.[68] After the Rajputs retreated onto Devil's Peak, they fought off a Japanese battalion that had optimistically assaulted their hastily prepared positions. An observer later reported, "The attack broke down in wire defences, and the enemy suffered heavy casualties."[69] Unwisely, Maltby abandoned this strong defensive position in the early hours

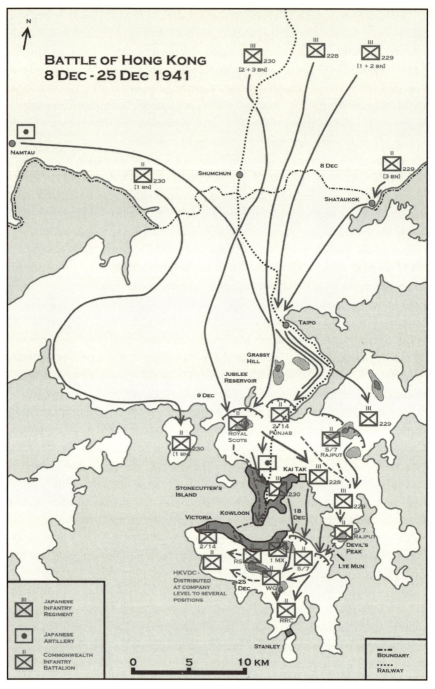

Figure 9.1. Japanese 23rd Army attack on Hong Kong, December 1941. (Based on data from LOC, Japanese Monograph No. 71, by Ishiwari; and Stacey, *Official History of the Canadian Army*.)

of 13 December, and the Rajputs withdrew to the island. Another American witness to the battle was U.S. Army air attaché Major Richard Grussendorff, who reported his surprise at these events. The Rajputs, he wrote in 1942, "were well entrenched on Devil's Peak [with] an excellent OP, and were successfully fighting off all Japanese attacks at great expense to the attacker."[70] In his criticism of the decision to withdraw, he added, "The value of this hill as an OP commanding the Japanese rear and to which telephone [communication] was still in operation cannot be underestimated . . . when the British still had nearly all their artillery available for use."[71]

Most of the Mainland Brigade was evacuated through Kowloon on the twelfth, but some artillery was destroyed or neutralized in the process. Royal Navy vessels had been moved to Aberdeen at the outset of the battle, but with the assistance of the 2nd MTB Flotilla, Stonecutters Island was evacuated that day, as was Kai Tak airfield and Devil's Peak. The Japanese followed up the British retreat and immediately occupied Kowloon. They soon brought forward their heavy 360mm siege guns to begin the bombardment of Hong Kong Island from inside the city and the hills immediately north. One of the first targets was the Hong Kong Dockyard, where HMS *Moth* was being refitted and could not be moved. Lacking effective means of targeting the Japanese guns, British counterbattery fire remained ineffective. General Magruder reported the evacuation to Washington.[72]

A temporary lull in ground operations brought a welcome respite, but additional problems emerged to eat away at the morale of the garrison. The presence of more than 750,000 civilians in Hong Kong created great difficulties for General Maltby and his officers. There were too many people to care for in the event of a long siege, and it quickly became apparent that there were many fifth columnists working on behalf of the Japanese. Sabotage and sniping constituted the bulk of their activity. Fifth columnists were associated with the Chinese puppet government headed by Wang Ching Wei or, alternatively, with a variety of criminal organizations and secret societies. Earlier in the year, the headquarters of a powerful puppet organization directing anticolonial operations in Malaya and the Dutch East Indies had been uncovered. Most were working simply for money or because family members had been physically threatened in some manner.[73]

Another worry for the men of the garrison was the damage inflicted on Royal Navy forces throughout the Far East. After the invasion of Malaya and the sinking of HMS *Prince of Wales* and HMS *Repulse* on 10 December, the specter of defeat became a reality, as relief from the south obviously became impossible. At Hong Kong, Japanese troops had already landed on Lamma Island, and with naval units patrolling nearby waters, the isolation of the garrison was complete. By 18 December, only the gunboat HMS *Cicala* and the remnants of the 2nd MTB Flotilla remained seaworthy and ready for battle.[74]

Prior to the Japanese assault on Hong Kong Island, the first of three surrender demands sent by General Sakai was rejected on 13 December, and Maltby reorganized his forces to prepare for an attack. East Brigade was commanded by Brigadier Wallis, whose forces included the Royal Rifles of Canada, the 5/7th Rajputs, two companies of the Middlesex Regiment, and two companies of the HKVDC. West Brigade was formed under Brigadier General Lawson. It comprised the Winnipeg Grenadiers, the 2/14th Punjabs, the remainder of the Middlesex Regiment, the Royal Scots, and five companies of the HKVDC.[75]

To meet the rapidly changing situation, the British command structure in Asia was also adjusted. On 14 December Brigadier General Grimsdale was made head of the British Military Mission to China, and General Dennys was ordered to take command of Detachment 204. General Archibald Wavell, commander in chief of India and head of the new ABDA (American-British-Dutch-Australian) Command, entered the thorny copse of Sino-British military relations by placing General Dennys's guerrilla forces under his overall authority.[76]

Prior to these adjustments, the Chinese government officially declared war on Japan on 9 December, and Allied arrangements for the relief of Hong Kong were put into action.[77] On that day, a meeting chaired by Chiang was attended by the U.S. and British ambassadors, along with their military attachés in Chungking. Magruder reported that Dennys attempted to allay some of Chiang's concerns by stating that the garrison at Hong Kong could hold with support. In response to Chiang's query:

The British Military Attaché informed him that the leased area or (territory) could be held for a month [and] also that if the Chinese would assist they could hold it longer than that. In regards to the island they could hold that for a much longer period. The Generalissimo assured the British attaché his entire and full support for Hongkong. He further stated he was moving his troops to the upper area about Canton. He stated that he could attack using a force of 3 corps—they are made up of 3 divisions each [Magruder substituted the more familiar U.S. designation of corps to describe a Chinese army]. This would take about 3 weeks to get his men there and ready.[78]

Chiang ordered guerrilla warfare to be initiated around Canton while regular army forces in Kwangtung began to advance on the Pearl River Delta.[79]

Additional details of the plan to relieve Hong Kong discussed at this meeting were recorded by British officers in the Detachment 204 War Diary:

> GOC attended conference under the chairmanship of General Ho Ying Chin, War Minister and attended by members of the British and American Military Missions, to discuss joint military action. The discussion was under two headings—direct and indirect assistance.
>
> Direct assistance to Hongkong: the Generalissimo ordered immediate preparations from the three armies under General Yu Han Mou to carry out an offensive from the East against general line of Kowloon-Canton Railway with the object of clearing the enemy West of the leased territory and joining up with the garrison at Hongkong. GOC stressed the importance of getting in supplies and evacuating civilians. A simultaneous attack to be made by three armies on Canton in order to contain Japanese reinforcements and guerilla action by one Division in the Swatow district. War Minister stated the action could commence on 1st January but would prefer 10th January; the Chinese considered the attack had a good chance of success if air support could be provided; they were, however, prepared to undertake the operations without air support. They urged that bombs for Area "B" should be sent in at once and promised to provide the necessary transport. Lieut. Col. Hughes was present during this discussion.[80]

Being closest to Canton, the Chinese 9th Independent Brigade, supported by two other regiments, commenced guerrilla operations by 14 December, while the 65th Army began its move to the south of the province and was scheduled to arrive on the twentieth.[81]

As part of this effort, Detachment 204 personnel worked with General

Yu's 7th War Zone Headquarters in Kukong to coordinate with Chinese army commanders north of the colony. Some of the officers involved were Lieutenant Colonel W. Lovat-Fraser, Lieutenant Colonel Count Bentick, Lieutenant Colonel Johnson, Major Munro-Faure, Major Gill Davies, and Major H. Chauvin. Lieutenant Colonel Owen Hughes was also serving as a liaison officer between Hong Kong and Kukong. Another officer attached to Detachment 204 was Flight Lieutenant James, who had arrived in Kweilin from Chungking to supervise the provisioning of aviation fuel to the airfields that were to be used in support of ground operations.[82] This plan to relieve Hong Kong was the only hope the garrison had, and Major General John Kennedy at the War Office acknowledged this fact in his memoirs by quoting a note he had penned to the chief of the Imperial General Staff, Field Marshal Alanbrooke:

> The garrison of Hong Kong is now in the process of withdrawing to the island. Here the only hope of a protracted defence is based on the feasibility of pressure by Chiang Kai Chek's troops on the mainland. This is not a strong hope. If a strong Chinese offensive does not materialize it seems fairly certain that Hong Kong will be captured within a month or six weeks at the outside.[83]

General Yu Han Mou, commander of the 7th War Zone, had a sizable force of more than 250,000 troops supported by twelve 150mm guns of the 14th Medium Artillery Regiment (in two battalions) and nineteen 150mm tubes of the 2nd Heavy Mortar Regiment. Additional artillery forces included twenty-eight Soviet guns and an antiaircraft battery with four 37mm guns. Yu issued orders for three armies to march on Hong Kong, along with a similar force to move for an attack on Canton. The earliest possible start date for the attack was set at 1 January 1942, but this was soon pushed back to the more realistic date of the tenth.[84] As events transpired, January was too late. Despite assurances that resistance on the mainland would last a month, the garrison was pushed out of Kowloon three days after the initial assault on the Gindrinkers' Line, and Hong Kong Island was immediately threatened with an amphibious assault.

Chinese forces south of the Yangtse River were deployed to meet an array of threats in several regions, but time was required to reach southern Kwangtung. Infrastructure problems contributed to the delay. Within a radius of approximately 100 miles from Canton, most roads, railways, and bridges had been destroyed, so there was no Chinese vehicular traffic of any kind within this area capable of reaching Hong Kong. Furthermore, all supplies had to be transported either by river craft or by carrier. Movement of troops and equipment was entirely on foot, and twenty-five miles per day was the most that could be expected.[85] The movement of Chinese divisions was a time-consuming endeavor.

Three armies of the 4th War Zone were also sent into Yunnan for possible use in Burma, but Anglo-Chinese friction was building steadily in the face of the worsening military situation, and Chiang had become frustrated over British delays in accepting Chinese ground forces in the colony. Because the British did not wish to increase their obligations to Chiang, they insisted on limiting Chinese help to indirect support in the form of guerrilla warfare in China. Recalling the previous withdrawal from Canton in October 1938, the War Office had low expectations of Chinese military forces. Hence, on 16 December General Magruder reported that because of the Japanese invasion of Burma and the threat posed to Rangoon, the British requested the use of Chinese Lend-Lease weapons still awaiting shipment north and the transfer of Chennault's AVG to serve in Burma. This only exacerbated relations with Chiang.[86] As the Far Eastern situation deteriorated, the British eventually reversed their policy, but by then, it was too late.

The attempted relief of Hong Kong continued nevertheless. On 13 December the Chinese air force began to bombard the Japanese main airfields at Canton with a force of about twenty bombers. By 20 December, two AVG squadrons arrived in Kunming from Burma. On the same day, at least one air strike was made against Japanese artillery positions in Kowloon.[87] On the ground, eight out of ten Chinese divisions of the 7th War Zone were en route to Canton and the lower East River to confront the Japanese Araki Detachment at Tamshui. These were elements of the 44th Army, which had originally been situated 200 kilometers north of Canton, and the 63rd Army, located about 140 kilometers northeast of the city at Sinfeng. The movement of these troops began on 16 December; following them were additional forces of the 2nd Army that were due to arrive on 31 December. By 20 December, approximately one and a half divisions had already arrived at Waichow, but the attack on the Araki Detachment was delayed until additional units arrived. The 4th and 74th Armies of the 4th War Zone were also dispatched from Kwangsi to an area north of Canton, while the victor of Changsha, General Hsueh Yueh, was ordered to take command of the situation. To encourage the defenders, General Yu Han

Mou sent a message to Governor Mark Young, stating that his troops were just a short distance from Hong Kong. The Chinese 80th Division in Fukien was also scheduled to attack Swatow by the end of December.[88]

General Sakai did not wait idly for Chinese forces to gather strength. After Governor Young rejected his call for surrender, Sakai readied his forces to assault Hong Kong Island, and an infantry brigade of the 18th Division, still headquartered at Shumchun, was brought forward to reinforce the 38th Division in Kowloon. An initial attempt to land on the island with one battalion occurred on the night of 15–16 December. This first effort to land at Pak Sha Wan ended in failure, resulting in many Japanese casualties, but hope that the garrison might hold did not last very long.[89]

After the British rejected a second surrender demand on 17 December, Sakai intensified his army's bombardment in preparation for a larger assault on the island the following night. Colonel Doi's 228th Regiment loaded onto collapsible assault boats on the eastern side of Kai Tak airfield, with each carrying approximately fourteen men. They crossed the harbor, along with elements of the 230th Regiment, to secure a western landing area near North Point. Tanaka's 229th Regiment was sent across farther east at Lye Mun, to attack the Rajputs covering Aldrich Bay and Sai Wan. Artillery had destroyed many defensive positions along the shoreline, and after a stealthy approach, the 229th Regiment rushed ashore at about 2030 hours. Though sustaining numerous casualties, they eliminated most of the surviving Rajputs. After the execution of prisoners at Lye Mun, the frequency and scale of Japanese atrocities only increased as the battle progressed. Landings near North Point were made, and by moving rapidly with the aid of fifth columnists, the assault forces converged in the center of the island at Wong Nei Chong Gap by dawn on 19 December. Night combat proficiency was a significant key to Japanese success.[90]

The fighting that occurred between 18 and 20 December 1941 was the most decisive of the battle. After advancing swiftly inland toward the center of the island, the Japanese 229th Regiment took Mount Parker and then Mount Butler to drive a wedge between East and West Brigades. In linking up with the 228th and 230th Regiments, however, the Japanese found themselves partially blocked at the Wong Nei Chong Gap. West Brigade had stubbornly refused to be pushed off this crossroad, and the heavy fighting that ensued resulted in large numbers of casualties on both sides. The defenders included the HKVDC, the Royal Scots, the Middlesex, a few surviving Indians, and various support troops without other duties to perform, but many of the men were from the Winnipeg Grenadiers. To clear the eastern half of the gap, Brigadier General Lawson ordered A Company of the Grenadiers to counterattack Colonel Tanaka's 229th Regiment on the morning of the nineteenth, but the effort turned into a costly failure. The company was encircled on Mount Butler and suffered many casualties, including Sergeant Major J. R. Osborn, who was posthumously awarded the Victoria Cross. Soon afterward, West Brigade's headquarters was also overrun, and Lawson himself was killed by machine gun fire during an attempted retreat. Colonel H. B. Rose would not be appointed as his replacement until the following day.[91] Losses among the Winnipeg Grenadiers were severe, and their experience of battle was a difficult one. Many of the men were new to the army, and quite a few brothers were killed in the fighting.

Despite ongoing Commonwealth resistance in the gap until 22 December, the Japanese 229th Regiment was able to swing units around the defenders and infiltrate farther south along the high ground east of the road. Their new positions were advantageous, as they dominated the north-south movement of Commonwealth units. On 20 December Japanese units were able to ambush reinforcements moving toward the fighting, including a force of three platoons of Royal Navy men reassigned as infantry. They were attacked in their trucks, and forty men were killed.[92]

Also ambushed were the men of the Hong Kong Chinese Regiment (HKCR). This small unit of about fifty Hong Kong Chinese was commanded by Major Mayer of the Middlesex Regiment, and the senior Chinese noncommissioned officer was Sergeant Chu Chan Mun. Recruitment for this unit had only begun in November, at the urging of American military officers posted to the colony. By the time the Japanese attacked Hong Kong, however, it was still only at platoon strength. Like the men of the HKVDC, these troops were eager to fight in defense of their families and homes. According to Captain R. Scriven, the men of the HKCR accredited themselves well during the battle and were spoken of highly by officers from other units. Unfortunately for the HKCR, most of the unit, including Second Lieutenant Pigott and Colour Sergeant Bond, were killed when they were ambushed south of the gap while retreating with a group of Canadians toward the Repulse Bay Hotel. One of the few survivors was Corporal Tong Po Hing, who managed to make his way back to the city of Victoria before the end of the battle and was ordered into hiding by

Scriven.[93] Had the recruitment of Hong Kong Chinese soldiers been started earlier and resulted in larger numbers, the HKCR might have had a greater impact on the battle. As it was, many Chinese were eager to aid in the defense of Hong Kong, but political considerations prevented the British from seeking greater Chinese support, and the opportunity to mount a more effective defense was lost.

By 22 December, the end of the battle was approaching. The Japanese were in command of the north-south axis bisecting the island, but their progress had been costly. After the war, Colonel Shoji explained some of his difficulties to Canadian officers in a passage quoted by Colonel Charles Stacey, author of the Canadian army's official history:

> The first assault wave by the troops to the right of our right flank came upon a powerful group of sheltered positions, provided with emplacements at the Eastern foot of Nicholson Hill. The enemy fire from those positions was so heavy that not only was the advance balked, but our troops were thrown into confusion. Our left flank units also faced heavy enemy fire from the defenders occupying a hotel on the Southern side of Tsu-Lo-Lan Hill, and their advance was impeded.[94]

Shoji claimed that his regiment suffered 800 casualties during this part of the battle. Japanese problems were compounded by the loss of many more men in the harbor. As Japanese troops pushed inland from their beachheads, reinforcements were ferried across in small boats, and these were attacked by the 2nd MTB Flotilla on 19 December. The attack was quite successful, with many boats being shot up and four being sunk. The remaining Japanese vessels steered hard for their starting point at Kai Tak, but Royal Navy losses mounted as they pressed forward in pursuit. Several MTBs sustained damage, and two were destroyed by shell fire. Unimpeded due to the lack of shore-based British artillery, the Japanese soon resumed their reinforcement operations and began to land their own guns on the island the following day.[95]

With the addition of this firepower, and with the defenders being split into two groups, the outcome of the battle was no longer in doubt. After the Japanese occupied the Repulse Bay Hotel on 22 December, Colonel Rose's brigade was pushed west along its entire front, while Tanaka's 229th Regiment advanced on Brigadier Wallis's East Brigade, pushing it

CHAPTER NINE

farther southeast into the village of Stanley. On Christmas Day, Company Sergeant Major George MacDonell led D Company of the Royal Rifles through the village in a final attack against Japanese forces, before the garrison finally laid down its arms.[96] Governor Young accepted defeat and surrendered Hong Kong that day, and the surviving defenders spent the remainder of the war in captivity under brutal conditions. The Japanese 23rd Army had won.

The end of the battle was a difficult time, and many of the worst Japanese atrocities were committed during these days. The slaughter of prisoners at places such as Eucliffe Castle was followed by the massacre of wounded troops and civilians at the hospital at St. Stephen's College. The rape and murder of civilian nurses at more than one location once again typified the bestial irrationality of Japanese methods.[97] One group that escaped did so by sea. A party of senior British and Chinese officials led by Admiral Chan Chak fled through Mirs Bay and continued on to Waichow. This group was guided by Major Francis Kendall, leader of the garrison's special operations Z Force detachment. The survivors of the garrison were marched into captivity, and many non-Chinese civilians were soon similarly interned. In all, roughly 1,560 Commonwealth troops were killed in battle, and twice that number died as prisoners of war. Approximately 2,000 Japanese were killed, and another 6,000 were wounded. The Foreign Office estimated that of the 4,000 civilian casualties, about 1,000 were killed. The Japanese 38th Division was quickly withdrawn from Hong Kong during January 1942, and a garrison of about 5,000 men was left to defend the island and the port. The 38th Division saw further combat in the Netherlands East Indies, including the battle for Amboina, but most of the unit was destroyed during the battle of Guadalcanal.[98]

Many problems contributed to the defeat of the Hong Kong garrison, but a lack of courage was certainly not one of them.[99] In the historiography of the battle, some authors have apportioned blame unfairly to one unit or another, but this is not useful, and it is certainly not accurate.[100] As Tony Banham rightly noted, "Casualty figures imply that all units fought with equal determination."[101] The impulse to place blame was likely inevitable due to the embarrassment associated with what was widely considered a rapid defeat. Although the defeat came before operations could be coordinated with the Chinese, it should be remembered that the length of the battle—eighteen days, or about two and a half weeks—was not much shorter than larger campaigns that occurred during the first two years of the war in Europe. Entire countries succumbed to invasion after only a few weeks or less. Still, the colony surrendered before a relief operation could be mounted, and resistance did not slow the Japanese advance south.[102] The problem with British Commonwealth forces originated not with the men on the ground but with the inadequate allocation of military resources by their respective governments during the interwar period, which resulted in an overall lack of preparedness. Given their limitations, the officers and men of the garrison performed admirably.

Commonwealth problems at Hong Kong were numerous and hastened the defeat, but from this battle, many military and diplomatic lessons can be learned. The unnecessary tragedy at Hong Kong exposed the fragility of British power, and to avoid shedding light on the geopolitical realities associated with the garrison's sacrifice (such as the cost of maintaining an alliance with the Soviet Union), officials in London and Ottawa focused primarily on military issues to diminish and divert unwanted public attention on questions of high policy—the most important being the purpose of the war. Maintaining popular support was the primary function of the Royal Canadian Commission of Inquiry headed by Sir Lyman Duff in the spring and early summer of 1942. The Duff Commission also served to contain domestic political damage by exonerating the government from blame and by helping Mackenzie King deflect opposition demands for the introduction of conscription.[103] An honest appraisal of Canada's involvement at Hong Kong, however, would have arrived at a different verdict. It would have explained that democratic countries are generally at a great disadvantage upon the outbreak of war with authoritarian states, but in doing so, it would have exposed the hypocrisy and culpability of those responsible for sending men into combat after years of embracing disarmament as a military policy. Unfortunately, this did not happen.

The battle of Hong Kong serves as a useful example of what often happens to weak military forces of democratic societies that pursue an aggressive foreign policy based on the principles of collective security. In Canada's case, lack of political will to maintain an adequately prepared army during peacetime, even when composed largely of reservists, meant that combat experience had to make up for shortfalls in equipment, training, and especially doctrine during the first years of the war. C Force was deficient in all these areas. To defeat the Axis, the Allies had to employ an effective combined-arms warfare doctrine that took years to develop, at the cost of many lives.[104] Canadian Lieutenant General Charles Foulkes, chief of the General Staff, commented on this when he recommended to the cabinet that the reinforcement issue remain closed following the release of the Maltby report in early 1948:

> I would strongly recommend that every effort should be made to avoid reopening this Hong Kong enquiry. Much of the evidence given at the time of the enquiry in respect to quality of training and equipment of these troops was based on the very limited experience of Canadian officers gained in the first two years of war before Canadian troops were actively engaged in operations. A great deal has been learned since then about training and equipment and it is very doubtful if the same officers who gave the evidence at the time of the Duff report would make similar statements in view of the lessons learnt from the last war. I doubt if Home, Price and others would agree now that they considered that these troops were adequately trained for war.[105]

Hong Kong's defenders were not the same soldiers as those who would serve in Normandy in 1944 or even those who would fight in North Africa beforehand. In 1941 many Canadian troops at Hong Kong were only partially trained, and officers with combat experience were, for the most part, ready to refight World War I. The garrison also lacked the cohesion to fight as a single force; it was a collection of units hastily cobbled together on an ad hoc basis without sufficient firepower. In contrast, according to General Martin Farndale, senior Japanese commanders were well trained at the operational level, as were the men of their units. The Japanese had also developed infiltration tactics and night-fighting capabilities to usher in a new form of infantry combat founded on both speed and stealth. Most important, they had been refining their methods against the Chinese for four and a half years.[106]

General Maltby's leadership and battle plan also hastened defeat.[107] Being roughly the size of an understrength division, or about 12,000 to 14,000 men, the garrison was too small to man the Gindrinkers' Line as well as a perimeter defense of the island.[108] Few good options were available to defend Hong Kong, but one possibility would have been to reduce the number of vulnerable troops manning beach defenses on the island and create a larger reserve with mobile artillery. Maintaining a defense of Devil's Peak and the southernmost built-up section of Kowloon would have made the Japanese advance more costly. Defending the island on the beach left insufficient troops to mount an effective counterattack. Command at the brigade level was also ineffective: Brigadier General Wallis lost confidence in Maltby's leadership, and both Wallis and Colonel W. J. Home most likely suffered from battle exhaustion during the final days.[109]

Other command problems were evident, such as Maltby's lack of diligence in preventing the loss of resources to the Japanese. Due to the presence of a nearby civil hospital, Maltby failed to ensure the destruction of strategically important oil storage tanks at Laichikok. Oil from Kowloon was subsequently used by the Japanese in Malaya. Furthermore, a two-year supply of drugs and medicine sufficient to meet the needs of the population of Hong Kong was seized and shipped to Japan.[110]

In contrast, combat experience and effective leadership were the main factors in the Allied victory in Hunan. The first indication of this came during the struggle for Wong Nei Chong Gap, when the Chinese correctly determined that the battle for Hong Kong had already been lost and General Hsueh redirected his energies and resources to the defense of Changsha. On 21 December 1941 the *New York Times* announced that the Chinese expected Hong Kong to fall, and most of the relieving forces marching in Kwangtung were brought to a halt.[111] Many in Hong Kong blamed the Chinese army for not coming to their aid, and some claimed there had been no attempt to do so, but this was not the case.[112] Hong Kong fell to the Japanese army earlier than expected and before Chinese forces could assemble for an attack.

The Reverend V. Mills was a credible eyewitness who explained this to Canadian authorities in September 1943. His statement indicates that the Chinese readied themselves to fight alongside their allies in defense of southern China, but their commanders were not inclined to commit troops to battle once defeat had already been assured. Mills was a young Canadian missionary who had been working along the East River since 1931, when he was eighteen years old. Born in Birmingham, Mills and his family moved to Winnipeg when he was only six. Considered reliable by future Canadian embassy officials, Mills also worked periodically for British intelligence, and he would eventually provide useful information to the USAAF 14th Air Force once the air war over southern China was fully under way.[113] Mills made the following statement:

> I witnessed for ten days and nights a continuous stream of men going to the front via the East River and other companies going across

country via Yungyuen making for Waichow with other troops travelling down the river making preparation to drive on Canton. At that time the morale of the Kwangtung soldiers was extremely high in spite of the fact that many had been walking for nine days, their feet covered with blisters and the majority of them had not enjoyed one night's good sleep during their long-trek. These men were pressing forward with an eagerness that I had never witnessed in the Kwangtung Army before. I never ascertained the strength of this army. However, I noticed that their equipment was very light. Besides their rifles, they had a good number of machine guns and a very small number of field pieces. One of the Chinese generals in charge was Chang Tek-nang, the brother of a very intimate friend of mine.

2. It was a great disappointment to these men when news was received that Hongkong had fallen. I never saw an army that looked so down in the dumps. After walking nine days and then told that they must recover their steps without even firing a shot at the Japs was almost more than these boys could bear.[114]

A Chinese offensive on Japanese lines of communication would have been useful in diverting 23rd Army resources, but the pace of events in Hong Kong made such an offensive an unnecessary expense.

Mills's statement also reveals the effect the fall of Hong Kong had on Chinese morale. For the first time since the start of the Sino-Japanese War, the Chinese were fighting as a full ally of Great Britain and the United States, and they were eager to assist the garrison at Hong Kong. The Chinese found themselves in a position to render direct material aid to Great Britain at a time when their country had become a significant theater of war.[115] Chiang had been assured that the colony could hold long enough for his armies to attack the Japanese rear, but with the fall of Hong Kong, Allied plans for southern China came to nothing. The defeat of British forces at Hong Kong, however, was only the first of a series of Allied military disasters leading to China's physical isolation.

Widespread expectations and plans for foreign intervention had started to disintegrate, and this greatly impacted Chinese morale over the next few months. The Dominions Office commented on the prospect of a separate peace in China as Hong Kong was falling to the Japanese, and Allied political leaders took note. On 25 December 1941 the Dominions Office sent the following message from London:

His Majesty's Ambassador at Chungking is concerned at the reaction of the Chinese to British reversals, particularly at Hong Kong and in Malaya. He reports that the Chinese were ready to write off the attacks at Pearl Harbour and on our ships, but are alarmed at the series of setbacks, particularly at Hong Kong where the quick deterioration of the situation has taken them by surprise, and where large numbers of the leading Chinese have their wives and families. His Majesty's Ambassador reports that Chiang Kai shek himself still remains rock-like in his faith and determination, but that if the fall of Hong Kong were to be followed by the occupation of Burma and the cutting of the Burma Road, there is the possibility of Japanese offer of quick peace which certain disillusioned elements in China might find it hard to resist.

3. United States Ambassador shares these fears, and agrees with Sir A. Clark Kerr that, to avert this possible danger, we should lose no time in signing pact for which Chiang Kai Shek has asked. Chinese are apparently working on a tentative text.[116]

The Chinese did not quit the war, but the fall of Hong Kong effectively brought Sino-British military cooperation to an end. Later in 1942, the China Commando Group and Detachment 204 would both be withdrawn.[117]

Before being transferred to the Soviet Union in February 1942, Ambassador Archibald Clark Kerr again commented on the political impact of Allied military reverses in Chungking. In one of his last official memorandums on China sent to Foreign Secretary Anthony Eden, he wrote:

When I first came to this country, early in the spring of 1938, the Central Government had been driven, bruised and breathless, from Nanking to Hankow. But the hesitations of the Japanese had given time for the licking of wounds, and already Government, armies and people alike had got their second wind and were showing striking signs of the spirit that had carried China, undaunted and unbeaten, through trials under which many another country would have collapsed.

. . . It was at that time that I ventured to express the opinion that, if they were given the help they sought and deserved, and so long as

Chiang Kai-shek was at their head, the people of China would hold, and would in the end themselves frustrate the Japanese attempt to subjugate them. From this opinion I have not swerved. But the Chinese are a mercurial people and at all times they have needed, as they will still need, careful nursing and sustained encouragement. Today this need is all the keener because they are fallen into a state of bewilderment and disillusionment.

. . . You will be aware that, since the earliest days of their struggle against Japan, the dearest hope of the Chinese has been to become the allies of ourselves and the Americans, for in this their salvation seemed to lie. . . . They felt that, if they could hold out until Great Britain and the United States became involved in their war, all would be well; that Japan would be disposed of in a few months and that they, who had borne the brunt of her attack for so many years alone, would be eased of their burden and would indeed be free to enjoy to the full the exquisite emotion of stamping on the corpse of the aggressor.

. . . To say that this hope was high falls short of reality. It was something so strong and so eager that upon it were built all Chinese plans. It was in some measure a part of the essence of their will to resist. Now it has been cruelly dashed by a series of tragic events which have followed each other in quick succession—Pearl Harbour, Hong Kong, Manila and today the disturbing threat to Singapore. For myself I feel that nevertheless they will survive all these blows, even the fall of Singapore. My anxiety would only become acute if Burma were to be overrun, for the effects of this might well be to stretch the threads of China's resistance to the point of breaking. If, therefore, the Chinese seem at the moment to waver and even to despair, we must not blame them. We must set about finding fresh and convincing means to sustain them both materially and morally. We still have good ground to work upon for their hearts are with us and set deep in the Grand Alliance, to which they are proud to belong.[118]

Chinese resolve to continue the war was buttressed by the faith in future American support, but another largely overlooked factor was the growing ability of their armed forces to contain the Japanese army.[119]

Anticipating another Japanese offensive against Changsha in support of the 23rd Army at Hong Kong, Chiang deployed four additional armies into Hunan to face the bulk of the 11th Army still based at Hankow and Yochow. General Anami wanted to draw Chinese forces north out of Kwangtung, and his plan for another foray into Hunan was approved in mid-November by Lieutenant General Ushiroku Jun, chief of staff of the China Expeditionary Army, as well as General Hata Shunroku, the senior Japanese commander in China. After licking its wounds from the earlier defeat in the fall, the 11th Army began to assemble its forces on 16 December 1941.[120]

The third battle of Changsha began in the second to last week of December 1941, and it would be the only significant Allied victory in Asia or the Pacific for the next several months. The battles of Changsha and Hong Kong were two elements of the same Japanese plan, but in the end, their victory in the Pearl River Delta did not compensate for the losses sustained or for the geopolitical impact of defeat in Hunan. The third battle of Changsha was much more damaging to the Japanese than either of the two previous battles for the city in 1939 and the fall of 1941, and although Chinese forces were withdrawn from Kwangtung to deal with the threat in Hunan, this occurred only after the defense of Hong Kong had virtually come to an end. In capturing Changsha, Anami hoped to force Chiang to negotiate and end the war, but instead, he achieved the opposite effect.[121]

As in September, the first stage of the battle went relatively well for the Japanese. Minor fighting preceded the attack in the northern portion of the province while the Japanese finalized their preparations. By 23 December 1941, the attack was fully under way, with the 11th Army advancing south to the Milo River. But unlike September's foray, fewer troops were assigned to this offensive. Japanese divisions included the 6th and 40th in the center, and eastern columns with elements of the 3rd farther west. The 9th Mixed Independent Brigade was also brought south from Hankow, along with the 14th Independent Brigade, to protect lines of communication back to Yochow. Defending Hunan under Hsueh were the 20th, 37th, and 99th Chinese Armies, while the 10th Army of General Li Yu Tang was positioned farther south at Changsha. The Chinese 79th Army's scheduled move from Hengyang to Kwangtung had already been abandoned, and the 58th Army was held in reserve to attack the Japanese eastern flank. To prevent a reverse similar to that experienced in the previous battle for Changsha, the Japanese 34th Division attacked in a southwesterly direction from Nanchang beginning on 24 December. The Japanese hoped to prevent a

CHAPTER NINE

Chinese move against the 11th Army's supply lines, but once again, Anami underestimated his opposition and attacked with insufficient forces.[122]

Japanese difficulties began with the crossing of the Milo River on 26 December 1941 (see figure 9.2). Weather conditions were almost as poor as they had been in September, and freezing temperatures combined with a violently turbulent river to make fording impossible. Crossing in strength required the use of several pontoon bridges. Opposing Anami's forces directly were the 99th and 37th Armies on the Chinese left and right, respectively, and they were dug in along the south side of the river. Fighting was heavy but brief, and the 37th Army was hit hard by the Japanese 6th and 40th Divisions. After several Japanese bridgeheads were established, the Chinese were ordered to withdraw from the river, but instead of falling back on Changsha, the 37th Army turned east and retreated toward the mountains. There it waited, along with the 58th Army farther north, for the Japanese to continue moving south.[123]

After breaching the Milo River line, few Chinese forces appeared to be blocking his line of advance, and General Anami pushed on to capture Changsha. The 11th Army's march was somewhat disorganized, however, as Anami did not wait for the assembly of all his forces. Nevertheless, by 29 December, the 3rd and 6th Divisions were closing on Changsha under the gaze of Chinese gunners perched atop Tamoshan. In bypassing this feature, Anami's western flank was left dangerously exposed, but the 40th Division followed close behind, leaving a few units to cover the tenuous line of communication back to Yochow. Once they were through the gap, the 3rd and 6th Divisions drove directly to Changsha, arriving at the city on 31 December. Its fall appeared certain to many foreign military and diplomatic officials.[124] Although Changsha was soon surrounded on three sides, the Chinese 10th Army was able to keep its western base along the river clear of Japanese troops. In doing so, General Li's line of supply remained secure.

Anami could not afford a protracted siege of Changsha, so a quick but ineffective assault was launched against the city's gates on New Year's Day. Some of the most serious fighting occurred between 1 and 3 January 1942, and unlike the second battle of Changsha, there was heavy urban combat during these three days. The city had been evacuated of most of its residents while troops constructed numerous fortified positions.[125] Dr. Winston Pettus of the Yale in China University Hospital described the situation to a colleague: "This time there was a pitched battle, first at the South Gate, then at the East, and finally at the North. The city itself was a maze

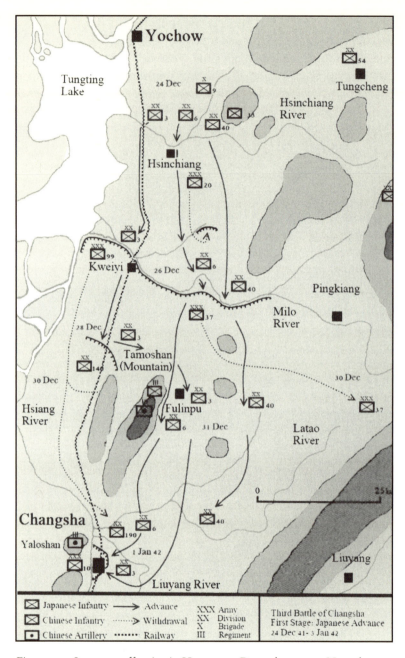

Figure 9.2. Japanese offensive in Hunan, 24 December 1941. Note that the Japanese referred to the September and December 1941 battles for Changsha as the first and second battles, respectively, whereas the Chinese identified the 1939 battle for Changsha as the first battle. (Based on data from LOC, Japanese Monograph No. 71, by Ishiwari; and Chang and Hsu, *History of the Sino-Japanese War [1937–1945]*.)

of barriers, trenches and blockades, which got thicker around the edges of the city."[126]

Anami's biggest problem was that 9th War Zone forces continued to enjoy artillery superiority from positions atop Yaloshan (Yuelu Hill), just west of the city, in addition to Tamoshan farther north. With Anami's infantry mired in the cold mud below, Chinese artillery units were able to rain fire down on them at will. One prominent structure that was not bombarded, even after two days of fierce combat, was the hospital located near the north gate. Many 9th War Zone officers were from Hunan, and they hoped to preserve the hospital for future use.[127] Conversely, the Japanese had great difficulty bringing their artillery south and were forced to assault Changsha without sufficient firepower. Japanese artillery problems began with the crossing of the Milo River. According to the *Times*, "The Chinese were able to shell the Japanese lines on the outskirts of Changsha without fear of reprisals, except from mortars and mountain guns, because the Japanese lost their artillery in the battle at the Milo River."[128] The entire force had just six mountain guns in total, and they had to rely on air strikes to make up for the shortfall in heavy weapons; however, with overcast weather conditions, this proved difficult.[129]

The bulk of the Japanese 3rd and 6th Divisions fought the Chinese 10th Army largely along the city's outer ring. Initially, fighting was heaviest on the southern rim against the 10th Division; then it became more intense against the 190th Division to the north. The Chinese 3rd Division was held in reserve. Street fighting continued, and casualties mounted in great numbers on both sides. Close-quarter combat was common, in conjunction with the widespread use of flamethrowers.[130]

As the battle for Changsha raged, pressure started to build in other regions of the 9th War Zone. On 4 January 1942 the Chinese 4th and 79th Armies arrived from Hengyang to break through to the 10th Army from the south. They were joined by the 26th and 78th Armies arriving from Kiangsi.[131] An area of dominant high ground southeast of the city—called Graveyard Hill by Western reporters—became another scene of heavy fighting, and the position changed hands eleven times. One Japanese regimental charge was wiped out during these engagements, and the Japanese 3rd Division sustained particularly high casualties.[132]

Much more dangerous, however, was the Chinese counterattack against Japanese lines of communication farther north. Once the assault on the city was under way, the Chinese quickly marched the 58th and 37th Armies out of the eastern mountains and advanced them in a westerly manner through the fields and along the rivers below. The Japanese 34th Division sent down from northern Kiangsi was supposed to prevent such a move, but it was halted by Chinese diversionary attacks to the north of Nanchang and by blocking forces along its line of advance. The Chinese 58th Army moved rapidly to take unoccupied positions along the north bank of the Milo River, while the 37th Army secured portions of the Latao River only a few miles northeast of Changsha. Defensive positions were prepared in anticipation of sustained combat. With the addition of the Chinese 99th and 73rd Armies moving in from the west, the Japanese retreat was also blocked along the Hsiang River running north into Tungting Lake. Subsequent combat between 99th Army forces and Japanese troops positioned at Kweiyi on the Milo River produced many additional casualties.[133]

Anami had overextended the 11th Army yet again, and consequently, the 3rd, 6th, and much of the 40th Divisions were cut off, with nine Chinese armies surrounding them. By positioning themselves astride the Latao and Liuyang rivers, elements of the Chinese 37th and 99th Armies had also managed to separate the 40th Division from the bulk of the 3rd and 6th Divisions, which were still fighting near the city. Japanese supplies ran out quickly, and airborne supply drops were required to prevent a catastrophe.[134] One prisoner by the name of Kyoshi Kowahara was captured near the eastern gate of the city after he tried to kill himself with a grenade, but it failed to explode. Kyoshi informed his captors that the cold and the rain were damaging morale, and he and his comrades had not eaten for three days. The prisoner also revealed that morale among most Japanese soldiers had not improved with the expansion of the war.[135]

The worst stage of the battle was set to begin. Between 4 and 11 January the Japanese 11th Army had to fight its way north from Changsha through numerous Chinese armies and over a total of four different rivers in muddy, icy conditions (see figure 9.3). Fighting was difficult, and severe casualties were the result. The retreat began on the very cold night of 3 January 1942, and as a parting gesture, the Japanese burned the university hospital after killing those wounded who could not be moved, along with several of the nursing staff. The fire was used as a funeral pyre. The first engagements occurred while the Japanese were crossing the Liuyang and Latao rivers running just north of the city. Rubber boats were used, but these were limited in number. Two bridgeheads were eventually secured on 4 and 5 January, but Chinese resistance was stiff, and only one of these routes could be used effectively. It was largely because of Japanese air-power that the divisions were able to extricate themselves at all. The Chinese air force rose to challenge Japanese air superiority, but on 6 January four Chinese planes were lost in exchange for a single Japanese fighter in a small air battle north of the city. No further air combat was reported after the Chinese squadron withdrew to Chengtu. While the 3rd and 6th Divisions fought their way across the first two rivers, elements of the Japanese 40th Division attacked from the northeast to reestablish a link between them south of the town of Fulinpu, which was approximately one-third of the way to Yochow. The two groups reestablished contact by 7 January, but casualties were severe.[136]

After breaking through the first set of Chinese defenses, the remnants of the 11th Army's main force reorganized to resume the advance northward in two separate columns. Only on 11 January 1942 were they able to link up with part of the 9th Independent Mixed Brigade, which had forced its way into Fulinpu. The 9th Brigade had been rushed south earlier to secure the town while the 40th Division was extricating the 3rd and 6th Divisions from Changsha, but in holding its position at Fulinpu, the 9th Brigade was subjected to heavy Chinese pressure.[137]

Other elements of the 40th Division farther north were already attacking across the all-important Milo River. These were aided by a battalion of the 9th Brigade that had been left behind to hit the defending Chinese forces from the rear. Battle for the north bank of the Milo intensified, and many Japanese soldiers drowned in the icy water, but again with the help of airpower, they were able to secure and defend two bridgeheads. The bulk of the 11th Army, however, was still fighting its way north to reach them. After crossing the Milo on 13 January, Anami's army was able to continue its retreat with diminished interference, but Japanese rearguard pockets cut off from the rest of the main body were less fortunate and sustained heavy casualties (see figure 9.4). The final river to be crossed before reaching their base at Yochow was the Hsinchiang, and this was completed by 15 January.[138] In summing up events, an article in the *Times* reported, "After suffering heavy losses of men and supplies during his abortive advance over four rivers, the frost-bitten [*sic*] enemy is now in full retreat across the wintry brown plains of northern Hunan."[139] When the Japanese reached Yochow the following day, the third battle of Changsha came to an end.

Japanese defeat was a result of several factors combined. The geography

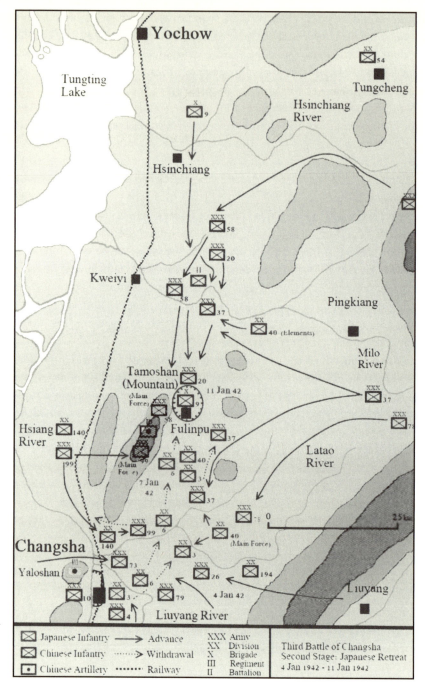

Figure 9.3. Japanese retreat in Hunan, 4 January 1942. (Based on data from LOC, Japanese Monograph No. 71, by Ishiwari; and Chang and Hsu, *History of the Sino-Japanese War [1937–1945]*.)

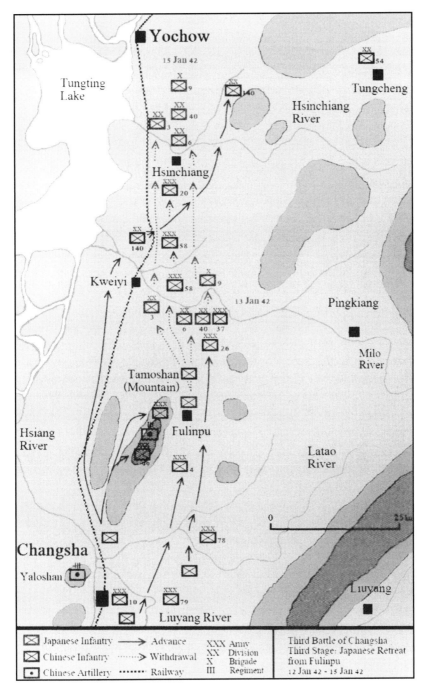

Figure 9.4. Japanese retreat in Hunan, 11 January 1942. (Based on data from LOC, Japanese Monograph No. 71, by Ishiwari; and Chang and Hsu, *History of the Sino-Japanese War [1937–1945]*.)

of Hunan and the poor weather conditions greatly aided the defense. Farther northwest, additional encouragement for a speedy retreat came in the form of another Chinese attack near Ichang in which a Japanese force suffered approximately 200 casualties. Most important, however, was General Anami's ineffective leadership. As in September 1941, the 11th Army was able to advance a considerable distance into Hunan, but again, Anami recklessly invited defeat by pushing ahead without his artillery and by overextending his forces. With Hong Kong already conquered, Anami should have ended his advance and returned to Yochow, but his search for glory resulted in disaster. Upon arriving at the gates of Changsha, Anami's men fruitlessly battled the Chinese 10th Army in the rubble-strewn outer ring of the city. Once encircled, he was forced to retreat as his army ran out of supplies. In 1945 Anami would serve as minister of war in Tokyo, and at that time he was the most senior official who advocated a continuation of hostilities after the bombing of Hiroshima and Nagasaki. Although his generalship in Hunan was less than inspiring, it can be said with some justice that his strongest characteristic was stubbornness.[140]

In contrast, the Chinese had a rare combination of superior firepower and leadership. Early in the battle Hsueh decided to cut Chinese losses in Kwangtung, and he wisely concentrated his 9th War Zone forces for the defense of Hunan. The garrison at Hong Kong was unable to hold, and Governor Young surrendered the colony on Christmas Day. As 7th War Zone forces under General Yu Han Mou were sufficiently strong to maintain the defense of northern Kwangtung, Hsueh's decision was sound. North of Changsha, Hsueh seized the initiative and counterattacked Anami's exposed lines of communication; he was able to do so because of General Li's stalwart defense of Changsha. Li had the respect of his men, and 10th Army morale was strong.[141] Hsueh's mountain-based artillery then took a terrible toll on the encircled Japanese 11th Army, which was forced to traverse the cold, muddy ground directly under their barrels. Some isolated units were wiped out through bombardment. In his memoirs, Major General Claire Chennault claimed that Hsueh was one of China's best generals and that later in the war, "Japanese intelligence reports rated Hsueh as the most capable war area-commander in China."[142] Because of this victory, Hsueh became known as the "Tiger" of Changsha.[143]

After the battle there was a great deal of evidence to support Chinese claims of victory. Many bodies and large quantities of damaged or abandoned equipment were seen by numerous eyewitnesses. The casualty figures reported publicly by both sides were grossly exaggerated, but reports filed by U.S. Army officers such as Lieutenant Colonel David Barrett provided more reliable estimates. Barrett traveled to Changsha and saw first-hand the extent of the damage as well as the unburied dead. By the time the Japanese crossed the Milo River, he reported that out of an original force of 80,000 men, somewhere between 10,000 and 20,000 Japanese dead were already accounted for. *Times* reporter Robert Payne also toured the region and noted that evidence for this number was vast. By the end of the battle, he estimated that the Japanese had sustained a total of 23,000 dead, and many of these were from the 3rd Division. Colonel Mayer reported Japanese casualties to be in the range of 10,000 to 15,000, and he estimated the number of Chinese killed at 4,000. Japanese losses could have been much higher, but Hsueh did not press home his advantage by pursuing Anami's army hard north of the Milo River. This may have been due in part to a limited offensive launched by the 23rd Army on 12 January toward Kukong, which required the presence of forces in Hunan that were capable of meeting any unexpected thrust in northern Kwangtung. In the absence of a pursuit, the bulk of the 11th Army was able to make good its escape.[144]

The primary significance of the battle was the psychological impact on Chinese morale. Japanese operations in Hunan and in the southwest Pacific were aimed at removing Western influence in Asia and forcing the Chinese to come to terms, but the third battle of Changsha helped prevent this.[145] The Chinese had been greatly shocked by the fall of Hong Kong, and U.S. Ambassador Clarence Gauss commented on this to the State Department when he recommended the approval of another loan: "Now that the Chinese have overcome the severe shock of our initial reverses, of which the fall of Hong Kong was psychologically the most serious, I feel that morale has steadied."[146] At the State Department's Far Eastern Desk in Washington, Stanley Hornbeck concurred. Changsha also helped mitigate the impact of the announcement by Churchill and Roosevelt that Allied grand strategy would be oriented toward the defeat of Germany first.[147] According to Chiang Kai Shek's son, Chiang Wego, the effect on morale was most important: "The psychological effect was tremendous. The Chinese rank and file felt that under the direction of our Generalissimo, they, too, could execute the Japanese favorite encircling maneuver and nearly annihilate our enemy in battle. Morale was boosted."[148] In the face of devastating Allied defeats in the Far East, the Chinese were able to

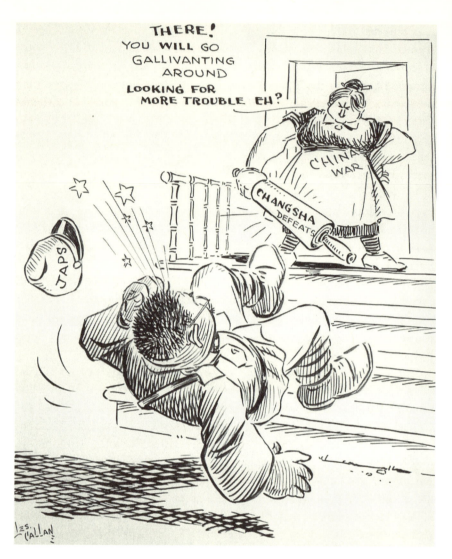

Figure 9.5. Newspaper cartoon about the third battle of Changsha. (LAC, Graphic, LAC 00243, Les Callan, "Been Neglecting the 'Little Woman' Lately, Mister?" *Toronto Daily Star*, 7 January 1942.)

beat the Japanese on their own, and by doing so, they were encouraged to maintain their resistance against Japan.[149]

In the aftermath of the battle, international reaction was often expressed in tones of positive surprise, and for a time, this too helped buoy Chinese morale. In Washington on 14 January 1942, General Dwight Eisenhower met with the Chinese military attaché, General Chu Shih Ming, and they discussed the recent victories at Changsha. In February, Wavell's chief of staff, General Henry Pownall, recorded that the British had underestimated both the Japanese and the Chinese.[150] As might be expected, the foreign media were eager to exaggerate any success because good news was scarce at the time (see figure 9.5).

It was George Orwell, however, who penned a relatively measured commentary while working for the BBC. On 10 January 1942 he wrote:

> The greatest military event of this week has occurred on a battlefield about which we have not lately heard so much, as we have heard about either Russia or Malaya, and that battlefield is China. The Japanese invaders have suffered a great defeat at the city of Changsha. . . .
>
> This event is not important only for the heroic defenders of China. It cannot be too much emphasized that this is a world war, and every success or failure upon each of the various fronts has its effect upon every other front, from Norway to the Philippine Islands.[151]

In February 1942 Richard Webb wrote that both Changsha and Hong Kong were part of the same Japanese operation, and he commented on the impact of these battles on the war:

> The price Japan paid for Hongkong must include the casualties she suffered at Changsha. . . .
>
> . . . the Changsha push was the biggest of a general Japanese offensive designed to prevent China from aiding the Allies. . . .
>
> The Japanese drive to eliminate British power in China was successful, but the effort to stop the movement of Chinese troops into Burma failed.[152]

The majority of newspaper reports and editorials, however, clearly sacrificed any pretense of objectivity in publicizing this Far Eastern success in order to boost home-front morale. Grossly inflated claims of Japanese casualties were common.

The Chinese also viewed Changsha as a contribution to the Allied effort. With the battle virtually over, General Hsueh discussed China's role in the war with journalists, and the *Times* reported on 12 January 1942 that the general drank a toast to Allied victory: "[He] said, 'I told my soldiers that we were fighting at Changsha not only for our own soil but also for a world cause.'"[153] The Japanese attack was intended to keep the Chinese from assisting Allied forces at Hong Kong and Burma, but Chiang had built up adequate forces to conduct operations in all three regions. The battle of Changsha did not cause a redirection of Chinese troops that led to the fall of Hong Kong. Chinese armies were assembling in Kwangtung as quickly as possible to begin their attacks on Canton as well as the Japanese rear at Hong Kong. These operations were set to begin by the second week of January, as agreed among Chiang, Dennys, and Magruder, but Hong Kong fell before the Chinese could help.[154] The Chinese moved in accordance with Allied plans, but once defeat at Hong Kong was obvious, they focused their attention on the threat in Hunan. Ultimately, it was more important to defend Hunan than it was to reinforce defeat at Hong Kong. Moreover, the military value of Hong Kong rested in its capacity to keep 9th War Zone forces supplied, and this could no longer be accomplished, even if the colony were relieved.

The battle of Changsha similarly did not prevent the Chinese from sending troops into Burma. This failure was the result of British hesitation to cooperate. As Hong Kong was falling to the Japanese, General Wavell met with Chiang and refused his offer of the Chinese 5th and 6th Armies for Burma. With the exception of some temporary help provided by Chennault's AVG, the British were reluctant to accept armed forces in the region because of concerns over Chiang's foreign policy ambitions. Chinese ground forces were accepted only when it was too late, and although the fall of Burma did not bring Chinese resistance to an end, without victory at Changsha, it had the potential to do so.[155]

The End of the Line

The fall and winter of 1941 was a critical period of the war marked by a series of devastating Allied defeats in the Far East, but the exception occurred in China. Despite the strongest Japanese efforts, the Chinese army did not break, and indirect support for the Soviet Far East was maintained when the Allied situation was most dire. The attack on Hong Kong and the third battle of Changsha were elements of the same Japanese operational plan, and partly because of their victory in Hunan, the Chinese were able to continue the war at a time when their morale was greatly undermined. In attacking Changsha, Japanese commanders wanted to demonstrate China's worthlessness as an ally, but the opposite effect was produced. The Japanese lacked sufficient troops to achieve a military victory, and once the Pacific war began, this problem did not improve.[156] Although the Chinese had many difficulties to contend with, the army was sufficiently strong to maintain a defense of the country. What they still required, however, was artillery. The third battle of Changsha demonstrated that even with limited firepower, the Chinese army was capable of defending some strategically important regions of the country virtually unaided. The victory at Changsha boosted Chinese morale, and even after the fall of Burma, they still expected that material shortages could be made up when America entered the war. Chinese faith rested on President Franklin Roosevelt's assurance of continued American aid. During the battles for Changsha, the Chinese evinced an ability to defend themselves, and Chiang's strategy of trading space for time appeared to be validated.[157]

For the Japanese, Hong Kong was a hollow victory spawned by a disastrously ineffective grand strategy. Success in Burma and Hong Kong made the Japanese army appear invincible for a time, but events in southern China ultimately made the Japanese situation worse. By attacking Hawaii as well as Hong Kong and Malaya, the Japanese started a suicidal war against the United States and Great Britain. The offensive into the southwest Pacific during December 1941 was one of the greatest strategic mistakes made by the Axis during the entire conflict, and according to Evan Mawdsley, Hitler later greatly regretted his encouragement of this Japanese action.[158] Instead of striking south, the Japanese would have been better off either coming to terms with Chiang or attacking the Soviet Union.[159] Many factors combined to bring about their fateful decision, and of these, the escalation of violence and Allied intervention in the Pearl River Delta was an important one that indicated time was running short. The addition of Canadian troops in November contributed to this problem. Hong Kong was a growing impediment to Japanese plans, and because of this, the colony became one of the first points of attack at the start of the Pacific war. After the battle of Midway in June 1942, the Empire of Japan would be destroyed, largely by U.S. forces, in a little over three years' time, but China served as the noose.

Defeats in Hong Kong, Burma, and Malaya were also disastrous to the British. The loss of prestige associated with these campaigns brought Britain's military role in China to an end. Sino-British military cooperation in the form of Detachment 204 and the China Commando Group did not survive the death of Major General Dennys. The general was appointed GOC China after the battle of Hong Kong, but he was killed in a CNAC plane crash after leaving Kunming on 14 February 1942.[160] Having had a positive working relationship with Chiang, Dennys might have been able to maintain better Sino-British relations and keep Detachment 204 operational, but this remains speculative.

British Far Eastern strategy would have been more effective if they had cooperated closely with the Chinese army or recruited large numbers of colonial Chinese soldiers to bolster the defense of Hong Kong. A prolonged battle of attrition in the Pearl River Delta would have tied up Japanese units and replacements that were badly needed farther south. However, given enough time and persistence, and even if the Hong Kong garrison had been relieved, Japanese naval and airpower advantages eventually would have reduced the defenders sufficiently to bring about the fall of the colony. In any case, in the absence of greater cooperation with China, Hong Kong should have been demilitarized at an earlier date.[161] If the New Territories were not worth buying in 1938–1939, Hong Kong was not worth defending in 1941.

The expansion of the war made the reduction of British global power a certainty. American entry into the conflict virtually ensured an Allied victory, but this came at British expense, both financially and imperially. During the postwar period, the British Empire would greatly diminish as one colony after another secured its independence. Decolonization would have been likely in any event, but an irony of the battle of Hong Kong was the return of the colony to British control in 1945. British credibility had been badly damaged in 1941–1942, but if Hong Kong had not been defended, it is doubtful that the Union Jack would have been hoisted there again. Ultimately, burgeoning Cold War realities emerged to encourage such an event to transpire.[162]

Also contributing to this outcome were the activities of the British Army Aid Group (BAAG), the only British military unit permitted to operate in China throughout the rest of the war. The BAAG, under the command of

CHAPTER NINE

Colonel Lindsay Ride, was headquartered in Kweilin but had a base at Waichow. The colonel was a medical professor at the University of Hong Kong, and he was one of the first prisoners of war to escape Japanese captivity. The BAAG was originally established to assist other escaping prisoners, and throughout the war it maintained positive relations with the people of Kwangtung. Because of the need to cooperate with the communist East River Brigade (ERB), friction with the Chinese army was common, but the BAAG soon evolved into an intelligence unit assisting General Chennault's 14th Air Force based in Kunming, and it was allowed to continue its work.[163]

A major beneficiary of the battle of Hong Kong and the war in China in general was the Chinese Communist Party. Following the battle and the subsequent withdrawal of the 38th Division, few Japanese troops remained in Hong Kong. The Chinese army maintained the 187th Division at its base in Waichow under the command of General Chan Kee, but Tamshui marked the farthest extent of central governmental authority south toward Hong Kong. The resulting power vacuum in the New Territories was filled by the ERB, which moved in from its base farther to the northeast. Some British and American military intelligence officers working in southern China believed that this expansion had been planned prior to the start of the battle. Most of the ERB's weapons were of British origin, and Major Kendall was the officer in contact with the ERB commander Tsang Shang.[164] The ERB enjoyed considerable popular support in the New Territories, as many in the region sought to join in order to defend their families and homes during the rest of the war.

The third battle for Changsha also effectively ended Soviet military aid to the Chinese central government, but Soviet Far Eastern security was maintained for the duration of the war, even as China became an American sphere of interest. Hard-pressed against the Germans, the Soviets could not spare resources for the Far East. Only a year after being sent to Chungking, General Vasilii Chuikov's mission to China was terminated, and he was ordered to return home in February 1942. Over the following winter, Chuikov became famous for his role in the defense of Stalingrad. In his memoirs he explained the primary rationale for the withdrawal of Soviet support: quite simply, he had completed his mission.[165] The Soviet Far East was secure.

■

Collective Insecurity: The Demise of Imperial Power in Asia

From the start of the German invasion of the USSR until U.S. entry into the war, the conflict in China assumed great geostrategic significance. Aided by difficult winter conditions, General Georgy Zhukov and the Red Army blunted the German offensive for Moscow on 6 December 1941 after launching a major counterattack against Field Marshal Fedor von Bock's Army Group Center. By using freshly organized forces, albeit of mixed quality, the Soviets won a decisive victory. Zhukov later claimed that he and other officers doubted their ability to hold in front of Moscow, but the addition of several strong divisions transferred across the country from Siberia was a significant factor that tipped the balance in his favor.[1] Had Stalin not been assured of the Japanese intention to strike south instead of north, it is doubtful these units would have been available in sufficient numbers to aid in the defense of Moscow. One of the most important reasons behind the Japanese decision to move south was the desire to bring the war in China to a close, but the increasing level of Anglo-American intervention meant that time was running short to achieve victory.

A clear example of Western commitment to China was the reinforcement of Hong Kong. The British colony was the primary point of entry for military supplies from abroad, which made it a significant Chinese military logistical base. The decision to strengthen the colony's garrison with Canadian soldiers in the fall of 1941 had far-reaching ramifications, but the impact of the deployment was far greater than that of the battle itself. The reinforcement of Hong Kong was the most significant geopolitical event in the colony's wartime experience. It demonstrated that the Anglo-American proxy war in China was designed primarily to keep the Japanese army bogged down and thereby provide indirect support to the Soviet Far East. Canadian reinforcements were sent to Hong Kong when the Soviets faced defeat in Europe, but this move was conducted largely because of American influence. A Japanese attack into Siberia during this time was a scenario the Allies wanted to avoid at all costs, and the reinforcement of Hong Kong was meant to prevent this eventuality by sustaining Chinese morale. As an exercise in collective security, its impact was felt globally. Indirect support was provided to the Soviet Union, and the deployment helped expand the scale of the war in the Far East. The battle of Hong Kong itself, however, was a direct Allied attempt to block Japanese aggression, but it was an event of regional significance. In the end, both events were hatched largely from a combination of dangerous military and foreign policies. These included limited British alternatives in implementing the Singapore strategy, successive years of disarmament, and a confrontational foreign policy based on the tenets of collective security. The result was a tragic disaster.

British alternatives included disengagement from the war in China and the demilitarization of Hong Kong. These options were largely discounted due to the country's economic interests in the region and the damaging impact on British influence. Another option was to hold their position in southern China with an overt military agreement that included the acceptance of Chiang's offer of 200,000 Chinese troops for the defense of Hong Kong. Airfields were available at Kweilin and elsewhere to support such a plan, but Sino-British cooperation was never fully developed. Instead, the proxy war in China was continued at great risk to British imperial security. Throughout this period the Chinese required substantial support, and Hong Kong remained the most vital logistical center for the importation of Western military supplies. With the Japanese lodged in Canton, low-intensity conflict against Britain in the Pearl River Delta became a significant factor in escalating the crisis toward the outbreak of the Pacific war—a prospect that grew following the invasion of southern Indochina.

Because of its military weakness, it was in Britain's interest to help broker a Sino-Japanese peace, but prior to 1941, numerous officials in Whitehall hoped that support for the Chinese war effort could be leveraged to encourage greater cooperation from Stalin against Hitler. When collaboration appeared possible, the transshipment of war supplies from Hong Kong was continued. When it did not, such as in mid-1940, the flow of weapons into China was restricted, as occurred during the closure of the Burma Road. Ultimately, the pursuit of collective security in southern China was a counterproductive endeavor as it failed to induce reciprocity from Stalin and helped ignite the Pacific war. By challenging the Japanese, Britain hoped to improve Anglo-Soviet relations, but it faced too many enemies from a position of military weakness to elicit external support, except at great cost. In the end, British power was sacrificed to the United States to safeguard the Soviet Union.

Anglo-American strategy during World War II also failed to adequately address the long-term implications of forging an alliance with the USSR. Intervention in southern China and Hong Kong helped secure the Soviet Far East, but by concentrating solely on the destruction of Nazi Germany while propping up Stalin, little was accomplished in promoting global peace and security. Despite the totalitarian nature of Stalin's rule in the USSR, Germany was considered the single most dangerous threat, and Anglo-American strategy was shaped around this belief. Foreign policy makers in the West were often deeply influenced by previous experience in the First World War, and many eyes remained closed to the long-term consequences of supporting Stalin.

Britain's China policy was flawed not only because it imperiled the long-term security of the empire but also because it was dishonestly formulated and falsely represented to the British public. The same can be said for Canada. Hong Kong was not reinforced and defended primarily to protect the British Empire or the Dominions, and the ulterior geopolitical issues underpinning events in the region were suppressed from public scrutiny. Commonwealth soldiers were expected to fight against Nazi totalitarianism only to help prop up a Soviet variation from Hong Kong. Had people been aware of the facts surrounding Allied efforts in China, governmental credibility and legitimacy would not be called into question, but official obfuscation makes this inevitable. Secrecy on this issue enabled the government to continue the war unhindered by intrusive questions about why it was being fought, even though the cost was exorbitant. In Britain's case, this amounted to an overall loss of global power, financial ruin at home, and the deaths of hundreds of thousands of servicemen. An informed public might have pressed for alternative solutions.

Results in China were similarly poor. In attempting to exploit the conflict enveloping Hong Kong, the Chinese were only partially successful in solidifying an anti-Japanese alliance. Britain and America finally became Chinese allies in large part because of events leading up to the battle of Hong Kong, but it took more than four years to accomplish this. Moreover, inter-Allied distrust prevented the development of effective large-scale military cooperation. The Chinese abandonment of Canton in 1938 did little to encourage Anglo-American officials. Conversely, the surrender of Hong Kong prior to the anticipated duration of resistance produced tremendous loss of prestige for the British in China. British reversals in Asia left China dangerously isolated by the spring of 1942, and had it not been for Chinese victory in the third battle of Changsha, resistance against Japan might have come to an end. The battles of Changsha demonstrated that large elements of the Chinese army were more combat effective than many foreign observers were willing to admit; nevertheless, the intensity of the war in China diminished after this point as Chinese logistical problems became acute. Some military supplies would be flown over the Himalayas by the USAAF, but from 1942 onward, the war in China declined in significance.[2]

Aside from logistical considerations, there were other reasons for the low priority assigned to the war in China, including the simple fact that the Chinese were physically exhausted. It was also understood that maintaining Chinese security was never as high a priority as maintaining China's ability to neutralize a large segment of the Japanese army. Respect for Chinese sovereignty was even less important, especially after the Americans assumed greater control of the war in the fall and winter of 1941. Although T. V. Soong had been appointed foreign minister because of his connections in America and to demonstrate solidarity with the Allied cause, Allied military reverses and the announcement of Roosevelt and Churchill's Europe-first strategy generated great criticism in China. The Chinese also expressed concern about Ambassador Clark Kerr's posting to the Soviet Union, as this further reflected the diminished significance London attached to the Far East, but anxiety over these events began to lessen by the summer of 1942.[3] Nevertheless, these problems created considerable drag on the Chinese war effort, which limited Allied enthusiasm for increased support. As time passed, the Chinese became less inclined to carry the fight to the Japanese because they were not accepted as a full partner of the alliance.

Despite China's military liabilities, another political issue motivated some Western officials to urge continued support. Racial divisions threatened to undermine the attainment of long-term alliance objectives, and this friction was aggravated by Japanese propaganda. The Japanese billed the war in China as a struggle against Asia's domination by white Europeans, and in February 1941 Japanese Foreign Minister Matsuoka Yosuke publicly demanded the expulsion of all white men from Oceania, with the exception of Australia and New Zealand.[4] After being assigned to Washington as head of the British Joint Staff Mission in America, Field Marshal Sir John Dill discussed this problem with Prime Minister W. L. Mackenzie King while in Ottawa. Mackenzie King recorded the following in his diary:

He [Dill] spoke feelingly of our losses at Hong Kong. They had been advised that a few detachments would be all that was needed. He is much concerned about China not holding on. Says that if the Japanese should demonstrate that they can destroy the British, take Singapore etc., it is altogether possible that they will come to make a peace with Japan on the basis of Asia for the Asiatics feeling that it is better to keep the white man out altogether. He agreed that this would certainly precipitate further difficulties in India.[5]

Although the idea of Pan-Asian unity was undone by Japanese conduct against civilians in occupied territories—such as that witnessed at Nanking in 1937 and the even worse barbarity exhibited by organizations such as Unit 731—fear of an anti-Caucasian front led by Tokyo persisted.[6] A formal peace between Japan and China would have been a political disaster for the Allies, and it would have given credence to Japanese claims of "Asia for the Asiatics."

Richard Webb also wrote on this subject for the Institute of Pacific Relations: "China's importance as an ally cannot be easily overestimated; her strategic position and man power [sic] are obvious. The political value of China's resistance is even more important—she makes Japan's claim to be leading Asiatic peoples a hollow mockery. American interest in China's fight is therefore fundamental."[7] A memorandum for the War Department's Operational Planning Division further emphasized the racial component later in the war: "Above all, the significance of the Asiatics resisting the encroachments of other Asiatics is of tremendous political and psychological importance. For all these reasons it is essential to uphold, even at considerable cost, the prestige and capacity to resist of Chiang Kai Shek."[8] Asian allies were needed because the Japanese claim to be fighting against white domination was supported by the internment of Canadian and American citizens of Japanese ancestry living in North America. Successful exploitation of such issues by the Japanese, resulting in the end of hostilities in China, would have been a blow to Allied prestige and an unwelcome shock to U.S. public opinion.[9]

Chinese confidence in Allied military power had been greatly shaken in the winter of 1941–1942, and after the fall of Hong Kong, the British were effectively pushed out of China. China in turn became a U.S. sphere of interest, and Roosevelt bolstered Chinese morale by strengthening Sino-American relations and promising greater material and diplomatic support. General Joseph Stilwell was dispatched to China to become the army chief of staff for Chiang Kai Shek, and the China-Burma-India (CBI) command was organized as a single Allied theater of operations.[10] To support China, however, Roosevelt turned to Mackenzie King for additional help.

Canada became involved in China because of White House pressure to support Allied collective security arrangements. Ultimately, the value of Canadian aid proved to be symbolic, and the costs incurred to help others meet international commitments in the Far East expanded. The sale of Bren guns to China in the summer and fall of 1941 was followed by the deployment of Canadian troops to Hong Kong.[11] It has been noted elsewhere that "U.S. Marines were not going to fight for Hong Kong."[12] This was indeed true, but soldiers from Winnipeg and Quebec were useful substitutes. Additional Canadian support consisted of the sale of heavy weapons. At Roosevelt's urging, Soong traveled by train from America, along with FDR's representative Lauchlin Currie, to meet Mackenzie King in Ottawa on 27 February 1942. Another meeting was held in Washington in April, with Supreme Court Justice Felix Frankfurter in attendance. During these visits, Mackenzie King and Soong established a close personal friendship, and the prime minister offered to extend all manner of assistance to China, including support for Chiang Kai Shek in his efforts to secure Indian independence, but only after the war was won. This pledge was well received, as was the assurance of American backing toward the same goal. Negotiations for military hardware went equally smoothly, at least initially; deals were concluded for the sale of 288 twenty-five-pounder guns with ammunition and artillery tractors.[13]

The short-term effect of these developments on Sino-Canadian relations was positive, but the long-term effects of collective security doctrine in Asia proved otherwise. After the winter of 1941–1942, Canadian support for China became less useful in fostering Allied cohesion or even in promoting U.S.-Canadian relations, as assistance from the two countries expanded along conflicting paths. Friction became evident the following year. The U.S. Army was quick to dominate the war effort in China by monopolizing Allied aid, and a degree of diplomatic tension emerged in Washington between the U.S. Army and Canadian authorities. Military supplies sent to China from Canada were included as part of the Mutual Aid plan implemented during 1942 and formally established at the Quebec conference in August 1943. This Canadian version of Lend-Lease was a billion-dollar military aid program designed primarily for the benefit of Great Britain and the USSR.[14] The Mutual Aid plan followed Canada's initial billion-dollar gift to Britain in early 1942. In addition to thirty-six U.S.-supplied Chinese divisions, ten armies would be created or upgraded with Mutual Aid weapons, each receiving twelve twenty-five-pounders. These plans ran afoul of General Stilwell during 1943, however, and few of these supplies were allowed to be flown into China over the Himalayan Hump. Canadian Mutual Aid weapons were earmarked for the Chinese central government without restriction on their use, but U.S. Lend-Lease material was administered by Stilwell for the forces under his command in Yunnan and India. Thus, shipment of the Canadian supplies was assigned a very low priority within CBI, and by early 1944, 12,500 tons of Canadian-produced weapons and vehicles had accumulated at storage depots in Karachi, awaiting delivery through the USSR. More supplies awaited shipment in Canada, and Soong pressed Roosevelt to facilitate their delivery. Soong's efforts failed, and the shipment of most of the Canadian-produced munitions was delayed until mid-1945 and 1946.[15]

Part of the reason that Canadian efforts were impeded was that Allied leaders and officials wanted to keep military support to the Chinese central government both limited and indirect. Allied collective security doctrine failed when applied in China because military aid was conditioned on Chungking's acquiescence to American interference in domestic affairs. Most prominent in this issue was General Stilwell, who, in seeking to regulate the Chinese army, kept much of the material flown into China between 1942 and 1944 under his direct control. He also wanted to supply CCP military forces in Yenan. Furthering this agenda were many Western foreign policy makers sympathetic to the communists; they were concerned that any heavy weapons supplied to Chiang, such as those stockpiled in Karachi, would be used against the CCP. In the south, Stilwell's lack of appreciation for the logistical limitations of the CBI theater also caused him to squander scarce transport capacity in an effort to create a Chinese military force in the image of the U.S. Army.[16] This was a wasted effort within the projected time frame of the war. What the Chinese army required, as the battles for Changsha proved, was a modest and sustainable artillery program. Field guns provided without restrictions, together with a minimal amount of gasoline and bombs for the air force, would have been sufficient to maintain Chinese morale and keep the country fighting.

Canada's Asian wartime experience illustrated that the disaster at Hong Kong was not an aberration of sound policy or bad luck; rather, it was the unsurprising consequence of prioritizing Soviet security over other Allied objectives. Despite the assistance provided to the USSR in China and elsewhere in previous years, Stalin worked against Allied strategy by destabilizing Sinkiang in 1943–1944. This greatly undermined morale in Chungking, as did Allied protection of the CCP. Because of this interference, Canadian military hardware destined for Chungking remained undelivered when it was needed most. During the 1944 Japanese offensive code-named Operation Ichigo, these weapons were not permitted to transit the overland route through Siberia, even though the psychological and material impact of their arrival in 1944 might have mitigated the morale problems contributing to the collapse of Chinese armies in the 4th and 9th War Zones.[17] The subsequent loss of south China resulted in the expulsion of U.S. ground and air forces from Kwangsi. Throughout this period, Stalin was not pressured to permit the passage of these weapons through Siberia. By yielding to Soviet security concerns in the Far East, the Allies failed to implement an effective strategy in China, and long-term Western interests were not served. Although Japan was eventually defeated in the Pacific, by the end of the war, the Chinese army remained undergunned, and the country's long-term security was at risk.

Even before the Mutual Aid fiasco, however, Canada's involvement in Far Eastern affairs had already proved to be a lopsided deal, and the fault lay with Mackenzie King. Despite Canada's efforts in China to safeguard Soviet security and its subsequent losses at Dieppe in August 1942 for the same reason, Stalin certainly did not reciprocate; nor did Canadian political leaders press him to do so. In early 1942, for example, a colleague with influence inside the USSR approached Mackenzie King about asking Stalin to pressure the Japanese to improve their treatment of Canadian prisoners of war; however, the scheme was quietly jettisoned in an attempt to limit the dictator's diplomatic leverage for a second front in France.[18] Official Sino-Canadian relations expanded as a result of Canada's support, and this was due in part to the close personal friendship between Soong and Mackenzie King. But in the framework of larger events, positive official relations did not amount to much. Ambassadors were exchanged by 1943, but Canada was not a great power and could do little to influence events in China on its own. In the end, once the Chinese communists assumed control of the country, Sino-Canadian relations were thoroughly disrupted, and by 1951, Canadian and Chinese soldiers would be killing each other in South Korea for control of the village of Kapyong (Gapyeong).[19]

The primary aim of this book has been to raise the level of understanding regarding Allied strategy during the Second World War. Some claim that critical arguments such as those presented here are formed with the benefit of hindsight. Likewise, many historians have suggested that because government officials and policy makers of the 1930s and 1940s had no way of knowing future events, especially the threat posed by Stalin during the Cold War, the alliance with the USSR was justified as a necessary expedient in opposing the fascist dictatorships. This argument is a canard. Aside from ideology, there was little choice between the fascist dictatorships and the USSR. It was not possible to maintain peace or security in the world by allying with the regime that existed in the Soviet Union. Furthermore, there was ample evidence of the true nature of Stalin's methods in the interwar period and during the war itself. Thus, aside from providing an expanded view of the war, this work also illustrates the danger of allowing ideological considerations to dominate the planning and execution of foreign and military policy. In doing so, it shows that Allied intervention in southern China and at Hong Kong made Anglo-American shortsightedness in forming an alliance with Moscow far most costly than was previously accepted.

British, U.S., and Soviet intervention in China during the Sino-Japanese War contributed to the start of a global conflagration by the end of 1941. This led to the destruction of imperial power in Asia. The war in southern China was integral to this process, particularly during the German invasion of the USSR. Because the conflict in southern China was fundamentally about the movement of munitions and supplies, it has been essential to examine the military logistics involved in sustaining Chinese resistance from Hong Kong. To understand the colony's importance, Hong Kong and southern China must be viewed as a single military theater of operations. The connection between the battle of Hong Kong and the third battle of Changsha as elements of the same Japanese plan demonstrates this reality. Until now, the geopolitical significance of Hong Kong has not been explained in this context because the role and impact of both Canada and the USSR in China have been largely ignored or downplayed. The fog of war was also thick in southern China. But in penetrating this cloud, the battle of Hong Kong assumes greater relevance because it helped consolidate the anti-Axis alliance. For the Japanese, the attack on Hong Kong and, more importantly, on Pearl Harbor marked the beginning of a reckless gamble aimed at bringing the war in China to a close. But it held little prospect of long-term success. The Japanese empire would be destroyed in less than four years. As for the British (or at least for some in Whitehall), they did not fight the battle of Hong Kong for the preservation of empire; instead, it helped bring about its end. For those seeking collective security, the battle of Hong Kong was an acceptable price to pay in chasing what was, and has always been, a dangerous illusion.

Notes

Abbreviations

BOMSC United Church of Canada Board of Overseas Missions, South China

CCJC Canton Committee for Justice to China

DHH Canadian Armed Forces Directorate of History and Heritage Archive

FDR Franklin Delano Roosevelt Presidential Library and Museum

FRUS U.S. Department of State, *Foreign Relations of the United States Diplomatic Papers, 1940, 1941,* and *1942* (Washington, DC: Historical Office, Bureau of Public Affairs, U.S. Department of State, 1955–1958)

HKU University of Hong Kong Archive

IWM Imperial War Museum (United Kingdom)

LAC Library and Archives Canada

LOC Library of Congress (United States)

NARA National Archives and Records Administration (United States)

TNA The National Archives (United Kingdom)

TRL Toronto Reference Library (Canada)

UCC United Church of Canada Archives, Toronto

USMIR *U.S. Military Intelligence Reports: China, 1911–1941,* ed. Paul Kesaris (Frederick, MD: University Publications of America, 1983)

USSDCF *Confidential U.S. State Department Central Files: China, Internal Affairs, 1930–1939* and *1940–1941,* ed. Paul Kesaris (Frederick, MD: University Publications of America, 1984)

Chapter 1. Collective Security in Asia

1. David Evans and Mark Peattie, *Kaigun: Strategy, Tactics, and Technology in the Imperial Japanese Navy, 1887–1941* (Annapolis, MD: Naval Institute Press, 1997), 460.

2. Dick Wilson, *When Tigers Fight: The Story of the Sino-Japanese War, 1937–1945* (New York: Viking Press, 1982), 62.

3. Vasilii Chuikov, *Mission to China: Memoirs of a Soviet Military Adviser to Chiang Kaishek*, trans. David Barrett (Norwalk, CT: EastBridge, 2004), 129.

4. John Foster Dulles, *War or Peace* (London: George G. Harrap, 1950), 98–99, 119; Eleanor Rathbone, *War Can Be Averted: The Achievability of Collective Security* (London: Victor Gollancz, 1938), 13–15, 88–89; Arthur Salter, *Security: Can We Retrieve It?* (London: Macmillan, 1939), 99–100, 164–166.

5. Correlli Barnett, *The Collapse of British Power* (London: Eyre Methuen, 1972), 354–356.

6. Rathbone, *War Can Be Averted*, 90–91, 174–178.

7. Jack Granatstein, *How Britain's Weakness Forced Canada into the Arms of the United States: The 1988 Joanne Goodman Lectures* (Toronto: University of Toronto Press, 1989); Galen Roger Perras, *Franklin Roosevelt and the Origins of the Canadian-American Security Alliance, 1933–1945: Necessary, but Not Necessary Enough* (Westport, CT: Praeger, 1998).

8. Keith Neilson, *The Permanent Under-Secretary for Foreign Affairs, 1854–1946* (London: Routledge, 2009), 244.

9. Franz Schurmann, *The Logic of World Power* (New York: Pantheon Books, 1974), 163–165, 415–416.

10. Ronald Spector, *Eagle against the Sun: The American War against Japan* (New York: Vintage Books, 1985), 224–225.

Chapter 2. Clearing the Decks

1. TNA, FO 371/22150 E 724 (1/12h/1938), Foreign Office General Correspondence—Political, 1938–1966, report by Commercial Counselor A. H. George, 7 September 1938. See also Hu Pu Yu, *A Brief History of the Sino-Japanese War (1937–1945)* (Taipei: Chung Wu Publishing, 1974), 42, 45.

2. LAC, RG 25, vol. 8517, file 6605-40, Foreign Office, biography of Pai Ch'ung-shi, 16 April 1943.

3. UCC, accession 83.046C, box 3, file 53, BOMSC, letter from R. D. Rees, 29 January 1937.

4. Ibid.

5. NARA, RG 165, entry 421, box 407, file China Campaign Plan, OPD, Operational Planning Division, Combined Staff Planners, A Plan of Campaign within China, CPS No. 107 D, 24 April 1944, 74.

6. David Bonavia, *China's Warlords* (New York: Oxford University Press, 1995), 119, 125.

7. LAC, RG 25, vol. 3277, file 6669-G-40—Kwangsi, memorandum, "Liang Kwang," by First Secretary Ralph E. Collins, 17 May 1944.

8. Eugene W. Levich, *The Kwangsi Way in Kuomintang China, 1931–1939* (London: East Gate, 1993), 164, 255.

9. LAC, RG 25, vol. 4717, file 50055-40 pt. 1, Political Situation in China, Report F 6046/1689/10 by Weightman, 27 August 1942.

10. Ibid. See also Robert L. Jarman, ed., *China: Political Reports, 1911–1960*, vol. 6, *1937–1941* (London: Public Record Office, 2001), 103, 109.

11. NARA, RG 165, M1444, Correspondence of the Military Intelligence Division Relating to General, Political, Economic, and Military Conditions in China, 1918–1941, reel 15, Report No. 7258 by First Lieutenant Helmar W. Lystad, 25 April 1928, Report No. 8480 by Lieutenant Colonel W. S. Drysdale, 13 January 1933, Report No. 9151 by Major S. V. Constant, 27 June 1935, Report No. 9343 by Captain Bernard A. Tormey, 22 April 1936, and Report No. 9518 by Colonel Joseph W. Stilwell, 19 February 1937.

12. LAC, RG 25, vol. 3277, file 6669-G-40—Kwangsi, "Liang Kwang" by Collins, 17 May 1944. See also Chang Jung and Jon Halliday, *Mao: The Unknown Story* (London: Vintage Books, 2006), 159, 203.

13. Hata Ikuhiko, "Marco Polo Bridge Incident," in *Japan's Road to the Pacific War: The China Quagmire: Japan's Expansion on the Asian Continent, 1933–1941*, ed. James Morley and David Lu (New York: Columbia University Press, 1983), 243–244. See also Shimada Toshihiko, "Designs on North China," ibid., 50, 103–107, 121–122.

14. NARA, RG 165, *USMIR*, reel 13, Report No. 9058 by Drysdale, 25 February 1935.

15. Martin H. Brice, *The Royal Navy and the Sino-Japanese Incident, 1937–41* (London: Ian Allan, 1973), 14.

16. LAC, RG 25, vol. 1687, file 1934 80-H, "Report on a Trip to the Philippine Islands and the China Coast—1935" by Hugh L. Keenleyside, 13 May 1935.

17. Ibid.

18. NARA, RG 165, M1444, reel 15, Report No. 7258. See also Shimada, "Designs on North China," 188.

19. NARA, RG 165, M1444, reel 15, Report No. 7967 by Lieutenant Colonel Nelson E. Margetts, 13 March 1931.

20. NARA, RG 165, M1444, reel 15, Report No. 9316 by Stilwell, 5 March 1936.

21. Ibid. See also Diana Lary, *Warlord Soldiers: Chinese Common Soldiers, 1911–1937* (Cambridge: Cambridge University Press, 1985), 40, and Dick Wilson, *When Tigers Fight: The Story of the Sino-Japanese War, 1937–1945* (New York: Viking Press, 1982), 9.

22. LAC, RG 25, vol. 3277, file 6669-G-40—Kwangsi, "Liang Kwang" by Collins, 17 May 1944.

23. Jarman, *China: Political Reports*, 82–83.

24. Ibid., 83.

25. NARA, RG 165, *USMIR*, reel 6, Report No. 9864 by Captain F. P. Munson, 3 April 1940. See also Jarman, *China: Political Reports*, 83, 104, and Hallett Abend, *My Life in China, 1926–1941* (New York: Harcourt, Brace, 1943), 128, 197–198.

26. Howard L. Boorman and Richard C. Howard, eds., *Biographical Dictionary of Republican China*, vol. 4 (New York: Columbia University Press, 1971), 61.

27. Jarman, *China: Political Reports,* 104.

28. Shimada, "Designs on North China," 188.

29. LAC, RG 25, vol. 8517, file 6605-40, biography of Pai Ch'ung-shi, 16 April 1943.

30. TNA, WO 106/5303 No. 293, Report on Visit to South China by Captain J. V. Davidson-Houston, 5 August 1938.

31. LAC, RG 25, vol. 3277, file 6669-G-40—Kwangsi, "Liang Kwang" by Collins, 17 May 1944; NARA, RG 165, *USMIR,* reel 6, Report No. 9864; TNA, WO 106/5356, HKIR No. 2/39 by Captain J. M. Sturgeon, 17 January 1939.

32. NARA, RG 165, M1444, reel 10, Report No. 9686 by Major David D. Barrett, 12 October 1938, and Report No. 9700 by Barrett, 8 December 1938; TNA, WO 106/5303 No. 289, Report on Visit to War Zone IV by Captain Charles R. Boxer and Captain H. Chauvin, 20 May 1939; TNA, WO 106/5356, HKIR No. 22/38, 25 October 1938. See also Wu T'ien Wei, "Contending Political Forces," in *China's Bitter Victory: The War with Japan, 1937–1945,* ed. James C. Hsiung and Steven I. Levine (London: M. E. Sharpe, 1992), 61.

33. LAC, RG 24, reel C-8301, file 5147, Report No. 33 on Canton by Major General F. S. G. Piggott, 18 November 1938. See also John W. Garver, "China's Wartime Diplomacy," in Hsiung and Levine, *China's Bitter Victory,* 11.

34. John H. Boyle, *China and Japan at War, 1937–1945: The Politics of Collaboration* (Stanford, CA: Stanford University Press, 1972), 44, 48–49. See also Shimada, "Designs on North China," 197–198.

35. Hata, "Marco Polo Bridge Incident," 244–250. See also Tsunoda Jun, "The Navy's Role in the Southern Strategy," trans. Robert A. Scalapino, in *The Fateful Choice: Japan's Road to the Pacific War: Japan's Advance into Southeast Asia, 1939–1941,* ed. James Morley (New York: Columbia University Press, 1980), 241.

36. Hata, "Marco Polo Bridge Incident," 244. See also Shimada, "Designs on North China," 184, 190–194.

37. David Evans and Mark Peattie, *Kaigun: Strategy, Tactics, and Technology in the Imperial Japanese Navy, 1887–1941* (Annapolis, MD: Naval Institute Press, 1997), 602n. See also Shimada, "Designs on North China," 190–194.

38. IWM, Conservation Shelf, "Thunder in the East" (1947) by Major General G. E. Grimsdale, 5. See also Brian P. Farrell, *The Basis and Making of British Grand Strategy: Was There a Plan?* (Lewiston, NY: Edwin Mellen Press, 1998), 11, 35, and Usui Katsumi, "The Politics of War," in Morley and Lu, *Japan's Road to the Pacific War,* 338.

39. Catherine Baxter, "Britain and the War in China, 1937–1945" (Ph.D. diss., University of Wales, 1993), 2–3, 6, 260–261. See also Shimada, "Designs on North China," 137–139.

40. V. H. Rothwell, "The Mission of Sir Frederick Leith-Ross to the Far East, 1935–1936," *Historical Journal* 18, 1 (1975): 149.

41. LAC, RG 25, vol. 1687, file 1934 80-H, "Report on a Trip to the Philippine Islands and the China Coast—1935" by Keenleyside, 13 May 1935.

42. Ibid.

43. FDR, Morgenthau Papers, box 268, file Correspondence 1933–1945 Hong Kong, Economic Situation in Hong Kong, report by Consul General C. L. Hoover, 21 August 1935; NARA, RG 165, *USMIR*, reel 2, Report No. 9108 by Drysdale, 28 April 1935. See also Shimada, "Designs on North China," 145–146, 167.

44. Chang and Halliday, *Mao*, 214– 219. See also NARA, RG 165, M1444, reel 15, Report No. 9316.

45. Chang and Halliday, *Mao*, 223, 226.

46. TNA, FO 371/27679 F 919/327/10, report by Consul General Berkeley E. F. Gage, 13 February 1941.

47. Farrell, *Basis and Making of British Grand Strategy*, 11, 35–37. See also Peter Lowe, "Retreat from Power: British Attitudes towards Japan, 1923–1941," in *War and Diplomacy across the Pacific, 1919–1952*, ed. Barry D. Hunt and A. Hamish Ion (Waterloo, ON: Wilfrid Laurier University Press, 1988), 48.

48. NARA, RG 165, M1513, reel 39, Naval Intelligence Report by Commander J. M. Creighton, 29 March 1941; NARA, RG 165, *USMIR*, reel 2, Report No. 9117 by Drysdale, 10 May 1935. See also Baxter, "Britain and the War in China," 145, and Brice, *Royal Navy and Sino-Japanese Incident*, 153–157.

49. TNA, CAB 121/718, file G/Hong Kong/1 (vol. 1), Telegram No. 444 by Air Ministry to C in C Far East, 14 January 1941. See also Brice, *Royal Navy and Sino-Japanese Incident*, 110, and Peter Lowe, *Great Britain and the Origins of the Pacific War: A Study of British Policy in East Asia, 1937–1941* (Oxford: Clarendon Press, 1977), 95.

50. IWM, "Thunder in the East" by Grimsdale, 10. See also Douglas Ford, *Britain's Secret War against Japan, 1937–1945* (New York: Routledge, 2006), 37–38.

51. DHH, file 352.019 (D1), statement by Brigadier General John Price, 27 January 1948; DHH, file 593.013 (D20), report by Major General A. H. Bartholomew, 20 August 1937; LAC, RG 24, vol. 20310, file 951.003 (D23), Report on the Policy for the Defence of Hong Kong, Committee of Imperial Defence, 15 July 1938; LAC, RG 25, vol. 1687, file 1934 80-H, "Report on a Trip to the Philippine Islands and the China Coast—1935" by Keenleyside, 13 May 1935; NARA, RG 165, M1513, reel 39, Report No. 0420, 11 December 1936, Report No. 478 by Consul Howard Donovan, 5 February 1937, Report No. 579 by Donovan, 2 July 1937, and Report No. 165 by Naval Attaché (Peking), 24 April 1937. See also Ford, *Britain's Secret War against Japan*, 17, and Christopher Bell, "'Our Most Exposed Outpost': Hong Kong and British Far Eastern Strategy, 1921–1941," *Journal of Military History* 60, 1 (1996): 70–73.

52. NARA, RG 165, M1513, reel 39, Report No. 165 by Naval Attaché (Peking), 24 April 1937; TNA, WO 106/5357, file Attendance of Chinese at Hong Kong Combined Defence Exercise, letter from Colonel Lance Dennys (War Office) to Colonel Burkhardt in Hong Kong, 14 May 1937, and letter from Captain Charles R. Boxer to Major General F. S. G. Piggott, 16 March 1937. See also Galen R. Perras, "'Our Position in the Far East Would Be Stronger without This Unsatisfactory Commitment': Britain, and the Reinforcement of Hong Kong, 1941," *Canadian Journal of History* 30, 2 (1995): 237.

53. Shimada, "Designs on North China," 188.

Chapter 3. The Sino-Japanese War Begins

1. Correlli Barnett, *The Collapse of British Power* (London: Eyre Methune, 1972), 505, 518.

2. LAC, RG 25, vol. 3233, file 5548-40C, memorandum by Lieutenant Colonel Hiram Wooster, 20 May 1944.

3. LAC, RG 24, reel C-8301, file 5147, Report No. 33 by Major General F. S. G. Piggott, 18 November 1938. See also NARA, RG 165, M1513, The Military Intelligence Division Regional File Relating to China, 1922–1944, reel 39, Report No. 86 by Commander H. E. Overesch, 3 December 1938.

4. LAC, RG 24, reel C-8301, file 5147, memorandum by Colonel W. Murray, 13 October 1943; NARA, RG 165, *USMIR*, reel 6, report by Major David Barrett, 1 August 1940. See also Diana Lary, *Warlord Soldiers: Chinese Common Soldiers, 1911–1937* (Cambridge: Cambridge University Press, 1985), 20–23.

5. NARA, RG 165, M1444, Correspondence of the Military Intelligence Division Relating to General, Political, Economic, and Military Conditions in China; 1918–1941, reel 15, Report No. 9316 by Colonel Joseph Stilwell, 5 March 1936.

6. TNA, WO 106/5303 No. 293, Report on Visit to South China July 1938, by Captain J. V. Davidson-Houston, 5 August 1938. See also Brigadier General J. M. Calvert, "Shanghai (1937)," in *The Mammoth Book of Battles: The Art and Science of Modern War*, ed. Jon E. Lewis (New York: Carroll and Graff, 1995), 124–125; Chang Jung and Jon Halliday, *Mao: The Unknown Story* (London: Vintage Books, 2006), 246–247; John W. Garver, "China's Wartime Diplomacy," in *China's Bitter Victory: The War with Japan, 1937–1945*, ed. James C. Hsiung and Steven I. Levine (London: M. E. Sharpe, 1992), 6–7; Billie K. Walsh, "The German Military Mission to China, 1928–1938," *Journal of Modern History* 46, 3 (1974): 509–510; and Dick Wilson, *When Tigers Fight: The Story of the Sino-Japanese War, 1937–1945* (New York: Viking Press, 1982), 36–38, 46.

7. UCC, accession 86.046C, box 1, file 4, Margaret H. Brown Collection, notes by Margaret Brown, 12 August 1937. See also Martin H. Brice, *The Royal Navy and the Sino-Japanese Incident, 1937–41* (London: Ian Allan, 1973), 36; Calvert, "Shanghai (1937)," 124–127; Garver, "China's Wartime Diplomacy," 11.

8. Hata Ikuhiko, "Marco Polo Bridge Incident," in *Japan's Road to the Pacific War: The China Quagmire: Japan's Expansion on the Asian Continent, 1933–1941*, ed. James Morley and David Lu (New York: Columbia University Press, 1983), 243, 269–277; and Hans Van de Ven, *War and Nationalism in China, 1925–1945* (London: RoutledgeCurzon, 2003), 218.

9. NARA, RG 38, M975, reel 2, file Probability of an Outbreak of War Documents N, Naval Attaché Tokyo, vol. 1, Report No. 153, 14 July 1938.

10. NARA, RG 165, *USMIR*, reel 2, Report No. 9623 by Barrett, 12 January 1938. See also John Toland, *The Rising Sun: The Decline and Fall of the Japanese Empire, 1936–1945* (New York: Random House, 1970), 46.

11. NARA, RG 165, *USMIR*, reel 2, Report No. 9633 by Barrett, 1 February 1938. See also Lu Suping, *They Were in Nanjing: The Nanjing Massacre Witnessed by American and British Nationals* (Hong Kong: Hong Kong University Press, 2004), 275–277.

12. NARA, RG 38, M975, reel 2, file Probability of an Outbreak of War Documents N, Naval Attaché Tokyo, vol. 1, Report No. 153, 14 July 1938.

13. NARA, RG 165, *USMIR*, reel 2, Report No. 9623 by Barrett, 12 January 1938.

14. IWM, Conservation Shelf, "Thunder in the East" by Grimsdale, 8–9. See also Hallett Abend, *My Life in China, 1926–1941* (New York: Harcourt, Brace, 1943), 271–272.

15. NARA, RG 165, *USMIR*, reel 2, Report No. 9633 by Barrett, 1 February 1938.

16. Wilson, *When Tigers Fight*, 89.

17. NARA, RG 165, *USMIR*, reel 2, Report No. 9667 by Stilwell, 25 June 1938.

18. NARA, RG 165, *USMIR*, reel 2, Report No. 9639 by Barrett, 20 February 1938; TNA, WO 106/5303 No. 293, report by Davidson-Houston, 5 August 1938. See also Van de Ven, *War and Nationalism in China*, 211, 225.

19. NARA, RG 165, M1444, reel 11, Report No. 9799 by Captain Edwin M. Sutherland, 29 September 1939; TNA, FO 371/22150 E 724 (1/12h/1938), report by Commercial Counsellor A. H. George, 7 September 1938; TNA, FO 371/22150 No. 727.E. (13/71/1938), report by Sir Archibald Clark Kerr, 1938. See also Hu Pu Yu, *A Brief History of the Sino-Japanese War (1937–1945)* (Taipei: Chung Wu Publishing, 1974), 39–41, 45; Annalee Jacoby and Theodore White, *Thunder Out of China* (New York: William Sloane Associates, 1961), 56–57, 70, 281–282; and Van de Ven, *War and Nationalism in China*, 225–226.

20. NARA, RG 165, entry 77, NM 84, box 1738, MID Regional File, Islands Hong Kong, report by Consul General Addison Southard, 13 December 1937; TNA, FO 371/22159 F 7617/4847/10, report by Governor Sir Geoffry Northcote, 14 July 1938.

21. NARA, RG 18, entry 300, box 934, file Misc A, USAAF Decimal Files, Oct 1942–44, memorandum by Captain John Griffith, 23 June 1938.

22. UCC, accession 83.046C, box 3, file 55, BOMSC, CCJC pamphlet, 10 December 1937.

23. LAC, RG 25, vol. 2661, file 6045-40C, Summary of News in China (January 1944), F 1003/34/10 by Ambassador Sir Horace Seymour, 7 February 1944; NARA, RG 59, M1221, General Records of the Department of State, Intelligence Reports, 1941–1961, OSS Research and Analysis Report No. 112; NARA, RG 165, *USMIR*, reel 3, Report No. 14 by Barrett, 1 March 1941; TNA, FO 371/22150 E 724 (1/12h/1938), report by George, 7 September 1938; Chan Lau Kit Ching, *China, Britain and Hong Kong, 1895–1945* (Hong Kong: Chinese University Press, 1990), 276–277.

24. TNA, FO 371/22150/53730/38, Colonial Office telegram to Northcote, 26 May 1938; TNA, WO 106/5303 No. 293, report by Davidson-Houston, 5 August 1938.

25. TNA, FO 371/22157 F 12885/2796/10, Telegram No. 192 from Consul General A. P. Blunt, 7 October 1938.

26. NARA, RG 165, *USMIR*, reel 2, Report No. 9623 by Barrett, 12 January 1938, and Report No. 9633 by Barrett, 1 February 1938; TNA, ADM 1/9568, file West River Flotilla, W.R. 124/38, HMS *Tarantula*, Report No. 38/181.A/38, 14 April 1938; TNA, CO 852/324/6, file War Trade Commodities, Wolfram, notation by B. Perry, 1 July 1940; TNA, FO 371/22150 E 724 (1/12h/1938), report by George, 7 September 1938; TNA WO 106/5303 No. 293, report by Davidson-Houston, 5 August 1938. See also

Chang and Halliday, *Mao,* 247; and Yu Maochun, *The Dragon's War: Allied Operations and the Fate of China* (Annapolis, MD: Naval Institute Press, 2006), 12.

27. NARA, RG 18, entry 300, box 914, file 300 B, USAAF Decimal Files, Oct 1942–44, Report on Land Routes between India and China, 12 April 1943; TNA, FO 371/27715 F 4787/3653/10, report by Ian Morrison on situation in China, 3 June 1941; TNA, WO 106/5303 No. 293, report by Davidson-Houston, 5 August 1938.

28. NARA, RG 18, entry 300, box 934, file Misc A, USAAF Decimal Files, Oct 1942–44, memorandum by Griffith, 23 June 1938; NARA, RG 38, entry 98A, box 705, F-6-c 23213 to F-6-e 22379, Naval Intelligence, May 1940 to 1 December 1941, Report No. 342 by Leland Harrison, 4 May 1938; NARA, RG 38, M975, Selected Naval Attaché Reports Relating to the World Crisis, 1937–1943, reel 2, Estimate of Potential Military Strength Documents G, Naval Attaché Tokyo, vol. 1, Report No. 91; NARA, RG 165, *USMIR,* reel 2, Report No. 9623 by Barrett, 12 January 1938, and Report No. 9633 by Barrett, 1 February 1938; TNA, WO 208/722, file Hong Kong Fortnightly Intelligence Reports January 1940 to October 1941, HKIR No. 4/40 by Major R. Giles, 31 March 1940. See also Claire L. Chennault, *Way of a Fighter: The Memoirs of Claire Lee Chennault, Major General, U.S. Army (Ret.)* (New York: G. P. Putnam's Sons, 1949), 61, and Yu, *Dragon's War,* 13.

29. NARA, RG 165, M1513, reel 39, Report No. 86 by Overesch, 3 December 1938. See also Michael Share, *Where Empires Collided: Russian and Soviet Relations with Hong Kong, Taiwan, and Macao* (Hong Kong: Chinese University Press, 2007), 100.

30. NARA, RG 165, *USMIR,* reel 2, Report No. 9623 by Barrett, 12 January 1938. See also Usui Katsumi, "The Politics of War," in Morley and Lu, *Japan's Road to the Pacific War,* 333.

31. NARA, RG 165, M1513, reel 39, Report No. 29 by Major Truman Martin, 3 February 1938, and report by Major E. W. Raley, 2 March 1938; Brice, *Royal Navy and Sino-Japanese Incident,* 92.

32. NARA, RG 165, M1513, reel 39, Report No. 86 by Overesch, 3 December 1938. See also TNA, WO 106/5303 No. 293, report by Davidson-Houston, 5 August 1938.

33. TNA, FO 371/22158 F 5194/3376/10, China Summary No. 3 by Clark Kerr, 5 April 1938. See also Catherine Baxter, "Britain and the War in China, 1937–1945" (Ph.D. diss., University of Wales, 1993), 78; John H. Boyle, *China and Japan at War, 1937–1945: The Politics of Collaboration* (Stanford, CA: Stanford University Press, 1972), 250–251; and Peter Lowe, *Great Britain and the Origins of the Pacific War: A Study of British Policy in East Asia, 1937–1941* (Oxford: Clarendon Press, 1977), 105.

34. NARA, RG 165, *USMIR,* reel 2, Report No. 9639 by Barrett, 20 February 1938; TNA, ADM 1/9568, file West River Flotilla, W.R. 124/38, HMS *Tarantula,* Report No. 20/181.A/38, 15 March 1938; TNA, FO 371/22157 F 3889/3376/10, China Summary No. 2 by Clark Kerr, 7 March 1938; TNA, WO 106/5303 No. 293, report by Davidson-Houston, 5 August 1938.

35. NARA, RG 165, *USMIR,* reel 2, Report No. 9639 by Barrett, 20 February 1938; TNA, ADM 1/9568, file West River Flotilla, W.R. 124/38, HMS *Tarantula,* Report No. 11/181.A/38, 12 February 1938, and HMS *Tarantula,* Report No. 20/181.A/38, 15 March 1938.

36. TNA, WO 106/5303 No. 293, report by Davidson-Houston, 5 August 1938; TNA, WO 106/5356, file Hong Kong Fortnightly Intelligence Reports, November 1938 to May 1939, HKIR No. 22/38, 25 October 1938.

37. TNA, WO 106/5303 No. 293, report by Davidson-Houston, 5 August 1938. See also Boyle, *China and Japan at War*, 179; Usui Katsumi, "Politics of War," 333, 379–380; and Wilson, *When Tigers Fight*, 84–85.

38. NARA, RG 165, *USMIR*, reel 2, Report No. 9618 by Barrett, 20 December 1937; Report No. 9623 by Barrett, 12 January 1938; and Report No. 9639 by Barrett, 20 February 1938. See also Usui Katsumi, "Politics of War," 333, and Wilson, *When Tigers Fight*, 84–85.

39. NARA, RG 165, M1513, reel 39, Report No. 86 by Overesch, 3 December 1938; TNA, FO 371/22153/410/123/70K/1938, report by Major General F. S. G. Piggott, 15 June 1938; TNA, FO 371/22153/464/132/70K/38, report by Piggott, 27 June 1938. See also Boyle, *China and Japan at War*, 139, 146, 149–150; Chan, *China, Britain and Hong Kong*, 277; and Usui Katsumi, "Politics of War," 336.

40. TNA, FO 371/22153/464/132/70K/38, report by Piggott, 27 June 1938; TNA, FO 371/22164 F 12289/12289/10, Telegram No. 399 from G. P. Young, 21 September 1938. See also Boyle, *China and Japan at War*, 134, 137–138, 153–154, 156–158, and Usui Katsumi, "Politics of War," 337–338.

41. NARA, RG 165, M1444, reel 15, memorandum by Colonel E. R. W. McCabe, 15 September 1937; TNA, WO 106/5356, HKIR No. 2/39, 17 January 1939; TNA, WO 106/5356, HKIR No. 4/39 by Edwards, 14 February 1939. See also Mark Peattie, *Sunburst: The Rise of Japanese Naval Air Power, 1909–1941* (Annapolis, MD: Naval Institute Press, 2001), 103, 114.

42. NARA, RG 18, entry 300, box 934, file Misc A, USAAF Decimal Files, Oct 1942–44, memorandum by Griffith, 23 June 1938; NARA, RG 165, M1444, reel 10, Report No. 9686 by Barrett, 12 October 1938; TNA, WO 208/722, HKIR No. 8/41 by Giles, 1 September 1941, and HKIR No. 10/40 by Giles, 30 September 1940. See also Chennault, *Way of a Fighter*, 64–65, 68, 79, and Peattie, *Sunburst*, 106, 111–116.

43. TNA, WO 106/5356, HKIR No. 22/38, 25 October 1938. See also Brice, *Royal Navy and Sino-Japanese Incident*, 92.

44. TNA, FO 371/22150 E 724 (1/12h/1938), report by George, 7 September 1938; TNA, FO 371/22158 F 5194/3376/10, China Summary No. 3 by Clark Kerr, 5 April 1938; TNA, WO 106/5303, No. 289, Report on Visit to IV War Zone Headquarters by Captain Charles Boxer and Captain H. Chauvin, 20 May 1939. See also Stephen MacKinnon, "The Tragedy of Wuhan, 1938," *Modern Asian Studies* 30, 4 (1996): 934, 936–937.

45. NARA, RG 165, M1444, reel 10, Report No. 9686 by Barrett, 12 October 1938; TNA, WO 106/5303, No. 289, Report by Boxer and Chauvin, 20 May 1939. See also Marvin Williamsen, "The Military Dimension, 1937–1941," in Hsiung and Levine, *China's Bitter Victory*, 136–137.

46. TNA, WO 106/5356, HKIR No. 22/38, 25 October 1938.

47. TNA, WO 106/5303, No. 289, Report by Boxer and Chauvin, 20 May 1939.

48. Ibid.

49. NARA, RG 165, M1444, reel 10, Report No. 9686 by Barrett, 12 October 1938.

50. Ibid.

51. TNA, WO 106/5356, HKIR No. 22/38, 25 October 1938.

52. Ibid.; NARA, RG 165, M1444, reel 10, Report No. 9694 by Barrett, 8 November 1938, and M1513, reel 39, Report No. 86 by Overesch, 3 December 1938. See also Wilson, *When Tigers Fight*, 130–131.

53. MacKinnon, "Tragedy of Wuhan," 933.

54. TNA, ADM 1/9568, file West River Flotilla, HMS *Tarantula*, July report, 12 August 1938.

55. LAC, RG 24, reel C-8301, file 5147, Telegram No. 41 from Randolph Bruce to External Affairs, 31 January 1938.

56. Hata, "Marco Polo Bridge Incident," 286.

57. LAC, RG 24, reel C-8301, file 5147, Telegram No. 41 from Bruce, 31 January 1938.

58. NARA, RG 165, *USMIR*, reel 2, Report No. 9623 by Barrett, 12 January 1938.

59. Ibid.

60. NARA, RG 165, *USMIR*, reel 2, Report No. 9639 by Barrett, 20 February 1938.

61. Brice, *Royal Navy and Sino-Japanese Incident,* 110; Peattie, *Sunburst,* 116.

62. LAC, RG 24, reel C-8301, file 5147, memorandum by Craigie, 8 June 1938. See also UCC, accession 83.046C, box 3, file 51, BOMSC, letter from Broadfoot to Arnup, 6 October 1937.

63. TNA, WO 106/5356, HKIR No. 1/39 by Edwards, 3 January 1939; TNA, WO 208/721, HKIR No. 13/39 by Edwards, 20 June 1939; TNA, WO 208/721, file Hong Kong Fortnightly Intelligence Reports January 1939 to December 1939, HKIR No. 26/39 by Giles, 19 December 1939.

64. LAC, RG 24, reel C-8301, file 5147, memorandum by Craigie, 8 June 1938; NARA, RG 165, M1513, reel 39, Report No. 27, 20 January 1938; NARA, RG 306, boxes 944–1000, Photographs, 1937–1949; TNA, CO 129/564/1, Northcote to Colonial Secretary W. G. A. Ormsby-Gore, 9 November 1937; UCC, accession 83.046C, box 3, file 55, BOMSC, CCJC pamphlet, October/November 1937, no. 1.

65. UCC, accession 83.046C, box 3, file 55, BOMSC, CCJC pamphlet, 10 December 1937.

66. TNA, ADM 1/9568, file West River Flotilla, HMS *Tarantula*, July report, 12 August 1938.

67. TNA, ADM 1/9568, file West River Flotilla, W.R. 124/38, HMS *Tarantula*, Report No. 11/181.A/38, 12 February 1938, and HMS *Tarantula*, Report No. 20/181.A/38, 15 March 1938. See also UCC, accession 83.046C, box 3, file 51, BOMSC, letter from Broadfoot to Arnup, 28 September 1937, letter from Reverend D. McRae to Arnup, 29 October 1937, and letter from McRae to Arnup, 23 December 1937; UCC, accession 83.046C, box 3, file 53, BOMSC, report by Dr. Jack Lind to UCC, 31 December 1937; and UCC, accession 83.046C, box 3, file 55, BOMSC, CCJC pamphlets, October/November 1937 and November 1937.

68. NARA, RG 38, M975, reel 2, Estimate of Potential Military Strength Documents G, vol. 1, Report No. 91.

69. LAC, RG 24, reel C-8301, file 5147, League of Nations memorandum, 3 March 1939; UCC, accession 83.046C, box 3, file 55, BOMSC, CCJC pamphlet, October/November 1937, no. 1, 10 December 1937. See also Brice, *Royal Navy and Sino-Japanese Incident*, 92; Hsu Shu Hsi, *Three Weeks of Canton Bombings* (Shanghai: Kelly and Walsh, 1939), 71–72; and Peattie, *Sunburst*, 116.

70. UCC, accession 83.046C, box 3, file 55, BOMSC, CCJC pamphlet, October/November 1937, no. 1.

71. TNA, WO 106/5303 No. 293, report by Davidson-Houston, 5 August 1938; UCC, accession 83.046C, box 3, file 57, BOMSC, letter from Thomson to *McGill News*, 18 June 1938.

72. UCC, accession 83.046C, box 3, file 57, BOMSC, letter from Thomson to *McGill News*, 18 June 1938.

73. LAC, RG 24, reel C-8301, file 5147, Craigie memorandum, 8 June 1938.

74. Ibid. See also LAC, RG 25, vol. 1866, file 226-A, *Ottawa Citizen* news article, 10 August 1938.

75. NARA, RG 165, *USMIR*, reel 10, Report No. 9667 by Stilwell, 25 June 1938.

76. Ibid.; TNA, FO 371/22150 E 724 (1/12h/1938), report by George, 7 September 1938; TNA, WO 106/5303 No. 293, report by Davidson-Houston, 5 August 1938. See also Chang Ming Kai and Hsu Long Hsuen, *History of the Sino-Japanese War (1937–1945)* (Taipei: Chung Wu Publishing, 1971), 262.

77. NARA, RG 165, *USMIR*, reel 10, Report No. 9667 by Stilwell, 25 June 1938.

78. TNA, WO 106/5356, HKIR No. 2/39, 17 January 1939.

79. TNA, WO 106/5303 No. 293, report by Davidson-Houston, 5 August 1938.

80. NARA, RG 165, *USMIR*, reel 10, Report No. 9667 by Stilwell, 25 June 1938.

81. UCC, accession 83.046C, box 3, file 57, BOMSC, letter from Thomson to Dr. Stephenson, 10 May 1938.

82. LAC, MG 26 J1, reel C-3732, vol. 247, no. 211153, Telegram No. 566 from Bruce to Mackenzie King, 8 September 1938; TNA, CO 129/564/1, newspaper clipping, 1 December 1937. See also Brice, *Royal Navy and Sino-Japanese Incident*, 81 (photo caption); Hu, *Brief History of Sino-Japanese War*, 46–47; and Share, *Where Empires Collided*, 101.

83. LAC, RG 25, vol. 3233, file 5548-40C, military situation memorandum by Lieutenant Colonel Hiram F. Wooster, 20 May 1944.

84. LAC, RG 24, reel C-8301, file 5147, Telegram No. 27 by Craigie, 26 February 1938, and Telegram No. 35 by Craigie, 8 March 1938; NARA, RG 165, *USMIR*, reel 2, Report No. 9623 by Barrett, 12 January 1938; TNA, CO 129/570/7, Admiralty telegram, 25 May 1938; TNA, CO 129/570/8, file cover notation; TNA, FO 371/27675 F 2616/317/10, Memorandum No. 1035 by Craigie, 25 January 1939.

85. TNA, CO 129/570/7, extract from newspaper article, 22 May 1938.

86. UCC, accession 83.046C, box 3, file 57, BOMSC, letter from Thomson to Dr. Stephenson, 10 May 1938.

87. UCC, accession 83.046C, box 3, file 57, BOMSC, letter from Thomson to *McGill News*, 18 June 1938.

88. TNA, FO 371/27674 F 9062/287/10, letter from Northcote, 14 May 1941.

89. Barnett, *Collapse of British Power*, 237–240, 298–299. See also Keith Neilson, *The Permanent Under-Secretary for Foreign Affairs, 1854–1946* (London: Routledge, 2009), 244.

90. Barnett, *Collapse of British Power*, 237–240, 422–423. See also R. A. Butler, *The Art of the Possible* (London: Hamish Hamilton, 1971), 63, 68.

91. Carroll Quigley, *The Anglo-American Establishment: From Rhodes to Cliveden* (San Pedro, CA: GSG and Associates, 1981), 10–11, 235–236, 253, 292–293.

92. Greg Kennedy, *Anglo-American Strategic Relations and the Far East, 1933–1939: Imperial Crossroads* (London: Frank Cass, 2002), 81.

93. Walter Krivitsky, *I Was Stalin's Agent* (London: Right Book Club, 1940), 19, 29–32, 37–38. See also Graham Ross, *The Foreign Office and the Kremlin: British Documents on Anglo-Soviet Relations, 1941–45* (Cambridge: Cambridge University Press, 1984), 4, and Nikolai Tolstoy, *Stalin's Secret War* (London: Jonathan Cape, 1981), 115, 172.

94. NARA, RG 165, *USMIR*, reel 3, Report No. 14 by Barrett, 1 March 1941.

95. Genrikh Borovik, *The Philby Files: The Secret Life of Master Spy Kim Philby*, ed. Phillip Knightley (Toronto: Little, Brown, 1994), 11–13; Donald Gillies, *Radical Diplomat: The Life of Archibald Clark Kerr, Lord Inverchapel, 1882–1951* (London: I. B. Tauris, 1999), 145; Krivitsky, *I Was Stalin's Agent*, 87–88. See also Tolstoy, *Stalin's Secret War*, 123.

96. NARA, RG 165, *USMIR*, reel 2, Report No. 9639 by Barrett, 20 February 1938. See also Barnett, *Collapse of British Power*, 237–240, 447, and Lynne Olson, *Troublesome Young Men: The Rebels Who Brought Churchill to Power and Helped Save England* (New York: Farrar, Straus and Giroux, 2008), 83.

97. LAC, Diaries of William Lyon Mackenzie King, 27 May 1937, 3, http://king.col lectionscanada.gc.ca/EN/default.asp.

98. TNA, FO 954/4, Anthony Eden Papers, letter from Francis Floud to Edward Harding, 28 February 1938.

99. TNA, FO 371/24667 F 3568/43/10, file cover, 8 July 1940.

100. S. Olu Agbi, "The Pacific War Controversy in Britain: Sir Robert Craigie versus the Foreign Office," *Modern Asian Studies* 17, 3 (1983): 504.

101. TNA, FO 371/22157 F 4832/3284/10, notation by J. Thyne Henderson, 13 June 1938.

102. NARA, RG 165, M1444, reel 15, report by Colonel E. McCabe, 15 September 1937. See also Baxter, "Britain and the War in China," 21, and Chan, *China, Britain and Hong Kong*, 274, 278–279.

103. Lowe, *Great Britain and Origins of the Pacific War*, 38–40.

104. IWM, "Thunder in the East" by Grimsdale, 6, 16.

105. TRL, Biographical Scrapbook, "Biographies of People," vol. 1, no. 457. See also Paul Dickson, "Crerar and the Decision to Garrison Hong Kong," *Canadian Military History* 3, 1 (1994): 98; Brereton Greenhous, *"C" Force to Hong Kong: A Canadian Catastrophe, 1941–1945* (Toronto: Dundurn Press, 1997), 7; and Galen R. Perras, "'Our Position in the Far East Would Be Stronger without This Unsatisfactory Commitment':

Britain, and the Reinforcement of Hong Kong, 1941," *Canadian Journal of History* 30, 2 (1995): 235.

106. Brice, *Royal Navy and Sino-Japanese Incident*, 110.

107. Chan, *China, Britain and Hong Kong*, 268.

108. LAC, RG 24, vol. 20310, file 951.003 (D23), CID, memorandum by the Chiefs of Staff Sub-Committee, Policy for the Defence of Hong Kong, 15 July 1938.

109. Ibid.

110. Ibid.

111. TNA, ADM 1/9568, file West River Flotilla, HMS *Tarantula*, Report No. 20/181.A/38, 15 March 1938, and Report No. 38/181.A/38, 14 April 1938; TNA, ADM 1/9568, file West River Flotilla, W.R. 124/38, HMS *Tarantula*, Report No. 923/2302, 7 June 1938. See also Brice, *Royal Navy and Sino-Japanese Incident*, 90; and http://www.naval-history.net/index.htm.

112. LAC, RG 24, vol. 20310, file 951.003 (D23), CID, Policy for the Defence of Hong Kong, 15 July 1938; TNA, CAB 121/718, Air Ministry Telegram No. 444, 14 January 1941. See also Christopher Bell, "'Our Most Exposed Outpost': Hong Kong and British Far Eastern Strategy, 1921–1941," *Journal of Military History* 60, 1 (1996): 70.

113. IWM, "Thunder in the East" by Grimsdale, 10; NARA, RG 165, M1513, reel 38, report on HKVDC, 1938. See also George Endacott, *Hong Kong Eclipse* (Oxford: Oxford University Press, 1978), 57; George Feifer, *The Battle of Okinawa: The Blood and the Bomb,* 2nd paperback ed. (Guilford, CT: Lyons Press, 2012), 203; Sir Martin Farndale, *History of the Royal Regiment of Artillery: The Far East Theatre, 1939–1946* (London: Brassey's, 2002), xxiii–xxv; and Oliver Lindsay, *The Battle for Hong Kong 1941–1945: Hostage to Fortune* (Hong Kong: Hong Kong University Press, 2005), 49.

114. HKU, BAAG series, vol. 2, Capture, Escape and the Early BAAG, Colonel Lindsay Ride report, Conditions in Hong Kong after Surrender, January 1942. See also Endacott, *Hong Kong Eclipse*, 95, 108.

115. HKU, BAAG series, vol. 2, Ride report, January 1942.

116. NARA, RG 165, entry 77, NM 84, box 1738, MID Regional File, Islands Hong Kong, Consul General Addison Southard report, 18 February 1938. See also Barnett, *Collapse of British Power*, 505, 518; Peter Wesley-Smith, *Unequal Treaty, 1898–1997: China, Great Britain and Hong Kong's New Territories* (Oxford: Oxford University Press, 1983), 160; and Russell Spurr, *Excellency: The Governors of Hong Kong* (Hong Kong: FormAsia Books, 1995), 171.

117. The following section on British discussions to purchase Hong Kong was first published as an article and is reprinted with permission: Franco David Macri, "Abandoning the Outpost: Rejection of the Hong Kong Purchase Scheme, 1938–39," *Journal of the Royal Asiatic Society Hong Kong Branch* 50 (2010): 303–316.

118. NARA, RG 165, *USMIR*, reel 2, Report No. 9633 by Barrett, 1 February 1938, and Report No. 9639 by Barrett, 20 February 1938; TNA, FO 371/22159 F 7617/4847/10, memorandum from Northcote to Colonial Secretary Malcolm MacDonald, 11 June 1938.

119. TNA, FO 371/22159 F 4847/4847/10, letter from Northcote to Ormsby-Gore, 13 April 1938.

120. TNA, FO 371/22159 F 4847/4847/10, letter from Nigel Ronald to Undersecretary Gerard E. Gent, 19 May 1938; TNA, FO 371/22159 F 7617/4847/10, letter from Northcote to MacDonald, 8 June 1938.

121. TNA, FO 371/22159 F 5994/4847/10, letter from Northcote to Ormsby-Gore, 7 May 1938.

122. TNA, FO 371/22159 F 7617/4847/10, memorandum from Northcote to MacDonald, 11 June 1938.

123. Ibid.

124. Ibid. See also TNA, ADM 1/9568, file West River Flotilla, HMS *Tarantula*, July report, 12 August 1938; and TNA, FO 371/22159 F 9184/4847/10, letter from Northcote to MacDonald, 4 August 1938.

125. TNA, FO 371/22159 F 7617/4847/10, memorandum from Foreign Office to Gent, 19 July 1938.

126. TNA, FO 371/22159 F 9516/4847/10, notes of meeting held at the Colonial Office, 26 August 1938.

127. TNA, FO 371/22159 F 9184/4847/10, file cover notation by Nigel Ronald, 26 August 1938.

128. TNA, FO 371/23513 F 1515/1515/10, letter from Northcote to Sir Henry Moore, 6 January 1939.

129. TNA, FO 371/23513 F 3280/1515/10, letter from Northcote to Moore, 27 February 1939.

130. TNA, FO 371/23513 F 1515/1515/10, file cover notation by Sir John Brenan, 23 February 1939.

131. TNA, FO 371/23513 F 2195/1515/10, file cover notation by Sir John Brenan, 8 March 1939.

132. TNA, FO 371/23513 F 3280/1515/10, letter from Northcote to Moore, 27 February 1939.

133. TNA, FO 371/23513 F 6050/1515/10, file cover notation, 21 June 1939.

134. TNA, FO 371/23513 F 6050/1515/10, letter from Northcote to Moore, 25 May 1939.

135. NARA, RG 165, M1444, reel 10, Report No. 9709 by Barrett, 6 January 1939; NARA, RG 165, *USMIR*, reel 3, Report No. 13 by Barrett, 31 January 1941; TNA, FO 371/22150 E 724 (1/12h/1938), report by George, 7 September 1938. See also Baxter, "Britain and the War in China," 276, 319, and Chennault, *Way of a Fighter*, 81–82.

136. NARA, RG 18, entry 300, box 934, file Misc A, USAAF Decimal Files, Oct 1942–44, memorandum by Griffith, 23 June 1938.

137. TNA, FO 371/22150 E 724 (1/12h/1938), report by George, 7 September 1938. See also Yu, *Dragon's War*, 5–6.

138. TNA, WO 208/722, HKIR No. 5/40 by Giles, 30 April 1940.

139. TNA, FO 371/22150 E 724 (1/12h/1938), report by George, 7 September 1938. See also TNA, WO 208/722, HKIR No. 3/40 by Giles, 29 February 1940.

140. NARA, RG 18, entry 300, box 934, file Misc A, USAAF Decimal Files, Oct 1942–44, memorandum by Griffith, 23 June 1938; TNA, FO 371/22150 E 724 (1/12h/1938), report by George, 7 September 1938; TNA, FO 371/22157 F 3284/3284/10,

memorandum from Northcote to Ormsby-Gore, 5 February 1938; TNA, FO 371/22157 F 13118/3284/10, telegram to Colonial Office, 9 December 1938. See also Chan, *China, Britain and Hong Kong*, 283–284.

141. TNA, FO 371/22206 F 7930/5217/87, Minutes of Ninth Meeting of the League of Nations Advisory Committee on Traffic in Opium and Other Dangerous Drugs, Twenty-Third Session by Colonel C. H. L. Sharman, 23 July 1938; TNA, FO 371/22194 F 7214/27/87, memorandum, 4 July 1938; TNA, FO 371/22194 F 8056/27/87, memorandum by R. A. Butler, 20 July 1938; TNA, FO 371/27653 F 5296/188/10, letter from Gent to Northcote, 17 June 1941.

142. TNA, ADM 1/9568, file West River Flotilla, HMS *Tarantula*, Report No. 20/181.A/38, 15 March 1938. See also ibid., Report No. 923/2302, 7 June 1938.

Chapter 4. The Trap Is Sprung

1. LAC, RG 24, reel C-8301, file 5147, Report No. 33 by Major General F. S. G. Piggott, 18 November 1938. See also NARA, RG 165, M1513, The Military Intelligence Division Regional File Relating to China, 1922–1944, reel 39, Report No. 86 by Commander H. E. Overesch, 3 December 1938.

2. NARA, RG 165, M1444, Correspondence of the Military Intelligence Division Relating to General, Political, Economic, and Military Conditions in China, 1918–1941, reel 10, Report No. 9694 by Major David Barrett, 8 November 1938.

3. NARA, RG 59, *USSDCF*, reel 10, Report No. 893.00 P. R. Canton/129 by Consul General Irving N. Linnell, 10 November 1938.

4. TNA, WO 106/5356, file Hong Kong Fortnightly Intelligence Reports, November 1938 to May 1939, HKIR No. 22/38, 25 October 1938.

5. NARA, RG 165, M1444, reel 10, Report No. 9686 by Barrett, 12 October 1938. See also TNA, WO 106/5356, HKIR No. 22/38, 25 October 1938.

6. NARA, RG 165, M1444, reel 10, Report No. 9694 by Barrett, 8 November 1938.

7. Ibid. See also TNA, WO 106/5356, HKIR No. 22/38, 25 October 1938.

8. TNA, WO 106/5356, HKIR No. 22/38, 25 October 1938.

9. Ibid.

10. NARA, RG 165, M1444, reel 10, Report No. 9694 by Barrett, 8 November 1938; NARA, RG 165, M1513, reel 39, Report No. 86 by Commander H. E. Overesch, 3 December 1938; NARA, RG 59, *USSDCF*, reel 10, Report No. 893.00 P. R. Canton/129 by Linnell, 10 November 1938. See also TNA, WO 106/5303, No. 289, Report on Visit to IV War Zone Headquarters by Captain Charles Boxer and Captain H. Chauvin, 20 May 1939; and TNA, WO 106/5356, HKIR No. 22/38, 25 October 1938.

11. NARA, RG 59, *USSDCF*, reel 10, Report No. 893.00 P. R. Canton/129 by Linnell, 10 November 1938; NARA, RG 165, M1444, reel 10, Report No. 9694 by Barrett, 8 November 1938; TNA, WO 106/5356, HKIR No. 22/38, 25 October 1938.

12. NARA, RG 59, *USSDCF*, reel 10, Report No. 893.00 P. R. Canton/129 by Linnell, 10 November 1938; NARA, RG 165, M1444, reel 10, Report No. 9694 by Barrett, 8 November 1938; TNA, WO 106/5356, HKIR No. 22/38, 25 October 1938.

13. NARA, RG 59, *USSDCF*, reel 10, Report No. 893.00 P. R. Canton/129 by Linnell, 10 November 1938.

14. Ibid.

15. LAC, RG 25, vol. 3233, file 5548-40C, military situation memorandum by Lieutenant Colonel Hiram F. Wooster, 20 May 1944; NARA, RG 59, *USSDCF*, reel 10, Report No. 893.00 P. R. Canton/129 by Linnell, 10 November 1938; NARA, RG 165, M1444, reel 10, Report No. 9694 by Barrett, 8 November 1938; TNA, WO 106/5356, HKIR No. 22/38, 25 October 1938.

16. TNA, FO 371/22158 F 13833/3376/10, China Summary No. 10 by Ambassador Sir Archibald Clark Kerr, 22 November 1938.

17. TNA, WO 106/5303, No. 289, Report on Visit to IV War Zone by Boxer and Chauvin, 20 May 1939.

18. Ibid.

19. NARA, RG 165, M1444, reel 10, Report No. 9694 by Barrett, 8 November 1938.

20. NARA, RG 165, M1513, reel 39, Report No. 86 by Overesch, 3 December 1938.

21. TNA, WO 106/5356, HKIR No. 22/38, 25 October 1938.

22. NARA, RG 59, *USSDCF*, reel 10, Report No. 893.00 P. R. Canton/129 by Linnell, 10 November 1938; NARA, RG 165, M1444, reel 10, Report No. 9694 by Barrett, 8 November 1938; NARA, RG 165, M1513, reel 39, Report No. 86 by Overesch, 3 December 1938.

23. TNA, WO 106/5356, HKIR No. 22/38, 25 October 1938.

24. NARA, RG 59, *USSDCF*, reel 10, Report No. 893.00 P. R. Canton/129 by Linnell, 10 November 1938; TNA, WO 106/5356, HKIR No. 22/38, 25 October 1938; TNA, WO 106/5356, HKIR No. 24/38 by Commander J. M. Sturgeon, 22 November 1938.

25. TNA, WO 106/5356, HKIR No. 24/38 by Sturgeon, 22 November 1938.

26. NARA, RG 165, M1444, reel 10, Report No. 9694 by Barrett, 8 November 1938.

27. Ibid.

28. TNA, WO 106/5356, HKIR No. 22/38, 25 October 1938.

29. NARA, RG 38, M975, Selected Naval Attaché Reports Relating to the World Crisis, 1937–1943, reel 2, Estimate of Potential Military Strength Documents G, Naval Attaché Tokyo, vol. 2, Report No. 236, 28 November 1938.

30. UCC, accession 83.046C, box 3, file 59, BOMSC, Reverend A. J. Fisher to J. E. Fisher, 8 November 1937.

31. Dick Wilson, *When Tigers Fight: The Story of the Sino-Japanese War, 1937–1945* (New York: Viking Press, 1982), 132–133.

32. NARA, RG 165, *USMIR*, reel 2, Report No. 9633 by Barrett, 1 February 1938. See also TNA, FO 371/22150 F 794/794/10, Report No. 1119 (3/15L/1937), 30 November 1937.

33. NARA, RG 165, M1513, reel 39, Report No. 29 by Major Truman Martin, 3 February 1938, and Report No. 9635 by Barrett, 16 February 1938.

34. NARA, RG 165, M1444, reel 10, Report No. 9700 by Major David Barrett, 8 December 1938. See also NARA, RG 165, *USMIR*, reel 2, Report No. 9633 by Barrett,

1 February 1938, and Report No. 9639 by Barrett, 20 February 1938; TNA, FO 371/23416 F 3704/14/10, HMS *Sandpiper* situation report, 1 January 1939; Stephen MacKinnon, "The Tragedy of Wuhan, 1938," *Modern Asian Studies* 30, 4 (1996): 934–935; and Wilson, *When Tigers Fight*, 115.

35. NARA, RG 59, *USSDCF*, reel 10, Report No. 893.00 P. R. Canton/129 by Linnell, 10 November 1938.

36. NARA, RG 165, M1513, reel 39, Report No. 86 by Overesch, 3 December 1938.

37. Ibid. See also United States Army Center of Military History, *The War against Japan* (Wilmington, DE: Scholarly Resources, 1998), reel 51, Statement No. 512 by Lieutenant Colonel Okada Yoshimasa, 12 December 1951.

38. LAC, RG 25, vol. 3233, file 5548-40C, Dr. George Patterson to External Affairs, 14 March 1945.

39. NARA, RG 226, entry 92, box 519, file 45, OSS Central Files Report, 2 March 1944.

40. LAC, RG 24, reel C-8301, file 5147, Report No. 33 by Piggott, 18 November 1938.

41. NARA, RG 165, M1513, reel 39, Report No. 86 by Overesch, 3 December 1938.

42. Ibid.

43. TNA, FO 371/23415 F 508/14/10, Report No. 110 by Acting Consul General C. E. Whitamore, 16 November 1938.

44. NARA, RG 59, *USSDCF*, reel 10, Report No. 893.00 P. R. Canton/129 by Linnell, 10 November 1938.

45. TNA, WO 106/5303, No. 289, Report on Visit to IV War Zone by Boxer and Chauvin, 20 May 1939.

46. Ibid.

47. NARA, RG 165, M1513, reel 39, Report No. 86 by Overesch, 3 December 1938. See also NARA, RG 165, *USMIR*, reel 6, Report No. 9864 by Captain F. P. Munson, 3 April 1940.

48. NARA, RG 165, M1444, reel 10, Report No. 9700 by Barrett, 8 December 1938. See also John W. Garver, "China's Wartime Diplomacy," in *China's Bitter Victory: The War with Japan, 1937–1945*, ed. James C. Hsiung and Steven I. Levine (London: M. E. Sharpe, 1992), 11; and Hans Van de Ven, *War and Nationalism in China, 1925–1945* (London: RoutledgeCurzon, 2003), 219–221.

49. NARA, RG 38, M975, reel 2, Estimate of Potential Military Strength Documents G, Naval Attaché Tokyo, vol. 2, Report No. 236, 28 November 1938; TNA, FO 371/22153 F 2136/2136/10, Memorandum No. 5 by Consul General A. P. Blunt, 12 January 1938; TNA, WO 106/5303 No. 293, Report on Visit to South China July 1938 by Captain J. V. Davidson-Houston, 5 August 1938. See also Garver, "China's Wartime Diplomacy," 10, 19; Peter Lowe, *Great Britain and the Origins of the Pacific War: A Study of British Policy in East Asia, 1937–1941* (Oxford: Clarendon Press, 1977), 59–60; Usui Katsumi, "The Politics of War," in *Japan's Road to the Pacific War: The China Quagmire: Japan's Expansion on the Asian Continent, 1933–1941*, ed. James

Morely and David Lu (New York: Columbia University Press, 1983), 350; Yu Maochun, "'In God We Trusted, in China We Busted': The China Commando Group of the Special Operations Executive (SOE)," *Intelligence and National Security* 16, 4 (2001): 38; and Yu Maochun, *The Dragon's War: Allied Operations and the Fate of China* (Annapolis, MD: Naval Institute Press, 2006), 46–47.

50. NARA, RG 165, M1444, reel 10, Report No. 9700 by Barrett, 8 December 1938; TNA, FO 371/23416 F 3704/14/10, HMS *Sandpiper* situation report, 1 January 1939; TNA, WO 106/5356, HKIR No. 24/38 by Sturgeon, 22 November 1938; Van de Ven, *War and Nationalism in China*, 228.

51. NARA, RG 165, M1444, reel 10, Report No. 9694 by Barrett, 8 November 1938, and Report No. 9700 by Barrett, 8 December 1938; TNA, WO 106/5356, HKIR No. 24/38 by Sturgeon, 22 November 1938, and HKIR No. 3/39 by Captain C. J. Edwards, 31 January 1939.

52. Church Missionary Society, sec. 1, East Asia Missions, pt. 20, Annual Letters, G1 AL, reel 444, letter from Hollis, 18 August 1945; TNA, FO 371/22164 F 12628/12582/10, Telegram No. 4726 from Lieutenant General Sir Arthur Grasett, 26 November 1938; TNA, FO 371/22164 F 12638/12582/10, Telegram Nos. 342 and 343 from Governor Sir Geoffry Northcote, 26 November 1938; TNA, FO 371/22164 F 12641/12582/10, Telegram No. 4728 from Grasett, 26 November 1938; TNA, FO 371/22164 F 12993/12582/10, Telegram No. 4747 from Grasett, 1 December 1938; TNA, FO 371/22164 F 13124/12582/10, telegram from Northcote, 3 December 1938; TNA, FO 371/27647 F 1783/178/10, Telegram No. 406 from Ambassador Sir Robert Craigie, 9 March 1941.

53. TNA, FO 371/24667 F 3597/43/10, Memorandum No. 1322 by Ambassador Lord Lothian, 12 July 1940. See also Lowe, *Great Britain and Origins of the Pacific War*, 268.

54. Peter Moreira, *Hemingway on the China Front: His WWII Spy Mission with Martha Gellhorn* (Washington, DC: Potomac Books, 2006), 121.

55. TNA, FO 371/27697 F 3707/846/10, report by Captain T. M. H. Pardoe, 30 April 1941. See also Chan Lau Kit Ching, *China, Britain and Hong Kong, 1895–1945* (Hong Kong: Chinese University Press, 1990), 276–277.

56. NARA, RG 165, M1444, reel 11, Report No. 9788 by Captain Edwin M. Sutherland, 12 August 1939; TNA, FO 371/24667 F 3584/43/10, memorandum, 11 July 1940; TNA, FO 371/27697 F 3707/846/10, report by Pardoe, 30 April 1941; William Grieve, "Belated Endeavor: The American Military Mission to China (AMMISCA) 1941–1942" (Ph.D. diss., University of Illinois, 1979), 35.

57. NARA, RG 165, M1444, reel 11, Report No. 9768 by Captain F. P. Munson, 5 May 1939. See also NARA, RG 165, *USMIR*, reel 3, Report No. 14 by Barrett, 1 March 1941.

58. TNA, FO 371/27715 F 4787/3653/10, memorandum by Ian Morrison, 3 June 1941.

59. LAC, RG 25, vol. 3233, file 5548-40C, Report No. 52 by Ambassador General Victor Odlum, 9 August 1943; NARA, RG 165, entry 184, box 959, radiogram by Barrett, 27 February 1941; NARA, RG 165, *USMIR*, reel 3, Report No. 11 by Barrett, 3

December 1940; TNA, WO 208/366, file Military Situation in China by Military Attaché, Oct 1941, report by Major General Lance Dennys, 22 November 1941.

60. NARA, RG 165, M1444, reel 10, Report No. 9709 by Barrett, 6 January 1939; NARA, RG 165, M1444, reel 11, Report No. 9788 by Sutherland, 12 August 1939, and Report No. 9793 by Sutherland, 8 September 1939; TNA, FO 371/22150 E 724 (1/12h/1938), report by Commercial Counsellor A. H. George, 7 September 1938; TNA, FO 371/23520 F 3668/3668/10, J. C. Hutchinson to A. H. George, 7 February 1939; TNA, WO 106/5356, HKIR No. 24/38 by Sturgeon, 22 November 1938, and HKIR No. 6/39 by Edwards, 14 March 1939; TNA, WO 208/721, file Hong Kong Fortnightly Intelligence Reports, January 1939 to December 1939, HKIR No. 14/39 by Edwards, 4 July 1939.

61. NARA, RG 165, M1444, reel 11, Report No. 9768 by Munson, 5 May 1939, Report No. 9793 by Sutherland, 8 September 1939, and Report No. 9799 by Sutherland, 29 September 1939; NARA, RG 165, USMIR, reel 3, Report No. 9844 by Major William Mayer, 11 January 1940; TNA, WO 106/5356, HKIR No. 9/39 by Edwards, 25 April 1939.

62. NARA, RG 38, M975, reel 2, Estimate of Potential Military Strength Documents G, Naval Attaché Tokyo, vol. 2, Report No. 189, 5 September 1939.

63. TNA, WO 208/722, file Hong Kong Fortnightly Intelligence Reports, January 1940 to October 1941, HKIR No. 11/40 by Major R. C. Giles, 31 October 1940.

64. NARA, RG 59, M1221, OSS Research and Analysis Report No. 112, July 1942. See also NARA, RG 165, USMIR, reel 3, Report No. 13 by Lieutenant Colonel David Barrett, 31 January 1941.

65. TNA, WO 208/722, HKIR No. 2/41 by Major R. C. Giles, 28 February 1941.

66. TNA, WO 106/5356, HKIR No. 2/39 by Sturgeon, 17 January 1939; TNA, WO 208/721, HKIR No. 17/39 by Edwards, 15 August 1939. See also Donald Gillies, *Radical Diplomat: The Life of Archibald Clark Kerr, Lord Inverchapel, 1882–1951* (London: I. B. Tauris, 1999), 99–100, and Lowe, *Great Britain and Origins of the Pacific War*, 50–53.

67. NARA, RG 165, M1444, reel 10, Report No. 9700 by Barrett, 8 December 1938.

68. Wilson, *When Tigers Fight*, 149–150.

69. NARA, RG 165, M1513, reel 39, Report No. 9713 by Captain Maxwell D. Taylor, 13 February 1939. See also TNA, WO 106/5356, HKIR No. 4/39 by Captain C. J. Edwards, 14 February 1939.

70. NARA, RG 165, M1513, reel 39, Report No. 9713 by Taylor, 13 February 1939; TNA, WO 106/5303 No. 290, Report on Visit to Canton and Shanghai, January to February 1939, by Major G. T. Wards, 11 March 1939; TNA, WO 106/5356, HKIR No. 2/39 by Sturgeon, 17 January 1939, HKIR No. 3/39 by Edwards, 31 January 1939, HKIR No. 4/39 by Edwards, 14 February 1939, HKIR No. 5/39 by Edwards, 28 February 1939, and HKIR No. 11/39 by Edwards, 23 May 1939.

71. TNA, WO 106/5356, HKIR No. 5/39 by Edwards, 28 February 1939, HKIR No. 6/39 by Edwards, 14 March 1939, and HKIR No. 8/39 by Edwards, 11 April 1939.

72. TNA, WO 106/5356, HKIR No. 4/39 by Edwards, 14 February 1939, and HKIR No. 5/39 by Edwards, 28 February 1939.

73. TNA, WO 106/5356, HKIR No. 5/39 by Edwards, 28 February 1939.

74. NARA, RG 59, *USSDCF*, reel 10, Report No. 893.00 P. R. Canton/129 by Linnell, 10 November 1938. See also TNA, WO 106/5356, HKIR No. 24/38 by Sturgeon, 22 November 1938.

75. TNA, FO 371/22153 F 12718/1155/10, Telegram No. 1391 by Craigie, 22 November 1938; TNA, WO 106/5356, HKIR No. 24/38 by Sturgeon, 22 November 1938.

76. TNA, WO 106/5356, HKIR No. 24/38 by Sturgeon, 22 November 1938.

77. Ibid.

78. TNA, FO 371/23415 F 508/14/10, Report No. 110 by Whitamore, 16 November 1938.

79. TNA, WO 106/5303 No. 290, Report on Visit to Canton by Wards, 11 March 1939.

80. Ibid.

81. Ibid.

82. TNA, FO 371/23514 F 3366/1696/10, Report on the Bombing of British Territory by Major General A. E. Grasett, 6 March 1939.

83. TNA, FO 371/23513 F 1696/1696/10, Telegram No. 75 by Northcote, 21 February1939; TNA, FO 371/23513 F 1709/1696/10, Telegram No. 4871 by Grasett, 21 February 1939; TNA, FO 371/23514 F 3366/1696/10, note of proceedings by Northcote, 8 March 1939; TNA, FO 371/23514 F 3437/1696/10, Northcote to H. R. Cowell, 8 March 1939.

84. TNA, FO 371/23513 F 1770/1696/10, Telegram No. 78 by Northcote, 23 February 1939; TNA, FO 371/23514 F 2808/1696/10, Telegram No. 64 by Blunt, 11 March 1939; TNA, FO 371/23514 F 3437/1696/10, Northcote to Cowell, 8 March 1939; TNA, WO 106/5356, HKIR No. 5/39 by Edwards, 28 February 1939.

85. TNA, WO 106/5303 No. 290, Report on Visit to Canton by Wards, 11 March 1939.

86. TNA, WO 106/5356, HKIR No. 9/39 by Edwards, 25 April 1939.

87. NARA, RG 165, entry 184, box 960, Intelligence Report No. 1 by Colonel E. R. W. McCabe, 18 August 1938.

88. Usui Katsumi, "Politics of War," 354–356.

89. LAC, MG 26 J1, reel C-3748, vol. 278, frame 234821, Malcolm Macdonald to External Affairs Canada, 11 January 1939; TNA, FO 371/23409 F 938/11/10, file cover notation by Nigel Ronald, 31 January 1939. See also S. Olu Agbi, "The Pacific War Controversy in Britain: Sir Robert Craigie versus the Foreign Office," *Modern Asian Studies* 17, 3 (1983): 504; Henry Gole, *The Road to Rainbow: Army Planning for Global War, 1934–1940* (Annapolis, MD: Naval Institute Press, 2003), xvi; Lowe, *Great Britain and Origins of the Pacific War*, 53, 60–61; and Yu, *Dragon's War*, 48.

90. TNA, FO 371/23513 F 3280/1515/10, file cover notation by Sir John Brenan, 13 April 1939.

91. NARA, RG 165, M1444, reel 10, Report No. 9700 by Barrett, 8 December 1938; TNA, WO 208/849, file Peace Overtures to China, September 1939 to February 1942, memorandum entitled "Japan's Peace Terms," 29 December 1938. See also Lowe, *Great Britain and Origins of the Pacific War*, 53, 60–62.

92. UCC, accession 83.046C, box 3, file 60, BOMSC, Reverend Duncan McRae to Reverend A. E. Armstrong, 8 February 1939.

93. NARA, RG 165, M1444, reel 10, Report No. 9709 by Barrett, 6 January 1939. See also TNA, WO 106/5356, HKIR No. 1/39 by Edwards, 3 January 1939; John H. Boyle, *China and Japan at War, 1937–1945: The Politics of Collaboration* (Stanford, CA: Stanford University Press, 1972), 222–223; and Usui Katsumi, "Politics of War," 382–384.

94. TNA, WO 106/5356, HKIR No. 2/39 by Sturgeon, 17 January 1939, and HKIR No. 3/39 by Edwards, 31 January 1939. See also Boyle, *China and Japan at War*, 224–225, 228.

95. UCC, accession 83.046C, box 3, file 60, BOMSC, Reverend Duncan McRae to Reverend A. E. Armstrong, 15 February 1939.

96. TNA, WO 106/5303, No. 289, Report on Visit to IV War Zone by Boxer and Chauvin, 20 May 1939.

97. UCC, accession 83.046C, box 3, file 60, BOMSC, McRae to Armstrong, 15 February 1939.

98. Sir Curtis Keeble, *Britain, the Soviet Union and Russia* (London: Macmillan Press, 2000), 143. See also R. Craig Nation, *Black Earth, Red Star: A History of Soviet Security Policy, 1917–1991* (Ithaca, NY: Cornell University Press, 1992), 98.

Chapter 5. Stalemate

1. LAC, RG 25, vol. 3029, file 3978-40C pt. 1, "Famine in Kwangtung," report by Ralph E. Collins, 9 May 1944.

2. Ibid. See also NARA, RG 165, M1444, Correspondence of the Military Intelligence Division Relating to General, Political, Economic, and Military Conditions in China, 1918–1941, reel 11, Report No. 9799 by Captain Edwin M. Sutherland, 29 September 1939; TNA, WO 106/5356, file Hong Kong Fortnightly Intelligence Reports, November 1938 to May 1939, HKIR No. 9/39 by Captain C. J. Edwards, 25 April 1939.

3. LAC, RG 25, vol. 3233, file 5548-40C, memorandum by Lieutenant-Colonel Hiram Wooster, 20 May 1944. See also NARA, RG 165, M1444, reel 10, Report No. 9700 by Major David Barrett, 8 December 1938; NARA, RG 341, entry 217, box 824, MIPI File No. 69404, photo reconnaissance report, 4 October 1944; UCC, accession 83.046C, box 3, file 60, BOMSC, Reverend Duncan McRae to Mr. Hockin, 20 January 1939, and McRae to Reverend A. E. Armstrong, 8 February 1939; UCC, accession 83.046C, box 3, file 61, BOMSC, Reverend Tom Broadfoot to Armstrong, 10 January 1939; and UCC, *Forward with China: The Story of the Missions of the United Church of Canada in China* (Toronto: United Church of Canada, 1928), 185.

4. TNA, WO 106/5356, HKIR No. 3/39 by Edwards, 31 January 1939. See also TNA, WO 106/5356, HKIR No. 4/39 by Edwards, 14 February 1939, and HKIR No. 5/39 by Edwards, 28 February 1939.

5. TNA, WO 106/5356, HKIR No. 9/39 by Edwards, 25 April 1939. See also Peter Vine, "Experiences as a War Crimes Prosecutor in Hong Kong," *Journal of the Hong Kong Branch of the Royal Asiatic Society* 35 (1995): 205–209.

6. NARA, RG 165, M1513, The Military Intelligence Division Regional File Relating to China, 1922–1944, reel 39, Report No. 9762 by Captain Elmer E. Count, 10 April 1939. See also TNA, WO 106/5356, HKIR No. 5/39 by Edwards, 28 February 1939, HKIR No. 6/39 by Edwards, 14 March 1939, and HKIR No. 9/39 by Edwards, 25 April 1939.

7. NARA, RG 38, entry 98A, box 705, F-6-c 23213 to F-6-e 22379, Report No. 1046-45, 28 February 1945; TNA, WO 106/5356, HKIR No. 1/39 by Edwards, 3 January 1939, and HKIR No. 5/39 by Edwards, 28 February 1939.

8. NARA, RG 165, *USMIR*, reel 13, Report No. 350.05-General by Lieutenant-Colonel Henry McLean, 14 October 1939. See also TNA, CO 129/563/5, Telegram No. 206, 15 December 1937; and TNA, WO 106/5303, No. 290, Report on Visit to Canton and Shanghai, January to February 1939, by Major G. T. Wards, 11 March 1939.

9. WO 106/5303, No. 290, report by Wards, 11 March 1939.

10. TNA, WO 106/5356, HKIR No. 8/39 by Edwards, 11 April 1939; TNA, WO 208/721, file Hong Kong Fortnightly Intelligence Reports, January 1939 to December 1939, HKIR No. 16/39 by Edwards, 1 August 1939. See also Martin H. Brice, *The Royal Navy and the Sino-Japanese Incident, 1937–41* (London: Ian Allan, 1973), 117.

11. NARA, RG 165, M1444, reel 11, Report No. 9768 by Captain F. P. Munson, 5 May 1939, and Report No. 9784 by Captain Edwin M. Sutherland, 14 July 1939. See also TNA, WO 106/5303, No. 290, report by Wards, 11 March 1939; TNA, WO 106/5356, HKIR No. 22/38, 25 October 1938; TNA, WO 106/5356, HKIR No. 11/39 by Edwards, 23 May 1939; TNA, WO 208/721, HKIR No. 12/39 by Edwards, 6 June 1939; UCC, accession 83.046C, box 3, file 60, BOMSC, McRae to Reverend Jesse Arnup, 6 May 1939; and Douglas Ford, *Britain's Secret War against Japan, 1937–1945* (New York: Routledge, 2006), 35.

12. NARA, RG 165, M1444, reel 11, Report No. 9768 by Munson, 5 May 1939; NARA, RG 165, M1513, reel 39, Report No. 9771 by Count, 24 April 1939. See also TNA, WO 106/5356, HKIR No. 6/39 by Edwards, 14 March 1939, and HKIR No. 9/39 by Edwards, 25 April 1939.

13. TNA, WO 106/5356, HKIR No. 9/39 by Edwards, 25 April 1939, and HKIR No. 11/39 by Edwards, 23 May 1939.

14. TNA, WO 106/5356, HKIR No. 8/39 by Edwards, 11 April 1939.

15. TNA, FO 371/23416 F 3639/14/10, Telegram No. 4984 by Lieutenant-General A. E. Grasett, 11 April 1939; TNA, WO 106/5356, HKIR No. 9/39 by Edwards, 25 April 1939. See also UCC, accession 83.046C, box 3, file 60, BOMSC, McRae to Armstrong, 28 April 1939, and McRae to Arnup, 6 May 1939; UCC, accession 83.046C, box 3, file 61, BOMSC, Broadfoot to Armstrong, 1 April 1939, and Broadfoot to Arnup, 6 May 1939.

16. LAC, MG 26 J1, reel C-3745, vol. 271, report by Ambassador Sir Archibald Clark Kerr, 8 May 1939. See also NARA, RG 165, M1444, reel 10, Report No. 9709 by Barrett, 6 January 1939; NARA, RG 165, M1444, reel 11, Report No. 9768 by Munson, 5 May 1939, and Report No. 9784 by Sutherland, 14 July 1939; NARA, RG 165, M1513, reel 39, Report No. 9762 by Count, 10 April 1939; TNA, FO 371/23473 F 8254/150/10, letter from Clark Kerr to Robert G. Howe, 10 June 1939; TNA, FO 371/

23473 F 8467/150/10, telegram from Consul General H. Prideaux-Brune, 4 August 1939; TNA, FO 371/23473 F 8514/150/10, Telegram No. 840 by Clark Kerr, 7 August 1939; TNA, FO 371/23473 F 8588/150/10, telegram from Senior Naval Officer China, 5 August 1939; TNA, FO 371/27675 F 2616/317/10, memorandum from Ambassador Sir Robert Craigie to Lord Halifax, 23 January 1941; TNA, WO 106/5356, HKIR No. 2/39 by Commander J. M. Sturgeon, 17 January 1939, HKIR No. 6/39 by Edwards, 14 March 1939, HKIR No. 7/39 by Edwards, 28 March 1939, HKIR No. 8/39 by Edwards, 11 April 1939, HKIR No. 10/39 by Edwards, 9 May 1939, and HKIR No. 11/39 by Edwards, 23 May 1939; TNA, WO 208/721, HKIR No. 12/39 by Edwards, 6 June 1939, HKIR No. 13/39 by Edwards, 20 June 1939, HKIR No. 14/39 by Edwards, 4 July 1939, HKIR No. 15/39 by Edwards, 18 July 1939, HKIR No. 16/39 by Edwards, 1 August 1939, HKIR No. 17/39 by Edwards, 15 August 1939, and HKIR No. 18/39 by Edwards, 30 August 1939; Claire L. Chennault, *Way of a Fighter: The Memoirs of Claire Lee Chennault, Major General, U.S. Army (Ret.)* (New York: G. P. Putnam's Sons, 1949), 87; and Mark Peattie, *Sunburst: The Rise of Japanese Naval Air Power, 1909–1941* (Annapolis, MD: Naval Institute Press, 2001), 116.

17. NARA, RG 165, M1513, reel 39, Report No. 9762 by Count, 10 April 1939. See also TNA, WO 106/5356, HKIR No. 8/39 by Edwards, 11 April 1939, and HKIR No. 9/39 by Edwards, 25 April 1939; Henry Gole, *The Road to Rainbow: Army Planning for Global War, 1934–1940* (Annapolis, MD: Naval Institute Press, 2003), 97; and Curtis Keeble, *Britain, the Soviet Union and Russia* (London: Macmillan Press, 2000), 143.

18. NARA, RG 165, M1444, reel 11, Report No. 9784 by Sutherland, 14 July 1939. See also TNA, FO 371/23416 F 5302/14/10, Telegram No. 3868, 30 May 1939; TNA, WO 106/5303, No. 290, report by Wards, 11 March 1939; TNA, WO 106/5356, HKIR No. 7/39 by Edwards, 28 March 1939; TNA, WO 208/721, HKIR No. 14/39 by Edwards, 4 July 1939, and HKIR No. 15/39 by Edwards, 18 July 1939; Chan Lau Kit Ching, *China, Britain and Hong Kong, 1895–1945* (Hong Kong: Chinese University Press, 1990), 282; and Tsunoda Jun, "The Navy's Role in the Southern Strategy," trans. Robert Scalapino, in *The Fateful Choice: Japan's Road to the Pacific War: Japan's Advance into Southeast Asia, 1939–1941*, ed. James Morley (New York: Columbia University Press, 1980), 263.

19. NARA, RG 165, M1444, reel 11, Report No. 9793 by Sutherland, 8 September 1939; NARA, RG 165, *USMIR*, reel 3, Report No. 9800 by Munson, 3 October 1939. See also TNA, WO 208/721, HKIR No. 20/39 by Edwards, 26 September 1939; and Hans Van de Ven, *War and Nationalism in China: 1925–1945* (London: RoutledgeCurzon, 2003), 227–228.

20. UCC, accession 83.046C, box 3, file 63, BOMSC, Dr. J. O. Thomson to Armstrong, 21 May 1939.

21. TNA, WO 208/721, HKIR No. 15/39 by Edwards, 18 July 1939.

22. Ibid.

23. TNA, WO 106/5356, HKIR No. 9/39 by Edwards, 25 April 1939.

24. TNA, WO 208/721, HKIR No. 15/39 by Edwards, 18 July 1939.

25. NARA, RG 165, *USMIR*, reel 3, Report No. 16 by Colonel David Barrett, 1

May 1941. See also NARA, RG 493, entry 531, box 51, Z Force Operations, Adjutant General Decimal File, report by Colonel David Barrett, 20 May 1944.

26. TNA, FO 371/22164 F 12980/12980/10, Report on Visit to Manchuria in September–October 1938 by Wards, 5 November 1938; TNA, FO 371/27715 F 4091/3653/10, file cover notation by A. L. Scott, 21 May 1941. See also TNA, WO 106/5356, HKIR No. 24/38 by Sturgeon, 22 November 1938; TNA, WO 208/849, file Peace Overtures to China, memorandum, 25 September 1939; UCC, accession 83.046C, box 3, file 60, BOMSC, McRae to Armstrong, 20 May 1939; and John H. Boyle, *China and Japan at War, 1937–1945: The Politics of Collaboration* (Stanford, CA: Stanford University Press, 1972), 83–84.

27. LAC, RG 25, vol. 3264, file 6161-40C, report by Reverend V. J. R. Mills, 27 September 1943. See also NARA, RG 38, M975, reel 2, Estimate of Potential Military Strength Documents G, Naval Attaché Tokyo, vol. 2, Report No. 189, 5 September 1939; TNA, WO 106/5356, HKIR No. 4/39 by Edwards, 14 February 1939, HKIR No. 5/39 by Edwards, 28 February 1939, HKIR No. 6/39 by Edwards, 14 March 1939, HKIR No. 8/39 by Edwards, 11 April 1939, HKIR No. 10/39 by Edwards, 9 May 1939, and HKIR No. 11/39 by Edwards, 23 May 1939; and TNA, WO 208/721, HKIR No. 12/39 by Edwards, 6 June 1939.

28. NARA, RG 38, entry 98A, box 705, F-6-c 23213 to F-6-e 22379, USS *Tulsa* Report No. A8-2(844), 27 July 1939. See also TNA, WO 106/5356, HKIR No. 9/39 by Edwards, 25 April 1939, and HKIR No. 11/39 by Edwards, 23 May 1939; and TNA, WO 208/721, HKIR No. 12/39 by Edwards, 6 June 1939.

29. TNA, WO 106/5356, HKIR No. 11/39 by Edwards, 23 May 1939.

30. TNA, WO 106/5356, HKIR No. 8/39 by Edwards, 11 April 1939, HKIR No. 10/39 by Edwards, 9 May 1939, and HKIR No. 11/39 by Edwards, 23 May 1939; TNA, WO 208/721, HKIR No. 12/39 by Edwards, 6 June 1939.

31. LAC, RG 25, vol. 3233, file 5548-40C, memorandum by Wooster, 20 May 1944. See also NARA, RG 165, M1444, reel 11, Report No. 9784 by Sutherland, 14 July 1939; and TNA, WO 208/721, HKIR No. 12/39 by Edwards, 6 June 1939, HKIR No. 13/39 by Edwards, 20 June 1939, HKIR No. 14/39 by Edwards, 4 July 1939, HKIR No. 15/39 by Edwards, 18 July 1939, HKIR No. 16/39 by Edwards, 1 August 1939, and HKIR No. 17/39 by Edwards, 15 August 1939.

32. NARA, RG 38, entry 98A, box 705, F-6-c 23213 to F-6-e 22379, USS *Tulsa* Report No. A8-2(844), 27 July 1939.

33. Ibid. See also TNA, FO 371/23520 F 3966/3905/10, Ambassador Quo Tai Chi to Halifax, 22 April 1939; TNA, FO 371/23520 F 3968/3905/10, Finance Minister H. H. Kung to Halifax, 22 April 1939; and TNA, WO 106/5356, HKIR No. 9/39 by Edwards, 25 April 1939, and HKIR No. 11/39 by Edwards, 23 May 1939.

34. TNA, WO 208/721, HKIR No. 12/39 by Edwards, 6 June 1939. See also TNA, WO 208/721, HKIR No. 14/39 by Edwards, 4 July 1939, HKIR No. 15/39 by Edwards, 18 July 1939, HKIR No. 16/39 by Edwards, 1 August 1939, HKIR No. 17/39 by Edwards, 15 August 1939, and HKIR No. 20/39 by Edwards, 26 September 1939.

35. TNA, WO 208/721, HKIR No. 16/39 by Edwards, 1 August 1939, HKIR No.

17/39 by Edwards, 15 August 1939, and HKIR No. 20/39 by Edwards, 26 September 1939.

36. TNA, FO 371/23416 F 5347/14/10, Telegram No. 5131 from Grasett to War Office, 1 June 1939. See also TNA, WO 106/5356, HKIR No. 5/39 by Edwards, 28 February 1939; TNA, WO 106/5356, HKIR No. 7/39 by Edwards, 28 March 1939, HKIR No. 9/39 by Edwards, 25 April 1939, HKIR No. 10/39 by Edwards, 9 May 1939, and HKIR No. 11/39 by Edwards, 23 May 1939; TNA, WO 208/721, HKIR No. 12/39 by Edwards, 6 June 1939, HKIR No. 16/39 by Edwards, 1 August 1939, and HKIR No. 18/39 by Edwards, 30 August 1939; TNA, WO 208/722, file Hong Kong Fortnightly Intelligence Reports, January 1940 to October 1941, HKIR No. 7/41 by Major R. Giles, 1 August 1941; UCC, accession 83.046C, box 3, file 61, BOMSC, Broadfoot to Arnup, 18 May 1939; Hata Ikuhiko, "The Army's Move into Northern Indochina," trans. Robert Scalapino, in Morley, *Fateful Choice*, 168; and B. H. Liddell Hart, *History of the Second World War* (New York: Cassell, 1971), 233.

37. TNA, WO 106/5303, No. 289, Report on Visit to IV War Zone Headquarters by Boxer and Chauvin, 20 May 1939. See also TNA, WO 106/5796, file Chinese Nationals: Yu Han Mou, Extract from Shanghai Military and Naval Intelligence Summary No. 47, 9 March 1939; and TNA, WO 208/721, HKIR No. 13/39 by Edwards, 20 June 1939, and HKIR No. 17/39 by Edwards, 15 August 1939.

38. TNA, WO 208/721, HKIR No. 12/39 by Edwards, 6 June 1939. See also TNA, WO 208/721, HKIR No. 15/39 by Edwards, 18 July 1939, HKIR No. 16/39 by Edwards, 1 August 1939, HKIR No. 17/39 by Edwards, 15 August 1939, and HKIR No. 18/39 by Edwards, 30 August 1939; and UCC, accession 83.046C, box 3, file 61, BOMSC, Broadfoot to Arnup, 16 July 1939, and Broadfoot to Arnup, 3 August 1939.

39. NARA, RG 165, M1513, reel 40, Report No. 9857 by Captain Eric Svensson, 2 August 1939. See also UCC, accession 83.046C, box 3, file 61, BOMSC, Broadfoot to Arnup, 28 June 1939.

40. NARA, RG 165, M1444, reel 11, Report No. 9788 by Sutherland, 12 August 1939.

41. UCC, accession 83.046C, box 3, file 61, BOMSC, Broadfoot to Arnup, 16 July 1939.

42. Church Missionary Society Archive (UK), sec. 1, East Asia Missions, pt. 20, Annual Letters 1917–1949, G1 AL, reel 445, letter from Wittenbach, 16 July 1940.

43. NARA, RG 38, entry 98A, box 705, F-6-c 23213 to F-6-e 22379, USS *Tulsa* Report No. A8-2(842) by Captain John Stapler, 27 July 1939. See also NARA, RG 165, M1444, reel 11, Report No. 9788 by Sutherland, 12 August 1939; and NARA, RG 165, M1513, reel 40, Report No. 9857 by Svensson, 2 August 1939.

44. UCC, accession 83.046C, box 3, file 60, BOMSC, McRae to Arnup, 28 August 1939; UCC, accession 83.046C, box 3, file 61, BOMSC, Broadfoot to Arnup, 3 August 1939. See also Boyle, *China and Japan at War*, 250–252.

45. NARA, RG 165, M1444, reel 11, Report No. 9799 by Sutherland, 29 September 1939. See also TNA, WO 208/721, HKIR No. 17/39 by Edwards, 15 August 1939,

and HKIR No. 20/39 by Edwards, 26 September 1939; and UCC, accession 83.046C, box 3, file 60, BOMSC, McRae to Arnup, 9 August 1939.

46. NARA, RG 165, M1444, reel 11, Report No. 9808 by Munson, 26 October 1939; NARA, RG 165, M1513, reel 40, Report No. 9930 by Svensson, 11 October 1939. See also TNA, WO 106/5356, HKIR No. 11/39 by Edwards, 23 May 1939; and TNA, WO 208/721, HKIR No. 21/39 by Edwards, 10 October 1939, and HKIR No. 22/39 by Giles, 23 October 1939.

47. NARA, RG 165, M1444, reel 11, Report No. 9808 by Munson, 26 October 1939; NARA, RG 165, M1513, reel 40, Report No. 9937 by Svensson, 26 October 1939. See also TNA, WO 106/5303, No. 289, Report on Visit to IV War Zone by Boxer and Chauvin, 20 May 1939; and TNA, WO 208/721, HKIR No. 22/39 by Giles, 23 October 1939.

48. TNA, WO 208/721, HKIR No. 22/39 by Giles, 23 October 1939.

49. NARA, RG 165, M1444, reel 11, Report No. 9784 by Sutherland, 14 July 1939, and Report No. 9788 by Sutherland, 12 August 1939. See also TNA, WO 208/721, HKIR No. 16/39 by Edwards, 1 August 1939, and HKIR No. 22/39 by Giles, 23 October 1939.

50. TNA, FO 371/22159 F 9516/4847/10, notes of meeting held at Colonial Office, 26 August 1938. See also TNA, WO 208/721, HKIR No. 19/39 by Edwards, 12 September 1939.

51. NARA, RG 165, M1444, reel 11, Report No. 9788 by Sutherland, 12 August 1939.

52. TNA, WO 106/5356, HKIR No. 8/39 by Edwards, 11 April 1939.

53. LAC, MG 26 J1, reel C-3745, vol. 272, Telegram No. 225 from Charges d'Affaires E. D'Arcy McGreer to Prime Minister William Lyon Mackenzie King, 28 July 1939; NARA, RG 165, M1444, reel 11, Report No. 9788 by Sutherland, 12 August 1939; TNA, WO 208/721, HKIR No. 18/39 by Edwards, 30 August 1939. See also Alan Lothian, "Khalkhin-Gol (1939)," in *The Mammoth Book of Battles: The Art and Science of Modern War*, ed. Jon Lewis (New York: Carroll and Graff, 1995), 140, and Keeble, *Britain, the Soviet Union and Russia*, 143.

54. NARA, RG 165, M1444, reel 11, Report No. 9788 by Sutherland, 12 August 1939, and Report No. 9793 by Sutherland, 8 September 1939. See also TNA, WO 208/721, HKIR No. 16/39 by Edwards, 1 August 1939, and HKIR No. 17/39 by Edwards, 15 August 1939.

55. NARA, RG 165, M1444, reel 11, Report No. 9784 by Sutherland, 14 July 1939. See also R. C. Raack, *Stalin's Drive to the West, 1938–1945: The Origins of the Cold War* (Stanford, CA: Stanford University Press, 1995), 21–23, and Yu Maochun, *The Dragon's War: Allied Operations and the Fate of China* (Annapolis, MD: Naval Institute Press, 2006), 14, 23.

56. NARA, RG 165, USMIR, reel 3, Report No. 9830 by Colonel William Mayer, 29 November 1939. See also TNA, WO 208/721, HKIR No. 21/39 by Edwards, 10 October 1939, HKIR No. 22/39 by Giles, 23 October 1939, and HKIR No. 24/39 by Giles, 21 November 1939; and Yu, *The Dragon's War*, 14.

57. TNA, WO 208/721, HKIR No. 21/39 by Edwards, 10 October 1939.

58. TNA, WO 208/721, HKIR No. 25/39 by Giles, 5 December 1939.

59. TNA, WO 106/5356, HKIR No. 11/39 by Edwards, 23 May 1939; TNA, WO 208/721, HKIR No. 25/39 by Giles, 5 December 1939.

60. NARA, RG 165, *USMIR*, reel 3, Report No. 9830 by Mayer, 29 November 1939; TNA, WO 208/721, HKIR No. 20/39 by Edwards, 26 September 1939. See also Boyle, *China and Japan at War*, 84, 257–258.

61. TNA, WO 208/849, file Peace Overtures to China, memorandum, 25 September 1939. See also Catherine Baxter, "Britain and the War in China, 1937–1945" (Ph.D. diss., University of Wales, 1993), 92.

62. TNA, WO 208/721, HKIR No. 17/39 by Edwards, 15 August 1939.

63. NARA, RG 165, M1513, reel 40, Report No. 70, 27 November 1939. See also TNA, CO 129/579/5, Lady Manton to Foreign Minister Lord Halifax, 7 February 1939, Hong Kong Police Report by Acting Sub-Inspector L. K. George, 23 April 1939, and aide memoire by Ambassador Sir Robert Craigie, 23 June 1939; TNA, WO 106/5356, HKIR No. 10/39 by Edwards, 9 May 1939; TNA, WO 208/721, HKIR No. 15/39 by Edwards, 18 July 1939, HKIR No. 17/39 by Edwards, 15 August 1939, HKIR No. 18/39 by Edwards, 30 August 1939, and HKIR No. 24/39 by Giles, 21 November 1939; UCC, accession 83.046C, box 3, file 63, BOMSC, Thomson to Armstrong, 17 November 1939; and Peter Moreira, *Hemingway on the China Front: His WWII Spy Mission with Martha Gellhorn* (Washington, DC: Potomac Books, 2006), 46–47.

64. IWM, Conservation Shelf, "Thunder in the East" by Grimsdale, 18–19. See also TNA, FO 371/23513 F 1597/1597/10, report by Governor Sir Geoffry Northcote, 16 January 1939; TNA, WO 106/5356, HKIR No. 1/39 by Edwards, 3 January 1939, and HKIR No. 5/39 by Edwards, 28 February 1939; and TNA, WO 208/721, HKIR No. 16/39 by Edwards, 1 August 1939.

65. NARA, RG 165, *USMIR*, reel 13, Report No. 350.05-General by McLean, 14 October 1939; TNA, WO 208/721, HKIR No. 18/39 by Edwards, 30 August 1939, HKIR No. 19/39 by Edwards, 12 September 1939, HKIR No. 20/39 by Edwards, 26 September 1939, HKIR No. 21/39 by Edwards, 10 October 1939, and HKIR No. 22/39 by Giles, 23 October 1939.

66. TNA, WO 208/721, HKIR No. 21/39 by Edwards, 10 October 1939.

67. TNA, WO 208/721, HKIR No. 19/39 by Edwards, 12 September 1939. See also Tsunoda, "Navy's Role in the Southern Strategy," 242–243.

68. Hosoya Chihiro, "The Japanese-Soviet Neutrality Pact," trans. Robert Scalapino, in Morley, *Fateful Choice*, 23.

69. NARA, RG 38, M975, reel 2, Estimate of Potential Military Strength Documents G, vol. 2, Report No. 189, 5 September 1939. See also TNA, FO 371/23514 F 9512/1696/10, Admiralty Telegram No. 1814/25, 24 August 1939; TNA, FO 371/23514 F 9739/1696/10, Telegram No. 160 from Acting Consul General Gerald Tyler to Governor Sir Geoffry Northcote, 22 August 1939; and TNA, WO 208/721, HKIR No. 18/39 by Edwards, 30 August 1939.

70. NARA, RG 165, M1444, reel 11, Report No. 9793 by Sutherland, 8 September 1939; NARA, RG 165, M1513, reel 40, Report No. 9895 by Captain Eric Svensson, 12 September 1939; TNA, FO 371/23514 F 9087/1696/10, telegram from Major General

A. E. Grasett to War Office, 16 August 1939; TNA, FO 371/23514 F 9467/1696/10, Telegram No. 954 from Ambassador Archibald Clark Kerr, 28 August 1939; TNA, FO 371/23514 F 9507/1696/10, telegram, 26 August 1939; TNA, WO 208/721, HKIR No. 18/39 by Edwards, 30 August 1939.

71. TNA, WO 208/721, HKIR No. 18/39 by Edwards, 30 August 1939. See also TNA, WO 208/721, HKIR No. 19/39 by Edwards, 12 September 1939; and UCC, accession 83.046C, box 3, file 63, BOMSC, Thomson to Arnup, 7 September 1939.

72. NARA, RG 165, M1444, reel 11, Report No. 9793 by Sutherland, 8 September 1939.

73. TNA, WO 208/721, HKIR No. 18/39 by Edwards, 30 August 1939.

74. Ibid.

75. NARA, RG 165, M1513, reel 40, Report No. 70, 27 November 1939; TNA, WO 208/721, HKIR No. 20/39 by Edwards, 26 September 1939, HKIR No. 21/39 by Edwards, 10 October 1939, and HKIR No. 22/39 by Giles, 23 October 1939.

76. NARA, RG 165, M1444, reel 11, Report No. 9808 by Munson, 26 October 1939; TNA, FO 371/23514 F 10769/1696/10, telegram, 2 October 1939. See also Boyle, China and Japan at War, 257–258, and Usui Katsumi, "The Politics of War," in Japan's Road to the Pacific War: The China Quagmire: Japan's Expansion on the Asian Continent, 1933–1941, ed. James Morley and David Lu (New York: Columbia University Press, 1983), 388–389.

77. NARA, RG 165, M1444, reel 11, Report No. 9808 by Munson, 26 October 1939; TNA, FO 371/23514 F 10769/1696/10, telegram, 2 October 1939; TNA, WO 208/721, HKIR No. 21/39 by Edwards, 10 October 1939.

78. NARA, RG 165, M1444, reel 11, Report No. 9793 by Sutherland, 8 September 1939, and Report No. 9799 by Sutherland, 29 September 1939. See also TNA, FO 371/23514 F 9467/1696/10, Telegram No. 954 by Clark Kerr, 28 August 1939; TNA, WO 208/721, HKIR No. 17/39 by Edwards, 15 August 1939, HKIR No. 18/39 by Edwards, 30 August 1939, HKIR No. 20/39 by Edwards, 26 September 1939, HKIR No. 22/39 by Giles, 23 October 1939, and HKIR No. 26/39 by Giles, 19 December 1939; Boyle, China and Japan at War, 258; Hosoya, "Japanese-Soviet Neutrality Pact," 18, 23–24; and Peter Lowe, Great Britain and the Origins of the Pacific War: A Study of British Policy in East Asia, 1937–1941 (Oxford: Clarendon Press, 1977), 100–102.

79. NARA, RG 165, entry 77 NM 84, box 1738, Military Intelligence Division Regional File: Islands, Hong Kong, report by Vice Consul John Pool, 15 July 1939; NARA, RG 165, USMIR, reel 13, Report No. 350.05-General by McLean, 14 October 1939. See also TNA, FO 371/23520 F 6814/3918/10, Telegram No. 5233 by Lieutenant General A. E. Grasett, 7 July 1939; TNA, FO 371/23520 F 12784/3661/10, file cover notation by A. L. Scott, 20 December 1939; Peter Elphick, Far Eastern File: The Intelligence War in the Far East, 1930–1945 (London: Hodder and Stoughton, 1997), 69–70, 73; George Endacott, Hong Kong Eclipse (Oxford: Oxford University Press, 1978), 43; Oliver Lindsay, The Lasting Honour (London: Hamish Hamilton, 1978), 5; Anne Ozorio, "The Myth of Unpreparedness: The Origins of Anti Japanese Resistance in Prewar Hong Kong," Journal of the Royal Asiatic Society Hong Kong Branch 42 (2003): 164–165; Philip Snow, The Fall of Hong Kong: Britain, China and the Japanese Occupa-

tion (New Haven, CT: Yale University Press, 2003), 48; and Andrew Whitfield, *Hong Kong, Empire and the Anglo-American Alliance at War, 1941–45* (Hong Kong: Hong Kong University Press, 2001), 227.

80. TNA, WO 208/721, HKIR No. 13/39 by Edwards, 20 June 1939; Lowe, *Great Britain and Origins of the Pacific War*, 95–96.

81. Castel Hopkins, *The Toronto Board of Trade, a Souvenir* (Toronto: Sabiston Lithographic and Publishing, 1893), 201.

82. TRL, "Biographies of People," Scrapbook vol. 1, frame no. 481, newspaper clipping.

83. Ibid., Scrapbook vol. 7, frame no. 602, newspaper clipping, 5 July 1935.

84. Ibid., Scrapbook vol. 1, frame no. 456, newspaper clipping, 15 May 1935, and Scrapbook vol. 5, frame no. 55, newspaper clipping, 17 March 1934.

85. Ibid., Scrapbook vol. 1, frame no. 457, newspaper clipping, 24 May 1938.

86. Arthur Tunnell, *The Canadian Who's Who*, vol. 12, *1970–1972* (Toronto: Who's Who Canadian Publications, 1972), 431.

87. TRL, "Biographies of People," Scrapbook vol. 1, frame no. 457, newspaper clipping, 24 May 1938.

88. Ibid.

89. Tunnell, *Canadian Who's Who*, 431.

90. TNA, FO 371/23513 F 6050/1515/10, file cover notation, 21 June 1939.

91. Ibid.

92. TNA, FO 371/27653 F 6607/188/10, file cover notation by A. L. Scott, 25 July 1941.

93. WM, War Diary, Royal Scots, 2nd Battalion, Hong Kong, December 1941; NARA, RG 226, entry 92, box 468, file 43, OSS Central Files, OSS memorandum by Lieutenant Colonel Kenneth Baker, 2 December 1943; NARA, RG 226, entry 139, box 169, OSS Field Station Files, OSS Investigative Report No. 11596, 3 December 1943; TNA, WO 199/1287, file Hong Kong, Siege Surrender and Occupation, report by Commander H. M. Montague, 16 January 1942; HKU, BAAG series, vol. 2, "Capture, Escape and the Early BAAG," "The Early BAAG," report by Colonel Lindsay Ride, 20 August 1942. See also Baxter, "Britain and the War in China," 231–232; Vasilii Chuikov, *Mission to China: Memoirs of a Soviet Military Adviser to Chiang Kaishek*, trans. David Barrett (Norwalk, CT: EastBridge, 2004), 157; Endacott, *Hong Kong Eclipse*, 78–79, 185; Compton Mackenzie, *Eastern Epic*, vol. 1, *September 1939–March 1943, Defence* (London: Chatto and Windus, 1951), 216; and Yu Maochun, "'In God We Trusted, in China We Busted': The China Commando Group of the Special Operations Executive (SOE)," *Intelligence and National Security* 16, 4 (2001): 54–55.

94. HKU, BAAG series, vol. 2, MI9 China Report by Squadron Leader Basil Russell (GHQ India), 31 August 1942; NARA, RG 226, entry 92, box 468, file 43, OSS Central Files, OSS memorandum by Baker, 2 December 1943. See also John Mendelsohn, ed., *Covert Warfare: Intelligence, Counterintelligence, and Military Deception during the World War II Era 8: The OSS-NKVD Relationship, 1943–1945* (New York: Garland Publishing, 1989), document 11; Charles Cruickshank, *SOE in the Far East* (Oxford: Oxford University Press, 1983), 154; Hamstat On Line, http://www.mwadui.com/Hong

Kong/Kendall.htm (1996); Roy MacLaren, *Canadians behind Enemy Lines, 1939–1945* (Vancouver: UBC Press, 2004), 186–187; Robert Wilcox, *Target: Patton, the Plot to Assassinate General George S. Patton* (Washington, DC: Regnery Publishing, 2008), 137–138; and Yu, "'In God We Trusted,'" 54–55.

95. TNA, WO 193/921, file Russia and the Far East, Telegram No. 1238, 12 October 1941.

96. IWM, "Thunder in the East" by Grimsdale, 15, 19–20.

97. Ibid., 14, 19–20; TNA, WO 208/721, HKIR No. 12/39 by Edwards, 6 June 1939; Elphick, *Far Eastern File*, 78.

98. IWM, "Thunder in the East" by Grimsdale, 9; LAC, MG 26 J1, reel C-3745, vol. 271, frame no. 229773, report by Ambassador Sir Robert Craigie, 3 March 1939; NARA, RG 165, *USMIR*, reel 3, Report No. 9800 by Munson, 3 October 1939; TNA, FO 371/23511 F 5298/1497/10, Telegram No. 65 by Archer, 1 June 1939; TNA, WO 208/721, HKIR No. 15/39 by Edwards, 18 July 1939, and HKIR No. 17/39 by Edwards, 15 August 1939. See also Baxter, "Britain and the War in China," 51–53, 56; Lowe, *Great Britain and Origins of the Pacific War*, 77; and Usui Katsumi, "Politics of War," 361.

99. Lowe, *Great Britain and Origins of the Pacific War*, 83–88, 105–107; Baxter, "Britain and the War in China," 43–44.

100. TNA, FO 371/23403 F 8061/1/10, file cover notation by Nigel Ronald, 15 August 1939.

101. TNA, WO 208/721, HKIR No. 17/39 by Edwards, 15 August 1939.

102. LAC, RG 25, vol. 4723, file 50056-40 pt. I, Telegram No. 211 by Ambassador Victor Odlum, 21 April 1944; TNA, FO 371/23520 F 10531/3661/10, telegram from Governor Sir Geoffry Northcote to Colonial Secretary Malcolm Macdonald, 26 September 1939; TNA, FO 371/23520 F 10793/3661/10, Telegram No. 332 from Northcote to Macdonald, 4 October 1939; TNA, FO 371/23520 F 11499/3661/10, telegram from Northcote to Macdonald, 13 October 1939; TNA, FO 371/23520 F 11173/3661/10, file cover notation, 23 October 1939; TNA, FO 371/23520 F 11499/3661/10, telegram from W. Donald to Witham, 28 September 1939; TNA, FO 371/23520 F 11499/3661/10, file cover notation, 7 November 1939; TNA, FO 371/23520 F 12017/3661/10, telegram from Northcote to Clark Kerr, 16 October 1939; TNA, FO 371/23520 F 12864/3661/10, telegram from Northcote to G. E. Gent, 24 November 1939; TNA, FO 371/27715 F 4787/3653/10, report by Ian Morrison on situation in China, 3 June 1941; TNA, WO 106/5356, HKIR No. 5/39 by Edwards, 28 February 1939.

103. TNA, FO 371/23520 F 11499/3661/10, telegram from W. Donald to Witham, 28 September 1939. See also TNA, FO 371/23520 F 12052/3661/10, Telegram No. 1275 by Clark Kerr, 21 November 1939; and TNA, FO 371/23520 F 12784/3661/10, file cover notation by A. L. Scott, 20 December 1939.

104. TNA, FO 371/23520 F 12784/3661/10, file cover notation by Scott, 20 December 1939.

105. Boyle, *China and Japan at War*, 251.

106. Peter Clarke, *The Cripps Version: The Life of Sir Stafford Cripps, 1889–1952* (London: Penguin, Allen Lane, 2002), 154.

107. Donald Gillies, *Radical Diplomat: The Life of Archibald Clark Kerr, Lord Inverchapel, 1882–1951* (London: I. B. Tauris, 1999), 126.

108. Keeble, *Britain, the Soviet Union and Russia*, 153–155.

109. Yu, *Dragon's War*, 48.

110. IWM, "Thunder in the East" by Grimsdale, 13; NARA, RG 165, *USMIR*, reel 3, Report No. 9830 by Mayer, 29 November 1939. See also Baxter, "Britain and the War in China," 90–93, and Frank Welsh, *A History of Hong Kong* (London: HarperCollins, 1993), 409–410.

111. TNA, WO 208/849, file Peace Overtures to China, memorandum, 25 September 1939.

112. Lowe, *Great Britain and Origins of the Pacific War*, 108–109.

113. NARA, RG 165, M1444, reel 11, Report No. 9784 by Sutherland, 14 July 1939, Report No. 9793 by Sutherland, 8 September 1939, and Report No. 9788 by Sutherland, 12 August 1939; NARA, RG 165, *USMIR*, reel 3, Report No. 9800 by Munson, 3 October 1939. See also TNA, WO 208/721, HKIR No. 16/39 by Edwards, 1 August 1939, HKIR No. 17/39 by Edwards, 15 August 1939, and HKIR No. 22/39 by Giles, 23 October 1939; Gole, *Road to Rainbow*, 14, 97; Lowe, *Great Britain and Origins of the Pacific War*, 97–98; and Jonathan Utley, *Going to War with Japan, 1937–1941* (Knoxville: University of Tennessee Press, 1985), 84–86.

114. NARA, RG 165, M1444, reel 11, Report No. 9808 by Munson, 26 October 1939; NARA, RG 165, M1444, reel 15, Report No. 7258 by First Lieutenant Helmar W. Lystad, 25 April 1928, and Report No. 9130 by Lieutenant Colonel W. S. Drysdale, 4 June 1935; NARA, RG 165, M1513, reel 38, report by Lieutenant Colonel Henry McLean, 25 October 1939; NARA, RG 165, M1513, reel 39, report, "First Battle of Changsha, Sept.–Oct., 1939," n.d.; NARA, RG 165, M1513, reel 57, telegram, 28 September 1941. See also TNA, WO 208/721, HKIR No. 16/39 by Edwards, 1 August 1939, and HKIR No. 21/39 by Edwards, 10 October 1939; and Edward Drea, *Japan's Imperial Army: Its Rise and Fall, 1853–1945* (Lawrence: University Press of Kansas, 2009), 207.

115. NARA, RG 165, M1513, reel 39, Report No. 9762 by Count, 10 April 1939; TNA, WO 106/5356, HKIR No. 8/39 by Edwards, 11 April 1939, and HKIR No. 10/39 by Edwards, 9 May 1939.

116. NARA, RG 165, M1444, reel 11, Report No. 9799 by Sutherland, 29 September 1939; TNA, WO 106/5303, No. 290, report by Wards, 11 March 1939, and No. 293, Report on Visit to South China July 1938 by Captain J. V. Davidson-Houston, 5 August 1938. See also TNA, WO 208/721, HKIR No. 20/39 by Edwards, 26 September 1939; TNA, WO 106/5356, HKIR No. 24/38 by Sturgeon, 22 November 1938; and Van de Ven, *War and Nationalism in China*, 228–229.

117. TNA, WO 106/5303, No. 289, Report on Visit to IV War Zone by Boxer and Chauvin, 20 May 1939.

118. NARA, RG 165, M1444, reel 11, Report No. 9784 by Sutherland, 14 July 1939, Report No. 9799 by Sutherland, 29 September 1939, and Report No. 9808 by Munson, 26 October 1939. See also TNA, WO 208/721, HKIR No. 21/39 by Edwards, 10 October 1939, and HKIR No. 22/39 by Giles, 23 October 1939; and Roy Stanley, *Prelude to Pearl Harbor* (New York: Charles Scribner's Sons, 1982), 123.

119. NARA, RG 165, M1513, reel 39, report, "First Battle of Changsha," October 1939. See also Stanley, *Prelude to Pearl Harbor*, 123.

120. NARA, RG 165, M1444, reel 11, Report No. 9808 by Munson, 26 October 1939; NARA, RG 165, M1513, reel 39, Report No. 9762 by Count, 10 April 1939; Van de Ven, *War and Nationalism in China*, 235, 237.

121. TNA, WO 208/721, HKIR No. 26/39 by Giles, 19 December 1939.

122. LOC, Japanese Monographs, "Japanese Monograph No. 71, Area Operations in China, December 1941–December 1943" by Heizo Ishiwari, 1963; LAC, RG 25, vol. 3233, file 5548-40C, report, "Changsha" by Ralph E. Collins, 8 June 1944. See also *New York Times*, 30 December 1941, 5; article by Robert Payne, *Times*, 1 January 1942, 3; and Richard E. Webb, "The War in China," *Far Eastern Survey* 11, 4 (1942): 49–50.

123. NARA, RG 165, M1444, reel 11, Report No. 9799 by Sutherland, 29 September 1939; TNA, WO 208/721, HKIR No. 20/39 by Edwards, 26 September 1939; TNA, WO 208/849, file Peace Overtures to China, memorandum, 25 September 1939. See also Chang Jung and Jon Halliday, *Mao: The Unknown Story* (London: Vintage Books, 2006), 268–270.

124. NARA, RG 165, *USMIR*, reel 3, Report No. 9810 by Colonel William Mayer, 1 November 1939.

125. TNA, WO 106/5356, HKIR No. 9/39 by Edwards, 25 April 1939; Van de Ven, *War and Nationalism in China*, 238.

126. TNA, WO 208/721, HKIR No. 21/39 by Edwards, 10 October 1939.

127. NARA, RG 165, *USMIR*, reel 3, Report No. 9810 by Mayer, 1 November 1939.

128. TNA, WO 208/721, HKIR No. 22/39 by Giles, 23 October 1939.

129. UCC, accession 83.046C, box 3, file 63, BOMSC, Thomson to Arnup, 18 October 1939.

130. Boyle, *China and Japan at War*, 270.

131. NARA, RG 165, M1444, reel 11, Report No. 9808 by Munson, 26 October 1939; TNA, WO 208/721, HKIR No. 22/39 by Giles, 23 October 1939, and HKIR No. 25/39 by Giles, 5 December 1939.

132. NARA, RG 165, M1444, reel 11, Report No. 9768 by Munson, 5 May 1939, Report No. 9788 by Sutherland, 12 August 1939, Report No. 9793 by Sutherland, 8 September 1939, and Report No. 9799 by Sutherland, 29 September 1939. See also TNA, WO 208/721, HKIR No. 15/39 by Edwards, 18 July 1939, HKIR No. 19/39 by Edwards, 12 September 1939, and HKIR No. 22/39 by Giles, 23 October 1939.

133. NARA, RG 165, M1444, reel 11, Report No. 9793 by Sutherland, 8 September 1939. See also TNA, WO 106/5356, HKIR No. 8/39 by Edwards, 11 April 1939, and HKIR No. 9/39 by Edwards, 25 April 1939.

134. TNA, WO 208/721, HKIR No. 19/39 by Edwards, 12 September 1939.

135. NARA, RG 38, entry 98A, box 705, F-6-c 23213 to F-6-e 22379, Report No. 1083-45, 12 March 1945; NARA, RG 165, M1444, reel 11, Report No. 9768 by Munson, 5 May 1939, and Report No. 9793 by Sutherland, 8 September 1939. See also TNA, WO 106/5356, HKIR No. 9/39 by Edwards, 25 April 1939; and TNA, WO 208/

721, HKIR No. 16/39 by Edwards, 1 August 1939, HKIR No. 17/39 by Edwards, 15 August 1939, HKIR No. 18/39 by Edwards, 30 August 1939, and HKIR No. 19/39 by Edwards, 12 September 1939.

136. TNA, WO 208/721, HKIR No. 15/39 by Edwards, 18 July 1939. See also Boyle, *China and Japan at War*, 227.

137. LAC, RG 25, vol. 1866, file 226-B pt. 1, Telegram No. 201 by Consul General H. Prideaux-Brune, 13 September 1939; NARA, RG 165, M1444, reel 11, Report No. 9788 by Sutherland, 12 August 1939, Report No. 9793 by Sutherland, 8 September 1939, and Report No. 9799 by Sutherland, 29 September 1939; NARA, RG 165, M1513, reel 40, report, 22 July 1939. See also TNA, WO 208/721, HKIR No. 16/39 by Edwards, 1 August 1939, HKIR No. 17/39 by Edwards, 15 August 1939, and HKIR No. 21/39 by Edwards, 10 October 1939.

138. TNA, WO 106/5356, HKIR No. 9/39 by Edwards, 25 April 1939.

139. NARA, RG 165, *USMIR*, reel 3, Report No. 7 by Major David Barrett, 22 July 1940.

Chapter 6. Impasse in Kwangsi and Japan's Failed Interdiction Strategy against Hong Kong

1. NARA, RG 165, M1513, The Military Intelligence Division Regional File Relating to China, 1922–1944, reel 40, Report No. 9962 by Captain Eric H. F. Svenssen, 20 November 1939. See also Hosoya Chihiro, "The Japanese-Soviet Neutrality Pact," trans. Robert Scalapino, in *The Fateful Choice: Japan's Road to the Pacific War: Japan's Advance into Southeast Asia, 1939–1941*, ed. James Morley (New York: Columbia University Press, 1980), 33; and Usui Katsumi, "The Politics of War," in *Japan's Road to the Pacific War: The China Quagmire: Japan's Expansion on the Asian Continent, 1933–1941*, ed. James Morley and David Lu (New York: Columbia University Press, 1983), 407.

2. Hata Ikuhiko, "The Army's Move into Northern Indochina," in Morley, *Fateful Choice*, 169.

3. Ibid., 156–158. See also NARA, RG 165, M1444, Correspondence of the Military Intelligence Division Relating to General, Political, Economic, and Military Conditions in China, 1918–1941, reel 11, Report No. 9799 by Captain Edwin M. Sutherland, 29 September 1939; NARA, RG 165, M1513, reel 40, Report No. 9962 by Svenssen, 20 November 1939; and TNA, WO 208/721, HKIR No. 22/39 by Captain R. Giles, 23 October 1939.

4. NARA, RG 165, M1444, reel 11, Report No. 9829 by Captain F. P. Munson, 29 November 1939; NARA, RG 165, M1513, reel 40, Report No. 70, 27 November 1939; NARA, RG 165, *USMIR*, reel 3, Report No. 9830 by Colonel William Mayer, 29 November 1939. See also TNA, WO 208/721, HKIR No. 24/39 by Giles, 21 November 1939, and HKIR No. 25/39 by Giles, 5 December 1939.

5. NARA, RG 165, M1444, reel 11, Report No. 9829 by Munson, 29 November 1939; NARA, RG 165, *USMIR*, reel 3, Report No. 9830 by Mayer, 29 November 1939. See also TNA, WO 208/721, HKIR No. 24/39 by Giles, 21 November 1939, and HKIR No. 25/39 by Giles, 5 December 1939.

6. NARA, RG 165, M1444, reel 11, Report No. 9829 by Munson, 29 November 1939, and Report No. 9842 by Munson, 11 January 1940; NARA, RG 165, *USMIR*, reel 3, Report No. 9830 by Mayer, 29 November 1939. See also TNA, WO 208/721, HKIR No. 25/39 by Giles, 5 December 1939, and HKIR No. 3/40 by Giles, 29 February 1940.

7. NARA, RG 59, M1221, OSS Research and Analysis Report No. 112, July 1942; NARA, RG 165, *USMIR*, reel 3, Report No. 9830 by Mayer, 29 November 1939. See also TNA, WO 208/721, HKIR No. 25/39 by Giles, 5 December 1939, HKIR No. 26/39 by Giles, 19 December 1939, and HKIR No. 3/40 by Giles, 29 February 1940.

8. TNA, WO 208/721, HKIR No. 25/39 by Giles, 5 December 1939.

9. NARA, RG 165, M1444, reel 11, Report No. 9856 by Captain Earl Mattice, 6 March 1940.

10. NARA, RG 165, M1444, reel 11, Report No. 9829 by Munson, 29 November 1939, Report No. 9856 by Mattice, 6 March 1940, and Report No. 9873 by Mattice, 1 May 1940. See also TNA, WO 208/721, HKIR No. 24/39 by Giles, 21 November 1939, HKIR No. 25/39 by Giles, 5 December 1939, and HKIR No. 26/39 by Giles, 19 December 1939; and TNA, WO 208/722, HKIR No. 7/40 by Giles, 30 June 1940.

11. NARA, RG 165, M1444, reel 11, Report No. 9842 by Munson, 11 January 1940, and Report No. 9849 by Mattice, 3 February 1940. See also TNA, WO 208/721, HKIR No. 26/39 by Giles, 19 December 1939; TNA, WO 208/722, HKIR No. 1/40 by Giles, 2 January 1940; and Hans Van de Ven, *War and Nationalism in China, 1925–1945* (London: RoutledgeCurzon, 2003), 242, 246.

12. TNA, WO 208/722, HKIR No. 2/40 by Giles, 31 January 1940. See also Chiang Wego, *How Generalissimo Chiang Kai-Shek Won the Eight-Year Sino-Japanese War, 1937–1945* (Taipei: Li Ming Culture Enterprise Co., 1979), 132–133.

13. TNA, WO 208/722, HKIR No. 3/40 by Giles, 29 February 1940.

14. NARA, RG 165, M1444, reel 11, Report No. 9842 by Munson, 11 January 1940, and Report No. 9856 by Munson, 6 March 1940; TNA, WO 208/722, HKIR No. 2/40 by Giles, 31 January 1940, HKIR No. 3/40 by Giles, 29 February 1940, and HKIR No. 4/40 by Giles, 31 March 1940; UCC, accession 83.046C, box 3, file 63, BOMSC, letter from Dr. J. Oscar Thomson to Reverend A. E. Armstrong, 17 November 1939. See also Troy L. Perkins, Telegram No. 18, in *FRUS 1940*, vol. 4, *The Far East*, 268.

15. NARA, RG 165, M1444, reel 11, Report No. 9849 by Mattice, 3 February 1940; TNA, WO 208/722, HKIR No. 2/40 by Giles, 31 January 1940, and HKIR No. 3/40 by Giles, 29 February 1940.

16. NARA, RG 165, M1444, reel 11, Report No. 9849 by Mattice, 3 February 1940, and Report No. 9856 by Munson, 6 March 1940; TNA, WO 208/722, HKIR No. 2/40 by Giles, 31 January 1940, and HKIR No. 7/40 by Giles, 30 June 1940.

17. NARA, RG 165, M1444, reel 11, Report No. 9849 by Mattice, 3 February 1940.

18. NARA, RG 165, M1444, reel 11, Report No. 9856 by Munson, 6 March 1940; TNA, WO 208/722, HKIR No. 3/40 by Giles, 29 February 1940.

19. NARA, RG 165, M1444, reel 11, Report No. 9856 by Munson, 6 March 1940. See also TNA, WO 208/722, HKIR No. 3/40 by Giles, 29 February 1940.

20. NARA, RG 38, entry 98A, box 705, F-6-c 23213 to F-6-e 22379, Report No. 1085-45, 12 March 1945; NARA, RG 165, M1444, reel 11, Report No. 9856 by Munson, 6 March 1940, Report No. 9862 by Mattice, 3 April 1940, and Report No. 9873 by Mattice, 1 May 1940; TNA, WO 208/721, HKIR No. 21/39 by Edwards, 10 October 1939; TNA, WO 208/722, HKIR No. 3/40 by Giles, 29 February 1940, HKIR No. 4/40 by Giles, 31 March 1940, HKIR No. 5/40 by Giles, 30 April 1940, and HKIR No. 11/40 by Giles, 31 October 1940. See also Hata, "Army's Move into Northern Indochina," 168.

21. NARA, RG 165, M1444, reel 11, Report No. 9849 by Mattice, 3 February 1940, and Report No. 9856 by Munson, 6 March 1940; NARA, RG 165, M1513, reel 40, Report No. 9995 by Svenssen, 20 November 1939. See also TNA, WO 208/722, HKIR No. 3/40 by Giles, 29 February 1940; and Ambassador William C. Bullitt, telegram, 15 January 1940, in *FRUS 1940*, vol. 4, *The Far East*, 263.

22. NARA, RG 165, M1444, reel 11, Report No. 9849 by Mattice, 3 February 1940.

23. NARA, RG 165, *USMIR*, reel 3, Report No. 9844 by Mayer, 11 January 1940. See also TNA, WO 208/722, HKIR No. 3/40 by Giles, 29 February 1940.

24. NARA, RG 165, *USMIR*, reel 3, Report No. 3 by Major David Barrett, 1 March 1940.

25. TNA, WO 208/722, HKIR No. 3/40 by Giles, 29 February 1940.

26. NARA, RG 165, *USMIR*, reel 3, Report No. 3 by Barrett, 1 March 1940; TNA, WO 208/722, HKIR No. 1/40 by Giles, 2 January 1940, HKIR No. 3/40 by Giles, 29 February 1940, HKIR No. 4/40 by Giles, 31 March 1940, and HKIR No. 5/40 by Giles, 30 April 1940. See also Ambassador Joseph Grew, telegram, 6 January 1940, in *FRUS 1940*, vol. 4, *The Far East*, 258; and Jonathan Utley, *Going to War with Japan, 1937–1941* (Knoxville: University of Tennessee Press, 1985), 80.

27. NARA, RG 165, *USMIR*, reel 3, report by Barrett, 20 April 1940; TNA, WO 208/722, HKIR No. 1/40 by Giles, 2 January 1940.

28. NARA, RG 59, *USSDCF*, reel 25, Report No. 893.20/714 by Krentz, 16 May 1940; NARA, RG 165, M1444, reel 11, Report No. 9849 by Mattice, 3 February 1940, and Report No. 9856 by Munson, 6 March 1940. See also NARA, RG 493, entry 531, box 51, Z Force Operations, Adjutant General, General Correspondence, Decimal File, memorandum by Brigadier General Malcolm F. Lindsey, 12 June 1944; and TNA, WO 208/722, HKIR No. 11/40 by Giles, 31 October 1940.

29. NARA, RG 165, *USMIR*, reel 3, Report No. 2 by Barrett, 2 February 1940.

30. Kurt Bloch, "China's Lifelines and the Indo-China Frontier," *Far Eastern Survey* 9, 4 (1940): 48.

31. TNA, WO 208/722, HKIR No. 1/40 by Giles, 2 January 1940, and HKIR No. 2/40 by Giles, 31 January 1940.

32. TNA, WO 208/722, HKIR No. 1/40 by Giles, 2 January 1940.

33. LAC, RG 24, vol. 20538, file 982.013 (D5), Historical Bulletin No. 249, History of the 38th Japanese Division; NARA, RG 165, M1444, reel 11, Report No. 9842 by Munson, 11 January 1940. See also TNA, WO 208/721, HKIR No. 24/39 by Giles, 21 November 1939; and TNA, WO 208/722, HKIR No. 2/40 by Giles, 31 January 1940, and HKIR No. 3/40 by Giles, 29 February 1940.

34. TNA, WO 208/722, HKIR No. 1/40 by Giles, 2 January 1940. See also TNA, WO 208/722, HKIR No. 2/40 by Giles, 31 January 1940, and HKIR No. 3/40 by Giles, 29 February 1940; and Peter Moreira, *Hemingway on the China Front: His WWII Spy Mission with Martha Gellhorn* (Washington, DC: Potomac Books, 2006), 87.

35. UCC, accession 83.046C, box 3, file 63, BOMSC, letter from Dr. J. Oscar Thomson to Reverend A. E. Armstrong, 14 December 1939.

36. NARA, RG 165, M1444, reel 11, Report No. 9842 by Munson, 11 January 1940, and Report No. 9849 by Mattice, 3 February 1940; TNA, WO 208/722, HKIR No. 1/40 by Giles, 2 January 1940, and HKIR No. 2/40 by Giles, 31 January 1940.

37. NARA, RG 165, M1444, reel 11, Report No. 9842 by Munson, 11 January 1940, and Report No. 9849 by Mattice, 3 February 1940; TNA, WO 208/722, HKIR No. 2/40 by Giles, 31 January 1940.

38. NARA, RG 165, M1444, reel 11, Report No. 9849 by Mattice, 3 February 1940. See also TNA, WO 208/722, HKIR No. 2/40 by Giles, 31 January 1940.

39. TNA, WO 208/722, HKIR No. 1/40 by Giles, 2 January 1940, HKIR No. 2/40 by Giles, 31 January 1940, and HKIR No. 5/40 by Giles, 30 April 1940.

40. TNA, WO 208/721, HKIR No. 26/39 by Giles, 19 December 1939; TNA, WO 208/722, HKIR No. 1/40 by Giles, 2 January 1940, and HKIR No. 2/40 by Giles, 31 January 1940.

41. TNA, WO 208/721, HKIR No. 22/39 by Giles, 23 October 1939, HKIR No. 24/39 by Giles, 21 November 1939, and HKIR No. 26/39 by Giles, 19 December 1939; TNA, WO 208/722, HKIR No. 1/40 by Giles, 2 January 1940, HKIR No. 2/40 by Giles, 31 January 1940, and HKIR No. 3/40 by Giles, 29 February 1940.

42. TNA, WO 208/721, HKIR No. 26/39 by Giles, 19 December 1939; TNA, WO 208/722, HKIR No. 3/40 by Giles, 29 February 1940, HKIR No. 4/40 by Giles, 31 March 1940, and HKIR No. 7/40 by Giles, 30 June 1940. See also UCC, accession 83.046C, box 3, file 63, BOMSC, letter from Thomson to Armstrong, 14 December 1939; UCC, accession 83.046C, box 4, file 65, BOMSC, letter from Reverend Duncan McRae to Dr. A. E. Armstrong, 24 February 1940, letter from Mrs. D. McRae to Jessie Arnup, 1 April 1940, and letter from Reverend Duncan McRae to Jessie Arnup, 17 April 1940; and UCC, accession 83.046C, box 4, file 66, BOMSC, letter from Reverend Tom Broadfoot to Jessie Arnup, 12 February 1940.

43. NARA, RG 165, *USMIR*, reel 3, Report No. 9866 by Munson, 4 April 1940; TNA, WO 208/722, HKIR No. 4/40 by Giles, 31 March 1940, and HKIR No. 5/40 by Giles, 30 April 1940; UCC, accession 83.046C, box 4, file 65, BOMSC, letter from Mrs. McRae to Arnup, 1 April 1940.

44. NARA, RG 38, entry 98A, box 705, F-6-c 23213 to F-6-e 22379, Report No. 128-40 by Lieutenant Commander D. J. McCallum, 3 September 1940; NARA, RG 38, entry 98A, box 705, Intelligence Division, Confidential Reports of Naval Attaches, 1940–1946, F-6-c 23213 to F-6-e 22379, "Southward Advance of the Japanese Navy"; NARA, RG 59, *USSDCF*, LM 183, reel 25, Report No. 893.1562/8 by Consul General M. Myers, 21 May 1940. See also TNA, FO 371/27636 F 1254/144/10, Canton Political Report—December Quarter, 1940 by Consul General A. P. Blunt, 31 December 1940; TNA, FO 371/27699 F 869/849/10, China Summary No. 11 by P. M. Broad-

mead, 14 February 1941; TNA, WO 208/721, HKIR No. 26/39 by Giles, 19 December 1939; TNA, WO 208/722, HKIR No. 5/40 by Giles, 30 April 1940; UCC, accession 83.046C, box 4, file 66, BOMSC, letter from Broadfoot to Arnup, 19 October 1940, and letter from Broadfoot to Arnup, 30 November 1940; Martin H. Brice, *The Royal Navy and the Sino-Japanese Incident, 1937–41* (London: Ian Allan, 1973), 139–140, 145; and Oliver Lindsay, *The Lasting Honour* (London: Hamish Hamilton, 1978), 3.

45. LAC, MG 26 J1, reel C-4574, vol. 295, no. 249963, Dominions Office Telegram No. B-16, 23 January 1940. See also TNA, WO 208/722, HKIR No. 1/40 by Giles, 2 January 1940, HKIR No. 3/40 by Giles, 29 February 1940, and HKIR No. 5/40 by Giles, 30 April 1940; Brice, *Royal Navy and Sino-Japanese Incident*, 141; and Sir Llewellyn Woodward, *British Foreign Policy in the Second World War*, vol. 2 (London: Her Majesty's Stationery Office, 1971), 89.

46. TNA, WO 208/722, HKIR No. 2/40 by Giles, 31 January 1940, HKIR No. 4/40 by Giles, 31 March 1940, HKIR No. 5/40 by Giles, 30 April 1940, and HKIR No. 6/40 by Giles, 31 May 1940.

47. NARA, RG 165, M1444, reel 11, Report No. 9873 by Mattice, 1 May 1940; NARA, RG 165, *USMIR*, reel 11, Report No. 9901 by Mayer, 10 June 1940. See also TNA, WO 208/722, HKIR No. 4/40 by Giles, 31 March 1940, HKIR No. 5/40 by Giles, 30 April 1940, and HKIR No. 6/40 by Giles, 31 May 1940; and UCC, accession 83.046C, box 4, file 68, BOMSC, letter from Thomson to Arnup, 9 May 1940.

48. TNA, WO 208/722, HKIR No. 2/40 by Giles, 31 January 1940, HKIR No. 4/40 by Giles, 31 March 1940, and HKIR No. 5/40 by Giles, 30 April 1940.

49. TNA, WO 208/721, HKIR No. 25/39 by Giles, 5 December 1939, and HKIR No. 26/39 by Giles, 19 December 1939; TNA, WO 208/722, HKIR No. 4/40 by Giles, 31 March 1940, and HKIR No. 8/40 by Giles, 31 July 1940; UCC, accession 83.046C, box 4, file 65, BOMSC, letter from McRae to Arnup, 17 April 1940.

50. NARA, RG 165, *USMIR*, reel 3, Report No. 10 by Barrett, 3 November 1940; TNA, WO 208/722, HKIR No. 2/40 by Giles, 31 January 1940, HKIR No. 5/40 by Giles, 30 April 1940, HKIR No. 6/40 by Giles, 31 May 1940, and HKIR No. 10/40 by Giles, 30 September 1940. See also UCC, accession 83.046C, box 4, file 66, BOMSC, letter from Broadfoot to Arnup, 12 February 1940; and UCC, accession 83.046C, box 4, file 68, BOMSC, letter from Thomson to Arnup, 12 February 1940, letter from Thomson to Arnup, 4 March 1940, letter from Thomson to Arnup, 27 May 1940, and letter from Thomson to Arnup, 1 October 1940.

51. NARA, RG 165, *USMIR*, reel 11, Report No. 9919 by Munson, 30 July 1940; TNA, FO 371/27623 F 110/110/10, Telegram No. 121 by Consul Ronald Hall, 14 November 1940.

52. NARA, RG 165, M1513, reel 58, report by Major K. K. Lau, 14 March 1944; NARA, RG 226, entry 140, box 54, "East River Dispatch, February 17th"; NARA, RG 226, entry 140, box 54, East River Column News Bulletin, vol. 3, no. 7, 24 March 1946; NARA, RG 226, entry 140, box 54, OSS Field Station Files, Kunming, East River Column News Bulletin, vol. 3, no. 7, 24 March 1946; HKU, BAAG series, vol. 4, "Advance Headquarters, Waichow, Field Operations Group," report, "The Hong Kong Guerillas: Background" by Major Ronnie Holmes, 12 July 1944.

53. Ibid.

54. TNA, WO 208/722, HKIR No. 4/40 by Giles, 31 March 1940.

Chapter 7. Leveraging War and Peace

1. David Marples, *Motherland: Russia in the 20th Century* (London: Pearson Education, 2002), 143. See also R. Craig Nation, *Black Earth, Red Star: A History of Soviet Security Policy, 1917–1991* (Ithaca, NY: Cornell University Press, 1992), 98, 105.

2. John Charmley, *Churchill: The End of Glory* (London: Hodder and Stoughton, 1993), 429–430. See also R. C. Raack, *Stalin's Drive to the West, 1938–1945: The Origins of the Cold War* (Stanford, CA: Stanford University Press, 1995), 21–22.

3. NARA, RG 165, M1513, The Military Intelligence Division Regional File Relating to China, 1922–1944, reel 54, Telegram No. 41 by Ambassador Nelson T. Johnson, 24 January 1941. See also David Evans and Mark Peattie, *Kaigun: Strategy, Tactics, and Technology in the Imperial Japanese Navy, 1887–1941* (Annapolis, MD: Naval Institute Press, 1997), 452–453, and Douglas Ford, *Britain's Secret War against Japan, 1937–1945* (New York: Routledge, 2006), 21.

4. Sir B. H. Liddell Hart, *The German Generals Talk* (London: Quill, 1979), 134–136.

5. Patrick Buchanan, *Churchill, Hitler, and the Unnecessary War: How Britain Lost Its Empire and the West Lost the World* (New York: Crown Publishers, 2008), 325.

6. John Lukacs, *The Duel, 10 May–31 July 1940: The Eighty-Day Struggle between Churchill and Hitler* (New York: Ticknor and Fields, 1991), 19.

7. LAC, RG 25, reel T-1791, vol. 774, file 355, Telegram No. 31, 5 November 1939; LAC, RG 25, reel T-1795, vol. 784, file 394, telegram from Prime Minister W. L. Mackenzie King to Prime Minister Winston Churchill, 8 August 1940. See also NARA, RG 38, entry 98, box 232, file Secret Naval Intelligence Reports, German War Aims, F-6-e No. 22839-F, Report No. 17,614 by Colonel B. R. Peyton, 9 October 1940. See also David Carlton, *Churchill and the Soviet Union* (Manchester: Manchester University Press, 2000), 79, and Charmley, *Churchill*, 423.

8. Brian D. Farrell, *The Basis and Making of British Grand Strategy: Was There a Plan?* (Lewiston, NY: Edwin Mellen Press), 60. See also Paul Kennedy, *The Rise and Fall of the Great Powers: Economic Change and Military Conflict from 1500 to 2000* (New York: Random House, 1987), 319, and Bernard Porter, *Britain, Europe and the World 1850–1982: Delusions of Grandeur* (London: George Allen and Unwin, 1983), 85, 103.

9. Correlli Barnett, *The Collapse of British Power* (London: Eyre Methuen, 1972), 564. See also Paul Kennedy, *The Contradiction between British Strategic Planning and Economic Requirements in the Era of Two World Wars* (Washington, DC: International Security Studies Program, Wilson Center, 1979), 15–17; B. H. Liddell Hart, *History of the Second World War* (New York: Cassell, 1971), 141; and Porter, *Britain, Europe and the World*, 104.

10. Galen Roger Perras, "'Our Position in the Far East Would Be Stronger without This Unsatisfactory Commitment': Britain, and the Reinforcement of Hong Kong, 1941," *Canadian Journal of History* 30, 2 (1995): 242.

11. Barnett, *Collapse of British Power*, 576. See also Buchanan, *Churchill, Hitler, and the Unnecessary War*, 359–360; Lukacs, *The Duel*, 8, 138–140; Lynne Olson, *Troublesome Young Men: The Rebels Who Brought Churchill to Power and Helped Save England* (New York: Farrar Straus and Giroux, 2008), 316; and Porter, *Britain, Europe and the World*, 102.

12. Barnett, *Collapse of British Power*, 588.

13. LAC, RG 25, reel T-1791, vol. 774, file 353, memorandum from Oscar Skelton to Prime Minister Mackenzie King, 30 April 1940. See also Charmley, *Churchill*, 411, 430, and Porter, *Britain, Europe and the World*, 102.

14. LAC, MG 31, E 46, Escott Reid Papers, vol. 27, file 7, CIIA 1939–1941, letter from John Baldwin to Escott Reid, 14 September 1939, and CIIA Policy Memorandum, 18 July 1940. See also Greg Donaghy and Stephane Roussel, *Escott Reid, Diplomat and Scholar* (Montreal: McGill-Queen's University Press, 2004), 5.

15. LAC, MG 31, E 46, Escott Reid Papers, vol. 27, file 7, CIIA 1939–1941, CIIA Policy Memorandum, 18 July 1940.

16. LAC, MG 31, E 46, Escott Reid Papers, vol. 13, file U.S. and Canada 12 January 1942–16 April 1943, CIIA Policy Memorandum, 12 January 1942. See also NARA, RG 165, entry 77, box 363, MID Regional File, *Washington Post* article, "Canada Is Pleased," 8 September 1940; and A. R. M. Lower, *Canada and the Far East—1940* (New York: Institute of Pacific Relations, 1940), 109, 117–119.

17. LAC, MG 31, E 46, Escott Reid Papers, vol. 27, file 7, note by Keenleyside, 29 October 1954. See also NARA, RG 165, entry 77, box 380, Canadian-American Defence Planning Report by W. Maddox, 15 November 1941.

18. Jonathan Utley, *Going to War with Japan, 1937–1941* (Knoxville: University of Tennessee Press, 1985), 68, 85.

19. NARA, RG 165, entry 77, box 363, MID Regional File, Telegram No. 97 from Daniel Roper to Secretary of State Cordell Hull, 24 June 1939. See also Paul D. Dickson, *A Thoroughly Canadian General: A Biography of General H. D. G. Crerar* (Toronto: University of Toronto Press, 2007), 91–93, 115.

20. NARA, RG 165, entry 77, box 363, MID Regional File, Telegram No. 97 from Roper to Hull, 24 June 1939.

21. Telegram from J. Pierrepont Moffat, in *FRUS 1940*, vol. 3, *The British Commonwealth, the Soviet Union, the Near East and Africa*, 13–14.

22. John English and Norman Hillmer, "Canada's American Alliance," in *Partners Nevertheless, Canadian-American Relations in the Twentieth Century*, ed. Norman Hillmer (Mississauga, ON: Copp Clark Pitman, 1989), 34, 42. See also Jack Granatstein, "Mackenzie King and Canada at Ogdensburg, August 1940," in *Fifty Years of Canada–United States Defense Cooperation*, ed. Joseph Jockel and Joel Sokolsky (Lewiston, NY: Edwin Mellen Press, 1992), 12–13; Arthur Menzies, "Canadian Views of United States Policy towards Japan, 1945–1952," in *War and Diplomacy across the Pacific, 1919–1952*, ed. Barry D. Hunt and A. Hamish Ion (Waterloo, ON: Wilfrid Laurier University Press, 1988), 158; Brian Nolan, *King's War: Mackenzie King and the Politics of War, 1939–1945* (Toronto: Random House, 1988), 51–53; Galen R. Perras, *Franklin Roosevelt and the Origins of the Canadian-American Security Alliance,*

1933–1945: Necessary, but Not Necessary Enough (Westport, CT: Praeger, 1998), 74; and Gordon Stewart, *The American Response to Canada since 1776* (East Lansing: Michigan State University Press, 1992), 153–155.

23. Jack Granatstein, *How Britain's Weakness Forced Canada into the Arms of the United States* (Toronto: University of Toronto Press, 1989), 29; Granatstein, "Mackenzie King and Canada," 16. See also Perras, *Franklin Roosevelt and the Canadian-American Security Alliance*, 78, 82, and Maurice Pope, *Soldiers and Politicians: The Memoirs of Lt.-Gen. Maurice A. Pope* (Toronto: University of Toronto Press, 1962), 150.

24. NARA, RG 165, entry 77, box 363, MID Regional File, Council on Foreign Relations Report No. T-B 15 by Philip E. Mosely, 18 July 1940; Stanley Hornbeck, Memorandum No. 793.94/16012, in *FRUS 1940*, vol. 4, *The Far East*, 361. See also Thomas Fleming, *The New Dealers' War: Franklin D. Roosevelt and the War within World War II* (New York: Perseus Books, 2001), 77; Henry G. Gole, *The Road to Rainbow: Army Planning for Global War, 1934–1940* (Annapolis, MD: Naval Institute Press, 2003), 14; Perras, *Franklin Roosevelt and the Canadian-American Security Alliance*, 75, 85–86; and Charles P. Stacey, *Arms, Men and Governments: The War Policies of Canada, 1939–1945* (Ottawa: Department of National Defence, 1970), 328–329.

25. LAC, Diaries of William Lyon Mackenzie King, 3 July 1940, 18 August 1940, 6 February 1941, and 28 August 1941, www.collectionscanada.gc.ca/databases/king/001059-100.01-e.php. See also LAC, MG 26 J4, reel C-4288, vol. 228, no. C155079, memorandum from Oscar Skelton to Prime Minister Mackenzie King, 23 August 1939; NARA, RG 165, entry 77, box 360, MID Regional File, Memorandum No. 97 by Consul Richard Ford, 5 October 1940; F. R. Scott, "A Policy of Neutrality for Canada," *Foreign Affairs* 17, 2 (January 1939): 404, 406, 408; and Stacey, *Arms, Men and Government*, 37.

26. LAC, Diaries of William Lyon Mackenzie King, 21 August 1941. See also "Canada 'With Us to the End,'" *Times*, 5 September 1941 and 17 February 1942; R. D. Cuff and Jack Granatstein, *Ties That Bind, Canadian-American Relations in Wartime from the Great War to the Cold War* (Toronto: Samuel Stevens Hakkert, 1977), 94; and Stacey, *Arms, Men and Government*, 149, 329.

27. LAC, Diaries of William Lyon Mackenzie King, 1 December 1941. See also LAC, MG 26 J1, reel C-3693, vol. 225, no. 193983, letter from W. L. Mackenzie King to J. D. Rockefeller Jr., 13 August 1936; LAC, MG 26 J1, reel C-3742, vol. 265, no. 225178, letter from W. L. Mackenzie King to Loring Christie, 13 January 1940; LAC, MG 26 J1, reel C-3748, vol. 277, no. 234225, letter from J. D. Rockefeller Jr. to W. L. Mackenzie King, 19 October 1939; LAC, MG 26 J1, reel C-6805, vol. 308, no. 273232, letter from David Carnegie to W. L. Mackenzie King, 24 November 1942; LAC, MG 26 J1, reel C-7046, vol. 353, no. 306670, letter from Major General George Vanier to W. L. Mackenzie King, 13 December 1943; LAC, MG 26 J1, reel C-9176, vol. 413, no. 373199, letter from W. L. Mackenzie King to J. D. Rockefeller Jr., 4 January 1946; Nolan, *King's War*, 6–7.

28. Utley, *Going to War with Japan*, 85.

29. LAC, MG 26 J1, reel C-3693, vol. 225, no. 193986, letter from W. L. Mackenzie King to J. D. Rockefeller Jr., 6 October 1936.

30. LAC, RG 25, vol. 3116, file 4526-40C, letter from Hugh Keenleyside to Major General Clayton Bissell, 16 January 1943. See also Claire L. Chennault, *Way of a Fighter: The Memoirs of Claire Lee Chennault, Major General, U.S. Army (Ret.)* (New York: G. P. Putnam's Sons, 1949), 168.

31. LAC, RG 25, vol. 1866, file 226-B pt. 2, letter from Reverend Jesse Arnup to Norman Robertson, 3 February 1941, and letter from Soong Mayling to Reverend Jesse Arnup, 4 March 1940. See also LAC, RG 25, vol. 2883, file 2172-40 pt. 1, External Affairs Memorandum, 19 June 1942; and UCC, accession 83.046C, box 3, file 61, BOMSC, Reverend A. E. Armstrong to Reverend Tom Broadfoot, 28 March 1939.

32. NARA, RG 165, *USMIR*, reel 3, Report No. 9844 by Colonel William Mayer, 11 January 1940. See also TNA, WO 208/721, HKIR No. 3/40 by Major R. Giles, 29 February 1940; Hosoya Chihiro, "The Japanese-Soviet Neutrality Pact," trans. Robert Scalapino, in *The Fateful Choice: Japan's Road to the Pacific War: Japan's Advance into Southeast Asia, 1939–1941,* ed. James Morley (New York: Columbia University Press, 1980), 18; and Roy Stanley, *Prelude to Pearl Harbor* (New York: Charles Scribner's Sons, 1982), 125.

33. TNA, WO 208/722, HKIR No. 4/40 by Giles, 31 March 1940.

34. TNA, WO 208/721, HKIR No. 3/40 by Giles, 29 February 1940.

35. TNA, WO 208/722, HKIR No. 4/40 by Giles, 31 March 1940.

36. NARA, RG 38, M975, Selected Naval Attaché Reports Relating to the World Crisis, 1937–1943, reel 2, file Probability of an Outbreak of War Documents N, Naval Attaché Tokyo, vol. 2, Report No. 29, 16 February 1940. See also NARA, RG 165, *USMIR*, reel 3, Report No. 9830 by Colonel William Mayer, 29 November 1939, and Report No. 2 by Barrett, 2 February 1940; TNA, WO 208/721, HKIR No. 26/39 by Giles, 19 December 1939; TNA, WO 208/722, HKIR No. 2/40 by Giles, 31 January 1940, HKIR No. 6/40 by Giles, 31 May 1940, HKIR No. 13/40 by Giles, 31 December 1940, and HKIR No. 7/41 by Giles, 31 August 1941; Ambassador Nelson T. Johnson, Telegram No. 13, in *FRUS 1940,* vol. 4, *The Far East,* 258–259; Evans and Peattie, *Kaigun,* 460, 463–464; Hosoya, "Japanese-Soviet Neutrality Pact," 32; and Tsunoda Jun, "The Navy's Role in the Southern Strategy," in Morley, *Fateful Choice,* 264.

37. NARA, RG 165, M1444, Correspondence of the Military Intelligence Division Relating to General, Political, Economic, and Military Conditions in China, 1918–1941, reel 11, Report No. 9829 by Captain F. P. Munson, 29 November 1939. See also Consul Richard Butrick, Telegram No. 793.94119/643, in *FRUS 1940,* vol. 4, *The Far East,* 360–361; Catherine Baxter, "Britain and the War in China, 1937–1945" (Ph.D. diss., University of Wales, 1993), 98–99; John H. Boyle, *China and Japan at War, 1937–1945: The Politics of Collaboration* (Stanford, CA: Stanford University Press, 1972), 289–290; Chan Lau Kit Ching, *China, Britain and Hong Kong, 1895–1945* (Hong Kong: Chinese University Press, 1990), 265–266; Peter Lowe, *Great Britain and the Origins of the Pacific War: A Study of British Policy in East Asia, 1937–1941* (Oxford: Clarendon Press, 1977), 209; and Usui Katsumi, "The Politics of War," in *Japan's Road to the Pacific War: The China Quagmire: Japan's Expansion on the Asian Continent, 1933–1941,* ed. James Morley and David Lu (New York: Columbia University Press, 1983), 409.

38. NARA, RG 165, *USMIR*, reel 3, Report No. 16 by Barrett, 1 May 1941; TNA, WO 208/722, HKIR No. 4/40 by Giles, 31 March 1940, and HKIR No. 5/40 by Giles, 30 April 1940. See also Boyle, *China and Japan at War*, 293, 297, and Usui, "Politics of War," 414.

39. NARA, RG 165, *USMIR*, reel 3, Report No. 9866 by Munson, 4 April 1940; TNA, WO 208/722, HKIR No. 5/40 by Giles, 30 April 1940; Usui, "Politics of War," 402.

40. Evans and Peattie, *Kaigun*, 475; Utley, *Going to War with Japan*, 80, 84–85.

41. NARA, RG 38, entry 98A, box 705, F-6-c 23213 to F-6-e 22379, Report No. 128 by Lieutenant Commander H. H. Smith-Hutton, 3 September 1940; NARA, RG 59, *USSDCF*, reel 8, Report No. 45, 893.00 N.I. Reports/247 by Captain F. J. Mc-Quillen, 10 June 1940. See also NARA, RG 165, *USMIR*, reel 11, Report No. 9901 by Colonel William Mayer, 11 June 1940, Report No. 9919 by Munson, 30 July 1940, Report No. 9924 by Munson, 21 August 1940, Report No. 9936 by Munson, 30 September 1940, and Report No. 9943 by Munson, 31 October 1940; TNA, FO 371/27624 F 685/125/10, Memorandum No. 105 by Major K. E. F. Millar to Air Ministry, 1 October 1940; TNA, FO 371/27624 F 981/125/10, Memorandum No. 96 by Wing Commander J. Warburton to Air Ministry, 1 September 1940; TNA, WO 208/722, HKIR No. 8/40 by Giles, 31 July 1940, HKIR No. 9/40 by Giles, 31 August 1940, and HKIR No. 10/40 by Giles, 30 September 1940; Ambassador Nelson T. Johnson, Telegram Nos. 793.94/15881 and 793.94/15938, in *FRUS 1940*, vol. 4, *The Far East*, 872, 877–878; Chang Jung and Jon Halliday, *Mao: The Unknown Story* (London: Vintage Books, 2006), 273; and Mark Peattie, *Sunburst: The Rise of Japanese Naval Air Power, 1909–1941* (Annapolis, MD: Naval Institute Press, 2001), 118–121.

42. NARA, RG 38, entry 98A, box 705, F-6-c 23213 to F-6-e 22379, Report No. 194 by Smith-Hutton, 20 November 1940; NARA, RG 165, *USMIR*, reel 3, Report No. 8 by Barrett, 21 August 1940, and Report No. 15 by Barrett, 31 March 1941. See also TNA, FO 371/27624 F 981/125/10, Memorandum No. 96 by Warburton to Air Ministry, 1 September 1940; TNA, WO 208/722, HKIR No. 5/40 by Giles, 30 April 1940, HKIR No. 6/40 by Giles, 31 May 1940, HKIR No. 7/40 by Giles, 30 June 1940, HKIR No. 8/40 by Giles, 31 July 1940, HKIR No. 9/40 by Giles, 31 August 1940, HKIR No. 10/40 by Giles, 30 September 1940, and HKIR No. 4/41 by Giles, 1 May 1941; Ambassador Nelson T. Johnson, Telegram Nos. 793.94/15953 and 793.94/15938, in *FRUS 1940*, vol. 4, *The Far East*, 881, 878; Chennault, *Way of a Fighter*, 89; Jerome Klinkowitz, *With the Tigers over China, 1941–1942* (Lexington: University Press of Kentucky, 1999), 41; and Peattie, *Sunburst*, 120.

43. TNA, FO 371/27675 F 2616/317/10, memorandum by A. L. Scott, 8 March 1941; TNA, WO 208/722, HKIR No. 6/40 by Giles, 31 May 1940, HKIR No. 7/40 by Giles, 30 June 1940, and HKIR No. 10/40 by Giles, 30 September 1940. See also Chang and Halliday, *Mao*, 273, and Chennault, *Way of a Fighter*, 90.

44. TNA, WO 208/722, HKIR No. 8/40 by Giles, 31 July 1940. See also Hosoya, "Japanese-Soviet Neutrality Pact," 43; Evans and Peattie, *Kaigun*, 453, 461; and Tsunoda, "Navy's Role in Southern Strategy," 247–248.

45. TNA, WO 208/722, HKIR No. 6/40 by Giles, 31 May 1940, and HKIR No. 9/40 by Giles, 31 August 1940.

46. Christopher Bell, "'Our Most Exposed Outpost': Hong Kong and British Far Eastern Strategy, 1921–1941," *Journal of Military History* 60, 1 (1996): 75–77.

47. LAC, MG 26 J4, reel H-1561, vol. 407, no. C286798, Chiefs of Staff Far Eastern Appraisal, 13 August 1940; NARA, RG 59, *USSDCF*, reel 8, Report No. 45 893.00 N.I. Reports/247 by McQuillen, 10 June 1940; NARA, RG 165, *USMIR*, reel 3; Report No. 9830 by Mayer, 29 November 1939. See also Saki Dockrill, "Britain's Grand Strategy and Anglo-American Leadership in the War Against Japan," in *British and Japanese Military Leadership in the Far Eastern War, 1941–1945*, ed. Bryan Bond and Kyoichi Takhikawa (New York: Frank Cass, 2004), 11; Farrell, *Basis and Making of British Grand Strategy*, 35–36, 45, 94–95, 99; and Sir Llewellyn Woodward, *British Foreign Policy in the Second World War*, vol. 2 (London: Her Majesty's Stationery Office, 1971), 91.

48. LAC, MG 26 J4, reel H-1561, vol. 407, no. C286798, Chiefs of Staff Far Eastern Appraisal, 13 August 1940.

49. Kent Fedorowich, "'Cocked Hats and Swords and Small, Little Garrisons': Britain, Canada and the Fall of Hong Kong, 1941," *Modern Asian Studies* 37, 1 (2003): 131. See also Oliver Lindsay, *The Battle for Hong Kong 1941–1945: Hostage to Fortune* (Hong Kong: Hong Kong University Press, 2005), 53; and Perras, "Our Position in the Far East," 245.

50. LAC, MG 26 J4, reel H-1561, vol. 407, no. C286798, Chiefs of Staff Far Eastern Appraisal, 13 August 1940. See also TNA, CAB 121/718, file G/Hong Kong/1 (vol. 1), Chiefs of Staff Report (40) 845, 18 October 1940.

51. Lowe, *Great Britain and Origins of the Pacific War*, 163.

52. LAC, RG 25, vol. 1881, file 862, External Affairs Memorandum, 17 April 1940; NARA, RG 165, *USMIR*, reel 3, Report No. 3 by Barrett, 1 March 1940, report by Barrett, 20 April 1940, and Report No. 9830 by Mayer, 29 November 1939; TNA, WO 208/722, HKIR No. 1/40 by Giles, 2 January 1940. See also Lindsay, *Battle for Hong Kong*, 53; Lowe, *Great Britain and Origins of the Pacific War*, 128, 130, 134; and Utley, *Going to War with Japan*, 43, 165.

53. NARA, RG 165, *USMIR*, reel 13, report by Lieutenant Colonel Henry C. McLean, 20 June 1940.

54. TNA, WO 208/722, HKIR No. 6/40 by Giles, 31 May 1940.

55. NARA, RG 165, *USMIR*, reel 13, report by McLean, 20 June 1940.

56. TNA, FO 371/27653 F 6607/188/10, file cover notation by A. L. Scott, 25 July 1941.

57. LAC, RG 25, reel T-1813, vol. 812, file 623, memorandum from Gerald Campbell to Mackenzie King, 9 October 1940.

58. Kent Fedorowich, "Decolonization Deferred? The Re-establishment of Colonial Rule in Hong Kong, 1942–45," *Journal of Imperial and Commonwealth History* 28, 3 (2000): 27.

59. Cuff and Granatstein, *Ties that Bind*, 95.

60. NARA, RG 165, *USMIR*, reel 11, Report No. 9919 by Munson, 30 July 1940; TNA, WO 208/722, HKIR No. 8/40 by Giles, 31 July 1940. See also Fedorowich, "Cocked Hats and Swords," 119; Perras, "Our Position in the Far East," 243–244; and Chan Lau Kit Ching, *China, Britain and Hong Kong*, 288.

61. NARA, RG 165, *USMIR*, reel 11, Report No. 9919 by Munson, 30 July 1940; TNA, FO 371/24667 F 3568/43/10, Circular D No. 319, 7 July 1940, and Telegram No. 1196 by Sir Robert Craigie, 9 July 1940. See also S. Olu Agbi, "The Pacific War Controversy in Britain: Sir Robert Craigie versus the Foreign Office," *Modern Asian Studies* 17, 3 (1983): 508–509; Boyle, *China and Japan at War*, 299; Lowe, *Great Britain and Origins of the Pacific War*, 143, 150; Peter Lowe, "Retreat from Power: British Attitudes towards Japan, 1923–1941," in Hunt and Ion, *War and Diplomacy across the Pacific*, 58–59; and Woodward, *British Foreign Policy in the Second World War*, 2:92–93, 99.

62. TNA, CO 967/70, letter from Governor Geoffry Northcote to Lord Moyne, 9 June 1941. See also TNA, FO 371/24668 F 3799/43/10, file cover notations by B. E. Gage and Ashley Clarke, 14 and 26 August 1940; TNA, FO 371/27664 F 10950/218/10, letter from Mr. Caine to Mr. G. C. Scott (Asiatic Petroleum Company), 16 October 1941; Lowe, *Great Britain and Origins of the Pacific War*, 141, 143–144; Utley, *Going to War with Japan*, 103; and Yu Maochun, "'In God We Trusted, in China We Busted': The China Commando Group of the Special Operations Executive (SOE)," *Intelligence and National Security* 16, 4 (2001): 40.

63. NARA, RG 165, M1513, reel 38, Memorandum No. 642 from Ambassador Nelson T. Johnson to Secretary of State Cordell Hull, 27 August 1940; NARA, RG 165, *USMIR*, reel 11, Report No. 9901 by Mayer, 11 June 1940, and Report No. 9919 by Munson, 30 July 1940; TNA, WO 208/722, HKIR No. 7/40 by Giles, 30 June 1940. See also Ambassador Nelson T. Johnson, Telegram No. 363, in *FRUS 1940*, vol. 4, *The Far East*, 409; and Dick Wilson, *When Tigers Fight: The Story of the Sino-Japanese War, 1937–1945* (New York: Viking Press, 1982), 175–176.

64. NARA, RG 59, *USSDCF*, reel 8, Report No. 45 893.00 N.I. Reports/247 by McQuillen, 10 June 1940; NARA, RG 165, *USMIR*, reel 3, Report No. 13 by Barrett, 31 January 1941; NARA, RG 165, *USMIR*, reel 11, Report No. 9901 by Mayer, 11 June 1940; TNA, FO 371/24667 F 3597/43/10, Telegram No. 1322 from Lord Lothian to Lord Halifax, 12 July 1940; TNA, WO 208/722, HKIR No. 7/40 by Giles, 30 June 1940. See also Usui, "Politics of War," 414; Hans Van de Ven, *War and Nationalism in China; 1925–1945* (London: RoutledgeCurzon, 2003), 246; and Wilson, *When Tigers Fight*, 173–176.

65. NARA, RG 59, M1221, General Records of the Department of State, Intelligence Reports, 1941–1961, OSS Research and Analysis Report No. 112; TNA, FO 371/24667 F 3597/43/10, Telegram No. 1322 from Lord Lothian to Lord Halifax, 12 July 1940. See also Boyle, *China and Japan at War*, 292; Edward Drea, *Japan's Imperial Army: Its Rise and Fall, 1853–1945* (Lawrence: University Press of Kansas, 2009), 209; and Usui, "Politics of War," 414–416.

66. Agbi, "Pacific War Controversy in Britain," 511. See also Farrell, *Basis and Making of British Grand Strategy*, 53–54; Barbara Tuchman, *Stilwell, and the American Experience in China, 1911–45* (New York: Macmillan, 1970), 219; and Utley, *Going to War with Japan*, 98, 133, 178.

67. TNA, FO 371/24667 F 3622/43/10, file cover notation by Ashley Clarke, 23 July 1940; TNA, FO 371/24668 F 3695/43/10, Telegram No. 55 by Mr. Broadmead, 1

August 1940; TNA, WO 208/722, HKIR No. 8/40 by Giles, 31 July 1940. See also Lowe, *Great Britain and Origins of the Pacific War*, 118, 144, 150–151; Nagaoka Shinjiro, "Economic Demands on Dutch East Indies," in Morley, *Fateful Choice,* 139–140; Usui, "Politics of War," 373–375; and Utley, *Going to War with Japan*, 97–99.

68. NARA, RG 59, M1221, OSS Research and Analysis Report No. 112. See also Farrell, *Basis and Making of British Grand Strategy*, 54–55; Gole, *Road to Rainbow*, 107, 114, 120; and William Grieve, "Belated Endeavor: The American Military Mission to China (AMMISCA) 1941–1942" (Ph.D. diss., University of Illinois, 1979), 16.

69. Chiang Kai Shek, *Soviet Russia in China* (New York: Noonday Press, 1957), 61. See also Donald Gillies, *Radical Diplomat: The Life of Archibald Clark Kerr, Lord Inverchapel, 1882–1951* (London: I. B. Tauris, 1999), 120; Martin Kitchen, *British Policy towards the Soviet Union during the Second World War* (London: Macmillan, 1986), 19–20; W. G. Krivitsky, *I Was Stalin's Agent* (London: Right Book Club, 1940), 19; Nation, *Black Earth, Red Star*, 98, 105; R. C. Raack, *Stalin's Drive to the West, 1938–1945: The Origins of the Cold War* (Stanford, CA: Stanford University Press, 1995), 23–24; and Nikolai Tolstoy, *Stalin's Secret War* (London: Jonathan Cape, 1981), 115.

70. LAC, MG 26 J4, reel H-1561, vol. 407, no. C286723, Telegram No. 950H-80 from Sir Gerald Campbell to Mackenzie King, 22 April 1940; LAC, RG 25, vol. 1994, file 1191 pt. 1, Dominions Office Circular D-43, 25 January 1940, and "League of Nations," n.d. See also Sir Curtis Keeble, *Britain, the Soviet Union and Russia* (London: Macmillan, 2000), 161; Kitchen, *British Policy towards the Soviet Union,* 34; Nagaoka Shinjiro, "Economic Demands on Dutch East Indies," 145; Nation, *Black Earth, Red Star*, 99; and Tolstoy, *Stalin's Secret War*, 108–109, 179, 247.

71. TNA, FO 371/24667 F 3584/43/10, Telegram No. 1286 from Lord Lothian to Foreign Office, 9 July 1940; TNA, FO 371/24667 F 3606/43/10, Telegram No. 276 from Lord Halifax to Sir Stafford Cripps, 25 July 1940. See also Chang and Halliday, *Mao*, 273–274.

72. TNA, WO 208/722, HKIR No. 2/40 by Giles, 31 January 1940.

73. TNA, FO 371/24667 F 3568/43/10, Telegram No. 1179 by Sir Robert Craigie, 8 July 1940.

74. TNA, WO 208/722, HKIR No. 11/40 by Giles, 31 October 1940. See also Hosoya Chihiro, "Japanese-Soviet Neutrality Pact," 39–40, 43; Keeble, *Britain, the Soviet Union and Russia*, 165; and Raack, *Stalin's Drive to the West*, 22.

75. TNA, FO 371/24667 F 3568/43/10, file cover notation, 10 July 1940.

76. TNA, FO 371/24667 F 3606/43/10, file cover notation by J. W. R. Maclean, 22 July 1940.

77. TNA, FO 371/24667 F 3606/43/10, file cover notation, 22 July 1940; Ambassador Joseph Grew, Telegram No. 793.94119/670, in *FRUS 1940*, vol. 4, *The Far East*, 420.

78. TNA, FO 371/24667 F 3606/43/10, telegram by J. Sterndale Bennett, 20 July 1940.

79. TNA, FO 371/24667 F 3606/43/10, Telegram No. 276 from Halifax to Cripps, 25 July 1940.

80. Peter Clarke, *The Cripps Version: The Life of Sir Stafford Cripps, 1889–1952* (London: Penguin, Allen Lane, 2002), 107. See also Kitchen, *British Policy towards the Soviet Union*, 15–16, 30–31.

81. Kitchen, *British Policy towards the Soviet Union,* 16.

82. Clarke, *Cripps Version,* 205. See also Kitchen, *British Policy towards the Soviet Union,* 42.

83. Kitchen, *British Policy towards the Soviet Union,* 50.

84. Clarke, *Cripps Version,* 190, 192. See also Tolstoy, *Stalin's Secret War,* 214.

85. Clarke, *Cripps Version,* 154.

86. NARA, RG 165, *USMIR,* reel 3, Report No. 14 by Barrett, 1 March, 1941.

87. NARA, RG 165, M1444, reel 11, Report No. 9793 by Captain Edwin M. Sutherland, 8 September 1939; NARA, RG 165, *USMIR,* reel 3, Report No. 3 by Barrett, 1 March 1940. See also TNA, CO 852/324/6, file notation by B. Perry, 1 July 1940; and TNA, WO 208/722, HKIR No. 4/40 by Giles, 31 March 1940.

88. NARA, RG 165, *USMIR,* reel 3, Report No. 3 by Barrett, 1 March 1940, and report by Barrett, 20 April 1940. See also TNA, CO 852/337/19, file notation by P. W. Davies, 17 May 1940; TNA, FO 371/27660 F 3189/198/10, letter from John Keswick to Counsellor W. C. Chen, 14 April 1941; TNA, FO 371/27660 F 3925/198/10, letter from John Keswick to Ashley Clarke, 10 May 1941; and TNA, FO 371/27660 F 4553/198/10, letter from Ashley Clarke to John Keswick, 27 May 1941.

89. TNA, CO 852/337/19, letter from Ministry of Supply to P. W. Davies, 15 May 1940; TNA, FO 371/27660 F 3187/198/10, letter from Ashley Clarke to B Perry, 17 April 1941; TNA, FO 371/27660 F 4875/198/10, Foreign Office memorandum to Clark Kerr; TNA, FO 371/27660 F 5208/198/10, Telegram No. 293 from Clark Kerr to Foreign Office, 12 June 1941; TNA, FO 371/27660 F 5754/198/10, file notation by S. Hebblethwaite, 27 June 1941; and TNA, FO 371/27660 F 8158/198/10, memorandum from Ministry of Economic Warfare to Ashley Clarke, 20 August 1941.

90. NARA, RG 165, *USMIR,* reel 3, report by Barrett, 22 July 1940, and Report No. 8 by Barrett, 21 August 1940; NARA, RG 165, *USMIR,* reel 11, Report No. 9936 by Munson, 30 September 1940. See also Baxter, "Britain and the War in China," 97; and Chang and Halliday, *Mao,* 273–274.

91. Drea, *Japan's Imperial Army,* 210.

92. NARA, RG 59, *USSDCF,* reel 8, Report No. 45, 893.00 N.I. Reports/247 by McQuillen, 10 June 1940. See also Evans and Peattie, *Kaigun,* 453; Hata Ikuhiko, "The Army's Move into Northern Indochina," in Morley, *Fateful Choice,* 165, 206–208; and Tsunoda, "Navy's Role in the Southern Strategy," 246, 248, 251, 269–270.

93. TNA, WO 208/721, HKIR No. 19/39 by Captain C. J. Edwards, 12 September 1939; TNA, WO 208/722, HKIR No. 9/40 by Giles, 31 August 1940, and HKIR No. 10/40 by Giles, 30 September 1940. See also Hata, "Army's Move into Northern Indochina," 166–167.

94. NARA, RG 165, *USMIR,* reel 11, Report No. 9936 by Munson, 30 September 1940; TNA, WO 208/722, HKIR No. 8/40 by Giles, 31 July 1940, HKIR No. 10/40 by Giles, 30 September 1940, and HKIR No. 12/40 by Giles, 30 November 1940. See also Drea, *Japan's Imperial Army,* 212; Hata, "Army's Move into Northern Indochina," 158–159, 173–175, 193–198; and Lowe, *Great Britain and Origins of the Pacific War,* 169.

95. LAC, MG 26 J1, reel C-4574, vol. 296, no. 251093, Dominions Office

Telegram No. D-470 to Mackenzie King, 16 September 1940; LAC, MG 26 J1, reel C-4574, vol. 296, no. 251105, Dominions Office Telegram No. D-474 to Mackenzie King, 18 September 1940. See also Tsunoda, "Navy's Role in the Southern Strategy," 254.

96. TNA, WO 208/722, HKIR No. 11/40 by Giles, 31 October 1940.

97. NARA, RG 165, *USMIR*, reel 3, Report No. 9 by Barrett, 24 September 1940. See also Tsunoda, "Navy's Role in the Southern Strategy," 249.

98. Drea, *Japan's Imperial Army*, 210. See also Hata, "Army's Move into Northern Indochina," 156, 199–200, 204, 206–208, and Tsunoda, "Navy's Role in the Southern Strategy," 252.

99. NARA, RG 165, *USMIR*, reel 11, Report No. 9936 by Munson, 30 September 1940. See also UCC, accession 83.046C, box 4, file 68, BOMSC, letter from Dr. Oscar Thomson to Reverend Jesse Arnup, 3 July 1940.

100. NARA, RG 165, *USMIR*, reel 11, Report No. 9936 by Munson, 30 September 1940.

101. TNA, WO 208/722, HKIR No. 11/40 by Giles, 31 October 1940. See also Hata, "Army's Move into Northern Indochina," 183, 204.

102. TNA, WO 208/722, HKIR No. 10/40 by Giles, 30 September 1940. See also Utley, *Going to War with Japan*, 136.

103. NARA, RG 38, entry 98A, box 705, F-6-c 23213 to F-6-e 22379, "Southward Advance of the Japanese Navy"; NARA, RG 165, *USMIR*, reel 3, Report No. 9944 by Munson, 31 October 1940, and Report No. 9957 by Mayer, 4 December 1940; TNA, CAB 84/20, J.P. (40) 519, 6 October 1940; TNA, WO 208/722, HKIR No. 8/40 by Giles, 31 July 1940, HKIR No. 10/40 by Giles, 30 September 1940, and HKIR No. 12/40 by Giles, 30 November 1940. See also Agbi, "Pacific War Controversy in Britain," 510; Boyle, *China and Japan at War*, 304; Brereton Greenhous, *"C" Force to Hong Kong: A Canadian Catastrophe: 1941–1945* (Toronto: Dundurn Press, 1997), 9; Lowe, *Great Britain and Origins of the Pacific War*, 167–170; Utley, *Going to War with Japan*, 95, 105; and Woodward, *British Foreign Policy in the Second World War*, 2:107.

104. NARA, RG 165, *USMIR*, reel 11, Report No. 9943 by Munson, 31 October 1940, and Report No. 10 by Lieutenant Colonel David Barrett, 3 November 1940. See also TNA, FO 371/27699 F 849/849/10, China Summary No. 10 by Ambassador Archibald Clark Kerr, 14 February 1941; Lowe, *Great Britain and Origins of the Pacific War*, 210; and Usui, "Politics of War," 414, 422.

105. TNA, WO 208/722, HKIR No. 11/40 by Giles, 31 October 1940.

106. TNA, WO 208/722, HKIR No. 7/40 by Giles, 30 June 1940, and HKIR No. 10/40 by Giles, 30 September 1940.

107. NARA, RG 165, *USMIR*, reel 3, Report No. 11 by Barrett, 3 December 1940, and Report No. 12 by Barrett, 31 December 1940; NARA, RG 165, *USMIR*, reel 11, Report No. 9956 by Munson, 5 December 1940.

108. TNA, FO 371/27637 F 11224/144/10, Chungking political report by Consul General A. J. Martin, 3 October 1940.

109. TNA, WO 208/722, HKIR No. 11/40 by Giles, 31 October 1940.

110. TNA, FO 371/27699 F 869/849/10, China Summary No. 11 by Clark Kerr to Lord Halifax, 14 February 1941; TNA, WO 208/722, HKIR No. 12/40 by Giles, 30

November 1940. See also First Secretary Smyth, Telegram No. 893.00/14554, in *FRUS 1940*, vol. 4, *The Far East*, 348–349; Ambassador Joseph Grew, Telegram No. 793/94119/694, ibid., 444–446; Boyle, *China and Japan at War*, 301; Tsunoda, "Navy's Role in the Southern Strategy," 260–262; and Usui, "Politics of War," 415, 417.

111. NARA, RG 165, *USMIR*, reel 11, Report No. 9943 by Munson, 31 October 1940; TNA, WO 208/722, HKIR No. 11/40 by Giles, 31 October 1940, and HKIR No. 13/40 by Giles, 31 December 1940.

112. LAC, MG 26 J1, reel C-4574, vol. 295, no. 249936, Dominions Office Telegram No. B-26 to Mackenzie King, 6 February 1940; NARA, RG 38, entry 98A, box 705, F-6-c 23213 to F-6-e 22379, Report No. 194 by Smith-Hutton, 20 November 1940; TNA, FO 371/27697 F 3707/846/10, report by Captain T. M. H. Pardoe, 17 October 1940; TNA, WO 208/721, HKIR No. 24/39 by Giles, 21 November 1939; TNA, WO 208/722, HKIR No. 6/40 by Giles, 31 May 1940, HKIR No. 10/40 by Giles, 30 September 1940, HKIR No. 11/40 by Giles, 31 October 1940, and HKIR No. 7/41 by Giles, 31 August 1941.

113. NARA, RG 38, entry 98A, box 705, F-6-c 23213 to F-6-e 22379, Report No. 194 by Smith-Hutton, 20 November 1940.

114. NARA, RG 38, entry 98A, box 705, F-6-c 23213 to F-6-e 22379, "Southward Advance of the Japanese Navy"; NARA, RG 165, *USMIR*, reel 11, Report No. 9924 by Munson, 21 August 1940; TNA, WO 208/722, HKIR No. 9/40 by Giles, 31 August 1940.

115. NARA, RG 165, M1444, reel 11, Report No. 9873 by Captain Earl Mattice, 1 May 1940; NARA, RG 165, M1513, reel 38, memorandum by Barrett, 1 October 1940.

116. Drea, *Japan's Imperial Army*, 213.

117. TNA, WO 208/722, HKIR No. 11/40 by Giles, 31 October 1940.

118. NARA, RG 165, *USMIR*, reel 3, Report No. 7 by Barrett, 22 July 1940. See also Hata, "Army's Move into Northern Indochina," 169.

119. TNA, WO 208/722, HKIR No. 6/40 by Giles, 31 May 1940.

120. NARA, RG 38, entry 98A, box 705, F-6-c 23213 to F-6-e 22379, Report No. 112-40, 29 July 1940; NARA, RG 59, *USSDCF*, reel 8, Report No. 45, 893.00 N.I. Reports/247 by McQuillen, 10 June 1940; NARA, RG 165, *USMIR*, reel 3, Report No. 7 by Barrett, 22 July 1940; NARA, RG 165, *USMIR*, reel 11, Report No. 9919 by Munson, 30 July 1940; TNA, WO 208/722, HKIR No. 7/40 by Giles, 30 June 1940; UCC, accession 83.046C, box 4, file 65, BOMSC, letter from Mrs. Susie H. McRae to Reverend Jesse Arnup, 2 July 1940. See also George Endacott, *Hong Kong Eclipse* (Oxford: Oxford University Press, 1978), 7–8, 14, and Hata, "Army's Move into Northern Indochina," 159, 169.

121. TNA, WO 208/722, HKIR No. 7/40 by Giles, 30 June 1940. See also TNA, WO 208/722, HKIR No. 8/40 by Giles, 31 July 1940.

122. TNA, WO 208/722, HKIR No. 8/40 by Giles, 31 July 1940.

123. NARA, RG 38, entry 98A, box 705, F-6-c 23213 to F-6-e 22379, "Southward Advance of the Japanese Navy"; NARA, RG 165, *USMIR*, reel 11, Report No. 9943 by Munson, 31 October 1940; TNA, FO 371/24667 F 3568/43/10, Telegram No. 184

from Major General A. E. Grasett to Admiralty, 6 July 1940; TNA, WO 208/722, HKIR No. 8/40 by Giles, 31 July 1940.

124. NARA, RG 38, entry 98A, box 705, F-6-c 23213 to F-6-e 22379, Report No. 128 by H. H. Smith-Hutton, 3 September 1940, and "Southward Advance of the Japanese Navy"; NARA, RG 59, *USSDCF*, reel 8, Report No. 45, 893.00 N.I. Reports/247 by McQuillen, 10 June 1940; NARA, RG 165, M1444, reel 11, Report No. 9856 by Mattice, 6 March 1940; TNA, WO 208/722, HKIR No. 8/40 by Giles, 31 July 1940, HKIR No. 10/40 by Giles, 30 September 1940, and HKIR No. 11/40 by Giles, 31 October 1940.

125. TNA, WO 208/722, HKIR No. 8/40 by Giles, 31 July 1940.

126. Ibid.; TNA, WO 208/722, HKIR No. 9/40 by Giles, 31 August 1940, HKIR No. 12/40 by Giles, 30 November 1940, and HKIR No. 13/40 by Giles, 31 December 1940.

127. LAC, RG 25, vol. 2813, file 1079-40, report by G. Goold, 17 September 1940; NARA, RG 38, entry 98A, box 705, F-6-c 23213 to F-6-e 22379, Report No. 194 by Smith-Hutton, 20 November 1940; TNA, FO 371/27683 F 561/561/10, letter from A. J. Bell to Brigadier General C. R. Woodroffe, 18 November 1940; TNA, WO 208/722, HKIR No. 8/40 by Giles, 31 July 1940, HKIR No. 10/40 by Giles, 30 September 1940, and HKIR No. 11/40 by Giles, 31 October 1940. See also Tony Banham, *Not the Slightest Chance: The Defence of Hong Kong, 1941* (Hong Kong: Hong Kong University Press, 2003), 6; and Peter Moreira, *Hemingway on the China Front: His WWII Spy Mission with Martha Gellhorn* (Washington, DC: Potomac Books, 2006), 46–47.

128. TNA, WO 208/722, HKIR No. 12/40 by Giles, 30 November 1940.

129. TNA, WO 208/722, HKIR No. 2/41 by Giles, 2 February 1941.

130. LAC, MG 26 J4, reel H-1561, vol. 407, no. C286798, Chiefs of Staff Far Eastern Appraisal, 13 August 1940; NARA, RG 38, M975, reel 2, Estimate of Potential Military Strength Documents G, Naval Attaché Tokyo, vol. 3, Report No. 160, 27 September 1940; NARA, RG 165, *USMIR*, reel 3, Report No. 10 by Barrett, 3 November 1940; TNA, FO 371/27624 F 1110/125/10, Telegram No. 9051 from Grasett to War Office, 18 February 1941; TNA, WO 106/5356, HKIR No. 8/39 by Edwards, 11 April 1939; TNA, WO 208/722, HKIR No. 10/40 by Giles, 30 September 1940, HKIR No. 11/40 by Giles, 31 October 1940, and HKIR No. 13/40 by Giles, 31 December 1940. See also Chennault, *Way of a Fighter*, 89, and Lowe, "Retreat from Power," 52.

131. LAC, RG 25, vol. 3233, file 5548-40C, military situation memorandum by Lieutenant Colonel Hiram F. Wooster, 20 May 1944; NARA, RG 38, entry 98A, box 705, F-6-c 23213 to F-6-e 22379, Report No. 845-44 by C. A. Perkins, 28 December 1944; TNA, WO 208/722, HKIR No. 13/40 by Giles, 31 December 1940. See also UCC, accession 83.046C, box 4, file 65, BOMSC, letter from Mrs. Susie H. McRae to Reverend Jesse Arnup, 1 April 1940, and letter from Reverend Duncan McRae to Reverend Jesse Arnup, 5 November 1940.

132. LAC, RG 25, reel T-1813, file British Press Service, Movements of Opinion in the USA, September 1940; TNA, WO 208/722, HKIR No. 9/40 by Giles, 31 August 1940, and HKIR No. 11/40 by Giles, 31 October 1940. See also Baxter, "Britain and the War in China," 98–99, 162; Charles Cruickshank, *SOE in the Far East* (Oxford: Oxford University Press, 1983), 77–78; Farrell, *Basis and Making of British Grand Strat-*

egy, 41, 54; Lowe, *Great Britain and Origins of the Pacific War*, 180, 187; and Yu, "In God We Trusted," 41, 44–46.

133. TNA, WO 208/722, HKIR No. 5/40 by Giles, 30 April 1940.

134. TNA, WO 208/721, HKIR No. 25/39 by Giles, 5 December 1939.

135. TNA, WO 106/2382, Telegram No. 8279 by Grasett, 26 October 1940, and Telegram No. 15741 by Air Chief Marshal Sir Robert Brooke-Popham, 13 February 1941. See also Greenhous, *"C" Force to Hong Kong*, 8, and Perras, "Our Position in the Far East," 247.

136. Endacott, *Hong Kong Eclipse*, 53.

137. TNA, CAB 84/20, COS (40) 549, 15 October 1940; TNA, CAB 121/718, COS (40) 843, 18 October 1940. See also Bell, "Our Most Exposed Outpost," 86, and Perras, "Our Position in the Far East," 245.

138. TNA, CAB 121/718, COS (40) 843, 18 October 1940.

139. TNA, CAB 84/20, COS (40) 549, 15 October 1940; TNA, CAB 121/718, COS (40) 875, 28 October 1940; TNA, WO 208/722, HKIR No. 7/40 by Giles, 30 June 1940.

140. TNA, WO 106/2389, Telegram No. 8204 from Grasett to War Office, 15 October 1940, Telegram No. 8260 from Grasett to War Office, 23 October 1940, and memorandum, 10 September 1941. See also Oliver Lindsay, *The Lasting Honour* (London: Hamish Hamilton, 1978), 5; and Philip Snow, *The Fall of Hong Kong: Britain, China and the Japanese Occupation* (New Haven, CT: Yale University Press, 2003), 48.

141. TNA, WO 106/2389, Telegram No. 8260 from Grasett to War Office, 23 October 1940.

142. TNA, WO 106/2389, Telegram No. 701 from Major General E. F. Norton to War Office, 3 November 1940.

143. TNA, WO 106/2389, Telegram No. 8260 from Grasett to War Office, 23 October 1940.

144. TNA, CO 967/69, letter from Governor Sir Mark Young to A. Parkinson, 14 October 1941; TNA, FO 371/23520 F 12017/3661/10, letter from Northcote to Clark Kerr, 16 October 1939; TNA, FO 371/27719 F 4526/4526/10, Telegram No. 95 from Clark Kerr to Northcote, 24 May 1941; TNA, FO 371/27719 F 4630/4526/10, Telegram No. 85 from Northcote to Clark Kerr, 29 May 1941; TNA, WO 208/720, Telegram No. 410 from Northcote to Lord Moyne, 19 May 1941. See also Endacott, *Hong Kong Eclipse*, 53.

145. Christopher Bayly and Tim Harper, *Forgotten Armies: The Fall of British Asia, 1941–1945* (London: Penguin Books, 2004), 114. See also Peter Elphick, *Far Eastern File: The Intelligence War in the Far East, 1930–1945* (London: Hodder and Stoughton, 1997), 256, 259.

146. TNA, FO 371/27653 F 3809/188/10, letter from Major General E. F. Norton to Lord Lloyd, 20 December 1940; TNA, FO 371/27653 F 4030/188/10, letter from Colonial Secretary N. L. Smith to Lord Moyne, 20 February 1941; TNA, FO 371/27653 F 7144/188/10, telegram from Naval Attaché, Tokyo, to Admiralty, 30 July 1941; TNA, WO 208/722, HKIR No. 11/40 by Giles, 31 October 1940.

Chapter 8. The Triumph of Collective Security

1. Richard Overy, *Why the Allies Won* (New York: W. W. Norton, 1995), 241.

2. Correlli Barnett, *The Collapse of British Power* (London: Eyre Methune, 1972), 592.

3. LAC, MG 26 J13, W. L. Mackenzie King Private Diary, "Missions to the Orient," vol. 1, 6 January, 12 and 13 February 1909.

4. This opinion was expressed in the *Ottawa Evening Citizen*, 19 November 1941.

5. LAC, MG 26 J1, reel C-4864, Telegram No. 405 from Mackenzie King to Roosevelt, 4 October 1941; *Times*, 5 September 1941. See also Henry Gole, *The Road to Rainbow: Army Planning for Global War, 1934–1940* (Annapolis, MD: Naval Institute Press, 2003), 15; Paul Kennedy, *The Contradiction between British Strategic Planning and Economic Requirements in the Era of Two World Wars* (Washington, DC: International Security Studies Program, Wilson Center, 1979), 14–15, 17; Priscilla Roberts, "The Transatlantic American Foreign Policy Elite: Its Evolution in Generational Perspective," *Journal of Transatlantic Studies* 7, 2 (2009): 172–173; and Charles P. Stacey, *Arms, Men and Governments: The War Policies of Canada, 1939–1945* (Ottawa: Department of National Defence, 1970), 148–149.

6. LAC, MG 30 D45, reel M-79, memorandum by Dexter, 29 January 1941; LAC, Diaries of William Lyon Mackenzie King, 3 February 1941, www.collectionscanada.gc .ca/databases/king/001059-100.01-e.php. See also David Carlton, *Churchill and the Soviet Union* (Manchester: Manchester University Press, 2000), 80–82; and Kennedy, *Contradiction between British Strategic Planning and Economic Requirements*, 14, 21.

7. John Charmley, *Churchill: The End of Glory* (London: Hodder and Stoughton, 1993), 437.

8. Brian P. Farrell, *The Basis and Making of British Grand Strategy, 1940–1943: Was There a Plan?* (Lewiston, NY: Edwin Mellen Press, 1998), 97; Thomas Fleming, *The New Dealers' War: Franklin D. Roosevelt and the War within World War II* (New York: Perseus Books, 2001), 83.

9. Charmley, *Churchill*, 438.

10. LAC, MG 26 J1, reel C-4872, letter from Wrong to Mackenzie King, 16 September 1941. See also *New York Times*, 11 November 1941; *Times*, 28 January 1942; and Charmley, *Churchill*, 438.

11. LAC, RG 25, vol. 3343, file 4929-F-40C pt. 3, British Mission memorandum, 20 May 1944. See also NARA, RG 493, entry 531, box 50, Z Force Journal; Barnett, *Collapse of British Power*, 590, 592; and Bernard Porter, *Britain, Europe and the World 1850–1982: Delusions of Grandeur* (London: George Allen and Unwin, 1983), 107.

12. Barbara Tuchman, *Stilwell and the American Experience in China, 1911–1945* (New York: Macmillan, 1970), 221.

13. FDR, Frederic A. Delano Papers, box 2, file China Defense Supplies; Department of State, Foreign Official Status Notification. See also NARA, RG 18, entry 300, box 934, file Miscellaneous A, letter from Boddis to Arnold, 9 September 1941; Daniel Ford, *Flying Tigers: Claire Chennault and His American Volunteers, 1941–1942*, 2nd ed. (New York: Smithsonian Books, 2007), 38.

14. LAC, Diaries of William Lyon Mackenzie King, 3 February, 25 August, and 9 October 1941. See also TNA, FO 954/31, letter from Smuts to Cranborne, 29 August 1941.

15. LAC, Diaries of William Lyon Mackenzie King, 9 October 1941; LAC, MG 26 J1, reel C-4864, Telegram No. 2917 by McCarthy, 26 September 1941. See also H. Montgomery Hyde, *The Quiet Canadian: The Secret Service Story of Sir William Stephenson* (London: Hamish Hamilton, 1962), 3, 30; and William Stephenson and Nigel West, *British Security Coordination: The Secret History of British Intelligence in the Americas, 1940–1945* (New York: Fromm International, 1999), xxvii, xxxiii.

16. LAC, MG 26 J1, reel C-4864, Telegram No. 2917 by McCarthy, 26 September 1941; LAC, MG 26 J1, reel C-4868, letter from Roosevelt to Mackenzie King, 23 January 1941, and letter from Mackenzie King to Roosevelt, 8 February 1941. See also LAC, MG 26 J1, reel C-4872, Memorandum No. 2295 by Wrong, 5 August 1941; LAC, MG 26 J4, vol. 424, file War Cabinet Minutes, July 1941–December 1941, minutes, 6 November 1941; and LAC, MG 31 E 47, vol. 27, file 7, Canadian Institute of International Affairs—Correspondence, letter from Baldwin to Reid, 14 September 1939.

17. LAC, MG 26 J1, reel C-4872, Memorandum No. 2775 by Wrong, 11 September 1941; TNA, FO 954/31, letter from Macdonald to Cranborne, 7 November 1941.

18. LAC, MG 26 J1, reel C-6805, letter from Currie to Mackenzie King, 4 December 1942; LAC, MG 30 D45, reel M-79, memorandum by Dexter, 21 April 1941; LAC, RG 25, reel T-1794, memorandum by Keenleyside, 27 December 1940; NARA, RG 165, entry 77, box 380, "Canadian-American Defence Planning," *Foreign Policy Reports* 17 (17) by William Maddox, 15 November 1941. See also *Times*, 5 January 1942, and Galen Roger Perras, *Franklin Roosevelt and the Origins of the Canadian-American Security Alliance, 1933–1945: Necessary, but Not Necessary Enough* (Westport, CT: Praeger, 1998), 97–98.

19. NARA, RG 165, entry 77, box 363, Report No. 1380 by Moffat, 25 April 1941, and *Baltimore Sun* article, 23 November 1941. See also NARA, RG 165, entry 77, box 380, "Canadian-American Defence Planning" by Maddox, 15 November 1941; *New York Times*, 4 November 1941.

20. LAC, Diaries of William Lyon Mackenzie King, 18 December 1941.

21. TNA, FO 371/27675 F 2617/317/10, file notation by Brenan, 12 March 1941. See also Thomas Buell, "American Strategy in the Pacific: Its Philosophy and Practice," in *War and Diplomacy across the Pacific, 1919–1952*, ed. Barry D. Hunt and A. Hamish Ion (Waterloo, ON: Wilfrid Laurier University Press, 1988), 147; Farrell, *Basis and Making of British Grand Strategy*, 133; and Peter Lowe, *Great Britain and the Origins of the Pacific War: A Study of British Policy in East Asia, 1937–1941* (Oxford: Clarendon Press, 1977), 189, 191, 201–202, 206.

22. LAC, MG 26 J4, vol. 422, file WWII Anglo-American Strategy ABC-1 1941, Joint Letter of Transmittal, 27 March 1941.

23. NARA, RG 165, entry 184, box 959, Telegram No. 35 by Lieutenant Colonel David Barrett, 21 March 1941. See also NARA, RG 165, *USMIR*, reel 3, Report Nos. 13, 14, and 15 by Barrett, 31 January, 1 and 31 March 1941; NARA, RG 165, *USMIR*, reel 11, Report No. 9972 by Captain F. P. Munson, 4 February 1941; Chang Jung and

Jon Halliday, *Mao: The Unknown Story* (London: Vintage Books, 2006), 275–277, 283–284; and Nagaoka Shinjiro, "The Drive into Southern Indochina and Thailand," trans. Robert Scalapino, in *The Fateful Choice: Japan's Road to the Pacific War: Japan's Advance into Southeast Asia, 1939–1941*, ed. James Morley (New York: Columbia University Press, 1980), 221, 226–227, 233–234.

24. NARA, RG 165, *USMIR*, reel 3, Report No. 15 by Barrett, 31 March 1941. See also Hosoya Chihiro, "The Japanese-Soviet Neutrality Pact," in Morley, *Fateful Choice*, 79–80.

25. LAC, MG 26 J4, reel H-1531, External Affairs memorandum, frame no. C243283, 1941.

26. TNA, WO 208/722, HKIR No. 1/41 by Major R. Giles, 31 January 1941.

27. LAC, MG 26 J1, reel C-4575, Dominions Office telegram D-605, 10 December 1940; LAC, RG 25, vol. 1881, file 862, Dominions Office telegram D-247, 29 April 1941; NARA, RG 165, *USMIR*, reel 3, Report No. 16 by Barrett, 1 May 1941. See also Hosoya, "Japanese-Soviet Neutrality Pact," 85; Tsunoda Jun, "The Navy's Role in the Southern Strategy," in Morley, *Fateful Choice*, 284, 288; and Sir Llewellyn Woodward, *British Foreign Policy in the Second World War*, vol. 2 (London: Her Majesty's Stationery Office, 1971), 117.

28. LAC, MG 26 J4, reel H-1561, memorandum, frame no. C286917, 4 January 1941; LAC, MG 30 D45, reel M-79, memorandum by Dexter, 22 April 1941; TNA, FO 371/27638 F 607/145/10, file notation by Gage, 10 February 1941. See also Annalee Jacoby and Theodore White, *Thunder Out of China* (New York: William Sloane Associates, 1961), 146.

29. LAC, MG 30 D45, reel M-79, memorandum by Dexter, 21 April 1941; TNA, FO 371/27638 F 1051/145/10, file notation by Scott, 21 February 1941. See also B. H. Liddell Hart, *History of the Second World War* (New York: Cassell, 1971), 231–232; Lowe, *Great Britain and Origins of the Pacific War*, 230–231; Peter Lowe, "Retreat from Power: British Attitudes towards Japan, 1923–1941," in Hunt and Ion, *War and Diplomacy across the Pacific*, 53; and Jonathan Utley, *Going to War with Japan, 1937–1941* (Knoxville: University of Tennessee Press, 1985), 148.

30. LAC, RG 25, vol. 2135, file 572-1943, letter from Pearson to Hickerson, 9 September 1943; NARA, RG 165, *USMIR*, reel 3, Report No. 11 by Barrett, 3 December 1940.

31. John Dugdale, "Hemingway Revealed as a Failed KGB Spy," *Guardian*, 9 July 2009. See also William Grieve, "Belated Endeavor: The American Military Mission to China (AMMISCA) 1941–1942" (Ph.D. diss., University of Illinois, 1979), 10–11; John Haynes, *Venona: Decoding Soviet Espionage in America* (New Haven, CT: Yale University Press, 1999), 145–146; Peter Moreira, *Hemingway on the China Front: His WWII Spy Mission with Martha Gellhorn* (Washington, DC: Potomac Books, 2006), 40; Nigel West, *Venona: The Greatest Secret of the Cold War* (London: HarperCollins, 1999), 294; and Yu Maochun, *The Dragon's War: Allied Operations and the Fate of China, 1937–1947* (Annapolis, MD: Naval Institute Press, 2006), 33–34.

32. NARA, RG 18, entry 300, box 934, file Misc A, letter from Currie to Stimson, 21 March 1941; NARA, RG 38, entry 98A, box 705, F-6-c 23213 to F-6-e 22379,

"Southward Advance of the Japanese Navy." See also Grieve, "Belated Endeavor," 11; Claire L. Chennault, *Way of a Fighter: The Memoirs of Clarie Lee Chennault, Major General, U.S. Army (Ret.)* (New York: G. P. Putnam's Sons, 1949), 99; Moreira, *Hemingway on the China Front,* 32–33, 74–75, 189–190; and Yu, *Dragon's War,* 34–35.

33. Philip Snow, *The Fall of Hong Kong: Britain, China and the Japanese Occupation* (New Haven, CT: Yale University Press, 2003), 41.

34. NARA, RG 84, entry 2685, box 98, Telegram No. 898 by Bruins, 29 April 1941; NARA, RG 319, entry 57, box 169, file 1, Telegram No. 734A, 8 October 1941.

35. Antony Beevor, *Crete: The Battle and the Resistance* (London: John Murray, 2005), 119; Galen Roger Perras, "'Our Position in the Far East Would Be Stronger without This Unsatisfactory Commitment': Britain, and the Reinforcement of Hong Kong, 1941," *Canadian Journal of History* 30, 2 (1995): 246–248.

36. Portions of this chapter dealing with Canadian intervention in China (such as this section on the delivery of infantry weapons) also appear in my forthcoming article for the *Journal of Military History.* See also C. D. Howe, in Hansard, *Dominion of Canada Official Report of Debates, House of Commons, Second Session, Nineteenth Parliament, 4-5 George VI, 1941,* vol. 1 (Ottawa: Government of Canada, 1941), 971; LAC, RG 24, reel C-5281, file 8865, letter from Currie to Howe, 29 August 1941, letter from Sheers to DesRosiers, 30 October 1941, letter from Ralston to Howe, 8 November 1941, and memorandum from Sifton to Crerar, 10 November 1941; NARA, RG 165, entry 184, box 959, Telegram No. 116 by Mayer, 6 July 1941; TNA, WO 208/366, note on the military situation in China by Dennys, 25 October 1941; and Gole, *Road to Rainbow,* 14.

37. LAC, RG 24, reel C-5281, file 8865, letter from Howe to Ralston, 15 November 1941; Franco David Macri, "Bren Guns for China: The Origins and Impact of Sino-Canadian Relations, 1941–1949," *International History Review* 34, 3 (2012): 5.

38. LAC, MG 30 D 45, reel M-79, memorandum by Dexter, 5 September 1941.

39. LAC, RG 25, vol. 3343, file 4929-F-40C pt. 3, Memorandum No. 61661 by Somervell, 6 July 1944.

40. NARA, RG 165, *USMIR,* reel 11, Report No. 9972 by Munson, 4 February 1941; TNA, FO 371/27655 F 544/196/10, Telegram No. 65 by Clark Kerr, 7 February 1941.

41. NARA, RG 38, entry 98A, box 705, Report No. 33-41 by Lieutenant Commander D. J. McCallum, 27 February 1941.

42. NARA, RG 38, entry 98A, box 705, Report No. 78-41 by Lieutenant Commander H. H. Smith-Hutton, 29 July 1941. See also TNA, FO 371/27637 F 8324/144/10, Report No. 17 by Prideaux-Brune, 22 April 1941; and TNA, WO 208/722, HKIR No. 1/41 by Giles, 31 January 1941, and HKIR No. 5/41 by Giles, 1 June 1941.

43. LAC, MG 26 J1, reel C-4865, Telegram No. Z-209 by MacDonald, 11 June 1941. See also LOC, Chennault Papers, reel 5, letter from Alsop to Chennault, November 1941; NARA, RG 165, entry 184, box 959, Telegram No. 37, 26 March 1941; NARA, RG 165, *USMIR,* reel 3, Report Nos. 10, 11, and 12 by Barrett, 3 November, 3 and 31 December 1940; TNA, FO 371/27596 F 4475/1/10, file notation by Scott, 27 May 1941; TNA, FO 371/27638 F 1198/145/10, Telegram No. A.4 18/2, 19 February

1941; TNA, FO 371/27638 F 1846/145/10, Telegram No. 312, 24 March 1941; TNA, FO 371/27639 F 4258/145/10, Telegram No. X.451, 16 June 1941; TNA, FO 371/27639 F 4381/145/10, file notation by Scott, 24 May 1941; Chennault, *Way of a Fighter*, 90, 99, 102; and Carroll Glines, *Chennault's Forgotten Warriors: The Saga of the 308th Bomb Group in China* (Atglen, PA: Schiffer, 1995), 18.

44. TNA, FO 371/27638 F 1073/145/10, file notation by Gage, 22 February 1941.

45. TNA, FO 371/27638 F 2035/145/10, file notation by Ronald, 19 March 1941.

46. TNA, FO 371/27638 F 1051/145/10, file notation by Scott, 21 February 1941.

47. TNA, FO 371/27638 F 2035/145/10, file notation, 20 March 1941.

48. TNA, FO 371/27638 F 1846/145/10, Telegram No. 312, 24 March 1941.

49. *New York Times*, 31 December 1941; *Times* (London), 31 December 1941. See also Stacey, *Arms, Men and Governments*, 329.

50. Timothy Wilford, *Canada's Road to the Pacific War: Intelligence, Strategy, and the Far East Crisis* (Vancouver: UBC Press, 2011), 40, 198.

51. LAC, MG 26 J1, reel C-4862, memorandum by Duff, 21 June 1941.

52. TNA, WO 208/722, HKIR No. 4/41 by Giles, 1 May 1941.

53. NARA, RG 38, entry 98A, box 705, Report No. 3-41 by McCallum, 24 February 1941, and "Southward Advance of the Japanese Navy." See also NARA, RG 165, *USMIR*, reel 3, Report No. 14 by Barrett, 1 March 1941.

54. TNA, FO 371/27639 F 5030/145/10, letter from Air Ministry to Clarke, 8 June 1941.

55. TNA, CAB 121/718, Telegram No. 135 6/1 by Brooke-Popham, 6 January 1941. See also Kent Fedorowich, "'Cocked Hats and Swords and Small, Little Garrisons': Britain, Canada and the Fall of Hong Kong, 1941," *Modern Asian Studies* 37, 1 (2003): 131; and Perras, "Our Position in the Far East," 248.

56. TNA, CAB 121/718, Memorandum No. D.9/1 by Churchill, 7 January 1941, as quoted by Christopher Bell, "'Our Most Exposed Outpost': Hong Kong and British Far Eastern Strategy, 1921–1941," *Journal of Military History* 60, 1 (1996): 80, and Perras, "Our Position in the Far East," 246–257.

57. DHH, file 593.013 (D21), Air Ministry telegram, 14 January 1941; TNA, CAB 121/718, COS (40) 843, memorandum, 18 October 1940. See also Bell, "Our Most Exposed Outpost," 80, and George Endacott, *Hong Kong Eclipse* (Oxford: Oxford University Press, 1978), 56.

58. TNA, CAB 121/718, COS (41) 51, memorandum, 22 January 1941.

59. LAC, MG 26 J1, reel C-4862, memorandum by Duff, 16 June 1941.

60. LAC, RG 24, reel C-8294, file 3507-4, Joint Intelligence Committee Report No. 154/2, 1 January 1944; NARA, RG 319, entry 57, box 164, file 6, Telegram No. 121 by Mayer, 20 December 1941; TNA, FO 371/27624 F 793/125/10, file notation by Scott, 13 February 1941; TNA, WO 208/722, HKIR No. 11/40 by Giles, 31 October 1940.

61. LAC, RG 25, vol. 3297, file "British Intelligence Agencies in China," report of interview with Reverend J. C. Mathieson, 4 October 1943. See also Vasilii Chuikov, *Mission to China: Memoirs of a Soviet Military Adviser to Chiang Kaishek*, trans. David Barrett (Norwalk, CT: EastBridge: 2004), 70–71, 157.

62. LAC, RG 24, vol. 20538, file 982.013 (D3), Operation Record in China The-

ater, December 1946; NARA, RG 38, entry 98A, box 705, Report No. 33-41 by Mc-Callum, 27 February 1941; TNA, FO 371/27636 F 4269/144/10, Canton Political Report—March Quarter 1941 by Blunt, 27 March 1941; TNA, FO 371/27706 F 5140/1386/10, file notation by Scott, 13 June 1941; TNA, WO 208/721, HKIR No. 17/39 by Edwards, 15 August 1939. See also Edward J. Drea, *Japan's Imperial Army: Its Rise and Fall, 1853–1945* (Lawrence: University Press of Kansas, 2009), 221.

63. TNA, WO 208/722, HKIR No. 1/41 by Giles, 31 January 1941.

64. TNA, FO 371/27626 F 5761/125/10, letter from Chapman, 29 June 1941.

65. LAC, RG 24, vol. 20538, file 982.013 (D3), Operation Record in China Theater, December 1946.

66. NARA, RG 165, entry 184, box 959, Telegram No. 20 by Barrett, 3 February 1941.

67. NARA, RG 38, entry 98A, box 705, Report No. 33-41 by McCallum, 27 February 1941, and "Southward Advance of the Japanese Navy"; NARA, RG 59, *USSDCF*, reel 10, Report No. 893.00 P. R. Canton/156 by Consul General M. Myers, 10 February 1941, Report No. 893.00 P. R. Canton/157 by Myers, 12 March 1941, and Report No. 893.00 P. R. Canton/161 by Myers, 10 July 1941; NARA, RG 165, M1513, reel 40, report by Myers, 30 April 1941. See also TNA, FO 371/27653 F 8529/188/10, report by Smith, 6 May 1941; TNA, FO 371/27637 F 10548/144/10, Canton Political Report No. 109 by Coates, 26 June 1941; TNA, WO 106/2384, Telegram No. 8972 by Grasett, 7 February 1941; TNA, WO 208/722, HKIR No. 12/40 by Giles, 30 November 1940, HKIR No. 13/40 by Giles, 31 December 1940, HKIR No. 2/41 by Giles, 28 February 1941, and HKIR No. 4/41 by Giles, 1 May 1941; UCC, accession 83.046C, box 4, file 71, BOMSC, letter from McRae to Arnup, 20 April 1941; and UCC, accession 83.046C, box 4, file 72, BOMSC, letter from Thomson to Arnup, 10 April 1941.

68. NARA, RG 38, entry 98A, box 705, "Southward Advance of the Japanese Navy"; NARA, RG 59, *USSDCF*, reel 10, Report No. 893.00 P. R. Canton/157 by Myers, 12 March 1941. See also TNA, WO 106/2384, Telegram Nos. 8972 and 8976 by Grasett, 7 February and 14 January 1941; TNA, WO 208/722, HKIR No. 12/40 by Giles, 30 November 1940, HKIR No. 13/40 by Giles, 31 December 1940, HKIR No. 1/41 by Giles, 31 January 1941, HKIR No. 2/41 by Giles, 28 February 1941, HKIR No. 6/41 by Giles, 1 July 1941, HKIR No. 9/41 by Giles, 1 October 1941, and HKIR No. 10/41 by Giles, 1 November 1941; UCC, accession 83.046C, box 4, file 71, BOMSC, letter from McRae to Arnup, 20 April 1941.

69. NARA, RG 38, entry 98A, box 705, Report No. 46-41 by Smith-Hutton, 24 March 1941, and "Southward Advance of the Japanese Navy." See also NARA, RG 59, *USSDCF*, reel 10, Report No. 893.00 P. R. Canton/161 by Myers, 10 July 1941; NARA, RG 165, M1513, reel 40, report by Major James McHugh, 11 March 1941; NARA, RG 165, *USMIR*, reel 3, Report No. 15 by Barrett, 31 March 1941; TNA, FO 371/27624 F 1812/125/10, Telegram No. 9202 by Grasett, 6 March 1941; and TNA, WO 208/722, HKIR No. 13/40 by Giles, 31 December 1940, HKIR No. 3/41 by Giles, 1 April 1941, and HKIR No. 4/41 by Giles, 1 May 1941.

70. NARA, RG 38, entry 98A, box 705, "Southward Advance of the Japanese Navy"; NARA, RG 165, entry 184, box 959, Telegram No. 23 by Barrett, 8 February

1941. See also TNA, FO 371/27624 F 1110/125/10, Telegram No. 9051 by Grasett, 17 February 1941; TNA, FO 371/27636 F 4269/144/10, Canton Political Report—March Quarter 1941 by Blunt, 27 March 1941; TNA, WO 106/2384, Telegram Nos. 8972 and 9147 by Grasett, 7 and 27 February 1941; TNA, WO 106/2384, War Office note, 10 February 1941; TNA, WO 208/722, HKIR No. 2/41 by Giles, 28 February 1941; and Chan Lau Kit Ching, *China, Britain and Hong Kong, 1895–1945* (Hong Kong: Chinese University Press, 1990), 288.

71. LAC, RG 24, vol. 3913, file 1037-5-3 vol. 1, Telegram FEW 21, 14 March 1941; NARA, RG 38, entry 98A, box 705, Report Nos. 60-41 and 78-41 by Smith-Hutton, 24 April and 29 July 1941. See also NARA, RG 38, entry 98A, box 705, "Southward Advance of the Japanese Navy"; NARA, RG 59, LM 65, reel 21, Report Nos. 893.23/97 and 893.23/98 by Consul General Addison Southard, 18 September and 7 October 1941; NARA, RG 59, *USSDCF*, reel 10, Report Nos. 893.00 P. R. Canton/160 and 893.00 P. R. Canton/163 by Myers, 11 June and 9 September 1941; NARA, RG 165, M1444, Correspondence of the Military Intelligence Division Relating to General, Political, Economic, and Military Conditions in China, 1918–1941, reel 11, Report No. 9990 by Major F. P. Munson, 11 May 1941; NARA, RG 165, M1513, reel 39, Telegram No. 1023 by Southard, 7 October 1941; NARA, RG 165, M1513, reel 40, Report No. 10477 by Major Stuart Wood, 28 July 1941; NARA, RG 165, *USMIR*, reel 3, Report No. 16 by Barrett, 1 May 1941; TNA, WO 106/2384, Telegram No. 9476 by Grasett, 12 April 1941; and TNA, WO 208/722, HKIR No. 3/41 by Giles, 1 April 1941, HKIR No. 4/41 by Giles, 1 May 1941, HKIR No. 5/41 by Giles, 1 June 1941, and HKIR No. 9/41 by Giles, 1 October 1941.

72. NARA, RG 165, M1513, reel 40, Telegram No. 9999 by Munson, 15 June 1941; TNA, WO 208/722, HKIR No. 3/41 by Giles, 1 April 1941, and HKIR No. 5/41 by Giles, 1 June 1941.

73. TNA, FO 371/27637 F 10548/144/10, Canton Political Report No. 109 by Coates, 26 June 1941; TNA, WO 106/2402, Telegram Nos. 9974, 9983, and 6 by Grasett, 15, 16, and 19 June 1941. See also TNA, WO 208/722, HKIR No. 13/40 by Giles, 31 December 1940.

74. LAC, RG 24, vol. 3913, file 1037-5-3 vol. 1, Telegram FEW 35, 19 June 1941; NARA, RG 38, entry 98A, box 705, "Southward Advance of the Japanese Navy"; NARA, RG 59, *USSDCF*, reel 10, Report No. 893.00 P. R. Canton/156 by Myers, 10 February 1941. See also TNA, FO 371/27653 F 5015/188/10, Telegram No. 501 by Northcote, 7 June 1941; TNA, FO 371/27653 F 12830/188/10, letter from Craigie to Toyoda, 10 September 1941; TNA, WO 106/2387, Telegram No. 9941 by Grasett, 10 June 1941; TNA, WO 106/2402, Telegram Nos. 45 and 331 by Grasett, 23 June and 24 July 1941; and TNA, WO 208/722, HKIR No. 4/41 by Giles, 1 May 1941, HKIR No. 5/41 by Giles, 1 June 1941, HKIR No. 6/41 by Giles, 1 July 1941, and HKIR No. 9/41 by Giles, 1 October 1941.

75. TNA, FO 371/27653 F 7144/188/10, Telegram No. 13, 30 July 1941; TNA, FO 371/27653 F 8529/188/10, letter from Northcote to Craigie, 6 May 1941; TNA, FO 371/27653 F 9206/188/10, Telegram No. 980 by N. L. Smith, 6 September 1941; TNA, FO 371/27653 F 12830/188/10, letter from Craigie to Toyoda, 10 September 1941;

TNA, FO 371/27706 F 5140/1386/10, Telegram No. 238/3 by Brooke-Popham, 11 June 1941; TNA, WO 106/2387, memorandum by Scott, 12 June 1941; TNA, WO 208/722, HKIR No. 3/41 by Giles, 1 April 1941, and HKIR No. 6/41 by Giles, 1 July 1941.

76. TNA, WO 106/2402, Telegram No. 837 by Grasett, 7 July 1941.

77. TNA, FO 371/27653 F 6996/188/10, telegram, 27 July 1941.

78. TNA, FO 371/27653 F 6607/188/10, Telegram No. 1226 by Craigie, 21 July 1941.

79. TNA, FO 371/27653 F 6607/188/10, file notation by Scott, 25 July 1941.

80. TNA, WO 106/2402, letter from Gent to Sterndale Bennett, 27 June 1941.

81. TNA, CAB 121/718, COS (41) 559, memorandum by Dill, 8 September 1941.

82. TNA, CO 967/70, letter from Northcote to Lord Moyne, 9 June 1941; TNA, WO 106/5360, Report No. 163 by Stacey, November 1946.

83. LAC, RG 24, vol. 20538, file 982.013 (D3), Operation Record in China Theater, December 1946; NARA, RG 38, entry 98A, box 705, "Southward Advance of the Japanese Navy"; NARA, RG 59, USSDCF, reel 10, Report No. 893.00 P. R. Canton/162 by Myers, 11 August 1941; NARA, RG 165, M1513, reel 38, telegram by Mayer, 6 August 1941; NARA, RG 319, entry 57, box 169, file 1, telegram by Captain Bernard Tormey, 4 August 1941. See also TNA, FO 371/27626 F 6765/125/10, Telegram No. 277 by Grasett, 18 July 1941; TNA, FO 371/27626 F 6961/125/10, telegram, 26 July 1941; TNA, FO 371/27627 F 7596/125/10, Telegram No. 440, 8 August 1941; TNA, FO 371/27627 F 8190/125/10, Telegram No. 547, 21 August 1941; TNA, FO 371/27627 F 9847/125/10, memorandum by Sterndale Bennett, 23 September 1941; TNA, WO 106/2402, Telegram No. 816 by Northcote, 7 August 1941; TNA, WO 208/722, HKIR No. 7/41 by Giles, 1 August 1941, and HKIR No. 8/41 by Giles, 1 September 1941; and Hallett Abend, New York Times, 25 July 1941.

84. TNA, FO 371/27627 F 7847/125/10, Telegram No. 486, 15 August 1941; TNA, FO 371/27627 F 8148/125/10, telegram, 22 August 1941; TNA, FO 371/27653 F 10742/188/10, Telegram No. 381 by Commodore A. C. Collinson, 13 October 1941; TNA, WO 106/2402, Telegram No. 1263 by Governor Sir Mark Young, 31 October 1941, and Telegram No. 1447 by Young, 4 December 1941. See also TNA, WO 208/722, HKIR No. 9/41 by Giles, 1 October 1941, and HKIR No. 10/41 by Giles, 1 November 1941.

85. LAC, RG 25, vol. 3264, file 6161-40C, Telegram No. 138 by Victor Odlum, enclosure report by V. J. R. Mills, 27 September 1943; NARA, RG 59, USSDCF, reel 10, Report No. 893.00 P. R. Canton/165 by Myers, 10 November 1941; NARA, RG 165, entry 184, box 959, Telegram No. 50 by Barrett, 30 September 1941; NARA, RG 165, M1513, reel 40, memorandum by Myers, 30 April 1941; NARA, RG 165, M1513, reel 40, Telegram No. 65/41 by McHugh, 17 October 1941; NARA, RG 165, M1513, reel 40, Report No. 10579 by Major C. Stanton Babcock, 22 October 1941; NARA, RG 319, entry 57, box 164, file 5, Telegram No. 54 by Barrett, 3 October 1941; NARA, RG 319, entry 57, box 164, file 6, Telegram No. 122 by Magruder, 23 December 1941. See also TNA, FO 371/27624 F 1812/125/10, Telegram No. 9202 by Grasett, 6 March 1941; TNA, WO 106/5303, No. 289, Report on Visit to IV War Zone Headquarters by

Boxer and Chauvin, 20 May 1939; TNA, WO 208/722, HKIR No. 9/41 by Giles, 1 October 1941; and Gole, *Road to Rainbow*, 9.

86. TNA, FO 371/27628 F 14340/125/10, file notation by JGW, 3 January 1942.

87. LAC, RG 25, vol. 3029, file 3978-40C pt. 1, Telegram No. 245 by Victor Odlum, enclosure no. 1, "Famine in Kwangtung" by R. Collins, 9 May 1944; NARA, RG 59, *USSDCF*, reel 3, Report No. 893.00/14801 by Myers, 29 August 1941; NARA, RG 59, *USSDCF*, reel 10, Report Nos. 893.00 P. R. Canton/160 and 893.000 P. R. Canton/162 by Myers, 11 June and 11 August 1941; TNA, FO 371/27682 F 12829/520/10, Telegram No. 1896 by Ambassador Joseph Grew, 6 September 1941; TNA, WO 106/2402, Telegram No. 816 by Northcote, 7 August 1941; TNA, WO 208/722, HKIR No. 11/40 by Giles, 31 October 1940. See also HKU, BAAG series, vol. 4, "Advance Headquarters, Waichow, Field Operations Group," report by E. D. G. Hooper, 14 August 1942, 152.

88. TNA, FO 371/27636 F 5072/144/10, quarterly report by Consul Hall, 3 April 1941.

89. LAC, RG 25, vol. 3356, file 25-G(s), Government of Hong Kong telegram, 15 June 1948; LAC, RG 25, vol. 8517, file 6605-40, FO biography of Tu Yueh-sen, 16 April 1943. See also NARA, RG 59, *USSDCF*, reel 10, Report No. 893.00 P. R. Canton/162 by Myers, 11 August 1941; and TNA, FO 371/27621 F 12172/91/10, report, 11 November 1941.

90. Fedorowich, "Cocked Hats and Swords," 119.

91. LAC, RG 25, vol. 2920, file 2670-A-40C-1, Telegram No. 2132 by Massey, 16 November 1941. See also H. Angus, *Canada and the Far East, 1940–1953* (Toronto: University of Toronto Press, 1953), 18.

92. *Toronto Daily Star*, 13 September 1941.

93. TNA, WO 208/366, note on the military situation in China by Dennys, 25 October 1941.

94. TNA, FO 371/27715 F 4787/3653/10, report by Morrison, 3 June 1941.

95. NARA, RG 18, entry 300, box 934, file Misc A, memorandum by Magruder, 18 August 1941. See also IWM, Conservation Shelf, "Thunder in the East" by Grimsdale, 35, 38.

96. TNA, FO 371/27640 F 6619/145/10, file notation by Sterndale Bennett, 10 July 1941.

97. Telegram No. 230 by Gauss, in *FRUS 1941*, vol. 4, *The Far East*, 712.

98. NARA, RG 165, entry 184, box 959, file Messages Incoming, telegram by Lee, 4 November 1941.

99. LAC, RG 2, vol. 3, file D-19-1 Pacific Area, Telegram No. 195 by Cranborne, 14 November 1941, and Telegram No. 349 by Chiang, 4 November 1941. See also NARA, RG 165, entry 184, box 959, file Messages Incoming, telegram by Mayer, 17 October 1941, and telegram by Lee, 10 November 1941; NARA, RG 165, M1513, reel 40, memorandum by Miles, 20 August 1941; TNA, FO 371/27627 F 9099/125/10, Telegram No. 580, 8 September 1941; TNA, FO 371/27715 F 4787/3653/10, report by Morrison, 3 June 1941; and TNA, HW 1/228, Message No. 097886, 19 November 1941.

100. TNA, FO 954/24B N 4840/78/G, Memorandum No. 216 by Eden, 26 August 1941. See also Rodric Braithwaite, *Moscow 1941: A City and Its People at War* (London: Profile Books, 2007), 93; Farrell, *Basis and Making of British Grand Strategy*, 153; Nagaoka, "Drive into Southern Indochina and Thailand," 235–236, 238; and Utley, *Going to War with Japan*, 151–153.

101. LAC, RG 25, vol. 2661, file 5940-40, Memorandum No. 393 by Halifax, 3 June 1942.

102. Hallett Abend, *My Life in China, 1926–1941* (New York: Harcourt, Brace, 1943), 361; Fleming, *New Dealers' War*, 23.

103. LAC, Diaries of William Lyon Mackenzie King, 30 November 1941.

104. LAC, RG 24, vol. 3913, file 1037-5-3 vol. 1, CIS telegram, 29 July 1941; NARA, RG 38, entry 98A, box 705, "Southward Advance of the Japanese Navy"; NARA, RG 165, entry 184, box 959, Telegram No. 131 by Barrett, 23 July 1941. See also *New York Times*, 1 October 1941; Chuikov, *Mission to China*, 150; Hosoya, "Japanese-Soviet Neutrality Pact," 97, 103–108; Drea, *Japan's Imperial Army*, 217; Curtis Keeble, *Britain, the Soviet Union and Russia* (London: Macmillan, 2000), 167; Mark Stoler, *Allies and Adversaries: The Joint Chiefs of Staff, the Grand Alliance, and U.S. Strategy in World War II* (Chapel Hill: University of North Carolina Press, 2000), 54–56; and Tuchman, *Stilwell*, 223.

105. Carl Boyd, *Hitler's Japanese Confidant: General Oshima Hiroshi and MAGIC Intelligence, 1941–1945* (Lawrence: University Press of Kansas, 1993), 58; Lowe, *Great Britain and Origins of the Pacific War*, 209.

106. Fleming, *New Dealers' War*, 21.

107. LAC, Diaries of William Lyon Mackenzie King, 9 October 1941.

108. Ibid., 10 October 1941.

109. Ibid., 16 October 1941.

110. Memorandum by Hornbeck, in *FRUS 1941*, vol. 4, *The Far East*, 427.

111. TNA, CAB 79/14/4, COS (41) 308, minutes, 3 September 1941.

112. Bell, "Our Most Exposed Outpost," 82; Fedorowich, "Cocked Hats and Swords," 155.

113. TNA, CAB 121/464, telegram by Stalin, 3 September 1941.

114. Nikolai Tolstoy, *Stalin's Secret War* (London: Jonathan Cape, 1981), 247.

115. TNA, CAB 121/464, telegram by Churchill, 29 August 1941.

116. Farrell, *Basis and Making of British Grand Strategy*, 305.

117. TNA, FO 954/24B N 5096/78/G, Memorandum No. 227 by Eden, 4 September 1941.

118. TNA, CAB 121/464, telegram by Stalin, 13 September 1941.

119. Carlton, *Churchill and the Soviet Union*, 89; Farrell, *Basis and Making of British Grand Strategy*, 163–164.

120. Peter Clarke, *The Cripps Version: The Life of Sir Stafford Cripps, 1889–1952* (London: Penguin, Allen Lane, 2002), 234.

121. LAC, MG 26 J4, vol. 424, file War Cabinet Minutes July 1941–December 1941, minutes, 10 and 18 September 1941. See also speech by Mackenzie King, *Times*, 5 September 1941; Brian Nolan, *King's War: Mackenzie King and the Politics of War, 1939–*

1945 (Toronto: Random House, 1988), 58; and Stacey, *Arms, Men and Governments,* 151.

122. Paul D. Dickson, *A Thoroughly Canadian General: A Biography of General H. D. G. Crerar* (Toronto: University of Toronto Press, 2007), 169–170.

123. LAC, MG 26 J4, vol. 424, file War Cabinet Minutes July 1941–December 1941, minutes, 2 October 1941.

124. Ibid.; Evan Mawdsley, *Thunder in the East: The Nazi-Soviet War, 1941–1945* (London: Hodder Arnold, 2005), 94.

125. Utley, *Going to War with Japan,* 161–162.

126. Editorial, *New York Times,* 18 October 1941.

127. TNA, CAB 121/464, memorandum by Davidson, 24 October 1941; TNA, WO 193/921, Telegram No. I/102, 10 December 1941. See also John Erickson, *The Road to Stalingrad: Stalin's War with Germany,* vol. 1 (London: Phoenix Giant, 1998), 218–220, 239; and Oliver Lindsay, *The Lasting Honour* (London: Hamish Hamilton, 1978), 11–12.

128. LAC, RG 25, vol. 2920, file 2670-C-40C, Telegram No. M-337 by Cranborne, 24 October 1941.

129. Ibid.

130. LAC, RG 25, vol. 2920, file 2670-C-40C, Telegram No. M-343 by Cranborne, 31 October 1941.

131. LAC, Diaries of William Lyon Mackenzie King, 6 November 1941.

132. TNA, CAB 120/570, note by Churchill, 7 January 1941.

133. LAC, Diaries of William Lyon Mackenzie King, 11 February and 13, 17, and 27 November 1941. See also LAC, MG 26 J1, reel C-4866, telegram by Mackenzie King, 3 May 1941.

134. LAC, MG 30 D45, reel M-79, letter from Dexter to Dafoe, 6 August 1941.

135. Ibid., 7 November 1941; Stacey, *Arms, Men and Governments,* 47.

136. LAC, Diaries of William Lyon Mackenzie King, 5 December 1941.

137. Ibid., 22 January 1942.

138. LAC, MG 30 D45, reel M-79, letter from Dexter to Dafoe, 22 April 1941; LAC, MG 26 J4, reel H-1561, Telegram No. Z-398 by Massey, 9 December 1940; LAC, RG 25, vol. 2920, file 2670-C-40C, Telegram No. 1000 by Crerar, 11 April 1942.

139. LAC, RG 25, vol. 2920, file 2670-C-40C, memorandum, 19 March 1942.

140. TNA, CAB 121/718, memorandum, 10 June 1942.

141. TNA, CAB 121/718, file notation, 10 June 1942.

142. LAC, RG 25, vol. 5769, file 152-A(s) pt. 1, Telegram No. 225 by Robertson, 26 February 1948.

143. TNA, FO 371/27622 F 11189/98/10, letter from Browne to Sterndale Bennett, 22 October 1941, and letter from Clarke to Nichol, 2 November 1941.

144. TNA, FO 371/27622 F 11189/98/10, file notation by Brenan, 28 October 1941.

145. TNA, FO 371/27622 F 11189/98/10, file notation by Evans, 30 October 1941.

146. LAC, RG 25, vol. 2920, file 2670-A-40C-1, Telegram No. 2132 by Massey, and "Hong Kong as Vital Bastion," *Daily Telegraph,* 11 November 1941.

147. LAC, MG 26 J4, vol. 422, file WWII Anglo-American Strategy ABC-1 1941,

Joint Letter of Transmittal, 27 March 1941; NARA, RG 165, entry 281, box 154, file 3793-161, memorandum by O'Rear, 16 December 1941; TNA, CAB 121/718, COS (41) 559, memorandum by Dill, 8 September 1941; TNA, FO 371/27622 F 10344/98/10, file notation by Sterndale Bennett, 6 October 1941. See also Bell, "Our Most Exposed Outpost," 79–80; Oliver Lindsay, *The Battle for Hong Kong 1941–1945: Hostage to Fortune* (Hong Kong: Hong Kong University Press, 2005), 56; and Perras, "Our Position in the Far East," 249.

148. Catherine Baxter, "Britain and the War in China, 1937–1945" (Ph.D. diss., University of Wales, 1993), 125.

149. "Japanese Monograph No. 71," in *Japanese Monographs: Area Operations in China, December 1941–December 1943* (Washington, DC: Library of Congress Photoduplication Service, 1963).

150. DHH, file 593.013 (D21), Telegram No. 1489 by Maltby, 19 November 1941, and notes on Telegram Nos. 192/6 and 243/6 by Brooke-Popham, 25 November 1941; NARA, RG 18, entry 300, box 934, file Misc A, Reinforcement Study, October 1941, and memorandum by Spaatz, 26 November 1941; NARA, RG 59, *USSDCF*, reel 25, Report No. 893.20/736 by Lee, 7 November 1941; NARA, RG 165, entry 184, box 959, Telegram No. 119 by Mayer, 8 July 1941; NARA, RG 165, entry 281, box 154, file 3793-161, memorandum by O'Rear, 16 December 1941. See also TNA, CAB 121/718, cabinet telegram (draft) to Brooke-Popham, 6 January 1941; TNA, FO 371/27596 F 4375/1/10, Telegram No. 345 by Brooke-Popham, 21 April 1941, and file notation by Gage, 26 May 1941; TNA, FO 371/27643 F 11410/145/10, telegram, 25 October 1941; TNA, FO 371/27678, Telegram No. 135 by Brooke-Popham, 6 January 1941; Baxter, "Britain and the War in China," 123–125; and Lowe, *Great Britain and Origins of the Pacific War*, 215.

151. TNA, FO 371/27624 F 1622/125/10, JPS report (41) 166, 1 March 1941; TNA, WO 106/2389, Telegram No. 701 by Smith, 3 November 1940. See also Charles Cruickshank, *SOE in the Far East* (Oxford: Oxford University Press, 1983), 75.

152. LAC, MG 26 J4, reel H-1561, Dominions Office Telegram No. M-476 pt. 2, 23 December 1941; NARA, RG 165, entry 184, box 959, Telegram Nos. 106 and 119 by Mayer, 25 June and 8 July 1941. See also TNA, FO 371/27638 F 3543/145/10, file notation by Brenan, 2 May 1941; TNA, FO 371/27639 F 4624/145/10, Telegram No. 104 by Dennys; TNA, FO 371/27639 F 4661/145/10, Telegram No. 142/3 by Brooke-Popham, 27 May 1941; TNA, FO 371/27639 F 5030/145/10, Air Ministry Telegram No. X.17, 8 June 1941; TNA, FO 371/27639 F 5248/145/10, minutes of interdepartmental meeting, 6 June 1941; TNA, FO 371/27640 F 5511/145/10, Telegram No. 293/3 by Dennys, 18 June 1941; Baxter, "Britain and the War in China," 105; and Lowe, *Great Britain and Origins of the Pacific War*, 214.

153. LAC, RG 25, vol. 5740, file 25-F(s), Dominions Office Telegram No. M-266, 25 August 1941; NARA, RG 18, entry 300, box 934, file Miscellaneous A, letter from Arnold to British Air Commission, 19 August 1941, and memorandum by Spaatz, 26 November 1941; NARA, RG 59, *USSDCF*, reel 25, Report No. 893.20/736 by Lee, 7 November 1941; NARA, RG 165, entry 184, box 959, Telegram No. 119 by Mayer, 8 July 1941; NARA, RG 319, entry 57, box 164, file 4, Telegram No. 49 by Barrett, 29

September 1941. See also TNA, FO 371/27640 F 5787/145/10, file notation by Gage, 16 August 1941; TNA, FO 371/27640 F 6092/145/10, file cover notation by Scott, 12 July 1941; TNA, FO 371/27640 F 6253/145/10, telegram, 14 July 1941; TNA, FO 371/27640 F 6327/145/10, telegram, 15 July 1941; TNA, FO 371/27640 F 6619/145/10, file notation by Sterndale Bennett, 10 July 1941; TNA, FO 371/27640 F 6619/145/10, file notation by Butler, 11 July 1941; TNA, FO 371/27641 F 7496/145/10, Telegram No. 171/4 by Brooke-Popham, 1 August 1941; and TNA, FO 371/27644 F 11824/145/10, WO Telegram No. 99905, 5 November 1941.

154. NARA, RG 59, decimal file no. 121.5493/214, box 269, file notation, 27 October 1941; NARA, RG 319, entry 57, box 164, file 6, Telegram No. C 112 by Mayer, 9 December 1941; NARA, RG 319, entry 57, box 169, file 1, Telegram No. 34, 27 September 1941, and Telegram Nos. 35 and 36 by Mayer, 27 September 1941.

155. DHH, file 593.013 (D21), notes on Telegram Nos. 192/6 and 243/6 by Brooke-Popham, 25 November 1941; LAC, RG 24, vol. 12299, reel T-17901, file 3/Cdn Ops OS/1, memorandum by Montague, 3 February 1942; NARA, RG 24, Deck Log of USS *Mindanao*, log entry, 1 December 1941.

156. Jacoby and White, *Thunder Out of China*, 156. See also Charles Romanus and Riley Sunderland, *United States Army in World War II, China-Burma-India Theater*, vol. 3, *Time Runs Out in CBI* (Washington, DC: U.S. Army, 1959), 355, 360.

157. LAC, RG 2, vol. 32, file D-19-1 1945-Aug 12, Falkland Islands, memorandum by Robertson, 13 March 1942; NARA, RG 165, entry 184, box 959, Telegram No. 106 by Mayer, 25 June 1941. See also Baxter, "Britain and the War in China," 167, and J. F. Hilliker, "Distant Ally: Canadian Relations with Australia during the Second World War," *Journal of Imperial and Commonwealth History* 13, 1 (1984): 53.

158. LAC, RG 2, vol. 32, file D-19-1 1945-Aug 12, letter from Robertson to Mac-Donald, 13 March 1942. See also Brian Villa, *Unauthorized Action: Mountbatten and the Dieppe Raid* (Oxford: Oxford University Press, 1994), 72; and Denis Whitaker, *Dieppe: Tragedy to Triumph* (Toronto: McGraw-Hill Ryerson, 1992), 111–112.

159. LAC, Diaries of William Lyon Mackenzie King, 11 February 1942.

160. Arthur Tunnell, *The Canadian Who's Who*, vol. 12, *1970–1972* (Toronto: Who's Who Canadian Publications, 1972), 431.

161. Eric Breindel and Herbert Romerstein, *The Venona Secrets: Exposing Soviet Espionage and America's Traitors* (Washington, DC: Regnery, 2000), 158, 512. See also Walter Krivitsky, *I Was Stalin's Agent* (London: Right Book Club, 1940), 131; and Pavel Sudoplatov, *Special Tasks: The Memoirs of an Unwanted Witness—A Soviet Spymaster* (New York: Little, Brown, 1994).

162. Nicholas Evan Sarantakes, *Allies against the Rising Sun: The United States, the British Nations, and the Defeat of Imperial Japan* (Lawrence: University Press of Kansas, 2009), 133.

Chapter 9. Empires Derailed

1. Edward J. Drea, *Japan's Imperial Army: Its Rise and Fall, 1853–1945* (Lawrence: University Press of Kansas, 2009), 217–218.

2. NARA, RG 165, entry 184, box 959, Telegram No. C-70 by Lieutenant Colonel

William Mayer, 17 October 1941. See also TNA, FO 371/27626 F 6700/125/10, Telegram No. 357 by Archibald Clark Kerr, 23 July 1941.

3. Drea, *Japan's Imperial Army*, 217.

4. Chi Hsi Sheng, "The Military Dimension, 1942–1945," in *China's Bitter Victory: The War with Japan, 1937–1945,* ed. James C. Hsiung and Steven I. Levine (London: M. E. Sharpe, 1992), 158.

5. LAC, RG 24, reel C-5281, file 8865, letter from Howe to Ralston, 15 November 1941. See also LAC, RG 25, vol. 2135, file 572-1943; and LAC, RG 25, vol. 3343, file 4929-F-40C pt. 1, letter from Sheils to Robertson, 14 April 1942.

6. LAC, MG 26 J1, reel C-6805, letter from Mackenzie King to Currie, 16 March 1942; LAC, MG 26 J1, reel C-6813, letter from Mackenzie King to Soong, 16 March 1942, and letter from Soong to Mackenzie King, 24 March 1942. See also LAC, Diaries of William Lyon Mackenzie King, 13 March 1942, www.collectionscanada.gc.ca/data bases/king/001059-100.01-e.php.

7. TNA, FO 371/27628 F 11035/125/10, Telegram No. 1510 by Major General Lance Dennys, 15 October 1941.

8. NARA, RG 319, entry 57, box 164, file 4, Telegram No. 44 by Lieutenant Colonel David D. Barrett, 25 September 1941. See also Vasilii Chuikov, *Mission to China: Memoirs of a Soviet Military Adviser to Chiang Kaishek,* trans. David Barrett (Norwalk, CT: EastBridge, 2004), 129–131.

9. Drea, *Japan's Imperial Army*, 219.

10. LAC, RG 25, vol. 3233, file 5548-40C, Report No. 291, enclosure 1 by Ralph Collins, 8 June 1944. See also NARA, RG 165, M1444, Correspondence of the Military Intelligence Division Relating to General, Political, Economic, and Military Conditions in China, 1918–1941, reel 15, Report No. 9130 by Lieutenant Colonel W. S. Drysdale, 4 June 1935; and Hans Van de Ven, *War and Nationalism in China, 1925–1945* (London: RoutledgeCurzon, 2003), 256–258, 263.

11. NARA, RG 165, USMIR, reel 3, Report No. 11 by Lieutenant Colonel David Barrett, 3 December 1940. See also TNA, WO 208/366, report by Major General Lance Dennys, 25 October 1941.

12. Brian P. Farrell, *The Basis and Making of British Grand Strategy, 1940–1943: Was There a Plan?* (Lewiston, NY: Edwin Mellen Press, 1998), 408–409.

13. TNA, FO 371/27715 F 4091/3653/10, file cover notation by A. L. Scott, 21 May 1941.

14. IWM, Conservation Shelf, "Thunder in the East" by Grimsdale, 87–88. See also LAC, RG 24, reel C-8301, file 5147, memorandum by Colonel W. Murray, 13 October 1943; NARA, RG 165, entry 184, box 959, Telegram No. 106 by Mayer, 25 June 1941; TNA, FO 371/27641 F 6700/145/10, Telegram No. 357 by Archibald Clark Kerr, 23 July 1941; TNA, FO 371/27643 F 10789/145/10, report by Major K. Millar, 23 July 1941; TNA, WO 208/722, HKIR No. 8/41 by Major R. Giles, 1 September 1941; and Catherine Baxter, "Britain and the War in China, 1937–1945" (Ph.D. diss., University of Wales, 1993), 115–116, 188–189.

15. LAC, RG 25, vol. 3233, file 5548-40C, Report No. 291, enclosure 1 by Collins, 8 June 1944. See also NARA, RG 165, M1444, reel 15, Report No. 9316 by Stilwell, 5

March 1936; NARA, RG 319, entry 57, box 164, file 5, Telegram No. 55 by Barrett, 6 October 1941; Baxter, "Britain and the War in China," 115–116; Diana Lary, *Warlord Soldiers: Chinese Common Soldiers, 1911–1937* (Cambridge: Cambridge University Press, 1985), 20; and Peter Lowe, *Great Britain and the Origins of the Pacific War: A Study of British Policy in East Asia, 1937–1941* (Oxford: Clarendon Press, 1977), 211.

16. TNA, FO 371/27643 F 10789/145/10, report by Millar, 23 July 1941.

17. NARA, RG 59, *USSDCF*, reel 3, Report No. 893.00/14809 by Mayer, 12 September 1941. See also TNA, WO 208/722, HKIR No. 8/41 by Giles, 1 September 1941.

18. TNA, WO 208/366, report by Dennys, 25 October 1941.

19. NARA, RG 165, M1513, Military Intelligence Division Regional File Relating to China, 1922–1944, reel 38, Report No. 9854 by Mayer, 28 February 1940. See also TNA, WO 208/366, report by Dennys, 25 October 1941.

20. TNA, FO 371/27627 F 10051/125/10, Telegram No. M.33 24/9 by Dennys, 25 September 1941.

21. NARA, RG 165, M1513, reel 57, memorandum, 28 September 1941.

22. NARA, RG 38, entry 98A, box 705, Report No. 70/41 by Major F. J. McQuillen, 4 November 1941; NARA, RG 319, entry 57, box 164, file 5, Telegram No. 53 by Barrett, 3 October 1941. See also TNA, FO 371/27627 F 10043/125/10; TNA, WO 208/366, report by Dennys, 25 October 1941; and Dick Wilson, *When Tigers Fight: The Story of the Sino-Japanese War, 1937–1945* (New York: Viking Press, 1982), 185.

23. NARA, RG 38, entry 98A, box 705, Report No. 86-41 by Lieutenant M. R. Stone, 23 August 1941. See also NARA, RG 165, entry 184, box 959, Telegram No. 31 by Barrett, 27 August 1941, Telegram No. 34 by Barrett, 19 March 1941, Telegram No. 37 by Barrett, 26 March 1941, and Telegram No. 97 by Mayer, 10 June 1941; TNA, FO 371/27626 F 5757/125/10, Telegram No. M.135 by Dennys, 26 June 1941; TNA, WO 208/722, HKIR No. 3/41 by Giles, 1 April 1941, HKIR No. 5/41 by Giles, 1 June 1941, and HKIR No. 8/41 by Giles, 1 September 1941; and Wilson, *When Tigers Fight*, 184.

24. NARA, RG 38, entry 98A, box 705, Report No. 70-41 by Major F. McQuillen, 4 November 1941; NARA, RG 165, entry 184, box 959, Telegram No. 42 by Barrett, 23 September 1941. See also NARA, RG 165, M1513, reel 40, Telegram No. 40 by Barrett, 24 September 1941, and Telegram No. 67 by Spiker, 24 September 1941; TNA, WO 208/366, report by Dennys, 25 October 1941; TNA, WO 208/722, HKIR No. 9/41 by Giles, 1 October 1941; and Chuikov, *Mission to China*, 128.

25. NARA, RG 38, entry 98A, box 705, Report No. 70-41 by McQuillen, 4 November 1941; NARA, RG 165, entry 184, box 959, Telegram No. 51 by Barrett, 30 September 1941. See also NARA, RG 165, M1513, reel 40, Telegram No. 57 by Barrett, 8 October 1941, and Report No. 10579 by Major C. S. Babcock, 22 October 1941; TNA, FO 371/27628 F 10705/125/10, Telegram No. M.82 by Dennys, 10 October 1941; TNA, WO 208/366, report by Dennys, 25 October 1941; and TNA, WO 208/722, HKIR No. 9/41 by Giles, 1 October 1941.

26. NARA, RG 165, entry 184, box 959, Telegram No. 50 by Barrett, 30 September 1941. See also NARA, RG 165, M1513, reel 40, Telegram No. 37 by Brink, 8 October 1941, Telegram No. 40 by Barrett, 24 September 1941, and Telegram No. 51 by Barrett, 1 October 1941; TNA, FO 371/27627 F 10252/125/10, Telegram M.43 by Dennys, 29

September 1941; TNA, WO 208/366, report by Dennys, 25 October 1941; TNA, WO 208/722, HKIR No. 10/41 by Major R. Giles, 1 November 1941; Edward Hume, *Dauntless Adventurer: The Story of Dr. Winston Pettus* (New Haven, CT: Yale-in-China Association, 1952), 98; and Wilson, *When Tigers Fight*, 186.

27. NARA, RG 165, entry 184, box 959, Telegram No. 50 by Barrett, 30 September 1941; NARA, RG 165, M1513, reel 40, Telegram No. 37 by Barrett, 8 October 1941. See also TNA, WO 208/366, report by Dennys, 25 October 1941; and Chuikov, *Mission to China*, 129.

28. NARA, RG 165, entry 184, box 959, AMMISCA Telegram No. 12 by Brigadier General John Magruder, 22 October 1941, and Telegram No. 59 by Barrett, 8 October 1941. See also NARA, RG 165, M1513, reel 38, Report No. 52 by Mayer, 21 December 1941; NARA, RG 165, M1513, reel 40, Telegram No. 44 by Barrett, 24 September 1941; TNA, WO 208/366, report by Dennys, 25 October 1941; and Claire L. Chennault, *Way of a Fighter: The Memoirs of Claire Lee Chennault, Major General, U.S. Army (Ret.)* (New York: G. P. Putnam's Sons, 1949), 223.

29. NARA, RG 165, entry 184, box 959, Telegram No. 6 by Mayer, 6 August 1941; TNA, WO 208/366, report by Dennys, 25 October 1941.

30. NARA, RG 165, M1513, reel 38, Report No. 67 by Mayer, 14 October 1941; NARA, RG 165, M1513, reel 40, Telegram No. 58 by Barrett, 8 October 1941; NARA, RG 319, entry 57, box 164, file 5, Telegram No. 68 by Mayer, 16 October 1941. See also TNA, FO 371/27628 F 10908/125/10; TNA, WO 208/366, report by Dennys, 25 October 1941; Chuikov, *Mission to China*, 134.

31. NARA, RG 165, entry 184, box 961, report by Colonel Ralph Smith, 12 November 1941; NARA, RG 165, entry 184, box 962, Weekly State Department Report, 9 October 1941; NARA, RG 165, M1513, reel 38, Report No. 33 by Mayer, 30 October 1941; NARA, RG 165, M1513, reel 40, Report No. 65-41 by Major J. M. McHugh, 17 October 1941; NARA, RG 319, entry 57, box 164, file 5, Telegram No. C-85 by Mayer, 30 October 1941. See also TNA, WO 208/366, report by Dennys, 25 October 1941.

32. NARA, RG 319, entry 57, box 164, file 6, Telegram No. 122 by Magruder, 22 December 1941.

33. NARA, RG 165, entry 184, box 962, Weekly State Department Report, 16 October 1941; NARA, RG 165, M1513, reel 38, Report No. 68 by Mayer, 15 October 1941. See also TNA, WO 208/366, report by Dennys, 25 October 1941.

34. NARA, RG 165, entry 184, box 959, Telegram No. 68 by Mayer, 15 October 1941. See also NARA, RG 165, M1513, reel 40, Telegram by Mayer, 15 October 1941, and Report No. 65-41 by McHugh, 17 October 1941; and TNA, WO 208/722, HKIR No. 10/41 by Giles, 1 November 1941.

35. TNA, WO 208/722, HKIR No. 10/41 by Giles, 1 November 1941.

36. NARA, RG 165, entry 184, box 959, Telegram No. C-70 by Mayer, 17 October 1941. See also NARA, RG 165, M1513, reel 40, telegram by Mayer, 15 October 1941, and Report No. 65-41 by McHugh, 17 October 1941; NARA, RG 319, entry 57, box 164, file 5, Original Telegram No. 68 by Mayer, 16 October 1941.

37. NARA, RG 165, M1513, reel 40, Report No. 65-41 by McHugh, 17 October 1941.

38. Chuikov, *Mission to China*, xxxvi, xli.

39. NARA, RG 165, M1513, reel 40, Report No. 65-41 by McHugh, 17 October 1941.

40. TNA, WO 208/366, report by Dennys, 25 October 1941. See also TNA, WO 208/722, HKIR No. 8/41 by Giles, 1 September 1941.

41. TNA, WO 208/366, report by Dennys, 25 October 1941.

42. Ibid.

43. Andrew Whitfield, *Hong Kong, Empire and the Anglo-American Alliance at War, 1941–45* (Hong Kong: Hong Kong University Press, 2001), 65.

44. TNA, FO 371/27641 F 6700/145/10, file cover notation by A .L. Scott, 26 July 1941, and file cover notation by J. Sterndale Bennett, 3 August 1941.

45. NARA, RG 165, entry 184, box 962, Weekly State Department Report, 2 October 1941; NARA, RG 165, *USMIR*, reel 3, Report No. 11 by Barrett, 3 December 1940; TNA, FO 371/27627 F 10051/125/10, Telegram No. M.33 24/9 by Dennys, 25 September 1941; TNA, FO 371/27627 F 10356/125/10, Telegram No. 640 by Dennys, 30 September 1941; TNA, WO 208/366, report by Dennys, 25 October 1941. See also Chuikov, *Mission to China*, 124–126, and Roy Stanley, *Prelude to Pearl Harbor* (New York: Charles Scribner's Sons, 1982), 128.

46. David Evans and Mark Peattie, *Kaigun: Strategy, Tactics, and Technology in the Imperial Japanese Navy, 1887–1941* (Annapolis, MD: Naval Institute Press, 1997), 493.

47. LOC, Japanese Monographs (microform), Japanese Monograph No. 71, Army Operations in China, December 1941–December 1943 by Lieutenant Colonel Ishiwari Heizo, Special Staff U.S. Army Historical Section, 1963, 54. See also Chennault, *Way of a Fighter*, 140, and Chi, "Military Dimension," 158.

48. LAC, RG 24, vol. 20538, file 982.013 (D3), Operation Record in China Theatre, vol. 2 by Colonel Shimoda Chiyoshi, December 1946; LAC, RG 24, vol. 20538, file 982.013 (D6), British Official History Report, appendix 5, Japanese Order of Battle, 17 February 1955; LAC, RG 24, vol. 20539, file 982.045 (D1), Report on the Japanese 38th Division Order of Battle, 30 July 1951.

49. LAC, RG 24, vol. 20538, file 982.013 (D5), History of the 38th Japanese Division; TNA, FO 371/27628 F 12048/125/10, Telegram No. 1356 by Maltby, 7 November 1941. See also Philip Snow, *The Fall of Hong Kong: Britain, China and the Japanese Occupation* (New Haven, CT: Yale University Press, 2003), 39.

50. LAC, RG 24, vol. 3913, file 1037-5-3 vol. 1, Telegram FEW 53, 22 October 1941; NARA, RG 165, entry 184, box 962, Weekly State Department Report, 30 October 1941; NARA, RG 165, M1513, reel 40, Telegram No. 83 by Mayer, 28 October 1941; TNA, FO 371/27628 F 11172/125/10, Telegram No. 1136 by Major General Christopher Maltby, 20 October 1941; TNA, FO 371/27628 F 11658/125/10, Telegram No. 25263, 1 November 1941; TNA, FO 371/27628 F 12898/125/10; TNA, FO 371/27628 F 12933/125/10; TNA, WO 208/722, HKIR No. 10/41 by Giles, 1 November 1941.

51. LAC, RG 24, vol. 20538, file 982.013 (D3), Operation Record in China Theatre, vol. 2 by Shimoda, December 1946; LAC, RG 24, vol. 20539, file 982.045 (D1), Report on the Japanese 38th Division Order of Battle, 30 July 1951; LOC, Japanese

Monographs, Japanese Monograph No. 71 by Ishiwari, 1963. See also TNA, FO 371/27628 F 10897/125/10, Telegram No. 1033 by Maltby, 13 October 1941; TNA, FO 371/27628 F 11033/125/10, Telegram No. 1057 by Maltby, 15 October 1941; TNA, FO 371/27628 F 11093/125/10, Telegram No. 1106 by Maltby, 18 October 1941; TNA, FO 371/27628 F 11172/125/10, Telegram No. 1136 by Maltby, 20 October 1941; TNA, FO 371/27628 F 12898/125/10; TNA, FO 371/27628 F 12933/125/10; and TNA, WO 208/722, HKIR No. 9/41 by Giles, 1 October 1941, and HKIR No. 10/41 by Giles, 1 November 1941.

52. LAC, RG 24, vol. 20538, file 982.013 (D3), Operation Record in China Theatre, vol. 2 by Shimoda, December 1946; LOC, Japanese Monographs, Japanese Monograph No. 71 by Ishiwari, 1963. See also NARA, RG 59, *USSDCF*, reel 10, Report No. 893.00 P. R. Canton/166 PS/TL by Consul General M. Myers, 16 August 1942; NARA, RG 165, entry 184, box 959, Summary of British Military Intelligence, 28 August 1941; NARA, RG 165, entry 184, box 962, Weekly State Department Report, 4 December 1941; TNA, FO 371/27628 F 13386/125/10, Telegram No. 1678 by Maltby, 4 December 1941; TNA, WO 106/2402, Telegram No. 919 by Governor Geoffry Northcote, 25 August 1941; and George Endacott, *Hong Kong Eclipse* (Oxford: Oxford University Press, 1978), 65–66.

53. LAC, RG 24, vol. 3913, file 1037-5-3 vol. 1, Telegram FEW 53, 22 October 1941; NARA, RG 319, entry 57, box 169, file 1, Telegram No. 48 by Major Reynolds Condon, 14 October 1941. See also TNA, FO 371/27628 F 10703/125/10, Telegram No. 1012 by Maltby, 10 October 1941; TNA, FO 371/27628 F 10897/125/10, Telegram No. 1033 by Maltby, 13 October 1941; TNA, FO 371/27628 F 12381/125/10, Telegram No. 1454 by Maltby, 14 November 1941; TNA, FO 371/27628 F 13192/125/10, Telegram No. 1658 by Maltby, 3 December 1941; TNA, FO 371/27628 F 13386/125/10, Telegram No. 1678 by Maltby, 4 December 1941; TNA, WO 106/2402, Telegram No. 1346 by Governor Mark Young, 15 November 1941; and TNA, WO 106/2402, Telegram No. 2198 by Ambassador Sir Robert Craigie, 2 November 1941.

54. TNA, FO 371/27622 F 11379/98/10, Telegram No. 24862, 23 October 1941.

55. TNA, FO 371/27628 F 13192/125/10, Telegram No. 1658 by Maltby, 3 December 1941.

56. NARA, RG 24, Deck Log of USS *Mindanao*, log entries, 4 December 1941 and 31 March 1942. See also NARA, RG 59, *USSDCF*, reel 3, Report No. 893.00/14828 by Ambassador Clarence Gauss, 6 December 1941; and TNA, FO 371/27628 F 13386/125/10, Telegram No. 1678 by Maltby, 4 December 1941.

57. Oliver Lindsay, *The Battle for Hong Kong 1941–1945: Hostage to Fortune* (Hong Kong: Hong Kong University Press, 2005), 64.

58. TNA, FO 371/27628 F 13447/125/10, Telegram No. 1704 by Maltby, 7 December 1941.

59. TNA, FO 371/27628 F 13452/125/10, Telegram No. 1705 by Maltby, 7 December 1941.

60. TNA, FO 371/27628 F 13452/125/10, file cover notation by Scott, 13 December 1941.

61. LAC, RG 25, vol. 8517, file 6605-40, FO Biographies, Tu Yueh-sen, 16 April 1943; LAC, RG 24, vol. 20539, file 982.045 (D1), Report on the Japanese 38th Division Order of Battle, 30 July 1951. See also NARA, RG 165, M1513, reel 40, report by Major Richard Grussendorf, 19 August 1942; NARA, RG 165, M1513, reel 58, telegram by Major Roberts, 9 December 1941; TNA, CAB 121/718, COS (41) 398, minutes, 26 November 1941; TNA, WO 106/5360, Report No. 163 by Colonel C. P. Stacey, November 1946; Tony Banham, *Not the Slightest Chance: The Defence of Hong Kong, 1941* (Hong Kong: Hong Kong University Press, 2003), 12.

62. LAC, RG 24, vol. 12299, reel T-17901, file 3/Cdn Ops OS/1, Telegram No. 1455 by Maltby, 18 November 1941. See also Endacott, *Hong Kong Eclipse*, 60, 79; Compton Mackenzie, *Eastern Epic*, vol. 1, *September 1939–March 1943, Defence* (London: Chatto and Windus, 1951), 199; and Carl Vincent, *No Reason Why: The Canadian Hong Kong Tragedy, an Examination* (Stittsville, ON: Canada's Wings, 1981), 106.

63. NARA, RG 165, entry 77 NM 84, box 1738, file Islands, Hong Kong, report by Major Reynolds Condon, 20 August 1942; TNA, WO 106/5360, Report No. 163 by Stacey, November 1946; Martin Farndale, *History of the Royal Regiment of Artillery: The Far East Theatre, 1939–1946* (London: Brassey's, 2002), 14.

64. LAC, RG 24, vol. 12299, reel T-17901, file 3/Cdn Ops OS/1, memorandum, 3 February 1942; LOC, Japanese Night Combat Study, pt. 3, U.S. Army Report by Lieutenant Colonel Tanaka Kengoro and Lieutenant Colonel Ida Masataka, 1962; TNA, WO 106/5360, Report No. 163 by Stacey, November 1946. See also Terry Copp, "The Defence of Hong Kong, December 1941," *Canadian Military History* 10, 4 (2001): 10; Endacott, *Hong Kong Eclipse*, 109; B. H. Liddell Hart, "The Ratio of Troops to Space," *Military Review* 40, 1 (1960): 8; Oliver Lindsay, *The Lasting Honour* (London: Hamish Hamilton, 1978), 95; and Lindsay, *Battle for Hong Kong*, 61.

65. NARA, RG 165, entry 77 NM 84, box 1738, file Islands, Hong Kong, report by Condon, 20 August 1942.

66. LAC, RG 24, vol. 20537, file 982.011 (D1), statement of Major General Shoji Toshishige, 18 November 1946; LAC, RG 24, vol. 20538, file 982.013 (D6), British Official History Report, appendix 5, Japanese Order of Battle, 17 February 1955. See also Copp, "Defence of Hong Kong," 10, and Farndale, *History of the Royal Regiment of Artillery,* 15.

67. IWM, War Diary of the 2nd Battalion, Royal Scots, 9–10 December 1941. See also DHH, file 593.013 (D7), statement by Major General Doi Teishichi, September 1952; Tim Carew, *Fall of Hong Kong* (London: Pan Books, 1963), 76–77; Copp, "Defence of Hong Kong," 11; and Lindsay, *Battle for Hong Kong*, 74–77.

68. Endacott, *Hong Kong Eclipse*, 75.

69. TNA, WO 106/5360, Report No. 163 by Stacey, November 1946.

70. NARA, RG 165, M1513, reel 40, report by Grussendorf, 19 August 1942.

71. Ibid.

72. LAC, RG 24, vol. 20538, file 982.013 (D3), Operation Record in China Theatre, vol. 2 by Shimoda, December 1946. See also NARA, RG 165, entry 77 NM 84, box 1738, file Islands, Hong Kong, report by Condon, 20 August 1942; NARA, RG 407, entry 360, box 736, file 400.3295 4-14-41 sec. 2, Telegram No. 100 by Magruder,

14 December 1941; TNA, ADM 199/1287, report by Commander H. M. Montague, 11 January 1942; and TNA, WO 106/5360, Report No. 163 by Stacey, November 1946.

73. LAC, RG 24, vol. 12299, reel T-17901, file 3/Cdn Ops OS/1, Canadian Military Headquarters Telegram No. GS 2877, 15 December 1941; NARA, RG 226, entry 92, box 130, file 4, report on Stanley Camp, 2 September 1942. See also TNA, FO 371/27752 F 14211/13456/10, Telegram No. 717 by Commodore Alfred Collinson, 22 December 1941; TNA, WO 106/5356, HKIR No. 10/39 by Captain C. J. Edwards, 9 May 1939; TNA, WO 208/720, Extract of Malaya Summary No. 27, 5 September 1941; and Wilson, *When Tigers Fight*, 142.

74. TNA, ADM 199/1287, report by Montague, 11 January 1942. See also Copp, "Defence of Hong Kong," and Mackenzie, *Eastern Epic*, 199.

75. TNA, FO 371/27752 F 13889/13456/10, telegram, 13 December 1941; Endacott, *Hong Kong Eclipse*, 184–186.

76. HKU, BAAG series, vol. 2, "Capture, Escape and the Early B.A.A.G.," Mission 204 War Diary, 14 and 15 December 1941.

77. TNA, FO 371/27628 F 13602/125/10, Telegram No. M.292 by Dennys, 9 December 1941. See also Wilson, *When Tigers Fight*, 192.

78. NARA, RG 407, entry 360, box 736, file 400.3295 4-14-41 sec. 2, Telegram No. 90 by Magruder, 9 December 1941.

79. LAC, RG 24, vol. 20538, file 982.013 (D3), Operation Record in China Theatre, vol. 2 by Shimoda, December 1946.

80. HKU, BAAG series, vol. 2, "Capture, Escape and the Early B.A.A.G.," Mission 204 War Diary, 9 December 1941.

81. NARA, RG 407, entry 360, box 736, file 400.3295 4-14-41 sec. 2, Telegram No. 101 by Magruder, 14 December 1941.

82. HKU, BAAG series, vol. 2, "Capture, Escape and the Early B.A.A.G.," Mission 204 War Diary, 8–9 December 1941.

83. John Kennedy, *The Business of War: The War Narrative of Major-General Sir John Kennedy* (London: Hutchinson, 1957), 186.

84. NARA, RG 165, M1513, reel 39, Report No. 53, 14 January 1942; TNA, FO 371/27628 F 13602/125/10, Telegram No. M.292 by Dennys, 9 December 1941.

85. LAC, RG 25, vol. 3233, file 5548-40C, military situation memorandum by Lieutenant Colonel Hiram F. Wooster, 20 May 1944.

86. LAC, RG 24, vol. 12299, reel T-17901, file 3/Cdn Ops OS/1, Canadian Military Headquarters Telegram No. GS 2868, 15 December 1941; FDR, Harry Hopkins Papers, box 135, file China, Telegram No. 124 by Magruder. See also NARA, RG 407, entry 360, box 736, file 400.3295 4-14-41 sec. 2, Telegram No. 105 by Magruder, 15 December 1941, and Telegram No. 106 by Magruder, 16 December 1941; Chennault, *Way of a Fighter*, 141; Chiang Wego, *How Generalissimo Chiang Kai-Shek Won the Eight-Year Sino-Japanese War, 1937–1945* (Taipei: Li Ming Culture Enterprise Co., 1979), 107; and B. H. Liddell Hart, *History of the Second World War* (New York: Cassell, 1971), 234–235.

87. HKU, BAAG series, vol. 2, "Capture, Escape and the Early B.A.A.G.," Mission 204 War Diary, 18 and 20 December 1941; IWM, War Diary of the 2nd Battalion,

Royal Scots, 20 December 1941; LAC, RG 2, vol. 80, file F-12 Hong Kong 1941–1949, Telegram No. 59713 by Governor Young, 23 December 1941; NARA, RG 165, entry 184, box 960, War Department Intelligence Journal of General Sherman Miles, 13 December 1941; TNA, FO 371/27752 F 14187/13456/10, Telegram No. 720 by Young, 22 December 1941.

88. DHH, file 593.013 (D21), memorandum, annex 1, 1 January 1942; LAC, RG 24, vol. 20538, file 982.013 (D3), Operation Record in China Theatre, vol. 2 by Shimoda, December 1946; LAC, RG 24, vol. 20538, file 982.013 (D6), British Official History Appendices, appendix 5, 17 February 1955; LAC, RG 25, vol. 2920, file 2670-A-40C-1, Telegram No. 720, 23 December 1941. See also NARA, RG 407, entry 360, box 736, file 400.3295 4-14-41 sec. 2, Telegram No. 101 by Magruder, 14 December 1941, and Telegram No. 107 by Magruder, 16 December 1941; TNA, FO 371/27628 F 13911/125/10, Telegram No. 687 by Clark Kerr, 17 December 1941; TNA, FO 371/27752 F 13765/13456/10, Telegram No. 1758 by Maltby, 14 December 1941; and Lindsay, *Battle for Hong Kong*, 87.

89. LAC, RG 25, vol. 2920, file 2670-A-40C-2, Diary of Rifleman S. Skelton, 16 December 1941; NARA, RG 407, entry 360, box 736, file 400.3295 4-14-41 sec. 2, Telegram No. 105 by Magruder, 15 December 1941; TNA, WO 208/722, HKIR No. 9/41 by Giles, 1 October 1941. See also Endacott, *Hong Kong Eclipse*, 81, and Evan Stewart, *Hong Kong Volunteers in Battle: A Record of the Actions of the Hongkong Volunteer Defence Corps in the Battle for Hong Kong December, 1941* (Hong Kong: RHKR [The Volunteers] Association Ltd. with Blacksmith Books, 2005), 20.

90. DHH, file 593.013 (D7), statement by Doi, September 1952; NARA, RG 226, entry 92, box 59, file 58, statement by S. E. Lavrov, 10 August 1942; TNA, ADM 199/1287, memorandum by W. G. Poy, 31 July 1942; TNA, FO 371/27752 F 14211/13456/10, Telegram No. 717 by Collinson, 22 December 1941. See also Endacott, *Hong Kong Eclipse*, 82, and Charles Stacey, *Official History of the Canadian Army in the Second World War*, vol. 1, *Six Years of War, the Army in Canada, Britain and the Pacific* (Ottawa: Department of National Defence, 1967), 471–472, 474.

91. Copp, "Defence of Hong Kong," 16–17; Endacott, *Hong Kong Eclipse*, 91, 93; Cameron Pulsifer, "John Robert Osborn, Canada's Hong Kong VC," *Canadian Military History* 6, 2 (1997): 88; Stacey, *Official History of the Canadian Army*, 480–481; Stewart, *Hong Kong Volunteers in Battle*, 26–30.

92. TNA, ADM 199/1287, report by Montague, 11 January 1942. See also TNA, CAB 106/88, Report on the Hong Kong Chinese Regiment, 25 July 1942.

93. NARA, RG 165, entry 77 NM 84, box 1738, file Islands, Hong Kong, report by Condon, 20 August 1942. See also TNA, CAB 106/88, Report on the Hong Kong Chinese Regiment, 25 July 1942; and Baxter, "Britain and the War in China," 388, 414.

94. Stacey, *Official History of the Canadian Army*, 482.

95. LAC, RG 24, vol. 3914, file 1037-5-14 vol. 2, Telegram No. 522, 23 December 1941; LAC, RG 24, vol. 20537, file 982.011 (D1), statement by Shoji, 18 November 1946; TNA, ADM 199/1287, report by Montague, 11 January 1942.

96. CSM George MacDonell, interview by the author, 3 August 2006. See also Copp, "Defence of Hong Kong," 18.

97. LAC, RG 24, vol. 12299, reel T-17901, file 3/Cdn Ops OS/1, Telegram M 407 by Grimsdale, 20 February 1942; Endacott, *Hong Kong Eclipse*, 97, 104–105.

98. LAC, RG 24, vol. 20538, file 982.013 (D5), History of the 38th Japanese Division; NARA, RG 165, M1513, reel 39, Report on Hong Kong Defences, 25 April 1942; TNA, ADM 199/1287, report by Montague, 11 January 1942; TNA, FO 371/27752 F 14206/13456/10, Telegram No. 740, 23 December 1941. See also *South China Morning Post*, 13 November 2009; Banham, *Not the Slightest Chance*, ix, 317–318; and Endacott, *Hong Kong Eclipse*, 185.

99. Farndale, *History of the Royal Regiment of Artillery*, 28.

100. Carew, *Fall of Hong Kong*, 76–77, 189, 200. See also Snow, *Fall of Hong Kong*, 65, and Whitfield, *Hong Kong*, 15, 219.

101. Banham, *Not the Slightest Chance*, 334.

102. Lindsay, *Battle for Hong Kong*, 143.

103. NARA, RG 165, entry 77, box 438, Report No. 1647 by Major R. Ervin, 17 July 1941, and Report on the Canadian Expeditionary Force to the Crown Colony of Hong Kong by Sir Lyman Duff, 4 June 1942.

104. Paul Dickson, "The Limits of Professionalism: General H. D. G. Crerar and the Canadian Army, 1914–1944" (Ph.D. diss., University of Guelph, 1993), 331. See also Douglas Ford, *Britain's Secret War against Japan, 1937–1945* (New York: Routledge, 2006), 57–59, 63–65, 118.

105. Laurier Centre for Military Strategic and Disarmament Studies (Waterloo, Canada), Hong Kong Papers, memorandum by Lieutenant General C. Foulkes, 9 February 1948.

106. Farndale, *History of the Royal Regiment of Artillery*, 28. See also Lindsay, *Battle for Hong Kong*, 83.

107. DHH, file 1-5-8 vol. 2, Memorandum HQS 1453-10 (DHS) by Stacey, 19 February 1951.

108. Copp, "Defence of Hong Kong," 10. See also Farndale, *History of the Royal Regiment of Artillery*, 15.

109. DHH, file 1-5-8 vol. 2, Memorandum HQS 1453-10 (DHS) by Stacey, 19 February 1951. See also Copp, "Defence of Hong Kong," 10, and Lindsay, *Battle for Hong Kong*, 138.

110. DHH, file 593.013 (D21), memorandum by G. E. Gent, 27 December 1941; NARA, RG 226, entry 92, box 128, file 4, memorandum by William Taylor, 10 September 1942; TNA, FO 371/27622 F 13284/98/10, file cover notation, 15 December 1941; John Toland, *But Not in Shame: The Six Months after Pearl Harbor* (New York: Random House, 1961), 138.

111. DHH, file 593.013 (D21), memorandum, annex 1, 1 January 1942. See also *New York Times*, 21 December 1941.

112. Baxter, "Britain and the War in China," 165.

113. LAC, RG 25, vol. 3264, file 6161-40C, Telegram No. 138 by Victor Odlum, 9 October 1943. See also ibid., Telegram No. 152 by Odlum, 18 October 1943.

114. LAC, RG 25, vol. 3264, file 6161-40C, Telegram No. 138 by Odlum, enclosure memorandum by V. J. R. Mills, 30 September 1943.

115. *New York Times*, 16 January 1942.

116. LAC, RG 25, vol. 5740, file 25-G(s), Dominions Office Telegram No. 769, 25 December 1941.

117. Baxter, "Britain and the War in China," 195. See also Yu Maochun, "'In God We Trusted, in China We Busted': The China Commando Group of the Special Operations Executive (SOE)," *Intelligence and National Security* 16, 4 (2001): 51–52.

118. LAC, RG 25, vol. 4717, file no. 50055-40 pt. 1, FO Document Page F 4351/113/10, memorandum by Clark Kerr, 3 February 1942.

119. Chiang, *How Generalissimo Chiang Kai-Shek Won*, 111–112.

120. Ibid., 107; LAC, RG 24, vol. 20538, file 982.013 (D3), Operation Record in China Theatre, vol. 2 by Shimoda, December 1946; LOC, Japanese Monographs, Japanese Monograph No. 71 by Ishiwari, 1963; TNA, WO 208/722, HKIR No. 4/41 by Giles, 1 May 1941, and HKIR No. 7/41 by Giles, 1 August 1941. See also Charles Romanus and Riley Sunderland, *United States Army in World War II, China-Burma-India Theater*, vol. 2, *Stilwell's Command Problems* (Washington, DC: U.S. Army, 1956), 372.

121. Chuikov, *Mission to China*, 161. See also Jay Taylor, *The Generalissimo: Chiang Kai-Shek and the Struggle for Modern China* (Cambridge, MA: Belknap Press, 2009), 189; and Richard Webb, "The War in China," *Far Eastern Survey* 11, 4 (1942): 49–50.

122. LAC, RG 24, vol. 20538, file 982.013 (D3), Operation Record in China Theatre, vol. 2 by Shimoda, December 1946; LOC, Japanese Monographs, Japanese Monograph No. 71 by Ishiwari, 1963; NARA, RG 165, M1513, reel 40, Report on Third Battle of Changsha, 7 January 1942; NARA, RG 319, entry 57, box 164, file 6, Telegram No. 123 by Magruder, 22 December 1941, and Telegram No. 125 by Magruder, 26 December 1941. See also Hume, *Dauntless Adventurer*, 95, and Robert Payne, *Chinese Diaries, 1941–1946* (New York: Weybright and Talley, 1970), 43.

123. LAC, RG 24, vol. 20538, file 982.013 (D3), Operation Record in China Theatre, vol. 2 by Shimoda, December 1946; LOC, Japanese Monographs, Japanese Monograph No. 71 by Ishiwari, 1963. See also Chang Ming Kai and Hsu Long Hsuen, *History of the Sino-Japanese War (1937–1945)*, trans. Wen Ha Hsiung (Taipei: Chung Wu Publishing, 1971), 366–367; Hume, *Dauntless Adventurer*, 98–99; and Payne, *Chinese Diaries*, 59.

124. LAC, RG 24, vol. 20538, file 982.013 (D3), Operation Record in China Theatre, vol. 2 by Shimoda, December 1946; LOC, Japanese Monographs, Japanese Monograph No. 71 by Ishiwari, 1963; NARA, RG 319, entry 57, box 164, file 6, telegram by Magruder, 30 December 1941; TNA, FO 371/27628 F 14368/125/10, Telegram No. M 405 by Dennys, 27 December 1941.

125. LAC, RG 24, vol. 20538, file 982.013 (D3), Operation Record in China Theatre, vol. 2 by Shimoda, December 1946. See also Hume, *Dauntless Adventurer*, 98, and Payne, *Chinese Diaries*, 43.

126. Hume, *Dauntless Adventurer*, 104.

127. Ibid., 114–115; Payne, *Chinese Diaries*, 50, 52.

128. *Times* (London), 12 January 1942.

129. NARA, RG 319, entry 57, box 164, file 7, Telegram No. 162 by Magruder, 3 January 1942.

130. NARA, RG 165, M1513, reel 40, Report on Third Battle of Changsha, 7 January 1942, and Report No. 15 by Mayer, 14 January 1942. See also *New York Times*, 3 January 1942.

131. Chang and Hsu, *History of the Sino-Japanese War*, 367, 369.

132. *New York Times*, 15 January 1942.

133. *New York Times*, 30 December 1941, 1 January 1942. See also Chang and Hsu, *History of the Sino-Japanese War*, 367, 369–371.

134. LAC, RG 24, vol. 20538, file 982.013 (D3), Operation Record in China Theatre, vol. 2 by Shimoda, December 1946. See also Chang and Hsu, *History of the Sino-Japanese War*, 371.

135. Payne, *Chinese Diaries*, 58–59, 62.

136. LAC, RG 24, vol. 20538, file 982.013 (D3), Operation Record in China Theatre, vol. 2 by Shimoda, December 1946; LOC, Japanese Monographs, Japanese Monograph No. 71 by Ishiwari, 1963; NARA, RG 165, M1513, reel 40, Report on Third Battle of Changsha, 7 January 1942; NARA, RG 319, entry 57, box 164, file 7, Telegram No. C 9 by Mayer, 11 January 1942. See also Payne, *Chinese Diaries*, 52, 55–57.

137. LOC, Japanese Monographs, Japanese Monograph No. 71 by Ishiwari, 1963; LAC, RG 24, vol. 20538, file 982.013 (D3), Operation Record in China Theatre, vol. 2 by Shimoda, December 1946.

138. LAC, RG 24, vol. 20538, file 982.013 (D3), Operation Record in China Theatre, vol. 2 by Shimoda, December 1946; LOC, Japanese Monographs, Japanese Monograph No. 71 by Ishiwari, 1963; NARA, RG 319, entry 57, box 164, file 7, Telegram No. 173 by Magruder, 11 January 1942. See also *New York Times*, 15 January 1942, and *Times* (London), 10 January 1942.

139. *Times* (London), 12 January 1942.

140. *New York Times*, 15 January 1942; *Times* (London), 10 January 1942. See also Drea, *Japan's Imperial Army*, 224, and Ienaga Saburo, *The Pacific War: World War II and the Japanese, 1931–1945* (New York: Pantheon, 1978), 232.

141. Payne, *Chinese Diaries*, 47.

142. Chennault, *Way of a Fighter*, 261.

143. *Times* (London), 12 January 1942.

144. LAC, RG 24, vol. 20538, file 982.013 (D3), Operation Record in China Theatre, vol. 2 by Shimoda, December 1946; NARA, RG 165, M1513, reel 40, Report on Third Battle of Changsha, 7 January 1942; NARA, RG 165, M1513, Report No. 15 by Mayer, 14 January 1942; NARA, RG 319, entry 57, box 164, file 7, Telegram No. 173 by Magruder, 11 January 1942, and Telegram No. C 15 by Mayer, 15 January 1942. See also *New York Times*, 15 January 1942; *Times* (London), 15 January 1942; Hume, *Dauntless Adventurer*, 104; and Payne, *Chinese Diaries*, 56–57.

145. LAC, RG 25, vol. 3233, file 5548-40C, Telegram No. 291, enclosure 1 by Collins, 8 June 1944. See also LAC, RG 24, vol. 20538, file 982.013 (D3), Operation Record in China Theatre, vol. 2 by Shimoda, December 1946.

146. Telegram by Ambassador Clarence Gauss, in *FRUS 1942, China*, 4–5.

147. Memorandum by Stanley Hornbeck, in *FRUS 1942, China*, 445. See also *New York Times*, 22 January 1942.

148. Chiang, *How Generalissimo Chiang Kai-Shek Won*, 111–112.

149. LAC, RG 25, vol. 5740, file 25-G(s), Dominions Office Telegram, 30 March 1942.

150. NARA, RG 165, M1513, reel 38, memorandum by Lieutenant Colonel F. Roberts, 14 January 1942. See also Lowe, *Great Britain and Origins of the Pacific War*, 280–281.

151. George Orwell, *All Propaganda Is Lies, 1941–1942: The Complete Works of George Orwell*, vol. 13 (London: Secker and Warburg, 1998), 121.

152. Webb, "War in China," 49–50.

153. *Times*, 12 January 1942.

154. NARA, RG 407, entry 360, box 736, file 400.3295 4-14-41 sec. 2, Telegram No. 90 by Magruder, 9 December 1941; TNA, FO 371/27628 F 13602/125/10, Telegram No. M.292 by Dennys, 9 December 1941.

155. NARA, RG 319, entry 57, box 164, file 7, Telegram No. C 11 by Mayer, 13 January 1942; NARA, RG 493, CBI AG Subject File, box 614, memorandum of Wavell-Chiang conference of 22 December 1941 by Colonel E. MacMorland, 23 December 1941. See also Christopher Bayly and Tim Harper, *Forgotten Armies: The Fall of British Asia, 1941–1945* (London: Penguin Books, 2004), 159; Chennault, *Way of a Fighter*, 140–142; and Webb, "War in China," 50.

156. Chuikov, *Mission to China*, xli, 124.

157. *New York Times*, 25 January 1942.

158. Evan Mawdsley. *Thunder in the East: The Nazi-Soviet War, 1941–1945* (London: Hodder Arnold, 2005), 16–17.

159. Henry Gole, *The Road to Rainbow: Army Planning for Global War, 1934–1940* (Annapolis, MD: Naval Institute Press, 2003), 151.

160. LAC, RG 25, vol. 2661, file 6045-40, Summary of News in China (March), F 3751/1689/10, by Ambassador Horace Seymour, 1 April 1942.

161. IWM, "Thunder in the East" by Grimsdale, 16.

162. LAC, RG 25, vol. 3345, file 6812-40C, Telegram No. 405 by Odlum, 16 September 1945. See also Kent Fedorowich, "Decolonization Deferred? The Re-establishment of Colonial Rule in Hong Kong, 1942–45," *Journal of Imperial and Commonwealth History* 28, 3 (2000): 44, and Lawrence Lai, "The Battle of Hong Kong: A Note on the Literature and the Effectiveness of the Defence," *Journal of the Royal Asiatic Society Hong Kong Branch* 39 (1999): 120–121.

163. HKU, BAAG series, vol. 2, "Capture, Escape and the Early B.A.A.G.," report by Colonel Lindsay Ride, 20 August 1942; HKU, BAAG series, vol. 7, "Coast Watching and the 'Red' Question," telegram by Captain E. Cooper, 7 June 1943; Fedorowich, "Decolonization Deferred," 43.

164. HKU, BAAG series, vol. 2, "Capture, Escape and the Early B.A.A.G.," report by Ride, 20 August 1942; HKU, BAAG series, vol. 4, "Advance Headquarters, Waichow, Field Operations Group," report by Major Ronnie Holmes, 6 December 1942, and report by Holmes, 12 July 1944. See also NARA, RG 493, entry 531, box 51, Z Force Report, 25 May 1944.

165. Chuikov, *Mission to China*, 20, 162–163.

1. Evan Mawdsley, *Thunder in the East: The Nazi-Soviet War, 1941–1945* (London: Hodder Arnold, 2005), 112, 116. See also "Soviet Commander Admits USSR Came Close to Defeat by Nazis," *Daily Telegraph* (London), 5 May 2010.

2. Yu Maochun, *The Dragon's War: Allied Operations and the Fate of China* (Annapolis, MD: Naval Institute Press, 2006), 92.

3. NARA, RG 165, entry 184, box 962, Weekly State Department Reports, 26 December 1941 and 22 January 1942; NARA, RG 165, entry 421, box 407, OPD ABC Files 1940–48, Joint Chiefs of Staff Memorandum No. 14, 4 July 1942; TNA, WO 208/849, Review of Foreign Press, No. 122, February 1942. See also *New York Times*, 18 January 1942, and Kent Fedorowich, "Decolonization Deferred? The Re-establishment of Colonial Rule in Hong Kong, 1942–45," *Journal of Imperial and Commonwealth History* 28, 3 (2000): 27.

4. NARA, RG 38, entry 98A, box 705, F-6-c 23213 to F-6-e 22379, "Southward Advance of the Japanese Navy"; NARA, RG 165, M1513, reel 58, Naval Intelligence Report, 30 June 1943.

5. LAC, Diaries of William Lyon Mackenzie King, 19 January 1942, www.collectionscanada.gc.ca/databases/king/001059-100.01-e.php.

6. John Dower, *War without Mercy: Race and Power in the Pacific War* (New York: Pantheon Books, 1986), 6–7; Hal Gold, *Unit 731: Testimony* (Tokyo: Yenbooks, 1996), 50–51.

7. Richard Webb, "The War in China," *Far Eastern Survey* 11, 4 (1942): 50.

8. NARA 165, entry 421, box 407, Joint Intelligence Committee Memorandum No. 201/1 by J. S. Lay, 2 August 1944.

9. NARA, RG 165, M1513, reel 58, Naval Intelligence Report, 30 June 1943.

10. NARA, RG 319, entry 57, box 164, file 6, Telegram No. 121 by Mayer, 20 December 1941. See also NARA, RG 493, entry 531, box 50, Z Force Journal.

11. LAC, RG 24, reel C-5281, file 8865, letter from Howe to Ralston, 15 November 1941; LAC, RG 25, vol. 3343, file 4929-F-40C pt. 1, letter from Sheils to Robertson, 14 April 1942.

12. Patrick Buchanan, *Churchill, Hitler, and the Unnecessary War: How Britain Lost Its Empire and the West Lost the World* (New York: Crown Publishers, 2008), 116.

13. LAC, Diaries of William Lyon Mackenzie King, 28 February and 13 March 1942. See also LAC, MG 26 J1, reel C-6805, letter from Mackenzie King to Currie, 16 March 1942; LAC, MG 26 J1, reel C-6813, letter from Mackenzie King to Soong, 16 March 1942, letter from Soong to Mackenzie King, 24 March 1942, and letter from Mackenzie King to Soong, 4 May 1942; LAC, RG 25, vol. 3343, file 4929-F-40C pt. 1, letter from Sheils to Robertson, 14 April 1942; and Franco David Macri, "Bren Guns for China: The Origin and Impact of Sino-Canadian Relations, 1941–1949," *International History Review* 34, 3 (2012): 8, 10.

14. LAC, MG 26 J1, reel C-7042, External Affairs Telegram No. 94 to Odlum, 15 October 1943; LAC, RG 25, vol. 3343, file 4929-F-40C pt. 1, Telegram No. 94, 15 October 1943; LAC, RG 25, vol. 3343, file 4929-F-40C pt. 2, memorandum, 27 March

1944. See also R. Warren James, *Wartime Economic Co-operation: A Study of Relations between Canada and the United States* (Toronto: Ryerson Press, 1949), 228–229.

15. LAC, MG 26 J4, reel H-1476, memorandum, 2 August 1944. See also LAC, RG 25, vol. 3343, file 4929-F-40C pt. 1, letter from Pearson to Robertson, 17 September 1943, Telegram No. 505 by Major General Maurice Pope, 17 September 1943, and letter from Robertson to Howe, 23 September 1943; LAC, RG 25, vol. 3343, file 4929-F-40C pt. 2, memorandum, 6 April 1944; LAC, RG 25, vol. 3343, file 4929-F-40C pt. 3, memorandum, 31 May 1944, file notation, 21 August 1944, and Telegram No. 109 by Odlum, 24 April 1945; LAC, RG 25, vol. 4201, file 4851-40 pt. 1, Telegram No. 1134 by Ronning, 22 October 1946; Kim Nossal, "Strange Bedfellows: Canada and China in War and Revolution, 1942–1947" (Ph.D. diss., University of Toronto, 1977), 220; and Macri, "Bren Guns for China," 10.

16. IWM, Conservation Shelf, "Thunder in the East" by Grimsdale, 76–77. See also LAC, MG 26 J4, vol. 244, reel H-1476, file China, Telegram No. 29 by Patterson, 31 January 1945; LAC, RG 25, vol. 3343, file 4929-F-40C pt. 2, memorandum by Arthur Menzies, 14 March 1944; Charles Romanus and Riley Sunderland, *United States Army in World War II, China-Burma-India Theater*, vol. 2, *Stilwell's Command Problems* (Washington, DC: U.S. Army, 1956), 452; Jay Taylor, *The Generalissimo: Chiang Kai-Shek and the Struggle for Modern China* (Cambridge, MA: Belknap Press, 2009), 235; and Barbara Tuchman, *Stilwell and the American Experience in China, 1911–1945* (New York: Macmillan, 1970), 495.

17. NARA, RG 160, entry 116, box 9, file 25/10/1943, Direct Lend Lease Aid to China, 25 October 1943. See also LAC, RG25, vol. 3343, file 4929-F-40C pt. 2, Telegram No. 789 by Massey, 8 April 1944.

18. LAC, MG 26 J1, reel C-6809, letter from Mackie to Mackenzie King, 28 March 1942. See also LAC, RG 25, vol. 3017, file 3722-40, External Affairs memoranda, 17 April and 5 May 1942.

19. LAC, MG 26 J1, reel C-6813, Soong–Mackenzie King correspondence, 3 March and 4 and 11 May 1942. See also LAC, MG 26 J1, reel C-7059, letter from Mackenzie King to Madame Laura Soong, 31 December 1944; LAC, MG 26 J1, reel C-11044, Soong–Mackenzie King correspondence, 30 January and 11 October 1947; Akira Ichikawa and Quo F. Q., "Sino-Canadian Relations: A New Chapter," *Asian Survey* 12, 5 (1972): 388.

■
Bibliography

Archival Sources

CANADA
Canadian War Museum
    Democracy at War: Canadian Newspapers and the Second World War. http://war
      museum.ca/cwm/exhibitions/newspapers/intro_e.shtml
    Diary of Captain Harry White
Laurier Centre for Military Strategic and Disarmament Studies
    Hong Kong Files
Library and Archives Canada
    Diaries of William Lyon Mackenzie King. http://king.collectionscanada.ca/EN/
      default.asp
    MG 26, Robert Borden Correspondence
    MG 26 J1, William Lyon Mackenzie King Fonds
    MG 26 J2, William Lyon Mackenzie King Fonds, Office Files
    MG 26 J4, William Lyon Mackenzie King Fonds, Memoranda and Notes
    MG 26 K, Richard Bennett Correspondence
    MG 30 D45, John Dafoe Papers
    MG 31 E46, Escott Reid Papers
    RG 2, Cabinet War Committee Records
    RG 12, Department of Transportation Fonds
    RG 13, Department of Justice Fonds
    RG 24, Army Central Registry Files
    RG 24, Army Headquarters Central Registry

RG 24, Canadian Military Headquarters, London
RG 25, Department of External Affairs Fonds
Metropolitan Toronto Reference Library
Biographies of People: Scrapbook vols. 1, 5, and 7
National Archives of the United Church of Canada
Accession number 83.046C, UCC Board of Overseas Missions, South China
National Defence and the Canadian Forces, Directorate of History and Heritage Library
Department of National Defence: Hong Kong Reports, 593 Series, and Kardex Files

GREAT BRITAIN
Imperial War Museum
Conservation Shelf
Grimsdale, G. E., "Thunder in the East," 1947
War Diary, Second Battalion, Royal Scots
The National Archives
ADM 1, Admiralty, and Ministry of Defence, Navy Department: Correspondence
and Papers
ADM 199, Admiralty: War History Cases and Papers, Second World War
CAB 79, War Cabinet and Cabinet: Chiefs of Staff Committee: Minutes
CAB 80, War Cabinet and Cabinet: Chiefs of Staff Committee: Memoranda
CAB 120, Cabinet Office: Minister of Defence Secretariat: Records
CAB 121, Cabinet Office: Special Secret Information Centre: Files
CO 129, War and Colonial Department and Colonial Office: Hong Kong, Original
Correspondence
FO 371, Confidential British Foreign Office Political Correspondence, China series
3: 1932–1945, pt. 4: 1939–1941
FO 371, Foreign Office General Correspondence—Political, 1938–1966, Hong
Kong
FO 954, Foreign Office: Private Office Papers of Sir Anthony Eden, Earl of Avon,
Secretary of State for Foreign Affairs
WO 106, War Office: Directorate of Military Operations and Military Intelligence,
and Predecessors: Correspondence and Papers
WO 208, War Office: Directorate of Military Operations and Intelligence, and Di-
rectorate of Military Intelligence; Ministry of Defence, Defence Intelligence
Staff: Files

HONG KONG
University of Hong Kong Archive
Ride, Elizabeth, ed., BAAG series, vols. 2, 4, and 7

UNITED STATES
Franklin D. Roosevelt Presidential Library and Museum
Frederic A. Delano Papers
Harry Hopkins Papers

Morgenthau Papers
President's Safe Files
President's Secretary's Files
Roosevelt Papers
Library of Congress
  Declassified Documents Reference System. *History of the JCS in World War II: The War against Japan*, vol. 1, *Pearl Harbor through Trident*. Chapter IX: "China-Burma-India, 1942, Supply and Support." Washington, DC: Department of Defense, 1953.
  Japanese Monographs. Washington, DC: Library of Congress Photoduplication Service, 1963.
  Japanese Night Combat Study, pts. 1–3. Washington, DC: Library of Congress Photoduplication Service, 1962.
National Archives and Records Administration, College Park, MD
  RG 18, Records of the Army Air Forces
  RG 24, Records of the Bureau of Naval Personnel
  RG 38, Records of the Office of the Chief of Naval Operations
  RG 38, M975, Selected Naval Attaché Reports Relating to the World Crisis, 1937–1943
  RG 59, *Confidential U.S. State Department Central Files: China, Internal Affairs, 1930–1939*, ed. Paul Kesaris. Frederick, MD: University Publications of America, 1984.
  RG 59, *Confidential U.S. State Department Central Files: China, Internal Affairs 1940–1944*, ed. Paul Kesaris. Frederick, MD: University Publications of America, 1984.
  RG 59, *Internal Affairs of China, 1940–1944*. Wilmington, DE: Scholarly Resources, 1985.
  RG 59, Records of the Department of State
  RG 84, Records of the Foreign Service Posts of the Department of State
  RG 111, Records of the Office of the Chief Signal Officer, 1860–1985
  RG 165, Records of the War Department General and Special Staffs
  RG 165, *U.S. Military Intelligence Reports: China, 1911–1941*, ed. Paul Kesaris. Frederick, MD: University Publications of America, 1983.
  RG 165, M1444, Correspondence of the Military Intelligence Division Relating to General, Political, Economic, and Military Conditions in China, 1918–1941
  RG 165, M1513, Military Intelligence Division Regional File Relating to China, 1922–1944: Records of the War Department General and Special Staffs
  RG 226, Records of the Office of Strategic Services 1940–1946
  RG 306, Records of the U.S. Information Agency, 1900–1992
  RG 319, Records of the Army Staff
  RG 341, Records of Headquarters U.S. Air Force (Air Staff), 1934–1989
  RG 407, Records of the Adjutant General's Office
  RG 493, Records of U.S. Army Forces in the China-Burma-India Theatres of Operations

Books, Articles, and Dissertations

Abend, Hallett. *My Life in China, 1926–1941.* New York: Harcourt, Brace, 1943.

Agbi, S. Olu. "The Pacific War Controversy in Britain: Sir Robert Craigie versus the Foreign Office." *Modern Asian Studies* 17, 3 (1983): 489–517.

Akira Ichikawa and Quo F. Q. "Sino-Canadian Relations: A New Chapter." *Asian Survey* 12, 5 (1972): 386–398.

Angus, H. *Canada and the Far East, 1940–1953.* Toronto: University of Toronto Press, 1953.

Banham, Tony. *Not the Slightest Chance: The Defence of Hong Kong, 1941.* Hong Kong: Hong Kong University Press, 2003.

Barnett, Correlli. *The Collapse of British Power.* London: Eyre Methuen, 1972.

Baxter, Catherine. "Britain and the War in China, 1937–1945." Ph.D. diss., University of Wales, 1993.

Bayly, Christopher, and Tim Harper. *Forgotten Armies: The Fall of British Asia, 1941–1945.* London: Penguin Books, 2004.

Beevor, Antony. *Crete: The Battle and the Resistance.* London: John Murray, 1991.

Bell, Christopher. "'Our Most Exposed Outpost': Hong Kong and British Far Eastern Strategy, 1921–1941." *Journal of Military History* 60, 1 (1996): 61–88.

Best, Antony. *British Intelligence and the Japanese Challenge in Asia, 1914–1941.* New York: Palgrave, 2002.

Bloch, Kurt. "China's Lifelines and the Indo-China Frontier." *Far Eastern Survey* 9, 4 (1940): 47–49.

Bonavia, David. *China's Warlords.* New York: Oxford University Press, 1995.

Bond, Bryan, and Kyoichi Takhikawa, eds. *British and Japanese Military Leadership in the Far Eastern War, 1941–1945.* New York: Frank Cass, 2004.

Boorman, Howard L., and Richard C. Howard, eds. *Biographical Dictionary of Republican China.* New York: Columbia University Press, 1971.

Borovik, Genrikh. *The Philby Files: The Secret Life of Master Spy Kim Philby,* ed. Phillip Knightley. Toronto: Little, Brown, 1994.

Boyd, Carl. *Hitler's Japanese Confidant: General Oshima Hiroshi and MAGIC Intelligence, 1941–1945.* Lawrence: University Press of Kansas, 1993.

Boyle, John H. *China and Japan at War, 1937–1945: The Politics of Collaboration.* Stanford, CA: Stanford University Press, 1972.

Braithwaite, Rodric. *Moscow 1941: A City and Its People at War.* London: Profile Books, 2007.

Breindel, Eric, and Herbert Romerstein. *The Venona Secrets: Exposing Soviet Espionage and America's Traitors.* Washington, DC: Regnery, 2000.

Brice, Martin. *The Royal Navy and the Sino-Japanese Incident: 1937–41.* London: Ian Allan, 1973.

Buchanan, Patrick. *Churchill, Hitler, and the Unnecessary War: How Britain Lost Its Empire and the West Lost the World.* New York: Crown Publishers, 2008.

Butler, R. A. *The Art of the Possible.* London: Hamish Hamilton, 1971.

Carew, Tim. *Fall of Hong Kong.* London: Pan Books, 1963.

Carlton, David. *Churchill and the Soviet Union*. Manchester: Manchester University Press, 2000.

Chan Lau Kit Ching. *China, Britain and Hong Kong, 1895–1945*. Hong Kong: Chinese University Press, 1990.

Chang Jung and Jon Halliday. *Mao: The Unknown Story*. London: Vintage Books, 2006.

Chang Ming Kai and Hsu Long Hsuen. *History of the Sino-Japanese War (1937–1945)*, trans. Wen Ha Hsiung. Taipei: Chung Wu Publishing, 1971.

Charmley, John. *Churchill: The End of Glory*. London: Hodder and Stoughton, 1993.

Chennault, Claire L. *Way of a Fighter: The Memoirs of Claire Lee Chennault, Major General, U.S. Army (Ret.)*. New York: G. P. Putnam's Sons, 1949.

Chiang Kai Shek. *Soviet Russia in China*. New York: Noonday Press, 1957.

Chiang Wego. *How Generalissimo Chiang Kai-Shek Won the Eight-Year Sino-Japanese War, 1937–1945*. Taipei: Li Ming Culture Enterprise Co., 1979.

Chuikov, Vasilii. *Mission to China: Memoirs of a Soviet Military Adviser to Chiang Kaishek*, trans. David P. Barrett. Norwalk, CT: EastBridge, 2004.

Clarke, Peter. *The Cripps Version: The Life of Sir Stafford Cripps, 1889–1952*. London: Penguin, Allen Lane, 2002.

Copp, Terry. "The Defence of Hong Kong: December, 1941." *Canadian Military History* 10, 4 (2001): 5–20.

Cruickshank, Charles. *SOE in the Far East*. Oxford: Oxford University Press, 1983.

Cuff, R. D., and Jack Granatstein. *Ties That Bind: Canadian-American Relations in Wartime from the Great War to the Cold War*. Toronto: Samuel Stevens Hakkert, 1977.

Dickson, Paul. "Crerar and the Decision to Garrison Hong Kong." *Canadian Military History* 3; 1 (1994): 97–110.

———. "The Limits of Professionalism: General H. D. G. Crerar and the Canadian Army, 1914–1944." Ph.D. diss., University of Guelph, 1993.

———. *A Thoroughly Canadian General: A Biography of General H. D. G. Crerar*. Toronto: University of Toronto Press, 2007.

Donaghy, Gerg, and Stephane Roussel. *Escott Reid, Diplomat and Scholar*. Montreal: McGill-Queen's University Press, 2004.

Dower, John. *War without Mercy: Race and Power in the Pacific War*. New York: Pantheon Books, 1986.

Drea, Edward. *Japan's Imperial Army: Its Rise and Fall, 1853–1945*. Lawrence: University Press of Kansas, 2009.

Duff, Lyman P. *Report on the Canadian Expeditionary Force to the Crown Colony of Hong Kong*. Ottawa: Government of Canada, 1942.

Dulles, John Foster. *War or Peace*. London: George G. Harrap, 1950.

Ellis, John. *Brute Force: Allied Strategy and Tactics in the Second World War*. New York: Viking, 1990.

Elphick, Peter. *Far Eastern File: The Intelligence War in the Far East, 1930–1945*. London: Hodder and Stoughton, 1997.

Endacott, George. *Hong Kong Eclipse*. Oxford: Oxford University Press, 1978.

Erickson, John. *The Road to Stalingrad: Stalin's War with Germany.* Vol. 1. London: Pheonix Giant, 1975.

Evans, David, and Mark Peattie. *Kaigun: Strategy, Tactics, and Technology in the Imperial Japanese Navy, 1887–1941.* Annapolis, MD: Naval Institute Press, 1997.

Farndale, Martin. *History of the Royal Regiment of Artillery: The Far East Theatre, 1939–1946.* London: Brassey's, 2002.

Farrell, Brian P. *The Basis and Making of British Grand Strategy: Was There a Plan?* Lewiston, NY: Edwin Mellen Press, 1998.

Fedorowich, Kent. "'Cocked Hats and Swords and Small, Little Garrisons': Britain, Canada and the Fall of Hong Kong, 1941." *Modern Asian Studies* 37, 1 (2003): 111–157.

———. "Decolonization Deferred? The Re-establishment of Colonial Rule in Hong Kong, 1942–45." *Journal of Imperial and Commonwealth History* 28, 3 (2000): 25–50.

Feifer, George. *The Battle of Okinawa: The Blood and the Bomb.* 2nd paperback ed. Guilford, CT: Lyons Press, 2012.

Fleming, Thomas. *The New Dealers' War: Franklin D. Roosevelt and the War within World War II.* New York: Perseus Books, 2001.

Ford, Daniel. *Flying Tigers: Claire Chennault and His American Volunteers, 1941–1942.* 2nd ed. New York: Smithsonian Books, 2007.

Ford, Douglas. *Britain's Secret War against Japan, 1937–1945.* New York: Routledge, 2006.

Gillies, Donald. *Radical Diplomat: The Life of Archibald Clark Kerr, Lord Inverchapel, 1882–1951.* London: I. B. Tauris, 1999.

Glines, Carroll. *Chennault's Forgotten Warriors: The Saga of the 308th Bomb Group in China.* Atglen, PA: Schiffer, 1995.

Gold, Hal. *Unit 731: Testimony.* Tokyo: Yenbooks, 1996.

Gole, Henry. *The Road to Rainbow: Army Planning for Global War, 1934–1940.* Annapolis, MD: Naval Institute Press, 2003.

Gordon, David. "Historiographical Essay: The China-Japan War, 1931–1945." *Journal of Military History* 70, 1 (2006): 137–182.

Graff, David, and Robin Higham, eds. *A Military History of China.* Boulder, CO: Westview Press, 2002.

Granatstein, Jack. *How Britain's Weakness Forced Canada into the Arms of the United States: The 1988 Joanne Goodman Lectures.* Toronto: University of Toronto Press, 1989.

Greenhous, Brereton. *"C" Force to Hong Kong: A Canadian Catastrophe, 1941–1945.* Toronto: Dundurn Press, 1997.

Grieve, William. "Belated Endeavor: The American Military Mission to China (AMMISCA) 1941–1942." Ph.D. diss., University of Illinois, 1979.

Hansard. *Dominion of Canada Official Report of Debates, House of Commons, Second Session: Nineteenth Parliament, 4-5 George VI, 1941.* Vol. 1. Ottawa: Government of Canada, 1941.

Haynes, John. *Venona: Decoding Soviet Espionage in America.* New Haven, CT: Yale University Press, 1999.

Hilliker, J. F. "Distant Ally: Canadian Relations with Australia during the Second World War." *Journal of Imperial and Commonwealth History* 13, 1 (1984): 46–67.

Hillmer, Norman, ed. *Partners Nevertheless: Canadian-American Relations in the Twentieth Century.* Mississauga, ON: Copp Clark Pitman, 1989.

Hopkins, Castell. *The Toronto Board of Trade, a Souvenir.* Toronto: Sabiston Lithographic and Publishing, 1893.

Hsiung, James C., and Steven I. Levine, eds. *China's Bitter Victory: The War with Japan, 1937–1945.* London: M. E. Sharpe, 1992.

Hsu Shu Hsi. *Three Weeks of Canton Bombings.* Shanghai: Kelly and Walsh, 1939.

Hu Pu Yu. *A Brief History of the Sino-Japanese War (1937–1945).* Taipei: Chung Wu Publishing, 1974.

Hume, Edward. *Dauntless Adventurer: The Story of Dr. Winston Pettus.* New Haven, CT: Yale-in-China Association, 1952.

Hunt, Barry D., and A. Hamish Ion, eds. *War and Diplomacy across the Pacific, 1919–1952.* Waterloo, ON: Wilfrid Laurier University Press, 1988.

Hyde, H. Montgomery. *The Quiet Canadian: The Secret Service Story of Sir William Stephenson.* London: Hamish Hamilton, 1962.

Ienaga Saburo. *The Pacific War: World War II and the Japanese, 1931–1945.* New York: Pantheon, 1978.

Jacoby, Annalee, and Theodore White. *Thunder Out of China.* New York: William Sloane Associates, 1961.

James, R. Warren. *Wartime Economic Co-operation: A Study of Relations between Canada and the United States.* Toronto: Ryerson Press, 1949.

Jarman, Robert, ed. *China: Political Reports, 1911–1960.* Vol. 6, *1937–1941.* London: Public Record Office, 2001.

Jockel, Joseph, and Joel Sokolsky, eds. *Fifty Years of Canada–United States Defense Co-operation.* Lewiston, NY: Edwin Mellen Press, 1992.

Johnson, J. K. ed. *The Canadian Directory of Parliament, 1867–1967.* Ottawa: Public Archives of Canada, 1968.

Keeble, Curtis. *Britain, the Soviet Union and Russia.* London: Macmillan, 2000.

Kennedy, Greg. *Anglo-American Strategic Relations and the Far East, 1933–1939: Imperial Crossroads.* London: Frank Cass, 2002.

Kennedy, John. *The Business of War: The War Narrative of Major-General Sir John Kennedy.* London: Hutchinson, 1957.

Kennedy, Paul. *The Contradiction between British Strategic Planning and Economic Requirements in the Era of Two World Wars.* Washington, DC: International Security Studies Program, Wilson Center, 1979.

———. *The Rise and Fall of the Great Powers: Economic Change and Military Conflict from 1500 to 2000.* New York: Random House, 1987.

Kitchen, Martin. *British Policy towards the Soviet Union during the Second World War.* London: Macmillan, 1986.

Klinkowitz, Jerome. *With the Tigers over China: 1941–1942*. Lexington: University Press of Kentucky, 1999.

Krivitsky, Walter. *I Was Stalin's Agent*. London: Right Book Club, 1940.

Lai, Lawrence. "The Battle of Hong Kong: A Note on the Literature and the Effectiveness of the Defence." *Journal of the Royal Asiatic Society Hong Kong Branch* 39 (1999): 115–136.

Lary, Diana. *Warlord Soldiers: Chinese Common Soldiers, 1911–1937*. Cambridge: Cambridge University Press, 1985.

Levich, Eugene. *The Kwangsi Way in Kuomintang China, 1931–1939*. London: East Gate, 1993.

Lewis, Jon, ed. *The Mammoth Book of Battles: The Art and Science of Modern War*. New York: Carroll and Graff, 1995.

Liddell Hart, Basil. *The German Generals Talk*. London: Quill, 1979.

———. *History of the Second World War*. New York: Cassell, 1971.

———. "The Ratio of Troops to Space." *Military Review* 40, 1 (1960): 3–14.

Lindsay, Oliver. *The Battle for Hong Kong 1941–1945: Hostage to Fortune*. Hong Kong: Hong Kong University Press, 2005.

———. *The Lasting Honour*. London: Hamish Hamilton, 1978.

Lowe, Peter. *Great Britain and the Origins of the Pacific War: A Study of British Policy in East Asia, 1937–1941*. Oxford: Clarendon Press, 1977.

Lower, A. R. M. *Canada and the Far East, 1940*. New York: Institute of Pacific Relations, 1940.

Lu Suping. *They Were in Nanjing: The Nanjing Massacre Witnessed by American and British Nationals*. Hong Kong: Hong Kong University Press, 2004.

Lukacs, John. *The Duel, 10 May–31 July, 1940: The Eighty-Day Struggle between Churchill and Hitler*. New York: Ticknor and Fields, 1991.

MacDonell, George. *One Soldier's Story 1939–1945: From the Fall of Hong Kong to the Defeat of Japan*. Toronto: Dundurn Press, 2002.

Mackenzie, Compton. *Eastern Epic*. Vol. 1, *September 1939–March 1943, Defence*. London: Chatto and Windus, 1951.

MacKinnon, Stephen. "The Tragedy of Wuhan, 1938." *Modern Asian Studies* 30, 4 (1996): 931–943.

MacLaren, Roy. *Canadians behind Enemy Lines, 1939–1945*. Vancouver: UBC Press, 2004.

Macri, Franco David. "Abandoning the Outpost: Rejection of the Hong Kong Purchase Scheme of 1938–39." *Journal of the Royal Asiatic Society Hong Kong Branch* 50 (2010): 303–316.

———. "Bren Guns for China: The Origin and Impact of Sino-Canadian Relations, 1941–1949." *International History Review* 34, 3 (2012): 1–17.

Maltby, Christopher. "Operations in Hong Kong from 8th to 25th December, 1941." *Supplement to the London Gazette* (1948): 699–726.

Marples, David. *Motherland: Russia in the 20th Century*. London: Pearson Education, 2002.

Mawdsley, Evan. *Thunder in the East: The Nazi-Soviet War, 1941–1945*. London: Hodder Arnold, 2005.

Mendelsohn, John, ed. *Covert Warfare: Intelligence, Counterintelligence, and Military Deception during the World War II Era 8: The OSS-NKVD Relationship, 1943–1945*. New York: Garland Publishing, 1989.

Molesworth, Carl. *Sharks over China: The 23rd Fighter Group in World War II*. Washington, DC: Brassey's, 1994.

Moreira, Peter. *Hemingway on the China Front: His WWII Spy Mission with Martha Gellhorn*. Washington, DC: Potomac Books, 2006.

Morley, James, ed. *The Fateful Choice: Japan's Road to the Pacific War: Japan's Advance into Southeast Asia, 1939–1941*. New York: Columbia University Press, 1980.

Morley, James, and David Lu, eds. *Japan's Road to the Pacific War: The China Quagmire: Japan's Expansion on the Asian Continent, 1933–1941*. New York: Columbia University Press, 1983.

Nation, R. Craig. *Black Earth, Red Star: A History of Soviet Security Policy, 1917–1991*. Ithaca, NY: Cornell University Press, 1992.

Neilson, Keith. *The Permanent Under-Secretary for Foreign Affairs, 1854–1946*. London: Routledge, 2009.

Nolan, Brian. *King's War: Mackenzie King and the Politics of War, 1939–1945*. Toronto: Random House, 1988.

Nossal, Kim. "Strange Bedfellows: Canada and China in War and Revolution, 1942–1947." Ph.D. diss., University of Toronto, 1977.

Olson, Lynne. *Troublesome Young Men: The Rebels Who Brought Churchill to Power and Helped Save England*. New York: Farrar, Straus and Giroux, 2008.

Orwell, George. *All Propaganda Is Lies, 1941–1942: The Complete Works of George Orwell*. Vol. 13. London: Secker and Warburg, 1998.

Overy, Richard. *Why the Allies Won*. New York: W. W. Norton, 1995.

Ozorio, Anne. "The Myth of Unpreparedness: The Origins of Anti-Japanese Resistance in Prewar Hong Kong." *Journal of the Royal Asiatic Society Hong Kong Branch* 42 (2003): 161–186.

Payne, Robert. *Chinese Diaries, 1941–1946*. New York: Weybright and Talley, 1970.

Peattie, Mark. *Sunburst: The Rise of Japanese Naval Air Power, 1909–1941*. Annapolis, MD: Naval Institute Press, 2001.

Perras, Galen Roger. *Franklin Roosevelt and the Origins of the Canadian-American Security Alliance, 1933–1945: Necessary, but Not Necessary Enough*. Westport, CT: Praeger, 1998.

———. "'Our Position in the Far East Would Be Stronger without This Unsatisfactory Commitment': Britain, and the Reinforcement of Hong Kong, 1941." *Canadian Journal of History* 30, 2 (1995): 231–259.

Pope, Maurice. *Soldiers and Politicians: The Memoirs of Lt.-Gen. Maurice A. Pope*. Toronto: University of Toronto Press, 1962.

Porter, Bernard. *Britain, Europe and the World 1850–1982: Delusions of Grandeur*. London: George Allen and Unwin, 1983.

Pulsifer, Cameron. "John Robert Osborn: Canada's Hong Kong VC." *Canadian Military History* 6, 2 (1997): 79–89.

Quigley, Carroll. *The Anglo-American Establishment: From Rhodes to Cliveden*. San Pedro, CA: GSG and Associates, 1981.

Raack, R. C. *Stalin's Drive to the West, 1938–1945: The Origins of the Cold War*. Stanford, CA: Stanford University Press, 1995.

Rathbone, Eleanor. *War Can Be Averted: The Achievability of Collective Security*. London: Victor Gollancz, 1938.

Roberts, Priscilla. "The Transatlantic American Foreign Policy Elite: Its Evolution in Generational Perspective." *Journal of Transatlantic Studies* 7, 2 (2009): 163–183.

Romanus, Charles, and Sunderland, Riley. *United States Army in World War II, China-Burma-India Theater*. Vol. 2, *Stilwell's Command Problems*. Washington, DC: U.S. Army, 1956.

———. *United States Army in World War II, China-Burma-India Theater*. Vol. 3, *Time Runs Out in CBI*. Washington, DC: U.S. Army, 1959.

Ross, Graham. *The Foreign Office and the Kremlin: British Documents on Anglo-Soviet Relations, 1941–45*. Cambridge: Cambridge University Press, 1984.

Rothwell, V. H. "The Mission of Sir Frederick Leith-Ross to the Far East, 1935–1936." *Historical Journal* 18, 1 (1975): 147–169.

Salter, Arthur. *Security: Can We Retrieve it?* London: Macmillan, 1939.

Sarantakes, Nicholas. *Allies against the Rising Sun: The United States, the British Nations, and the Defeat of Imperial Japan*. Lawrence: University Press of Kansas, 2009.

Schurmann, Franz. *The Logic of World Power*. New York: Pantheon Books, 1974.

Scott, F. R. "A Policy of Neutrality for Canada." *Foreign Affairs* 17, 2 (1939): 402–416.

Share, Michael. *Where Empires Collided: Russian and Soviet Relations with Hong Kong, Taiwan, and Macao*. Hong Kong: Chinese University Press, 2007.

Snow, Philip. *The Fall of Hong Kong: Britain, China, and the Japanese Occupation*. New Haven, CT: Yale University Press, 2003.

Spector, Ronald. *Eagle against the Sun: The American War against Japan*. New York: Vintage Books, 1985.

Spurr, Russell. *Excellency: The Governors of Hong Kong*. Hong Kong: FormAsia Books, 1995.

Stacey, Charles. *Arms, Men and Governments: The War Policies of Canada, 1939–1945*. Ottawa: Department of National Defence, 1974.

———. *Official History of the Canadian Army in the Second World War*. Vol. 1, *Six Years of War, the Army in Canada, Britain and the Pacific*. Ottawa: Department of National Defence, 1967.

Stanley, Roy. *Prelude to Pearl Harbor*. New York: Charles Scribner's Sons, 1982.

Stephenson, William, and Nigel West. *British Security Coordination: The Secret History of British Intelligence in the Americas, 1940–1945*. New York: Fromm International, 1999.

Stewart, Evan. *Hong Kong Volunteers in Battle: A Record of the Actions of the Hongkong Volunteer Defence Corps in the Battle for Hong Kong December, 1941*.

BIBLIOGRAPHY

Hong Kong: RHKR (The Volunteers) Association Ltd. with Blacksmith Books, 2005.

Stewart, Gordon. *The American Response to Canada since 1776*. East Lansing: Michigan State University Press, 1992.

Stoler, Mark. *Allies and Adversaries: The Joint Chiefs of Staff, the Grand Alliance, and U.S. Strategy in World War II*. Chapel Hill: University of North Carolina Press, 2000.

Sudoplatov, Pavel. *Special Tasks, the Memoirs of an Unwanted Witness—A Soviet Spymaster*. New York: Little, Brown, 1994.

Taylor, Jay. *The Generalissimo: Chiang Kai-Shek and the Struggle for Modern China*. Cambridge, MA: Belknap Press, 2009.

Toland, John. *But Not in Shame: The Six Months after Pearl Harbor*. New York: Random House, 1961.

———. *The Rising Sun: The Decline and Fall of the Japanese Empire, 1936–1945*. New York: Random House. 1970.

Tolstoy, Nikolai. *Stalin's Secret War*. London: Jonathan Cape, 1981.

Trist, George. "Report on the Part Played by the Winnipeg Grenadiers in the Defence of Hong Kong." *Canadian Military History* 10, 4 (2001): 21–26.

Tuchman, Barbara. *Stilwell and the American Experience in China, 1911–45*. New York: Macmillan, 1970.

Tunnell, Arthur. *The Canadian Who's Who*. Vol. 12, *1970–1972*. Toronto: Who's Who Canadian Publications, 1972.

U.S. Department of State. *Foreign Relations of the United States Diplomatic Papers, 1940*. Vol. 3, *The British Commonwealth, the Soviet Union, the Near East and Africa*. Washington, DC: Historical Office, Bureau of Public Affairs, U.S. Department of State, 1958.

———. *Foreign Relations of the United States Diplomatic Papers, 1940*. Vol. 4, *The Far East*. Washington, DC: Historical Office, Bureau of Public Affairs, U.S. Department of State, 1955.

———. *Foreign Relations of the United States Diplomatic Papers, 1941*. Vol. 4, *The Far East*. Washington, DC: Historical Office, Bureau of Public Affairs, U.S. Department of State, 1956.

———. *Foreign Relations of the United States Diplomatic Papers, 1942. China*. Washington, DC: Historical Office, Bureau of Public Affairs, U.S. Department of State, 1956.

Utley, Jonathan. *Going to War with Japan, 1937–1941*. Knoxville: University of Tennessee Press, 1985.

Van de Ven, Hans. *War and Nationalism in China, 1925–1945*. London: RoutledgeCurzon, 2003.

Villa, Brian. *Unauthorized Action: Mountbatten and the Dieppe Raid*. Oxford: Oxford University Press, 1994.

Vincent, Carl. *No Reason Why: The Canadian Hong Kong Tragedy, an Examination*. Stittsville, ON: Canada's Wings, 1981.

Vine, Peter. "Experiences as a War Crimes Prosecutor in Hong Kong." *Journal of the Royal Asiatic Society Hong Kong Branch* 35 (1995): 205–209.

Walsh, Billie. "The German Military Mission to China, 1928–1938." *Journal of Modern History* 46, 3 (1974): 502–513.

Webb, Richard. "The War in China." *Far Eastern Survey* 11, 4 (1942): 49–50.

Welsh, Frank. *A History of Hong Kong.* London: HarperCollins, 1993.

Wesley-Smith, Peter. *Unequal Treaty, 1898–1997: China, Great Britain and Hong Kong's New Territories.* Oxford: Oxford University Press, 1983.

West, Nigel. *Venona: The Greatest Secret of the Cold War.* London: HarperCollins, 1999.

Whitaker, Denis. *Dieppe, Tragedy to Triumph.* Toronto: McGraw-Hill Ryerson, 1992.

Whitfield, Andrew. *Hong Kong, Empire and the Anglo-American Alliance at War, 1941–45.* Hong Kong: Hong Kong University Press, 2001.

Wilcox, Robert. *Target: Patton, the Plot to Assassinate General George S. Patton.* Washington, DC: Regnery, 2008.

Wilford, Timothy. *Canada's Road to the Pacific War: Intelligence, Strategy, and the Far East Crisis.* Vancouver: UBC Press, 2011.

Wilson, Dick. *When Tigers Fight: The Story of the Sino-Japanese War, 1937–1945.* New York: Viking Press, 1982.

Woodward, Llewellyn. *British Foreign Policy in the Second World War.* Vol. 2. London: Her Majesty's Stationery Office, 1971.

Yu Maochun. *The Dragon's War: Allied Operations and the Fate of China.* Annapolis, MD: Naval Institute Press, 2006.

———. "'In God We Trusted, in China We Busted': The China Commando Group of the Special Operations Executive (SOE)." *Intelligence and National Security* 16, 4 (2001): 37–60.

Index

Abe Noboyuki, Prime Minister and General, 154, 209
Allied powers
China, significance of, 269, 273, 276, 284, 340
coalition building, 2, 12, 14, 72, 75, 164, 248, 250–251
Hong Kong, sacrifice of, 215–216, 241, 244
Hong Kong demilitarization, impact on, 215, 241, 260–261, 279, 282
southern China defense plan, 280–282, 292
American British Dutch Australian (ABDA) Command, 276, 310
American Volunteer Group (AVG), 11, 255
in Burma, 313, 336
creation of, 257, 271
deployment of, 281, 289
Hong Kong relief plan and, 280–281
Amoy, 134
bombardment of, 66, 135
ground operations at, 198
Japanese garrison, 236
Japanese naval forces, 95, 135, 211, 265
Kulangsu incident, 135
occupation of, 113

Anami Korechika, General, 288
Changsha, second battle of, 290, 292
Changsha, third battle of, 324–325, 328–329, 332
Ando Rikichi, General, 133, 137–138, 141, 151, 161, 200
meets with British officials, 115–117, 158–159
failure in Kwangsi, 183, 188–189
in Nanning, 186
in northern French Indochina, 227–229
objectives, 115–117, 176, 181, 190, 197
relations with Imperial General Headquarters, 152
removed from command, 229
treatment of civilians, 114, 179, 189
Anglo-American relations, 9, 71–72, 90, 119–121, 123–124, 215, 269
adherence to American policy, 258–259, 271–272, 276–277
British impetus in, 204, 218, 230, 239
British covert activities, 248, 250–251, 259
destroyers for bases deal, 207
Anglo-American strategic cooperation and planning, 164, 217, 239, 342
ABC-1 talks, 252

Anglo-American strategic cooperation and
  planning, *continued*
  and Burma Road, 220, 230, 255
  impact of Axis victories, 259, 270–271
  Europe first strategy, 252, 254, 279, 333,
    343
  impact of intelligence on, 272
  Rainbow 5 plan, 221
  priority of Soviet security, 248, 270–271,
    276, 279, 284, 347
  XYZ Plan, 281–282
  see also strategic planning, Great Britain
Anglo-Chinese relations, 46, 73–74, 80
  British Military Mission, 291, 310–311
  British relations with communists, 157,
    159, 164, 199, 339
  intelligence ties, 154–155, 164, 261, 281
  lack of formal alliance, 76, 103
  mistrust, 158, 290–291, 343
  overt military cooperation, 46, 82, 122,
    124, 161, 205, 215, 217, 280, 338
  rupture in, 301, 313, 322, 345
  see also British support for China
Anglo-Japanese agreement, 160, 162
Anglo-Japanese antagonism, 7–8, 32, 38,
    43, 80, 116, 126, 129, 132
  British support for China, 148, 151,
    161–162, 164
  Chiang's influence, 47–48, 104–105
  invasion of Hainan, 111, 119
  invasion of northern Indochina, 234,
    245
  Japanese terror bombing, 213
  low-intensity conflict, 67–69, 104, 135,
    237, 260–262, 288, 300
  Tientsin crisis, 135–136, 148, 158–162,
    214–215
Anglo-Portuguese relations, 86
Anglo-Soviet relations, 83, 102, 132, 146
  British Military Mission, 158
  British support for USSR, 12, 71, 73, 82,
    90, 160, 163, 246, 274, 276, 284
  closure of Burma Road, 221, 342
  collective security, 90, 119, 123, 154
  cooperation in China, 72, 132, 144, 161,
    218, 341–342
  friction in, 123, 126, 147, 174, 202,
    214, 221
  rupture in, 223–226
Arnup, Jesse, 209
Asaka Yasuhiko, Prince, 42

assassination, 52, 67, 135, 148, 160–161, 262
Atlantic Charter, 272
atrocities, 4, 42, 112, 133, 196, 198–199,
    221, 344. *See also* Chinese morale;
    Hong Kong; Nanking (Nanjing)
Attlee, Prime Minister Clement, 278–279
Australia, 208, 226, 282, 344
Axis Pact - Tripartite Pact, 132, 253
  Japan joins, 227, 230

Babbington, Air Marshal John T., 155
Baltic States, 224
Banham, Tony, 317
Bank of Canada, 251
Barbosa, Artur Tamagnini de Sousa, 86, 139
Barnett, Correlli, 205
Barrett, Colonel David, 42, 57, 60, 71, 110,
    187
  British embassy relations with
    communists, 225
  Chinese-Japanese trade, 133, 211
  fall of Canton, 95, 98
  Japanese brutality, 189
  third battle of Changsha, 332–333
Bartholomew, Major General A. H., 33–34,
    76
Bates, F., 64
Baxter, Catherine, 280
Beaverbrook, Lord, (Max Aitken), 250, 255,
    274
Bedniakoff, Colonel, 297
Bertram, James, 225
Bissell, Major General Clayton, 208
Blunt, A. P., 118, 149
Bocca Tigris, 91, 93, 95
  Chinese defenses, 49–50
  Japanese defenses, 138
  Japanese reinforcements at, 264,
    302–303
  radio intelligence net, 242, 303
Bond, Colour Sergeant, 315
Bourne, Captain G. K., 80
Boxer, Major Charles R., 35, 57, 95, 117,
    131, 265
  tour of 4th War Zone, 101–102
  liaison to Chinese army, 155, 242
Brenan, Sir John, 71
  Hong Kong purchase scheme, 80–81,
    120
  on Hong Kong in Anglo-U.S. policy, 279
Brice, Martin, 74

British Admiralty, 33–34, 80
British Air Ministry, 80
British Army Aid Group, 77, 338
British Broadcasting Corporation, 335
British Chiefs of Staff, 33, 75, 148,
    159–160, 215
  Hong Kong defense, 217, 312
  Hong Kong demilitarization, 260, 341
  Hong Kong reinforcement, 255, 260,
    273–274
  Hong Kong relief plan, 282
  Hong Kong, sacrifice of, 241, 245
  US policy, adherence to, 258
British Colonial Office, 29, 46, 79–80, 266
British Committee of Imperial Defence,
    74–75, 162
British Commonwealth army regiments, 76
  5th Anti-Aircraft Regiment, Royal
    Artillery, 305
  7th Rajput Regiment, 306–310, 314
  14th Punjab Regiment, 306, 310
  Hong Kong and Singapore Royal
    Artillery, 34, 306
  Hong Kong Chinese Regiment, 315–316
  Kumaon Rifles, 34, 153, 235–236
  Middlesex Regiment, 104, 306, 310,
    314–315
  Royal Irish Rifles, 34
  Royal Rifles of Canada, 310, 317, 345
  Royal Scots, 117, 306–307, 310, 314
  Royal Welch Fusiliers, 34, 41
  Seaforth Highlanders, 34
  Winnipeg Grenadiers, 310, 314–315, 345
  see also Hong Kong Volunteer Defence
    Corps
British Dominions Office, 275, 277, 279,
    321
British economic warfare, 29–31, 43, 119,
    159
  bankruptcy, 204, 248–249
  loans to China, 90, 119–121, 123, 146,
    253
British Far East Command, 240
British Foreign Office, 9, 13, 29, 46, 74,
    106, 157, 220, 241, 266, 268
  China-Soviet trade, disruption of, 226
  collective security, 9, 37–38, 72–73, 87,
    123–124, 132, 226, 270, 279, 291
  communists, support for, 71, 159,
    162–164, 224
  Hong Kong, battle of, 305, 317

Hong Kong purchase scheme, 78–80, 82,
    120
Hong Kong, sacrifice of, 241, 245, 299
  leadership change, 71–72
  peace in China, exploitation of,
    202–203, 218
  peace in China, rejection of, 165, 171, 175
  proxy war, disruption of, 214, 218, 221,
    223
  proxy war, support for, 17–18, 37, 41,
    72–73, 87, 257–258, 261
  Sian incident, 31–32
  Tientsin crisis, 159–161
  U.S., cooperation with, 119, 279
  war policy, Far East, 66, 87, 122, 258
British House of Commons, 9, 60, 71, 123,
    224
British Joint Staff Mission, 344
British military weakness, 10, 33, 71–72,
    74, 77, 81–82, 204, 260, 341
  Japanese reactions, 154, 164, 226–227,
    284–285
British officials
  divergent policies, 13, 280
  lack of confidence in Chinese military,
    101–102, 122, 159, 257–258, 291,
    312–313
British Security Coordination (BSC), 250
British support for China, 33, 43, 73–75,
    116–117, 124
  after Japanese invasion of northern
    Indochina, 234
  after German invasion of USSR, 274
  after second battle of Changsha,
    299–300
  diminishes as priority, 257–259
  through Hong Kong, 46, 83, 110, 163
  see also Anglo-Chinese relations
British Treasury, 29, 31, 80, 82, 249
British War Cabinet
  Burma Road policy, 219
  Anglo-German peace, 204, 227, 230
British War Office, 80, 158–159, 209
  support for proxy war, 163, 261–262
  see also Hong Kong
Broadfoot, Martin, 139
Brooke, Field Marshal Sir Alan F., 312
Brooke-Popham, Air Chief Marshal Sir
    Robert, 240, 255, 260–261, 281
  appointment, 240
  meets with Grasett, 260

Burma, 11, 138, 283, 301, 336
    as logistical base, 76, 174, 177, 200
    railway construction, 106, 171
Burma Road, 7, 83, 174, 176
    in Allied strategy, 280
    closure of, 9, 106, 202–203, 218–220,
        226, 271
    construction of, 46, 105
    disadvantages of, 106–107, 172
    Mackenzie King's views on, 283
    reopening of, 230, 257
    United States interest in, 164 255, 289
Butler, Richard Austen (RAB), 224

C Force, 275–276, 277–279, 281–283, 306,
        318–319
    prisoners, 348
Cadogan, Sir Alexander, 73
Cairncross, John, 71
Caldecott, Governor Sir Andrew, 34
California, 211
Cambridge Five, 71
Camranh Bay, 227
Canada, 11, 247, 272–273
    aid to Britain, 249, 346
    Department of External Affairs, 205,
        207, 279
    foreign policy, 207–208, 247–248, 259,
        269, 273, 284
Canada-China relations, 209, 259
    aid to China, 11–12, 269, 288
Canada-U.S. relations
    Canada as U.S. proxy, 289, 345–346
    Canadian geopolitical realignment, 11,
        203–208, 245, 247, 251, 278
    Conference on Canadian-American
        Affairs, 206
    intelligence links, 250–251, 278
Canadian China policy
    Chinese morale, 283, 285, 288
    coalition cohesion, 209, 259, 269,
        275–276, 278–279, 283–284, 341
    deepens U.S. involvement, 248, 256,
        288
    fulfillment of U.S. obligations, 256, 259,
        282, 288
    Grasett-Crerar meeting, 267
    military intervention, 11, 203, 275
    military aid, 248, 255–256, 285, 288,
        345–346
    Mutual Aid Plan, 346–347

Soviet Far Eastern security, 269, 275,
        279, 285, 341
    U.S. origins of, 208–209, 248–249,
        255–256, 269, 341, 345
Canadian Institute of International Affairs,
        205–206, 208
Canton
    18th Japanese Army Division in, 262
    104th Japanese Army Division in, 228,
        302–303
    airfields, 76, 137, 199, 239, 242, 313,
        341
    bombardment of, 61, 64–65, 86
    Chamber of Commerce, 121
    destruction of, 93–95
    fall of, 80–81, 86, 90, 93, 96, 105, 119
    Japanese relations with civilians,
        114–115, 118, 121, 132, 195,
        198–199, 267
    occupation and Chinese logistics, 84,
        110, 115, 197
    Shameen Island, 65, 115
    strategic significance of, 18–19
    troop revolt, 122
Canton, New York, 206
Cape Town, 249
Catroux, General Georges, 227
Central Trust China Corporation, 160
Chamberlain, Prime Minister Neville, 71,
        73, 159–160
Chan Chak, Admiral, 157, 317
Chang Fa Kwei, General, 91, 180, 234, 290
Chang Hsueh-liang (Zhang Xueliang),
        Young Marshal, 31–32
Chang Wai Chang (Cheung Wai Cheung),
        General, 128, 130–131, 138, 141,
        143–144
Changkufeng, 90
Changsha
    center of resistance, 58, 89, 103
    destruction of, 103–104
    impact of battles on Chinese morale,
        125, 137, 144, 165, 168–170
    strategic significance, 6, 14, 19,
        102–103, 125
Changsha, first battle of, 125–126, 137,
        144, 146–147, 166–170
    casualties, 165
    geopolitical impact, 168–169, 203
    see also Hsueh Yueh, General
Changsha, second battle of, 268, 281, 325

7th Chinese War Zone, 294
9th Chinese War Zone, 289, 292–293, 295, 300
11th Japanese Army, 289, 292, 294
23rd Japanese army, 294
geopolitical impact, 287, 289–290, 297–300
impact on Chinese morale of, 289, 296
Japanese airpower, 293–294
Japanese army communications during, 289, 294
Japanese retreat, 294
Milo River, 292–294
Tamoshan, 294
Tungting Lake and, 292–295
weather, 294
see also Anami Korechika, General; Chiang Kai Shek (Jiang Jieshi), Chairman and Generalissimo; Chuikov, Marshal Vasily; Hsueh Yueh, General; Li Tsung Ren (Li Zhongren), General; Yochow
Changsha, third battle of, 168, 301
9th Chinese War Zone, 327, 332
11th Japanese army, 288, 323–325, 328–329, 332–333
airpower, 328–329
casualties, 333
geopolitical impact, 287–288, 324, 333, 335–337, 339, 343
as diversion, 323–324
fighting in built up area, 325, 327
impact on Chinese morale of, 301, 332–333, 337
Japanese army communications during, 324, 327–328
and Japanese attack on Hong Kong, 280, 287, 324, 336–337
Japanese POW, information from, 328
Milo River, 324–325, 327–329, 333
Tamoshan, 325, 327
Tungting Lake and, 328
weather, 325, 328
Yaloshan, 327
see also Anami Korechika, General; Barrett, Colonel David; Hsueh Yueh, General; Yochow
Chang Tek Nang, General, 321
Chan Kee, General, 339
Chan Shu Tang, General, 98
Chaoyang, 302

Charmley, John, 249
Chauvin, Lieutenant Colonel H., 57, 95, 101–102, 312
Chehnankuan, 179
Chekiang, 109–110, 136, 165, 236, 264
chemical weapons, 57, 268
at Ichang, 296
Chen Cheng, General, 166, 219, 295
Chen Chi Tang, General, 19, 25, 50, 98
Chen Chung Fu, 50
Chennault, Major General Claire, 11, 54, 84, 213, 313, 332, 336
search to equip AVG, 257
Cheung, Victoria, 64–65
Chiang Kai Shek (Jiang Jieshi), Chairman and Generalissimo
Americans, relations with, 253–254, 271, 344–345
army improvements, 102–103
British, relations with, 59, 82, 103, 110, 119, 253
Canadians, relations with, 288, 345
Canton, sacrifice of, 48–49, 58, 86, 96, 99–101, 124
Changsha, second battle of, 295
collective security, support for, 161
communists, war with, 23, 200, 252
Dennys, meets with, 280–282, 310, 336
difficulties securing foreign allies, 102, 122, 162, 343
efforts to secure foreign allies, 41, 86–87, 89–90, 100, 193, 200–201, 204, 213
generals, execution of, 98–99
Grasett, coordinates with, 155, 242–243
in Kwangsi, 184
Kwangtung, maintains control in, 130
Magruder, meets with, 310, 336
offensive military action, restricts, 297, 300
peace with Japan, potential for, 210, 220, 231, 270–271, 277, 322
political leadership, 5, 20–21, 55, 102, 234, 322
popular support, 232
rice hoarding ban, 300
James Roosevelt, meets with, 255
Shanghai, in battle of, 38
Sian incident 31
southern provinces, war with, 25–26
strategic planning, 3, 8, 27–28, 144

Chiang Kai Shek (Jiang Jieshi), Chairman
    and Generalissimo, *continued*
    strategic withdrawal, 43–44, 58, 102,
        337
Chiang Wego, 333
Chi Chi Ching, 121
Chienkiang, 184
China
    central government legitimacy, 5, 38, 40,
        49, 102, 121, 168–169
    civil war in south, 25–26
    corruption, 51, 59, 97–98, 127,
        172–173, 232, 236
    declaration of war, 310
    foreign military support, origins of 17,
        37
    geography, 5, 18–19, 84, 329
    New Life Movement, 23
    regional political autonomy, 4–5, 19–20,
        23, 26, 179–180
    southern provinces, strategic importance,
        87–88, 124, 173
China, naval blockade of, 38, 113, 68, 126,
        190, 245
    establishment, 60
    intensifies, 263–265
    Pearl River, 196
    Swatow, 135–136
China-Burma-India (CBI) theater, 208, 255,
        259, 280, 345–346
    development of unconventional warfare,
        13–14, 239–240, 280–282
    low priority in Allied grand strategy,
        253, 343
    Operation Carbonado, 282
China Commando Group, 158, 163, 240,
        280, 291, 322, 338
China Defense Supplies, 249–250
China National Aviation Corporation
        (CNAC), 67, 183, 237–238, 257,
        263, 305, 338
Chinese air force
    creation of AVG, 257
    destruction of, 257
    losses at Changsha, 328–329
    losses at Chengdu (1941), 293
    mixed quality, 66
    requirements, 45, 238
    strength, 53, 131, 182, 231–232, 238
    training, 84–85
    see also American Volunteer Group (AVG)

Chinese armies
    2nd, 313
    4th, 57, 101–102, 293, 327
    5th (semi-mechanized), 181, 291, 336
    6th, 336
    10th, 293, 324–325, 327, 332
    16th, 178
    20th, 293, 324
    26th, 293, 327
    35th, 99
    37th, 293, 324–325, 327
    44th, 313
    46th, 178
    53rd, 99
    58th, 293, 324–325, 327
    61st, 99
    63rd, 313
    65th, 311
    72nd, 293
    73rd, 328
    74th, 293
    78th, 327
    79th, 293, 324, 327
    99th, 293, 324–325, 327
Chinese army
    April offensive, 130
    armored forces, 179, 181, 292
    British delays of relief, 281–282,
        299–300, 313
    casualties, 59
    improvements and success, 57, 73, 200,
        287, 291, 297–299, 301, 323
    Kwangsi, counterattacks in, 181–186
    Kwangtung, battle of, 190–193
    militia, 92, 112, 130, 137, 139, 141,
        143, 170, 198
    organization, 40
    winter offensive, 181, 220
Chinese artillery
    7th War Zone, 101, 312
    9th War Zone, 289–290, 294, 327, 332
    at Canton, 66
    destruction of, 41
    in Kwangsi, 234
    requirements, 347
    shortages, 40, 49, 130, 337
    see also Ichang, battle of
Chinese brigade
    9th Independent, 311
Chinese collaborationist governments, 22,
        48–49, 116, 122, 126, 136, 143, 160

armed forces, 128, 138–139, 143, 195,
197–200
armed forces, 20th Division, 264
failure, 122, 131, 141, 144, 152,
169–170, 177
Japanese military defeat, impact of, 169,
177, 203
Japanese support for, 52–53, 87, 116,
119, 121, 133
national government, recognition of,
210–211, 232–233
national government inauguration, 126,
143, 153–154
peace, potential for, 59, 100, 119, 137,
262
popular support, 130, 141
see also Hong Kong
Chinese divisions
2nd, 184
3rd, 327
10th, 327
13th, 184
17th, 184
19th, 178–179
45th, 184
75th, 184, 198
78th, 184
80th, 314
84th, 184
92nd, 184
93rd, 184
103rd, 184
110th, 184
115th, 184
135th, 178, 184
145th, 184
151st, 92, 104, 130, 191
152nd, 130, 139, 264
153rd, 92, 191, 237
154th, 130, 191
155th, 184
156th, 184
157th, 130, 191, 237, 262
158th, 130
159th, 112, 130, 235, 237
160th, 130, 191, 264
165th, 237
168th, 191
170th, 178
175th, 178
187th, 191, 339

188th, 178
190th, 327
301st, 184
302nd, 184
303rd, 184
Chinese group armies
9th, 101, 137–138
12th, 55, 90–92, 97, 104, 130, 137,
152–153, 170
12th, weaknesses of, 101, 193
16th, 101, 138
31st, 166, 293
33rd, 166, 293
Chinese guerillas, 43, 102, 162, 165, 210
in Hainan, 112
in Kiangsi, 291
in Kwangsi, 183
in Kwangtung, 153, 195, 239, 262,
311
piracy and banditry, 122, 130
popular support, 133
training, 152
Chinese Maritime Customs Service,
266
Chinese military logistics, 2, 7, 44, 83, 124,
261
crisis, 343
provocation to Japan, 89
see also Mirs Bay supply route
Chinese military weakness, 3–4, 39–40, 66,
102–103, 148, 167, 200
Chinese morale, 5, 11, 54–55, 101, 120,
145, 335
aerial bombardment, 212, 270–271
Allied military defeat, 301, 321–322,
333, 337, 343
Anglo-American involvement in East
Asia, 230–231, 234, 271, 345
atrocities, 133
and battle of Hong Kong, 321
and battle of Shekki, 143–144
British, 74–75, 271, 273, 279, 284
Canadian involvement in East Asia, 269,
273, 282
economy, 231–232, 300
German invasion of USSR, 231
logistical support, Burma and Hong
Kong, 177, 200, 220–221, 235
Chinese navy, 138, 200
Hai Chi, 32
tactics, 68–69

Chinese war zones
    4th, 91–92, 122, 130, 180, 234, 313,
        347
    5th, 295–296
    6th, 219, 295–296
    7th, 99, 234, 263, 332
    9th, 7, 168, 287, 336, 347
Chichibu, Prince, 95–96
Chiao Fu Sa, 51
Chinchow Bay, 178
Chow, Sir Shouson, 78–79, 81, 120
Chu Chan Mun, Sergeant, 315
Chuchow, 66, 103, 294
Chuikov, Marshal Vasily
    Soviet Military Mission, 157, 261, 339
    Changsha, second battle of, 289, 295,
        297–298
Chunghsiu, 109
Chungking
    aerial bombardment of, 131, 173,
        212–213
    defensive advantages, 219–220
Chungshan district, 125
    38th Japanese Army Division in, 239,
        262
    aerial bombardment of, 139
    ground combat in, 130–131, 137–139,
        141–144, 150, 196
    Japanese reinforcements in, 151, 153,
        239, 302
    Japanese withdrawal from, 267
Churchill, Prime Minister Winston, 204,
        209, 278
    British neutrality, 205
    Chiang, relations with, 271
    Hong Kong as fortress, 277
    Hong Kong reinforcement, 255, 260
    Mackenzie King, relations with, 207,
        274
    Roosevelt, relations with, 220
    Singapore as fortress, 215, 254
    United States alliance, 248–249
    USSR, support for 274
Chu Shih Ming, General, 335
Chu Teh, Marshal, 261
Claggett, Brigadier General Henry, 254–255
Clark, Clifford, 251
Clarke, Peter, 225, 274
Clark Kerr, Sir Archibald, 52, 95, 258, 343
    Chiang at Hankow, 103, 119
    Chinese breaking point, 322–323

Chinese communists, 225
    David Kung incident, 160–162
    French officials, meets with, 172
    Grasett, support for, 243–244, 283
    Hong Kong purchase scheme, 78–79
    security, breach of, 161–162
    Stalin, relations with, 162
    USSR, support for, 71, 224
Cockfield, Richard, 65
Cohen, Major General, Morris, 254
collective security, 2, 9–12, 37, 71–72,
        123–124
    critical period, 271–272
    Soviet security, 301, 341
    see also Hong Kong, battle of
Compton, E. G., 80
communists, Chinese, 21, 42, 120–121, 162
    army, 157, 199, 226, 252, 339
    in Kwangtung, 50, 157
    intelligence network, 261
    Soviet support for, 147
Condon, Colonel Reynolds, 306
Cowell, H. R., 80
Craig, Lieutenant Commander D. L. C., 86
Craigie, Sir Robert, 52–53, 65, 67–68, 266
    Burma Road, 219
    China policy, 73
    Lo Wu incident, 117–118
    Soviet-Japanese relations, 222
    Tientsin crisis, 159–160
Cranborne, Robert G. C., Marquess of
        Salisbury, 217, 275–276
Crerar, General Harry D. G., 206–207, 267,
        278
Cripps, Sir Stafford, 224–225, 274
Currie, Lauchlin
    envoy to Chiang, 254–255
    in Canada, 256, 345
    Soviet intelligence, 254
Curtis Wright Corporation, 85
Czechoslovakia, 123, 132, 145

Daily Telegraph, 279
Davidson-Houston, Brigadier General James
        V., 49, 51
Davies, Major Gill, 312
Dawson, Lieutenant Colonel W., 33
Decoux, Admiral Jean, 155, 172, 227
Delano, Frederic Adrian, 250
Dennys, Major General Lance, 35, 270,
        280–282

Chinese army, 291–292, 298–299
  death, 338
  Detachment 204, 310
  recommends support, 298–299
Detachment 204, 163, 240, 280–281, 291,
    310, 322, 338
  in relief of Hong Kong, 311–312
Dexter, Grant, 206, 256, 278
Dieppe, 282–283, 347
Dill, Field Marshal Sir John, 219, 254, 344
disarmament, 2, 12, 32, 71, 318, 341
Doi Teihichi, Lieutenant Colonel, 307, 314
Doihara Kenji, General, 22, 30
Donald, William H., 31, 160–161
Dong Dang, 179
Donovan, Brigadier General William,
    250–251
Doson, 227
Duff, Sir Lyman, 278, 318–319
Dulles, John Foster, 206
Dunkirk, 204

economics and power
  Great Depression, 29
  new world order, 10, 71, 163, 206–207,
    251, 274
Eden, Prime Minister Sir Anthony, 37, 60,
    71–73, 271, 322
Edwards, Captain C. J., 113, 131, 133,
    147–148, 150, 152, 169
Egypt, 254
Eisenhower, General and President Dwight
    D., 335
escalation of war, 8–9, 15, 33
  Allied reinforcements, 211, 248, 279,
    340–341
  British covert warfare, 154–155, 161,
    164, 240, 259
  British military weakness, 205, 213–214,
    226–227, 286
  Changsha, second battle of, 287
  economic warfare, 164, 287
  fall of France, 126, 177, 190, 201, 204,
    206, 213, 215, 217–218, 227
  frontier shooting incidents, 267
  German invasion of USSR, 267,
    269–271, 340
  German pressure in Tokyo, 253
  Hainan, invasion of, 111, 113, 119, 123
  insubordination of British officials, 67,
    155, 244, 260, 266, 269, 272

insubordination of Japanese officials,
    148, 210, 227–228, 265
Japanese bombing, 38–39, 48, 109, 188,
    212
Japanese entry to Axis Pact, 230, 234
Kwangsi, invasion of, 188–189
low-intensity conflict, 67–68, 137, 174,
    214, 235, 247, 260–262, 288, 300
military stalemate, 170, 173, 177, 269
naval blockade, 59–60, 126, 136, 148,
    150–151, 245, 247, 265–266
north Indochina invasion, 234
opium trade, 85
Pakhoi incident, 28
policy divergence of British officials, 70,
    77–78, 155, 158–159
policy divergence of Japanese officials,
    133, 210
south China invasion, 53, 55, 70, 83, 89,
    124
south Indochina invasion, 267, 269,
    271
Soviet-Japanese neutrality pact, 253
submarine incident, 266
Eucliffe Castle, 317
Eurasian Aviation Corporation, 67
Evans, F. E., 279

Fahsien, 152, 170
Falkland Islands, 282
famine, 127, 268
Far East Combined Bureau (FECB), 74,
    158–159
Farndale, General Sir Martin B., 319
Farrell, Brian, 274
Fatshan, 138, 190
Federal Reserve Bank, 251, 254
Feng Chan Hai, General, 99
Feng Ti, General, 104
Finland, 147, 221–222, 224
Foochow, 109, 129, 264, 302
  bombardment of, 134
  occupation of, 126, 132
  trade at, 134
Formosa, 68, 141
Foshan, 302
Foster, Wing Commander R. M., 80
Foulkes, Lieutenant General Charles, 318
France
  air force, 84–85, 227
  army, 72, 147, 227–229

France, *continued*
China, support for, 85, 107, 155, 172–173, 200
defeat in Europe, 11, 84, 215, 219, 222, 227, 269
impact on Japan of French defeat, 126, 177, 190, 201, 203, 213, 218, 227
Japan, relations with, 67, 188, 213, 218, 227
navy, 75, 172, 215, 227–228
Frankfurter, Felix, 345
French Indochina, 7, 83, 126, 200, 203
5th Japanese Army Division in, 228, 233
airbases, 233
Japanese interdiction base (northern Indochina), 234, 257
Japanese occupation of north, 227–228, 233
Japanese occupation of south, 259–260, 267, 269
military forces, 227
railway, 84, 106–109, 171, 173, 176, 187–188, 219, 233
South China Expeditionary Force (Japanese Field Army) in, 227, 229
strategic resources, restrictions on, 226
Thailand, war with, 253
French naval vessels
Argus, 75, 172
Lamotte Picquet, 172
Suffren, 172
Fujii Yoji, General, 191, 263
Fukien, 109–110, 150, 198, 264, 314
Fu Tso Yi, General, 99
Fulinpu, 329

Gage, Sir Berkeley E. F., 31–32, 257
Gandhi, Mahatma, 156
Gauss, Clarence, 271, 322, 333
Gent, Gerard, 266
German-Japanese relations, 213
Germany, 71–74, 81, 90, 119, 132, 175, 204–205, 218, 280
Anglo-American planning, 251–252, 254, 279, 333, 343
autarky, 204, 207–208
China peace effort, 51–52
Europe, control of, 239
HMS *Liverpool* incident, 196
Japan, pressure on, 253
Military Mission to China, 6, 23, 40

Soviet support for, 146–147, 221, 226
SS *Automedon*, 244
see also Hitler, Chancellor Adolph
Gia Lam airfield, 233
Giles, Major R., 109, 143, 168, 180–182, 190, 201, 209, 216, 231–232, 235–238
Gorgulho, Captain Carlos de Souza, 86
Grasett, Lieutenant General Arthur Edward, 131, 217, 265
ability, 303
aggressiveness, 217, 245, 247, 260, 266
biographical data, 156
bravery, 156
and British involvement in China, 155, 242–243, 260, 267, 281
Chiefs of Staff, 273–274
Chinese intelligence links, 242–243
commando, 241
and Crerar, 267
Hong Kong reinforcements, 241, 244, 267, 255, 260
independent action, 14, 74, 155, 157–158, 241–242, 245
insubordinate action, 155, 242, 266
Lo Wu incident, 117–118, 151
Mayer, cooperation with, 255
propaganda, 240
Roosevelt, James, 255
Soviet medal, 283
Greater East Asian Co-Prosperity Sphere, 176, 214
New Order in East Asia, 110, 119
Greece, 253, 258
battle of Crete, 255
collective security and, 278
Grew, Joseph, 164, 168
Grimsdale, Major General Gordon E., 73–74, 149, 158, 310
Grussendorf, Major Richard, 309
Guadalcanal, 38th Japanese Army Division at, 317
Guan Lin Cheng, General, 166

Hachung, 91–92
Hainan, 90, 118, 129, 138, 157, 168
Formosan Force (28th Japanese Army Division) in, 111–112
interdiction base, Japanese, 61–63, 109, 111, 172, 239
invasion of, 110–113, 125

Haiphong, 2, 28, 83–84, 105, 107, 149,
171–172, 189
Hakka (Chinese minority), 50, 157
Halifax, Viscount, (E. F. L. Wood), 71–72,
79, 204, 250, 271–272
Hamamoto Kisaburo, Lieutenant General,
138
Han Fu Chu, General, 99
Hangchow, 85
Hankow, 58, 89, 101, 105, 115, 119
air action at, 54, 66, 147
air bases at, 131, 212
national government, seat of, 55, 59
strategic center, 44, 166, 296, 323
Hanoi, 83, 107, 228, 233
Hara Mamoru, General, 237, 263
Harvard University, 161, 208
Hata Shunroku, General, 52, 209–210, 298,
324
Hawaii, 211, 254, 337
Hemingway, Ernest, tour of 7th Chinese
War Zone, 254. *See also* Yu Han
Mou, General
Henderson, J. Thyne, 73
Hengyang, 292, 324–325
Hikojiro Suga, Rear Admiral, 263
Himalayas, 5, 84, 233, 343, 346
Hingning, 109
Hiranuma Kiichiro, Prime Minister, Baron,
154
Hirohito, Emperor, 64
Hiroshima, 332
Hitler, Chancellor Adolf, 15, 72, 144–147,
279, 337
British neutrality, 204
peace in China, 51
relations with Stalin, 144, 146–147, 171,
202, 218, 221, 245
see also Germany
Home, Brigadier General William,
319–320
Homma Masaharu, General, 148, 160
Hong Kong
7th Chinese War Zone, and relief of,
311–313
activities of Chinese collaborationist
governments in, 265, 309
Angle-Japanese antagonism and, 52, 60,
73, 103, 118, 122, 151
artillery, 34, 76, 216
atrocities at, 314, 317

arrangements for relief of, 280, 310,
320–321
British War Cabinet and, 241, 244
China-Japan peace negotiations in, 210
Chinese bombardment of, 313
Chinese covert operations, 160–161, 244
conscription, 83, 154, 157
corruption, 77
Deep Bay, 237
defense plan, 76–77, 216–217, 279
economic importance, 31, 76, 79, 81–82,
144, 232
garrison training exercises, 34–35, 77
Gindrinkers' Line, 76
internment of Chinese soldiers at, 105
Kai Tak airfield, 45, 237, 263
Kowloon, 309, 312–313, 320
Lamma Island, 310
Lo Wu incident, 89, 117, 148–149, 151
Mackenzie King, Prime Minister William
Lyon, in, 247
New Territories purchase scheme, 38,
78–82, 120, 338
opium, 268
radio transmitters (Chinese), 152, 160,
244
Roosevelt, President Franklin Delano,
and reinforcement of, 255, 279
Shataukok incident, 104–105, 151
Stonecutters Island, 34, 155, 172
U.S. military involvement, 255, 279–280
war scare, 30, 129, 151–152, 235
Z Force, 157, 281
see also Brenan, Sir John; British Foreign
Office; Churchill, Prime Minister
Winston; Clark Kerr, Sir Archibald;
Grasett, Lieutenant General Arthur
Edward; Northcote, Governor Sir
Geoffry
Hong Kong, battle of, 305, 307, 316
23rd Japanese Army and, 301, 317
18th Japanese Army Division and border
of, 235, 263, 265, 302, 314
38th Japanese Army Division and, 307,
314
104th Japanese Army Division and
border of, 237
amphibious assault, 314
Anglo-American strategic cooperation
and planning and, 255, 261, 275
anti-aircraft defenses, 305

Hong Kong, battle of, *continued*
  artillery, 306
  casualties, 317
  Chiang Kai Shek offers troops for, 155,
    161–162, 205, 217, 281, 341
  civilians and, 311
  collective security and, 318
  defense plan, 306, 319–320
  defenses of, and British War Office,
    33–34, 216, 241
  Devil's Peak, 307–309
  East Brigade, 310, 314, 316
  evacuation of mainland, 307
  fifth columnists, 303, 309, 314
  garrison troop strength, 306–307, 319
  geopolitical impact, 288, 301
  Gindrinkers' Line, 306, 312, 319
  Japanese Southern Advance and,
    261–263
  Kai Tak, 305, 309, 314
  Mainland Brigade, 306, 309
  South China Expeditionary Force
    (Japanese Field Army) and planning
    of, 235
  St. Stephen's College, 317
  Stanley, 316
  Stonecutters Island, 309
  surrender, 287, 310, 314, 317
  West Brigade, 310, 314–316
  Wong Nei Chong Gap, 314–316, 320
  Z Force, 307, 317
  see also American Volunteer Group
    (AVG); British Chiefs of Staff;
    Churchill, Prime Minister Winston;
    Grasett, Lieutenant General Arthur
    Edward; strategy, Great Britain; Yu
    Han Mou, General
Hong Kong, blockade of, 113, 118, 126,
    132, 148–149, 190, 195–196
  after invasion of southern Indochina,
    247, 260, 263–265
  after liberation of Kwangsi, 234–237,
    245, 262
Hong Kong, civilians in, 235, 242, 261,
    322
  British responsibility, 70, 190
  Japanese shootings of, 267
Hong Kong, logistical infrastructure, 36, 38,
    45
  aviation, 45, 67, 149, 237
Hong Kong, low-intensity conflict at, 14,

    27, 38, 59–61, 87, 111, 123, 137,
    288
  airspace violations, 67, 117, 148–149,
    263, 267, 303
  attacks on junks, 68, 85, 126, 149–150,
    197, 245, 265–267
  food supplies, 127, 129, 139, 148, 150,
    160, 196, 235, 239, 266
  territorial violations, 68, 104, 149, 197,
    267
  war, 300
Hong Kong, military function of, 41, 75,
    164
Hong Kong, strategic logistical significance,
    17, 36–38, 45–46, 74, 84, 105, 261,
    264, 163
  after battle of Shanghai, 88
  with Burma Road, 219, 235, 246–247,
    262, 323, 336
  after fall of France, 203, 214
  after invasion of Kwangtung, 105, 110,
    124–126
  after invasion of northern Indochina,
    234
  due to stalemate in Kwangsi, 176, 200
Hong Kong, strategic military liability, 75,
    81–83, 154, 214–215, 226, 239, 252,
    261
Hong Kong border tensions, 137, 150–151,
    153–154, 190, 235–237, 265
  shootings, 267
Hong Kong demilitarization, 8, 33, 74, 81,
    157, 205, 214–215, 241
  rejected, 260, 338, 341
Hong Kong officials, 67, 70, 118, 157, 164,
    241–243, 289
  civil-military relations, 244
  policy divergence from Whitehall, 61,
    117, 158, 242, 280
Hong Kong reinforcement, 10–11, 75, 203
  Allied policy, 207, 209, 247, 251–252,
    255, 279, 282
  deterrent value, lack of, 75, 260, 279, 285
  Grasett's efforts, 267
  provocation, 10, 248, 279, 285, 337
  sacrifice of garrison, 318
Hong Kong Volunteer Defence Corps, 34, 76
  strengthened, 154
  at war, 306, 310, 314–315
  see also British Commonwealth army
    regiments

Hoover, C., 31
Hopkins, Harry, 249
Hornbeck, Stanley, 333
Howard, F. J., 80
Howe, Clarence D., 255–256
Howe, Robert G., 73
Ho Ying Chin, General, 311
Hsiatung, 184
Hsia Wei, General, 138
Hsi Chao Tzu, 50
Hsinkai, 193
Hsiukwan, 109
Hsueh Yueh, General, 55, 313
   battlefield success, 57, 168
   Changsha, first battle of, 166–168
   Changsha, second battle of, 289, 295
   Changsha, third battle of, 324, 332–333,
     336
   political leadership, 290
Huang Ta Wei, General, 198
Hudson, Captain, E. J., 282
Hull, Cordell, 221–222, 275, 284, 286
Hughes, Lieutenant Colonel Owen,
   311–312
Hunan, 166, 280, 286–287, 290, 292
   logistical connections, 110, 165
   Red Army advisors in, 103, 289,
     294–298
   strategic significance, 5–6, 89, 102–103,
     165, 168
Hyde Park agreement, 247, 251
Hyakutake Harukichi, Lieutenant General,
   262

Ichang, 131, 168, 219, 281, 332
   air bases, 212, 220
   effect on Chinese morale of fall of, 220
   logistics, 220, 226
Ichang, battle of, 289, 295–298, 300
   chemical weapons, 296
   Chiang's withdrawal order, 296–297
   Chinese artillery at, 295–296
   geopolitical impact, 297–300
   Japanese counterattack, 296
   Soviet advisers, 296–298
Iida Shojiro, Lieutenant General, 138
Imamura Hitochi, General, 181
imperial decline, Great Britain, 2–3, 10, 16,
   226
   collective security, 71, 87, 120, 123, 175,
     338, 341–342

Far East, 39, 82, 201, 205, 318, 337–338
   proxy war policy, 144, 175, 288
   U.S. impact, 203–205, 213–214, 245,
     247–249
Imperial Defence College, 156
Imperial General Staff, 219, 254, 312
India, 8, 156, 288, 290, 344–346
industry, 44, 103
Inglis, John and Company, 255
Institute of Pacific Relations, 344
Internment of Japanese in North America,
   345
Ishii Itaro, 52
Ismay, General Hastings, 260, 278
Itagaki Seishiro, General, 22, 28, 210–211,
   232
   Ichang offensive, 219–220
   see also Ichang, battle of
Italy, 72, 215, 218
Ito Takeo, Lieutenant General, 263, 307
Ivanov, Combrig, 145

Japan
   arrest of British nationals, 236
   cabinet, 52, 110, 124, 154, 203, 209,
     213, 275
   corruption, 85, 134, 232, 236
   economic warfare, 30, 136, 146, 300
   empire, destruction of, 2–3, 16, 39, 87,
     170, 201, 301, 337
   failure in China, 209–211
   failure in grand strategy, 301, 337
   Imperial General Headquarters, 290, 301
   Kiri project, 210–211, 213, 220, 232,
     245
   littoral warfare, 111, 122, 126, 134,
     233, 263–264
   maritime shipping companies, 91
   military advantages, 4, 41, 138, 154,
     179, 183, 216–217
   military inter-service rivalry, 28, 60, 122,
     132, 229
   north China, expansion in, 22, 41, 209
   peace negotiations, Chinese central
     government, 163, 200, 202
   insubordination among senior military
     officers, 42–43, 147–148, 213,
     228–229
   personal ambition and autonomy of
     senior military officers, 3, 22, 38, 49,
     52–53, 115, 132, 148, 199

Japanese air forces
  Chungking bombing campaign, 212–213
  doctrine, 54
  Nanning, battle of, 182–183
  Shekki incident, 263
  strength, 53, 173, 238–239
  women, 212
Japanese air units
  5th Air Regiment, 263
  11th Air Fleet, 301
  21st Air Flotilla, 301
  23rd Air Flotilla, 301
  45th Light Bomber Regiment, 305
  Mihoro Air Group, 64
  Naval Wing 13, 212
  Naval Wing 15, 212
  Wild Eagles, 257
Japanese armies
  6th, 145–147
  11th, 166–167, 183, 193, 268, 327, 329
  15th, 138
  21st, 111, 114, 117, 138
  23rd, 267, 300, 302, 323, 333
Japanese army
  armored forces, 93, 111–112, 138, 141,
    151, 166, 197
  cavalry, 239, 294
  doctrine, 319
  ground operations north of Canton, 130,
    152, 190–193, 197, 262–263
  Kempeitai, 128
  Kwangsi operations, 178–180, 187
  Kwangtung, battle of south-central,
    189–193
  lines of communication, 167, 183,
    191–193
  logistical limitations, 55, 57, 118, 166
  losses, 132, 168, 297
  mobilization, 267
  morale, 110, 144, 147–148, 170, 176,
    328
  Nanning, battle of, 181–186
  operation Ichigo, 100, 282, 347
  troop shortage, 195, 200
  Unit 731, 344
Japanese army brigades
  1st Imperial Guards (Mixed)
  2nd Imperial Guards (Mixed), 239
  9th Mixed Independent, 324, 329
  14th Mixed Independent, 324
  19th Mixed Independent, 302

  23rd, 151, 262
  107th, 190
  Formosan, 143, 183
Japanese army divisions
  2nd, 55
  3rd, 166, 292, 294, 324–325, 327–329
  4th, 292–293
  5th, 104, 264
  6th, 58, 166, 292, 294, 324–325,
    327–329
  9th, 166
  13th, 166, 219, 292, 296
  18th, 91–92, 95, 111, 138, 151
  26th, 228
  27th, 148
  33rd, 166, 292–294
  34th, 324, 327–328
  38th, 191, 195, 197, 263–264, 302–305,
    339
  39th, 296
  40th, 293–294, 324–325, 328–329
  51st, 302
  101st, 27, 55
  104th, 138, 263, 267
  106th, 27, 55, 57
  110th, 228
  112th, 111
  Formosan Force (28th Division), 264
Japanese army group
  China Expeditionary Force, 298, 324
Japanese army regiments
  13th, 57
  55th, 151–152
  66th (Araki Detachment), 302, 313
  115th, 264
  124th, 235–236, 263–264
  136th, 197
  137th, 237
  147th, 57
  228th, 307, 314
  229th, 263, 307, 314–315
  230th, 263, 307, 314
Japanese field armies
  Central China Expeditionary Army, 42,
    166, 169
  Kwantung Army, 22, 148
  South China Expeditionary Force, 114,
    152, 197, 200, 210, 230, 233, 262,
    267
Japanese interdiction campaign, 7–8, 39, 86,
  116, 119

attacks on aircraft, 67, 149, 237, 257,
 263
bombardment of Kwangsi, 64, 91, 95,
 109, 111, 171–173, 187, 200
bombardment of roads and rail lines,
 129–130, 235–236, 263–264
bombardment of Yunnan, 172, 200,
 233–234, 256–257
ineffectiveness, 65–66, 91, 130, 136,
 172, 177, 200, 263
Lace Bridge bombing incident, 187–188
naval operations, 135–136, 149–150,
 196
Osumi incident, 263
West River ground operations, 128, 131,
 137, 190, 195–196, 239, 262
see also Mirs Bay supply route,
 bombardment of
Japanese naval fleets
 2nd China Expeditionary Fleet, 228,
 265, 301
 5th Fleet (South China Fleet), 91, 111,
 132, 137–138, 154, 195
 Combined Fleet, 91, 211
Japanese naval flotillas
 5th Destroyer Flotilla, 138
 23rd Destroyer Flotilla, 138
 45th Destroyer Flotilla, 138
Japanese naval squadrons
 8th Cruiser, 91
 2nd Destroyer, 91
Japanese naval vessels
 Akagi, 178, 211
 Chiyoda, 135
 Enoshima, 138
 Ento, 138
 Fuso, 178
 Hiryu, 211, 264
 Izuzu, 266
 Jintsu, 91
 Kaga, 61, 64, 91, 95, 111–112, 150,
 178
 Kamikawa Maru, 135
 Mizuho, 138, 263
 Myoko, 111, 135, 149–150
 Nagara, 135
 Natori, 135
 Ryujo, 91, 211
 Saga, 138–139
 Soryu, 91, 211
Japanese navy, 91, 111–112, 211

blockade of China, 61–63, 68–69, 122,
 239
use of Tungting Lake, 166
Japanese strategy
 civil-military relations, 133, 210, 213
 disunity, 3, 28, 38, 59–60, 121–122,
 132, 203, 286
 Kwangtung and West River operations,
 122, 239
 north-south indecision, 11, 41, 87, 132,
 210
 northern Indochina, 229
Japanese strategy, northern advance, 210
 planning, 272
 potential for, 275–278
 reinforcement of Manchuria, 260, 286
Japanese strategy, southern advance, 210,
 227, 245–247
 adoption of, 201–202, 204, 213, 302
 miscalculation, 337
 Osumi incident, 263
 planning, 227
 preparations, 228, 233–235, 259, 271,
 276, 302
 southern China, significance of, 235,
 269, 276
 southern Indochina, invasion of, 247,
 253, 259–262, 271, 286
 see also Changsha, third Battle of
Jarrett, C. G., 80
Johnson, Nelson T., 199, 255

Kaipong Island group, 265
Kalgan, 159, 161–162
Kamei Chudo, Captain, 233
Kanchow, 109
Kao Tsung Wu, 51
Karachi, 346–347
Katajima, Lieutenant General, 265, 302
Kato Tateo, Major General, 302
Kawaguchi Kiyotako, Major General, 264
Keenleyside, Hugh, 30, 205–206, 208–209
Kendall, Major Francis, 157, 199, 317, 339
Kennedy, Major General Sir John, 312
Kent, W. C., 237–238
Keswick, Sir John, 158
Kiangsi, 109–110, 134, 138, 165–166, 261,
 327–328
 guerillas, 291
Kiev, 273
King, Captain J., 71

Kingston, 156, 206
Kishan, 139
Kiungchow, 112
Knatchbull-Hugessen, Sir Hughe, 42
Knox, Frank, 257
Kondo Nobutake, Admiral, 111, 132, 134,
    136–137, 154, 171, 195
Konoye Fumimaro, Prime Minister, Prince,
    41, 51–52, 110, 121, 124, 213, 275
  northern Indochina, 228
  power of, 253
Kongmoon, 61, 64, 95, 127, 137
  ground combat, 131, 139, 141,
    195–196, 262
Korean troops, 122, 135
Kotewall, Sir Robert, 79
Kowkong, 141
Koyiu, 138
Kuhn, Loeb and Company, 119
Kukong (Shiukwan), 333
  7th War Zone headquarters, 254
  bombing target, 63
  logistical center, 110, 261, 287
  provincial capital, 93, 101, 190
Kung, David, 126, 160–161, 244
Kung, H. H., 31, 51, 120, 160
Kunlunkwan Pass, 181, 184, 186
Kunming
  air strikes against, 109, 257
  aviation, 84–85, 237–238, 280, 339
  logistics center, 106–107, 174
  transportation, center, 7, 83–84
Kuno Seiichi, Lieutenant General, 138
Kun Shaan, 195
Kuomintang, 5, 52, 120, 173, 244
Kuribayashi Tadamichi, General, 301–302
Kwangchowan (Fort Bayard), 107, 172,
    227
Kwanghan, 84
Kwangsi, 19, 83, 92, 113, 219
  1st Imperial Guards (Mixed), Japanese
    Army Brigade in, 138, 183–184, 186,
    197
  5th Japanese Army Division in, 178,
    181, 186, 197,
  18th Japanese Army Division in,
    183–184, 186
  21st Japanese army operations at, 176,
    178
  armaments production, 103
  anti-Japanese movement, 30

Formosan Force (28th Japanese Army
    Division) in, 178, 186, 197, 233
government effectiveness, 20
invasion of, 126, 174, 176–179
Japanese failure, 177, 188
Nanning, battle of, 181–186
rebellion in, 25–26
Red Army advisors in, 182–183
reinforcement of, 178, 234
road network, 106–107, 177, 180
Japanese withdrawal, 187, 233
South China Expeditionary Force
    (Japanese Field Army) operations in,
    186
Kwangsi army, 50, 99, 103, 138, 143, 178
  artillery, 178
Kwangsi army divisions, 178
Kwangtung
  5th Japanese Army Division and, 91–93,
    95, 114
  12th Chinese Group Army and, 190–193
  21st Japanese Army and, 91–95
  104th Japanese Army Division and,
    91–92, 95, 190, 192, 197
  antagonism to central government, 59,
    66, 86, 97
  anti-Japanese movement, 30
  battle of south-central, 190–193
  Bias Bay, 90–91, 96, 136, 150, 263–264
  civil strife, 48, 50, 59, 85, 130, 141,
    198–199, 267–269
  corruption, 97, 127
  coup d'état, 48–50, 66, 78, 86, 97, 98
  Formosan Force (28th Japanese Army
    Division) and, 135, 138, 143, 151,
    302
  geography, 19
  invasion of, 48–49, 58, 83, 89–95, 123
  Japanese aerial bombardment of roads
    and rail lines at, 46, 48, 61–65, 91,
    172, 195, 197, 256–257
  Japanese Army Brigade, 1st Imperial
    Guards (Mixed) and, 190–192
  Japanese Field Army, South China
    Expeditionary Force in, 191, 193,
    262–263
  military forces in, 138
  political destabilization of, 38, 48, 50, 86
  political reliability of, 99–100
  popular morale in, 28, 50, 58–59, 63,
    97, 122

rebellion in, 25–26
South China Expeditionary Force
(Japanese Field Army) operations in,
191, 193, 262–263
see also Chiang Kai Shek (Jiang Jieshi),
Chairman and Generalissimo;
Chinese Army; Chinese Guerillas;
communists, Chinese;
Kwangtung army, 54, 58, 99, 101
7th Division, 191
armored forces, 92–93, 181
Kweichow, 181
aerial interdiction of, 257
base of resistance, 44
Kweilin, 6, 107
airbase, 280, 341
BAAG headquarters, 338
Soviet military personnel, 146, 182
transportation center, 171
Kweiyi, 328
Kwonghai Bay, 239

Lanchow, 46
Soviet base at, 146–147, 173
Langkow, 191
Langson, 173, 228–229
Laokay, 233
Laolung, 109
Lashio, 106
Lattimore, Owen, 206, 208
Laurier, Prime Minister Sir Wilfrid, 247
Lawson, Brigadier General John K., 306,
310
killed, 315
requests additional forces, 281
Lay Chan Ming, General, 197
League of Nations, 44, 60, 64, 208, 221
Leith-Ross, Sir Frederick, 29, 31
Leningrad, 146
Li Au Yat, 264
Li Chai Sum, Marshal, 97
Li Chi Shen, 50
Liddel Hart, Captain Sir Basil, 204
Li Fook Lam, 50
Li Fu Ying, General, 99
Lind, Jack, 65
Linnell, Irving N., 93, 95, 97, 101
Litang, 184
Li Tsung Ren (Li Zhongren), General, 19,
177
rebellion, 25–26

relations with Chiang, 55, 173, 180
Changsha, second battle of, 295
Liuchow, 109, 182–183
Li Yu Tang, General, 324–325, 332
Lo Kuan, 104
Lockheed Aircraft Corporation, 250
Loiwing, 233
Lothian, Lord (Philip Kerr), 249
Louvet, Lieutenant Colonel, 228
Lovat-Fraser, Lieutenant Colonel W. A., 312
Lowe, Peter, 215
Lower, Arthur R. M., 206
Lukacs, John, 204
Lung Yun, General, 23, 27, 84, 173, 177,
180, 188, 290
Lungchow, 229
Lungchuan, 109
Lungmoon, 191–192
Lutien, 191

Macau, 26, 125, 127
armed forces, 128–129, 196
Banco Nacional Ultramarino, 85
China-Japan peace talks in, 128, 210
Japanese intimidation, 86, 149, 196
Kuomintang counterintelligence, 244
logistical center, 85, 131, 139
low intensity conflict, 67, 85, 237
opium, 85, 268
Portuguese officials, 69, 85–86, 129
war scare, 48–49
MacDonald, Malcolm, 79
MacDonell, Sergeant Major George, 317
MacDougall, Brigadier General David, 299
Mackenzie King, Prime Minister William
Lyon, 72
aid to Stalin, 282
British covert action, 250–251
C Force, sacrifice of, 277–278, 284,
318
Dill, meets with, 344
in London, 274
Roosevelt, relations with, 207, 259, 278
Singapore, significance of, 283
Soong friendship, 289, 345, 348
Soviet collapse, 272–275, 277
U.S. alliance, 205
U.S. policy in China, 288, 345
worldview, 207–208
MacLean, J. W., 223
Magill, Roswell, 206

Magruder, Brigadier General John, 221, 254, 296, 309, 313
Malaya, 309, 320, 322, 337
   Japanese objective, 253
Maltby, Major-General Christopher, 282, 309
   garrison readiness, 307
   ineffectiveness, 303–305, 319–320
   post-war battle report, 279
Manchiang, 291
Manchoukuo, 3–4, 85, 286
Mansion House, 208, 274
Mao, General P. T., 257
Mao Tse Tung (Mao Zedong), Chairman, 21, 31, 159
Maisky, Ivan, 224, 274
Marco Polo Bridge Incident, 3, 40, 209
Mariana Islands, 95, 111, 302
maritime civilian vessels
   MS *Asama Maru*, 196
   SS *Asian*, 68
   SS *Automedon*, 244
   SS *Awatea*, 275
   SS *Bertram*, 132
   SS *Empress of Asia*, 237
   SS *Haitan*, 150
   SS *Hauk*, 147
   SS *Lalita*, 91
   SS *Maron*, 41
   SS *Ranpura*, 149–150
   SS *Sagres*, 91, 135
   SS *Salenga*, 226
   SS *Vladimir Mayakovsky*, 226
   SS *Wosang*, 149
Martin, A. J., 232
Martin, General Maurice, 155
Matsui Iwane, General, 41–43, 52
Matsumoto Shigeharu, 51
Matsuoka Yosuke, 213, 344
   northern advance, 272
   Soviet-Japanese neutrality pact, 253
Mattice, Captain Earl, 184, 187
Mawdsley, Evan, 337
Mayer, Major (Hong Kong Chinese Regiment), 315
Mayer, Lieutenant Colonel William, 168–169, 179, 199, 333
   commando unit, 281
   cooperation with Grasett, 255
Maymyo, 281
McHugh, Lieutenant Colonel James, 297, 298

McLean, Lieutenant Colonel Henry C., 216–217
McNaughton, General Andrew, 283
McRae, Duncan, 64
Meihsien, 109
Mencheong, 112–113
Merrill, Major General Frank, 281
Middle East, 253
Midway, battle of, 337
Millar, Major K., 291–292
Mills, V., 320
Mirs Bay supply route, 27, 106, 109–110, 163, 176, 219
   significance, 84, 170, 261
   bombardment of, 263
   see also Chinese military logistics; Japanese interdiction campaign
Moffat, Jay Pierrepont, 206
Molotov, Vyacheslav, 222, 224
Moore, Sir Henry, 82
Morgenthau, Henry, 31, 221, 249, 251, 257
Mori, Lieutenant, 265
Morrison, Ian, 106
Mosley, Sir Oswald, 224
Mountbatten, Admiral Louis, 1st Earl of Burma, 161
Mukden Special Service Agency, 22
Munich Agreement, 90
Munro-Faure, Major, 312
Munson, Captain F. P., 106, 229
Mussolini, Prime Minister Benito, 72

Nagasaki, 332
Nakahara Yoshimasa, Vice-Admiral, 28
Nakajima Tokutaro, Colonel, 151
Nakamura Aketo, Lieutenant General, 228–229
Nakamura Toyokazu, 51, 64
Namao Island, 66
Namtau, 93, 130, 151, 153, 191, 235
   Japanese anti-aircraft guns, 237
   Japanese reinforcements at, 264, 302–304
Namyung, 66
Nanchang, 66, 101, 165–166, 324, 327
   air action at, 54
Nanking (Nanjing), 99, 148, 211, 233
   atrocities at, 4, 42, 344
Nanning, 191
   air base, 179, 239
   battle of, 181–186

civilians, 179
logistics center, 107, 179
occupation of, 125, 138, 171, 174, 176,
179
reclaimed, 233–234
see also Ando Rikichi, General; Japanese
Air Forces; Japanese Army; Kwangsi
nationalism, Chinese, 3, 116, 173, 189
Nazi-Soviet Pact, 9, 123, 145–147
impact on Britain, 155, 162–163, 202,
214
impact on Japan, 146, 150–151,
168–169, 174, 209, 272
impact on Poland, 221
impact on USSR, 146–147
Netherlands East Indies, 228, 236, 252,
276, 309
air force, 238
Amboina, 317
New York Times, 275, 320
New Zealand, 226, 344
Ng Kei Wai, General, 101, 137–138
Niimi Masaichi, Admiral, 265
Ningpo, 109–110, 232, 236, 238, 264
Nishihara Issaku, Lieutenant General,
228–229
Nishimura Takuma, Lieutenant General,
229–230
Nishio Toshizo, General, 148, 209–210
Nishi Yoshiaki, 51
Noble, Admiral Sir Percy, 79
Nomura Kichisaburo, Admiral, 271, 284,
286
Norton, Major General E. F., 242, 244
Nomizo, Colonel, 235
Nomonhan (Khalkhin Gol), 47, 125–126,
137, 144–147, 154, 164, 168
geopolitical impact, 169, 174, 176,
222
resolution of, 235
North Africa, 254
Northcote, Governor Sir Geoffry, 34, 59,
76–77, 157, 267
absence of, 242
David Kung incident, 160
and demilitarization, 241
Hong Kong purchase scheme, 78–82
Lo Wu incident, 117–118
policy divergence from Grasett, 244
Norway, 213
nuclear weapons, 246, 332

Office of the Coordinator of Information,
250
Office of Strategic Services (OSS), 100, 158,
250
Ogdensburg Agreement, 207
Ohira Hideo, Lieutenant Colonel, 115
Oikawa Koshiro, Admiral, 233
Okamura Yasuji, General, 166, 193
Okazaki Katsuo, 118, 149
Operation Barbarossa, 11, 14, 146, 226,
231, 246, 259–260, 276, 340
Army Group Center, 275, 340
impact on Japan, 267, 269, 271
see also Germany
opium, 22, 23–24, 39–40, 85, 199, 210,
250, 268
Ormsby-Gore, William, 78
Orwell, George, 335
Osborn, Sergeant Major John R., 315
Osumi Mineo, Admiral, 263
Ou Yang Chen, General, 55, 57, 101
Outaokang, 91
Overesch, Commander H. E., 49, 96,
99–101

Pacific war, start of, 305
Pai Chung Hsi (Bai Zhongxi), 19–20, 107,
177, 179–180
Chiang, relations with, 55, 173,
179–180
Nanning, battle of, 181, 188
rebellion, 25–26
Pakhoi, 28, 61, 107, 171–172
airbase, 187
Kwangsi, invasion of, 178
occupation, 186
Pawley, William, 85
Payne, Robert, 333
Pearl Harbor, 12, 211, 272, 278, 301, 305,
322
Peffers, Brigadier, 265
Permanent Joint Board of Defence,
207–208, 247, 251
Persia, 85
Pettus, Dr. Winston, 325
Philippines, 216
military forces in, 132, 280
preparations for war in, 164, 271, 289,
304
U.S. interests in, 10, 120
Phulangtong, 233

Phuto, 233
Piggott, Major-General Francis S. G., 27, 35, 52, 100, 114, 160
Pigott, Second Lieutenant (Hong Kong Chinese Regiment), 315
Pingkiang, 293
Pingshan, 92, 95, 104, 200
Pingwu, 152
Pinyang, 184, 186
piracy, 75, 104, 122
Poklo, 93
Pokut, 237
POL (petroleum, oil, lubricants), 45, 84, 100, 106, 163, 179, 188, 200, 218–219, 264
Poland, 147, 168, 171, 175, 224
    Katyn Forest, 221
Poon, Colonel, 57
Pope, Lieutenant General Maurice, 207
Porter, Bernard, 205
Pownall, Lieutenant General Henry, 335
Poyang, Lake, 55

Québec, 207
Québec Conference (Quadrant), 346
Queen's University, 206

racial geopolitics, 344–345
railway lines, 7, 17–19, 63, 83, 87–88
    Hunan-Kwangtung railway, 61, 84, 107, 261, 174, 166
    military operational significance, 287, 292
    northern China, 4, 44
    southern provinces, impact on, 23–24, 35, 79, 173
Ralston, James L., 255–256
Rangoon, 2, 9, 105, 132, 174, 203, 226, 232
    aviation, 237
    Japanese threat to, 313
Rebello, Commodore, 86
Red Army
    advisers in China, 7, 146–147, 231, 339
    destruction of, 11, 246, 270–271, 284
    Moscow, battle of, 11, 231, 275, 277, 297, 340
    Nomonhan, 145
    purge of, 146
    Siberian divisions, 11, 272, 275, 340
    see also Hunan; Ichang; Kwangsi; USSR

Red Cross, 268
Rees, R.D., 18
Reeve, Brigadier General, 105, 306
Reid, Escott, 205
Repulse Bay Hotel, 51, 315
Ride, Colonel Lindsay, 77, 338
roads, 4, 7, 18, 44, 83–84, 171, 177, 233
Rockefeller III, John D., 208
Rogers, P., 80
Rommel, Field Marshal Erwin, 254
Ronald, Sir Nigel, 78, 80, 160, 258
Roosevelt, President Franklin Delano, 9, 120, 275, 337, 346
    American entry to war, 207, 248, 250–251, 272
    AVG, 257
    Chiang, relations with, 271
    family background, 250
    personal diplomacy, 207, 211, 220, 250, 259, 278, 345
    reelection, 214, 230, 239, 248–249, 257
    silver policy, 29–30
    worldview, 10, 206, 259, 269
Roosevelt, Brigadier General James, 250
    meets with Chiang, 255
    meets with Grasett, 255
Rose, Colonel H. B., 315–316
Roshchin, Colonel N. V., 261
Royal Air Force, 34, 148, 238, 280
    battle of Britain, 205, 230, 238, 249
    Kwangtung reconnaissance, 303
    losses, 305
Royal Institute of International Affairs, 71
Royal Military College of Canada, 156, 206
Royal Navy, 41, 72, 75–76, 135, 150, 196, 207
    ground forces, 315
    mining, 266
Royal Navy vessels
    HMS *Bee*, 42
    HMS *Cicala*, 75, 149, 310
    HMS *Cumberland*, 75
    HMS *Delight*, 172
    HMS *Dorsetshire*, 150
    HMS *Eagle*, 67
    HMS *Falcon*, 187
    HMS *Folkestone*, 135
    HMS *Kent*, 75
    HMS *Ladybird*, 42–43
    HMS *Liverpool*, 196
    HMS *Moth*, 75, 115, 309

HMS *Prince of Wales*, 309
HMS *Repulse*, 309
HMS *Robin*, 75
HMS *Seamew*, 75, 86
HMS *Tamar*, 32
HMS *Tarantula*, 75, 78, 86
HMS *Tenedos*, 136
HMS *Thracian*, 75, 135
RFA *Pearleaf,* 150
Royal Navy flotillas
    2nd Motor Torpedo Boat Flotilla, 32,
      75, 149–150, 267, 309–310, 316
    4th Submarine Flotilla, 75
    21st Destroyer Flotilla, 75
    West River Flotilla, 32, 75, 86
Royal Navy squadrons
    5th Cruiser Squadron, 75
    China Squadron, 196
Rybalko, Marshal Pavel, 231

Saint George, Lieutenant Commander
    Ruyneau de, 172
Sakai Takashi, Lieutenant General, 302,
    310, 314
Samah Bay (Hainan), 111, 259
Samma (Kwangtung), 101
Samshui, 95, 104, 127, 138, 190, 302
Samson, George, 220
Sanchau Island, 137, 149, 239
San Francisco, 205
Sano Tadayoshi, Lieutenant General, 302,
    307
Sawamoto Yorio, Vice-Admiral, 264–265
Schurmann, Franz, 13
Scott, A. L., 157, 161–162, 258, 266, 291,
    305
Scriven, Captain, R., 315
secrecy in government, 12–13, 15, 119, 248,
    269, 272, 278–279, 284, 342
Sekiya, Captain, 265
Seymour, Sir Horace, 45
Shanghai, 97, 161, 232
    battle of, 3–4, 40–41, 73, 100, 109
    Chapei district, 22, 41
    Kuomintang counterintelligence
      operations, 244
    withdrawal of British garrison, 219
Shataukok, 104–105, 152–153, 235, 265,
    267
Shayuchang, 197, 235
Shekki, 139

air attacks on, 127, 141
    battle of, 125–126, 137, 139, 141, 170
    Japanese air loss, 263
    reoccupied, 239
Sheklung, 91–93, 95, 138, 151–152, 199
Shenkang, 192
Shihlingpu, 130
Shimada Shigetaro, Admiral, 265
Shimoda, General, 262
Shiratori Toshio, 151
Shoji Toshishige, Major General, 307, 316
Shotwell, James, T., 206
Shumchun, 26, 104–105, 151, 191, 199,
    235–236, 265
    Japanese deployments to Hong Kong
      from, 302, 304, 314
Shum Hang Chung, 244
Shum Sung, 160
Siangtan, 103
Sian incident, 31–32
Sinfeng, 313
Singapore, 252, 254, 303–304
    Allied conferences and meetings at, 155,
      240, 261, 279
    Far East Command headquarters, 240
    Japanese objective, 253
    naval base, 196, 207
Singapore strategy, 29, 32–33, 35, 74–76,
    144, 214–215, 279–280, 341
    Hong Kong relief from, 241, 260
Sinkiang, 347
    supply routes, 46–47, 106, 203
Sino-Japanese peace, 11, 51, 78, 90, 102,
    120, 123–124, 126
    Anglo-American intervention, 231–232,
      271
    Burma Road, impact of, 283, 322
    Canadian intervention, 269
    negotiations, 202, 210, 213
    rejected, 165, 171, 174, 210, 232
    Soviet collapse, potential impact of,
      270–271
    through trade, 133–134
    war weariness, potential due to, 163,
      213, 220–221, 226, 270, 277,
      284
    USSR, potential impact on, 271, 277
Sino-Soviet barter agreements, 226
Sino-Soviet Non-Aggression Pact, 46
Skelton, Oscar D., 207
Smith, Norman L., 73, 244

Smuts, Prime Minister and Field Marshal
  Jan, 250
Somervell, General Brehon B., 256
Soong Ai Ling, 78
Soong Ching Ling, 78
Soong Mei Ling (Madame Chiang), 78, 209
Soong, T. V., 99, 343, 346
  AVG, 257
  China Defense Supplies, 249–250
  Chinese National Bonds Subscription
    Branch Society, 78
  Mackenzie King, friendship with, 289,
    345, 348
  Military Affairs Commission, 45
  South-West Transportation Commission,
    45, 106, 164, 172
Sorge, Richard, 275
Soviet-Japanese relations, 145, 176
  improvements, 222–223, 231
  neutrality, 147, 154, 164, 168, 209
  Soviet-Japanese neutrality pact, 253, 271
South East Asia Command (SEAC), 161
Spear, Lieutenant Colonel C. R., 149,
  159–162
Special Operations Executive (SOE), 158,
  240
Stacey, Colonel Charles P., 206, 316
Stalin, General Secretary Josef, 72, 279, 340
  British, relations with, 83, 102, 132,
    145, 174, 221–222
  Clark Kerr, relations with, 283
  Hitler, relations with, 144, 146, 171,
    202, 218, 221, 245
  Japanese southern advance, 222, 253
  Mao, relations with, 31, 225
  proxy war, support for, 17, 46, 144–148,
    162, 297
  repression by, 15, 71, 147, 221, 342
  second front, 273–274, 348
  Western powers, antagonism to, 10, 123,
    146–147, 202, 218, 221, 347–348
Stalingrad, battle of, 339
Stapler, Captain John, 136
strategic resources (e.g. tungsten), 21, 46,
  147, 149, 221, 225–226
  at Hunan, 5–6, 165, 290
  seized by Japanese, 264
  Toishan, 134, 268
  transshipped through Hong Kong, 132,
    151, 238, 261, 263
strategic planning, Great Britain

disarray, 202, 218, 259
with French, 155, 172
options, 73–74, 148, 245, 341
with United States, 164, 221, 239, 272,
  276
see also Anglo-American strategic
  cooperation and planning
strategy, Great Britain
covert actions, 158, 161–164, 239–240,
  257–258, 271
disunity, 17, 29, 38, 87, 164, 241
guerilla warfare, 162, 313
Hong Kong purchase scheme, 77, 80, 82,
  87, 120
neutrality in Europe, 8, 74, 202,
  204–205, 213, 220–222
proxy war, 8–9, 75, 124, 202, 230,
  245–246, 271, 273, 341–342
southern Indochina, 244
Stephenson, Captain Sir William, 250
Sterndale Bennett, Sir John, 223, 270–271,
  279
Stilwell, General Joseph, 23, 40, 43–44, 65,
  120, 345–347
Stuart, John L., 210–211
Sturgeon, Commander J. M., 114–115
Suefuji Tomofumi, Major General,
  263–254
Suetsugu Nobumasa, Admiral, 60
Sullivan, Wing Commander Ginger, 305
Sun Fo, 46, 132
Sunwui, 139, 141,
  railway destroyed, 239
Sun Yat Sen, 46, 78, 137, 141, 143
Sutherland, Captain, Edwin M., 106, 139,
  145
Swabue, 109, 136, 139, 264
Swatow, 101, 109, 129, 157, 267
  bombardment, 66, 134–135
  garrison, Japanese, 138, 190, 195, 197,
    236
  ground operations, 198, 264, 311, 314
  occupation, 126, 132, 135–136, 151
  opium, 268
  trade, 134
Szechwan
  air strikes, 131
  air combat, 293
  defensive stronghold, 176
  national government base, 44
  political reliability, 290

rice hoarding, 300
threat of Japanese offensive, 219
Sze Yap district, 127, 239

Taierhchuang (Taierzhuang), 4, 73
Tai Li, General, 55, 158, 261
Takasu Shiro, Admiral, 154, 195, 211
Tamshui, 91–92, 197, 200, 238, 264, 268,
    302, 313, 339
Tanaka Hisaichi, Lieutenant General, 117
Tanaka Ryosaburo, Lieutenant Colonel,
    307, 314–315
Tang, General K. C., 160
Tan Moon, 263
Tchangyi, 238
Tehan, 27, 55–59, 92, 101, 143
Terauchi Hisaichi, Field Marshal, 210
Thailand, 252–253, 276
Thomson, Oscar, 66, 69, 133, 191, 199
Tienchiachen, 58
Tientsin, 119, 126, 135–136, 145, 148,
    154–155, 158–162
    Anglo-French garrison, 163
Tieshih, 143
The Times, 327, 329, 333
Toishan, 63–64, 127, 134
    occupied, 239, 268
    railway destroyed, 239
Tojo Hideki, Prime Minister and General
    anti-Soviet view, 223
    Kwantung Army, 28
    northern advance, 272, 275
    South China Area Army commanders,
    229
Tonkin, Gulf of, 95, 113, 172–173
Tong Po Hing, Corporal, 315
Toronto, 65, 156, 209, 255
Trautmann, Oscar, 51–52
Tsai Ting Kai, General, 100
Tsang Shang, 199, 339
Tsengcheng, 130, 191–192
Tseng Yang Fu, 51
Tsuchihashi Yuichi, Lieutenant General,
    195
Tsungfa, 95, 152, 170, 190, 192, 197, 263
Tuchman, Barbara, 249–250
Tungcheng, 293
Tungkunghsien, 93
Tung Tao Ning, 51
Turkey, 253, 278
Tu Yueh Sheng, 268, 305

Ueda Kenkichi, General, 148
Ugaki Kazushige, General, 51–53
Umezu Yoshijiro, General, 148
United Church of Canada, 65, 209
United Nations, 205
United States
    congress, 247, 272, 284
    conscription, 207
    eastern establishment, 208, 248
    Neutrality Act, 60, 164
    State Department, 271, 333
    Treasury Department, 254
    War Department, 344
United States Army
    advisers in China, 164
    Merrill's Marauders, 281
United States Army Air Force
    10th Air Force, 208
    14th Air Force, 320, 339
United States Marine Corps, 255, 297, 345
United States Navy
    Asiatic Fleet, 282
    Pacific Fleet, 33, 75, 163, 211, 217, 252,
    254
    USS *Mindanao*, 282, 304
    USS *Panay*, 42–43
    USS *Tulsa*, 136, 281
Universal Trading Corporation, 249
University of Hong Kong, 338
U.S.-China relations, 2, 9–11, 116, 132,
    234, 254, 259, 271
    China as US sphere of interest, 254, 269,
    288, 339, 345
    Chinese sovereignty, 231–232, 234, 247,
    252, 343, 346,
U.S. coalition leadership, 11, 203, 206, 208,
    221, 259, 272, 276, 288
    Allied strategic planning, 252
    northern Indochina, 230–231, 245–247
    Roosevelt reelection, 248, 251, 254, 284
U.S. economic warfare
    Lend-Lease, 10–11, 221, 247–249, 251,
    254–255 313, 346
    loans to China, 90, 119, 121, 123, 188,
    211, 230, 253–254, 284, 333
    sanctions, 154, 164, 168, 220–221, 230,
    247, 271, 276, 287
U.S. foreign relations, 9, 163, 218, 259
    collective security, 223
    communists, support for, 346–347
    evacuation order, 230

U.S. foreign relations, *continued*
  officials, independent action of, 11, 13,
    255, 257, 280–281
  USSR, support for, 12, 223, 247, 269,
    284
Ushiroku Jun, General, 210, 229, 324
U.S.-Japanese relations, 116, 188, 228, 230,
    234, 245–246
  commercial treaty, 164, 168
  deterrence, 10, 33, 75, 163–164
U.S. Military Missions, 221, 254–255, 311
USSR
  air units at Nanning, 182–183
  Changsha events, 287, 336, 339
  collective security, 224
  Far Eastern security, 15, 90, 132,
    144–145, 162, 221
  influence in China, 163
  interests in China, 269, 297
  intelligence, 275
  intervention in China, 90, 145–146,
    296–297
  key to Allied grand strategy, 231,
    246–247, 269, 277, 284, 341
  NKVD, 71, 158, 221, 274, 283
  potential of defeat against Germany, 272
  repression in, 10, 221, 274
  see also Red Army
USSR, support for China, 2, 6, 9, 37, 46,
    106, 124, 126, 145–147
  airpower, 47, 53–54, 131–132, 146, 165,
    173, 182–183, 238, 257
  artillery, 47, 66, 146, 167, 294, 312, 327
  diminishes, 231
  terminated, 339
U.S. support for proxy war, 10, 90, 116,
    230, 234
  with British, 255, 271, 279
Utley, Jonathan, 206, 208

Vladivostok, 47, 72, 90, 146–147, 226
von Bock, Field Marshal Fedor, 340
von Falkenhausen, General Baron
    Alexander, 40
von Kleist, Field Marshal Baron Paul L.E.,
    204

Wada Shinzo, Lieutenant, 128
Waichow, 104, 197
  18th Japanese Army Division in, 264
  Chinese garrison, 237, 262

escape and evasion route, 157, 317,
    338–339
  and invasion of Kwangtung, 92–93,
    95–96
  Japanese occupation, 264
  logistical center, 84, 106, 109, 174, 238,
    261
  relief of Hong Kong, 313, 321
  threat to Japanese flank, 152–153,
    264–265
Wallis, Brigadier General Cedric, 306, 310,
    316, 320
Warburg, James, 250
Wan Fu Lin, General, 99
Wang Ching Wei, President, 120, 160, 162,
    177, 309
  defection of, 59, 121, 124
  discredited, 169–170, 174
  failure of, 49, 170
  Japanese support for, mixed, 133, 148,
    154
  lack of popular support , 141, 152–153,
    198
  official recognition of government,
    210–211, 233
  potential for success, 262
Wangmoon, 141, 143
Wardley, D. J., 80
Wards, Major G. T., 115–117, 119, 128
Wavell, Field Marshal and Viceroy Sir
    Archibald P., 283, 310, 335
Webb, Richard, 335, 344–345
Wedemeyer, General Albert C., 282
Weichow Island, 61, 149, 172
Wenchow, 134, 136, 264
Whitaker, Brigadier General Denis,
    282–283
Whitamore, C. E., 101, 115
White, Lieutenant Colonel Simon, 307
Whitfield, Andrew, 299
Wittenbach, Harry, 139
Wonglik, 93
Wong Ngai, General, 112
Wuchow, 138, 178
Wuming, 184, 186
Wu Teh Chen, General, 46, 50–51, 97, 261

Yale in China University, 325
Yamada Otozo, General, 166, 169
Yamamoto Isoroku, Commander-in-Chief,
    Admiral, 211

464   INDEX

Yamchow (Chinchow), 178, 183–184,
    186–187
Yanagawa Heisuke, Lieutenant General, 210
Yingtak, 104, 190
Yochow, 165–166,
    Changsha, second battle, 292–294
    Changsha, third battle, 324–325, 329,
    332
Yonai Mitsumasa, Prime Minister, Admiral,
    60, 209, 213
Young, Governor Sir Mark, 313–314, 317,
    332
Yu Han Mou, General, 95–96, 99, 130,
    137, 234, 263, 332
    coup suppression, 50–51
    loyalty, 21, 25–27, 50, 66, 97, 99–100,
    102
    meets with Hemingway, 254
    military commander, effectiveness as, 55,
    90, 92, 99–101, 152–153, 170, 193

relief of Hong Kong, 311–314, 320
treason, accusations of, 96–99, 144
Yugoslavia, 278
Yungshun, 184
Yungyun, 190–191
Yunnan, 7, 83, 176, 219
    air bases, 85
    army, 55
    attacks on aircraft, 237–238
    base of military resistance, 44, 84–85
    Lace Bridge bombing incident,
        187–188
    logistical network, 107, 174, 181, 233
    political reliability, 25, 173, 181, 188,
        290
    political autonomy, 23, 84, 180–181
    reinforcement of, 178, 181, 313
    threats of invasion, 229, 271

Zhukov, Marshal Georgy, 340